# History of Music Theory

# History of Music Theory

Books I and II

*Polyphonic Theory to the Sixteenth Century*

by

HUGO RIEMANN

*Translated, with a preface, commentary, and notes*

by

RAYMOND H. HAGGH

University of Nebraska Press · Lincoln · 1962

The publication of this book was assisted by a grant from the Ford Foundation.

*Publishers on the Plains*

**UNP**

Printed in the United States of America

For Hilde, Barbara, and Karen

# *Translator's Preface*

A HISTORY of polyphonic theory needs no excuse for being. Riemann's *Geschichte der Musiktheorie* appeared in its second edition forty years ago[1] and is no longer available except in libraries with well developed collections. The present work is based upon the need for a comprehensive revision of the first two books of Riemann's *Geschichte*, at the same time making this valuable publication again available for general reference. These two books cover the earliest appearances of polyphony to the counterpoint manuals of Tinctoris, Gafurius, Aron, and Vicentino. Studies and interest in the musico-theoretical aspect of Western musical culture are growing, and the works of the theorists are being employed for their contributions in clarifying practices of distant periods and as an aid for the solution of many problems encountered in the study of extant musical monuments.[2] A study of the history of music theory belongs to the history of ideas as well as to the history of music; it is not an attempt to set up music theory as authoritative for every phase of past musical practice but to show how men accounted for the musical practice of their time.

The relationship between theory and practice is by no means so distant as Riemann would like us to believe. It is better to say that the relationship of any art and its theory has certain characteristics and definite limitations. The theorist of music accounts for the tonal system and musical practice in a systematic way; he may even initiate new concepts,

---

[1] Hugo Riemann, *Geschichte der Musiktheorie im IX.–XIX. Jahrhundert* (2nd ed.; Berlin, 1920). This translation is of the first two books only.

[2] New editions as well as translations of theoretical sources are listed among *Sources* in the bibliography. Translations into English of theoretical treatises and writings on music theory are in a convenient bibliography in James Coover, "Music Theory in Translation," *JMT* III: 70–96. Gustave Reese, in footnotes to his *Music in the Middle Ages* and *Music in the Renaissance*, gives comprehensive bibliographical coverage of translations of treatises into modern languages. See also Reese's *Fourscore Classics of Music Literature* (1957), a review of important treatises and references to various editions.

indulge in speculation, and on certain premises that he has established apply these as a basis for evaluative criticism.[3] We cannot expect the theorist to account for every variation encountered in practice, but we can expect him to give us the fundamentals of this practice and a systematic presentation of the materials available to it, enabling us to observe their influence in the composition and performance of music. This the theorists of all periods have done, and it is not without good reason that we approach them for the information they can give us as an aid in the reconstruction of the music of past times.

Riemann's *Geschichte der Musiktheorie* has been used as a source for a half-century. It contains a number of errors based upon preconceptions common in the 19th century, but in spite of these errors this work, of all of Riemann's prolific contributions to the science of musicology, continues to have an active life in the footnotes and contents of musicological publications and dissertations, in the United States as well as in Europe. What accounts for this vitality? The fact is that despite the definite slant of some of Riemann's arguments and despite his attempts to prove something for which he had no evidence in actual fact, the *Geschichte* is a demonstration of his thorough mastery of the literature of music theory, of his perception and skill in gathering the important information contained in these works, and of his insistence, in most cases, on allowing the sources to speak for themselves. He quotes extensively, and to a remarkable degree he has richly documented the developing theory of polyphony from the earliest known sources (some of these are conjectural, as will be shown in the commentary) to the 16th century immediately before the advent of harmonic theory in the treatises of Gioseffo Zarlino. It is necessary, therefore, to discuss Riemann's convictions in the light of present knowledge in order to make use of his valuable work.

The reader of the *Geschichte der Musiktheorie* will quickly become aware that Riemann had certain convictions which recur constantly, like leading motives, throughout the first two books. These convictions were part of the traditions of the 19th century, and even with his more scientific approach he was not able to resist them.[4] The quest for origins and the evolution of ideas occupied Riemann's attention in the *Geschichte*. The former led Riemann to several hypotheses for which no proof can exist. Nineteenth-century music history, and Riemann too, seemed anxious to use folk practice as a specific basis for its theories of origins. That folk

[3] Theorists in the Middle Ages and the Renaissance did not hesitate to evaluate the musical practice of their times. The *Speculum musicae* (see Chapter X) of Jacobus of Liège, and works of Tinctoris, Gafurius, Aron, and Vicentino, passed judgments on the basis of standards they established for past or present practice.

[4] For a detailed study of the philosophies of 19th-century music history see Warren D. Allen, *Philosophies of Music History*, pp. 86–127, pp. 177–342, *et passim*.

music is important in this regard must be true to some extent, yet folk practice is a "compliant *deus ex machina*,"[5] and one can attribute to such a practice what one wants in order to support some particular theory. Readers of 19th-century literature dealing with music are familar with references to that obscure and ambiguous group, the "Folk," existing before recorded evidence of their activities (or ignored by those who recorded such evidence), out of which came the fresh, untainted, and natural utterances based upon the rightness of natural instinct. The third (particularly the major third), which Riemann regarded as the necessary harmonic component of a higher level of polyphony, was an example of a natural element, an interval of "nature" which had been intuitively recognized by the "Folk," and which had probably always existed as a part of "folk polyphony." The thought never suggested itself to Riemann that popular or folk practice might conceivably have been influenced at some time by art music.

Fauxbourdon and English discant, in Riemann's opinion, are the late civilized products of folk art, of the natural polyphony (*naturwüchsige Mehrstimmigkeit*) that must have been in existence much earlier. The polyphony of art music resulted from a series of refinements of this practice, and the theory of polyphony—the real laggard—not only came into being last of all, but also altered the natural and instinctive proclivities for certain sounds (thirds) to conform to theoretical preconceptions and inherited authority. Thus, the early medieval writers on polyphony (Hucbald and his anonymous contemporaries) in deference to antique theory adopted the fourth as a fundamental consonance, ignoring the fuller and richer beauty of the natural third, which was a dissonance according to the theoretical viewpoint these writers represented. Organum, too, was a theoretical crystallization of existing practice, and parallel organum a purely theoretical form. From this theoretical beginning, Riemann attempted to trace an evolution in theory which finally resulted in recognition of the third, in counterpoint having the third as a basic interval, and finally in harmonic theory based upon the triad. This evolution took place in theoretical writings only, theory gradually overcoming its reticence to recognize what already existed in popular practice. Since we have more early music available to us for examination than did Riemann, we can only conclude, in opposition to him, that theory in all likelihood followed practice at a reasonably close distance, particularly with regard to the third or a triadic formation. The third and its relation to folk practice have been investigated by a number of scholars, and they have shown that no unequivocal evidence exists to support this assumption.[6]

[5] W. Apel, *Notation of Polyphonic Music*, p. 221.
[6] See Chapter II, Note *7.

We can concur, however, with Riemann's statement that England was the mother of a contrapuntal style based on the third, since the earliest records of such a usage are from English sources, yet we have no basis for dating the advent of this style as early as he does.[7]

Riemann presents his main ideas concisely and clearly in the introduction to the *Geschichte*, and the reader of this work should be familiar with them. He was of the opinion that polyphony did not exist in antiquity, and he did not regard as tenable the citations given as proof for a Greek polyphonic practice.[8] Polyphony, according to him, very likely came into being in the early centuries following the death of Christ, and intervals other than the octave and fifth must have been used. According to Giraldus Cambrensis, a real polyphonic folk practice must have existed very early in North Scotland, brought there very likely from Scandinavia. Riemann felt that further historical research would bring to light the fact that:

...Germanic nations were the first to bring the crude beginnings of natural polyphony to a definite artistic level; England became the actual cradle of a completely developed technique of counterpoint. The third as a basis of polyphony was far removed, even unthinkable, for those who grew up under the influence of the ideas of antique theory; this wholesome kernel of harmonic music could not be found by way of speculation. Rather, those to whom the third was for centuries an established fact in their practice were called upon to bring order and reason to the theory and practice of the musical art, a fact which the heirs of antique culture, in endeavoring to assimilate what was foreign to them, had at first entirely misrepresented.

Romanic nations, participating in this development, forced natural polyphony into rigid confines following the patterns of early polyphonic theory under the domination of antique concepts. Fauxbourdon appeared as a correction of this stylization, a correction based upon the musical instincts of Nordic nations, which required no theoretical justification for the consonance of the third, for it was known to them as an actual, natural, and existing fact. Riemann continues:

Above all, the final amalgamation of the developed artistic technique of *déchant* (including diminutions) with naturalistic fauxbourdon led to true counterpoint, which in turn was more a theoretical cultivation of fauxbourdon than a further development of *déchant*.

The nature of harmony, according to Riemann, was made apparent in fauxbourdon; however, this was first clearly perceived not by a Germanic mind but by a thinker from Romanic lands, Gioseffo Zarlino:

[7] See the article "Gymel" in *MGG* V: 1139–1146.
[8] See Gustave Reese, *Music in the Middle Ages*, pp. 50–51.

...for the Romanic peoples were still the bearers of culture and the thinkers, whereas the Germanic peoples were only the conveyors of this wholesome material which was available for assimilation.

Riemann warns against regarding the theorists as those who were the agents responsible for this development. It is possible, he points out, to indicate theorists who were noted as composers in their time, particularly in the period between 1475 and 1520 (Adam von Fulda, Gafurius, and Tinctoris). Even as early as Philippe de Vitry, Franco, and Johannes de Garlandia, these men were known not only as theorists but also as skilled composers of their time. Nevertheless, the theorists are by no means the ones who provided the stimulus for musical development.

We finally go back to the period when the practice of polyphony is in such a primitive state that "theory appears to be the actual agent of progress." This can be considered true of the time of Guido of Arezzo, and even of Hucbald of St. Amand, theorists who were seeking formulations for a type of polyphony that was being practiced on a purely intuitive basis, and which in its inner logic was very likely far superior to the theoretical products of the time.

Riemann concludes the introduction as follows:

Since we are not examining the history of music but that of music theory, the most extreme deviations from the right paths, which were in greatest contradiction to practice, provide material of great interest for our scrutiny and strengthen the gratifying impressions we receive from the knowledge which is gradually dissipating the obscurity of the past, until we shall come to the time when extant monuments of the best musical art will put us in a position to examine further the works of the theorists in order to evaluate them with even greater certainty.

As medieval theory does not appear to us today to be an infallible revelation of the spirit of those early church melodies, some of which were created even centuries earlier, so is it equally difficult to believe without reservation that musical practice after the rise of polyphony corresponded very closely to a theory which was at first so very clumsy, and which struggled so much with its terminology. But it is exactly this observation of the attempts to force into conceptual forms what natural musical instinct had created which is the real object of our investigation. Because of the lack of any reliable tradition, what goes beyond this can only be hypothesis.

In this way Riemann introduces us to the material he has gathered for us in the *Geschichte*. We can no longer follow many of his premises. Lack of knowledge of musical sources not known in his time left gaps in Riemann's work, and in the case of fauxbourdon led him to a number of false conclusions. These false conclusions, discussed throughout the commentary, were strengthened by the preconceptions which have been pointed out. Others, such as the assumption that binary meter preceded ternary, and that secular music always exerted a beneficial influence on ecclesiastical music, can also be traced back to these convictions. In addition, some of the sources used by Riemann as evidence are so ambiguous that they must also be discounted. It is with the correction of these defects that Riemann's work can be restored to great usefulness; therefore this material is dealt with in detail throughout the commentary.

The first two books of the *Geschichte* appear here for the first time in complete translation.[9] (The third book deals with harmonic theory, a history of which has been made available in a more recent work.[10]) A commentary has been added to this study which attempts to bring the contents of each chapter into correspondence with the findings of contemporary scholarship. The annotated bibliography contains items which relate to the contents of the first two books of the *Geschichte* and which have been published since this work appeared. Only items covering topics in the original text which are extensive enough to constitute additional information, or which contain emendations of the material in the original, have been included. Recent publications of original sources have been cited as much as possible; all printed treatises discussed by Riemann have been included with their original publication dates, since these are now available on microcard or microfilm reproduction, or the originals may be inspected, at several major libraries in the United States.[11]

Riemann left a great many Latin quotations untranslated which have been translated for this edition; the Latin texts are included in an appendix at the end of each chapter. Latin quotations which are translated in the body of the text appear in their original form in the footnotes. The texts of Gerbert and Coussemaker are well known for their unreliability; therefore, whenever revised editions of these texts were available, they were utilized. For this reason, in many cases the Latin text in an appendix or footnote does not agree with the versions given in the *Geschichte*. The emended versions used are cited in the commentary. All texts quoted by Riemann have been checked for errors and corrected.

The translation of some of the Latin texts proved difficult, so, since the aim was to provide a rendition as objective and as close to the original as possible, it was often necessary to include explanations within the translation. These and all other interpolations by the translator are enclosed in

---

[9] Chapter XI of the *Geschichte der Musiktheorie* and the introduction have been published in English translation by John F. Pratt, *Florida State University Studies*, 18:41–128, including a preface by the translator.

[10] Matthew Shirlaw, *The Theory of Harmony* (2nd ed.; 1955), pp. 484.

[11] The Library of Congress has a comprehensive collection of printed treatises from the Renaissance which were consulted by the writer.

brackets, while Riemann's brackets have been changed to parentheses wherever possible in order to avoid confusion.

The musical examples in the text have been emended whenever a better version was available; such changes are indicated in the commentary. Otherwise, Riemann's original examples have been retained.

Riemann's footnotes are indicated by asterisks in the original edition, but have been numbered in this translation. References to notes in the commentary are also numbered, but these numbers are preceded by an asterisk (e.g., *1).

The following abbreviations have been used:

| | |
|---|---|
| *AfMF* | *Archiv für Musikforschung* |
| *AfMW* | *Archiv für Musikwissenschaft* |
| *AM* | *Acta Musicologica* |
| *HAM* | *The Harvard Anthology of Music*, vol. 1 |
| *HD* | *The Harvard Dictionary of Music* |
| *JAMS* | *Journal of the American Musicological Society* |
| *JMT* | *Journal of Music Theory* |
| *KMJ* | *Kirchenmusikalisches Jahrbuch* |
| *MD* | *Musica Disciplina* |
| *MF* | *Die Musikforschung* |
| *MGG* | *Die Musik in Geschichte und Gegenwart*, vols. 1–8 |
| *MQ* | *The Musical Quarterly* |
| *NOHM* | *The New Oxford History of Music* |
| *SIMG* | *Sammelbände der Internationalen Musikgesellschaft* |
| *VfMW* | *Vierteljahrsschrift für Musikwissenschaft* |
| *ZfMW* | *Zeitschrift für Musikwissenschaft* |

# Acknowledgment

I WISH to express my gratitude to Dr. Charles Kent, now dean of the Peabody Conservatory of Music, for his advice, assistance, and encouragement in the several stages of development of this manuscript. I am deeply indebted to my wife, who gave much help in the translation of difficult passages from the German and who accomplished the arduous task of preparing four drafts of this work, including the final manuscript, with the greatest care and precision. I wish also to express my thanks to the following: Dr. Dorothy Seay of Memphis State University for her gracious help in the translation of many Latin passages not translated by Riemann, to my father-in-law, Mr. Ernst-Günther Wentzlaff-Eggebert, for similar assistance, to Mr. Hugh Birmingham of Memphis State University for assistance in problems concerning early mensural notation, and to Dr. Frederic Homan of Texas Lutheran College for his kindness in securing information enabling me to complete documentation.

I am grateful for the use of materials in the Library of Congress as well as for microfilms furnished by them, for microfilms furnished by the New York Public Library, and for the use of resources in the Indiana School of Music Library, the Memphis State University Library, and Love Memorial Library of the University of Nebraska.

Permission has been secured from the publishers, Max Hesses Verlag, Berlin, Germany, for the use of the second original German edition of Riemann's *Geschichte der Musiktheorie* from which this translation was made.

R. H. H.

# Table of Contents

# Introduction

IF WE undertake the history of the origin and development of systematic polyphonic composition following the theoretical expositions of its principles which have come down to us, we must, from the beginning, limit the boundaries of our investigation as far as the earliest periods are concerned. We are therefore not considering the music of classical antiquity. There is still no definite answer to the question of whether or not the Greeks knew polyphony in the same sense that we know it, in spite of the mass of literature from the last two centuries devoted to this problem. Even highly respected historians, such as François-Auguste Gevaert of Brussels, believe the question can be answered in the affirmative. Nevertheless a new examination of this problem is not made here, since according to a majority of the historians who have disputed it, rules of composition are not to be found in the works of any of the antique writers. It is unnecessary to prove that in antiquity as well as today, men and women and young men and girls or boys sang together in octaves, unaware they were singing in different registers. The oft-cited evidence for the existence of a type of polyphony, taken from Plato's *De legibus* VII:812, is actually proof of the contrary viewpoint, for the teacher playing, at the octave, the same melody that his student plays, embellishing it in a virtuoso manner, is the exact opposite of what we understand today as genuine polyphony. Plutarch's report that certain steps of the seven-tone scale were avoided in the melody but performed by the accompanying instrument may, without any difficulty, be understood in a similar sense, namely, that these tones were played in between by the latter, while the voice was either silent or sustaining a tone. In any case, it is quite impossible to reconstruct tangible rules for the simultaneous motion of several voices from such isolated assertions, even if they might be interpreted as indicating a kind of contrapuntal practice. Probably the fifth, as well as the octave and perhaps other intervals, came into conscious employment in the early Christian period; however, as far as clear-cut

xvii

evidence for this kind of usage is concerned, we can look no earlier than the 9th century. With some degree of probability it may be assumed, in accord with the convictions of many historians, that the elements of an intentionally differentiated and melodically independent movement of two or more singing voices (foreign to antique practice) were brought into musical practice by peoples of northern ancestry overflowing southern Europe (dating from the 2nd century before Christ). In his *Descriptio Cambriae*, a witness, Giraldus Cambrensis, from what is, to be sure, a comparatively later time (12th century), important nevertheless because polyphony was then still in its infancy, ascribes a polyphonic practice to the natives of northern Scotland, with voices independent in melody and movement. He even maintains that children were fluent in this practice and employed it as a matter of course; apparently this type of singing was brought to Scotland very early from Scandinavia. We have every reason to believe that this popular polyphony must have been chiefly a singing in thirds and sixths, even though this is still difficult to prove. It is not without reason to assume that the first attempts at a theory of polyphony (the so-called organum) were stimulated by this natural polyphony. It is also hardly circumstantial that historical research is bringing more and more to light the fact that Germanic nations were the first to bring the crude beginnings of natural polyphony to a definite artistic level; England became the actual cradle of a completely developed technique of counterpoint. The third as a basis of polyphony was far removed, even unthinkable, for those who grew up under the influence of the ideas of antique theory; this wholesome kernel of harmonic music could not be found by way of speculation. Rather, those to whom the third was for centuries an established fact in their practice were called upon to bring order and reason to the theory and practice of the musical art, a fact which the heirs of antique culture, in endeavoring to assimilate what was foreign to them, had at first entirely misrepresented. We should not be surprised if our investigations lead to the conclusion that there were several rather sudden developments which can be convincingly explained as being caused by the intervention of peoples of other nations. If the *déchant* of the Romanic peoples is explained as a radical but reactionary transformation of the vague principles of early organum (influenced by the antique teaching that the octave and the fifth were the sole consonances), then fauxbourdon appears as a similarly radical correction effected by the musical instincts of Nordic nations for whom the consonance of the third was a natural fact requiring no scholarly demonstration of its validity. Above all, the final amalgamation of the developed artistic technique of *déchant* (including diminutions) with naturalistic fauxbourdon led to true counterpoint, which in turn was more a theoretical cultivation of fauxbourdon than a further development of *déchant*. Indeed, it was several centuries after this penetration of fauxbourdon with elements of *déchant* before harmony, whose presence is first revealed in fauxbourdon, comes into its full realization. It is further only natural that a definition of the nature of harmony was first formulated not by a Germanic but by a Romanic mind (Zarlino), for the Romanic peoples were still the bearers of culture and the thinkers, whereas the Germanic peoples were only the conveyors of this wholesome material which was available for assimilation. A long time was required to make thinkers χατ ἐξοχὴν of our ancestors. However, they seized upon theory, after allowing it initial entry, with the same tenacity with which they held it off in the beginning, and therewith became the bearers of the last great advance. This advance, which was made manifest by the development in evidence in the history of music theory, was the complete penetration of the nature of harmony and the complete exploitation of its means. We look among the theorists in vain for the individual responsible for this last advance; his name was not Rameau, Tartini, or Hauptmann, but J. S. Bach.

It would certainly be a great mistake if we regarded the theorists of earlier centuries who were responsible for the gradual development of the theory of composition as responsible, at the same time, for the advances. At least this is not the case for the great age in which polyphony or counterpoint reached its culmination. The most important creative masters of the 16th century, and I will name only Palestrina and di Lasso, were not theorists; the greatest theorist of this time, Zarlino, is scarcely known to us today as a composer, though he was highly esteemed as such in his time. The further we go back before 1500, the more the great theorists appear to be the most famous composers; around 1475–1520 we meet with figures like Adam of Fulda, Gafurius, and Tinctoris as masters of almost equal stature with purely practicing composers like Dufay, Heinrich Isaac, Heinrich Finck, Paul Hofhaimer, Josquin des Pres, and many others. Even earlier, figures like Philippe de Vitry, Franco of Cologne, and Johannes de Garlandia are simultaneously representatives of the productive ability of their time. We finally come to a period in which creative efforts in polyphonic music are still of such a primitive nature that theory appears to be the actual agent of progress. We will assume, for the period of Guido of Arezzo, and earlier of Hucbald of St. Amand, that theorists searched for formulations for a type of polyphony which was practiced in a purely natural and empirical manner, perhaps even more advanced in inner logic than the products of an ever-watchful theory. This may have been the case especially with secular music, which was deliberately suppressed by theorists in holy orders. Unfortunately for us, only theory with its dry pedagogical examples exists from that early time. However, we can conclude from the exquisite musical quality of extant Troubador and Minnesinger melodies that very likely even the uncultivated secular polyphony of this time must have been of greater distinction than the theoretical examples. Of course we cannot prove this. Shall we then, as a result, first discover how theorists through the centuries tried to reduce a type of polyphony, which may have corresponded to our present-day folk polyphony, to fixed rules and often went astray in doing so? Since we are not examining the history of music but that of music theory, the most extreme deviations from the right paths, which were in the greatest contradiction to practice, provide material of great interest for our scrutiny and strengthen the gratifying impressions we receive from the knowledge which is gradually dissipating the obscurity of the past, until we shall come to the time when extant monuments of the best musical art will put us in a position to examine further the works of the theorists in order to evaluate them with even greater certainty.

As medieval theory does not appear to us today to be an infallible revelation of the spirit of those early church melodies, some of which were created even centuries earlier, so is it equally difficult to believe without reservation that musical practice after the rise of polyphony corresponded very closely to a theory which was at first so very clumsy, and which struggled so much with its terminology. But it is exactly this observation of the attempts to force into conceptual forms what natural musical instinct had created which is the real object of our investigation. Because of the lack of any reliable tradition, what goes beyond this can only be hypothesis.

# BOOK I

## ORGANUM — DISCANT — FAUXBOURDON

## CHAPTER I

# The Ecclesiastical Modal System

ALTHOUGH the particular object of our inquiry is the historical evolution of the principles of polyphonic composition, we must nevertheless preface this study with a brief consideration of the system of eight ecclesiastical modes which determined the melodic material of the first attempts at polyphony. Without this knowledge an understanding of the theories of Hucbald and Guido, among others, is hardly possible. The historical origin of the ecclesiastical modes is undoubtedly to be found in the old Greek scales; in what way the simple diatonic system, known since the 8th century in Western civilization, grew out of the highly developed chromatic-enharmonic one of the Greeks is difficult to demonstrate and lies beyond the boundaries of the present investigation.*1 Many medieval theorists continued to rely upon the Latin representation of the antique tonal system from Boethius, whose influence began to wane only in the 10th century. It is essential, therefore, to show the two-octave *Systema teleion metabolon* (Greater Perfect System) of Greek theory which, according to his synthesis, is composed of similarly constructed tetrachords.*2 Not even Hucbald was able to escape from the idea that each series of four degrees is a strict unity, and even the hexachord of Guido of Arezzo can be regarded as the interlocking of the three possible species of the tetrachord contained within the limits of a perfect fourth:*3

$$c \quad d \quad e\tfrac{1}{2}f \quad g \quad a$$

III  
   II  
      I

Of these three, the Greeks regarded the first (e f g a) as the standard and constructed their basic system of two octaves by placing several of this species of tetrachord side by side in either disjunct relationship (distance of a whole-tone between tetrachords—*diazeuxis*) or conjunct relationship (tetrachords sharing a common connecting tone—*synaphe*). This system was completed by the addition of a tone two octaves below the highest tone; the system which was so limited or bounded, the *systema teleion ametabolon* (incapable of modulation) was made capable of modulation (*metabolon*) through the interpolation of still another tetrachord of the same species placed in the middle of the system (*tetrachordum synemmenon*):

*Systema teleion metabolon*

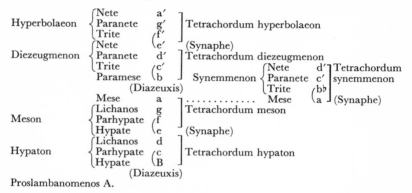

With this system (and without the use of the *tetrachordum synemmenon*) the Greeks demonstrated the various possible octave species,*[4] that is to say, melodic ranges the distance of an octave, whose individual patterns differed according to the various locations of the semitones, namely:

*Octave Species*

1. B c d ef g a b       = Semitones 1 2 and 4 5. Mixolydian
2. c d ef g a b c′      = Semitones 3 4 and 7 8. Lydian
3. d ef g a b c′ d′     = Semitones 2 3 and 6 7. Phrygian
4. ef g a b c′ d′ e′     = Semitones 1 2 and 5 6. Dorian (Hypomixolydian)
5. f g a b c′ d′ e′f′   = Semitones 4 5 and 7 8. Hypolydian
6. g a b c′ d′ e′f′ g′ = Semitones 3 4 and 6 7. Hypophrygian (Ionian)
7. a b c′ d′ e′f′ g′ a′ = Semitones 2 3 and 5 6. Hypodorian (Aeolian)

These same seven octave species were also formed by the Greeks by retuning individually the tones of the middle octave e—e′; they regarded these various tunings of the middle octave as sections from the customary transpositions of the complete *systema ametabolon*. According to the only correct way of reading Greek notation,[1] which regards the Dorian tuning

---

[1] First accounted for in my study *Notenschrift und Notendruck* (Leipzig, 1896), pp. 2–5. The circumstance that the core of the Greek vocal notation extended from f′ to e out of the intact alphabet was interpreted by Bellermann and Fortlage in such a way that

as the basic scale (without chromatic alterations), these seven transpositions correspond to our minor scales up to five sharps (G♯ minor) along with the scale corresponding to D minor at the very beginning of the *systema teleion metabolon*, which, through the *tetrachordum synemmenon* (with b♭), makes available modulation to a subdominant key:*5

*Transposition Scales:*

```
 ┌d″
 │c″
 │b♭′                                    ┌b′ ················         ┌c♯″
 └a′       ┌a′ ················          │a′ ················         │b′
 ┌g′       │g′ ················          │g′ ················         │a′                    ┌g♯′
 │f′       │f′ ················          └f♯′        ┌f♯′ ······      │g♯′        ┌f♯′ ······ │f♯′
 └e′ ┐     └e′ ┐       ┌e′ ┐       ┌e′ ┐       ┌e′ ┐       ┌e′ ┐     └d♯′        ┌e′ ┐
 ══  │     ┌d′ │       │d′ │       │d′ │       │d′ │       │d′ │                 │d♯′
 ┌d′ │     │c′ │       │c′ │       └c♯′│       └c♯′│    ══             ┌c♯′       │c♯′
 │c′ │     └b  │   ══  │   ══  │   ┌b  │   ┌b  │     ┌c♯′│             │b
 │b♭ │ 1.  ══  │ 4.┌a  │ 7.┌b  │ 3.│a  │ 6.│b  │ 2. │b  │ 5. ┌a♯
 └a  │     ┌a  │   │g  │   │a  │   └g♯ │   └g♯ │     │a  │     ══
 ┌g  │     │g  │   └f♯ │   │g  │    ══            │g♯ │     ┌g♯
 │f  │     │f  │    ══   │   └f♯ │    ┌f♯′│       │f♯ │     │f♯
 └e  ┘     └e  ┘    ┌e  ┘   ┌e  ┘   │e  ┘   ┌e  ┘     │e  ┘     │e  ┘
 ══       ┌d       │d       │d       │d       │d       └d♯       ┌d♯
  d        │c       │c       │c       └c♯      │c       ══        │c♯
           └B       └B       └c       ┌B       └c♯                └B
```

(Note: this diagram shows seven transposition scale ranges labeled 1., 4., 7., 3., 6., 2., 5.)

```
   M     ══        A      B      A      c♯     B
   i      A        G            └G♯     L     └A♯
   x               └F♯     P    ══      y     ══
   o      D      ══        h     F♯     d      G♯
   l      o        E       r     ══     i
   y      r      ══        y     H      a      H
   d      i        H       g     y      n      y
   i      a        y       i     p             p
   a      n        p       a     o             o
   n               o       n     p             l
                   d             h             y
                   o             r             d
                   r             y             i
                   i             g             a
                   a             i             n
                   n             a
                                 n
```

The seven transposition scales shown above were the only ones recognized by Ptolemy (II. ι′, although they had been increased by other theorists to scales containing as many as six sharps and six flats).*6 They played an important role in medieval theory due to the arrangement of them conveyed to the Middle Ages by Boethius (*de Musica* IV. 15). This arrangement became the cause of a grave error as far as the indications

---

f′–f would be the basic scale (with the extension of the semitone from f–e below). With that the Dorian would be a scale with five flats or seven sharps (B minor or A♯ minor). My interpretation, which views the middle section as e′–e with the extension of the semitone f′–e′, also regards this as the basic scale (A minor).

concerning the pitch locations were concerned (compare the lowest tones, the *proslambanomenoi*):

| | | |
|---|---|---|
| (e | Hypermixolydian) | *7 |
| | | 1 |
| d | Mixolydian | |
| | | N.B.½ |
| c♯ | Lydian | |
| | | 1 |
| B | Phrygian | |
| | | 1 |
| A | Dorian | |
| | | ½ |
| G♯ | Hypolydian | |
| | | 1 |
| F♯ | Hypophrygian | |
| | | 1 |
| E | Hypodorian | |

These were mistakenly related to the octave species (cf. page 4), whose pitch locations had within the system almost exactly the opposite order:

| | |
|---|---|
| Hypophrygian | g–g′ |
| Hypolydian | f–f′ |
| Dorian | e–e′ |
| Phrygian | d–d′ |
| Lydian | c–c′ |
| Mixolydian | B–b |
| Hypodorian | A–a |

Unfortunately someone (the author of the *Alia musica*, who is identified in Gerbert, *Scriptores* I:125 as Hucbald and who probably belongs in his period), misinterpreting Ptolemy or more likely Boethius, conceived the idea of calling the ecclesiastical modes then in use by the names of the antique scales, an idea which unluckily found general acceptance.*8 Thus it came about that the scale names of antiquity again came into circulation, but with completely changed meanings, and they continued to be known by their new appellations:

| | | | | |
|---|---|---|---|---|
| | IV. Mixolydian | g–g′ | | |
| | | N.B.1 | | |
| Authentic | III. Lydian | f–f′ | | |
| Modes | | ½ | | |
| | II. Phrygian | e–e′ | | |
| | | 1 | | |
| | I. Dorian (=Hypomixolydian) | d–d′ | IV | |
| | | 1 | | |
| | Hypolydian | c–c′ | III | Plagal |
| | | ½ | | Modes |
| | Hypophrygian | B–b | II | |
| | | 1 | | |
| | Hypodorian | A–a | I | |

Although not even the arrangement of the whole-tones and semitones of the ecclesiastical scales corresponded with those of the Greek transposition scales (compare the two systems given in the examples), it was thought that in these scales of the ecclesiastical chant the old Greek ones had been rediscovered.*⁹

The first mention of the ecclesiastical scales (without the above names, however) is found in Western sources in a treatise of an 8th century author, Flaccus Alcuin (Gerbert, *Scriptores* 1:26); he does not define their construction (relative to the location of the semitones) but does enumerate them as Protus, Deuterus, Tritus, and Tetrachius (for Tetrardus!), with reference to the Greeks, and differentiates between their principal forms as *authentici* and their secondary forms as *plagii* (*obliqui*, also *laterales*). The latter name is supposed to indicate that the mode "includes a part which lies lower than the authentic but does not differ from it, rather being the same in a lower position."² The 9th-century writer Aurelianus Reomensis (Gerbert, *op. cit.*, 1:28 ff.) discusses the ecclesiastical modes in greater detail by at first copying Flaccus Alcuin almost word for word and then quoting numerous examples from the liturgy for each individual mode; unfortunately, there are neither notated examples nor any mention of scalar construction.*¹⁰ These are first to be found in the already mentioned *Alia musica*, to whose contents I should like to attribute an early origin as a consequence of G. Jacobsthal's study, *Die chromatische Alteration im liturgischen Gesange der abendländischen Kirche*, 1897, p. 3.

The unfortunately anonymous author of this *Alia musica*, who was made immortal by his new but improper application of the Greek scale names, was apparently a contemporary of Hucbald, for he sets himself in unmistakable opposition to Hucbald's principles, which we shall presently discuss.³ He establishes the pitch level of each individual tone with the Greek *systema teleion* as a basis and defines the relationship of the plagal to the authentic modes as that of the lower fourth.⁴ However, he makes use

---

² "This name (*plagii*) is said to mean the lower part of these (Protus, Deuterus, Tritus, and 'Tetrachius') because they (the *plagii*) are four in number. They do not completely withdraw from the former (Protus, Deuterus, etc.) and are lower because their sound is more depressed than that of the higher ones."

³ Gerbert 1:127: "Either by separation or by conjunction of the tetrachords, the same kind (of interval) returns every fourth or every fifth degree, yet the diapente does not always follow itself in the same order." This certainly refers to Hucbald's artificial succession of consecutive fifths (cf. Chapter II). On the contrary, Hucbald's method of singing out the names which designated the functions of the tones in the tetrachord (Gerbert I:154) seemed to the author to be useful (Gerbert I:133): "This is also of great benefit to the tones (*soni*) which they called Protus, Deuterus, and the rest."

⁴ Gerbert, p. 127a: "The first and lowest mode of all is known as the Hypodorian from the first species of diapason and ends on that middle tone (*media nervo*) which is called *mese*." (127b): "Therefore, this first species (of diapason) uses a semitone in the third and sixth place." This is also said for the other modes.

of what is to a certain extent misleading terminology when he says, for example, that the *proslambanomenos* of the Dorian scale is the *lichanos meson* of the Hypodorian, and the *mese* of the Dorian is the *paranete diezeugmenon* of the Hypodorian, this also applying to the other scales, while he designates the steps of the plagal scales according to the *systema teleion* A–a' (for example e as *hypate meson* of the Hypophrygian).*[11] For the boundary tones of the authentic octave-scales, however, he employs the names *proslambanomenos* and *mese* as terms, so that all four finals d e f g appear as *proslambanomenoi* and their octaves as *mesai*. In this work there still appears to be a striving towards new means of expression, which compels one to regard the treatise as quite old. As the author knows no other means of establishing the absolute pitch level other than by using the Greek tone names and the letters of the Boethian monochord, he is, without doubt, from the period of Hucbald (around 900). That he refers to the eight ecclesiastical modes as either *tropi* or *modi*, and not as *toni*—as can already be found in Aurelianus Reomensis and in Hucbald's *Institutio harmonica*—is probably an insufficient basis for estimating his age as even older than that of Hucbald,[5] since the *Scholia* of the *Musica enchiriadis* stresses that *tropi* or *modi* are also wrongly called *toni*.*[12] The writer of the *Alia musica* calls the first plagal mode the second (as Hucbald has done in the *Institutio harmonica*) (Gerbert, *Script.* 1:19) and the second plagal mode the fourth, continuing this from I to VIII.

The plagal modal scales without question had the same final tone, the so-called *finalis*, as the authentic scales with which they were paired from the beginning. Even if Flaccus Alcuin does not say this directly, it is nevertheless clearly implied in the passage cited above, which states that the plagal scales can never really be separated from the authentic (*non recedunt*). Nor does Aurelianus express himself any more clearly; he demonstrates much more than Alcuin, however, by citing plainsong examples with which he supposes the reader is familiar. That there are only four finals is first definitely expressed by Hucbald,[6] who also states that each one governs a pair of the ecclesiastical modes, namely, an authentic mode (*authentus*) and its plagal counterpart (*plagis, subjugalis, lateralis*):

I. Authentus protus

A B c d e f g a b c'd'   (Finalis d)

II. Plagis proti

---

[5] Hucbald says (Gerbert I: 119): "There are four *modi* or *tropi* which they now call *tonos*."

[6] (Gerbert I:119): "And each one of these four tones (*lichanos hypaton, hypate meson, parhypate meson, lichanos meson*) governs a trope like itself but inferior to it, for which reason these same tones are called finals, because all that which is sung, finds a conclusion in them."

III. Authentus deuterus

B c d e f g a b c′ d′ e′  (Finalis e)

IV. Plagis deuteri

V. Authentus tritus

c d e f g a b c′ d′ e′ f′  (Finalis f)

VI. Plagis triti

VII. Authentus tetrardus

d e f g a b c′ d′ e′ f′ g′  (Finalis g)

VIII. Plagis tetrardi

The oldest detailed consideration of the ecclesiastical modes is, however, probably the *Alia musica*, to which the fragment found in Gerbert I:124b–125b (directly before the inscription *Alia musica*) belongs.[7] If one agrees with Gerbert that the end of this fragment is a commentary on the missing beginning, then the whole seems to take on a certain unity. Unfortunately, the text is very corrupt, although it is apparent that the author established the extent of the individual modes according to the tetrachords of the *systema teleion* of the Greeks. The differences are enumerated in detail under the name *distinctiones*, as they were in the later sections of the *Alia musica*, except that in the latter (Gerbert I:130 f.), as today, they are called *differentiae* and are further subdivided into *loca*. Present terminology defines *differentiae* as the several different possible closing formations of the Psalm tones and the final *saeculorum amen* (*evovae*) in the individual modes. A detailed examination of this antiquated representation of the modal system, with its awkward terminology still firmly based on the *Systema teleion* for single tones as well as for intervals, is made more difficult because of the many mistakes in the text. A complete emendation can scarcely be hoped for, since only one manuscript copy exists (the Cod. lat. 14 272 of the Munich *Hof- und Staatsbibliothek*), but a critical examination of this codex would be of special interest for the study of the history of ecclesiastical modal theory. The burdensome playing with numbers, as for example the indication of the interval of the fifth as V because the sum of the numbers of the ratio 3/2 is V, as well as the indication of VII ($=4/3$) for the fourth, or even $XXI = 12/9$ ($4/3$) and $XX = 12/8$ for the fifth ($3/2$), etc., are not so insurmountable that one should shy away from this treatise (or this collection of treatises) for that reason. I must, however, forego such an attempt, particularly because the investigation would

---

[7] Compare also Anonymous II in Gerbert's *Scriptores* I:338 ff., and especially p. 341b, which is, at least, helpful in deciphering the *Alia musica*. It probably also belongs to approximately the same period.

hold us up too long, and leave the completion of such a task to some future
doctoral dissertation.[8] The exposition of the old system of the ecclesiastical
modes to the extent which I have given it is, for our purposes, completely
sufficient. A further pursuit of the antecedents of the modal system, which
would necessarily lead to the *Troparion* of the Byzantine church, must also
be dismissed at this time.*[13] For the further development of ecclesiastical
modal theory enough material will present itself in the course of our study.

[8] Such a work has, in the meantime, appeared: W. Mühlmann's *Die Alia musica*
(Leipzig, 1914). During the period of transition to the time when neumes were notated
on lines, a method of notating formulas of the eight ecclesiastical modes for memorization
appears, making use of colored lines (for Protus and its plagal, red; for Deuterus and its
plagal, green; for the two Tritus modes, yellow; and for the two Tetrardus modes,
purple). This is first found in the *Quaestiones in musica* (Ms. Darmstadt 1988 and Brussels,
Kgl. Bibl. 10162–10166). See the dissertation of Rudolf Steglich, *Die Quaestiones in musica
und ihr mutmasslicher Verfasser Rudolph von St. Trond* (1070–1138) (Leipzig; Breitkopf und
Härtel, 1911) (I F, II D, III G, IV E, V a, VI F, VII ♭, VIII g).

### APPENDIX

FOOTNOTE 2: "Quod nomen significare dicitur pars sive inferiores eorum: quia videlicet quatuor quaedam partes sunt eorum, dum ab eis ex toto non recedunt, et inferiores,
quia sonus eorum pressior est, quam superiorum."

FOOTNOTE 3: Gerbert I:127: "Semperque sive per disjunctum, sive per conjunctum
tetrachordum quartis locis eadem species redit [aut] quintis locis; non tamen semper
diapente sibi invicem succedit." ...Gerbert I:133: "Ad id quoque multum soni prosunt,
quos dicunt protum deuterum et reliqua."

FOOTNOTE 4: Gerbert, p. 127a: "Erit ergo (igitur) primus modus omnium gravissimus
hypodorius ex prima specie diapason et terminatur eo, qui meses dicitur, medio nervo."
(127b): "Prima itaque species [diapason] tertio et sexto loco utitur semitonio."

FOOTNOTE 5: Hucbald says (Gerbert I:119): "Quatuor modis vel tropis, quos nunc
tonos dicunt."

FOOTNOTE 6: Gerbert I:119: "Ita ut singulae earum quatuor chordarum (lichanos
hypaton, hypate meson, parhypate meson, lichanos meson) geminos sibi tropos regant
subjectos...unde et eaedem finales appellatae, quod finem in ipsis cuncta, quae canun-
tur, accipiant."

CHAPTER II

# The Theory of Organum in the 9th and 10th Centuries

As THE result of a casual observation made by Martin Gerbert in the preface to the first volume of his *Scriptores* (fol. c 2 r), the opinion has been promulgated that Hucbald not only was the first writer to deal with the crude beginnings of polyphony, but also that he himself first introduced organum as a purely theoretical concept. Disregarding at first the fact that Hucbald's authorship of the treatise containing the most detailed report about organum is disputed on what seems to be weighty evidence, the earliest accounts of this primitive type of polyphony extend back even farther than the period of Hucbald—the monk of the cloister of Saint Amand sur l'Elnon in Flanders (Monachus Elnonensis).[*1]

A report of Ademar of Chavannes,[1] the monk of Angoulême[2] (Ademar died in 1034 and was therefore younger than Hucbald), who tells in his chronicle that "Roman singers gave Frankish singers instruction in *Ars organandi*," I should like to interpret as dealing with instruction in the playing of the organ. Other evidence of such early activity in polyphonic music by the Romans is completely lacking. Nevertheless it appears that in the 9th century[3] the art of organ playing was more advanced in Germany than in Italy. I cannot agree with Hans Müller[4] that organum, like the organ from which organum probably got its name, was of Greek origin and had its beginnings in antique heterophony, an effect which at times occurred as the result of instruments deviating from the vocal line which they were accompanying.[*2]

The testimonial of the philosopher Scotus Erigena (about the middle of the 9th century) cannot, on the contrary, be misinterpreted. In his treatise *De divisione naturae* he gives a competent, though brief, description

[1] *Monumenta Germaniae* IV:118: "Similiter eruderunt Romani cantores supradicti cantores Francorum in arte organandi."

[2] Duchesne, *Hist. Franc. script.* II:75.

[3] Letter of Pope John VIII (872–880) to Bishop Arno of Freysing (Baluze, *Miscell.* V:480).

[4] *Hucbald's echte und unechte Schriften über Musik* (Leipzig, 1884), p. 78.

11

of organum which, through the more detailed writings of later authors yet to be discussed, is not only clearly understandable but has been proved to be entirely correct. He says: [5]

> The singing called organum consists of voices of different kinds and ranges which are soon separated from one another at wider intervals sounding in well-measured ratio. Soon these come together according to certain rational rules of art which, in conformity with one or the other of the modes, yields a natural and agreeable concord of sound.*[3]

The definition of Regino of Prüm (died 915) is of less consequence: [6]

> Concentus (monophonic song? unison?) is the uniform fusion of the same melodies; succentus (polyphonic voice? accompanying voice?), on the other hand, is the best possible combination of different tones, which one can see in organum.

The third witness is Hucbald in the treatise *De harmonica institutione* which is generally attributed to him: [7]

> Consonance is the rational and harmonious combination of two tones which happens only when two voices from different sources form a concord of sounds, as, for example, when a boy's voice and a man's voice sing the same thing, or as in the so-called organum.

A complete theory of organum is generally assumed to occur first in a 10th-century treatise, *De organo*, which is found in a number of manuscripts, the oldest of which (10th century) is in the possession of the Cathedral Chapter Library at Cologne. Hans Müller regards this work as an earlier source which the author of the chief work on organum, the *Musica enchiriadis*, was able to use. Müller's argumentation against the authorship of Hucbald is, incidentally, not so convincing in spite of his comprehensive comparison of the manuscripts. It must not be regarded as impossible that Hucbald, who was born in 840, ordained as priest in 880 and who died in 930 or 932 in his nineties, could not have written the *Harmonica institutione* around 880, and in his advanced years the *Musica enchiriadis* in 920. If one accepts this latter thesis, however, then every

---

[5] "Organicum melos ex diversis qualitatibus et quantitatibus conficitur dum viritim separatimque sentiuntur voces longe a se discrepantibus intensionis et remissionis proportionibus segregatae dum vero sibi invicem coaptantur secundum certas rationabilesque artis musicae regulas per singulos tropos naturalem quandam dulcedinem reddentibus."

[6] Gerbert, *Script.* I:234: "Concentus est similium vocum adunata societas; succentus vero est: varii soni sibi maxime convenientes sicut videmus in organo." *Concentus*, according to official liturgical terminology, means chanting in unison, in contrast to the *accentus* which indicates a recitation tone chanted by an individual priest.

[7] Gerbert, *Script.* I:107: "Consonantia siquidem est duorum sonorum rata et concordabilis permixtio, quae non aliter constabit, nisi duo altrinsecus editi soni in unam simul modulationem conveniant, ut fit, cum virilis ac puerilis vox pariter sonuerit; vel etiam in eo, quod consuete organizationem vocant."

reason to regard the treatise *De organo* as being considerably older than the *Musica enchiriadis* is invalidated. The many similarities of terminology mark the three treatises as belonging to a closely related group too strongly to allow their origins to be unhesitatingly separated over the period of a century or more. The Cologne treatise *De organo* reads as follows:[8]

Diaphony or organum is, as is known, based on the consonance of the fourth, only if the two voices moving at this interval blend harmoniously. In this connection it follows that:

According to the *first rule*, the voices must, tone by tone, continue at the distance of a fourth; but further,

According to the *second rule*, at the end of most melodic sections the two voices separated from each other must come together on the same note, namely, where the end of a section occurs on the final of a mode or on one of its two neighboring tones the step above or below. In order that the voices may come together in a suitable fashion in this manner in the closes, it is necessary,

According to the *third rule*, that whenever the chief voice (at one of these sections) descends to a final or one of the aforenamed neighbor tones, the accompanying or organal voice can not descend lower than that tone which is a step below the final. Therefore, it often happens that this third rule makes it impossible to follow the first one, and thus continuation of the organum at the interval of a fourth is not always attainable.*[4]

It is further to be remarked that, according to its position, one differentiates between middle, high, and low organum. The middle moves to the final itself, the high to the fifth above, the low to the lower fourth. All three types are of equal significance. It may also happen that one must, in certain melodic sections,

---

[8] "Diaphoniam seu organum constat(!) ex diatessaron symphonia naturaliter derivari. Diatessaron autem est per quartanas regiones suavis vocum commixtio. Ergo ex hac conlatione una quidem principali lege producitur, ut in quartanis locis vox voci resultet, altera autem ut in plerisque particulis ad finem sese voces diversae conjungant, videlicet ubi colon (MS. cola) in finali rectore consistit vel in lateralibus ejus id est in subsecundo ipsius aut in supersecundo. Verum ut in finalitatibus vox ad vocem apte convenire possit, tertia quoque lex accedit quatinus ubi colon vel commatis positio ad finalem usque rectorem descendit seu in alium ex praedictis lateralibus suis, organum inferius descendere non possit quam in illum usque sonum, qui finali rectori fuerit subsecundus. Unde fit ut plerumque haec lex tertia primae legi obviet et hoc obstante limite organum non semper quartanas regiones obtineat. Praeterea organum tres sibi sedes constituit ut sit organum medium, organum superius, organum inferius. Medium vocatur organum, quod moratur circa finalem rectorem; organum superius quod circa socialem ejus superiorem, organum inferius, quod circa socialem ejus inferiorem. Constant singula autem organa eodem legum jure. Est interdum ubi deficientibus naturalibus spaciis tertiana et secundana etiam conlatione per quaedam membra abusivum organum ponimus. Poscit autem semper organum diligenti et modesta morositate fieri et honestissime sacris canticis adhibetur." (According to Eccles. metropolit. Coloniensis Codd. Mss., Jaffé & Wattenbach, 1874, Appendix VII, 109, contained in Hans Müller's *Hucbald's echte und unechte Schriften über Musik* [1884], p. 79.)

set the organum in thirds and seconds because the distance of a fourth is not at one's disposal. This is, then, an irregular organum.

Organum always requires a careful and deliberate tempo, and is justly employed for sacred singing.

Here the elements of organum are clearly and concisely explained, as are those which are developed in later, more detailed expositions (to be considered presently), at least as far as two-voiced organum is concerned —the only type of which the older sources speak. Hucbald already emphasizes the identity of octave tones in the *Harmonica institutio* (when men and boys sing the same note), so three- and four-voiced organum results, as we shall see, only from augmenting the number of voices in two-voiced organum by octave doubling.

Since Scotus Erigena already speaks of the coming together of other-wise separated voices at the close, we must give this definition special consideration. Regino and Hucbald (in the *Harmonica institutio*) at least do not contradict the possibility of such voice-leading in their much too brief descriptions. It must, then, be understood that in no way is strict parallel movement of the voices in fourths or fifths characteristic of organum, but rather the distinguishing quality is an alternation of move-ments going apart and coming together to a unison.*5 We shall find confirmation of this in all further accounts of the theorists.[9]

Nevertheless, organum remains for us today an unusual phenomenon, since the fourth is indicated as the chief interval involved in the moving apart and parallel motion of the voices.*6

The treatise *De organo* differentiates *organum medium*, which moves around the final, from *organum superius*, which moves around the fifth above and *organum inferius* which moves around the lower fourth, for the upper "associate" of the final is undoubtedly the octave above the lower "associate"—both are the outer or delimiting tones of the plagal form of the mode. Since we find the four authentic modes with their plagal forms discussed earlier in the 8th century by Flaccus Alcuin (Gerbert, *Script.* I:26), we can probably assume that for the first mode on d, the upper associate a was probably at that time already established in musical

[9] The two-part vocal composition published in photographic facsimile by the Plain-song and Medieval Society in 1890, presumably written in the 10th century in Cornwallis in a two-octave letter notation (a–p), is well suited to serve as a verification of the results of our inquiry to the effect that the nature of organum corresponds with practice. I do not wish to regard this piece as a specimen of polyphonic folk singing but rather as a specimen of organum (probably making some use of a folk melody) as English monks were wont to practice it in the 10th century in imitation of folk song. The relationship of the principal melody (in the upper voice) to that of *Sumer is icumen in*, as well as the similarity in tonality (F major) and voice movement of the two pieces, is striking. Cf. Oskar Fleischer's felicitous discussion of this piece in *VfMW* (1890).

practice, although we find the division of the scale into a fifth and a fourth:

authentic:   d – a – d'

plagal:       A – d – a

first by the author of the treatise *Alia musica* (printed under Hucbald's name by Gerbert in *Script.* I : 125) in a form somewhat confused by number mysticism, and then presented systematically and clearly by Pseudo-Bernelinus, around the year 1000. Since, for example, d is the final of the plagal Protus, it is at least firmly established that the division of the plagal mode is accomplished through the interval of the fourth. The close relationship of the plagal modes to the authentic modes gives prominence to the outer tones of the former, so that no other tones but these may be understood as the *socialis* of the final, either above or below.

One is at first tempted to regard *organum superius* and *organum inferius* as organum at the upper fifth and organum at the lower fourth, which leaves the meaning of *organum medium* a mystery. The term organum in the treatise, however, does not refer to the organal voice in this case but rather the composition which results from the combination of two voices whose closing sections may find their conclusions in one of three places. This distinction has nothing to do with the differentiation to be discussed later between *organum sub voce* and *organum supra vocem*. A passage in Hucbald's *Institutio harmonica* shows that the *socialis* is really intended to be the fifth above or the fourth below. This treatise is possibly from the same period as the treatise *De organo*, or in all probability even older. It reads, after the establishment of the four finals d e f g (Gerbert I : 119) : [10]

After the model or pattern set by this tetrachord composed of four finals (d e͡ f g) are arranged the intervals and the relationships of the tones of the four remaining tetrachords (one which is found under this one, and three above). If one does not consider the tetrachord *synemmenon* (a͡ b♭ c' d'), the fifths found above the four finals stand in such close relationship with them that many chants

[10] "Ad quarum exemplar (sc. quatuor finalium vocum) caetera nihilominus tetrachorda, quorum unum inferius, tria superius eminent, spatia, vel qualitatem deducunt sonorum. Illud nihil (?) attendendum, quod synemmenon tetrachordo summoto, quinta semper loca his quatuor superiora quadam sibi connexionis unione junguntur, adeo, ut pleraque etiam in eis quasi regulariter mela inveniantur desinere, nec rationi ob hoc vel sensui quid contraire et sub eodem modo vel tropo recte decurrere. Hac ergo socialitate continentur lichanos hypaton cum mese; hypate meson cum paramese; parypate meson cum trite diezeugmenon (lichanos meson cum paranete diezeugmenon) (quae quinto scilicet loco singulae a se separantur [Gerbert: disparantur]). [The phrases enclosed in parentheses are reversed in Gerbert.] Cum inferioribus quoque quartis (et in quibusdam quintis) parem quodammodo obtinent habitudinem quamvis non fini sed initiis deputentur."

regularly close on them [the fifths above] without reason or instinct taking offense, because these upper fifths appear to be following in the same mode or trope (transposed). Such a close relationship (*socialitas*) unites a with d, b♮ with e, c′ with f, and d′ with g. The finals stand in this relationship to their fourths below (and partly to the fifths below), not for the closes, however, but only for the beginnings of chants.

This passage is also of special interest because it provides strong evidence for Hucbald's authorship of the *Musica enchiriadis* in its maintenance of a similar succession of whole- and half-steps in the four remaining tetra-chords, namely:

G A̅ B♭ c, ... a b̅♮ c′ d′, e′ f̅♯′ g′ a′, b′ c̅♯″ d″ e″

(or instead, A B̅ c d, ... a b̅ c′ d′, d′ e̅′ f′ g′, a′ b̅′ c″ d″?)

This will be further discussed later.

This demonstration of the *socialitas* of the fifth above and the fourth below with the finals provides sufficient reason to believe that these are the tones which are meant by the *sociales superiores* and *inferiores* of the *Cologne* treatise.

The, to us, somewhat enigmatic preference for the fourth as the major consonance of organum probably had its basis in imitation of Greek theory—not in the sense of organum finding its roots in Greek musical practice, but rather in the fact that Hucbald and his contemporaries, still under the spell of Boethius and his teachings, were accustomed to give special importance to the tetrachords. If what Gerald de Barri (Giraldus Cambrensis) [11] reports is true—that polyphonic singing had been popular since primitive times—then this naturally developed polyphony would

[11] *Descriptio Cambriae* I. VI:189 (Rerum Britannicarum medii aevi Scriptores I: XXXVI.): "Concerning symphonies, how they are rendered and the organization of their rendering. In their singing of music they do not sing their songs in unison as else-where, but in many different parts, so that you hear as many songs as there are heads in the group of singers (as is customary in this nation), finally uniting with harmony in one consonance under the soft sweetness of B-flat.

"Indeed, in the northern parts of Greater Britain, beyond the Humber around York-shire, the people who live there use the same kind of symphonious harmonies in their singing but in only two different parts, one murmuring below and the other soothing and delighting the ear above. Yet it is not by art that each nation has acquired this skill, but by long custom, so that this practice has become natural and familiar. This way of singing has become so deeply rooted that nothing here is sung in unison but in parts. In Wales they sing at least in two parts, and in the North in (several) parts; and what is more wonderful, children and even infants when they first turn from crying to song observe the same practice. The English as a whole do not use this method of singing, but only those of the North, I believe, because they derived it from the Danes and Norwegians, who often occupied their lands and held them rather long, just as they caught likenesses in speech."

scarcely correspond to the organum which Hucbald (assuming him to be author of the treatises *De organo* and *Musica enchiriadis*) reduced to rules, but would probably show a preference for the intervals of the sixth and third over those of the fourth and fifth. It is very understandable, however, that a theorist who is endeavoring to prove that such natural singing in parts is based upon rules, and who is steeped in the traditional definitions of consonance, cannot very well represent intervals other than the octave, the fifth, and the fourth as structural supports of part-movement which uses other intervals as well. That he is thinking mainly of the fourth leads one to the conclusion that in such natural singing, the third—which neighbors on the fourth—was given the main role.*[7] Already the Cologne treatise *De organo* raises thirds to the status of permissible intervals, although together with seconds.

If we now turn to detailed investigations of the *Musica enchiriadis* and its *Scholia*, we must first point out that the *Musica enchiriadis* in its teachings goes further in some points than the treatise *De organo*, but not to the extent that both could not be by the same author.

Some manuscripts of the *Musica enchiriadis* (those in Paris, Florence, and Bruges) contain in place of Chapters XIII to XVIII found in the other manuscripts (corresponding to those printed in Gerbert, *Script.* I) the treatise *De organo*,[12] which we shall call the Paris treatise in order to distinguish it from the Cologne treatise of Hans Müller. This Paris treatise *De organo* is unmistakably closer to the Cologne than to those chapters of the *Musica enchiriadis* already indicated. This is especially true in the sense that the Paris treatise again mentions the rule[13] which the Cologne treatise sets up for the deviation of organum from the interval of the fourth and for coming to rest on a unison, namely, the third rule, which states that the organal voice must never go lower than a step below the final. Among other things the Paris treatise contains one sentence which is difficult to interpret and which does not appear elsewhere with similar wording.[14] One could interpret this sentence to mean that the octave is preferred to the fifth and fourth, since it is consonant as one sound (*in unum*) as well as in sequence (*consequenter*), while the same effect would be produced by the fifth only in sequence and by the fourth only as one

---

[12] Printed in Coussemaker, *Script.* II:74 ff.

[13] "The rule by which fourths are combined has its own limits, for it pertains to the tone which in any mode is a second below the final (immediately following the final tone of the mode). For on this sound the organum remains, nor is it allowed to go lower. From this sound the other part at the beginning ascends and returns to it in the end, since it is forbidden that the organum go lower."

[14] Symphonia diapason sicut major ceteris ita prae ceteris obtinet (principatum), ut et in unum et (Couss. sed) consequenter dicendo consonantiam faciat; diapente non in unum sed consequenter, diatessaron non consequenter sed in unum."

sound. Such an interpretation, however, is not possible in view of all the definitions of consonance which stem from the same time or earlier. These always place the fifth between the octave and the fourth, all three being consonances of equal value. On this point Hucbald says, in his *Harmonica institutio*, immediately following his mention of organum:[15] "Within the octave only two consonant relationships exist, namely, the fourth and the fifth, both tones of which appearing together are apprehended as consonant." The meaning of such an enigmatic sentence can be determined with certainty, however, by a study of the *Scholia* of the *Musica enchiriadis* (Gerbert I:191), where it is definitely stated that progressions of similar tropes (*iidem tropi*) are to be found only at intervals of the fifth but not at intervals of the fourth;*[8] this is evident at least in the important middle section of the melodic gamut employed:

Fifths:
g  a  b♮ c′  d′  e′     The same three forms of the perfect fourth
                        [TTS, TST, STT] are found in both series of
c  d  e  f  g  a        tones.

Fourths:
f  g  a  b♮ c  d        Here the relationships differ because of the
                        shifted position of the semitone; note the
c  d  e  f  g  a        *tritonus* f–b♮.

We shall soon see, however, that the *Musica enchiriadis* follows this relationship throughout its entire tonal system, for in proceeding through its gamut at the interval of a fifth, sequences of similar fifths will always result, but at the interval of a fourth a number of deviations occur. The questionable passage in the Paris treatise *De organo* says that only at the interval of a fifth are these consonances possible consecutively (*consequenter*), but such is not the case at the distance of a fourth. The octave as an interval is not dealt with in the *Harmonica institutio*, nor in the *Musica enchiriadis*, nor even in the *De organo* treatises standing midway between them. They regard it only as the reproduction of a similar tone in another species, so that octave doublings of both voices in organum in the gamut (presently to be discussed) designed to allow for a uniform succession of perfect fifths, with its chromatic octaves, are out of the question. The meaning of the sentence is clear only in relation to organum of more than

---

[15] Gerbert, *Script.* I:107a: "Quarum consonantiarum intervalla tantummodo inter haec praedicta spatia duo sola reperiri possunt, id est, diatessaron diapente, in quinta videlicet ac septima specie, et si duae ipsarum voculae simul enuntientur, consonantiam reddunt."

two voices in which only octaves and fourths constitute consonances, the latter as normal intervals, the former as reproductions in other tonal regions (as we have seen and which we shall continue to emphasize). On the contrary, the consonance of the fifth is only a secondary (*non in unum*) result occurring between two of the voices, of which one is the octave doubling and the other the organal voice a fourth below the principal voice, or the *cantus firmus*. This passage again demonstrates a close connection between the *Harmonica institutio* and the *Musica enchiriadis* in its identity of conception.*[9] Above all, it is necessary to note that in the Paris treatise organum at the fifth does not as yet exist.

The Paris treatise does speak of the doubling of one or both voices [16] of the organum and contains relevant statements about organum in medium, high, and low registers. Toward the end of the treatise the following appears, written in a detailed and authoritative manner: "Accordingly, middle organum can find its conclusion only in the final itself or the tone above or below it. The higher organum has its endings instead on the third, fourth, or fifth step above the final, the lower one on the third, fourth, or fifth step below the final."

Coussemaker's version of the Paris treatise is unfortunately full of errors and very incomplete, since almost all examples are missing. It is nearly impossible, therefore, to make use of this version only. Enough can be ascertained from it, however, to enable us to say that the use of parallel fourths or fifths is as foreign to it as to the Cologne treatise.

This theory of uninterrupted parallel voice-leading is to be found first in the *Scholia* of the *Musica enchiriadis*. Even the *Musica enchiriadis* starts with the fourth as the preferred interval and first deals with the organum at the fourth, without placing a limitation on parallel voice-leadings (Chapter XIII). It then shows how the number of voices is increased and how the attainment of a full sonority through octave doublings of the principal voice, as well as of the organal voice, is gained. Even six voices

---

[16] That octave doubling of one voice of the organum was already practiced around the year 900 can be assumed from an interpretation of a passage from Martianus Capella by Regino of Prüm (Gerbert I:234a): "In Apollon's sacred groves the forest echoes the melodies of the god, the tops of the trees with the original high placement of the melody, the lower hanging branches with the lower octave, the middle branches with a medium tone which divides the octave into its fifth and fourth." It would not have been necessary to relate this to organum, since it could be satisfactorily explained as having to do with the old Pythagorean theories of consonance, had not Regino, especially in this place, according to our interpretation, referred to organum. The middle tone (*media*) is, of course, according to Regino, the antique *mese*, that is, the fifth below the upper tone. The three-voiced appearance of organum which here appears is then equivalent to the second form of organum (doubling of the organal voice at the octave) described in the text above.*[10]

are deemed possible—with the aid of instruments, however.*[11] It is said here that even with octave doubling of only one voice, organum of the fifth must result next to that of the fourth:

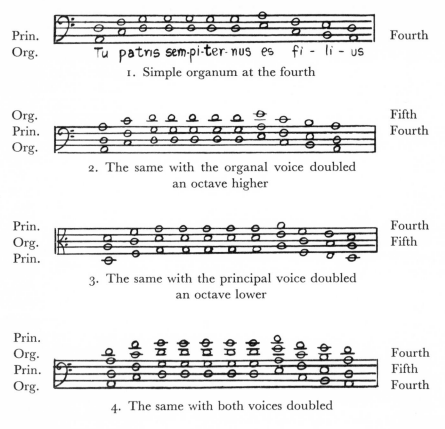

Prin.
Org.                                                                    Fourth

Tu patris sem-pi-ter-nus es fi - li - us

1. Simple organum at the fourth

Org.                                                                    Fifth
Prin.                                                                   Fourth
Org.

2. The same with the organal voice doubled
an octave higher

Prin.                                                                   Fourth
Org.                                                                    Fifth
Prin.

3. The same with the principal voice doubled
an octave lower

Prin.
Org.                                                                    Fourth
Prin.                                                                   Fifth
Org.                                                                    Fourth

4. The same with both voices doubled

The *Musica enchiriadis* does not yet speak of an independent system of organum in fifths.*[12] This is demonstrated only as a secondary result of octave doublings. The following example from Chapter XII of the *Musica enchiriadis*, which immediately precedes the actual explanation of organum,

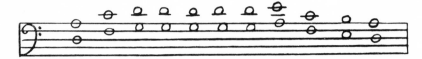

shows that only at distances of the fifth do the same tonal relationships reappear, but in the same sense in which the identity of octave tones is demonstrated in Chapter XI, as in the following example:

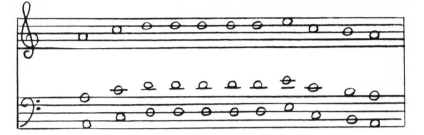

Presumably a complete organum at the fourth with the addition of a third, fourth, and even more voices through octave doubling, as well as organum at the fifth, which also results from this doubling, is only the schematic result of an attempt to subject to theoretical procedure a certain kind of primitive polyphonic singing which may have been imported from England and which appeared in northwest Europe between the 9th and 11th centuries. In order to ascertain the uncertain age of the *Musica enchiriadis*—which can by no means be placed before Hucbald's time, since it contains, as has been already mentioned, some of Hucbald's premises—we must consider the short report of Scotus Erigena, which in this connection is especially important. Scotus Erigena does not even mention strict parallel movement, but talks somewhat laboriously of a "coming together of voices for an ending," following certain artistic rules.*[13] As the Cologne treatise speaks only of the fact that organum is based on the consonance of the fourth (mentioning nothing of continued parallel movement at this interval and also nothing about movement in fifths), and as these theories are not to be found in the Paris treatise (which has proved to be closely connected to the Cologne treatise), we apparently have reason enough to regard as more important, foreshadowing the practical application of organum, that which the *Musica enchiriadis* and the Paris treatise say about organum which uses different intervals. It is unfortunate that the Paris treatise has not been better preserved. The examples which appear toward the end contain many errors, and it is often not even clear in the notation what voice is in what position. The examples seem to contain, strikingly enough, many thirds, which seems to me to be of importance.

We have so far ascertained from the Cologne treatise that, following a fundamental rule, if the voices are to come together in unison at the close of organum, that voice which follows in parallel motion at the lower fourth must never descend lower than the degree below the final. This general rule is still to be found in the Paris treatise and says in effect: In the neighborhood of a close or a partial close, c is the lowest tone of organum for the first authentic mode, Dorian, with d as its final. The lowest tone is d for the second authentic mode, Phrygian, which is based on e; e for the third authentic mode, Lydian, based on f; and f for the fourth, Mixolydian, based on g. Implicit instructions governing the beginnings of organum are also contained, the essential facts of which had so far been missing. The following is quoted from the preface (Coussemaker, *Script.* II: 75–76): [17]

> As long as the *cantus* does not ascend above the final, organum is not yet present (that is to say it is in unison with the *cantus*), and even as long as the *cantus* does not attain the third above the final, organum cannot develop. For the third above the final, however, organum intones the step below the final. With further ascension above the final, organum follows the *cantus* at the lower fourth. As in the beginning, the step below the final constitutes the lower limit of organum as far as the close is concerned, excepting those cases in which the *cantus* has a cadence three, four, or five steps below the final, which constitutes *organum inferius*.

The following is one of the examples found toward the end of the treatise (in Mode I):

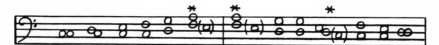

The notes given in parentheses, however, would have to be inserted for those indicated at the places marked with an asterisk, as there is no justification in the text for reading it as given.

The Paris treatise uses without special explanation the unusual system of notation, explained in the *Musica enchiriadis*, which is now referred to as Daseian notation. To use this as a basis for concluding that the author of the *Musica enchiriadis* is also the author of the Paris treatise does not

---

[17] "Antequam particula ejus (sc. finalis rectoris) locum transscendat profecto organum legitimum silet. Si non ultra quam ad secundam supra terminalem (Couss. tertium) pertingit ibi similiter sesponso organi caret. Ubi vero trium spatiorum fuerit a terminali suo ibi primus qui terminali proximus subest quarta(na) collatione organum dicitur. Similiter sursum vel deorsum flectendo quatuor a terminali fuerit spatiorum (tunc aut alter ex praedictis aut utrique organum faciunt et terminus scilicet ei 'subhaerens.' Porro ubi quinque aut sex spatia a terminali habuerint, quotis sonis ei eadem particula ultra eum qui quartus est a terminali disceditur, totis sonis a terminali organum comitando sequitur). . . . Non potest . . . ab inferiori quolibet sono organum in elevando incipere nec in descendendo (in) inferiori (Couss. inferiorem) deponi quam qui (Couss. quam quam) in quovis toni genere proximus (Couss. proximo) terminali subjacet excepto cum positio particulae in tertio vel quarto vel quinto sub terminali constiterit, quod inferioris est organi."

seem imperative; however, the Paris treatise must under no circumstances be dated later than the *Musica enchiriadis*. It might be correct to assume that either the writer or the compiler of the first draft (to which the Parisian, Florentine, and Bruges manuscripts refer) preferred to retain this older version in place of the final chapter of the *Musica enchiriadis* dealing with organum. There are plausible reasons for this assumption, as we shall see later. In this case one would have to assume that the writer left out the explanation of Daseian notation, which would have to have been included in a treatise introducing such notation for the first time, since the *Musica enchiriadis* had already explained this in its first chapter. On the other hand, it seems to me to be an even more tenable assumption that we are here making the acquaintance of an older version of the *Musica enchiriadis* in this group of manuscripts which is estimated as being of little importance by Hans Müller. As these manuscripts (at least the Parisian and Bruges MSS) attribute the work to a so-called Uchubaldus Francigena,*[14] the possibility of Hucbald's authorship of the *Musica enchiriadis* grows considerably. A further factor in favor of this conclusion is that the *Scholia* is missing in all three manuscripts. I cannot agree with Hans Müller that the *Scholia* was from the first a part of the *Musica enchiriadis*. However, I do not wish to maintain at the same time that the commentator who wrote the *Scholia* must necessarily be someone other than the author of the main work. Hucbald lived to be ninety years old. Why is it not possible that the same man should, during such a long life, lead his own devised system through those stages of development known to us? On closer examination of these theoretical writings, Hans Müller's following statement (refer to Müller, *op. cit.* p. 98) is not justified:

No extensive self-contained theory of tone-system, modes, and polyphony can have existed around the year 900, when we see writers of the 9th century and the beginning of the 10th, such as Aurelianus, Remigius Altisiodorensis, Regino, and Hucbald in his first writing, *De harmonica institutione*, making only clumsy attempts.

That organum was already in common use around the time when Hucbald was young (he was born in 840) and was written according to well-established rules is proved by the testimony of Scotus Erigena which has not been and probably never can be disproved.*[15] The system of ecclesiastical modes had also been entirely developed by Hucbald's time, and even much earlier (in the time of Flaccus Alcuin, during the 8th century).*[16] The formulas for the *tropi* of each of the ecclesiastical modes, which are traceable back to the early medieval Byzantine tonal system and which have not even to this day been satisfactorily explained (*noeane, nonaneane, nonanoeane*),*[17] first appear in the writings of Aurelianus Reomensis, a 9th-century author who sometimes follows Flaccus Alcuin word for word. They are also to be found in the *Scholia* of the *Musica enchiriadis* (the commentary of Remigius on Martianus Capella has no connection with the theoretical systems of its period and is of no importance to us at this time). All of the concepts of the *Musica enchiriadis* fit well into the 9th and 10th centuries, as they are based exclusively upon tetrachord division and moreover, as we shall soon see, a system of tetrachord mutation is developed. The *Musica enchiriadis* uses a slightly larger range in its tonal system than the *Harmonica institutio*, as is seen in the following scale of Daseian signs, which shows in its two upper notes, the *residui*, two steps which are still missing in the Paris treatise:

| I | II | III | IV | I | II | III | IV | I | II | III | IV | I | II | III | IV | I | II |
|---|----|-----|----|---|----|-----|----|---|----|-----|----|---|----|-----|----|---|----|
| *Graves* | | | | *Finales* | | | | *Superiores* | | | | *Excellentes* | | | | *Residui* | |

These signs are explained in the first and second chapters of the *Musica enchiriadis*, which state that the four highest are related to the four lowest at the distance of two octaves and that each group of four tones should have the same interval relationship as the next group of four tones. In other words, the relationships between the four finals (d e f g) should also be found to exist in the four-tone sequences of the *graves*, *superiores*, and *excellentes*, with the two *residui* tones constituting the beginning of a fifth similarly constructed tetrachord. The following gamut gives this result, as Phillip Spitta [18] has shown in detail:

| G | A | Bb | c | d | e | f | g | a | b | c′ | d′ | e′ | f#′ | g′ | a′ | b′ | c#″ |
|---|---|----|---|---|---|---|---|---|---|----|----|----|-----|----|----|----|-----|
| I | II | III | IV | I | II | III | IV | I | II | III | IV | I | II | III | IV | I | II |

This gamut, however, stands in obvious contrast to the antique two-octave system which Hucbald expounds in his *Harmonica institutio* (Gerbert I:111) and which is built of antique Dorian tetrachords having the STT pattern:

A ‖ B c d e f g a ‖ b c′ d′ e′ f′ g′ a′

This gamut is used as a basis for the tonal system in later periods (as in Odo, Berno, and Guido) but its range is extended higher and is divided according to octaves rather than tetrachords. This system, however, still indicates no awareness of the Bb *gravium* nor the f#′ *excellentium*, let alone the c#″ *residuorum*. As has been intimated, however, the example cited above from the *Harmonica institutio* (Gerbert I:119) probably implies a chain of tetrachords, each of whose tones are arranged intervallically to correspond to those of the tetrachord formed by the four finals (antique

[18] *VfMW* V:443 ff. (1889). Cf. Rowbotham, *History of Music*, III:366 ff. (1887).

Phrygian). Unfortunately this passage is not explicit enough to allow us to decide whether Hucbald was thinking in terms of the Greek row of tetrachords or of the order which U. Kornmüller[19] believed to be that of the Daseian signs of the *Musica enchiriadis*:

$$A \ \overset{\frown}{B \ c} \ d \qquad \| \ a \ \overset{\frown}{b \ c'} \ d'$$
$$d \ \overset{\frown}{e \ f} \ g\| \qquad d' \ \overset{\frown}{e' \ f'} \ g'$$

This explanation is possible if one interprets Hucbald as placing three tetrachords of the order TST above the d (final of the first mode) and one below. The analogy to the construction of the Greek system, which Hucbald had dealt with previously (Gerbert, p. 111), seems to demand this interpretation, since, with reference to the similarity of the tetrachords, the same wording is used in each case.[20] Also, in imitation of the Greek *proslambanomenos*, one could derive the missing lower G which Hucbald presupposes[21] as the lower fifth of the *finalis proti*. However, an upper note is then missing which Hucbald requires, for he supposes enough range for a ninth above each authentic tone;[22] this would require a' for the *tetrardus* on g. (In one statement about the organ, which he calls *hydraulia vel organalia*, and about another instrument having many strings [probably the Rotta], he speaks of a range of three octaves, starting at C, customarily without the chromatic b♭ [p. 113]). Since we must consequently discard the interpretation in the sense of connected and disconnected tetrachords, we can do nothing else but assume for Hucbald's four or five (?) similarly constructed tetrachords (p. 119) an order of tones which, even if optional, was available for a special purpose as stipulated in the *Musica enchiriadis*. This special purpose is none other than the production of a series of perfect fifths in succession throughout the entire gamut.

This constitutes another proof that there is no principal difference between the *Harmonica institutio* and the *Musica enchiriadis*, or, first of all, between the Cologne and Paris treatises *De organo*. Both the *Harmonica*

19 *Allgemeine Musikalische Zeitung* (1880), Sp. 433 ff.

20 Gerbert I:111: "Following the example of one (combination) the relationship of the other tetrachords proceeds." Page 119: "After the model or pattern set by this (tetrachord composed of four finals) are arranged the relationship of the tones of the four remaining tetrachords."

21 Gerbert, p. 119: "A mode is without exception neither able to arrange itself higher than the fifth above nor lower than the fifth below its final." Page 121: "From the final, which is *lichanos meson*, there is an extension into the fifth sound on either side (authentic tetrardus)."

22 Gerbert I:116: "Every authentic mode ascends from its final as far as the ninth tone (above). Moreover, it descends to what is next to itself and sometimes to the semiditone or to the third below."

*institutio* (Gerbert I:119) and the Paris treatise require that the points of rest in the various sections (*tropi*, differences) have sufficient range available between the fourth below and the fifth above the final. But another point demands special attention. The *Harmonica institutio* does not have a proper ending. Gerbert's version skips on page 121 in the middle of the line (without a break) to an organ-pipe measurement (without a heading) to which are further appended two directions for the division of a monochord. Scarcely two pages before this, Hucbald says:[23]

> After we have come so far, we must further explain (for everything pointed to this from the beginning) that which follows from what we have discussed and what the fruits are which the seed shall yield. After we have determined the intervals of the modes according to their distances as found in the tetrachords, and furthermore illuminated the names and notation of single tones, we must now begin to demonstrate how these elements join with each other and what effect they have within the single modes.

Does the meager output of the following two pages really serve to fulfil this promise? Or is this only a transition to a second part dealing especially with polyphony, possibly the Paris treatise, which does not have a beginning, but presupposes a first part by saying: "After having spoken of the normal distances between the tones within the tetrachords and after having deduced from them the four tones or *modi*...."?! Thus a hypothesis seems to suggest itself which would bring both treatises into the closest connection. But let us look further into the *Musica enchiriadis* to see what new material it will present to us.

One especially striking innovation is the changed motivation for the digression of the organal voice from its movement in fourths. A passage from the seventeenth chapter (Gerbert I:169) reads:[24]

[23] Gerbert, p. 119: "His igitur hucusque productis, quo jam inde ab initio cuncta prospectant; quod his procreetur, quodque sparsorum fructus assurgat seminum, planius abhinc declarandum. Spatiis quippe vocum primo punctorum discrimine post tetrachordum, dehinc ipsarum chordarum nominibus, postremo notis earundem dispositis ad purum; qualiter haec eadem sibi commisceantur, seu qualiter in diversos modos procedant, jam locus est aperire." In connection with this, should special importance not be attached to the *vocum commixtio* in the beginning of the Cologne treatise?

[24] "At in diatessaron, quoniam non per omnem sonorum seriem quartis locis suaviter sibi phthongi concordant, ideo nec absolute ut in caeteris symphonica editur cantilena. Ergo in hoc genere cantionis sua quadam lege vocibus voces divinitus accommodantur; per omnem enim sonorum seriem tritus subquartus a deutero solus a symphonia deficit et inconsonus ei efficitur eo quod solus diatessaron symphoniae mensuram excedens, tribus integris tonis a praefato sono elongatur, cui extat subquartus. Quapropter et vox, quae organalis dicitur, vocem alteram, quae vocatur principalis, eo modo comitari solet, ut in quolibet tetrachordo, in qualibet particula nec infra tetrardum sonum descendat positione, nec inchoatione levetur, obstante triti soni inconsonantia, qui tetrardo est subsecundus."

As movement in fourth does not result in consonant relationships throughout the entire gamut, as does movement in fifths, the joining of voices in this kind of polyphony (namely, organum) is solved in a marvellous manner by an appropriate rule. Everywhere in the entire gamut the *tritus* III [third step in any tetrachord] appears in dissonance against *deuterus* II [second step in the tetrachord above] which is four steps higher, the distance being greater (by a half-step) than that of a perfect fourth and comprising three whole tones (*tritonus*). As a result, the relationship of the organal voice to the principal voice is regulated in such a manner that the organal voice in any melodic section does not go below *tetrardus* IV [fourth step of a tetrachord] of the relevant tetrachord nor start under the same step in ascending, because the dissonance occurring on *tritus* III which lies below *tetrardus* stands in the way:

Rex  coe - li  do - mi - nus ma - ris  un - di - so - ni
2.  Ti - ta - nis,  ni - ti - di  squa - li - di - que  so - li

Since Spitta explained the proper form which Hucbald (whom we shall henceforth call the author of the *Musica enchiriadis*) claimed for the organum gamut, it has become clear why, in the preceding example, an accompaniment in perfect fourths "has become impossible because of the obstacle which the *tritonus* constitutes." A succession of fourths within this basic scale appears as follows:

The tritone relationship occurs every fifth note (reckoning downwards) between *tritus* III of the organal voice and *deuterus* II of the higher principal voice. Therefore, in Chapter XVIII it is correctly stated [25] that the organal voice has only a distance of three, or at the most four, steps available to it. But as the principal voice frequently changes its position in

[25] Gerbert, p. 170: "Because the organum is restricted to a narrow interval (*diastemate*) being limited in its movement by the tone C (𝄐), and has a range of only three or four tones in which to move about, it therefore changes its position following the movement of the tones of the other voice [the *principalis*]. For if the tones of the other voice move here and there, and the *cantilena* [i.e., the melody of the *principalis*] soon ascends and then soon descends, the tones of the *cantilena* first being in a higher range around the *superiores* and then in a lower range bordering on the *finales* or around the *graves*, the organal voice then follows this *cantilena* only with the restriction that it never go below the fourth tone (*tetrardus* [of the next lower tetrachord]) if this boundary is reached by the *cantilena*, for it can neither begin nor end correctly on the notes lying directly below this boundary tone."

the various sections of the melody, the organal voice also assumes other positions in which it is always governed by the same laws, namely, neither to move below the Tetrardus of the tetrachord in which it is located (*gravium, finalium, superiorum*), nor to begin below it, as is demonstrated in the following example:

Te   hu - mi - les   fa - mu - li   mo - du - lis   ve - ne - ran-do  pi - is
Se   ju - be - as  fla-gi -tant   va - ri - is   li - be-ra-re  ma-lis

(N.B. Here the need for a fifth e b♮ on *modulis* is not explained in the text, but we shall mention this later.)

The considerable difference between the two methods of effecting the movement of voices apart and their convergence, namely, the differences in method of the Cologne and Paris treatises (and even of Scotus Erigena —halting on the step below the final), and those of the *Musica enchiriadis* (*horror tritoni*), is quite remarkable. The difference not only consists in another type of formulation, but also implies varying results as far as the setting is concerned. From the standpoint of the older definitions, continuing parallel movement in fourths, even at the cadences, would be out of the question. According to one definition movement in fourths is still possible, but according to another it is absolutely forbidden. As the few examples from the Paris treatise cannot, unfortunately, be used for purposes of demonstration, we shall illustrate the differences with an example from the *Musica enchiriadis* which leads the *Tu patris sempiternus es filius* through all four authentic modes in order to determine the influence of the impeding tritone upon the shaping of the organal voice.

1. *Authentic tone*

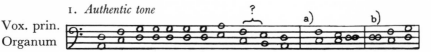

Vox. prin.
Organum

Here parallel movement in fourths is carried out to the end, but it is in contradiction to the text of the *Musica enchiriadis*, which states quite rightly that accompaniment in fourths is possible in the beginning only because the *absonia* (that is, the error-producing effect of the tritone, B♭–e) does not occur (since the *vox principalis* skips the step on e). At the end, however, the organal voice should not descend below Tetrardus (c) for the same (or rather the opposite) reason. Therefore, the ending must be changed to that shown in *a*. According to the older version of these theories, the ending would be the same, but the A in the beginning could not be used, and the organum would begin in unison with the *cantus*, as in *b*. Everything else corresponds to the procedures of both methods.

2. *Authentic tone*          ?                    a)

The text offers us no help in connection with the questionable tritone F–b♮ found in Example 2, but remarks in passing only that the fourth below the beginning and ending tones is necessarily lacking because the B♭ would create a dissonance against the e. Should an F♯ be used with the b♮ of the *cantus* (since b♭ in the Deuterus mode is out of the question in this case)? Admittedly, we do not know what the older school would have done with the b♮,[26] but we do know that according to practice the ending would have to appear as in *a*—which would certainly enhance the effect.*[18]

3. *Authentic tone*

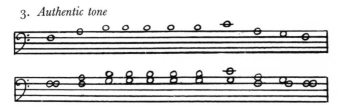

In this example, according to the explanations in the text, the use of any type of organum is rendered impossible by the b♮ repeated five times. An observation of Hucbald's, which stresses the repeated use of b♭ (*synemmenon*) for the Tritus mode, makes this conclusion unnecessary, and in this case removes all difficulties. Our reference to the f–b♮ relationship, however, is of special interest to us here because it confirms our doubts about the f–b♮ in *Te humiles* (p. 28). Or is it possible that f♯ would be possible for organum in Deuterus but not in Tritus? It is possible, but is nowhere commented upon.*[19] According to the older theories, organum would not be impossible, since the missing fourth would require a third (a) (cf. the Cologne treatise, as quoted on p. 13 above).

4. *Authentic tone*

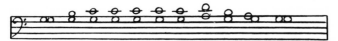

[26] Spitta (p. 454), who recognized the error, remarks that the organum must either remain on e or ascend to g (*tetrardus superiorum*). The latter is probably correct, as movement in fifths is out of the question. Compare this example, however, with the example *Te humiles* (p. 28).

In Example 4, the organum must begin on g, since beginning on d would not then allow an f against the second tone of the *cantus*. Therefore f♯ does not seem to enter into the question here and does not seem intended for the Deuterus. According to the older school, which does not deal with the tritone at all (but seems to have it in mind), the beginning and ending would sound the same in the case of a *deficientibus naturalibus spatiis*.

The problematic f b♮ also appears in the principal example of the first book of the *Scholia* to the *Musica enchiriadis*. Regarding the many Daseian signs which precede the examples in this book, one should note that the symbols for the upper octave are not employed for octave doublings, but that the same symbols are used for the octave position which contains both voices representing only a two-voiced form. This at least partially solves the problem of how Hucbald, in his scale of Daseian signs, could place B♭ in one octave and b♮ in the other, and f♮ in one but f♯' in another.*[20] This explanation is proved conclusively by the three letters A H P[27] of the so-called Boethian notation in the first table (Gerbert I:185), which stand for one note (A) and its octave (H) and double octave (P).

The *Scholia*, moreover, presents an organum of fifths as the basic

---

[27] If we assume Hucbald to be the author of the *Scholia* to the *Musica enchiriadis*, he probably must also be regarded as the creator of Latin letter notation; his works, at least, are the oldest in which traces of this notation can be found. Although the text of the *Harmonica institutio* makes no reference to this notation, a later addition can and must be assumed (in explanation of the Greek notation in Gerbert, p. 118). This is so since the repetition of the same letter notation for the upper octave already shows an apparently later development, which cannot be found in the earlier *Harmonica institutio*. It is not found even in the Scholia of the *Musica enchiriadis*. This also does not apply to the *Musica enchiriadis*, in the eleventh chapter of which appears one of the familiar diagrammatic contrivances in the middle of a representation of a scale:

A B C D E F G A B C D E F G A
t s t t s t t t s t t s t t

This is the basis of the later meaning which letter notation will have (and which first appears in Odo's *Dialog*); for this reason it is probably an addition, a substitute for another notation, presumably a Daseian sign notation. In the same chapter, however, the identical scale, without the tones and semitones indicated, is made use of (running from top to bottom) to demonstrate a melody (*Tu patris sempiternus es filius*) which is accompanied at the octave and the double octave. This scale, therefore, is used in a completely different sense.

In the beginning of the second part of the *Scholia*, on the contrary, there is a reference in the text (Gerbert, pp. 184–185) to the following letter notation:

A B C D E F G H I K L M N O P

Diapason remissum    Diapason intensum
("tamquam si ab H deponatur in A, vel ab H levetur in P.")

organum and not as an organum which appears secondarily through octave doublings of an organum of fourths. This is not the procedure in the *Musica enchiriadis*, as I have already indicated. While the *Musica enchiriadis* uses voice-leading in fifths only to demonstrate that these intervals may appear in this form, the *Scholia* constructs forms in which the number of voices is increased from the basic two-part texture in fifths. Nevertheless, it is not necessary to assume another author for the *Scholia*; it is very likely that as the same theorist became more and more deeply involved in using a system of strict parallelism as the real basis for organum, he gradually attributed more and more importance to the fifth, especially after he had once erected his system of equally built tetrachords. The assumption of an independent organum of fifths can certainly be verified by a few examples in Daseian notation, shown in Gerbert I:187:

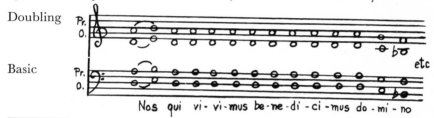

Doubling

Basic

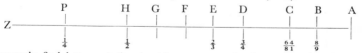

Nos qui vi- vi-mus be-ne-di-ci-mus do-mi-no

Immediately over the above-mentioned explanatory illustration of the significance of the letters A H P and three notations (one above the other) of the same example in Daseian signs, the following chart is found (at the end of the third part, Gerbert, p. 209):

| A | B | C | D | E | F | G | H | I | K | L | M | N | O | P |
|---|---|---|---|---|---|---|---|---|---|---|---|---|---|---|
| t | t | s | t | t | t | s | t | t | s | t | t | t | s | |
| Diatessaron | | | Diapente | | | Diatessaron | | | Diapente | | | | | |

Thus, according to the evidence given by the placement of the t and the s in the sense of a major mode, this bears a close relationship to the text (A=full string, H=one-half of the string, P=one-fourth, D=three-fourths, and E=two-thirds, etc.).

$$Z \quad \overset{P}{|} \qquad \overset{H}{|} \quad \overset{G}{|} \quad \overset{F}{|} \quad \overset{E}{|} \quad \overset{D}{|} \qquad \overset{C}{|} \quad \overset{B}{|} \qquad \overset{A}{|}$$

$$\tfrac{1}{4} \qquad \tfrac{1}{2} \qquad \tfrac{2}{3} \quad \tfrac{3}{4} \qquad \tfrac{64}{81} \quad \tfrac{8}{9}$$

We frequently find letter notation in this same sense in the 10th and 11th centuries (A=the later C). Since this development is found almost at the end of the *Scholia*, it is certainly possible that the first incentive toward notation with these letters occurred here, and that this must be accredited to Hucbald. Since several small treatises found in Gerbert under Hucbald's name make use of this "Frankish" notation, this can only serve to strengthen such a conviction.

The treatises of Anonymous I and II in the first volume of Gerbert's *Scriptores* use this letter notation in the later (present) sense. Anon. I from A–S (with H I K L for the tetrachord *synemmenon*), Anon. II from A–P for A–aa.*21

The example (p. 186) which precedes this, however, arranges the signs in accordance with organum in fourths and at the beginning, the questionable progression in fourths $\begin{smallmatrix} a & b\natural & a \\ e & f & e \end{smallmatrix}$ appears (the upper voice is the *vox principalis* in the first mode, ending on d) without explanation, in which case it is necessary to sing b♭ instead of b♮. This is according to an old tradition, the "*una voce super LA semper canendum esse FA*," based upon Guido's terminology, which without doubt follows an even older usage. It is and remains puzzling, however, that nothing is said about this, and that the symbol which means b♮ and not b♭ is used without hesitation. One can only assume that the use of b♭ was regarded as self-evident and that the Daseian symbols, in spite of their usefulness for the explanation of mutations (modulations, which we shall shortly discuss), could not be used as a practical means of notation without some confusion resulting.

That b♭ (*synemmenon*) was used as a matter of course may also be assumed for the observations which follow and which deal with real organum in fourths and its limitations as far as the use of parallel movement is concerned:

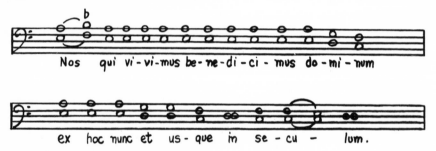

Nos  qui vi-vi-mus be-ne-di-ci-mus do-mi-num

ex  hoc nunc et  us-que  in  se - cu - lum.

Not much progress can be observed in moving from the older organum to that of the *Musica enchiriadis*, unless one so considers the strict parallelism of the latter. What is most interesting in the *Scholia* of the *Musica enchiriadis* is, however (Gerbert, *Scriptores* I: 175 ff.), a type of solmization with the aid of Daseian signs. These, however, served only the theoretical purpose of defining chromatic tones which were not then in use. In his work *Die chromatische Alteration im liturgischen Gesang der abendländischen Kirche* (1897), Gustav Jacobsthal places too much importance upon this method of solmization in assuming that it was a form of instruction in modulation (through mutation of tetrachords, as in the later solmization by mutation of hexachords). That this did not occur to Hucbald is proved by the fact that he did not use this aid to explain the difference between his series of fifths and the diatonic series with the b♭ and b♮ which was then in use.

The nature of tetrachord mutation is as follows:[28] The individual tones
are given names which indicate their position in the tetrachord composed
of the finals, or one of its counterparts: I *archoos* (=*protos*), II *deuteros*, III
*tritos*, IV *tetrardos* (for which we shall employ I, II, III, IV from now on)
and the name of the tetrachord, i.e., *gravium* (gra.), *finalium* (fin.), *superiorum* (sup.), *excellentium* (ex.). These tones are to be sung while pronouncing
these names (leaving only one step further to solmization with single
syllables; however, Hucbald does not take this step!), in order that one
will be conscious of each tone in the system at all times. In case of doubt
it should be remembered that in each tetrachord the relationship between
*deuteros* and *tritos* is that of a semitone.[29] It is stated that

the correct placement of the semitones gives the individual tones their special
significance....If the distance between two succeeding tones is judged wrongly,
it immediately takes on a different significance and disturbs the order which has
been begun.[30]

This can happen in such a way that a tone which is not rightly intoned will not
change the mode but will only appear to be wrong, or it can occur in such a
manner that it will bring about a new order, that is to say, it will cause a transposition.[31]

Something of a similar nature is stated at the beginning of the *Scholia*,
where three kinds of *absonia* are enumerated:[32]

[28] Cf. *Handbuch der Musikgeschichte* I, 1st and 2nd editions, p. 205 ff., for the connection
between Hucbald's Daseian notation and the memorization formulas *noeane*, etc., and
the antique solmization (tah, tā, toh, teh).*22 Also, the *Martyrien* of Byzantine notation
serve the same purpose of making it easier to remember the position of the semitones.

[29] Gerbert I:154: "For this purpose it is of no little profit when one sings each individual tone and those next to it in the proper order, using their Greek names in the
following manner:

*archoos    deuteros    tritos    tetrardos*

If every tone is sung in this manner, with its own name, one will perceive with ease
which this one or that one is."

[30] Gerbert I:175: "Semitonia...suo loco posita et suam sonis proprietatem tribuunt
...at si falso metiatur sonus a sono, in aliam mox qualitatem migrat, coeptumque
transvertit ordinem."

[31] Gerbert I:212: "Atque idcirco dum in alieno loco quid sumitur, aut tropi qualitatem retinens discrepat ab eo quod praecedit, dum sui ordinis positionem non invenit; aut
alieno cedens ordini tropi qualitatem transpositione convertit."

[32] Gerbert I:173–174: "(Fit haec absonia in phthongis) si aut ignavius pronuntientur,
aut acutius, quam oportet....Quod vitium in quibuslibet musicis instrumentis nequit
fieri: eo quod, dispositio semel phthongorum ordine, vox sua sonis singulis manet. Alia
fit dissonantia, quando sonus a sono falso metitur, id est, alius pro alio. Tertia dissonantia
fit, quando sonus non respondet sono, quoto loco oportet. Et haec duo vitia ex eadem
quidem causa nascuntur; sed in hoc differunt, quod illud in eadem fit neuma, hoc vero in
praecinendo et respondendo."

1. If the intonation of a tone is too high or too low, thereby causing the whole melody to suffer. This does not occur with instruments, the intonations of which are already firmly established.
2. If the interval is misjudged as to distance, so that another interval comes into being which does not belong to the gamut.
3. If a joint sound does not consist of the proper interval.

The second type of *absonia*, when a whole-step is replaced by a half-step (or vice versa), causing a transposition in the course of a melodic phrase, occurs when, for example, c d e♭ f g is sung instead of c d e f g. This Hucbald refers to as the principle governing mutation, which says that the *tritus finalium* follows the *archoos finalium* (d) directly, the *tritus finalium*, according to this principle, always being the upper tone of the half-step interval (i.e., only if Daseian notation is used for such theoretical purposes):

IV. gr. I fin.

(= II) III IV I sup.

The succession I III means that the second degree is moved the distance of a half-step, so that instead of e, e♭ appear in the series. The movement back through the same five tones (g f e♭ d c) appears, then, completely in the manner of notation characteristic of a Protus melody: I. sup. IV III II I fin. Thus, the Daseian signs entirely lose their original pitch designations and assume new ones (*archoos finalium* is no longer d, but c).

Other such mutations, which are shown in the *Scholia* to the *Musica enchiriadis*, are as follows:

2. c d e f♯ g instead of: c d e f g = IV gr. I II fin.

(= I) II III fin.

backwards: III II I fin. IV III gr., with e as *archoos finalium*.

3. a g f♯ e d instead of: a g f e d = I sup. IV

(= III) II I IV gr.

backwards: IV gr. I II III IV fin., with e as *archoos finalium*.

4. a g f e♭ d instead of: a g f e d = I sup. IV III

(= IV) III II fin.

backwards: II III IV fin. I II sup., with c as *archoos finalium*.

Credit belongs to Gustav Jacobsthal for being the first to offer these new interpretations, despite the difficulties arising from the errors contained in Gerbert's version. These interpretations, however, lie entirely outside the theory of organum and are not used even to supply the reason for the introduction of the B♭ *gravium* or f♯' *excellentium* into the series of fifths, although this certainly would have been possible. Also, the introduction of the middle b♭ instead of b♮, in cases which we have discussed earlier, could easily have been defined as the succession I III *sup.* in the manner of the later FA *contra* MI. This, however, was not done. Therefore, we must view carefully, and perhaps rather skeptically, the far-reaching conclusions which G. Jacobsthal draws from the discussion of *absonia*. Without stretching the point too far, it is possible, and indeed necessary, to interpret the *absonia* of Hucbald, which have all been discussed, simply as "wrong intonations" or as "mistakes," the character of which must be clearly ascertained. This also holds true for the third kind of *absonia*, which occurs when a *vox principalis* is confronted with an organal voice at another distance than that of the octave (doubling), the upper fifth (organum at the fifth), or the lower fourth (organum at the fourth). This third *absonia* was entirely misinterpreted by Jacobsthal. The term *abson* can already be found in the Paris treatise, although it applies only to a nonexistent tone, that is, to the lower fourth of the *Deuterus gravium*, an e which lies beyond the limit of the tonal system and is, therefore, called *abson*.[33]

The incongruity of the purely theoretical gamut of Daseian notation with the demands of a musical practice which required above all the agreement of tones at the distance of an octave (while Hucbald constructed his gamut to achieve a consecutive series of perfect fifths) can be solved by the already mentioned exemption of the octave from the rank of essential intervals:

> Although in simple singing and in the tonal gamut the same function is given not to the eighth step but to the ninth step (through the same placement in the tetrachord, and the same importance I, I ; II, II), in polyphonic singing, tones of equal importance, not only at the distance of an octave but also at the distance of the double octave, can be found through a marvelous mutation.[34]

We have concerned ourselves more extensively with the character of organum during the 9th and 10th centuries in order to refute the opinion

[33] Coussemaker, *Script.* II:75: "If the fourth below (*Deutero gravium*) responds as organum to this tone, having crossed the natural boundary, it will result in an error."

[34] Gerbert I:164: "Attendenda quoque in hoc mira ratio ut quamvis absolute canendo vel in ordine sonos rimando, idem inveniuntur noni ad nonos, non octavi ad octavos: in symphonia tamen non modo diapason, quae octava incedit regione sed et bisdiapason mutatione mirabili octavi et octavi idem sunt."

that the theory of the *Musica enchiriadis* was so much more highly developed than that of Hucbald's time that it would seem inadmissable to attribute the authorship of the *Musica enchiriadis* to Hucbald himself. I feel that I have succeeded in this refutation. A detailed knowledge of the older teachings, however, will be of great service to us in understanding further developments.

The attempt to interpret organum not as the simultaneous performance of several voices, but rather as a type of alternating singing, or as a kind of predecessor to fugal composition, will not concern me here. Since earlier writers [35] speak quite unmistakably of real accorded singing (sounding together), no doubt can remain, in the light of its further development. The new theory of Oskar Paul, contained in the *Wiener Rezensionen*, no. 25 (1865), and in his *Geschichte des Klaviers*, p. 234, is based on the appearance of expressions such as *praecinere* and *respondere*, *subsequi*, *responsio*, etc. Organum is always concerned with a melody which is already present, a *cantus prius factus*, as later mensural composers call it, to which is added the accompanying voice, or rather, the voice which follows. In such a sense the principal voice really is a "preceding" voice which is followed by the organal voice.

[35] Cf. especially the remarks of Regino (Gerbert I:237), who unmistakably indicates that by the term *consonantia* he means the simultaneous sounding together of tones: "Consonance is the concordance of unlike tones into one sound. Or, consonance is the mixture of high and low tones falling sweetly and uniformly upon the ears. On the other hand, dissonance is the sound of two tones coming to the ear roughly and unpleasantly. ...Whenever two strings are stretched and one sounds lower and the other higher, if they are struck at the same time and give a rather mixed and pleasing sound, the two sounds being united in one blending, there is made that which is called consonance. But if being struck at the same time each tries to go contrary to the other, and they do not blend for the ear in a soft and pleasing sound as one composed of two, then is made what is called dissonance."

## APPENDIX

Footnote 11: Descriptio Cambriae I. VI:189 (Rerum Britannicarum medii aevi Scriptores I:XXXVI.) "De symphonicis, eorum cantibus et cantilenis organicis. In musico modulamine non uniformiter ut alibi, sed multipliciter multisque modis et modulis cantilenas emittunt, adeo ut in turba canentium, sicut huic genti mos est, quot videas capita tot audias carmina, discriminaque vocum varia, in unam denique sub B mollis (!) dulcedine blanda consonantiam et organicam convenienta cantilenam. In borealibus quoque majoris Britanniae partibus, trans Humbrian scilicet Eboracique finibus, Anglorum populi qui partes illas inhabitant simili canendo symphonica utuntur harmonia: binis tamen solummodo tonorum differentiis et vocum modulando varietatibus, una inferius submurmurante, altera vero superne demulcente pariter et delectante. Nec arte tamen sed usu longaevo et quasi in naturam mora diutina jam converso, haec vel illa sibi gens hanc specialitatem comparavit. Qui adeo apud utramque invaluit et altas jam radices posuit, ut nihil hic simpliciter nihil nisi multipliciter ut apud priores (the inhabitants of Wales) vel saltem dupliciter ut apud sequentes (the inhabitants of Northumberland) melice proferri consueverit, pueris etiam, quod magis admirandum, et fere infantibus cum primum a fletibus in cantus erumpunt eandem modulationem observantibus. Angli vero, quoniam non generaliter omnes sed boreales solum hujusmodi vocum utuntur modulationibus, credo quod a Dacis et Norwagiensibus qui partes illas insulae frequentius occupare ac diutius obtinere solebant, sicut loquendi affinitatem, sic et canendi proprietatem contraxerunt." [Quoted from NOHM II:315–316.]

FOOTNOTE 13: "Haec quartanae conlationis lex suos limites habet; nam usque ad illum sonum pertingit, qui in quolibet modo sub sono finali fuerit subsecundus (quem cujusque modi sonus finalis habuerit subsecundum). In hoc enim sono stat organum nec inferius descendere licitum est. A quo sono incipit in levatione particulae in eo subsistit in depositione et inferius organum progredi prohibetur."

FOOTNOTE 20: Gerbert I:111: "Ad unius autem exemplar caeterorum status tetrachordorum procedit." Page 119: "Ad quarum (sc. vocum finalium) exemplar caetera nihilominus tetrachorda...qualitatem deducunt sonorum."

FOOTNOTE 21: Gerbert, p. 119: "Et omnis omnino tonus a finali suo nec supra quintum superiorem, nec infra quintum inferiorem umquam ordiendi facultatem habebit." Page 121: "A finali, quae est lichanos meson, in quintum phthongum utraque regione deductus protenditur (authentus tetrardus)."

FOOTNOTE 22: Gerbert I:116: "Unusquisque tonus authentus a suo finali usque in nonum sonum ascendit. Descendit autem in sibi vicinum et aliquando ad semiditonum (Gerbert: semitonium) vel ad tertium."

FOOTNOTE 25: Gerbert, p. 170: "Ergo quoniam praedicti limits (sc. triti, subquarti deuteri) oppositione brevi diastemate coarctatur, et nisi in tribus vel quatuor sonis organalis vox spatium habet; idcirco secundum particularum positionem et loca mutat; vagantibus enim particulis, dum modo cantilena in sursum prodeat, modo in ima deponatur, et nunc quaelibet particula positionem habeat circa superiores, aliquando circa graves semper vox organalis positionum finalitatem eo jure subsequitur, ut subtus tetrardum sonum, in quem vel finalitas particulae pervenerit (Gerbert: devenerit) vel qui proximus ipsi finalitati suberit, nec ordiri levationem valeat, nec rite finalitatem deponere."

FOOTNOTE 29: Gerbert I:154: "Non parum enim ad investigationem hanc proficit, dum singulorum ipsorum per vicinos sonos graeca suo ordine modulantur vocabula hoc modo: archoos (f., gr., sup., exc.), deuteros (f., gr., sup., exc.), tritos (f., gr., sup., exc.), tetrardos (f., gr., sup., exc.). Sic itaque sonus quisque dum suo semetipsum nomine canit, facile in canendo sentitur, quis ille vel ille sit."

FOOTNOTE 33: Coussemaker, *Script.* II:75: "Etenim si quartus sub (deutero gravium) se sonus organum ei respondeat, transgresso naturali termino absonum fiet."

FOOTNOTE 35: Gerbert I:237: "Consonantia est dissimilium inter se vocum in unum redacta concordia. Aliter: consonantia est acuti soni gravisque mixtura, suaviter uniformiterque auribus accidens. Et contra dissonantia est duorum sonorum sibimet permixtorum ad aurem veniens aspera atque injucunda percussio.... Quotiens enim duae chordae intenduntur et una ex his gravius, altera acutius resonat, simulque pulsae reddunt permixtum quodammodo et suavem sonum, duaeque voces in unum quasi conjunctae coalescunt, tunc fit ea, quae dicitur consonantia. Cum vero simul pulsis sibi quisque contraire nititur, nec permiscent ad aurem suavem atque unum ex duobus compositum sonum, tunc est quae dicitur dissonantia."

CHAPTER III

# Odo of Cluny. Berno of Reichenau. Hermannus Contractus

O̲U̲R̲ contemporaries delight in using historical criticism, often very farfetched, to deny credit to those men upon whom tradition bestows it for special accomplishments. By such methods, and in particular through the work of Hans Müller, Hucbald has been reduced to an insignificant music-loving monk whose principal achievement consisted of the composition of a few hymns in honor of Saint Amand, patron saint of his cloister, and one poem in praise of bald heads, addressed to Charles the Bald. How wrong it is to assume that internal reasons show the author of *Harmonica institutio* not to be the author of *Musica enchiriadis* and finally the author of the *Scholia*, was shown us by a closer examination of the contents of the last two works. Hucbald was by no means unnoticed by his contemporaries, even though one could assume so according to Müller. This is proved by the fact that Berno of Reichenau, who lived more than a century after Hucbald, did not hesitate to copy from Hucbald on a grand scale—not from the *Musica enchiriadis* but from the *Harmonica institutio*, which has always been regarded as of lesser importance. This, however, was noticed neither by Hans Müller nor by Wilhelm Brambach, a specialist in the work of the Reichenau school.[1]*[1] This fact is of greater importance than the rarity of the manuscripts of the *Institutio harmonica*.[2] It seems almost as though it were now Berno's turn

[1] Only Jacobsthal has realized that Berno copied Hucbald (refer to Jacobsthal, *op. cit.*, p. 183), but even he did not realize the degree of Berno's dependence.

[2] It may be worth while to compare parts of the *Prologus in tonarium* of Berno (Gerbert II:62 ff.) which are borrowed from Hucbald with the respective parts of the *Institutio harmonica*:

(Concerning intervals):

| HUCBALD*[2] | BERNO |
|---|---|
| *De harmonica institutione* | *Prologus in tonarium* |
| (Gerbert I:105a): | (Gerbert II:64a): |
| The first type occurs when two notes divided by the briefest interval cling together so that scarcely any difference is | The first type consists of the briefest interval between two tones and results in the semitone, as this is clearly illustrated |

39

felt between them as in the antiphon "Missus est Gabriel" in the place "Mariam" or again in "Virginem."

The second type is readily perceived as in "Missus est," again in "Mariam Virginem," and again in "Angelus."

The third type is a little more drawn out as in "Missus est Gabriel ad Mariam Virginem."

The fourth type is also more extended as in the antiphon "Beati qui ambulant."

The fifth type is of even greater extent as in "Ne timeas Maria" and in "In illa die fluent."

The sixth type is nevertheless greater as in the responses "Iam corpus ejus" and "Cujus pater feminam" and again the response "Isti sunt dies, quos observare debetis temporibus."

The seventh type advances beyond these also into its own space as in the antiphon "Beata Agnes in medio flammarum minas."

The eighth type is truly found in "Tu vir Symphoriane suspende in tormentis."

The ninth type is of more extended space than all others, and is divided in this way: for you will never find one greater than the one just spoken of, nor one narrower than the first. And it is found in this antiphon "Ad te levavi animam meam. Deus meus in te." Response "Inter natus mulierum non."

Beyond this is then the most extreme division if you are looking for tones more

in low and high in this antiphon "Missus est Gabriel" in the place "Mariam" and again "Virginem."

The second type is a more perceptible interval and results in a whole tone as in this antiphon "Missus est."

The third type is a little more drawn out than this having a tone and semitone as in this antiphon "Missus est Gabriel ad Mariam Virginem."

The fourth type is also more extended and has two tones as in this "Beati qui ambulant."

The fifth type is still more spacious, that is, it has two tones and a half as in this "Ne timeas Maria" and again in the antiphon "In illa die fluent."

The sixth type is yet larger and it has three continuous tones as in the responses "Iam corpus ejus" and "Cujus pater feminam."

The seventh type surpasses this in space consisting of three tones and a semitone as in the antiphon "Beata Agnes in medio minas."

The eighth type, which is the rarer one, you will find in four tones not yet full as in the response "Tu vir Symphoriane suspende in tormenta . . ." (a correction of the explanation follows).

The ninth is more extended in space than all others and is divided in this way, for you will neither find any division of musical tones greater than this nor more closely observed. It consists of four tones and a semitone and you have an example in this antiphon "Ad te levavi animam meam Deus meus" and again in the response "Inter natos mulierum non," and in the responses "Haec est virgo" and "Introivit," and to the highest degree in the antiphon "Iste cognovit" at "et inventus est in."

Beyond this is then the most extreme division if you should seek for any tones widely separated. You will neither find these in any rational melody nor will such a movement be humanly possible, so that the voice could easily execute it from the highest tone to the lowest at one stroke, unless there was a change into a new voice.

separated from each other by a more distant sound... until you come to a consonant diapason where it is the permutation of a voice rather than a progression of a larger kind. For the latter does not admit of human execution, so that a suitable sound could be made for those tones differing from each other by so great an interval.

Consonance is the rational and harmonious combination of two tones which happens only when two voices from different sources form a concord of sounds, as, for example, when a boy's voice and a man's voice sing the same thing, or as in the so-called organum.

And consonance happens when men's and boy's voices sound together, or rather in that sort of singing which is usually called organum. In the rest of the intervals not accounted for as consonances, indeed, there is not consonance, but intervals and a certain difference of tones.

(Ecclesiastical modes):

(p. 119): If one does not consider the tetrachord *synemmenon*, the fifths above the four finals stand in such close relationship with them that many chants close regularly on them [the fifths above] without reason or instinct taking offense because these upper fifths appear to be following in the same mode or trope.

(p. 74b): It may be truly noted that in the place a fifth above or below the final, there is always a concord, as something sweet is to be found in these, as if they closed regularly.

Such a close relationship unites *lichanos hypaton* with *mese*; *hypate meson* with *paramese*; *parypate meson* with *trite diezeugmenon*; *lichanos meson* with *paranete diezeugmenon*. The finals stand in this relationship to their fourths below (and partly to the fifths below), not for the closes, however, but only for the beginnings of chants.

This kind of agreement in association unites *lichanos hypaton* with *mese*, *hypaton meson* with *paramese*, *parypate meson* with *trite diezeugmenon*, *lichanos meson* with *paranete diezeugmenon*.

The finals stand in this relationship to their fourths below (and partly to the fifths below) although not so much at the beginning as at the end. (Here follows an independent reference to the transposition of the *modi* to the upper fourth.)

And in every case every tone can be used at the beginning or the end in relation to the final, not ever lower than the fifth below, nor higher than the fifth above, but within these nine tones, or sometimes eight, partly authentic or partly plagal.

(p. 74): And this is their rule for beginning any melody. They do not begin it at any place higher than the fifth above the final nor lower than the fifth below, but make their beginning among these eight or sometimes nine tones.

(Musical tones):

(p. 107b): The ancients wished to call those sounds *phthongos*, which possessed certain qualities they considered as be-

(p. 63): Truly every *cantilena* is not woven together of any kind of sound, but of certain and determined sounds which

to appear less significant; even Brambach has considerably reduced Berno's achievements by showing a number of interpolations from other sources in other passages of his works.[3] Concerning the theory of organum, Berno says nothing other than that which he plagiarized from the *Institutio harmonica* of Hucbald.

The learned abbot Odo of Cluny, who died in 943 and who is often referred to during the later Middle Ages, has suffered a fate similar to that of Hucbald.*[3] According to Jacobsthal (*Die chromatische Alteration* [1897], p. 228), "Probably no one today doubts that Odo of Cluny is not the author of the *Dialogus de musica* (Gerbert I: 152 ff.). But whoever the author may be, which Odo he is, or even whether he is an Odo at all, has not been proved." Similarly, Hans Müller and Brambach (*Die Musikliteratur des Mittelalters* [1883], p. 13) doubt whether Odo had anything to do with the treatises which Gerbert published under Odo's name.

The claim that the *Dialogus* (which was labeled *Musica enchiridionis* by Gerbert in the last of the group of treatises which he compares with the Admontensian manuscript) is not by Odo is based, and rightly so, on the fact that in the text of this treatise the Domnus Odo is cited as the authority.[4] This testimonial alone provides the same degree of proof of the genuineness of the *Prooemium tonarii* (Gerbert I:248 ff.) and that of the *Tonarius* itself (which unfortunately has not yet been published), for the rectification of the mode of the antiphon "O beatum pontificem" is

----

longing to music. These were not just any sort of sounds, but only those which were rationally separated and determined by quantity. Being suited to the melody, they laid the surest foundation for the whole *cantilena*. For this reason they called these same elements *phthongos*, because from the elements of letters the whole multiplicity of words is gathered and whatever can be said is made clear by these letters, so the *phthongi* are varied from their likeness to speaking. . . .

the Greeks called *phthongos* because of their likeness to speaking and

. . .arranged and set into order in the same way as speech is made of a series of the elements of letters.

Those who do not find enough proof in the above examples may find other less significant references in Hucbald, p. 104a, third paragraph, and Berno, p. 63a, third paragraph, as well as Hucbald, p. 116a and Berno, p. 72a, etc.

[3] Gerbert II:67b–69a, 70a–71b=Anon. I, Gerbert (I:353 and 337).

[4] Gerbert I:256: "As in the antiphon 'O beatum pontificem,' which, although beginning and ending in the second mode, was corrected and changed to the first mode with the greatest care by Dom Odo, merely because of the ascent of the melody on the words 'O Martine dulcedo.'"

actually contained in this work.[5] That the author holds high rank is proved by the use of the imperative case throughout this treatise (see the beginning after which it appears as though Odo only dictated [*scribere procuravi*] the *Tonarius*. In addition, see line 8 of the *Admoneo autem omnes cantores*, etc., p. 248b, which contains expressions of indignation concerning the arrogance of singers, and especially the *praecipio*, p. 249a, line 10). The authorship of Odo is also proved by the special heading of the ninetieth chapter[6] of the manuscript of Monte Cassino, which belongs to the 11th century and consists of a large collection of music theory treatises.

Since proofs of the existence of any other abbot named Odo living in the same era are lacking, we must, accordingly, regard the abbot Odo of Cluny as the author of that treatise on modes (with its unusual terminology) which appears in a fragmentary fashion between each division of the *Tonarius*. In it the modes appear with their following characteristics:

I. Tone: Dorius, Authentus protus. Vox odax. Metrum:
Lichanos hypaton.
Organum anoton. Chorda: Scembs. Schema D.
(Range: III–VIII (IX)).

II. Tone: Hypoiastius, Plagis proti. Vox odax. Metrum:
Lichanos hypaton.
Organum ysaton. Chorda: Scembs. Schema D.
(Range: I–VI).

III. Tone: Aeolius semitonius, Authentus deuterus. Vox jubilo.
Metrum: Hypate meson.
Organum chamilon. Chorda: Caphe. Schema E.
(Range: IV–XI).

IV. Tone: Cantus (?), Plagis deuteri. Vox jubilo. Metrum:
Hypate meson.
Organum salpion. Chorda: Caemar. Schema E.
(Range: III–VII).

V. Tone: Parmenus, Authentus tritus. Vox excelsa. Metrum:
Parhypate meson.
Organum cuphos. Chorda: Asel. Schema F.
(Range: VI–XI).

[5] Gerbert I:249a: "And finally, no one thinks that every antiphon in its beginning is the same as the beginning of the psalm. For the most part they wish the psalm to begin where the antiphon ends as is true of the antiphon 'O beatum pontificem,' which many consider as being in the second tone. They are mistaken, however, since it is in the first and of the seventh difference."

[6] "Also the *tonora*, the order of its differences which we have nobly emended and explained by Dom Odo, pious abbot who was learned in the art of music."

VI. Tone: Epyniceus semitonius, Plagis triti. Vox excelsa.

Metrum: Parhypate meson.

Organum bubos. Chorda: Neth. Schema F.

(Range: III–VIII).

VII. Tone: Adonta, Authentus tetrardus. Vox stridens. Metrum:

Lichanos meson.

Organum strigon. Chorda: Suggesse. Schema G.

(Range: VII–XII).

VIII. Tone: Theticon. Plagis tetrardi. Vox stridens. Metrum:

Lichanos meson.

Organum fonicon. Chorda: Neth. Schema G.

(Range: VI–XI).

We must not concern ourselves unnecessarily with the curious names of the modes, which are mostly Greek and among which only *Dorius* is familiar. Also we must not be troubled about the different implications of the word "organum," the meaning of which we cannot even guess from its usage here. The word *vox* possibly indicates the characteristics of the pitch range, *odax* could mean "biting," *jubilo* probably means "jubilant," *excelsus* "high," and *stridens* "hissing" (very high!). The *metrum* determines the *finalis* according to its position in the *systema teleion*; the *schema* tells us the new names of the tones in Odo's system. Where the barbaric names *scembs*, *caphe*, etc., come from is entirely unknown. The definition of the range of the modes creates a system extending from A to e' and discloses further barbaric tone names (apparently with a few changes) which seem to play a role in the definition of the finals of the modes:*4

| (A) | (B) | (c) | (d) | (e) | (f) |
|---|---|---|---|---|---|
| I. Buc | II. ? ? | III. Re | IV. Scembs | V. Caemar | VI. Neth |
| (g) | (a) | (b) | (c') | (d') | (e') |
| VII. Uciche | VIII. Asel | IX. Caphe | X. ? ? | XI. Suggesse | XII. Nar. |

For the first time we encounter the use of Latin letters (as they were later used) to indicate pitches, namely D E F G for the four finals; for this reason it seems feasible to maintain that it was Odo who brought about the shift in meaning of pitch indications.

It is difficult to present Odo's system in its entirety due to the peculiar characteristics of his presentation of the ecclesiastical modes. I presume it likely that the learned abbot preserved here only a portion of the theory of the early Middle Ages, a vestige of earlier concepts which go back, perhaps, beyond Flaccus Alcuin (the expressions *chamilon*, *anoton*, *ysaton*, and *cuphos* point to Byzantine music theory). The barbaric pitch names may even be derived from old Gallic tone-indications. The narrow boundaries of the system decisively indicate that this is a treatise of early origin, although Aribo Scholasticus in the 11th century still describes all the properties of the eight modes within the same interval of a sixth (C–a).

The *Dialogus* was not, apparently, written by Odo himself; however, it does belong to a group of treatises which might be called Odonic, since it uses the same order of pitch names which are first to be found in Odo's works. These are not of the older type found in the *Musica enchiriadis*, which simply indicate certain points on the monochord. This new method of designating pitch is intended as a real notation by the use of which a melody can be precisely defined and read at sight. Gerbert assumes the author to be Odo without any particular reason (the titles in the manuscripts indicate the *Domnus* Odo [Vienna], *Domnus* Odo Abbas [St. Emmeran], and name *Domnus* Odo Abbas *primus Cluniacensis coenobii* [Admont] as the author, and probably rightly so; the reforms set down in this work are very likely due to the work of Odo of Cluny). The author is not a little proud of the surprising success of his method, which made possible practicing new chants at sight without the necessity of having them first sung. The arrangement of the system in the *Dialogus* is as follows:

$$\Gamma \quad A \quad B \quad C \quad D \quad E \quad F \quad G \quad a \quad b\flat \quad b\natural \quad c \quad d \quad e \quad f \quad g \quad \genfrac{}{}{0pt}{}{a}{a}$$

For the first time this system uses large and small letters to indicate the difference between the two octaves whose tones are similarly named; it also adds the $\Gamma$ for the lowest G and an octave doubling of a for the highest tone. The monochord diagram printed by Gerbert, the *Monochordum Guidonis* $\left(\text{with a range extending to } \genfrac{}{}{0pt}{}{a \ b\flat \ b\natural \ c \ d}{a \ b\flat \ b\natural \ c \ d}\right)$ is naturally of later origin. The *Monochordum enchiriadis Odonis*, with Hucbald's Daseian signs and tetrachord arrangements, including both *residui*, probably did not originally belong in the treatise. The text, at least, gives no evidence for its inclusion.

There are no traces of Greek names for the ecclesiastical modes in the *Dialogus*, and the ranges of the modes are expanded, in contrast to the treatise in *Tonarius*, as follows:

I. C–d    II. $\Gamma$–$\natural$    III. D–e    IV. A–c

V. E–f    VI. C–d    VII. F–$\genfrac{}{}{0pt}{}{a}{a}$    VIII. C–e

Odo's *Dialogus* attributes special importance to the dual aspect of the ninth step, b♭ being the first ninth step (*nona prima*) and b♮ being the second (*nona secunda*). Neither stands in the relationship of a half-step or a whole-step to the other [for they are not related to one another in Odo's thinking]; they divide the distance between the eighth and ninth step in two different ways,*[5] namely:

$$a \quad b\flat \quad c \qquad \text{and} \qquad a \quad b\natural \quad c$$
$$\tfrac{1}{2} \quad \text{I} \qquad\qquad\qquad \text{I} \quad \tfrac{1}{2}$$

Although there is no mention of the Greeks or even of Boethius in the *Dialogus*, and the tone-names of the *systema teleion* have been completely dropped, nevertheless a vestige of the antique system can be clearly seen in the use of the b♭ adjoining b♮. The avoidance of the name *synemmenon*, however, shows a conscious effort to throw off the burdensome fetters of the old theoretical system. Even the ecclesiastical names *Protus, Deuterus, Tritus,* and *Tetrardus,* with their division into *authentus* and *plaga,* have been discarded in favor of simple numbering: Modes I and II, III and IV, V and VI, VII and VIII (p. 259a). The author of the *Dialogus* makes an important observation concerning the transposition of modes (Gerbert, p. 262):[7]

> For it is well known to us that the modes are not, as narrow-minded music teachers would have it, differentiated from one another by absolute pitch levels; for nothing prevents any favorite mode from being sung high or low. Only the various arrangements of whole- and half-tones on which the remaining intervals are dependent define the distinctions and peculiarities of the individual modes.

A similar commentary is found in the *Commemoratio brevis de tonis et psalmis modulandis* (Gerbert I:227):[8]

> Although the Psalms and all other chants (melodies) are to be sung higher or lower according to either the festive season or the large or small number of singers, it is not to be regarded as imperative that a chant prescribed for a certain festival be sung at one and the same pitch. Rather one must, for example, differentiate between the intoning of the *Laudes* at a higher pitch for the joyous mood of the morning, and at a lower pitch for the hushed composure of nocturnal vigils.

These two testimonials are sufficient evidence of the fact that in the century prior to the establishment of a fixed notation of the chant on lines, the modes were not to be sung at any fixed pitch location. The theoretical expositions were concerned (in the diatonic *systema teleion* as

---

[7] "Non enim, ut stultissimi cantores putant, gravitate vel acumine unum modum ab alio discrepare scimus; nihil enim impedit, quemcumque volueris modum si acute vel graviter decantaveris: sed tonorum et semitoniorum quibus et aliae consonantiae fiant, diversa positio diversos ab invicem ac differentes modos constituunt."

[8] "Praeterea quemadmodum psalmi vel alia quaelibet melodia ad rationem causae vel temporis, pro paucitate vero seu multitudine cantorum celsius vel humilius canendi sunt; nec enim indifferenti altitudinis modo cantum cujusque temporis modulari oportet, verbi gratia, matutina laetitia elatiore canore celebranda, quam nocturna synaxis."

well as in the diatonic system now indicated by Latin letters) with the internal structure rather than with any absolute pitch location. Nevertheless, through this particular arrangement of the modes, the concept of a variety of pitch regions was formed, as is shown by incidental observations concerning the extent of the vocal range possible to attain. The Odonic *Dialogus* also regarded as senseless the notation of chants in the seventh mode with a b♭, since this particular arrangement was available in the notation of the first mode from D to d (Gerbert I:262). From this standpoint it becomes clear why Hucbald found nothing noteworthy in the fact that his Daseian signs through mutation could be transferred to another pitch region (cf. p. 34).

A third Odonic treatise exists under the name of Berno of Reichenau as part of a Leipzig manuscript, but it cannot be ascribed to him in any case; it was found by Gerbert (I:265 ff.) in a St. Blasien manuscript (now no longer in existence) appended to the *Dialogus* of Odo.*6 This treatise helps to give us an even more profound insight into the theoretical thinking of the time by means of a table which is very similar to a passage in the *Dialogus* (which thereby gains in interest). Special attention is given to the four divisions of the monochord (I:254), and the following intervals are determined:

1. the whole tone (9/8)
2. the fourth     (4/3)
3. the fifth      (3/2)
4. the octave     (2/1)

The author of this Odonic treatise, which begins with the words "*Musica artis disciplina*," measures these intervals from all tones of the [characteristic medieval] regular monochord. This, contrary to the *Dialogus*, increases the range by three steps and extends one step above Hucbald's Daseian scale. The following letters are used:

Γ  A  B♭  C  D  E  F  G  a  b♭  b♮  c  d  e  f  g  α  β  χ  Δ

The author of this treatise acknowledges himself expressly as the originator of these extensions.[9] Naturally the measurement of the intervals

[9] Gerbert I:272: "Although these are rarely found, they are not to be utterly ignored. When in a monochord we think that a tone should be placed before the first one, we call it not the first but rather the adjunct, because of its rare usage. We do not designate it with the first letter A but we draw the Greek letter GAMMA." (Page 272b): "We moreover add four tones after the last because the *cantus* runs over, yet you will scarcely or never find it ascending to these tones." (Page 273a): "The third verse, indeed (= the third letter of the alphabet) which is believed superfluous is rather noted by the Greek letters (α β χ Δ) having five tones; of which two (β, ♮♮), in the likeness of the former (♭ ♮) (the diapasons of which are measured by size) are accepted as one letter, although divided."

of a whole-tone, fourth, and fifth results in the division of the regular monochord, that is to say, the customarily used scale of the antique *systema teleion metabolon* with the addition of a step below and three foreign chromatic steps above. The author of the treatise, however, does not recognize the chromatic steps as justifiable;[10] he argues that these half-steps, which are outside of the range of a regular monochord, should be eliminated rather than imitated, since their use in melody is faulty, rambling in effect, and insignificant. Special pains must be taken that singers will not introduce these chromatic tones by mistake in going from one scale to another (transposing). This would constitute a faulty progression, even though it had been already "satisfactorily" explained by teachers (referring to Hucbald's explanation of the *absonia* which are called *dissonantia* by this author). Two whole-steps must always be followed by a half-step, and a half-step always followed by two whole-steps. As it is only possible, however, to avoid that which one can recognize, the author incorporates five such half-steps into his division of the monochord, which naturally fall outside of the normal scale. First, he incorporates the octave below the *nona prima*, B♭, then the octave above the *nona prima* (β), as well as the fourth above the low B♭ (E♭) and its octave (e♭). Drawings of the monochord with these tones are missing. Two pages further on a table also includes a fifth and a sixth chromatic step: the fifth above the low B♮ (=F♯) and its octave (f♯), as well as finally also a seventh, eighth, and ninth step, the whole-tone above B♮ (=C♯), b♮ an octave higher (=c♯), and the highest b♮ (c♯'); in all, ten chromatic tones appear, i.e., the following half-tone progressions:

A B♭, C♯ D, D E♭, F♯ G | α♭, c♯ d, d e♭, f♯ g | α β, c♯' d'

The text speaks of two kinds of signs for chromatic tones, both of which

[10] Gerbert I:272: "Praeterea aliquando vitiosa et maxime lasciviens et nimium delicata harmonia plura, quam diximus, semitonia quaerit, et quae nos posuimus, renuit, quod magis corrigi, quam imitari oportet. Cavendum est autem, ne per musici incuriam hoc fiat, cum cantum aliter, quam compositus est, incipiat atque perficiat; ipsa enim dissonantia (=absonia!) sicut magistri (Hucbald!) probant, repugnat, neque post duos tonos aliud quam semitonium; neque post semitonium aliud, quam duos tonos debere poni. Nos autem quia evitari non potest vitium, nisi fuerit cognitum, quinque hujusmodi semitonia sed extra praefixam regulam, in monochordo ponimus; unum quidem post primam, a quo ad finem medius ille post octavam stat semitonus; quae nos quoque recipimus: uterque tamen semitonii charactere; sed dissimili, formatur. Alter quoque qui ab ipso, qui est post octavam, medius simili, sed graeco charactere pingitur, Item post quartam alius notatur, qui ab eo, qui est post primam, quaternaria divisione colligitur; a quo alius post undecimam medius invenitur. Sed ambo hi aspirationis littera fiunt, sed dissimili: quare graeci per eam litteram hemitonium dicunt et scribunt. De quibus eum qui est post octavam vel medium ejus recipimus, alios potius cavendos quam recipiendos monemus."

are to be represented by the sign for the aspirate ( ⌐? ᶜ? ch, χ? ) with which the Greeks represented the half-tone (?). The table shows only m and m̃, the former for F#, f#, C#, c#, and c#', the latter only for e♭, in the uppermost row in which distances are indicated with T and S (*tonus* and *semitonium*), between ♮ and β♮♮, and only for F# a ch is written below the m. The m, without doubt, signifies "*medius*" (intermediate tone).

Jacobsthal, who was the first to mention this table (*op. cit.*, p. 30), uses it to prove the existence of these chromatic tones in the ecclesiastical modal chants, a hypothesis with which I do not agree.*[7] The table (Gerbert I:274) appears as follows:

| | | T | T | S | T | T | S | T | T | S | m̃ | S | T | T | S | T | T | S | m̃ | S | T |
|---|---|---|---|---|---|---|---|---|---|---|---|---|---|---|---|---|---|---|---|---|---|---|
| Litterae monochordi per ordinem | Γ | A | B | C | D | E | F | G | a | ♭ | ♮ | c | d | e | f | g | α | β | ♮♮ | χ | Δ |
| La divisio per IX. id est epogdous tonus | A | B | m | D | E | m (ch) | G | a | ♮ | c | m | d | e | m | g | α | ♮♮ | χ | m | Δ | Novem |
| Divisio prior per IV. id est diatessaron | C | D | E | F | G | a | ♭ | c | d | m̃ | e | f | g | a | β | χ | Δ | Quator | | | |
| Divisio prior per III. id est diapente | D | E | m | G | a | ♮ | c | d | e | f | m | g | α | ♮♮ | χ | Δ | Tria | | | | |
| Divisio prior per II. id est diapason | G | a | ♮ | c | d | e | f | g | α | β | ♮♮ | χ | Δ | Duo vel medietas | | | | | | | |

In addition, the following remark is found:[11]

If you consider studiously and tenaciously that which we have written, you shall find the way to comprehend many even more complicated relationships between tones. I shall not further concern myself with these in order to avoid the suspicion that I am feeding the youthful reader with superfluous dishes instead of simple milk.

The remark of Guido of Arezzo toward the end of his famous letter *De ignoto cantu*, directed to the monk Michael (at the end of the *Prologus in tonarium*), may also refer to this table:[12]

Those who wish to learn more should take my *Micrologus* in hand and also read again the *Enchiridion* written with such clarity by the most reverend Abbot Odo, from whose example I have departed only in the forms of the notes, in conde-

[11] "Et si ea, quae dicta sunt, sollicitius assidua mente revolvas, ad alia quamplura et altiora numerorum mysteria sensum protendere poteris. Quae nos ideo praetermisimus ne tenerum lectorem magis suffocare superfluis cibis quam lacte nutrire videremur."

[12] (Gerbert, *Script.* II:50): "Qui autem curiosus fuerit, libellum nostrum, cui nomen Micrologus est, quaerat, librum quoque Enchiridion, quem Reverendissimus Oddo Abbas luculentissime composuit, perlegat, cujus exemplum in solis figuris sonorum dimisi, quia parvulis condescendi, Boetium in hoc non sequens, cujus liber non cantoribus sed solis philosophis utilis est."

scension to young beginners. I have not followed Boethius, whose book is of no use to singers but only to scholars.

That the *Dialogus* and also the treatise *Musicae artis disciplina* were influenced by Odo is made even more probable by a passage in the *Rhythmimachia Domni Oddonis* (Gerbert I:285 ff.), which apparently also alludes to possible intermediate chromatic tones (p. 293a). This passage appears toward the end, written in intricate allegorical terms: "Quot etiam camporum spatiis vel etiam quas in partes singulas liceat species producere, qui minoris formae, qui rotundae quive quadratae debeant existere...."

The importance of the Odonic writings, among which also occur a whole series of small monochord measurements (including one from A to P, also semitone distances between B♮ and C, E and F in Gerbert I:342), organ pipe dimensions, etc., lies in the rearrangement of the letter scale, in the use of different letter forms for different octave positions, and in the establishment of b as *b-rotundum* and *quadratum* (compare with the passage from the *Rhythmimachia*), which provided the first basis for the later system of transposition. An insight into the nature of transposition, together with a strong distaste for all that which goes beyond the limits of the simple diatonic, stamps the spiritual founder of these writings (whom we must still call Odo, the abbot of Cluny, since proof to the contrary is lacking) as a personality of firm will and clear judgment. The treatise *Musicae artis disciplina*, which is appended to the *Dialogus* and which includes an interesting table of chromatic tones, also contains a comprehensive discussion of elementary melodic construction. Guido of Arezzo refers to this treatise frequently in his *Micrologus* (he uses the following terminology: *syllaba, pars, distinctio; arsis, thesis,* etc.).

The Odonic treatises, however, contain no information concerning the theory of polyphony. The same is true of the treatises by Berno of Reichenau, whose *Prologus in tonarium* contains very little original material, especially when one first eliminates those passages added later (and lacking in several codices) which use the Odonic (or Guidonian) tone letters and, second, attributes those passages containing the systematic dissection of octaves into fourths and fifths to an anonymous writer before Berno's time (Pseudo-Bernelinus; see paragraph in Gerbert I:313). Even if Berno's additions to Hucbald's text of the *Harmonica institutio* are numerous, though small, these can hardly be regarded as original contributions of Berno. When this is done, little more remains than the *Tonarius* itself and a few remarks concerning the classification of chants in the same work, which are valuable only as far as the history of liturgy is concerned.

The division of the ecclesiastical modes into fifths and fourths, and the proof that the two parts of the octave [the authentic division into a fifth and fourth] are reversed in the plagal modes was, as we have already seen, undoubtedly older than Berno. I am even convinced that this concept is as old as Hucbald, since the *Alia musica* deals with this subject;*[8] the language, however, is involved and unfortunately rather difficult to understand. The exposition of Pseudo-Bernelinus is, on the contrary, to the point and short; one can readily surmise that it aroused a great deal of attention and was well received. It also became the standard reference for the enumeration of the species of fourths and fifths. Although the author of the *Alia musica* lists the octave species ascending from a,

|     |      |      |
|-----|------|------|
| I. Hypodorius | II. Hypophrygius | III. Hypolydius |
| IV. Dorius | V. Phrygius | VI. Lydius |
| VII. Mixolydius | VIII. Hypermixolydius | |

he still notates species of fourths in the antique manner:

*Alia musica:* I. e′ d′ c͡′ b          Boethius: I. a g f͡ e
    (semitone in third place)

      II. d′ c͡′ b a          II. g f͡ e d
    (semitone in second place)

      III. c͡′ b a g          III. f͡ e d c
    (semitone in first place)

      (IV. b a g f͡ (with half-steps outside the tetrachord)

as well as the species of fifths descending from *nete diezeugmenon* (developing them from species of fourths by adding a tone below):

*Alia musica:* I. e′ d′ c͡′ b‖a

      II. d′ c͡′ b a‖g

      III. c͡′ b a g‖f

      IV. b a g f͡‖e

(Boethius reckons fourths downwards from the *mese* [a], which results in the same order as far as the position of the semitone is concerned. The ancient Greeks, however, thought of the species of fourths, as well as the octave species, as progressing upwards from *hypate hypaton* [B♮].)

As a consequence, Bernelinus also lists the species of fourths downwards from A, or actually from a (!), but does not attempt to develop the fifth in the antique manner by the addition of a whole-tone to the fourth. He adopts the ecclesiastical modal system in its entirety as his basis and establishes the different species of fifths and fourths by division of the four authentic modes. (We must assume that Bernelinus was not familiar with a similar division of the antique octave-species into fifths and fourths by Gaudentios, as the latter wrote in Greek.)

|  |  |  |
|---|---|---|
|  | I   I | I   I |
|  | I. D͡a d | I. A͡D͡a |
|  | II  II | II II |
| authentic | II. E͡b͡e | II. B͡E͡b |
|  | III III | III III    plagal |
|  | III. F͡c f | III. C͡F͡c |
|  | IV  I    (N.B.) | I  IV |
|  | IV. G͡d͡g | IV. D͡G͡d |

Bernelinus discovers internal structural similarities occurring in the four authentic modes. These he finds by comparing pairs of species in similar and opposite order:

| | | |
|---|---|---|
| 1. authentic D E͡ F G a (ascending) | The fifths are shown in opposite order; the fourths of both are the same structure and order. | a b͡ c d |
| 4. authentic d c͡ b a G (descending) |  | D E͡ F G |
| 2. authentic E͡ F G a b | Fifths and fourths are shown in opposite order. | b c d e |
| 3. authentic c͡ b a G F |  | f e͡ d c |

If the authorship of Bernelinus cannot be upheld (see Brambach, *Die Musikliteratur des Mittelalters*, p. 14), then the author whom Berno had to thank for these innovations unfortunately has faded into oblivion. The same observations, however, are found in the Anonymous I treatise of Gerbert (I:330) for which we must assume an early origin because of the manner in which the author uses the tone letters A–S for A–$\frac{a}{a'}$, with H I K L for the *tetrachord synemmenon*. Anonymous I undoubtedly belongs in the period of the Odonic treatises, for he recognized the similarity of octave tones, but did not differentiate between them by using different letter forms, rather preferring to continue further in the alphabet.[13] His three species of diatessaron are:

1. A B C D = T S T
2. B C D E = S T T
3. C D E F = T T S

"These three species you will encounter again and again in those

[13] Gerbert I:335a: "For, however, there are seven different notes, namely A B C D E F G, but when you come to the eighth, which is H, you find it the same as the first."

remaining, only not between F M (=F ♮), and I P (=♭ e)." The four
species of diapente are:

1. D E F G A
2. E F G H M  (M=b♮ since H I K L=a ♭ c d is interpolated for
          the tetrachord *synemmenon*)
3. F G H M N
4. G H M N O

"These four species appear again and again in those remaining, except
between B F (=♮ – F), E I (=E – ♭), and M Q (=♮ – f)."

The seven octave species finally are:

1. A – H  (first fourth and first fifth).
2. B – M  (second fourth and second fifth).
3. C – N  (third fourth–third fifth).
4. D – O  (first fifth and first fourth).
5. E – P  (second fifth and second fourth).
6. F – Q  (third fifth and third fourth).
7. G – R  (fourth fifth and first fourth).

Berno offers us another method of determining species of fourths and
fifths which lies between this new method (which was the standard for
the period to follow) and the older transitional method contained in the
*Alia musica:*

corresponding
to the middle fifth
of the four modes

This was still quoted as the standard by Engelbert of Admont (Gerbert,
*Script.* II:315) around 1300.

Berno prefers, and rightly so, the newer method, since it shows most clearly the nature of the four ecclesiastical modes (compare Gerbert I:67 and 69 f., as well as pp. 78 f.). Berno explicitly states on p. 78b that it was not he himself who instituted these innovations, and refers to a *quidam sapiens* [a certain philosopher] (Pseudo-Bernelinus).

Berno's contemporary, Hermann Graf von Vehringen, called Hermannus Contractus (died 1054), a monk in the cloister at Reichenau, has nothing to say about organum and does not offer any independent contribution as far as the tonal system is concerned. His treatise *Musica clarissimi viri Herimanni*,*[9] which is printed in Gerbert (II:125 ff.) is chiefly noteworthy for a certain practical simplicity in the development of concepts which had been established by his predecessors. Hermann demonstrates the fourth, the fifth, the octave, and the double octave through simple division of a string:

| 4/4 | 3/4 | 2/4 | 1/4 |
|---|---|---|---|
| A | D | a | a |
|   |   |   | a |
|   | fourth | fifth | octave |

octave

double octave

He further differentiates between two ways of dividing the gamut into tetrachords: one which is applicable to the antique measurement of the monochord, descending from right to left with tetrachords having a T T S pattern (for example: e d c ♮), and the other suitable for determining the ecclesiastical modes (*troporum constitutioni*), with tetrachords having a T S T pattern in an ascending direction:

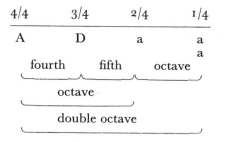

Graves                    Excellentes

$\Gamma \parallel$ A B̂ C D          d ê f g $\parallel$ a / a (superacuta)

D Ê F G $\parallel$ a ♮̂ c d
Finales $\parallel$ Superiores

Hermannus then finds the various species of fourths existing between tones having the same position in the *graves* and *finales* tetrachords (in the course of which he makes use of the terms *prima*, *secunda*, *tertia*, *quarta* [*gravium, finalium,* etc.], apparently with regard to Hucbald's tonal nomenclature in the *Musica enchiriadis*):

1. A–D =    I gravium –    I finalium
2. B–E =   II gravium –   II finalium
3. C–F = III gravium – III finalium
(4. D–G =    I gravium –    I finalium)

Hermannus is rather proud of the fact that he can easily continue in this manner, while the above-mentioned older method which Berno discusses, starting with D–G and ascending, must omit F–♮ and cite G–c as a third species.

Hermannus, however, demonstrates the species of fifths as those existing between tones of the *finales* and *superiores* tetrachords having the same number:

1. D–a =    I finalium –    I superiorum
2. E–♮ =   II finalium –   II superiorum
3. F–c = III finalium – III superiorum
4. G–d = IV finalium – IV superiorum

and the octave species as those existing between tones having the same number in the *graves* and *superiores* and the *finales* and *excellentes* tetrachords (the D–d octave species appearing twice):

Plagal
- 1. A–a =    I gravium –    I superiorum
- 2. B–♮ =   II gravium –   II superiorum
- 3. C–c = III gravium – III superiorum
- 4. D–d = IV gravium – IV superiorum

and:

Authentic
- 1. D–d =    I finalium –    I excellentium
- 2. E–e =   II finalium –   II excellentium
- 3. F–f = III finalium – III excellentium
- 4. G–g = IV finalium – IV excellentium

Can there be anything more pleasing and reliable than this established order of octaves, fifths, and fourths in which all first species are formed by the first letters of the tetrachords, all the second species by the second letters, all the third species by the third letters, and all the fourth species by the fourth letters?! (Page 132a)

This, admittedly, constitutes a very practical and undeniably useful application of Hucbald's tone names according to their placement in the normal tetrachord (that one composed of finals). Hermannus knows the Greek scale names, introduced by the author of the *Alia musica* with their new meaning, considers them genuinely Ptolemaic, but discards the Hypermixolydian $\left(a-\dfrac{a}{a}\right)$ after a humorous refutation and replaces it with the Hypomixolydian (D–d with final G).

Hermannus regards his double enumeration of the D and d as the fourth plagal mode in the lower tetrachord and the first authentic mode in the higher tetrachord as a personal achievement. This might, nevertheless, be counted as an additional, though not necessary, proof that Hucbald's tetrachords of "equal structure" were not meant in such an order. On the other hand, one must not overlook the fact that the Odonic treatise (referred to above) with which the *Musica artis disciplina* begins contains a table which might refute Hermannus' claim to originality (Gerbert I:267):

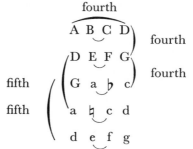

Unfortunately the accompanying text is not completely in order; it does, however, clearly refer to the intervals of fourths and fifths occurring between the tetrachords.

In addition, the treatise printed under the name of Bernelinus by Gerbert (I:313) shows the same system of determining species of fourths and fifths and their arrangement in the octave species; so Hermannus can lay claim only to the transcription of this system to tonal letters and a skillful and complete presentation.

Hermannus is not very kindly disposed toward Hucbald's Daseian notation.[14] He understood the gamut in the same manner as Spitta, the

---

[14] (Gerbert, *Script.* II:144):*[10] "Wherefore those persons are a long way from the truth who almost everywhere put the same signs in the fifth place, as if there were a perfect consonance at this point, and who through this error find that, contrary to the general opinion of all musicians—nay, contrary to the laws of nature herself, the same signs occur in the ninth place rather than the eighth; and thus the characters alone and not the pitches are equal, which is absolutely absurd. Wherefore, those who linger in the study of such an arrangement should consider that where almost no truth, no certainty exists, due to the disorganized operation of the principal pitches, the confused system of the species, and the disturbed order of the modes, they know that they themselves will accomplish nothing that is true or certain. To make this clearer, let us lay out this same arrangement before your eyes."

first scholar to correctly reinterpret it, since he refers throughout to the interval of a semitone between the second and third tone of each tetrachord, and assumes a whole-tone distance between the two outer tones of the tetrachords. In order to clarify the disparity which he feels exists in the Daseian notation, and to show that unity should exist between symbols, he makes use of four letters: A (for all Proti), B (for all Deuteri), C (for all Triti), and D (for all Tetrardi). He is filled with indignation that the ninth, not the octave, carries the corresponding symbol (although he did not notice that Hucbald also used the same symbol for octave doublings)*[11] and expresses his disgust with these words:

Whoever wastes time with the study of this tonal system should realize that in it the value of the basic gamut as well as the order of the interval successions is anulled, that the nature of the ecclesiastical modes is destroyed, and that almost nothing true and reliable remains.

Hermannus is chiefly renowned for his attempt to clarify the neumatic notation of intervals by the substitution of his own interval notation, which used the beginning letters of interval names to identify them (Gerbert II: 149 ff.: cf. my *Studien zur Geschichte der Notenschrift*, p. 108).

For our purposes this attempt of Hermannus, which naturally met with little approval, is without significance.

APPENDIX

FOOTNOTE 2:

| HUCBALD | BERNO |
|---|---|
| *De harmonica institutione* | *Prologus in tonarium* |
| (Gerbert I: 105a): | (Gerbert II: 64a): |
| Primus modus est, cum sibi duae voces brevissimi spatii divisione cohaerent, adeo, ut vix discrimen sentiatur inter eas, ut in antiphona, "Missus est Gabriel" ad id loci "Mariam" item "Virginem." | Primus modus est in brevissimo duarum vocum spatio et fit in semitonio ut hoc liquet exemplo in gravitate et acumine in illa antiph. "Missus est Gabriel" ad id loci "Mariam" item "Virginem." |
| Secundus jam perceptibilioris est, ut in hoc "Missus est" item ad "Mariam Virginem" item "Angelus." | Secundus jam perceptibilioris est intervalli et fit in tono ut in hac antiph. "Missus est." |
| Tertius adhuc parvo diductiori ut in hoc: "Missus est Gabriel ad Mariam Virginem." | Tertius adhuc parvo diductior hoc est in tono et semitonio, ut in hac ant. "Missus est Gabriel ad Mariam virginem." |
| Quartus hoc quoque protensior: ut in hac antiphona: "Beati qui ambulant." | Quartus hoc quoque protensior, qui fit in duobus tonis ut in hac "Beati qui ambulant." |
| Quintus adhuc spatiosior: ut in hoc "Ne timeas Maria" et "In illa die fluent." | Quintus adhuc spatiosior id est duobus tonis et semitonio ut in hac "Ne timeas Maria" item ant. "In illa die fluent." |

Sextus nihilominus amplior: ut in hoc responso: "Iam corpus ejus" "Cujus pater feminam" item R., "Isti sunt dies, quos observare debetis temporibus."

Septimus hos quoque spatio proprio supervadit, ut in hac antiphona: "Beata Agnes in medio flammarum minas."

Octavum vero in hoc reperies: "Tu vir Symphoriane suspende in tormentis."

Nonus prolixiori super omnes tensus spatio metam hujusmodi divisionum sortitur: nam nec amplius isto, nec strictius primo umquam vocum reperies divisionem. Et est ipse in hac antiphona "Ad te levavi animam meam. Deus meus in te." R. "Inter natos mulierum non."

Ultra hunc enim novissimum divisionis, si quas adhuc amplius distantiae continentes voces quaesieris, nec in aliquo id rationabili cantu reperies, nec possibilitas humani appulsus hic accommoda erit: ut in tam longe distantibus vocibus uno quasi ictu tam facile e summo ad infima reflectatur, quin potius pene in novam permutatio erit vocem....

Consonantia...non aliter constabit, nisi duo altrinsecus editi soni in unam simul modulationem conveniant, ut fit, cum virilis et puerilis vox pariter sonuerit; vel etiam in eo, quod consuete organizationem vocant.

Sextus nihilominus amplior id est tribus tonis continuis ut in hoc R. "Iam corpus ejus." "Cujus pater feminam."

Septimus hos quoque spatio supervadit, constans tribus tonis et semitonio ut haec ant. "Beata Agnes in medio minas."

Octavam ac si rarius in quatuor tonis non tamen plenis, reperies, ut in hoc R. "Tu vir Symphoriane suspende in tormenta...(a correction of the explanation follows).

Nonus prolixiori super omnes spatio tensus metam hujusmodi divisionum sortitur; nam nec ampliorem isto nec strictiorem primo ullam musicarum vocum reperies divisionem; constat enim quatuor sonis et semitonio; et habes exemplum in hac ant. "Ad te levavi animam meam Deus meus," item R. "Inter natos mulierum non," item R. "Haec est virgo." "Introivit." Item in acumine ant. "Iste cognovit" in hoc loco "et inventus est in."

Ultra hunc enim novissimum modum si quas voces inter se subalterna percussione distantes quaesieris...donec ad diapason consonantiam pervenias ubi magis est nova permutatio vocis, quam progressio modi amplioris: quia nec ipsa humani appulsus possibilitas admittit ut intervallum tam longe inter se distantibus aliquis aptus reddatur sonus.

Et tunc consonantiae fiunt, quando altrinsecus virilis ac puerilis vox pariter sonuerit: vel potius eo cantandi genere, quod consuete dicitur organizare. In reliquis vero non sunt consonantiae, sed intervalla, et quaedam vocum discrimina.

(Ecclesiastical modes):

(p. 119): Illud nihil (?) attendendum, quod synemmenon tetrachordo summoto, quinta semper loca his quatuor superiora quadam sibi connexionis unione junguntur, adeo, ut pleraque etiam in eis quasi regulatirer mela inveniantur desinere, nec rationi ob hoc vel sensui quid contraire, et sub eodem modo vel tropo recte decurrere.

(p. 74b): Notandum vero est, quod quinto semper loco superioribus cum inferioribus finalibus quaedem talis concordia est, ut aliqua mela in eis quasi regulariter inveniantur finire....

Hac ergo socialitate continentur lichanos hypaton cum mese; hypate meson cum paramese; parypate meson cum trite diezeugmenon; lichanos meson cum paranete diezeugmenon, quae quinto scilicet loco singulae a se disparantur.... Cum inferioribus quoque quartis, et in quibusdam quintis, parem quodammodo obtinent habitudinem, quamvis non fini, sed initiis deputentur....

Hoc ergo socialitatis foedus obtinet lichanos hypaton cum mese, hypate meson cum paramese, parypate meson cum trite diezeugmenon, lichanos meson cum paranete diezeugmenon. Cum inferioribus quoque quartis et in quibusdam quintis, parem habitudinem habent, quamvis hoc magis ad initia illorum quam ad finem pertinere soleat (here an independent reference to the transposition of the *modi* to the upper fourth follows).

Et omnis omnino tonus a finali suo nec supra quintum superiorem, nec infra quintum inferiorem umquam ordiendi facultatem habebit, sed intra eas novem voces, vel aliquando octo partim principales, partim laterales, fines vel initia cohibebunt.

(p. 74): Et haec est eorum regula ad quodlibet melum inchoandum ut nec supra quintum superiorem, nec infra quintum inferiorem locum aliquando incipiant, sed inter eas octo voces vel aliquando novem initia sua cohibeant.

(Musical tones):

(p. 107b): Sonos, quibus per quaedam veluti elementa ad Musicam prisci aestimaverunt ingrediendum, graeco nomine phthongos voluerunt appellare, id est, non qualescumque sonos... sed eos tantum, quos rationabili discretos ac determinatos quantitate, quique melodiae apti existerent, ipsi certissima totius cantilenae fundamenta jecerunt. Unde et elementa vel phthongos eosdem nuncupaverunt: quod scilicet, quemadmodum litterarum elementis sermonum cuncta multiplicitas coarctatur et quidquid dici potest, per eas digeritur;... dicti autem phthongi... a similitudine loquendi....

(p. 63): Verum quia omnis cantilena non quibuscumque vocibus sed certis et determinatis sonis, quos Graeci phthongos quasi a similitudine loquendi vocant, ordinabiliter contexitur, ut....

quemadmodum litterarum elementis omnis sermonum series digeritur....

FOOTNOTE 4: Gerbert I:256: "Ut haec antiphona: 'O beatum pontificem!' quae cum in principio et fine secundi modi esset, propter illius tantum vocis elevationem, ubi dicitur: 'O Martine dulcedo' in primo tono a Domno Oddone curiosissime est emendata'."

FOOTNOTE 5: Gerbert I:249a: "Nullus denique putet, quod omnes antiphonae in suo principio se conveniant cum initio psalmi; majorem autem partem antiphonarum in fine volunt sibi incipere psalmum, sicut antiphona: 'O beatum pontificem,' quam multi faciunt de secundo tono; sed fallunt, cum sit de primo et de septima differentia."

FOOTNOTE 6: "Item Tonora per ordinem cum suis differentiis, quos habemus honorifice emendatos et patefactos a Domno Oddone religioso Abbate, qui fuit peritus in arte musica."

FOOTNOTE 9: Gerbert I:272: "Quamvis haec raro inveniantur, non tamen penitus ignoranda sunt. Unde in monochordo ante primam unam vocem ponendam censuimus, quam propter rarum usum...non primam, sed magis adjunctam vocamus. Neque eam per primam litteram (A) designamus sed per graecum Gamma $\Gamma$ depingimus...." (p. 272b): "Addimus praeterea quatuor voces post ultimam, sive propter superfluos cantus, quos tamen aut vix aut nunquam reperies ad eas ascendere...." (p. 273a): "Tertius vero versus (=Alphabetum tertium), quia superfluus creditur, graecarum potius litterarum forma notatur ($\alpha \beta \chi \Delta$), habens voces quinque; de quibus duo ($\beta$,♮♮) ad earum similitudinem, quarum diapason dimensione fiunt (♭♮), pro una accipiuntur littera, quamvis divisa."

FOOTNOTE 13: Gerbert I:335a: "Nam septem dumtaxat sunt vocum distantiae, videlicet A B C D E F G, quodsi octavam, quae est H tetigeris, eandem invenies primae."

FOOTNOTE 14: Gerbert, *Script.* II:144: "Unde longe a veritate discordant, qui fere ubique in quintis locis eadem signa quasi ibi perfecta concordia sit ponunt. Quibus etiam hoc vitio contingit, ut contra communem omnium musicorum consensum immo contra ipsius jura naturae eadem signa in nona potius quam octava regione veniant, sicque quod nimis absurdum est characteres tantum non voces aequalitatem habeant. Quo circa talis dispositionis studio immorantibus considerandum est, quod ubi dissipata principalium chordarum operatione perturbata specierum constitutione, disjecto troporum ordine nil fere veritatis nil pene certitudinis constat, nihil se verum, nihil certum acturos sciant. Quod ut manifestius fiat; eandem suboculis dispositionem ponamus:

```
     t  s  t    t  t  s  t    t  t  s  t    t  t  s  t    t  s
   A B C D ‖ A B C D ‖ A B C D ‖ A B C D ‖ A B
```

## CHAPTER IV

# Organum in the 10th and 11th Centuries

THE first writer after Hucbald (assuming him to be the author of the *Musica enchiriadis* and its *Scholia*) to concern himself in detail with the theory of organum and to alter this theory was Guido of Arezzo (died 1050). His greatest accomplishment was, of course, the placing of neumes on lines, or in other words, founding our present system of notation.*[1]

The theory of strict parallel organum, developed to its limits in the *Musica enchiriadis*, was available to Guido in its complete form; he begins his expositions (in Chapter XVIII of the *Micrologus*; Gerbert, *Script.* II:21)[1] with a short description of parallel organum and its composite forms:*[2]

[1] (Cap. XVIII. De diaphonia i.e. organi praecepto): "Diaphonia vocum disjunctio sonat, quam nos organum vocamus, cum disjunctae ab invicem voces et concorditer dissonant et dissonanter concordant. Qua quidam ita utuntur, ut canenti semper quarta chorda succedat, ut .A. ad .D. ubi si organum per acutum .a. duplices, ut sit .A.D.a., resonabit .A. ad .D. diatessaron, ad .a. diapason; .D. vero ad utrumque .A. a., diatessaron et diapente; .a. acutum ad graviores diapente et diapason. Et quia hae tres species tanta se ad organum societate ac ideo suavitate permiscent, ut superius vocum similitudines fecisse monstratae sunt symphoniae, id est aptae vocum copulationes dicuntur, cum symphonia et de omni cantu dicatur. Dictae autem diaphoniae hoc est exemplum ('Miserere mei Deus'):

```
Diapente     c d e c    d e d    c c c ♮ a G c d e d d c
Diapason     F G a F    G a G    F F F E D C F G a G G F
Miserere       me-i    De-us
Diatessaron  C D E C    D E D    C C C B Γ C D E D D C
```

"(Haec autem figura aperte emendata continet praecedentes voces hujus antiphonae 'Miserere mei Deus,' subsequentes organizando per diatessaron, quod vulgariter dicitur organum sub voce, id est, subter praecedentes; acutas voces retinet organizantes per diapente quod organum dicitur supra vocem....) Potes et cantum cum organo et organum quantum libuerit duplicare per diapason; ubicumque enim ejus concordia fuerit, dicta symphoniarum aptatio non cessabit.

"Cum itaque jam satis vocum patefacta sit duplicatio, gravem a canente succentum, more quo nos utimur, explicemus. Superior nempe diaphoniae modus durus est, noster vero mollis, ad quem semitonium et diapente non admittimus; tonum vero et ditonum et semiditonum cum diatessaron recipimus, sed semiditonus in his infimatum, diatessaron vero obtinet principatum. His itaque quatuor concordiis diaphonia cantum subsequitur.

"Troporum vero alii apti, alii aptiores, alii aptissimi existunt. Apti sunt qui per solam diatessaron quartis a se vocibus organum reddunt, ut deuterus in .B. et .E.; aptiores sunt qui non solum quartis, sed tertiis et secundis per tonum et semiditonum, licet raro respondent, ut protus in .A. et .D. Aptissimi vero, qui saepissime suaviusque id faciunt, ut tetrardus et tritus in .C. et .F. et .G. Hae enim tono et ditono et diatessaron obsequuntur. Quorum a trito, in quem vel finis distinctionum advenerit, vel qui proximus ipsi finalitati suberit subsecutor numquam tamen descendere debet nisi illo inferiores voces cantor admiserit. A trito enim infimo aut infimis proxime substituto deponi organum numquam licet. Cum vero inferiores voces admiserit congruo loco, et per diatessaron organum deponatur; moxque ut illa distinctionis gravitas ita deseritur ut repeti non speretur, quem prius habuerat locum subsecutor repetat, ut finali voci si in se devenerit commaneat, et si super se e vicino decenter occurrat. Qui occursus tono melius fit, ditono non adeo, semiditono numquam. A diatessaron vero vix fit occursus, cum gravis magis placet illo loco succentus; quod tamen ne in ultima symphoniae distinctione eveniat est cavendum. Saepe autem cum inferiores trito voces cantor admiserit, organum suspensum tenemus in trito; tunc vero opus est ut cantor in inferioribus distinctionem non faciat, sed discurrentibus sub celeritate vocibus praestolanti trito redeundo subveniat, et suum et illius laborem facta in superioribus distinctione repellat. Item cum occursus fit tono diutinus fit tenor finis, ut ei et partim subsequatur et partim concinatur; cum vero ditono diutior, ut saepe per intermissam vocem dum vel parva sit subsecutio, etiam toni non desit occursio. Quod quia tunc fit cum harmonia finitur deutero; si cantus non speratur ultra ad tritum descendere, utile tunc erit proto vim organi occupare, subsequentibus subsequi, finique per tonum decenter occurrere. Item cum plus diatessaron sejungi non liceat, opus est, cum plus se cantor intenderit, subsecutor ascendat, ut videlicet .C. sequatur .F., et .D. .G., et .E.a. et reliqua. Denique praeter ♮ quadratam singulis vocibus diatessaron subest, unde in quibus distinctionibus illa fuerit, .G. vim organi possidebit. Quod cum fit, si aut cantus ad .F. descendat, aut in .G. distinctionem faciat, ad .G. et .a. congruis locis .F. subsequitur; si in .G. vero cantus non terminet, .F. cum cantu vim organi amittit. Cum vero .b. mollis versatur in cantu, .F. organalis erit. Cum ergo tritus adeo diaphoniae obtineat principatum ut aptissimum supra caeteros obtineat locum, videmus eum a Gregorio non immerito plus caeteris vocibus adamatum. Ei enim multa melorum principia et plurimas repercussiones dedit, ut saepe si de ejus cantu triti .F. et .C. subtrahas, prope medietatem tulisse videaris. Diaphoniae praecepta donata sunt, quae si exemplis probes, perfecte cognosces.

"(Cap. XIX. Dictae Diaphoniae per exempla probatio.) Igitur a trito non deponimus organum sive in eo sive in sequentibus finiatur, hoc modo:

| F | FG | GFF | DEFEDC |
|---|----|-----|--------|
| I- | psi | so- | li |
| C | CD | DCC | CCCCCC |

Ecce finis in trito C,

| F | G | GaG | GF |
|---|---|-----|----|
| Ser-vo | fi- | dem | |
| C | D | DED | DC |

Ecce alia distinctio in trito .F. in quo et quartis vocibus per diatessaron subsequimur, et diatessaron succentus plusquam occursus placet,

| F | FE | D | FG | F |
|---|----|---|----|---|
| I- | psi | me | to- | ta |
| C | CC | C | CD | C |

Diaphony means the rendering independent of the voices, and is also called organum, this occurring when several voices moving at different pitch levels form a harmonious combination of two sounds. This is the same as a concord of sounds containing elements which are possible to distinguish from each other. This happens, consequently, when the accompanying voice follows the melody at the distance of a fourth, for example, singing an A to a D.

If one doubles the organal voice by the addition of the a above so that the concord A D a results, A will make a fourth with D and an octave with a. D, however, will stand in the relationship of a fourth and a fifth to A and a, and the

Ecce alia ejusdem modi,

| F | F | F | FE | G | FE | D | D |
|---|---|---|----|---|----|---|---|
| De | vo- | ti- | o- | ne | com- | mitto | |
| C | C | C | CC | D | CC | C | D |

Ecce alia distinctio in proto .D., in qua et toni occursus ad finem patet.

Item

| C | D | F | F | F | F | F | FE | DE | E |
|---|---|---|---|---|---|---|----|----|---|
| Ho | mo | e-rat | in | Ihe- | ru- | sa- | lem | | |
| C | C | C | C | C | C | C | CC | CC | E |

aut ita

| F | FE | DE | E |
|---|----|----|---|
| Ihe- | ru- | sa- | lem |
| C | CC | CD | E |

Ecce distinctio in deutero .E. in qua ditoni occursus vel simplex vel per intermissas patet.

| CF | F | F | D | E | CD | | DCBA | C | DF | | E | C | E | D |
|----|---|---|---|---|----|--|------|---|----|--|---|---|---|---|
| Ve- | ni | ad | docendum | | | | nos | | vi-am | | prudenti- | ae | | |
| CC | C | C | C | C | CC | | AΓΓA | C | CC | | C | C | C | D |

Distinctio in proto A. In hac distinctione inferiores trito .C., qui fini proxime subest .D., voces admissae sunt, et locus prior finita gravitate repetitus est [ubi diximus 'viam prudentiae']. Et in hac similiter:

| F | FG | | GFF | D | DC | FG | | a | G | | F | G | | FFEDCFGaGF |
|---|----|--|-----|---|----|----|--|---|---|--|---|---|--|------------|
| Sexta | | | ho- | ra | se- | dit | | super | | | pute- | um | | |
| C | CD | | DCC | C | CC | CD | | E | D | | C | D | | CCCCCFFFFF |

Ecce ut ascendit organum, ne in ultima distinctione succineret cavens.

| F | FG | | GF | FD | | DC | FG | | a | G | | F | G | | FFEDCFGaGF |
|---|----|--|----|----|--|----|----|--|---|---|--|---|---|--|------------|
| Sexta | | | ho- | ra | | se- | dit | | super | | | puteum | | | |
| F | FF | | FF | FF | | FF | FF | | F | F | | F | F | | FFFFFFFFFF |

Ecce quomodo admittente cantore graves voces organum suspensum tenemus in trito .F.

| c | c | d | c | a | c | ♮ | c | a | G | F | GG |
|---|---|---|---|---|---|---|---|---|---|---|----|
| Victor | | a- | scendit | coelos | | unde | descenderat | | | | |
| G | G | a | G | GG | G | G | F | F | F | FG | |

Ecce ut .F. ad .G. et .a. in finem subsequitur. Idem in plagali trito invenies usurpatum videlicet, ut ad .c. et .d. ita .b. subsequatur, sicut ad .G. et .a. subsequitur .F., hoc modo:

| e | c | d | dedc | d | d | c |
|---|---|---|------|---|---|---|
| Ve-ni-te | | | ad- | or-em-us | | |
| c | c | c | cccc | b | b | c |

higher a will form a fifth and an octave with the two lower tones. Since these three individual tones blend to form the harmonious union of organum, corresponding to our demonstration of the agreement of consonance, one rightly calls such tone relationships *copulatio*, whereas the expression *symphonia* is applicable to all melodic tone relationships. The following is an example of such a *copulatio*:

This clearly representative example has for its *cantus* the melody of the antiphon *Miserere mei Deus* and as accompaniment an organal voice at the fourth below, commonly called *organum sub voce*. In addition, there is an organal voice a fifth above the *cantus*, commonly called *organum supra vocem*. . . . It is also possible, at one's discretion, to double the *cantus* with an organal voice at the octave, or, in other words, to let an organal voice proceed in octaves with the *cantus* without destroying the blend of the concord which has already been described.

Thus far Guido has achieved nothing new other than the differentiation of *organum supra vocem* (the organum of the fifth above which was first established as an independent type of the *Scholia* of the *Musica enchiriadis*) from the organum of the fourth below, now called *organum sub voce*. But Guido does not build his exposition upon this product of Hucbaldian theory:

With this the doubling of the voices is sufficiently and clearly shown. I shall now try to explain in what manner we set the lower organal voice today. The type of diaphony which we have described is somewhat rigid, and ours is, on the contrary, softer. We exclude the fifth and the semitone from the series of intervals available to us for concords, and allow outside of the fourth only the whole-tone and the major and minor third to be used. Of these the minor third has the lowest rank and the fourth the highest. The diaphony of the *cantus* results from the use of these four intervals.

Of the ecclesiastical modes (*tropi*) some are only usable, others better suited, and still others especially adaptable (for the composition of organum). Those which are merely usable allow organum to proceed exclusively at the distance of a fourth, as Deuterus in B and E; those better suited allow the introduction of thirds and seconds (namely, whole-tones and minor thirds) in the organal voice, such as Protus on A and D. Especially adaptable, however, are those in which this occurs in rich measure and with the most beautiful effect, such as in Tritus and Tetrardus in C, F, and G. For these accompany with whole-tones, major thirds and fourths. In these the organum may never be allowed to go below Tritus (on which either a distinction may find its conclusion, or which may be the tone below the final), unless the *cantus* itself goes lower (that is to say, a transition to an *organum inferius* results). It is, therefore, forbidden that the organum should go below Tritus, which is itself either a lowest possible tone, or the second below a lowest possible tone. If the *cantus* descends even further, the organum may in certain cases be placed a fourth lower. If the *cantus* descends even lower, organum may—in certain cases and if appropriate—also be placed a fourth lower. As soon as the organum leaves this lower position, having no intention of ever returning to it again, the organal voice should take its earlier position again in order to rest on the final of the *cantus* in case the *cantus* descends to it. If the *cantus* remains in a higher position, it should move gracefully toward it with the use of a neighboring tone. Such coming together of the voices is done best with a whole-tone, less well with a major third, but never with a minor third (as penultimate interval). The fourth as penultimate interval before the concluding unison can scarcely be allowed. In such a case, the interval of a fourth is more appropriate to the final; however, this must never happen at the end of the entire composition.

Sometimes organum may also rest on Tritus, if the *cantus* descends below Tritus. Then, however, the *cantus* must not rest on any of the lower tones, but must quickly run through them and rejoin the organal voice on Tritus which is waiting for it, in order to rectify its position and that of the organum through the accomplishment of a close in a higher position.

If the coming together of the voices starts from a whole-tone, the final of the *cantus* (tenor) is lengthened, so that the organum sings a tone foreign to it for a time, but then sings the same tone in another part. Such an extension of the *cantus* occurs more frequently when the coming together starts with the ditone, so that, even though the note value be short, the whole-tone is also touched upon which lies in between. This happens when the melody ends on Deuterus. As the *cantus* usually does not descend to Tritus in this case, it is recommended that the organum rest on Protus, and remain fixed in this position against further tones in order to allow it to enter into the final from the interval of a whole-tone. Since any interval other than the fourth is not allowed when the *cantus* ascends higher, organum must follow in such a manner that it unites C to F, D to G, and E to A, etc. Finally, we must remark that a perfect fourth lies below all tones with the exception of b♮; to all parts of the melody where this b♮ occurs, the organum must add G. If, in this case, the *cantus* descends to F or concludes on G, the organum adds F to G and a, should this be appropriate. If the ending does not rest on G, *cantus* and organum come together on F. If b♭ occurs in the *cantus*, then F is the organal tone. As Tritus dominates diaphony to such an extent that it occupies the highest place, we see that it is also preferred in Gregorian chant, as is its due. Beginnings and repercussions of many chants were allotted to it, so that if one removes the F and c of the Tritus, one removes almost half of all available tones.*[3]

These are the rules governing diaphony, which may become clearer through some examples:

Here we find an example in Tritus C.

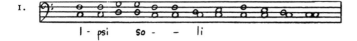

1.

I - psi    so - - li

Partial close in Tritus F with accompaniment in fourths of the organum even at the final, since this is more pleasant than coming together from the fourth.

2.

ser - vo  fi - - dem

As above:

3.

I - psi      me  to - ta

Partial close in Protus D as an example of the coming together of voices.

4.

De - vo - ti - o - ne com - mit - to

Partial close in Deuterus E, the simple or divided *occursus* beginning with the major third.

5.

Ho - mo — erat in Ihe - ru - sa - lem      Ihe - ru - sa - iem
                                        or:

Partial close in Protus A.*4 At the first point of rest (in the middle, on *nos*) a lower tone than that of Tritus C (the second below the final) is allowed (namely A) which again ascends (on *viam prudentiae*) into its former position.

6.

Ve - ni ad do - cen - dum   nos           vi - - am pru - den - ti - ae

Here the organum ascends in order not to end on the fourth below the final at the conclusion.

7.

Sex - ta   ho - - ra se - dit   super pu - te - um

A case where the *cantus* descends lower, but the organum remains on Tritus F.

8.

Sex - ta   ho - - ra se - dit   su - per pu - te - um

Here organum adds the tone F to G and a. It may also be found that in the plagal *Tritus* the tone b♭ (b♮ is apparently an error)*5 is added to c and d as the tone F is added to G and a:

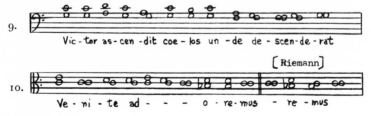

9.

Vic - tor as - cen - dit coe - los un - de de - scen - de - rat

[Riemann]

10.

Ve - ni - te ad - - - - o - re - mus - re - mus

The reason I have quoted Guido's treatise on organum in full is not only because of his great individual significance but also because I wish to show as distinctly as possible how close Guido's exposition comes to the older treatises with which we dealt at length.*6 This strengthens the assumption that strict parallel organum, especially organum at the fifth, is a product of that theory whose gradual evolution we have been able to follow.

That the practical use of organum was not becoming obsolete in Guido's time is shown by his remark that organum at the fourth (as lower organum, *organum sub voce*) was called *vulgariter*, or that which was in general use. It is probably not by accident that *vulgariter* defines only the organum at the fourth, which, from the very beginning, occupied a place in the foreground (in Hucbald). G. Jacobsthal (*Die chromatische Alteration...*, p. 271) was not very perceptive when he claimed the fifth to be the most important interval in organum and explained organum at the fourth as a deviation of actual organum, a theory which demanded quite a number of concessions. Organum at the fifth is of no particular importance before the *Scholia* of the *Musica enchiriadis*,*7 and its continuous parallel movement of fifths only the consequence of Hucbald's teachings in the *Scholia*. It is, however, completely rejected by Guido, for he mentions it only briefly as *organum supra vocem* and begins his remarks by treating of organum at the fourth. Even in this he shows continued parallelism to be a defect. I do not maintain that Guido used *modus noster* as a term of approval to define that form of organum which was then in general use. It may very well be that strict parallel organum became esteemed and widespread as a result of the writings of Hucbald, and that Guido was speaking of his own new version when he refers to *modus noster*, which was meant to oppose the former.

Guido strictly rejects the use of the fifth for organum. Furthermore, he does not subsequently speak of octave doublings, so one must assume that he did not regard them very highly. It is rather remarkable that the different modes are evaluated according to how well they favor the use of parallel fourths. This is entirely opposed to Hucbald's interpretation, inasmuch as the modes which are found especially suited for organum are those which require the most deviations from parallel motion. Nevertheless Guido clings theoretically to the fourth as his preferred interval, most probably under the forceful pressure of tradition. It must not be overlooked that the major modes are those which are found to be especially suitable: Tritus and Tetrardus on C, F, and G. In spite of the "♭ *mollis dulcedine*" of Giraldus Cambrensis, it may probably be assumed that the first development of polyphonic music was furthered by the gradual infiltration of concepts dominated by a feeling for the major mode, rather than for the minor mode, which had predominated in antiquity.

The halting of the organum (the organal voice) on C *gravium* we already know from the *Musica enchiriadis*, which, however, gave another reason and another rule for this. In the Daseian gamut, with its continued succession of fifths (p. 24), C is not Tritus, but Tetrardus, and the *Musica enchiriadis* forbids the stepwise descent of organum under Tetrardus because of the tritone which stands in the way. By this it means not only under C, but actually not under every Tetrardus, above all, the G. According to Hucbald's terminology the halting of organum on Tritus would be entirely impossible. In Guido's treatise those tones on which organum preferably cadences appear as F, G, and C, the finals of Tritus and Tetrardus, and the lower *socialis* of the final of Tritus. The reason for these cadence points is, supposedly, that under these three tones the intervals of a half-step and a minor third are found, from which an *occursus* is not allowed. This theory of the *occursus* is entirely new and thoroughly Guidonian. It reminds us, however, of the oldest descriptions of organum in Scotus Erigena as well as those in the Cologne and Paris treatises, which especially emphasize the coming together of voices to a unison in endings and partial endings. Apparently Guido is not satisfied with the new explanations, in the *Musica enchiriadis* and its *Scholia*, which replace the old ones and which often place the organal voice on one tone while the *cantus* continues to move. He seeks another explanation and achieves results similar to those contained in the Cologne and Paris treatises. He apparently did not know these older explanations and was presumably considering musical practice which might have often contradicted the theory of the *Musica enchiriadis*. The Cologne and Paris treatises generally require the organum to remain on the second below the final so that it can move to the unison together with the principal voice, which, for the most part, descends stepwise to the final. The organal voice would then move to the unison by ascending a second. Guido, however, at first requires only that the organal voice remain on C, the *Tritus gravium*. For Protus this agrees with the older teachings. Afterwards, however, he says that when melodies in Deuterus are concerned, the organal voice should remain on D in order to ascend to E at the final. He offers no explanation for this rule and must have based it upon practice alone, for under Deuterus we find the desirable major third (C D E) and nothing to prevent what was regarded as a normal *occursus* from being used. For the Tritus closing on F and the Tetrardus closing on G, on the other hand, he does not require stopping on the second below. The ninth example closes on G and the organum is placed on F, but as it uses b♭, it should be regarded as being in the transposed Protus, where F must play the role which C plays otherwise, a condition which Guido expressly demands (*cum vero .b. mollis versatur in cantu, F organalis erit*).*8 Guido also solves the problem which arises in Hucbald's *Musica enchiriadis* concerning the use of organum with b♮, when this occurs in the principal voice, and prescribes correction of those examples which were transcribed erroneously: G is the organal tone for b♮ (*vim organi possidet*). We find unmistakable proof for our conception of the real nature of organum in Guido's remark that organum often stops on a higher tone (especially the Tritus F), in order to avoid ending on the fourth below the final, this being allowed only for partial closes. The *Musica enchiriadis* evidences no such fear of a discrepancy in the voices at endings, but this apprehension is found in the three older versions (Scotus Erigena: "*sibi invicem coaptantur*"; Cologne treatise: "*ad finem sese voces diversae conjungant*" and "*ut vox ad vocem apte convenire possit*"; while the Paris treatise indicates not the purpose but only the means to its achievement). Guido's definition does not show clearly to what extent Tritus F in the Lydian mode (the authentic Tritus) may be used as a held tone in the organal voice, that is, the tone which is forbidden by Hucbald for use in descending from Tetrardus G while the tritone (b♮) is above it. It almost seems as if Guido considered it self-evident to either use b♭ or to avoid using b♮. For as a means of moving through the unsatisfactory *occursus* to F and G, the following

does not help to remove the difficulty connected with the tritone. As we have seen, this was also considered a problem by Guido, since he requires G for the organum whenever the *cantus* has a b♮ (it is certainly the *horror tritoni* which was one of the main reasons for the appearance of hexachord mutation, which dates at least back to Guido).

That the *cantus* may descend below the organal voice if the latter stops on Tritus is an entirely new concept. Crossing of voices is not found in any of the older authors. Compared with the older versions of the theory of organum, the more numerous occurrences of the prolongation of the organal voice in Guido is worthy of note. One may assume that organum belonging to the time in which the beginnings of mensural music are found (cf. Chapter IX), in which the tenor consists of only a few long sustained tones, evolved directly from that type which Guido describes.*9

It is probably not by chance that we note the appearance of instruments around the same time that organum developed, or only slightly later; these imply a similar kind of primitive polyphony. One of these instruments is the *organistrum*, which may be compared with the *Drehleier* (hurdy-gurdy), now becoming obsolete. Furthermore, stringed instruments are found with bourdon strings, next to the finger board, which are always plucked during the playing of the instruments. One can assume also that the bagpipe, which can be traced throughout the entire Middle Ages, acquired bourdons around this time. To base theories on these facts would be daring; such an obvious analogy, however, can hardly be disregarded. The *organistrum* points rather clearly to the *organizatio* because of its name.*[10] I mention these curiosities of music history at this time, for, following Guido, the theory of organum rapidly pursues other courses and leads directly to the theory of discant.

Special attention must be given to only one more post-Guidonian theorist before we shall be led through Johannes Cotton to the theory of discant. This is the anonymous author of the treatise *Ad organum faciendum* (found in Coussemaker's *Histoire de l'harmonie au moyen-âge*, pp. 229 ff.), which belongs to an 11th- or 12th-century MS of the Library Ambrosiana in Milan, and which we shall call the Milan treatise to distinguish it from the Cologne and Paris treatises. Since this treatise at the outset refers directly to Guido's theory of organum, the author is certainly post-Guidonian. Internal evidence, however, compels us to regard it as having been written around 1100, at the latest. The author first deplores the fact that Pythagorean teachings have been made more complicated and hard to understand by Boethius. He goes on to say that Guido's instructions on organum were contradicted by his examples (?), which made them hard to appreciate and difficult to remember. He then enumerates five ways of leading the organum (*quinque modos organizandi*), or rather, five elements of organum: the beginning interval, the transition interval to the middle, the actual middle interval (between beginning and end), the transition interval to the final interval, and the final interval.

The author is thorough and systematic. He finds it necessary to note that if (a member of) organum discloses six tones (intervals), five of these are not superfluous (but are required to prove the necessity for his establishment of five elements!).

Then, after having copied Guido's introduction almost word for word, and even having copied Guido's reference to the formerly mentioned (!) fusion (*similitudo*) of consonances (which reference was only applicable to Guido), he establishes his own theory, which, to our surprise, shows hardly any similarity to Guido's.

The rules of the Milan treatise are as follows:[2]

[2] (Coussemaker, *Histoire*, p. 232): "Prima vox organi aut manebit conjuncta cum praecedente per diapason vel in eadem, aut disjuncta (per) diapente et diatessaron; mediae vero voces diapente et diatessaron discurrunt.

"Cum autem cantus praestolatur organum, copulatio fit quolibet modo; et ita, cum quatuor voces tantum subsequentes sint, una organalis dicitur; nam prima quandoque jungitur, secunda semper disjungitur, tertia intuens praestolantem, ut habilem copulam tribuat quartae voci cum qualibet consonantia.

The beginning of the organal voice forms its connection either with the *cantus* at the octave or in unison, or by its division at the interval of a fifth or fourth. All middle tones (on distinctions [partial cadences determined in the chant by the ends of phrases] in the text) follow in fourths and fifths with the *cantus*.

But whenever the *cantus* awaits the organal voice (i.e., in all divisions or part endings), both unite (in unison) in the same manner.

Whenever there are only four tones to put below, then only one of these is the real organal tone, because the first, according to the rule, goes with the *cantus* (at the octave or in unison), the second always occurs in contrast to it (at the fifth or the fourth), and the third determines its position by the final tone, in order to come easily to a unison by the means of a consonance.

Groups of only three tones have a beginning and an end (*inceptio* and *copulatio*), with an interval in between which serves to make beginning and end recognizable, as for instance (1) octave or unison, (2) fifth or fourth, (3) octave or unison; groups of only two tones do not have the opportunity to develop into contrast, i.e., the voices stay conjunct (at the octave or in unison).

The differentiation between beginning-, middle-, and final tones is indispensable

---

"Cum tres voces perspiciuntur, ibi est tantum inceptio et copulatio, duabus autem sola conjunctio. Nam differentia primae et mediae et ultimae vocis ideo praeponitur, ut cum ad tractatum perveniremus, ad dandas consonantias earum non conturbet nos ignorantia earum. Sed ut cuncta facilius colliquescant, paulo altius ordinandum est, videlicet a primo et a secundo et a caeteris.

"Primus modus organizandi est quando prima vox copulatur cum praecedenti.

"Secundus fit per disjunctionem ipsius vocis; nam differentia est conjunctio respectu disjunctionis.

"Tertius modus sumitur a mediis vocibus quae mutantur per diatessaron si sunt in diapente et e converso.

"Quartus fit a diverso principio, vel a diverso medio; non tantum ab uno, sed ab utroque.

"Quintus per multiplicationem oppositarum vocum, augendo vel auferendo.

"Quod autem dictum est verbis, ostendemus exemplis:

|     |     |     |     | a?  |     |     |     |     |     |     |
|-----|-----|-----|-----|-----|-----|-----|-----|-----|-----|-----|
| c   | a   | b   | G   | F   | e   | c   | d   | c   | a   | b   | G   |
| C   | D   | F   | D   | F   | E   | F   | G   | F   | E   | F   | G   |
| Al- | le  | —   | —   | —   | lu  | —   | —   | —   | —   | ia  |     |

"Quando prima vox copulatur cum praecedenti.
"Per disjunctionem ipsius vocis, ut:

|     |     |     |     |     |     |     |     |     |     |     |
|-----|-----|-----|-----|-----|-----|-----|-----|-----|-----|-----|
| F   | a   | c   | G   | F   | a   | F   | C   | D   | E   | C   | C   |
| Al- | le  | —   | —   | —   | lu  | —   | —   | —   | —   | ia  |     |

|     | a?  |     |     |     |     |     |     |     |     | G?  |
|-----|-----|-----|-----|-----|-----|-----|-----|-----|-----|-----|
| F   | d   | c   | G   | ♭   | a   | c   | d   | c   | a   | b   | c   |
| Al- | le  | —   | —   | —   | lu  | —   | —   | —   | —   |     | ia  |

|     |     |     |     |     |     |     |     |     |     |     |     |
|-----|-----|-----|-----|-----|-----|-----|-----|-----|-----|-----|-----|
| c   | a   | c   | d   | b   | a   | c   | d   | c   | G   | F   | D   | C   | D   | E   |
| Al- | le  | —   | —   | lu  | —   | —   | —   | —   | —   | —   | ia." |

in order to determine the correct consonances for them. More specifically, the relationships are as follows:

The first tone of the organal voice occurs at the octave or in unison with the *cantus*.

The second tone appears in contrast to the *cantus* (i.e., at the interval of a fifth or fourth).

The third tone appears at the interval of a fifth, if the second tone was at the interval of a fourth, and, vice versa, at the interval of a fourth if the second tone was at the interval of a fifth. All other middle tones keep the same interval as the third tone (fifth or fourth).

The fourth (whenever there are no more than five, otherwise the next to the last) again changes the form of the disjunct interval (fourth instead of fifth, fifth instead of fourth) and leads in such a manner to the end, in unison or at the octave.

A fifth element consists of ("rhythmic") deviations of organum from the *cantus* by the introduction of longer or shorter tones(?).*11

The first example demonstrates the above rules best:

Of the three following polyphonic settings of the same *cantus* (which, it should be noted, is now characteristically the lower voice), it is possible in two of these to set the first note of the organal voice at the interval of a fourth:

The third setting proceeds again from the octave, but seems to contain errors, as the counter voice is longer than the principal voice.

Here the name *organum* is still employed, as is the coming together of voices at distinctions, but for the first time a counter voice is seen which is placed above the *cantus*, employing the preferred intervals of the fourth or fifth—apparently an outcome of the organum at the fifth—and the octave as well as the unison for the beginning and final tones of a distinction.

The unmistakable indications of the voices coming together from the octave to the fifth, and then to the distance of a fourth, or the moving apart from the unison to the fourth and then the fifth show a strong tendency toward considering contrary motion as the leading principle. However, the rule for continued parallel motion in fifths or fourths for the *mediae* of individual distinctions remains so strongly under the dictates of organum that one is tempted to derive also the rules for the movement from the unison into the fifth or from the fifth into the unison from organum as it was then practiced. The inclusion of the octave among the intervals used by two-voiced organum is entirely new. Following Hucbald's reasoning, and other detailed arguments justifying the use of octave doublings since octave tones are identical, the substitution of the octave for the unison is not unusual. This might, however, be a result of personal initiative on the part of the anonymous author of the Milan treatise. The consistent change between fifth and fourth in such a way that the *mediae* are fifths when the second interval and the penultimate interval are fourths, and vice versa, is also not elsewhere found.

The examples prefaced to the treatise probably belong to it. The first may be included here, although it does not entirely correspond to the rules:

Cun-cti-po-tens ge-ni-tor de-us, om-ni-cre-a-tor, e - - - - ley-son!

Chri-ste De-i splendor, vir-tus pa-tris-que so-phi-a, e - - - ley-son.

Am-bo-rum sa-crum spi-ra-men, ne-xus a-mor-que, e - - - - - ley-son.

In this example we notice that the transition to contrary motion is carried even further.

The Latin rhymed verses which follow the treatise are in part borrowed from Guido's *Regulae rhythmicae* (Gerbert II:25 ff.), although they are in part original. They conform in the beginning to the teachings of Anonymous and speak of the alternation of the fifth and fourth, as well as of the lovely closes in unison or at the octave.

The examples described in the verses are:

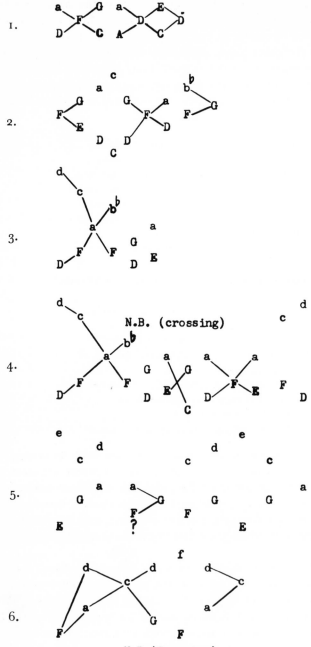

Even more clearly than Anonymous' rules, these examples show how organum threw off the fetters of parallel motion more and more and developed gradually into discant.*[12] The fact that the Milan treatise shows the organum as an upper voice which occasionally takes the liberty of descending below the *cantus*, is very important for this further development. Guido, on the other hand, still allows the *cantus* to descend occasionally below the organum, which is fixed. Thus polyphony is already on its way to making the *cantus firmus* a subsidiary voice and to giving melodic emphasis to the added voice. The closing verses of the Milan treatise celebrate organum as the victorious contestant:

Organum acquirit totum sursum et inferius,
Currit valde delectando ut miles fortissimus,
Frangit voces velut princeps senior et dominus,
Qua de causa applicando sonat multum dulcius.
Cantus manet ut subjectus praecedendi gratia
Quia quod praecedit tantum minus quam sequentia (!)
Ut Boetius praedicit sic in dialectica,
Ergo organum excedit majori potentia.

(Organum acquires all of the rise and fall [of tones],
It runs on joyously like a brave soldier,
It bursts into notes, like a powerful sovereign
  subjecting the other voice to its mastery,
And, in doing so, it sounds much sweeter.
The cantus remains as if subjected, because of
  precedence,
For that which goes ahead [i.e., the *cantus*] is of
  lesser worth than that which follows,
As Boethius excels in dialectic,
So organum surpasses by its greater power.)

It appears as if with *frangit voces* we are concerned with movement in shorter note values, that is, *diminutio organi*, which is borne out even by the last sentence of the fragment of the prose text which we have given above. The rules given in the prose portion of the treatise, however, are not quite liberal enough for such free voice-leading, and for this reason I cannot at all subscribe to the view that the rhymed portion stems from the same author.

That the assertions in the Milan treatise (*Ad organum faciendum*) are not the result of an individual search for greater knowledge, but that during the course of the 11th century parallel organum gradually changed to discant and even relinquished its preference of the fourth for the middle part of each melodic section, is proved with certainty by the musical treatise of the Englishman John Cotton (Gerbert II:230 ff.), which must have been written in the 11th century, or at any rate must be dated around 1100. I shall give his brief treatment of our subject in its entirety, since the report of such a fine writer, who is thoroughly informed of and refers to works by Guido, Berno, and Hermannus Contractus, must be of special value to us (Chapter XXIII, *De Diaphonia*, i.e., *Organo*):[3]

We wish to speak briefly about Diaphony, in order to satisfy the hunger for wisdom in the reader even in this respect.

Diaphony is a well-ordered combination of different tones presented by at least two singers; one does not deviate from the *cantus firmus*, but the other uses different tones with which he moves around the same [*cantus firmus*] according to certain rules whereby both singers come together, either in unison or at the octave, at certain points of rest. Diaphony means as much as two-voiced harmony. Before we present special rules for the leading of organum (*organizandi*) we must speak first about the types of movement (melodic steps) of the single voices.

Here follows a treatment of simple and compound neumes which corresponds with that of Guido in *Micrologus* (Chapter XVI, Gerbert II:17), for which we found a source in the Odonic tract, *Musica artis disciplina* (Gerbert I:265 ff.).

After this short explanation we return to diaphony. This is practiced (!) in different manners, but the simplest one to understand is the one in which special emphasis is placed on contrary motion, in which the organizing voice moves downward while the *cantus firmus* moves upward, and vice versa. If the *cantus* comes to an ending in a low position, then the organizing voice should be above it and rise to the octave; if the *cantus* ends in a higher position, then the organizing

---

[3] "Breviter nunc et succincte de diaphonia disserere volumus, quatenus lectoris aviditati in hac quoque re satisfaciamus quantum possumus.

"Est ergo diaphonia congrua vocum dissonantia quae ad minus per duos cantantes agitur, ita scilicet ut altero rectam modulationem tenente, alter per alienos sonos apte circueat, et in singulis respirationibus ambo in eadem voce vel per diapason conveniant. Qui canendi modus vulgariter organum dicitur, eo quod vox humana apte dissonans similitudinem exprimat instrumenti quod organum vocatur. Interpretatur autem diaphonia dualis vox sive dissonantia.

"Sed antequam organizandi praecepta demus, de motibus vocum, quorum consideratio ad hoc negotium utilis est, pauca perstringere volumus.

"...His ita compendiose insertis ad diaphoniam redeamus.

"Ea diversi diverse utuntur. Caeterum hic facillimus ejus usus est, si motuum varietas diligenter consideretur; ut ubi in recta modulatione est elevatio, ibi in organica fiat depositio et e converso. Providendum quoque est organizanti, ut si recta modulatio in gravibus moram fecerit, ipse in acutis canenti per diapason occurrat; sin vero in acutis, ipse in gravibus per diapason concordiam faciat: cantui autem in mese vel circa mese pausationes facienti in eadem voce respondeat.

"Observandumque est ut organum ita texatur, ut nunc in eadem voce, nunc per diapason alternatim fiat, saepius tamen et commodius in eadem voce."

voice seeks the lower octave; but if the *cantus* ends in middle position, then both voices must come together in unison. A well-considered treatment of the organum will take care that endings in unison will alternate with those at the octave, with preference to the former.

The conclusion of Cotton's treatment of organum, which unfortunately lacks musical examples,*[13] but for which the examples of the Milan treatise could serve as illustrations (especially those in the preface and those described in the rhymed second part), consists of a passage, the interpretation of which is doubtful:

Animadvertere etiam debes, quod quamvis ego in simplicibus motibus simplex organum posuerim [probably in the missing examples] cuilibet tamen organizanti simplices motus duplicare vel triplicare vel quovis modo competenter conglobare si voluerit licet.

(You must also take notice that, although I have shown only simple organum with simple movements in the voices, it is possible that any composer of organum who desires may double or triple the voices, or may at his discretion increase them in any way.)

This sentence may have reference to the possibility of octave doubling of both voices, since the "*ad minus per duos cantantes*" points to the more-than-two-voiced forms of organum; it is even more plausible, however, that *motus* refers to what Cotton has previously described in more detail, namely, the simple and compound neumes. With this interpretation a whole new perspective opens. The interpretation of *frangit voces* in the Milan treatise to mean "a richer, more figurative treatment of the *organalis*" gains a firmer foundation.*[14] Neither Cotton nor the Milan Anonymous, however, give us any information as to the "how" of such figurative treatment. The surplus notes found in the organizing voice in the fourth setting of the *Alleluia* in the first part of the Milan treatise are difficult to understand, in this sense, since the ending is obviously incorrect (a third), although it is not impossible that in the ending an illustration of such figuration is present which is now not clearly ascertainable.

Before we pursue our subject further, I wish briefly to call attention to the fact that in and before Cotton's time it is impossible to find an f♯ in Tetrardus endings or a c♯ in Protus endings. Gustav Jacobsthal's work, *Die chromatische Alteration im liturgischen Gesange der abendländischen Kirche* (1897), is very likely to lead to such a misapprehension, especially considering his remark on page 22:

Accordingly, there must have existed a general feeling (already during the 9th and 10th centuries, around the time of the writing of *Alia musica*!), that the association of F♯ to G was something peculiar to Tetrardus melodies and that with this association the impression of this mode group [VII and VIII] was connected.

This remark is highly questionable and likely to confuse the reader. It is sufficient, however, to point to Guido's teachings concerning the *occursus* in order to show the complete untenability of the assumption of a *subsemitonium* at such an early time. That Cotton holds a similar viewpoint is proved by his remark (Gerbert II:245) that the authentic Tritus does not, as do the other authentic modes, regard the second (under the final) as belonging to its normal ambitus, for this second is only a half-step away from the final ("[*Authento trito*] *nulla infra finalem descensio attributa est, non aliam ob causam nisi quod semitonii imperfectio competentem fieri descensum non permittit*"). Also Cotton's directions (Gerbert II:249) (which have been used by Jacobsthal for his theory of chromatic alteration) that many Protus melodies should not be set in the normal position (D–d), but a fifth higher, since they would otherwise lack the necessary whole-tone (!) under C and also under F, and that even Tritus melodies occasionally are not usable in normal position for the same reason, show the same marked aversion toward the *subsemitonium* of the *finalis*.

The minor third before the unison, which later developed so naturally (and, respectively, the major sixth before the octave), was still completely unknown at that time. Cotton maintains a difference in rank between the major and minor third for the closing intervals of organum; the former appears to have gradually acquired recognition as a consonance, the latter not for the time being. The second part of the Milan treatise also shows this reluctance concerning the *semiditonus*:

> Est quaedam consonantia de qua parum reliquimus,
> De A ad c, de D ad F, hoc est semiditonus,
> Causa cujus depravatur organum superius.
> Namque saliendo vadit ut ornetur melius.
> Stricte sonat inter mixta ascendendo organum,
> Quapropter non tenet legem nisi sit per circulum!

> (There is a certain consonance [interval] to which
>     we have paid too little attention,
> Which is A to c and D to F, that is a semiditone [minor third],
> By means of which the organum above is made to move lower.
> For the organum goes forward in leaps in order to make
>     a better effect,
> By ascending, the organum sounds more clearly among the
>     various sounds [intervals, literally "mixed sounds"],
> Therefore it does not keep a rule unless it be in a circle!)

The last line seems to indicate that the minor third is permissible as a consonance only when both voices are introduced to and leave the minor third by step, as in the second example of the second versified part (cf. p. 74):

```
                              a
                      G
              F
                  E
                      D
```

The major third, however, finds favor and is even compared to a *dulcis fistula* [a sweet-sounding pipe] a few lines later.

I do not wish to suppress the assumption that the concept of the *subsemitonium* under UT[4] came about only gradually through the hexachord teachings of Guido and his successors; that is to say that the two positions (hexachords) C D E F G a and F G a b♭ c d have this *subsemitonium* (B̂ C, Ê F), and that the same may have asserted itself for G a b♮ c d e. The carrying over of the same practice from the major modes (C, F, G) to the minor modes (D, a) occurred, on the other hand, long afterward. For Deuterus (E) which had the *semitonium* above the *finalis*, the *subsemitonium* was naturally out of the question.

[4] Cf. p. 140 (Garlandia I).

## CHAPTER V

# The Discant during the 12th Century

JUST as we saw in the strict parallel organum of the *Musica enchiriadis* the probable result of subjecting a naturally developed primitive polyphony to the restraining confines of a theoretical system (which had constant difficulty in completely ignoring its prototype), so we find during the 12th century the first manifestations of a new form, discant (*déchant*), which constituted a second type of crystallization issuing from the test tubes of the theorists.*[1] The antique teachings of consonance receive recognition again in this pure form of discant, with the result that even the fourth, the preferred interval of organum, disappears entirely and only the first two consonances, the octave (or the unison) and the fifth are regarded as permissible intervals. These are to be used as much as possible in constant alternation and in contrary motion. As was the case with organum, when discant first appears the two voices are joined by their simultaneous use of the same text, but contrary motion from interval to interval occurs using only the unison (octave) and the fifth (twelfth). Since the rules for leading the counter-voice were so mechanical, notation was as unnecessary here as it was for parallel organum; rather, as long as these rules were in existence, the discant was simply improvised (*chant sur le livre*, i.e., extemporation of the counter-voice on the basis of the notated *cantus firmus*). The fully-written-out polyphonic composition known as *res facta* [meaning "completed work"], distinguished from that which is improvised,*[2] and whose beginning may be seen in the 12th century, was based, however, upon deviations from such strict norms. For such a purpose new methods of written notation were needed (to indicate rhythmic values and rests) which would make conceivable the freeing of voices from the necessity of singing the same textual syllables simultaneously. Figuration (diminution) was possible in pure *déchant* as well as in Cotton's organum and that of the Milan treatise, but only in the form of a richer, melismatic treatment of single syllables. The syllables, with their traditional rhythmic delivery, are the real leaders of voices singing together as long as the principle of note values indicated by the particular shapes of notes is not used.

Those rules for the *déchant* which we now have in our possession for the most part say nothing at all about mensural notation, but do contain instructions (some without any examples of notation) for individual cases written in dry and rather complicated language. These instructions are almost superfluous when one keeps in mind the rule that the unison (octave) and fifth should constantly alternate.

The oldest of these accounts still contains traces of theories of organum in a later stage of its development, as may be seen in the rule which says that the *mediae voces* should continue in parallel movements of fifths. They are:

1. An Old French treatise, "*Quiconques veut deschanter*" (Coussemaker, *Histoire de l'harmonie au moyen-âge*, pp. 245–246)

2. A Latin reworking of the same (second part of the Anonymous III in Coussemaker, *Script.* I: 324 ff.)

In order to convey to the reader an idea of how the rules for (improvised) *déchant* are stated, we shall here include the apparently oldest instructions (first named above), found in manuscript number 813 of the Paris National Library, fol. 269r and 270r, written in the margin:[1]

Whoever would like to discant must know above all what a fifth and an octave are. A fifth is the fifth note, an octave the eighth.

Furthermore, it must be kept in mind whether the *cantus* (in the beginning) ascends or descends: If it ascends, one must begin with the octave, if it descends, with the fifth.

[1] *Libellus in gallico de arte discantandi*: "Quiconques veut deschanter, li doit premiers savoir qu'est quins et doubles; quins est la quinte note et doubles est la witisme; et doit regarder se li chans monte ou avale.

"Se il monte, nous devons prendre la double note; se il avale, nous devons prendre la quinte note.

"Se li chans monte d'une note si come UT–RE, on doit prendre le deschant du double deseure et descendre deux notes; si come il appert (the examples are missing):

"Se li chant monte deux notes si come UT–MI[MI]SOL, nous devons prendre le descant en hutisme note et descendre une note;...si demourra li deschans ou quint comme il appert:

"Si li chans monte trois notes si come UT–FA, nous devons prendre la witisme note et nous tenir ou point; si demourra li descans ou quint si come il appert:

If the *cantus* ascends one step, i.e., UT–RE, the *déchant* must begin with a higher octave and descend two steps, as shown in example 1 (examples missing):

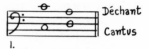

If the *cantus* ascends two steps, i.e., UT–MI (or MI–)SOL the *déchant* must take the octave and descend one step in order that it may end on the fifth, as shown in example 2:

If the *cantus* rises three steps, i.e., UT–FA, we must take the octave and remain upon the same tone; in this case the *déchant* will constitute the fifth of the *cantus*, as shown in example 3:

If the *cantus* rises four steps, i.e., UT–SOL, we must take the octave and ascend one step, in order that we reach the fifth, as shown in example 4:

"Se li chans monte quatre notes UT–SOL, nous devons prendre ou double et monter une note, si sera li descans ou quint:

"Et si devons savoir que de toutes les montées qui sont, nous devons mettre la premiere note ou double et toutes les autres ou quint et monter ensi come li cans.

"Se li chans descent une note si come FA–MI, nous devons prendre ou quint... monter deux notes, si sera li deschans ou double:

"(Se li chans descent deux notes, si come FA–RE, nous devons prendre ou quint et monter une note, si sera li deschans ou double):

"Se li chans descent trois notes si come FA–UT, nous devons prendre ou quint et nous tenir ou point; si demourra la première ou quint et l'autre ou double:

"Se li chans descent quatre note, si come SOL–UT, nous devons prendre ou quint et descendre une note; si sera la première ou quint et l'autre ou double:

"Et si devons savoir que de toutes les avalées nous devons prendre le quint et chanter tout ensi que le plain-chant, et mettre la daaraine ou double."

Furthermore, we must note that as often as the *cantus* ascends in succession (stepwise), we must take the octave first, but must then lead successive fifths parallel with the *cantus*, as shown in example 5:

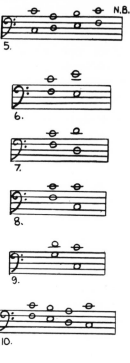

If the *cantus* falls one step, i.e., FA–MI, we must take the fifth and go two steps higher in order that the *déchant* is an octave removed from the *cantus*, as shown in example 6:

If the *cantus* falls two steps, i.e., FA–RE, we then take the fifth and go one step higher in order that the *déchant* reaches the octave, as shown in example 7:

If the *cantus* falls three steps, i.e., FA–UT, we must take the fifth and remain upon the same tone in order that we bring the octave after the fifth, as shown in example 8:

If the *cantus* falls four steps, i.e., SOL–UT, we must take the fifth and descend one step, in order that the fifth is followed by the octave, as in example 9:

Finally, we must note that as often as the *cantus* descends continually (stepwise), we must follow the *cantus* in fifths and add the octave only to the last tone, as shown in example 10.

The Latin text of Anonymous III contained in the first volume of Coussemaker's *Scriptores* (found in a later MS in the library of St. Dié, which, among other items, already contains the *Lucidarium* of Marchettus of Padua) agrees almost literally with the one in Old French which we included here. The two passages concerning parallel fifths read:

Nota quod si cantus ascendat duos tonos (sive duos cum dimidio) aut tres aut quatuor, debemus incipere in diapason et descendere in diapente, hoc est dicere, quod debemus incipere in duplo et descendere in quintum et ascendere sicut cantus ascendit ut hic patet exemplo:

Discant
Cantus

Si cantus descendit gradatim ditonum vel tritonum omnes descendentes debent esse in diapente praeter ultimam quae debet esse in diapason ut hic patet:

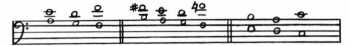

(Take note that when there are two tones ascending in the *cantus* (a whole-tone apart, or two tones a semitone apart) or three or four, we may begin at the octave and descend to the fifth, that is to say, we begin by doubling the *cantus* at the octave and descend to the fifth. Then we ascend as the *cantus* ascends as shown in the example [see above]:

When the *cantus* descends by step all of the other descending groups of two or three tones (in the discant) must be at the fifth with the exception of the last which must be at the octave, as in the example [see above]:)

The penultimate example is of such questionable character that it casts suspicion on the genuineness of the notated examples. On the other hand, it is apparent that this Latin treatise is a translation of the French because it contains clarifying additions to the French text. In spite of the doubts concerning the genuineness of the notational examples which I mentioned, I do not wish to omit pointing out that they are of interest because of their introduction of the *duplicatio, triplicatio,* and chiefly the *conglobatio* following Cotton's expositions.*[3] Almost throughout the entire treatise diminutions are added to the note-against-note contrapuntal settings, as is required by the rules, a few examples of which may be appended here (compare the numbers of these examples with those of the French treatise):

The notation of the examples appears to be mensural; at least we must interpret them as such if the *opposita proprietas* ( ) were so intended. The ligatures, with the exception of those in examples 5 (with *opposita proprietas*), 3a and 9 (*conjunctura* 🎵 ) have, however, only the form of chant ligatures (*cum proprietate et perfectione*). For this reason it is obvious that we must not yet transcribe them according to Franco's mensural theories, but recognize in them only a *conglobatio* of several tones on one syllable. If this assumption is correct, the single notes of the *cantus* should be placed under the beginning notes of the ligatures. The arrangement which I have given above attempts to show clearly the strictness of a contrapuntal setting embellished by interpolated tones, the rhythmic order of which is doubtful. As the codex could not have been written before 1300, it is very possible that these diminutions are a later addition. The application of mensural rules for the solution encounters such difficulties, however, that I am inclined to assume that the *opposita proprietas* is not intended, although there is a reference to the same in the preceding first part of Anonymous III (the explanation of notes). The parts are probably entirely independent of each other and were joined only by accident.

It must be further noted that in both treatises the unison is not dealt with. This is not the case, however, in a third treatise treating of the *déchantier* rules. This treatise must be regarded as belonging to the older group of characteristic treatments of *déchant* because of its admittance of parallel fifths. This is the treatise *De arte discantandi*, reprinted by Coussemaker in his *Histoire de l'harmonie au moyen-âge*, pp. 262 ff. (Codex 813 of the Paris National Library). The passages concerning fifths read:

Cum tres vel quatuor vel plures ascendant una post aliam, omnes possunt esse in quinto praeter (primam et) ultimam (this should, of course, also be added to the two excerpts mentioned above); prima debet esse in duplo et ultima potest redire ad cantum:

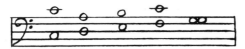

Quando tres notae vel quatuor vel plures descendunt una post aliam, omnes possunt esse in quinto praeter ultimam, quae debet esse in duplo:

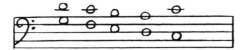

(In groups of three, four, or more [tones] one [voice] ascends after the other. Both voices must be at the fifth with the exception of the [first and the] last. The first [tone of the *cantus*] may be doubled [at the octave] and the last [tone of the discant] can come together in unison with the *cantus*:

When there are three, four, or more tones descending, one after the other, both voices may be at the fifth with the exception of the last tone which must be doubled [at the octave].)

The word *possunt*, in contrast to the *devons* and *debemus* (i.e., *debent*) of the two first versions, is of great significance, for the treatise gives other rules which allow parallel fifths only on a limited scale. A number of passages in this treatise are concerned with cases where three tones of the *cantus* appear in ascending or descending stepwise order; it allows for these either the normal alternation between the octave and the fifth, or stepwise motion in the discant:

At e the descending of the discant under the *cantus* is intended in both cases, and at d a succession of parallel fifths is found. At a, however, the avoidance of parallel fifths through the alternation of the octave and the fifth is introduced. Stepwise motion to or from the unison and also motion to and from the octave is already known to us from the instructions for organum contained in the Milan treatise (cf. pp. 70–75). In that treatise we also found transition from the unison to the fifth or from the fifth to the unison already established as a fixed rule.

We see here (in *De arte discantandi*) a remarkable multiformity together with wise innovations, the character of which might persuade us to connect the treatise with the teachings of Franco, if it were not so obvious that it is still connected with the last formulations of diaphony.

These beginnings of stepwise contrary motion [of discant] disappear entirely in a series of versions of this theory which must also be placed in the 12th century. Of these, that of Guido de Caroli Loco (Gui de Châlis) is probably the oldest (called *De Organo* and printed in Coussemaker, *Histoire*, pp. 255 ff. and *Scriptores* II: 191 ff.). For the first time we meet here the exclusion of parallel motion on principle and the exclusive limitation of concords to the intervals of the octave (unison) and the fifth. It is not necessary to repeat the individual rules here word for word. It suffices to show in examples which interval combinations Guido requires for the individual steps of the *cantus* (Guido interprets [*ascendere* or *descendere*] *duas voces* to mean the second, *tres voces* the third, etc., while earlier writers do not count the first step and regard *duas voces* as the third, etc.):

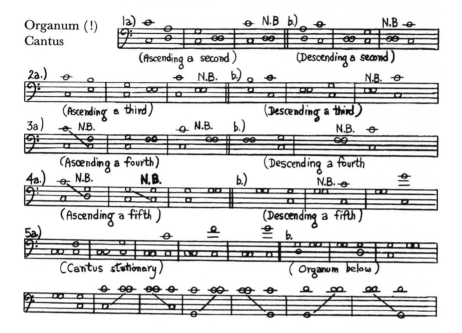

It is not entirely apparent, however, how the fourth is accounted for in these instructions. It seems, according to the examples marked 3a, 4a, and 5b, that it develops because the organum (this name, oddly enough, is still used by Guido) descends below the *cantus* instead of the *cantus* taking the fifth from above. In example 5a, on the other hand, the fourth even appears above the *cantus*, an isolated instance to which we should probably not attach any special significance.

In its purest form the *déchant* theory appears in the anonymous treatise *De organo*, which Coussemaker printed in the second volume of the *Scriptores* (pp. 494 ff.) from a Louvain codex. The Louvain treatise is without doubt closely connected to the treatise of Gui de Châlis (from the library of St. Geneviève) and is probably a reworking of the same. It also refers to the third as *tres voces*, etc., and employs almost the same wording. It uses the Greek names for intervals (*diapente, diapason*) rather than the Latin (*quinta, octava* [*duplex vox*], etc.) and instead of tone letters it uses solmization syllables based on two hexachords:

| G | a | b | c | d | e |
|----|----|----|----|-----|----|
| UT | RE | MI | FA | SOL | LA |
| C | D | E | F | G | a |

There are, however, no fourths to be found in the Louvain treatise, either above or below the *cantus*. On the other hand, it develops [movement] in the middle part, as does organum; i.e., it leads the discant voice from the octave or fifth to the unison in order to reach a fifth or octave by contrary motion, starting from this unison:

Coussemaker is mistaken in looking for a similar manipulation in which the *cantus* descends a fifth, since this would not result in contrary motion:

In place of the organum moving to the lower fourth of the *cantus* (in the crossing of voices and starting from the unison), the Louvain treatise substitutes motion to the lower fifth of the *cantus*:

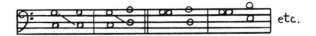

etc.

Here we really meet contrary motion *à tout prix* [at any cost] excluding all intervals other than the unison, octave and fifth. One might feel the absence here of the possibility of contrary motion in which the *cantus* ascends from the unison by octave skip.

It is probably very likely that this extreme theoretical position based upon contrary motion never achieved common acceptance in wider circles. Rather, we find in all further sources containing discant rules similar motion from the octave to the fifth, and vice versa, as characteristic procedures. The most important trait of real discant, and that which separates it from earlier as well as later types of compositions, is the limitation of intervals to octaves, unisons, and fifths. This is demonstrated by the treatise *Quaedam de arte discantandi*, which belong to the 12th century and is to be found in Coussemaker's *Histoire*, pp. 274 ff. (from Codex 812 of the Paris National Library). This treatise contains sections which deal with mensural notation; however, discant rules are separated from any reference to this notation. I quote here only a few examples to show the correspondence to older expositions:

This treatise in its terminology stands in contrast to the two others mentioned above, since it does not count the beginning tone when reckoning intervals ("Et nota quod quando dicitur: ascende vel descende sic vel sic prima vox non computatur"). This reference permits us to regard these treatises as belonging to approximately the same period. The same sentence (on p. 312, "et nota quod...") is also found in Anonymous II (which belongs, as does Anonymous III, to the St. Dié MS), found in Coussemaker's *Scriptores* I:303 ff. It is a completely independent section dealing with rules of discant and begins on p. 312 with "Sciendum est...." Anonymous IIc also contains one of the most unalloyed presentations of the teachings of discant. The fact that every skip is "filled out" stepwise diatonically is probably not meant to imply figuration but is rather intended to clarify the interval distance:

The same holds true of the discant rules in the first part (IIa, up to p. 211 at "Sequitur de discantu"). This part is different from the third (IIc) in that the method of reckoning intervals mentioned above is missing. The middle part (IIb) probably belongs to the oldest set of treatises which regard thirds as consonances.

Gradually the overabundance of movement in contrary motion from the octave to the unison and vice versa (cf. p. 87) disappears, after having been explained at length by Guido of Châlis and after having been dealt with for each step of the *cantus* by the last-named treatises. It is not even mentioned in the *Discantus positio vulgaris* (in Coussemaker's *Scriptores* I:94 ff. in the treatise of Hieronymus de Moravia). This treatise, which Hieronymus de Moravia calls the oldest of all (*antiquior omnibus*), and which during his time (middle of the 13th century) was regarded as an old anonymous treatise, proposes, on the basis of the discant rules with which we are now familiar, a useful interpolation of tones in the discant. The result is as follows:

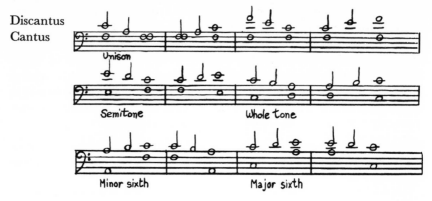

In the last four examples we again meet similar motion from the octave to the fifth, or vice versa.

The *Compendium*[2] *Magistri Franconis* (Coussemaker, *Script.* I:154 ff.), in spite of its beginning with "*Ego Franco de Colonia,*" is probably not an independent work of Franco, but a school manual for oral instruction. Its first part is in no way different from the treatises which have just been discussed; it even includes the octave-unison progression (in contrary motion), as well as similar motion from the octave to the fifth when the *cantus* moves up a fifth $\left(\begin{smallmatrix} c & d \\ C & G \end{smallmatrix}\right)$. Up to this point the treatise is definitely not specifically Franconian, but gives the pre-Franconian rules unchanged. The third chapter, however, belongs to Franconian theory. It introduces the third before the fifth and the unison, and the sixth before the octave. Specific permission sometimes to lead the discant parallel with the *cantus* is indicative of the reaction, which began at this time, against the inflexible theory of continued contrary motion.

Anonymous 4*[4] (Coussemaker, *Script.* I:354 ff.), who in many respects is very interesting, teaches us, by the way, either that parallel chanting was not entirely obsolete at his time (after 1250) or that it had taken on a new form (Fauxbourdon? This codex is of English origin):

Et differentia est inter istos et discantores qui dicuntur plani cantores, quoniam plani discantores si tenor ascendit ipsi ascendunt, si tenor descendit et ipsi descendunt (356).

(The difference between singers of discant and the vagrant singers, who are

[2] (Cf. p. 97f.) The *Compendium* is probably by Franco of Cologne, but the *Ars cantus mensurabilis* by Franco of Paris. *[5]

also *discantores*, is that if the tenor rises for the latter group, they sing the upper part higher also, and if it falls, they also sing the upper voice lower in pitch.)

We have good reason to believe that the greater importance which this period generally ascribes to major and minor thirds was based upon the renewed influence of primitive popular polyphony, which, as we mentioned before, may have influenced also the first attempts at artistic polyphony, namely, organum. This time, however, a new stimulus is not involved, rather a thorough emendation which will only slowly achieve perfection. Anonymous IV also tells us the basis for the higher esteem in which the thirds were held. As far as the mention of consonance or nonconsonance of thirds is concerned, this treatise says:

Tamen apud organistas optimos et prout in quibusdam terris sicut in Anglia, in patria quae dicitur Westcuntre[3] optimae concordantiae dicuntur, quoniam apud tales magis sunt in usu (358).

(Thus there are excellent composers of polyphonic music in certain places such as England, in that part which is called Westcountry, who consider these to be the best possible consonances since they use them so much.)

This reference increases the importance of the report of Giraldus Cambrensis (cf. p. 16) and at the same time heightens the probability that gymel and fauxbourdon are a great deal older than the period of Guilelmus Monachus, in whose treatise they are first described.

[3] Hawkins, *History* II: 199, assumes that Anonymous wrote *Westcuntre* instead of *North Country*, which would, in this case, serve as proof of the information given by Giraldus Cambrensis.

# The Transformation of the Theory of Consonance and Dissonance during the 13th Century

E VEN though sufficient grounds exist for the assumption that parallel singing in thirds—perhaps even in thirds and sixths—appeared on the continent as early as the 12th century, having come from England, and that gymel and fauxbourdon probably provided the first impetus toward a formation of the theory of organum, we must nevertheless defer the discussion of this possibly oldest kind of parallel singing until we meet with it in reliable theoretical sources.*[1] In approaching those works to be discussed chronologically we meet first an extensive series of treatises. Already in these treatises appears a revision of the theories of polyphonic music (organum and déchant) which originated on the continent (in the Netherlands, France, and Italy). These revisions direct our attention to native practices of polyphony which, although probably much older, still had not been definitely formulated. The first revision is the designation of thirds and sixths as consonances next to octaves and fifths, even though they remain for centuries "imperfect" consonances. The darkness of those minds which are still concerned with the antique theories of consonance is suddenly illuminated; it appears that thirds actually do not sound bad at all and that they add pleasant variety to attempts which hitherto included only the octave, fifth, and fourth. The dulcis fistula of the Milan Anonymous, however, already presages such a development during the 11th century, and Guido of Arezzo also shows a preference for those modes which lend themselves to the introduction of thirds.*[2] This is an important symptom of a gradually increasing consciousness of the fact that being limited only to the consonances recognized by antiquity amounted to the suppression of natural musical instinct. At this point, however, there was still a long way to go before thirds were theoretically recognized as being of equal importance with the other consonances. Only toward the end of the 15th century were thirds finally considered legitimate; until then they were allowed only against better judgment (or what was thought to be better judgment) under a kind of artistic license.

Who it was who first said that thirds were "imperfect consonances" cannot be clearly proved. The Greek music theorist Gaudentios (who probably lived during the second century A.D.) indicates an intermediate position between consonance and dissonance for the major third (*ditonus*), regarding it as a so-called *paraphone* interval when it occurs in connection with the *tritonus* (!), while he does not mention the minor third, the *trihemitonium*, at all. This is reason enough for us to attribute no importance whatsoever to his writings as far as the theory of polyphonic music is concerned. Fétis committed this error and looked for the oldest traces of organum in Gaudentios, whom he assumed to be two centuries earlier than he was. According to general research, Franco of Cologne is regarded as the originator of the new theory of consonance. It is, however, even more probable that it was one of the early masters of more-than-two-voiced settings who is mentioned in the music-historical sketch of Anonymous IV, printed in Coussemaker, *Script.* I, namely, Leoninus, Perotinus, Robert of Sabilon, Petrus (de Cruce), or Johannes Primarius (de Garlandia [!]). Because of the lack of other sources, we can find proof for this in the categorical manner in which this author, who himself belongs in the 13th century, in several places cites these masters chronologically (pp. 341 and 342). According to him, mensural notation must have appeared in France. Therefore, one would also like to attribute the revised version of the theory of consonance to one of those early masters who unfortunately left no treatise bearing a name. Anonymous IV explicitly remarks, however (p. 344), that the differentiation of note values through the shapes of notes was at first not a thoroughly developed system,[1] especially the ligatures, and that only during the course of time (*in longo tempore*) did specific rules evolve. These sentences we must regard as true in view of the many discrepancies contained in the earliest versions of mensural theory.

The treatise on discant which Hieronymus de Moravia (who lived in the middle of the 13th century) called the oldest, and which Coussemaker entitles *Discantus positio vulgaris* in *Script.* I:94 ff., does not yet recognize

---

[1] Coussemaker I:341: "This was so during and after the time of Perotinus the Great. Nevertheless, they did not know how to distinguish these notes from those which will be presented shortly. This was so even since the time of Leo, because two ligated notes were put for the durational value of a *brevis longus*, and in a similar manner, three ligated notes were quite often used for a *longa brevis, longa* (p. 344). Concerning what we have just discussed, the greater part of the knowledge of the ancients did not take into consideration the formal shapes of notes. They based their knowledge of consonances on entire melodies ...and they said: The upper voice must form a good consonance with the lower part, and that is enough."

thirds as consonances, but does suggest that thirds are no longer regarded as really dissonant (p. 95):[2]

> Consonance is the amalgamation of several voices singing the same or different notes. Of the concordances, three are better than the others, namely the unison, the fifth, and the octave. The remaining intervals are more dissonant than consonant, and are separately graded, inasmuch as the second (*tonus*) seems to be more dissonant than all other intervals.

If Walter Odington (who writes an extremely curious discussion of this question and who comes very close to the results of Bartolomeo de Ramis [1482!]) really was the same person as Walter of Eynsham, who was made Archbishop of Canterbury in 1229, we should have to attribute authorship of this new theory to him. Since it has been proved, however, that Walter Odington, the monk of Evesham, has nothing more in common with this person than the first name Walter (see Grove's *Dictionary of Music* IV: 734), this assumption must be regarded as untenable. Odington is, on the other hand, identical with the mathematician of the same name who taught in Oxford in the year 1316. For this reason, his treatise must be dated 1275 at the earliest. The treatise *De musica libellus* (Coussemaker, Anonymous VII, *Script.* I: 378) must undoubtedly be of the same age as the *Discantus positio vulgaris*, which must be dated before Franco and Garlandia. The author of *De musica libellus*, who may be Robertus de Sabilone, must be seriously considered at this time.*[3] He says simply and briefly (p. 382):[3]

> It is further to be noted that the most necessary intervals are the unison, the minor, and the major third, the fourth, the fifth, and the octave, as the discant always keeps its relationship with the tenor by one of these intervals. The unison and the octave are perfect consonances; the minor and major third imperfect, the fourth and fifth intermediate ones.

He does not mention the sixth; otherwise one could assume that the author was one of the early English teachers mentioned in Anonymous IV.

So far we do not know enough—in spite of what is contained in Anonymous IV—about the time relationship between Johannes de Garlandia and Franco of Cologne, the two most important theorists of this time, because we are not exactly certain when Franco of Cologne lived. There

---

[2] "Item consonantia est diversarum vocum in eodem sono vel in pluribus concordia. Inter concordantias autem tres sunt ceteris meliores scilicet unisonus diapente et diapason. Ceteri vero modi magis sunt dissonantiae quam consonantiae, tamen secundum magis et minus, unde major videtur dissonantia in tono quam in aliquo alio modo."

[3] "Et notandum quod unisonus, semiditonus, ditonus, diatessaron, diapente et diapason sunt magis necessariae species quam aliae, quia omnis discantus cum tenore suo in aliqua istarum consonantiarum. Notandum est quod unisonus et diapason sunt consonantiae perfectae, ditonus et semiditonus sunt imperfectae, diatessaron et diapente dicuntur mediae."

is absolutely no doubt that the Scholastic Franco of Lüttich (11th century) is not concerned here; it is also not probable that the Franco who was prior of the Benedictine abbey of Cologne in 1190 was the author of *Ars cantus mensurabilis*, especially since, according to Anonymous IV, Franco of Cologne also worked in Paris. In order to heighten the confusion, Hieronymus de Moravia directly denies Franco the authorship of *Ars cantus mensurabilis* and mentions as author a Johannes de Burgundia, who seems to have been his teacher.[4]

Johannes de Garlandia, according to Coussemaker, *Script*. III, page VII, was born around 1190 in England (!), educated in Oxford, studied around 1210 at the University of Paris, and established in Paris *in septo Garlandiae* a school, which gave him his name "*de Garlandia*." In 1229 he was schoolmaster at the newly established University of Toulouse, and in 1232 was back at his school in Paris. To regard Franco of Cologne as having lived *before* Garlandia is impossible. Those parts of the *Ars cantus mensurabilis* which sometimes agree word for word with the treatise of Garlandia given by Hieronymus de Moravia were probably taken over by Franco, who may have written between 1230 and 1250. The mensural theory of *Ars cantus mensurabilis* is much more advanced and stable than that of Garlandia. If both teachers lived in Paris, a direct connection between the one and the other would be self-evident. The importance of the older Franco (of Paris), who is mentioned in Coussemaker's Anonymous IV, can unfortunately no longer be estimated. Posterity has merely succeeded in confusing the existence of the two Francos. The testimony of Anonymous IV, who was a contemporary of the second Franco, is not to be disregarded, however, and W. Nagel's assumption of a "Legend of Franco of Paris," therefore, is certainly doubtful. An *Arbor* of Johannes de Burgundia is incidentally mentioned by Petrus Picardus (Coussemaker I: 136 and 137), along with the *Ars cantus mensurabilis* of Franco of Cologne, as an independent work. For this reason we must not attach too much importance to the doubt cast by Hieronymus de Moravia on Franco's authorship of the *Ars cantus mensurabilis*.*[4]

In the second half of the treatise *De musica mensurabili* of Johannes de Garlandia, printed in Coussemaker, *Script*. I:97 ff., beginning on page 104 (which half is missing in the second printing of the same treatise in Coussemaker I:175 ff.), the consonances (*concordantiae*) are divided into perfect (unison and octave), intermediate (fifth and fourth), and imperfect (major and minor third). The dissonances (*discordantiae*) are similarly divided into perfect (semitone, *tritonus*, and major seventh),

---

[4] (Page 117): "There follows a third standpoint (*positio*) which we heard from the lips of Johannes of Burgundy, or which, according to common opinion, was said by Franco of Cologne."

intermediate (whole-tone and minor sixth [*semitonium cum diapente*]), and imperfect (major sixth and minor seventh). The treatise also contains the sentence specifying that a dissonance must never appear before a perfect consonance, other than for the purpose of adding *color*. By *color* is meant figuration, so the sentence means that no dissonance is to appear as an independent combination of the two voices before a perfect consonance (here belong, rather, the imperfect and intermediate consonances). Garlandia further states, in that part of his treatise dealing with a discussion of the *triplum* (Couss. I:116), that a dissonance exists between the twelfth and the double octave which "achieves a fine consonance," apparently meaning the enlargement of the major sixth by an octave (the examples are not usable).

Garlandia's definition agrees almost verbatim with the definition which is found in the *Ars cantus mensurabilis*, Chapter XI (Gerbert III:11) and which reads the same in Couss. I:129 (H. de Moravia): "There exist three kinds of consonances: perfect, imperfect, and intermediate. Those consonances are perfect when one can scarcely distinguish the individual tones because of their perfect blending."[5] The elements of the

[5] "There exist three kinds of consonances: perfect, imperfect, and intermediate. Those consonances are perfect when one can scarcely distinguish the individual tones because of their perfect blending. Of these there are two: unison and diapason. (Examples are from Gerbert):

"Those consonances are imperfect when the ear distinguishes two sounds which are quite different, yet are not discordant. Of these there are two: ditone and semiditone.

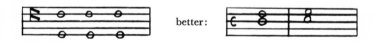

"Those consonances are intermediate when they produce a better sound in combination than the imperfect, but not better than the perfect. Of these there are two: diapente and diatessaron.

"As to why one concord is more consonant than another, this must be decided by plainsong. There are two species of discords, one perfect and the other imperfect. Those discords are perfect when the two sounds in combination are heard by the ear to dis-

three groups are the same as those given by Garlandia. Franco, however, divides the dissonances only into perfect and imperfect groups, and includes the intermediate with the perfect dissonances so that the remaining imperfect dissonances are only the whole-tone, the major sixth, and the minor seventh. "The extension of the consonant and dissonant intervals by the addition of the octave does not alter the fact that such intervals are synonymous with those not so altered." In addition, the following rule is given: "Be it known that immediately before a consonance any imperfect dissonance is in the right place." I shall leave as undecided the question as to whether the minor deviations which were pointed out constitute a step forward, a revision of the other possibly older version, or not. On the other hand, the deviations found in the *Compendium discantus*, which starts *Ego Franco de Colonia* (Coussemaker I:154), are so pronounced that another author must probably be assumed:[6][*5]

There are six pure dissonances: the minor and major second, the *tritonus*, the minor sixth (*semitonium cum diapente*), and the minor and major seventh. There are three perfect consonances, namely the unison, the octave, and the fifth; three become consonances by chance (*per accidens*), namely, the minor and major third when progressing to the fifth or the unison, and the major sixth when progressing

---

agree with one another. Of these there are four: semitone, tritone, ditone plus diapente, and semitone plus diapente.

better:

"Those discords are imperfect when the two sounds in combination are heard by the ear to agree to a certain extent, but are still discordant. Of these there are three: tone, tone plus diapente, and semiditone plus diapente.

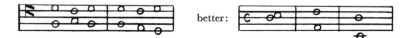

better:

"Please note that both concords and discords may be infinitely extended as in diapente plus diapason, diatessaron plus diapason...and in the same way by adding the double and triple diapason, if possible for the voice. It must also be known that any imperfect discord concords well before a concord."

[6] "Dissonantiae pure sunt sex, scilicet: semitonium, tonus, tritonus, semitonium cum diapente, ditonus cum diapente, semiditonus cum diapente. Consonantiarum sunt tres per se, et perfectae, scilicet: unisonus, diapason et diapente; tres sunt per accidens scilicet: semiditonus, ditonus in ordine ad diapente vel unisonum, (tonus) cum diapente in ordine ad diapason; una est perfecta et non (perfecta) per accidens (scilicet diatessaron)."

to the octave. One is in itself consonant, but becomes a dissonance in progression (N.B., the fourth!).

This exceptional treatment of the fourth is very striking and already points to a strongly developed feeling for harmony in the sense of using thirds as consonances.*[6] (Perhaps the Parisian Franco is rather the author of the *Ars cantus mensurabilis* and Franco of Cologne the author of the *Compendium*?!)

The strict separation of the major and minor sixths strikes one as strange in these definitions, in which the first is said to be really dissonant, but has an effect similar to that of a consonance, while the second is regarded as entirely dissonant. A similar distinction is made almost one hundred years later by Simon Tunstede (1351) in IV. *principale*,*[7] which Coussemaker printed in vol. III of the *Scriptores* as Anonymous I. (Dr. W. Nagel, *op. cit.*, vol. I:62, is in error not only in doubting the relationship of the Anonymous I to the *Quatuor principalia* of Tunstede, but also in determining that the Anonymous I treatise is approximately thirty years older than Tunstede's work and was a source for the same; the proof of its identity is contained in the Anonymous itself, on page 354, in the words *secundum principale*, a proof which Nagel overlooked.)[7] Tunstede rightly calls the whole-tone, the fourth, and the minor sixth imperfect dissonances, the major and minor third and the major sixth, however, imperfect consonances.[8]

Despite the fact the Walter Odington did not write before 1275 (as was mentioned before), his appraisal of thirds (and sixths) is of such an unusual nature that it is of great interest to us. The discrepancy between theory and practice which becomes apparent here, and which was, apparently, rather extensive, strengthens our hypothesis that during Odington's time the treatment of thirds as consonances had already been long established, at least in English practice.*[8] Mathematical speculation leads Odington to the conclusion (Couss. I:191) that the acoustical determination of the fifth as 3/2 is a result of the combination of the ratios 5/4 and 6/5:

$$5/4 \times 6/5 = 30/20 = 3/2$$

and he seriously considers whether or not the major third might be regarded as the ratio 5/4 and the minor third as the ratio 6/5. He notes,

---

[7] Cf. Coussemaker III:356, the reference to the III. *principale*.

[8] (Couss., *Script*. III:356 with reference to IV:280): "An imperfect concord is rightly called because of its own instability which changes from place to place and which is found in no certain proportions, for such are the semitone, the ditone, and the whole-tone plus a *diapente*. The semiditone and ditone which are thirds vary in different ways according to whether the *cantus* is ascending or descending (!)...The sixth is sometimes made of a *diapente* plus a whole tone or a *diapente* plus a semitone (...an imperfect discord)."

however, that two whole-tones of the ratio 9/8 are not exactly equal to the ratio of a third, 5/4:

Sesquioctava (9/8)  Sesquioctava (9/8)

| LXIII | LXXII | LXXX | LXXXI | XCVI |
|-------|-------|------|-------|------|

Sesquiquarta (5/4)          Sesquiquinta (6/5)

Sesquialtera (3/2)

and finds (p. 198) that the *ditonus* consisting of two whole-tones of the ratio 9/8 is larger (by 81/80) than the major third derived by a harmonic division of the fifth as 5/4. He also finds that the *semiditonus* is smaller (by 81/80) than the minor third which carries the ratio of 6/5. But as the former (p. 199) comes close to the ratio of the thirds defined as 5/4 and 6/5, most people are of the opinion that they are consonant; and although their consonance is not apparent in their numerical ratios, the human singing voice achieves their blending in a wonderful way.[9] Odington retains the major sixth as a dissonance (p. 200) and explains its frequent appearance by the fine effect which is achieved by its resolution to the octave.[10] Even he does not mention the minor sixth. He is, however, probably the first to point (p. 202) to the consonance of the triad, even with octave doublings.[11]

The short middle section (pp. 311–312) of Anonymous II in Coussemaker, *Script.* I (St. Dié), which apparently still belongs to Franco's time, contains some rules for the *Ars sciendi componere et profere discantum ex improviso* [the art of composing and leading the discant by improvisation]. Contrary motion is a standing rule; however, occasional parallel motion is allowed. Consonances are the basis, and dissonances are occasionally added for embellishment, as foils for the consonances. The major and minor third and the major sixth are imperfect consonances when the former [thirds] appear before fifths or unisons, and the latter [major sixths] appear before the octave. The minor sixth is expressly regarded as

[9] "But yet, because the *sesquiquarta* [5/4] and *sesquiquinta* [6/5], when placed together, so united make a *diapente*, therefore many think they are consonant. If the consonance is not found in the numbers, nevertheless, the voices of men bring them together with skill in a pleasing blend...." As late as 1496 Faber Stapulensis makes similar statements.

[10] "Nevertheless, in cantilenas of this time, they very often make use of a *diapente* plus a whole-tone as a concord, which, when it happens, is sweeter because it is rarer."

[11] "Without having to be of the same kind, when all these lower tones are compared: the ditone or semiditone (!), the *diapente*, the *diapason*, the *diapason* plus ditone or semiditone (!), the *diapason* plus *diapente*, and the *disdiapason*, as in the following numbers, they become apparent in this formula: 64, 81 (Couss. 73!), 96, 128, 162, 192, 256 (= C E G c e g c)."

a dissonance. It seems that this Anonymous is the earliest writer to regard the major sixth as an imperfect consonance. The point of view of Franco, on the other hand, is also taken by Coussemaker's Anonymous I (*Script.* I: 296 ff.), who simply quotes the *Ars cantus mensurabilis* and adds only one original statement, namely, that the minor third is a better consonance than the major third (because in moving to the unison, to which it resolves, one of its two tones needs to move only the distance of a half-step).

In the treatise of Anonymous IV (which dates back to the Franconian epoch, and whose author we already know is an Englishman) we search in vain for more details concerning the nature of early English polyphony. After this writer concerns himself briefly with the various meanings of the term *organum* (*organum purum*, the organ, *organum triplum* and *quadruplum*), and questions in part the validity of these meanings, he continues:

> Finally, there is a kind of organum so called by the ancients when they set tones in harmony with other tones. This is the common name for conducts in simple ligatures for two parts and mensurable music of all types. This common usage may be explained in the following manner: we proceed from the same tone sung twice, i.e., when the tenor (*cantus*) sings the C *gravium* twice, then the organum can sing the c which is an octave higher, twice, or it can proceed from c to G, or to F, or to E, or also to E-flat (*deutera synemmenon* [!]).

In this way, in a purely mechanical fashion, beginning with C G, C F, C E, and C E♭ as first consonances, the steps to the other consonances within the range of the octave are indicated. The other possible steps of the *cantus* (movements by seconds, thirds, etc.) are then indicated, and in a similarly mechanical fashion the possibilities of forming consonances are developed, including the use of parallel octaves and fifths. The whole thing is an unnecessarily detailed table of consonances which is only of interest to us in that it, too, includes the major and minor thirds and, furthermore, the sixths, without indicating any reasons for not including them. It must be noted, however, that the sixths appear only in places using binary measure (*pares*; the text mentions only the octave, the unison, the fifth, the fourth, and the major and minor third for ternary measure, in which all dissonances are allowed according to this treatise). Anonymous, however, says that many *organistae* use the major and minor third for endings, although only the octave, the unison, the fifth, and as an exception in more-than-two-voiced settings, the fourth, are permissible.[12]

---

[12] Coussemaker, *Script.* I: 354. "The rule which the best composers follow for every natural harmonic progression is to begin with a unison, octave, fifth, fourth, or either the major or minor third. Properly speaking, however, a composition does not end with a

The rules concerning the discant (p. 356) state that for the beginning note any consonance may be chosen; this means, in other words, that besides the octave, the fifth, and the fourth, the major and minor third, or the unison (this is mentioned last) may also be used. The rules further demand that all ternary-value *puncta* (i.e., notes on stressed places, actually principal notes) must be consonant, while all others (those falling on unstressed places) may be dissonant (*indifferenter ponuntur*). At this time especially (toward the end of the 13th century), all types of methods were probably used, as indicated by the distinguishing between three types of *discantores* (p. 356). In general, the rule is established (p. 358) that the ternary *puncti* (stressed notes) of the first *modus* must be consonances, i.e., unison, octave, fourth, fifth, or a major or minor third. The sixths are not mentioned (!).

Chronologically speaking, the position of the writer assuming the pseudonym Aristotle (Couss. I:260)*[9] is rather difficult to understand. This writer—contrary person that he is—calls [13] the semitone, whole-tone, and *tritonus* imperfect dissonances (and notes in passing that the roughness of the dissonances is ameliorated the farther apart the tones producing the dissonances are), the major and minor third intermediate dissonances, and major and minor sixths perfect dissonances (*discordantiae perfectae*). In using this terminology he wishes to express the fact that the last-mentioned dissonances are closest to the consonances (fourth, fifth, and octave). It is of great interest that such an early writer places the same value on both types of sixths, and one might be tempted to place this author later than Franco, if his mensural theory were not definitely pre-Franconian. The preference of sixths over thirds, however, is typical of his pseudo-Aristotelian contrariness.

Anonymous XIII writes with surprising clarity (Coussemaker, *Script.* II:496); his is a treatise in Old French dealing with discant written during the 13th century.*[10] Comparing it with the *Libellus in gallico le arte discantandi*, discussed on pages 81–83, it shows clearly in which direction the theory of polyphony moved when thirds and sixths were regarded as consonances.

---

major or minor third, although thére are some persons who use these improper sounds at the end. Every composition should end with an octave, fifth, fourth, or unison. It should be noted, however, that two-voiced compositions rarely end with a fourth, whereas three- and four-voiced compositions use this interval in conjunction with other consonances."

[13] "Quarum autem (discordantiarum) quaedam dicuntur imperfectae, quaedam mediae et quaedam perfectae. Imperfectae vero sunt tonus, semitonium et tritonus, quia quanto propiores inveniantur eo tanto pejores, et quanto remotiores tanto meliores. Mediae vero sunt ditonus et semiditonus (Couss. semitonium). Perfectae sunt tonus cum diapente et semitonium cum diapente."

The treatise[14] begins with the (incomplete) enumeration of the

[14] "Qui veult savoir l'art de deschant, il doit savoir qu'ils sont XIII espèces de chant c'est assavoir: unisson, demi-ton, (ton), ton et demi, deux tons, deux tons et demi, trois tons, trois tons et demi (lesquelez font une quinte) (demiton avec quinte, ton avec quinte, ton et demi avec quinte), deux tons (avec quinte), deux tons et demi avecque quinte (lesquelz font une double)...

"Encore est à savoir que de ces XIII espèces devant dites sont fais XIII acors, III parfais et IIII imparfais et VI dissonans. Les III parfais sont: unisson, quinte et double. Les IIII imparfais sont II tierces et II sixtes. Les VI dissonans sont II secondes II quartes et II septimes...

"La tierce de ton et demiton requiert unisson après li et celle de deux tons quinte après li.

"La sixte de demi ton avuec quinte requiert après li quinte et celle d'un ton avuec quinte requiert double après li.

"Qui veult prendre double contre sa teneur, il doibt dire contre UT: FA, contre RE: SOL, contre MI: LA, VIII notes de sus la teneur ou que soit... contre FA SOL LA... UT RE MI; car FA SOL LA est réputés pour UT RE MI.

"Qui veult prendre quinte contre sa teneur, il doibt dire contre UT: SOL, contre RE: LA et tout ainsi comme la teneur V notes de sus etc. etc....

"Qui veult faire bon deschant, il doit commenchier et finir par acort parfait, c'est à scavoir par unisson, quinte ou double; doibt regarder comme la teneur se gouverne; se elle monte à son commencement, si comme UT RE MI etc., la première doibt estre double, et se la teneur descent, si comme RE UT ou MI UT ou LA FA ou LA SOL, la première doibt estre quinte, mes que ce soit sur notes appendans; et ne doibt on point faire ne dire II quintes ne deux doubles l'une apres l'autre ne monter ne descendre avec sa teneur car ils sont parfais (!); mais par accors imparfais, tierces et sixtes, peut-on bien monter ou descendre II ou III notes ou plus se besoing est, mais que ce soit sur notes appendans. Car il sont III manières de notes, c'est ascavoir appendans, non appendans et désirans appendans.

"Notes appendans sont comme ici: (missing) sur lesquelles on doibt dire tierce-quinte ou sixte-double tant en commencement de déchant comme en moyen, item... (illegible)

"Notes non appendans: (missing) sur lesquelles on doit dire double-quinte ou quinte-tierce. Item sur les(quelles) on doit dire double-tierce.

"Notes désirans appendans sont quand la teneur monte une note ou II, ou III en droit degré et en la fin soit une appendant, toutes celles par devant sont désirans appendans; si come yci: (missing)

"Se c'est en commencement de chant la première et la darrenière doibt être double et les moiennes sixtes, ou la première et la darrenière quinte et les moiennes tierces. (Se) c'est en moyen chant, les premières sont sixtes et la darrenière double, ou les premières sont tierces et la darrenière quinte. Et ne doibt-on faire que II ou III tierces ou sixtes l'une après l'autre sans moyen etc.

"Item, se la teneur monte III notes en droit degré ou hors degré comme icy:

la première doibt être double, la seconde quinte; se c'est fin de chant la darrenière unisson, se c'est moyen chant la darrenière tierce.

°"Si la teneur montoit IIII notes en degré comme icy:

se c'est fin de chant, double, quinte, tierce, unisson; se c'est moyen, double, tierce ou quinte et les autres tierces.

thirteen intervals (*espèces de chant*) from the unison to the octave (0–12 semitones). Of the thirteen intervals which are made up of combinations of these tones (*accors*), three are perfect (*parfais*), four imperfect (*imparfais*), and six dissonant (*dissonans*), namely:

> *Accors parfais: unisson, quinte et double*
> *imparfais: 2 tierces et 2 sixtes*
> *dissonans: 2 secondes, 2 quartes* (!), *2 septimes*

In addition, these rules:

The minor third requires that a unison follow, the major third requires the fifth. The minor sixth requires the fifth to follow and the major sixth requires the octave.

"Item se la darrenière est hors de degré comme icy:

double, quinte, tierce et la darrenière tierce dessous la teneur ou la première double et les aultres moyennes sixtes et la darrenière tierce, et se c'est fin de chant, la dernière unisson.

"En toute ligature montant, se la teneur montoit V ou VI notes entir, on doit prendre la ordonnance des III ou quatres dessus dites etc.

"Item se la teneur descendoit III notes en droit degré, comme icy:

se c'est commencement de chant, double-sixte-double ou quinte-tierce-quinte; se c'est en moyen sixte-sixte-double ou tierce-tierce-quinte ou tierce-sixte-double etc. Si c'est hors de degré comme icy:

tierce-quinte-double, ou ainsi

tierce-sixte-double.

"Se la teneur descendoit IIII notes en droit degré, comme icy:

se c'est commencement de chant, il y a III déchants, c'est escavoir: double-sixte-(sixte)-double ou quinte-tierce-tierce-quinte ou quinte-tierce-sixte-double. Se c'est en moyen chant il y a six déchants, III sixtes et la darrenière double, ou trois tierces et la darrenière quinte, ou sixte-double-sixte-double ou tierce-quinte (-tierce-quinte) ou tierce-tierce-sixte-double (? ou tierce-sixte-sixte-double?); se la teneur descendoit V ou VI notes, on poet l'ordenance de III ou de IV devant dicte.

"Item, en chant a III exceptions dont la première est, se la teneur avoit RE FA (RE) etc. ou (MI) SOL MI comme icy:

et le deschant fust double-quinte-double lequel serait SOL FA SOL ou LA SOL LA.

"La seconde est se la teneur descendoit II tons et demi, comme icy:

se la première estoit tierce, il doibt et veul mielx descendre une pour avoir quinte que monter II pour avoir double, car la tierce est en parchon et en flours (?).

"Item la tierce exception est, se le teneur montoit II tons et demi comme icy:

Se la première estoit disième, il laist et veult mieulx monter une pour avoir double que descendre deux pour avoir quinte."

The treatise uses the terminology of Guidonian solmization, based on the two hexachords C–a and G–e:

| | | | | | | | | | | | |
|---|---|---|---|---|---|---|---|---|---|---|---|
| UT | RE | MI | FA | SOL | LA | | UT | RE | MI | FA | SOL LA |
| | UT | RE | MI | FA | SOL | LA | | UT | RE | MI | FA SOL LA |

$\Gamma$    A    B    C    D    E    F    G    a    ♮    c    d    e    f    g    a
                                                                                 a

Octaves are then UT–FA (C–c), RE–SOL (D–d), MI–LA (E–e), or in combination:

$$\text{combination:}\quad \begin{matrix} \text{FA} & \text{SOL} & \text{LA} \\ \text{UT} & \text{RE} & \text{MI} \end{matrix} = \begin{bmatrix} c & d & e \\ C & D & E \end{bmatrix}.$$

Fifths are UT–SOL (C–g), RE–LA (D–a), MI–MI (E–♮), FA–FA (F–c), etc.

The actual rules for the setting are as follows:

Whoever wishes to compose a good *déchant* must begin and end with a perfect consonance, i.e., with the unison, the fifth, or the octave. He has to take note, however, in which direction the tenor moves in the beginning: If the tenor ascends (i.e., C D E), one must begin with the octave; if it descends (i.e., D C or E C or a F or a G), one must begin with the fifth, assuming that movement from the fifth will be stepwise in contrary motion. One must never use two fifths or two octaves in succession*[11] with either ascending or descending tenor, because these are perfect consonances (!). On the other hand, one may take two, three, and, if necessary, more steps with the tenor using imperfect consonances, namely, thirds and sixths, assuming that these lead to stepwise movements in contrary motion.

The anonymous author distinguishes between successions of intervals (two at a time) in the following manner:

1. Interval connections which may be achieved by moving stepwise in contrary motion (*appendans*—to that which is appended), namely, the (major) third to the fifth and the (major) sixth to the octave, or vice versa, the fifth to the (major) third and the octave to the (major) sixth. In spite of the incomplete text, the successions of the (minor) third to the unison and the unison to the (minor) third must be included as is shown in the introduction to this treatise.

2. Intervals in which connection by step is missing or available in only one voice (*non appendans*), whether in similar or contrary motion, namely, an octave to a fifth (in contrary or similar motion), a fifth to a third (in similar motion or oblique motion?) and an octave to a third (in contrary motion).

3. Intervals which may be connected by step in both voices in parallel motion (*désirans appendans*), which must, however, always lead to a stepwise ending in contrary motion, or, in other words, a stepwise succession

of sixths ending in the octave, or a stepwise succession of thirds ending in the fifth or unison; that is:

1. *Appendans:*

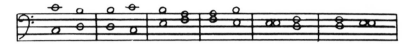

2. *Non appendans:*

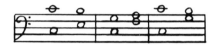

3. *Désirans appendans:*

It should be noted that the minor sixth which leads to the fifth is missing, although it was mentioned in the introductory list of practical rules. At any rate, one of the two voices must remain on the same tone if the sixth moves to the fifth, a situation which is not discussed but which must, however, appear frequently. Outside of the introduction, differentiation between the major and minor sixth is not made. Also, a definite rule to the effect that the *appendans* must always move a half-step in one of the voices is not to be found, although this is probably implied. We shall refer to this again. The continuation of the special instructions, because of its clearness, directness, and musical practicability, is of enough interest to be included here in its entirety:

In the beginning of a melodic section the first and the last interval must be an octave, and the middle intervals then are sixths; or the first and the last are fifths and the middle ones are thirds; in the middle of a melodic section the first intervals (of a ligature? a distinction?) are sixths and the last one is an octave, or the first are thirds and the last is an octave, or the first are thirds and the last is a fifth. One should not, however, place (unnecessarily) more than two or three thirds or sixths in succession without another interval in between (*moyen*).

If the *cantus firmus* (*teneur*) ascends through three tones stepwise or even by skips, the first interval shall be an octave, the second a fifth, and the last, if it occurs at the end of the melody, a unison, but if it occurs in the middle of the melody, it shall be a third.

(Here it can plainly be seen that we are concerned with neumes consisting of several tones, namely *syllabae*, using Odo's and Guido's
terminology):

If the tenor ascends four steps, it should be done as follows: place an octave-
fifth-third and unison, wherever a close occurs, and an octave-fifth (or third) and
continue in thirds, in the middle of a melodic section:

If the tenor skips to its last tone, one must place an octave-fifth-third and third
below, or octave-sixth-sixth-third and, where a close occurs, place instead of the
third a unison:

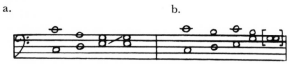

If the tenor ascends by five or six steps, the rules governing movements of three
or four steps must apply, i.e.:

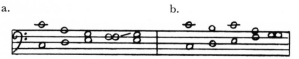

If the tenor descends through three tones stepwise, one must place in the beginning of the melody an octave-sixth-octave, or a fifth-third-fifth (a), in the middle
of a melodic section, however, a third-third-fifth, or a third-sixth-octave (b); if
the tenor skips at the end, one must place third-fifth-octave (c), if it skips at the
beginning, a third-sixth-octave (d):

If the tenor descends stepwise through four tones, at the beginning of a melodic section, there are three kinds of *déchant* available, namely, the octave-sixth-sixth-octave, or fifth-third-third-fifth, or fifth-third-sixth-octave (a). In the middle of a melodic section there are six kinds of *déchant*: three sixths and one octave; three thirds and one fifth; sixth-octave-sixth-octave; third-fifth-third-fifth; two thirds-sixth-octave (and third-two sixths-octave) (b):

a.                                             b.

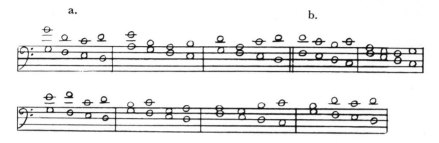

If the tenor descends five or six notes, the rules governing three- or four-note movements are applicable.

Furthermore, there are three exceptions (*exceptions*):

1. If the tenor shows RE–FA–RE or SOL–MI–SOL respectively, and the *déchant* takes in addition the octave-fifth-octave with SOL–FA–SOL or LA–SOL–LA respectively, then the middle note will not (!) be chromatically changed:[15]

2. If the tenor descends a fourth, then the *déchant*, if it places a third above the first note, takes the fifth in similar motion, rather than the third ascending to the octave, because the third is then (*en parchon* (?) *et en flours*). (This florid figure of speech which is untranslatable seems to indicate that the connection becomes more fluid, delicate):

not:

etc.

3. If the tenor ascends a fourth, the *déchant*, if it is a tenth (!) above the first

---

[15] We shall repeatedly find the term *soustenir* or *sustinere* as it applies to chromatic change (*sustentio*). It seems to have appeared toward the beginning of the 14th century, but is still used in 1555 by Vicentino (*sustentar*).

See Joh. de Muris, *Ars discantus* (Couss. III:73): "It is noteworthy that no other notes are altered in counterpoint except these three: SOL, FA, and UT."

tone, finds it more appropriate to move in parallel motion to the octave for its
second tone, rather than descend a third and take the fifth:

Unfortunately, the date of origin for this treatise is doubtful. The
Codex *fonds latin* 1474 of the Paris National Library (formerly *fonds* St.
Victor 665), from which Coussemaker took it, also contains a catechism
according to Johannes de Muris (contained in Gerbert, *Script.* III:301),
which naturally belongs in the 14th century. Since Anonymous XIII
makes no reference at all to mensural theory he unquestionably belongs
to the literature treating of *déchant sur le livre*, or extemporized counterpoint, which *déchant* in its first stages, having evolved directly from
organum, undoubtedly is. In this practice Anonymous XIII occupies an
important position, for he modified the old rules to such a large degree, in
order to include the new concepts of dissonance and consonance, that
these almost meet the demands of strict contrapuntal writing of note
against note. If the treatise is older than the codex—which is entirely
possible, according to our experience with the other treatises we have
discussed—then the rule forbidding parallel fifths and parallel octaves
becomes a highly important one. It would, then, be a question of whether
the teachers of the *Ars nova* independently set up this rule or whether they
merely carried it over from the reformed practice of the *déchanteurs*.

The treatise of Anonymous V (Coussemaker, *Script.* I:366), which is
found in a 14th-century MS in the British Museum in London, also belongs to the same group of treatises.*[12] Since this Anonymous, however, is
not yet familiar with the forms of the smaller note values (*minima* and
*semiminima*), which were already established and had been in use since
about 1320, one must assume that his treatise is much earlier. Whatever
the case may be, this treatise is still clearly founded upon the *déchantier*
rules and shows significant deviations from Anonymous XIII.

To show this, the definition of consonances must be included here:
"Some consonances are pure (*clarae*), namely, the fifth and the twelfth,
others less pure (*minus clarae*), namely, the third, sixth, and tenth, and others
extremely pure (*clarissimae*), namely, the unison, the octave, and the
double octave."

A remark about the common practice of singing [16] (of the English?) is

---

[16] "Nota quod totus generalis modus cantandi consistat aut in octavo aut in sexto.
Similiter est notandum, quod in illo modo cantandi generaliter incipiendum est in octavo;
tamen quandoque potest fieri in sexto; et semper est in octavo pausandum, nisi planus
cantus pauset in MI descendente."

also of interest; this practice, according to this Anonymous, is based entirely upon the intervals of the octave and the sixth (!); he says: "This general practice of singing begins usually with an octave, and rarely with the sixth, and it must always close with the octave, except when the *cantus planus* (main voice) ends on FA–MI." In this case, however, as we find further on, the discant comes to this close from the major second below (RE), or in other words, from the minor third to the unison:

A detailed discussion of these possibilities leads also to other possibilities of closing formations (*pausatio*): A close may occur at the fifth or twelfth instead of at the octave (this occurring less often). Furthermore, in some exceptions, if the *cantus planus* closes in ascending on MI, an ending may occur on the (major) tenth (below the *cantus*), and, less often, if the descending *cantus* closes on MI, a close may occur on the sixth (above the *cantus*):

A close in the unison also occurs if the *cantus* descends one step to the final:

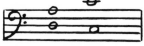

Generally, the *penultima* (the next to the last interval) in closes on the octave consists of the sixth; but it may sometimes be a fifth, when the *cantus* ascends by a third:

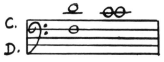

or even a tenth, when the *cantus* descends a second:

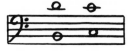

Before closes on the fifth, the *penultima* is usually an octave, when the *cantus* descends a third (a), or a third when the *cantus* ascends a second (b):

 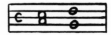

Before closes on the twelfth, the *penultima* is usually a tenth (the intervals of the aforementioned combination increased by an octave) or an octave, if the *cantus* ascends a whole-tone. Occasionally, however, it is a sixth or a fifth, when the *cantus* ascends a third, fourth, or fifth at the close:

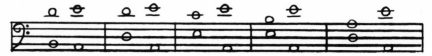

Before closes on the tenth, which occur only when the *cantus* ascends by a whole-tone or a major third, the *penultima* is a fifth or sixth, and less often an octave, the latter only when the *cantus* ascends by a whole-tone:

Before closes at the sixth which only occur when the *cantus* descends by semitone to the final, the *penultima* shall be an octave:

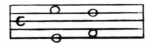

Before closes at the unison, which only occur when the *cantus* descends a semitone to the close, the *penultima* is a (minor) third:

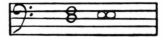

Note well that in addition there are four possibilities of descending with the *cantus*: from the third to the fifth, from the fifth to the octave, from the sixth to the octave, and from the tenth to the twelfth:

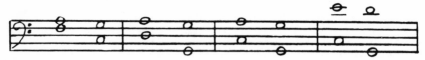

Accordingly, there are four possibilities of ascending above a stationary *cantus*: unison-fifth, fifth-octave, octave-twelfth, and twelfth-double octave, the last being little used:

One should note that in many of the cases which are dealt with in this treatise, the *cantus firmus* is placed above the counter-voice.

The end of the treatise consists of some rules for avoiding the MI *contra* FA, of the intervals having no harmonic value (*relationes non harmonicae*). A fifth, octave, twelfth, or double octave shall never appear as MI *contra* FA (the diminished fifth is also entirely excluded).*13

This treatise also contains in its beginning the rule forbidding parallel octaves, but in a version which deviates from that of Anonymous XIII. It says:17

> Bear in mind that in beginning with the unison, octave, and double octave, one must never—either ascending or descending—continue in the same intervals with the *cantus planus*, except when the *cantus* uses wider steps than those of a third or when one or both voices pause between two intervals of the same kind.

This, then, is only a prohibition of parallel octaves, although they are allowed if movements of larger intervals occur in the voices. In addition, stepwise octaves may be written if the counter-voice disguises these octaves by the inclusion of figurative tones (*frangendo*):

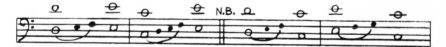

This treatise, however, does not look as though it had been written after the time of Philippe de Vitry. One must, rather, assume that the treatise of Anonymous V, even if not earlier in its origin, is nevertheless earlier than the treatise of Anonymous XIII in the point of view its contents reflect.

The *De contrapuncto quaedam regulae utiles* of the Magister Philippotus Andreas, printed in Coussemaker III:116 f., was probably written at the earliest during the 14th century (the notational examples in white notes even point to the 15th century), but its contents indicate that it belongs to the period of discant rules. Andreas' rules speak only of arranging

---

17 Coussemaker I:366: "Nota quod ab unisono vel ab octavo vel quintodecimo numquam ascendendo vel descendendo (est) cum plano cantu per consimilem quantitatem nisi planus cantus ascendat vel descendat ultra tertium gradum, vel facta fuerit aliqua pausatio aut ex parte unius aut amborum."

octaves, sixths, thirds, twelfths, and fifths (singly) in a manner which even today cannot be disputed, for example (*cantus firmus* lies in the lower voice):

Finally, we must also include Marchettus of Padua in the discussion in this chapter. His final work, the *Lucidarium musicae planae* (which overlaps with the Franconian period), was written, according to its own testimony, in 1274 in Cesena and Verona.*[14] It shows that his change in attitude toward accepting the new views was only partial, inasmuch as he continues to limit his classification of consonances to the fourth, fifth, octave, eleventh, twelfth, and double octave in this following earlier usage. He concedes to the third, sixth, and tenth (!) an exceptional position among the dissonances or the diaphonies only under the pretext of their "compatibility."[18] He goes on to say:[19]

These and similar dissonances (i.e., their compound forms [these intervals enlarged by an octave]) are agreeable in the judgment of our ear because they prove to be nearest neighbors of consonances when both of their tones move at the same time, one ascending and the other descending. It is, therefore, ruled (!) that two tones may be regarded as dissonances tolerated by the ear when they allow that kind of progression in moving toward a consonance in which one tone moves up and the other down. This type of dissonance then finds itself occupying a position neighboring the consonance (*distando per minorem distantiam*), which relationship is not found in the other dissonances.

Marchettus himself, incidentally, proves to be a daring innovator, because he is the first to allow chromatic progression of the voices, which

[18] Gerbert III:80: "*Dissonantia,* moreover, and *diaphonia* are the same; for as Isidore says, diaphony is voices that are discordant or dissonant, in which there is not a pleasant but a rough sound.

Some of these diaphonies or dissonances are arranged according to hearing and reason and others are not. These consist primarily of three: the third, sixth, and tenth."

[19] *Ibid*: "Hae autem dissonantiae et his similes ideo compatiuntur ab auditu, quia sunt magis propinquae consonantiis, cum moventur sursum et deorsum. Dicitur enim, quod ...duae voces sunt in dissonantia, quae compatitur ab auditu, quando ipsarum quaelibet requirens consonantiam, moveatur ita: videlicet ut si una in sursum tendit, reliqua in deorsum semper distando per minorem distantiam a consonantia, ad quam tendit. Aliae vero dissonantiae sive diaphoniae ideo non compatiuntur ab auditu, quia etsi moveantur sursum et deorsum: non tamen ante consonantias per minorem distantiam sunt distantes."

he defends intelligently. In this he is far ahead of his time. Even though we find tone-steps regarded as having a dual aspect (that is, tone-steps other than b♭ and b♮) as far back as John Cotton, Odo, and even Hucbald (in the *Musica enchiriadis*), for a long time the rule persisted forbidding a change from MI into FA on the grounds that they do not constitute the same tone. Marchettus is the first, through his knowledge of Boetius, to conceive the idea of attempting something similar to that of the chromaticism and enharmonicism of the ancients and to achieve satisfying results with these attempts. In the second chapter of treatise VIII in the *Lucidarium* he first establishes in musical terminology the concept of the "*permutatio*," which means changing the name of a note which occupies the same place on a line or in a space in order to indicate another pitch. This he does by dividing the whole-tone into a diatonic and an enharmonic semitone, or into a chromatic semitone and a *diesis*, in order to demonstrate clearly the possibility of the consonances (*propter consonantiam*).[20]

In doing this, he does not seem to be aware of the fact that his restraint in recognizing thirds and sixths is robbed of its reason for being:

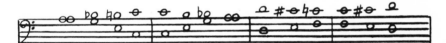

The chromatic tones which he introduces (cf. pp. 73–75), f♯, c♯, and g♯ are not at all foreign to his time but have even been given certain designations:[21]

[20] (Page 89): "*Permutatio* is a variation in the name of a note which takes place on the same line or in the same space and has a different sound. For a change is made when a whole-tone is divided for the sake of consonance into a diatonic or enharmonic semitone or in a chromatic semitone or a *diesis*, or the contrary as shown here:

[21] "Signa autem, quibus notis innuitur permutationem facere, sunt tria, scilicet ♮ quadrum, ♭ rotundum et aliud signum, quod a vulgo falsa musica nominatur: de quibus videre oportet. Prima namque duo signa, scilicet ♮ et ♭ sunt, vel esse possunt in quolibet cantu plano ac etiam mensurato. Tertium verso signum solum in cantu ponitur mensurato, vel in plano, qui aut colorate cantatur, aut in mensuratum transit, puta in tenoribus Motetorum seu aliorum cantuum mensuratorum. De primis duobus signis ait Richardus Normandus: ubicumque ponitur ♮ quadrum, dicimus vocem MI, ubicumque vero ♭ rotundum, dicimus vocem FA."

There are three designations which may bring about such a permutation, namely, the ♮ *quadrum*, the ♭ *rotundum*, and a third, which is called *falsa musica*. The first two (♮ and ♭) are found or can be found in chant of the ecclesiastical liturgy and also in mensural music; the third (♯) appears only in mensural music, although it may appear in the *cantus planus*, if that is sung in coloration and used in a mensurated way, as in the motet and other forms of mensural music.

Here he refers to a Richard of Normandy (Richardus Normandus), who says: "Everywhere where we find the ♮ *quadrum*, we shall say MI, and wherever we find the ♭ *rotundum*, FA." Marchettus, in order to achieve certain consonances, or rather dissonances, fights against the practice of not differentiating between ♮ and ♯ and maintains that ♮♭ divides the whole-tone into one enharmonic and one diatonic interval, but that ♯, on the other hand, divides it into one chromatic and one *diesis* (! p. 89; again he remembers his definition of intervals, unfortunately at the wrong time, for here it weakens his demonstration). This differentiation is, of course, an error, for (at least in general use) the ♯ merely reverses the order of the two types of semitones found when the ♭ is in the same place (f:f♯:g = 128/125:16/15, a:♭:♮ = 16/15:128/125). Marchettus did not and could not know this, as he was unaware that between c and d and between g and a there is another interval, determined by mathematical acoustics as 25/24 (=c:c♯ and g:g♯). It should be noted how Marchettus determines the various ratios of the three kinds of semitone[22] (page 75): "The enharmonic semitone (a–♭) consists of two *dieses*, the diatonic (♭–♮) three, the chromatic (c–c♯) four."

This runs contrary to present-day procedures, according to which the diatonic semitone (which Marchettus calls enharmonic) is the largest interval of the three:

G–g♯ = 25/24,   in logarithms with a base of 2 = 0.05889[*15]
b♭–b♮ = 135/128, in logarithms with a base of 2 = 0.07681
b♮–c = 16/15,   in logarithms with a base of 2 = 0.09311

(that is, approximately of the relationship 4:5:6). We must note first

[22] "For, from a *acuto* to *primum* ♭, that is, the *rotundum*, is an enharmonic semitone, which as was said, is minor. From the first [*primo*] ♭ to the ♮ following, that is, the *quadratum*, is a diatonic semitone which is called major. In the second example, from the first ♭ to the ♮ following is a diatonic semitone and from the ♮ to c *acuto* is an enharmonic semitone. With this it becomes evident how the whole-tone, from a *acuto* to the ♮ following, is divided into an enharmonic and diatonic semitone, and how the whole-tone which extends from the first ♭ to c is divided into diatonic and enharmonic.

"From the enharmonic semitone and the *diesis* arises the diatonic semitone: from the diatonic semitone and the *diesis* the chromatic semitone, and from the chromatic semitone and the *diesis* the whole-tone. Therefore, the enharmonic semitone contains two *dieses*, the diatonic three, and the chromatic four; the whole-tone truly consists of five *dieses*."

that the entire Middle Ages and Antiquity, following the designation of the diatonic semitone as the remainder of the fourth after deduction from it of two whole-tones of the ratio 9/8, regarded the diatonic semitone as smaller than the chromatic. Secondly, we are aware of the tendency of musicians even today to move a leading-tone closer to its tonic, in order to make this interval smaller, so that the designation of a–♭ as a combination of two *dieses*, and c♯–d as only one *diesis* does not seem so strange after all.

It is striking to note some refinements in the use of certain kinds of voice-leading (p. 75):

One reads:

Such a division of the whole-tone was regarded as coloration (and in this instance we learn the exact meaning of *color*: the introduction of the *subsemitonium* as a neighboring tone!)*16 and was executed in such a manner that the singer, when singing the first interval downward, which was a *diesis*, bears in mind that he will return to the same note (!). In such a situation the third consonance (the fifth; the interval of a fourth which Gerbert uses in the second case is an error) follows less naturally and obviously.23

Is this not an exceptionally fine explanation of such deceptive voice-leading?

We stand here apparently at the threshold of a new epoch; a strong harmonic feeling appears, even if only in occasional instances, for which the point of view held by the Romanic people during the preceding centuries was unable to furnish an explanation. This new epoch shows clearly a definite breakthrough of harmonic principles which were common knowledge among the musicians of the entire Occident, and which probably had been in use for centuries in the north of Europe.

Without doubt, since the end of the 12th century, the gradual freeing of polyphony from the constricting fetters of the necessity of simultaneously chanting the same words of a text did much to make the nature of harmony apparent. This new freedom became possible with the establishment of a notation which could also represent rhythmic values. The nature of harmony shows itself at first in the placement of different values on the

23 "Hic enim bipartitio toni debet fieri cum colore fictitio, ut qui eam profert, fingat in primo descensu, qui est diesis, ac si vellet post talem descensum sursum redire: post haec chromaticum descendat, et sic consonantia (tertia) licet minus naturaliter et proprie, subsequitur."

various intervals for purposes of musical logic and for the creation of normal, well-ordered musical procedures. Some of the findings which we have just discussed are the result of this. Organum undoubtedly contained from its very beginnings elements of a harmonic nature in its clear movement from the unison back into the unison at the beginning and end of each melodic section. Guido's reference to the impossibility of ending organum with the principal voice a fourth below is proof of the fact that originally the unisons at the beginning and end were characteristic of organum, and that parallel organum was able to evolve only as the result of a theory based upon false premises.

Before we proceed with the first development of mensural music, however, we must investigate another curious form of singing in parallel intervals with two or even three (!) voices. The origin of this form cannot be shown, however, though, according to the testimonies, it was first practiced in England. Undoubtedly it was closer to the natural polyphonic singing of the Nordic races, even in its latest formulations, than parallel organum. This form is the so-called fauxbourdon.

## APPENDIX

FOOTNOTE 1: Coussemaker I:341: "A tempore (Couss. parte) et in suo tempore Perotini Magni; sed nesciebant numerare (Couss. narrare) ipsas cum quibusdam aliis postpositis et semper a tempore Leonini (Couss. Leonis) pro parte, quoniam duae ligatae tunc temporis pro brevi longa ponebantur et tres ligatae simili modo in pluribus locis pro longa brevi, longa." Page 344: "Maxima pars cognitionis antiquorum fuit a praedictis sine materiali significatione, quod ipsi habebant notitiam concordantiarum melodie complete...et dicebant: punctus ille superior sic concordat cum inferiori, et sufficiebat eis."

FOOTNOTE 4: (Page 117): "Subsequitur positio tertia, Johannis videlicet De Burgundia, ut ex ore ipsius audivimus vel secundum vulgarem opinionem Franconis de Colonia."

FOOTNOTE 5: "Concordantiarum tres sunt species, scilicet perfecta, imperfecta et media. Perfecta concordantia dicitur quando plures voces conjunguntur ita, quod una ab alia vix accipitur differre percipitur propter concordantiam. Et tales sunt duae scilicet unisonus et diapason ut hic. (Examples according to Gerbert):

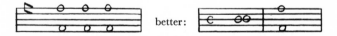

"Imperfecta dicitur quando duae voces multum differre percipiuntur ab auditu, non tamen discordant. Et sunt duae, scilicet ditonus et semiditonus, ut hic:

"Mediae vero concordantiae dicuntur, quando duae voces conjunguntur (majorem) meliorem concordantiam habentes quam praedictae, non tamen ut perfectae: et sunt duae scilicet diapente et diatessaron, ut hic patet:

better:

"Quare autem una concordantia magis concordat quam alia, planae musicae relinquatur. Discordantiarum duae sunt species, perfecta et imperfecta. Perfecta discordantia dicitur, quando duae voces sic conjunguntur, quod se compati non possunt secundum auditum. Et sunt quatuor, scilicet semitonium, tritonus, ditonus cum diapente et semitonium cum diapente ut hic apparet:

better:

"Imperfectae discordantiae dicuntur, quando duae voces se quodammodo compati possunt secundum auditum, sed discordant. Et sunt tres species, scilicet tonus, tonus cum diapente et semiditonus cum diapente ut hic:

better:

"Et nota, quod tam concordantiae quam discordantiae possunt sumi in infinitum, ut diapente cum diapason, diatessaron cum diapason....Et sic in duplici diapason et triplici, si possibile esset in voce. Item sciendum, quod omnis imperfecta discordantia immediate ante concordantiam bene concordat."

FOOTNOTE 8: (Coussemaker, *Script.* III:356 and IV:280): "Imperfecta concordantia ab instabilitate sua merito denominatur, quae de loco movetur in locum et per se inter nullas certas invenitur proportiones. Tales enim sunt semiditonus, ditonus et tonus cum diapente; nam semiditonus et ditonus quae tertiam sonant (Couss. tenent) vocem diversimode variantur, prout cantus ascendit et descendit (!)...sexta vox aliquando fit in dyapente cum tono et aliquando in dyapente cum semitonio (...discordantia imperfecta)."

FOOTNOTE 9: "Verumtamen quia vicine sunt sesquiquarte et sesquiquinte habitudinibus, quarum unitas facit diapente (Couss. differentiam), idcirco plurimi estimant consonas esse [ditonum et semiditonum]. Et si in numeris non reperiantur consone, voces tamen hominum subtilitate ipsos ducunt in mixturam suavem."

FOOTNOTE 10: "Verumtamen per diapente cum tono (Couss. toto) proceditur (Couss. procedetur) multoties in cantilenis istius temporis quod fit ut concordia, cum acciderit, quia rara est, fiat suavior."

FOOTNOTE 11: "Compatientur ergo se simul, si eidem voci gravi comparentur, ditonus vel semiditonus (!), diapente, diapason, diapason cum ditono vel semiditono (!) diapason cum diapente, bis diapason ut in his numeris patet sub hac formula: 64, 81 (Couss. 73!), 96, 128, 162, 192, 256 (=C E G c e g c)."

Footnote 12: Couss., *Script.* I:354: "Unde regula: omnis inceptio naturalis armonica inter organistas optimos est autem in unisono vel diapason, vel diapente vel diatessaron, vel semiditono vel ditono. Sed finis proprie loquendo non est in semiditono vel ditono, quamvis aliqui ibidem sonos suos improprie terminant; sed omnis finis in diapason vel diapente vel diatessaron et unisono. Nota quod diatessaron raro in duplicibus terminatur; sed saepius eis triplicibus et quadruplicibus bene cum alia consonantia."

Footnote 15: Couss. III:73: "Et est notandum quod in contrapunctu nullae aliae notae sustinentur, nisi istae tres, scilicet: SOL, FA et UT."

Footnote 18: Gerbert III:80: "Dissonantia autem et diaphonia idem sunt; nam ut dicit Isidorus, diaphoniae sunt voces discrepantes sive dissonae, in quibus non est jocundus sed asperus sonus."

"Harum autem diaphoniarum seu dissonantiarum aliae compatiuntur secundum auditum et rationem, et aliae non. Quae vero compatiuntur sunt tres principaliter scilicet tertia, sexta, decima."

Footnote 20: (Page 89): "Permutatio est variatio nominis vocis seu notae in eodem spatio seu linea in diverso sono; fit enim permutatio, ubi tonus dividitur propter consonantiam in diatonicum et enarmonicum aut in chromaticum et diesim, vel e contrario, ut hic:..."

Footnote 22: "Nam ab a acuto ad primum ♭, scilicet rotundum est semitonium enarmonicum, quod, ut praedicitur, minus est. A primo ♭ ad secundum ♮ scilicet quadratum, est semitonium diatonicum, quod dicitur majus. In secunda figura a primo ♭ ad secundum ♮ diatonicum semitonium est: a secundo vero ♮ ad c acutum semitonium enarmonicum est. Sicque patet, quomodo tonus qui est ab a acuto in secundum ♮, in enarmonicum et diatonicum semitonium dividatur, et tonus, qui est a primo ♭ ad c praedictum in diatonicum et enarmonicum.

"Ex enarmonico et diesi consurgit diatonicum; ex diatonico et diesi chromaticum, ex chromatico et diesi tonus. Continet itaque enarmonicum duas dieses, diatonicum tres, chromaticum quatuor; tonus vero ex quinque diesibus est formatus."

## CHAPTER VII

# Gymel and Fauxbourdon*[1]

WE FIRST meet the term *fauxbourdon* as referring to a special kind of polyphonic technique in the literature of the 15th century or even of the latter 14th century. Toward the end of the 15th century we find references concerning fauxbourdon in Johannes Tinctoris, Adam of Fulda, and Franchinus Gafurius; these speak of the use of the fourth as a consonance in connection with the sixth. More references to the *faberdon* might doubtless be found in sources which are not of a purely musical nature, such as that of the Meistersinger Hanns Rosenpluet, 1447, in his *Spruchgedichten: "mit Contratenor und Faberdon."*

The word *bordunus* in the present-day sense of the term *bourdon* (for the *bourdons* of the bagpipe and the hurdy-gurdy) was used by Hieronymus de Moravia (middle of the 13th century) to indicate the drone strings of the *viella* (because they were located next to the finger board) and may also have been used to name the strings of the *chrotta* which were located next to the finger board. Anonymous IV (whom Coussemaker erroneously dates around 1200) uses the expression *bordunus organorum* for a tone in the tenor voice which is sustained or plucked again and again (following the practice of organum in which one voice remains on the second below the final, i.e., on a Tritus). We shall not concern ourselves here as to whether Anonymous means the organ as the instrument or organum. At any rate, he makes use of an extension of the meaning of a word which originally referred to the position of the strings (*bordunus* derived from *bord*; *bordo* = edge). As the same author mentions the *plani cantores* (see p. 90 f. above), which runs parallel with the tenor, it is very probable that in actuality fauxbourdon was in use even at that time; final proof is missing, since Anonymous IV does not employ this word.*[2]

The oldest source known to us in which this name can be found is an Old English treatise mentioned by Hawkins on pp. 227–229 of the second volume of his *General History of Music* (1776), a treatise which for some reason has never been noted by our historians. The author of this treatise is a certain Chilston, the dates of whose life we do not know.*[3] His period, however, may with some certainty be placed around 1375–1400, which can be proved by the language he employs and also by the close connection of his treatise with another treatise preceding his in the same codex (MS of Waltham Holy Cross). The latter is written by Lionel Power, who is known to us as one of the earliest English contrapuntists (before Dunstable) through Haberl's discovery and description of the Bologna and Trent mensural codices dating from the beginning of the 15th century. The detailed remarks contained in these two treatises (in which only Chilston uses the expression *faburden* or *faburdun*) shed a completely different light upon the treatise of Guilelmus Monachus (the age of which cannot be exactly determined), which thus far has been regarded as the main source for fauxbourdon. At the same time, our findings so far concerning the common practice of singing in thirds and sixths in England are corroborated by these two English treatises. It should by no means be assumed that the theory of fauxbourdon in England came about as a result of continental attempts at polyphonic music. This is disproved by a special terminology, and even by a special manner of notation found in England which perhaps only partially appeared on the continent. The idea that fauxbourdon may have appeared during the exile of the Roman Curia in Avignon (1305–1376) is, therefore, scarcely tenable. It is possible, however, that the Papal choir there became acquainted with the English manner of parallel singing and took it with them to Rome. The manuscript repertories which we have already mentioned seem to prove that toward the end of the exile the compositions of the old English masters were being disseminated on the continent.[*4]

The passage of the treatise written by Lionel Power (called Lionello Polbero in the Trent codices) concerning discant is given by Hawkins as follows:[*5]

This treatise is written about the Great Scale for those who will be singers or composers or teachers.

For first of all they must know how many intervals they may use in harmonizing the mean, treble, and quatreble parts with the plainsong or tenor part. As old men have told us and as men practice singing nowadays, there are nine. But no one who wishes to sing well will sing a fifteenth above the plainsong except in the quatreble part, for a fifteenth befits no man's voice. And so there are only eight intervals used today, with the above exception; no composer may employ more than eight intervals. These eight extend from the unison to the thirteenth. But in contrapuntal singing in which there is a quatreble part there are nine intervals: unison, and the third, fifth, sixth, eighth, tenth, twelfth, and fifteenth (above the plainsong). Of these nine intervals five are perfect and four are imperfect. The five perfect are: unison and the fifth, eighth, twelfth, and fifteenth. The four imperfect are: the third, sixth, tenth, and thirteenth. When you sing a descant part, you may ascend or descend from one interval to another, but you may not sing the same perfect interval twice in direct sequence—that is, you may not sing two unisons in direct sequence, or two fifths, or two eighths, or two twelfths, or two fifteenths. You may not sing two such perfect accords in ascending or descending sequence. You must use certain intervals in conjunction with certain others, as I shall teach you. First you shall use a fifth with a third, an eighth with a sixth, a twelfth with a tenth, and a fifteenth with a thirteenth. In descent, one may extemporize three parts [three sights] with the nine intervals just mentioned. The parts are the mean sight, treble sight, and quatreble sight. There is another matter to take up in connection with the nine intervals, namely, how you shall visualize the notes of the part you are extemporizing in relation to the notes of the plainsong (which are the only ones actually written on the sheet of music). Here follows an example. First, to instruct a child to extemporize a part, you must teach him to visualize a note in his part in unison with a note in the plainsong as written an eighth below it, a note a third above a note in the plainsong as written a sixth beneath it, a note a fifth above as written a fourth beneath, a sixth above as written a third beneath, an eighth above as written a unison, a tenth above as written a third above, a twelfth above as written a fifth above, a thirteenth above as written a sixth above, a fifteenth above as written an eighth above.

Chilston's treatise continues, as we have mentioned before, directly where Lionel Power left off, and adds to it as follows:*6

Here follows a little treatise which deals with the sight of descant in the manner of the first treatise and which also deals with the singing of the parts of counter, countertenor, and *faburdon*.

After repeating the definitions of consonance (the nine *accordis*) almost verbatim, he continues:

Also one should know, that there are three parts to improvise in descant, namely, the quatreble sight, the treble sight, and the mean sight. The mean begins a fifth above the plainsong in voice and is with the plainsong in sight.

The treble begins an eighth above the plainsong [in voice], and the eighth is visualized as a unison [in sight] by the singer of that part. The quatreble begins a twelfth above the plainsong [in voice], and the twelfth is visualized as a unison [in sight] by the singer of that part.

In singing the mean part, one may use five intervals, namely, the unison, third, fifth, sixth, and eighth; in singing the treble part, one may use five intervals, namely, the fifth, sixth, eighth, tenth, and twelfth; and in singing the quatreble part, one may use five intervals, namely, the eighth, tenth, twelfth, thirteenth, and fifteenth. Furthermore, one should know that some of the intervals used in these parts in descant are visualized above the plainsong, some beneath, and some in unison with the plainsong.

The descanter who takes the mean part must begin it in sight with the plainsong and with a fifth above the plainsong in voice and he shall end his part with

a third and a fifth above the plainsong, if the plainsong descends at the end as in
FA, MI, MI, RE, RE, UT. A note in the mean part a sixth above the plainsong
[in voice] is visualized as a second above [in sight], the third below in sight is a
third above in voice, the fourth above in sight is an eighth above in voice, the
sixth above in sight is the tenth above in voice, which tenth may be sung by
the descanter, who takes the mean part if the plainsong is low. There are only
five intervals which belong to the mean part, as has been said above.

($\bigcirc$ = *cantus planus*
● = *mene* sight
◇ = actual sound of the same)

Furthermore:

Also you must know that when you sing a perfect interval to FA in the plainsong, you must make that note a FA, as MI, FA, SOL, LA. (Example not further
explained, probably thus:)

And it is well-sounding and pleasant to repeat an imperfect interval many times
in direct sequence in one part, as three or four or five thirds followed by a fifth
or a unison, or as many tenths followed by a twelfth, or as many thirteenths
followed by a fifteenth. This way of singing is pleasant both to the singer and to
the hearer.

Chilston writes the following concerning fauxbourdon:

The mode of singing [sight] called *faburden* with its intervals [accords]. For the
least process of sights natural and most in use, is expedient to declare the Sight of
*Faburden* the which hath but two Sights: a third above the plainsong in Sight
which is a sixth from the Treble in voice, and an even [and in unison] with the
plainsong in Sight, the which is an octave from the Treble in voice. These two
accords the Faburdener must rule by the Mean of the plainsong. For when he
shall begin his Faburden, he must set his Sight even with the plainsong and his
Voice in a fifth beneath the plainsong.

And after that, whether the plainsong ascend or descend [he ought] to set his
Sight always, both in rule and space, above the plainsong in a third. And after
that if the plainsong haunteth his course either in *acutis* from *g solreut* above to
*G Solreut* beneath, [he ought] to close downward in Sight even upon the plainsong upon one of these keys: *D Lasolre*, *C Solfaut*, *A Lamire* or *G Solreut* beneath.
And if the plainsong haunt his course from *G Solreut* beneath down toward *A Re*,
[he ought] conveniently then to see before where he may close, with two or three
or four thirds before, either in *F Faut* beneath, or *D Solre*, or *C Faut*, or *A Re*. And
all these closes [are] gladly to be sung and closed at the last end of a word. And

as often as he will [he ought] to touch the plainsong—and void therefrom—
except twice together, for that may not be, inasmuch as the plainsong Sight is an
octave to the Treble and a fifth to the Mean, and so to every degree he is a perfect
chord; and two perfect chords of one nature may not be sung together in no
degree of discant.

It is easy to see that both treatises deal mainly with the *déchant sur le
livre*, or extemporaneous counterpoint; the meaning of the term *sights*
being the different point of view with which one looks at the same melody,
which is the *cantus firmus* taken from plainchant (*sight* is among others a
technical term for the sight of firearms). We are not confronted here with
several different manners of notation for single voices, but with several
different manners of reading one and the same notation. The appearance
of an indication through notation to point out progressions which deviate
from the normal is only secondary. This indication presupposes a special
manner of reading (in other words, a transposed notation). Guido Adler's
*Studie zur Geschichte der Harmonie* (1881) does not mention these "sights,"
although fauxbourdon is the main subject of his work.*[7] He concerns himself only with the treatise of Guilelmus Monachus, to which we shall refer
again quite extensively.[1]

The three "sights"[2] which Lionel Power mentions are:

1. The manner of reading the *mene*, i.e., the alto voice or the middle
voice (*mene* = mean) of a three-part setting, which intones the first note of
the *cantus planus* a fifth higher. This occurs only with the beginning note;

[1] The oldest reference to the treble sight is probably that of Johannes de Garlandia
(*ca.* 1200!) in Couss., *Script.* I:114: "*Triplum* in its stricter sense must be consonant,
though at a greater distance with the first and second voice, if one does not represent the
intervals reduced by one octave, which, however, means the same." Anonymous IV,
Couss. (*Script.* I), probably also has the three "sights" in mind when he writes the
following (p. 357): "It should be noted that the real *discantores* have three ways of composing a melody. The first method makes use of the neighboring consonances, that is, the
lower fourth and fifth. The other method employs the more remote intervals, which include
the lower octave along with the others. The third method utilizes the most distant intervals,
such as the lower twelfth and fifteenth, or even larger ones."*[8]

[2] Johannes de Grocheo (*ca.* 1300) speaks (*SIMG* I:106 f.) of the three sights (without
actually mentioning them) when he establishes the relationship of the *motetus* and the
*triplum* to the tenor. "The tenor is that part on which all other parts are established, as
that part of a house or edifice which rests on its foundation. It [the tenor] regulates them
[the other parts] and gives them proportion as bones give proportion to the body. The
*motetus* is that voice which is placed immediately above the tenor. It begins usually at
the interval of the fifth and continues in the same relation at which it began, or ascends
to the octave. In hockets it is called *magistrans* by many. The *triplum* is that voice which
begins above the tenor at the distance of an octave and continues for the most part in
the same relationship. I say for the most part because sometimes for greater euphony it
descends to the *motetus* or the fifth, as the *motetus* sometimes ascends to the octave."

all following tones until the partial closes (here we meet again the *cola* and *commata* of the Cologne treatise, the *distinctiones, partes,* and *syllabae* of Guido, etc.), for which the sight must be sung "pure" again, accompany the *cantus planus* a third lower than the fifth, so that they sound a third higher. The distance of a fifth continues to be in effect as the difference between the actual sound and the note which is read. The lower third is therefore to be read so that the one singing can continually imagine the actual sounded note and find himself in unison with that which is notated at the beginning. Only slight deviations are made during the course of individual melodic sections according to simple rules covering such situations.

2. The manner of reading the "treble," or the soprano (treble to this day refers to the soprano voice in England, the treble clef being the equivalent of the German *Violinschlüssel*), which intones the notes of the *cantus planus* one octave higher, again only with the beginning and closing notes of each melodic section. All middle notes are likewise accompanied a third lower than the octave; however, the lower thirds sound a sixth higher than the *cantus planus* because of deviation in sounding the unison (for which the octave is substituted).

3. The manner of reading the "quatreble," i.e., a supersoprano, which to all appearances takes on the role of the *mene* in the higher octave, but probably was only used in two-voiced writing. Unfortunately, all further discussions of this are missing.

It is very understandable that such a method of reading in which the notation of the *cantus planus* underwent a quasi-transposition made it easier on the discanters. But this must have resulted, on occasion, in other intonations of the *mene* (and quatreble) than the unaltered notation in the same place. For instance, a C B D of the mene "in sight" had to be changed to G F♯ a because it sounded a fifth higher:

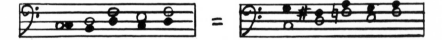

Perhaps this realization became the reason that later the *mene* sight was no more used (in Guilelmus Monachus we no longer find any mention of this).

The practice of fauxbourdon, however, was not as simple as it seems when looking at these basic precepts: accompaniment of all the inter- mediate tones of single melodic sections with parallel sixths chords (the third and sixth above the *cantus planus*). Parallel motion was not even used consistently as long as the movement of the *cantus planus* continued in seconds. Even Chilston prescribes that in cases where the *cantus planus* has continuous motion the discant has to make use of other intervals, i.e., sixths, and even finally tenths instead of thirds, in order not to go to a register which was too low for the voice. And because these rules were general, it means for a treble a movement from sixths to tenths and thirteenths above the *cantus planus*,*9 for which reason each voice also may use five consonances (the perfect consonances for the partial closes and transitions from one position to another).

With the accounts of Lionel Power and Chilston in mind, older treatments of *déchant* using the imperfect consonances (Anonymous XIII and V of Coussemaker) become more interesting and achieve real significance. They tell us how *déchant* in thirds and sixths moved, with octaves, fifths, and unisons occurring here and there, and what was to be done when skips occurred in the *cantus planus*, etc. The "commonly used manner" of singing of Anonymous V as well as the *appendans* and *désirans appendans* of Anonymous XIII are so close to the core of Power's and Chilston's teachings that one should regard both treatises in a category with the older treatises concerning English discant. The Anonymous XIII could possibly be regarded as an independent French formulation of this theory. The well-known six-voiced double canon "Sumer is icumen in," which (according to detailed proofs in Grove's *Dictionary of Music* III: 765–68 and IV: 1–3), was written between 1226 and 1240 by the monk John of Fornsete in the Abbey of Reading, and which is even today listened to with pleasure despite some parallel fifths and octaves (caused by the fifth voice, the third voice of the main canon), no longer seems difficult to interpret in the light of our recent investigations.*10 In its time it must have been a curiosity, because we find no mention anywhere of such a climax in polyphony. The *pes* of the canon, an obstinate little canon in its own right between both bass voices,

and even the beginning of the melody of the four-voiced main canon in its connection with both bass voices points clearly to fauxbourdon:

This wonderwork may have grown out of a simple fauxbourdon version of a folk song, for which undying fame is naturally due to the monk of Reading.

We now rapidly approach actual counterpoint, i.e., that elaboration of polyphony which was dictated by an instinctive comprehension of harmonic laws which to this day give pleasure and full satisfaction to those with any appreciation of music. Before we come to the place which rhythm occupied in this perfection of style, we shall look briefly at the treatise of Guilelmus Monachus, which apparently belongs to the 15th century, since it uses white notation (⎅ ◻ ◇ ◊ instead of ◣ ■ ◆ ♩) which appeared only after 1400; nevertheless, it has a direct relationship to the older versions of the English discant, so that we shall not find a better place for its treatment than here.

The treatise *De praeceptis artis musicae et practicae compendiosus libellus* (reprinted by Coussemaker, III:273 ff., from a MS in the St. Mark's Library in Venice), written by a monk Guilelmus, whose age or nationality has not yet been established,[*11] discusses the compositional manner of the English (*de modis Anglicorum*), for which he had an obvious predilection, in great detail. From this we may assume that he himself was either an Englishman or that he became thoroughly acquainted with the English manner of writing as a result of a long stay in that country. From the fact that he uses the words *apud nos* several times, contrary to English and French usage, we can assume that he was not living in England at the time this treatise was written. His nationality, however, is of no importance to us.

The fifth chapter, with which we are first concerned, explains fauxbourdon in the way Chilston does and claims nowhere that fauxbourdon is to be notated in a different manner. It says simply that it must be interpreted in the sense of the "sights:"

The soprano (*supranus*) begins in unison with the tenor but is instead thought of as being an octave higher. It moves a third below the tenor but actually sounds in sixths above. It then returns to the unison, sounding the octave. The *contra*, on the other hand, has the fifth above the tenor as a beginning consonance, and, following this, thirds above the tenor to the close which is again at the fifth above:[*12]

*Contra*
*Tenor*
*Supranus*

This is not meant as notation, but is meant to clarify the relationship of the voices to the tenor (*cantus planus*). The "sight" of the *mene* seems to have been abandoned, because it is no longer required that the thirds above be represented as thirds below; the fifth above is actually represented as the third above (the soprano is needlessly notated in still another system as it actually sounds).

The English, however, have yet another manner (of discant) which is called "gymel."*[13] This is sung in two voices, in thirds above and thirds below, by also representing the octaves and sixths an octave lower so that the voices move (according to actual sound) in octaves and sixths.

The last example which is given here shows, in line with the explanation, not only thirds below, but also thirds above, which is not unusual in the light of our other experiences:

 i.e.:

(A dot is missing after the antepenultimate note of the tenor, or else the penultimate note should not have a stem; the clef is probably wrong, or a b♭ would have to be supposed because of the tritone progression in the soprano.) The sixth chapter which follows does not concern itself with gymel and fauxbourdon over a tenor *cantus planus*, but teaches a three-voiced compositional technique without transposition of the voices (the voices sound where they are actually written); it still supplies the key to such transposing, however, from thirds below to thirds above:

Compose a conjunct soprano voice (*non disjunctum*) [3] in any mode. Add thereto a second soprano which begins in unison and then moves in as many thirds below as are desired; however, the two tones before the final tone require a third above, if they lead to the final tone in a descending manner, which must end in the unison; then continue again with thirds below and close in unison.

This is to say, as the unison is required for the voices at the close, then the second discant must be so placed that it may move in contrary motion to the first from the third above or third below into the unison:

This relationship between the voices is to exist beginning with the antepenultimate tones, in this way:

not:  but:

[3] Here, as well as in Chapter XII, one should read *disjunctum* and not *distinctum*.

There is probably no need of pointing out here that gymel (there has been no explanation of this term as yet) [4] probably constitutes the oldest form of English polyphony, from which the three-voiced *fauxbourdon* must have developed.

We shall concern ourselves at greater length with the following chapters of Guilelmus Monachus, since they represent the viewpoints of contrapuntal theories around 1450.

Treble sight is probably mentioned for the last time by the Englishman John Hothby in his very short *Regulae supra contrapunctum*, printed in Coussemaker, *Script.* III:333 ff.: "Secundum quosdam Anglicos iste modus canendi vocatur discantus visibilis (According to certain Englishmen this mode of singing is called *discantus visibilis*)." The word *visibilis* is apparently a literal translation of "with (treble) sight"; the treatise itself is of no value. Treble sight is mentioned as well by the Italian Nicolaus Burtius (given in Ambros, *Geschichte* II:164: "Erit tertia ad visum, sexta vero quantum ad sonum [There will be a third to be seen, but a sixth as far as sound is concerned]," etc., which Ambros quotes without realizing its meaning). Davey (see p. 58) claims that the term "sight" was used until the year 1620, for which claim, however, he has no proof.

[4] Among the different ways of writing this word which are shown in H. Davey's *History of English Music* (1895, p. 57) is also found *gemellum* (Eton MS), which would provide a simple solution to this riddle (twin song).

### APPENDIX

FOOTNOTE 1: Coussemaker, *Script.* I:114: "Triplum specialiter sumptum debet ex remoto concordare primo et secundo cantui, nisi fuerit concordantia insimul per sonum reductum, quod sibi aequipollet." And: Coussemaker, *Script.* I:357: "Notandum quod duplex (triplex) est modus faciendi discantum secundum veros cantores. Primus modus est propinquis proportionibus hoc est infra diatessaron et diapente; alius modus est ex remotioribus quae continentur sub diapason cum praedictis; tertius modus est ex remotissimis infra diapente cum diapason vel duplex diapason vel ultra."

FOOTNOTE 2: *SIMG* I:106 f.: "Tenor autem est illa pars, supra quam omnes aliae fundantur quemadmodum partes domus vel aedificii super suum fundamentum. Et eas regulat et eis dat quantitatem, quemadmodum ossa partibus aliis. Motetus vero est cantus ille, qui supra tenorem immediate ordinatur. Et in diapente ut plurimum incipit et in eadem proportione, in qua incipit, continuatur vel in diapason ascendit, et in hoquetis ab aliquibus dicitur magistrans. Triplum vero est cantus ille, qui supra tenorem in diapason proportione incipere debet et in eadem proportione ut plurimum continuari. Dico autem, ut plurimum, quia aliquoties in motetum [Wolf: tenore] vel diapente descendit propter euphoniam, quemadmodum motetus aliquando in diapason ascendit."

BOOK II

# MENSURAL THEORY AND SYSTEMATIC COUNTERPOINT

# CHAPTER VIII

# *Mensural Theory to the Beginning of the 14th Century*

THE free rhythm of early ecclesiastical chant, which is gradually coming to light as a result of present-day research, remained at least partially influential even during the time of the first attempts at rhythmic notation, i.e., the representation of tonal duration through the shape of notes. In finding one's way through the maze of contradictory remarks referring to the value of single notes within tonal groups, joined through notation to form firm units of ligatures and *conjuncturae*, it seems impossible not to assume some effect remaining from earlier traditions. There is no doubt that hymn-singing possessed a strict metric nature which was continually dependent upon the spoken rhythm of the text, following the practice of antiquity. This is also probably true of the sequence, modelled after the hymn—especially the rhymed sequence, which, if not strictly measured, had very definite patterns of syllables. The sequences in turn perhaps produced secular songs, unless, on the other hand, sequences appeared as a more or less conscious imitation of a popular element.*[1] Apart from this entire songlike literature with its regular scansion and rhythmically marked melody corresponding to a strictly measured text (a characteristic which particularly marks the troubadour and minnesinger melodies), we must be cognizant of the fact that in medieval music melodies of a very early origin (probably originating in part in Hebraic psalm-singing) were joined to texts whose inherent rhythm not only prevented the creation of melodies, but also had no affinity for them.*[2] In my *Studien zur Geschichte der Notenschrift*, 1878 (p. 143 ff.), I pointed out that in such adaptations the melodies in many instances suffer major changes, for in setting them to a text rich in syllables, groups of neumes are often separated into single neumes. On the contrary, in setting melodies to a shorter text, single neumes were fused into groups, and very often tone repetitions had to be included or disappear from the texture.[1] The melodies, so to speak, had a kind of special

[1] See O. Fleischer, *Neumenstudien*, 1895, 1897, II: 19 ff. I do not wish to state, in making this reference, that I regard as successful Fleischer's attempt to provide a key to what pitch designations (and even rhythm) the neumes indicate. Any firm foundation seems to be lacking for the establishment of absolute pitch distances in the *tonus currens*, and the same for the intervals which make up the rising and falling motion at the cadence.

existence outside of the texts (which came about through their association with the original texts), but were modified in each single case according to the demands of meaningful textual declamation and possible conservation of their original musical structure. To what extent these original melodies have come down intact, in spite of the course of centuries, with more than a thousand years of insufficient notation, to a period using a more definite notation (around A.D. 1000) is not possible to establish and is not the subject of our investigation. Competent authorities are now working in large numbers to solve these questions with all the aids of modern scientific research. I include here especially the names of Dom Pothier (*Les Mélodies grégoriennes*, 1880), and Dom Mocquereau (editor of the "*Paléographie musicale*" of the Benedictine monastery of Solesmes), Fr. Aug. Gevaert (*Les origines du chant liturgique de l'église latine*, 1890, and *La mélopée antique dans le chant de l'eglise latine*, 1895), G. Houdard (*Le rhythme du chant dit grégorien d'après la notation neumatique*, 1898), and A. Dechevrens (*Etudes science musicale*, 1898).[*3] On the other hand, it is of the greatest interest, in relation to our subject, to know what rhythmic theory or established practice in the rhythmic structure of ecclesiastical singing existed at the time of the beginnings of mensural notation. The sixth chapter of my *Studien zur Geschichte der Notenschrift* (pp. 189–205) includes an almost complete collection of remarks of writers up to the 12th century, in which evidence can be found that a continued succession of equal values before the appearance of mensural music was never maintained for ecclesiastical vocal music, even though complaints concerning the disintegration of rhythm are not lacking from the 9th century on.[*4]

The *Commemoratio brevis de tonis et psalmis modulandis* ascribed to Hucbald (belonging, at any rate, to the 10th century), which uses Daseian notation combined with neumes, remarks, after stating that not only the pitch level but also the tempo of the singing must vary according to festivities and occasion:[2] "Regardless of singing fast or slowly, it is always to be observed that the neumes are accented truly and completely at the proper speed and are neither drawn out too much nor sung too rapidly from lack of piety." He also speaks of customary retards in the right proportion ("Legitimis inter se morulis numerose canere"), of extending verse beginnings and endings, and expressly of the ratio 2:1 between long and short tones ("semper unum alterum duplo superet").

All those passages which we met with during the course of our investigations which dealt with *cola, commata, membra, incisiones, distinctiones, fines particularum*, etc., now assume importance in connection with recognizing

---

[2] (Gerbert I:227): "Verum sive morosius, sive celerius dicantur, hoc attendi semper debet, ut honestis et plenis neumis congruo celeritatis pronuntientur modo, ut nec nimiae productionis taedeat, nec eos irreverenti festinantia os ignobiliter canem ebulliat."

the rhythmical nature of the old manner of chanting, if we regard them in the light of the comprehensive summary available to us from the second half of the 10th century in a part of the often-cited Odonic treatise, *Musicae artis disciplina*. The relevant passage, however, is found only in the St. Blasien codex (from the 12th century) which Gerbert used as a source; nevertheless, this passage, with reference to its terminology, agrees with the undoubtedly original text, which directly follows. The entire contents agree so well with all earlier information on the same subject that I do not hesitate to regard the brief formulation found in this passage as the most significant expression of thought prevalent in the 9th and 10th centuries.*5 It reads:3

For the study of singing it is of utmost value to know how tones are joined. Because, as in speaking, two or three or four letters usually constitute a syllable, or a single (vowel) represents one syllable, as in *a-mo tem-plum*, in the same manner in music either a single tone is sounded by itself, or two, three, or four connected ones constitute a unit, which we may name a musical syllable. And as one single syllable or two, three, or even more constitute a meaningful part of speech (a word), as in *mors, est, vita, gloria, benignitas, beatitudo*, in the same manner one, two, or more musical syllables having the tonal range of a second, fourth, or fifth are joined in melody, the form and measure of which we understand and admire and which we call a member of a musical setting. A section of the musical setting (*distinctio*) extends to the place where a point of rest is reached.

If we add to this the rules of Guido of Arezzo in the fifteenth chapter of the Micrologus,4

All neume groups (parts of settings, *partes*) are to be notated and performed as a single or closed unit (compressed, *compresses*), especially the single neumes (*syllabae*). The extension of the final note, though only slight in a single syllable, is more pronounced at the end of a part [*parte*], but most pronounced at the end of a distinction.

---

3 (Gerbert I:275): "Ad cantandi scientiam nosse quibus modis ad se invicem voces jungantur summa utilitas est. Nam sicut duae plerumque litterae aut tres aut quatuor unam faciunt syllabam, sive sola littera pro syllaba accipitur, ut a-mo, tem-plum: ita quoque et in musica plerumque sola vox per se pronuntiatur, plerumque duae aut tres vel quatuor cohaerentes unam consonantiam reddunt: quod juxta aliquem modum musicam syllabam nominare possumus. Item sicut sola syllaba aut duae vel tres vel etiam plures unam partem locutionis faciunt, quae aliquid significat, ut mors, est, vita, gloria, benignitas beatitudo; ita quoque et una vel duae vel plures musicae syllabae tonum, diatessaron, diapente jungunt, quarum dum et melodiam sentimus et mensuram intelligentes miramur, musicae partes, quae aliquid significant, non incongrue nominavimus. Distinctio vero in musica est quantum de quolibet cantu continuamus, quae ubi vox requieverit pronuntiatur."

4 (Gerbert, *Script.* II:14): "Tota pars compresse et notanda et exprimenda est, syllaba vero compressius. Tenor vero, id est mora ultimae vocis, qui in syllaba quantuluscumque est, amplior in parte, diutissimus vero in distinctione."

then we have firm evidence for the division of a melody into single neumes. Different only in its terminology, the *Musica enchiriadis* speaks of a colon (=*distinctio*) which is formed from several *commata* (=*partes*).

I am not including the fifteenth chapter of the *Micrologus* here since I have already done so in my *Studien zur Geschichte der Notenschrift* (pp. 196–199), and I also do not wish to take Guido's rules of the correspondence of neumes (*syllabae*), parts (*partes*), and distinctions (*distinctiones*) too much at face value; these have been explained in even further detail by Aribo Scholasticus (see *ibid.*, pp. 199–200). The sentence cited above is certainly not Guido's invention but established tradition.

This "united presentation" of tones combined into one neume is actually found only in the oldest known extant versions of mensural theory; however, the lengthening of the final note constitutes the point of departure for designating the values of the tones in the ligatures. The presentation of syllables of the text which are provided only with single notes has undoubtedly always been connected with the natural stress of the text, even if not in the strict scanning manner which Guido seems to require,[5] "so that the presentation of the melody takes place according to the manner of metric units in verse." He even assumes such measurements within the neumes, remarking "that one neume progresses in the dactylic, the other in spondaic or iambic meter." As late as Hieronymus de Moravia (*ca.* 1250) we find a rhythmic interpretation of ecclesiastical chant similar to this, and we must especially point out his curious theory of embellishments (*flores*) (Coussemaker, *Script.* I:91). This refers simply to the five notes which are differentiated from others as being "long ones" (*principalitas*, that is, a beginning note, but only if it is the *finalis*; a *secunda nota* in the case where this is not true; the *penultima*, apparently only in feminine endings; the *ultima*; and as the fifth a single note with *plica*). If the text is set with single notes, the meter of the text is of the most importance throughout.[6]*[6]

It seems as though during the 11th and 12th centuries a more schematic rhythmic system gradually developed in place of the earlier free rhythms. This also applied to the performance of ecclesiastical chants.*[7] The so-called *modi* of the earliest mensural theorists are for that reason not actually to be regarded as something new, but are only a convenient point of departure for this new technique. It was naturally an overwhelming

[5] (Gerbert, *Script.* II:15): "Sicque opus est ut quasi metricis pedibus cantilena plaudatur, et aliae voces ab aliis morulam duplo longiorem vel duplo breviorem...habeant... utpote ista neuma dactylico, illa vero spondaico, illa iambico more decurrit, et distinctionem nunc tetrametram nunc pentametram."

[6] (Coussemaker, *Script.* I:91): "Quandocumque extra syllabas et dictiones, metro scilicet interrupto..."

recommendation for the new signs (or more correctly, the new use for the old signs) that these could be employed in the most simple, direct, and comprehensible manner for the representation of rhythm, when formerly they had been explained in a rather roundabout way. For this reason, as a rule, there is contained in the beginning of these oldest treatises covering mensural music an enumeration of five or six or even more *modi.*[8]

The "earliest" explanation of this theory, according to the testimonial of Hieronymus de Moravia (*Discantus positio vulgaris*, second part [b], in Coussemaker, *Histoire*, p. 247, and *Script.* I:94 ff.) shows the following order:

|   |   |   |
|---|---|---|
| I. Modus (trochaic): | ▮ ▪ ▮ ▪ | etc. |
| II. Modus (iambic): | ▪ ▮ ▪ ▮ | etc. |
| III. Modus (dactylic): | ▮ ▪ ▪ ▮ ▪ ▪ | etc. |
| IV. Modus (anapestic): | ▪ ▪ ▮ ▪ ▪ ▮ | etc. |
| V. Modus ("long notes") (spondaic): | ▮ ▮ ▮ ▮ | etc. |
| VI. Modus ("short notes") (tribrachic): | ▪ ▪ ▪ ▪ ▪ ▪ | etc. |
| or: | ♦ ♦ ♦ ♦ ♦ ♦ | etc. |

This is treated in the same manner by Anonymous VII (Coussemaker, *Script.* I:378 ff.), apparently one of the earliest writers on mensural notation, and by Johannes de Garlandia (Coussemaker, *Script.* I:97 ff. and 175 ff.), who, however, already speaks of a listing of further *modi* or *maneries*, which he regards as superfluous. We shall not concern ourselves with this any further, as the differences and the reasons for these are without importance. We must, however, note that Garlandia (in the second version, Couss. I:175) calls the first, second, and sixth modes *mensurabiles*; the third, fourth, and fifth ones, on the other hand, he calls *ultra mensurabiles*. *Ultra mensuram* is, according to Garlandia, the same as *ultra mensuram rectae longae*, that is, it uses perfect longas [equal to three breves], which Garlandia also calls *longae obliquae*. The treatise *Discantus positio vulgaris* (Couss., *Script.* I:94) calls all values which are longer than two units (breves) or shorter than one (!) *ultra mensuram*.

Unfortunately, the mensuralists immediately turn up with obligatory triple meter and write that formerly the longa consisted regularly of only two breves (see *Studien zur Geschichte der Notenschrift*, pp. 205 ff.),[9] although originally the third and fourth *modus* (dactylic and anapestic) must have certainly corresponded with our ♩ ♪ ♪ | ♪ ♪ ♪ etc., and ♪ ♪ | ♪ ♪ ♪ | ♪ etc. We find them in Garlandia having the following meaning:

3/4 ♩· | ♪ ♪ | ♩· | ♪ ♪ and: ♪ ♪ | ♩· | ♪ ♪ | ♩·

We are now concerned, for the entire time up to the rehabilitation of simple [imperfect] meter in the beginning of the 14th century, with only one single meter, which we would today write as 3/4, for which, however, the epoch we are now dealing with, thinking in terms of breves (■), adopted the value of the perfect longa as a unit, the so-called *perfectio*.

Several idiosyncrasies of early mensural terminology betray the fight against simple [imperfect] meter, which mystical speculation (with express reference to the Holy Trinity) tried to banish entirely. In this regard the *Discantus positio vulgaris* states:[7] "The consonant tones are more consonant on odd-numbered notes, and the dissonances less (?) dissonant, than on even-numbered notes." Because the *modi* are not dealt with in these discant rules (they are mentioned only in the second part, which is a short study of form), this concerns simply the differences between the (first, strong) tones which enter with the tones of the *cantus firmus* and the (second, weak) notes which are placed between them by the discant. In Garlandia the same terminology is to be found in direct reference to the *modi*:[8] "Odd-numbered notes call for consonance (between discant and tenor) in the first as well as in the second or third (etc.) *modus*." The younger Anonymous IV (Couss., *Script.* I), who is, however, acquainted with the oldest rules, uses the same expression (*puncta imparia*) for the strong values:[9] "All odd numbers of notes in the first mode are longas and must form consonances with the tenor. The remainder of the notes, the even-numbered ones, may be composed without regard to consonance."

That the terms *longa recta* and *recta mensura* for the imperfect longa, and *longa obliqua* or *per ultra mensuram* for the perfect longa, are actually contrary to the principle that triple meter and the perfection of the longa are acceptable, is first evident to the author called Quidam Aristoteles, who also belongs among the earliest mensural authors (also known as Pseudo-Beda). For this reason he attacks this old terminology with rather weak logic:[10]*[10]

[7] (Couss., *Script.* I:95): "Sciendum insuper, quod omnes notae impares, hae quae consonant, melius consonant, quae vero dissonant, minus dissonant quam pares."

[8] (Couss., *Script.* I:107): "Omne quod fit in (im)pari debet concordari cum omni illo, quod fit in impari si sit in primo vel secundo vel tertio modo."

[9] (Couss., *Script.* I:356): "Omnia puncta imparia primi modi sunt longae et cum tenore concordare debent. Reliqua vero indifferenter ponuntur."

[10] (Couss., *Script.* I:271): "Unde si quaerat aliquis, utrum posset fieri modus sive cantus naturalis de omnibus imperfectis sicut fit de omnibus perfectis. Responsio cum probatione, quod non; cum puras imperfectas nemo pronunciare possit. Verumtamen quidam in artibus suis referunt, perfectam figuram se habere per ultra mensuram; et quosdam etiam modos sicut primum et quartum esse per ultra mensurabiles, id est non rectam mensuram habentes, quod falsum est; quia si verum esset, tunc posset fieri cantus naturalis de omnibus imperfectis, quoniam imperfectam dicunt esse perfectam." Here a reference to the Trinity follows: "Anything that is shaped into the likeness of divine

Should anyone ask whether or not a *modus*, that is, a natural melodic formation with nothing but imperfect *longae*, be also possible in the same manner as it is possible with nothing but perfect ones, one must with justice answer: No! For no one can sing isolated imperfect notes. If, therefore, some people ascertain in their artistic rules that a perfect note exceeds the measure in length, and if they assert of some *modi*, as the third and fourth, that they are measured with such "extended" values, that is, do not have the right measure, then this is incorrect. Because if this were true, then singing with nothing but imperfect values should be possible, which they regarded as perfect ones.

As a matter of fact, it was soon possible to remove these troubling reminiscences of imperfect meter from musical practice entirely.

While the rules for the perfect and imperfect value of the longa and the doubling of the value (alteration) of the breve are presented by the first mensuralists in the same form which is found in Franco and all later writers, great uncertainty and variety exist for a long time in the designation of the note values of the ligatures, as well as in the use of the smallest note values. Undoubtedly this still shows the influence of performances using the *neumae compositae*. In the beginning (in the *Discantus positio vulgaris*, in the treatise by Anonymous VII, Couss., *Script.* I, and also in the historical report of Anonymous IV on earlier teaching, Couss., *Script.* I), the ligatures exist only in shapes characteristic of the *cantus planus*:[*11]

$$\textbf{◖} = Pes \quad \text{and} \quad \textbf{◗} = Clivis$$

These have the meaning of the *mora ultimae vocis*, that is, the value of the breve-longa (with the exception found in the *Discantus positio vulgaris*, when the first note is larger: ◣). Ligatures consisting of three and more tones also have, at the beginning and end, shapes which are theirs in *musica plana*. The ligatures consisting of three tones[*12]

are measured as longa-breve-longa (with the exception, also found in the *Discantus positio vulgaris*, when they are preceded by a longa: the first two notes are then read as breves). In ligatures of four notes all four are breves.

---

nature consists of three, so in voices and sounds three kinds of consonance exist (octave, fifth, fourth. See p. 101). Thus every mensurated *cantus* is found to be in three in likeness to divine nature, whose approval is evident in *mensura* where the third number creates that which is perfect."

Further, Franco, *Ars cantus mensurabilis* (Couss., *Script.* I:119): "From this it follows that those who call (an imperfect longa) proper are mistaken, for something proper may stand by itself."

Ligatures of five notes are no longer measured exactly according to the *Discantus positio vulgaris*, but are sung (!) at will. Anonymous VII gives these an upward stem at the beginning:

but still does not mention the significance of *opposita proprietas*. He states the general rule that all ligatures containing more than three notes have the same value as one that has only three, as in:

Naturally, the perfect or imperfect value of the final note depends upon the value which follows the ligature.

Anonymous IV (Couss., *Script.* I), who preserved so much of historical value for us, describes (pp. 327–336) at first the various possibilities of representing the six *modi* and their different *ordines* (shorter or longer series of notes bounded by rests) with single notes of full value and ligatures consisting of two and three notes, as we have discussed above. He goes on to show, however (pp. 337–339), how it is possible at any point to diminish (*frangere*) longas through *currentes* (*semibreves*, whereby apparently the number of the values is greatly increased), i.e.:

instead of:        which is equivalent to: 3/4            or:

instead of:        which is equivalent to: 3/4            . He also declares that it means the same when one uses five notes in one ligature, in which case the three first notes are read as a longa followed by two *currentes*, which diminish it:

          which is equivalent to:

It seems that this was the manner of notation that Leoninus used (also Leonis instead of Leonini); according to the report of Anonymous IV (p. 327 and p. 341), it was used in Paris during the time of the great Perotinus and also of Robertus de Sabilone, until the time of Petrus (de Cruce? Since Petrus Trothun from Orleans is said not to have understood much about the measurement of time [p. 344b], he is probably not the one who is meant by the designation *optimus notator*). This kind of notation was also used in the time of Thomas de Sancto Juliano (the old Parisian) and another (Thomas), the "Englishman" who also used the English manner of notation and taught some things according to the

English manner, as well as Johannes the Elder (*primarius*, most probably Johannes de Garlandia). There were especially the two Francos (the Elder [Parisian] and Franco de Colonia), who appeared and set up new rules.*13 Anonymous IV also mentions some further contemporaries of Franco: Master Theobaldus Gallicus, Master Simon de Sacalia, Master (Johannes) de Burgundia, also a *probus* (an honest man) from Picardy with the name of Johannes Le Fauconer, and in addition the especially famous English masters Johannes *filius dei*, Makeblite of Winchester, and Blakesmith of the "court of the last Henry" (III).

There are a number of names here which might possibly be identified with the Anonymi; whoever makes the choice, however, must accept the consequences. At any rate, the *Discantus positio vulgaris* seems to represent the practice of Leoninus; Anonymous VII might possibly be the "English" Thomas, if the sixth were not missing in his enumeration of consonances (although we know [see p. 120 ff.] that Englishmen—at least later—represented the sixths as thirds!).

Johannes de Garlandia, Pseudo-Aristotle [Magister Lambert], and the Karlsruhe Anonymous (Dietericus? See Hans Müller, *Eine Abhandlung über Mensuralmusik*, 1886) already show different shapes of ligatures;11 the upward tail of the beginning note, which makes the two first notes semibreves (*opposita proprietas*), is introduced, as well as the forms *sine proprietate* and *sine perfectione*:*14

The first is to some extent still ambiguous, however, because of the persisting influence of the earlier manner of measuring ligatures consisting of more than one tone. Garlandia still clings to the concept that ligatures consisting of more than three tones count as much as those having only three tones, and still recognizes the diminution of the longa and breve (!) through attached semibreves.12 Important information concerning the real nature of the third and fourth *modi* (◀ ■ ■ and ■ ■ ◀) is contained in the remark (p. 107) that in these, two notes are counted for one value*15 (namely, the imperfect or unaccented value), and therefore one or the

---

11 [This footnote is not indicated by an asterisk in the text.] See W. Niemann, *Über die abweichende Bedeutung der Ligaturen in der Mensuraltheorie vor Joh. de Garlandia* [Leipzig, 1902].

12 (Coussemaker, *Script.* I:103): "Therefore it should be noted that whenever there is found a multitude of breves, that is, semibreves, they always share with that which has gone before, because the preceding note together with these semibreves is not considered being worth more than that value which is like the preceding note."

other may frequently be treated as a dissonance.[13] Furthermore, the examples prove that in the second *modus* (■ ◗), not the first but the second note is understood as perfect (*impar*), i.e., the first short value is always interpreted as an upbeat, and consonance, even here, is required for the downbeat or strong beat, namely, the value represented by the longa:[*16]

In the light of all this material we cannot expect too much that is new of Franco of Cologne. In fact it appears that he, as was true in the case of Berno, Guido, and others, was made the representative of an epoch by posterity because he had the good fortune to bring a gradual process of clarification, then in progress, to a temporary conclusion. His personal merit as far as mensural theory is concerned seems to consist only in the removal of the remaining traditions in the reading of ligatures which had followed the manner of *musica plana*. The establishment of thirds as imperfect consonances and that of the major sixth as an imperfect dissonance is, as we have already seen, definitely pre-Franconian; also, the differentiation between strong and weak values as basis for rules of composition is proved to have existed before Franco. Even the descriptions of the most important of the new art forms of the music of the early mensural period are already found in the *Discantus positio vulgaris* and in Garlandia. The latter also informs us (Couss., *Script.* I:115) about the introduction of the *subsemitonium* (F♯) in order to avoid the tritone in a stepwise descent from b♮, when the turn occurs on F, that is, the reverse of *una voce super LA*:

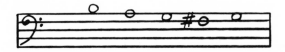

Evidently Garlandia is referring to trills used at the cadence (*op. cit.*) when he says the following:[14] "In closes, the penultimate note is embellished whether it is at the distance of a semitone or a whole-tone from the

---

[13] (*Op. cit.*, p. 107): "But two puncti may be taken here (that is, in the third mode) in the place of one; sometimes one of them causes a discord because of the *color* of the music, and this may be the first or the second. And it is quite permitted by the authorities and approved. This also is found in organum in many places and especially in motets."

[14] "Super quietem penultima proportio minuitur sive fuerit semitonium sive tonus."

final note." That this is not a venturesome rule but a necessary one is proved by the remarks of Anonymous IV, which are of a somewhat later date,[15] and especially by those of Hieronymus de Moravia concerning the art of embellishments. The latter even goes into detail describing how the trill is accomplished on the organ by remaining on one tone and intermittently striking its (minor or major) neighbor.[16] From these remarks we may conclude that by means of the circuitous route of embellishments (or the *color*) the *subsemitonium* was gradually established during the 12th century, the former antipathy toward it having vanished. The *Introductio secundum Johannem de Garlandia*, which, even though it was not written by Garlandia himself, still refers to him (it apparently belongs in the 13th century, and was reprinted by Coussemaker [*Script.* I: 157 ff.] from a MS of St. Dié), asserts the possibility and necessity for dividing all

[15] (Coussemaker, *Script.* I:359): "There are certain people who heap discords on discords before a perfect consonance, such as before the octave, and for this reason they are at the same time both greatly praised and derided. This may be seen by those who write accordingly, namely:

in superiori: d f c ♮ c B♭ c (Couss. ♭ c ♭ c)
in inferiori: D D E F E D C

[16] (Couss., *Script.* I:91): "There is a beautiful flower of harmony of the sounds of the voice and the very swift vibration of trills...long ornaments [*flores*] are those whose vibration is slow and which do not go beyond the bounds of the semitone. The open ornaments are those whose vibration is not slow (nor sudden but something in between) and which do not exceed the bounds of a tone....Sudden ornaments are those whose vibration is slow in the beginning and fastest in the middle and the end and whose vibration does not exceed a semitone. Long ornaments ought to occur on the first, penultimate, and final notes, in an ascending semitone; if something else occurs in descending, these other things constitute open ornaments, which the second note of a syllable ought to have. But sudden ornaments are none other than the *plica* and the longa, among which and immediately following which the shortest are placed for the beauty of the harmony." (Page 93: I have perhaps discovered the earliest differentiation between the three registers of the human voice.) "Speaking not naturally but commonly (!), certain voices are of the chest (chest voice), certain of the throat (middle voice), and some are indeed of the head itself. Chest voices are strong in low notes, those of the throat in high notes, but those of the head in very high notes." The passage concerning instrumental trills is as follows (p. 91): "If when we play some sort of song on the organ we wish to decorate a note of this same song, we strike G in the low notes, then keep it down and held firmly, restraining ourselves from going lower than this note, then we strike F in the low notes, but somewhat higher we vibrate a high a; from this there arises a most beautiful and suitable harmony which we call a harmonic flower [ornament].

"When, therefore, a *clavis* [a pitch-name] is stationary and when the vibrations of the semitone cease, and when this vibration itself is slow, then this is the ornament called long. When, moreover, the ornament includes a tone and the vibration is neither slow nor sudden but midway between the two, then it is an open ornament. When the semitone is determined, but the vibration in the beginning is slow, however, in progress and in coming to an end very fast, then we have the ornament which is called sudden."

whole-tones into two semitones. This would be especially indispensable for instruments (organ), and therefore the use of chromatic signs (flat, sharp) could be extended to all steps of the scale.[17]

That greater motion was already present in instrumental music toward the beginning of the 13th century is proved by the repeated remarks of authors concerning the more numerous use of chromatic tones and embellishments created by the breaking of long notes into circumscribing figuration (see also Anonymous IV in Coussemaker, *Script.* I:328).[18]

Undoubtedly the figure of Franco of Cologne (i.e., the author of the *Ars cantus mensurabilis*)*[17] stands out significantly among the numerous mensural composers of the 13th century. The certainty of his bearing, the categorical manner in which he asserts himself as a teacher, is still as impressive to us as it was to his contemporaries, especially in the light of the caution with which his predecessors acted. His terminology was rapidly and generally accepted in the musical world, and the *Ars cantus mensurabilis* was everywhere copied, excerpted, and commented upon. The introduction to his little work is a masterwork of rhetoric, a first speech, so to speak, given by the master as he accepts the office of his new calling as a teacher. He mentions only Boethius, Gregor, and Guido (of Arezzo) as those who have done well in their teaching of the *musica plana*. Then, after having been urged by some people of high rank (*magnatum*), he decides to write something proper concerning mensural music. This one should not interpret as arrogance on his part, for it is not the result of egotism, but rather "it is in order to alleviate a generally recognized need." It is also to facilitate the understanding of musical works while hearing them, as well as for the better information of composers themselves. As he had seen how earlier and recent masters had said many good things about mensural music in their instructions, but in some aspects showed marked errors in that which was necessary to this art, he decides, in the interest of the arts, to alleviate this situation and to write this compendium himself concerning mensural music. Those things which were said well by his predecessors he will, without hesitation,

---

[17] (Page 166): "It must be noted about *falsa musica* that it is very necessary in musical instruments, especially in organs. *Falsa musica* is when we make a tone from a semitone or vice versa. Every tone is divisible into two semitones and consequently the signs denoting semitones can be employed in all tones." (See p. 212.)

[18] "There are other modes like those mentioned above which split the breve or breves into two, three, or four notes, as in instrumental music....A tone of one durational unit may be defined as a sound which is not held for the minimum or maximum length of time possible, but which, though sufficiently short, may yet be split into two, three, or four rapid notes; further division is not possible in vocal music, although this is feasible in instrumental music."

include in his work, but he will also destroy and prevent errors and substantiate sufficiently the new theories which he proposes.[19]

This preface is certainly proof enough that Franco was not the first mensural theorist[20] but was able to use a whole series of preparatory works. Hans Müller rightly points out (in *Eine Abhandlung über Mensural-musik*, etc.), that one should be careful of "regarding authors who actually were source material for Franco as post-Franconian, because they wrote down the same rules and definitions as the most well-known writer among the earlier mensural writers." Led astray by his earlier incorrect assumption of Walter Odington's identity with the archbishop Walter of Eynesham, however, he went too far in assuming him also as a source for Franco. Even though Odington did not adopt all of Franco's innovations, he nevertheless seems to have been acquainted with the *Ars cantus mensurabilis*; this is certainly possible, since Franco wrote around 1230–1250 but Odington probably not before 1275. There still remains the possibility that Odington took over that which seems Franconian to us from Franco's immediate predecessors. By no stretch of the imagination can Franco be said to have used Odington [as a source].

An early although rather insignificant innovation of Franco is the

[19] (Couss., *Script.* I:117): "Now that philosophers have treated sufficiently of plain-song and have fully explained it to us both theoretically and practically (theoretically above all Boethius, practically, on the other hand, Guido Monachus and, as to the ecclesiastical tropes, especially the blessed Gregory), supposing plainsong to have been most perfectly transmitted by the philosophers already mentioned, we propose—in accordance with the entreaties of certain influential persons and without losing sight of the natural order—to treat of mensurable music, which plainsong precedes as the principal the subaltern.

"Let no one say that we began this work out of arrogance or merely for our own convenience, but rather out of evident necessity, for the ready apprehension of our auditors and the most perfect instruction of all writers of mensurable music. For when we see many, both moderns and ancients, saying good things about mensurable music in their 'arts' and on the other hand deficient and in error in many respects, especially in the details of the science, we think their opinions are to be assisted, lest perchance as a result of their deficiency and error the science be exposed to harm.

"We accordingly propose to expound mensurable music in a compendium, in which we shall not hesitate to introduce things well said by others or to disprove and avoid their errors and, if we have discovered some new thing, to uphold it and prove it with good reasons."

[20] Heinrich Bellermann in his very recent work "Geschichtliche Bemerkungen über die Notation" (in Haberl's *Kirchenmusikalisches Jahrbuch für das Jahr* 1898, p. 5) writes: "The earliest writer on polyphonic music (!) is Franco of Cologne, who, in all probability, lived in the second half of the 12th century (!)." Our remarks are sufficient proof of the unacceptability of Bellermann's attempt (*Allgemeine Musikalische Zeitung*, 1868, and also 1874 in the program of the *Graues Kloster Gymnasium*, and separately) to read into the 11th chapter of the *Ars cantus mensurabilis* the evaluation of the minor and major sixth as being similar.

elimination of the fifth [rhythmic] mode by subordinating it to the first:

❚ ❚ ❚  or:  ❚ ■ ❚ ■ ❚

The reason for this, Franco indicates, is his intention of settling the discord between earlier and more recent theorists.[21] This also pre-Franconian manner of regarding the original fifth mode (only perfect longas) as first and the former first mode (❚ ■) as second is used by pseudo-Aristotle. Even Garlandia was acquainted with this practice but rejected it for practical reasons, although he did not find it unreasonable.[22] Franco's adjustment was a happy one insofar as it removed the confusion created by moving the numbers by one place; yet his purpose, which was the replacement of the old fifth mode, was accomplished. (Movement in nothing but long notes is as little an actual mode as movement in nothing but short ones.)

The *Discantus positio vulgaris* and Anonymous VII are acquainted with rests only as they are found in *cantus planus*, i.e., as caesuras between sections of the melody (*distinctiones*); rests, however, according to whether they appear in place of a longa or breve (all *modi* are generally catalectic, that is, they have a "missing value" at the end) are held for different lengths.[23] In the first mode the last short note is generally missing, in the second one the last long note, in the third and fourth the catalexis [the time value which is filled by a pause] has the value of a perfect longa; all these values are simply indicated by a line for the rest, but this line does not yet indicate its value through its length.

In Garlandia, however, we meet with rests of different shapes (*signa significantia demissionem vocis*): for the breve a rest fills one space (*pausa rectae brevis*); for the imperfect longa it fills two spaces (*pausa rectae longae*). The rest sign which extends through three or even more spaces is called *divisio modi* and is no longer to be regarded as an actual rest (the final line

---

[21] (Couss., *Script.* I:118): "The modes are diversely numbered by different persons; some allow six and others seven. We admit only five, however, since all the others may be reduced to these. The first mode proceeds entirely in longas; we combine this mode with the one which proceeds by longas and breves for two reasons: first, because the rests are found in both of these, and second, to put an end to the controversy between the ancients and some of the moderns."

[22] (Couss., *Script.* I:98): "But some wish that the fifth mode be first of all and for good reason, because all our modes proceed through this mode. But as far as *tempora* is concerned, you must know a *modus rectus* from a *modus non rectus*, and so it is not right when it is said that the fifth is first."

[23] (Couss., *Script.* I:96) regarding the first mode: "The pause of each voice (that is the *tenoris* and the *moteti* [in three-voice settings]) is valued at one breve unless each voice pauses along with the *tripla*. Then the pauses of ecclesiastical chant are taken at one's pleasure." Anonymous VII (Couss., *Script.* I:378) writes: "Such is a pause when it is a *penultima*" (cf. also p. 379).

drawn through all the spaces in *musica plana*). Also, the little line through the lowest staff line, called *divisio sillabarum*, is not an actual rest; for the same reason the *suspiratio*, the breathing mark, is not a rest of definite value, but is only what we now call a "Luftpause" (*apparens pausa et non existens*—apparent pause and one that does not exist).

Pseudo-Aristotle proceeded quite naturally in his unique style and first established the terms *recta vox* for note and *omissa vox* for rest, which Franco then took over from him. His rest marks and the values which they indicated are: through all four spaces (*pausa perfecta*) = perfect longa; through three spaces (*pausula imperfecta*) = imperfect longa or *brevis altera*; through two spaces (*suspirium breve*) = a single breve; through one space (*semisuspirium majus*) = a large semibreve (2/3 of a breve); through a half of one space on a line (*semisuspirium minus*) = a small semibreve (1/3 of a breve). This system met with no approval.

A more sensible way is discussed by the Karlsruhe Anonymous (H. Müller's *Dietericus*):

value:        1      2      3    *tempora*

no more and no less! Naturally, this Anonymous presupposes acquaintance with the *finis punctorum* (final line, through all staff lines) but does not mention it since it is not mensural. In this respect also there is not much left for Franco to do: he continues to use the rest marks which he inherited (with the exception of those of the stubborn Aristotle) and which are in agreement with the Karlsruhe Anonymous, adding special forms for the larger and smaller semibreve ( = 2/3 or 1/3 of a space):

2/3       1/3

Franco did not introduce new note-symbols but stopped with the semibreve, differentiating between two kinds, the *semibrevis major* and the *semibrevis minor*, sometimes reckoning as many as nine semibreves to one breve ( = 1 *tempus*; see Gerbert, *Script.* III:5). This nomenclature he also found in Aristotle, although in the latter the *semibrevis major* always equals 2/3 of a breve, and the *semibrevis minor* equals 1/3 of a breve.

According to the ingeniously conceived dialogue treatise of Robert de Handlo (in the year of 1326, in which the teachers Johannes de Garlandia, Petrus de Cruce, Petrus le Viser, Franco [the Parisian, according to Coussemaker] and Handlo are introduced speaking for themselves, and

who add comments on the individual concepts of theory which we owe
to them), the *punctum divisionis* seems to have been the invention of
Johannes de Garlandia (?) or of Petrus de Cruce. Both employ the
*punctum divisionis*, although in Handlo they use it only to divide larger
groups of semibreves. Petrus de Cruce does this in the shape of a filled dot,
Garlandia in the shape of a small circle. Since the same Garlandia appears
in Handlo as the originator of distinguishing note values smaller than the
semibreve according to name and shape, and as nothing is to be found
concerning the *signum divisionis* in the two treatises of the pre-Franconian
Garlandia (printed by Coussemaker in *Script.* I), for the first time the
thought presents itself that in addition to the Garlandia teaching in the
beginning of the 13th century there is another one by the same name one
hundred years later, for which assumption we shall encounter more
weighty evidence as we proceed. Thus the introduction of the *punctum
divisionis* remains as an attribution of the *optimus notator* Petrus de Cruce,
whose treatise concerning mensural notation is unfortunately not preserved. Perhaps credit belongs to Franco for having continued the use of
the *signum divisionis* (used by de Cruce to group semibreves) and also for
the separation of larger note values. At any rate, the *Discantus positio
vulgaris*, Anonymous VII, Garlandia, Pseudo-Aristotle, and the Karlsruhe
Anonymous do not yet know of the possibility that of two breves standing
between two longas, the first breve could belong to the first longa and the
second breve to the following longa, or that a single breve between two
longas makes the second and not the first imperfect.[24]

If we pursue further the thought that Walter Odington lived later than
the two Francos, but perhaps still did not know the *Ars cantus mensurabilis*,
then not only does each deviation of his rules from those of this work
achieve significance, but we also receive further evidence of the merits of
Petrus de Cruce, and (if the *Ars cantus mensurabilis* really comes from
Franco of Cologne) of the older Franco. We must then admit that Franco
of Cologne is further divested of some of his merits. Odington speaks of
the possible division of the breve into six and even seven semibreves (but
not nine as in Franco); however, he attacks the custom of calling them
semibreves: "I divide the semibreve into three parts and call these parts
*minutae*, while keeping the shape of the semibreve for the same, in order
not to deviate from the custom of musicians."[25] In the light of his admitted eclecticism, if the author of the *Ars cantus mensurabilis* had known

---

[24] The *punctum divisionis* assumes special significance in the *Compendium de discantu
mensurabili*, written in 1336 by Petrus Dictus Palma Ociosa. See p. 197.

[25] (Couss., *Script.* I:236): "Therefore, just as the longa is divided in breves, and breves
are divided into semibreves, so I divide a semibreve into three parts which I call *minutae*,
retaining the form of a semibreve for them lest I appear to disagree with other musicians.

this proposal of Odington, he would in all probability have accepted it. Odington also uses the term minima by chance in one place; this later became generally accepted in order to describe the division of the semibreve. Odington uses the dot and circle to group the smaller note values (see remarks) in the same way as Petrus de Cruce and the doubtful Johannes de Garlandia in Handlo's *Dialogue*. He also uses the *signum perfectionis* (the point of division directly by the *longa*) and also the *signum divisionis* between two breves belonging to different perfections. He calls rests *tempora vocum tacita* and explains them in the same manner as the Karlsruhe Anonymous and Franco, but still does not include the third-space rest for the smaller semibreve (he designates a half-space rest for the semibreve). The expression *longa omissa* (p. 238) for *pausa longae* indicates his acquaintance with the treatise of Pseudo-Aristotle. Odington enumerates the *modi* in the old manner, but apparently knows of the attempt at reform by Aristotle, for he ends, somewhat angrily: "This is the order according to the older and also the modern habit and usage!"

The short explanation of note values in ligatures is especially well worded (p. 243);[26] if this should stem from the older Franco or another of the predecessors of Franco of Cologne, then it would diminish the merit of the latter. It may have been the personal accomplishment of Odington himself, whose great aptitude as a theorist should not be underestimated.

---

But when the breve, divided into two semibreves, follows one divided in three parts or, on the contrary [divided] in three parts and two, place the division thus:

$$(\phantom{x} = \Diamond\,\square \;|\; \Diamond\,\Diamond\,\Diamond \;|\; \Diamond\,\square \;|\; \mathbf{I}$$

"When the breve has been divided into four, five, or even more parts, it is not called a division but is known by a little circle which is also the sign of division, thus:

$$(\phantom{x} = \Diamond\,\Diamond\,\lozenge\,\lozenge \;|\; \Diamond\,\lozenge\,\lozenge\,\lozenge\,\lozenge \;|\; \Diamond\,\Diamond\,\lozenge\,\lozenge\,\lozenge\,\lozenge\,)$$

"There are two from the first four *semibreves minores*; and these are followed by two *minutae* which are like minimas or the swiftest, and so of the others." Here Odington uses the *signum divisionis* for the simpler divisions according to the usage of Petrus de Cruce, and the small circle for the more complicated ones, according to the usage of the (younger) Garlandia in Handlo. It appears almost as though Handlo has made an error here and that Odington is the innovator of this new usage which Handlo, who writes only a little after Odington, attributed to his contemporary, the younger Garlandia.

[26] "All propriety is expressed in breves, impropriety in longas. Opposite propriety is made by two semibreves [opposite propriety occurs when an upward tail is attached to the beginning of a ligature causing the first two notes of the ligature to become semibreves] because one [semibreve] does not make a ligature; more than two are not required. If more little notes should occur to a division, however (that is, when a ligature encompasses more than two notes), it is done in the following manner: all perfection is in longas, imperfection is in breves, but the breve is always in the middle, except that which is in opposite propriety, this being in semibreves. In these just as in the simple kind there are perfect and imperfect longas; and *rectas* breves are made and altered."

Odington also discusses (as does Anonymous IV) several curious ways of enumerating notes and ligatures during the transition period (which we have already partially touched upon) and concludes: "Patet igitur, quod usus quem prius acceptavi, certior est atque acceptior (It is therefore evident that what I formerly accepted is surer and more acceptable)," thus again rejecting all innovations.

From the theoretical treatment of the *plica*, that embellishment of a single note (longa or breve) which has been so much disputed, or from the treatment of the final note of a ligature, evidence may also be found for the succession and the age relationships of the various writers; this, however, leads to the same results. It need only be mentioned here that the *Discantus positio vulgaris* does not mention the *plica* and that Anonymous VII is not yet acquainted with it in connection with ligatures, but that Garlandia does treat it in this combination, although rather awkwardly.

The *modi*, as represented by the shapes of ligatures, have a similar history. Attempts to signify the *modus* by the note shapes, as well as by the shapes of the ligatures, manifest themselves early. The *Discantus positio vulgaris* and Anonymous VII do not enter this field as yet; Garlandia, however, establishes firm rules and also develops the *ordines* of the individual *modi*:

The first *modus* might start with a *ligatura ternaria* ($- \cup -$) and then might progress (if tonal repetitions do not make the use of ligatures impossible) with *ligatura binariae* ($\cup -$) to the end.

(The first *ordo* of the first *modus* might possibly introduce a *pausa brevis*, always after a *ligatura ternaria*.)

The second *modus* might move from the beginning and continue in *ligaturae binariae* [$\cup -$] and end with a *ternaria sine proprietate cum perfectione*, which, however, is to be measured as $\cup - \cup$. Garlandia's three-note ligatures do not yet correspond to the later [Franconian]: and

are still called, as in Franco, *sine proprietate et cum perfectione*, but are measured as $\cup - \cup$!

(The first *ordo* of the second *modus* is: *ligatura ternaria* [$\cup - \cup$ as before], with a rest having the value of a longa following, this pattern being continually repeated.)

The third *modus* first uses a *longa simplex* and then continually moves in *ligaturae ternariae*, but *cum proprietate et cum perfectione*, which is to be measured as $\cup \cup -$. The final rest (and this might be an error) is not the usual perfect longa.

The fourth *modus* differs from the third because of the fact that the *longa simplex* is missing at the beginning, and because it ends with two "imperfects" and one *longa pausatio*.

The fifth *modus* moves only in single longas or, as in the first *ordo*, in *ligaturae ternariae cum proprietate et cum perfectione*, but with a *pausa longae perfectae* following; this, again, is a very arbitrary rule designed only to establish a difference between the first and fourth *modi* in the note picture. Since the first *modus* has ligatures of the same shape in the first *ordo*, but breve rests, the second has *ligaturae ternariae sine proprietate*, the third has *ternariae* of the same shape preceded by a *longa simplex*, and the fourth differs in the two "imperfects" before the pause.

The sixth *modus*, whose characteristic distinction is the accumulation of short values, cannot be confused with the other *modi* as long as they do not become identical with it by the division of the longas into breves.

The catalectic *modi* are called perfect, the acatalectic imperfect; the latter also have a different note picture, and the differentiations are even more complicated and do not have to be touched upon at this place, since in general only catalectic modes appear. The examples are, incidentally, interspersed with rests; these seem designated only for the *cantus truncatus* (*hoketus*) which was then widely esteemed.

Apparently, then, the varying shapes of the beginning and ending notes of ligatures were used not to indicate other values, but rather only to distinguish the *modi* in the note picture. The curious ambiguity of the same forms of the *ligaturae ternariae* we also find in Pseudo-Aristotle; we would also undoubtedly find them in the Karlsruhe Anonymous, if the latter had dealt more in detail with the *modi*. On the other hand, Odington (Couss., *Script.* I:244) opposes the form ▪▪▪ for — ∪ — of the *indecens et rationi dissonum* and replaces it by ▪▪▪, which is again proof either that he already knew the teachings of Franco or that Franco had already incorporated those innovations from his predecessors.

The most explicit representation of the different *ordines* of the *modi perfecti* and *imperfecti* is found in Anonymous IV (Couss., *Script.* I:328 ff.). He also presents valuable material for the history of these representations, and is certainly one of the most important sources of music history for the 12th and 13th centuries. He probably lived into the time of Franco of Cologne and was approximately the same age as Odington. He gives the same rules concerning ligatures which remain constant for some time after, but in addition he also offers clarifications of earlier, irregular values, as we have already seen.

It hardly needs to be emphasized how important the changes in interpretation of ligatures (and *conjuncturae*), which we have already briefly discussed, are for the attempts at deciphering compositions from the 12th and 13th centuries. Many inadequacies of former transcriptions might be exchanged for more satisfying solutions if, in individual cases, correct methods of transcription could be used. We know definitely, for instance, that the Franconian mensural rules cannot be applied to the compositions of Perotinus. Certainly much labor and effort will be required of musicology in order to solve these riddles fully.

The most important innovation of mensural theory for the technique of musical composition is the conscious and continuous distinction between strong and weak values, which we met with first as *impares* and *pares* in the *Discantus positio vulgaris*, in Johannes de Garlandia, and in Anonymous IV. Garlandia's remark (Couss., *Script.* I:114), "Omne id quod accidit in aliquo (modo) secundum virtutem consonantiarum dicitur longum (Everything that meets with another according to the virtue of consonances is said to be long)," probably also means the contrary, that the longa in all *modi* is that part of the value upon which the consonances belong.*[18] Therefore when, as a result of *aequipollentia* (division into equal values), two breves appear in the place of a longa, the breve which is placed on the first part of a longa is entitled to a consonance. The expression *aliquid aequipollens* in this sense already appears in the *Discantus positio vulgaris* (Couss., *Script.* I:95 and 96); Anonymous VII also says (Couss., *Script.* I:379) that the *aequipollentia* is possible for all *modi* and uses this expression repeatedly.

In place of the *pares* and *impares*, whose contrast continually regulates the relationship between two voices, Pseudo-Aristotle first introduces the idea of the *perfectio* as a regulative factor for the connection between voices singing at the same time:[27]

Temporal measurement (in contrast to the *localis mensura*—the measurement of the vertical distance between tones) is the equality of two or more series of tones, according to the number which is measured according to the *perfectio*. For if anyone wishes to be certain whether in the relationship of two or three voices consonance is correctly used in any one place, then he must start at a known point (where all voices are together) and count up to the place in question in groups of

[27] (Couss., *Script.* I:278): "Temporalis, autem, [mensura] ut hic sumitur, est duarum trium vel plurium figurarum, secundum quod sunt in numero, ad aliquam perfectionem relata aequalitas; nam ut si quis aliquam proportionem justam, seu consonantiam duorum cantuum sive trium diversorum generum, alicujus loci determinati scire desiderat, ab aliquo sibi noto principio ad locum usque deputatum per tria tempora vel per aequipollentiam semper ad perfectionem figuram diligenter studeat computando referre." Whoever has ever transcribed old notation without measure bars knows that this procedure is the only reliable one (even today) in the discovery of mistakes. Prosdocimus de Beldemandis gives similar advice (Couss., *Script.* III:228): "If you wish to know in what measure any *cantus* which is placed before you is, you ought to sing it yourself or do something else proportionate to it, such as counting its counterpoint. Through this, without mistake, you can come into a knowledge of any *cantus* which is proposed to you, if you are willing to work."

three *tempora*, or values the same as those *tempora*, and count the notes together in perfections.

This early manner of counting the *tempora* (the beat)*[19] is shown to have existed even as late as Walter Odington. As we have already stated, however, with the use of the *signum divisionis* and *signum perfectionis*, which are basically similar to our bar lines, it appears at this time that Franco (in the *Ars cantus mensurabilis*) used the *perfectio* in the sense of our modern beat rather consistently. The sentence (which is a landmark in the history of music theory, though less by its contents than by its setting), providing the first basis for the normal treatment of dissonance as contrasted with consonance, is as follows:[28] "In all *modi*, consonances are to be used at the beginning of every measure [unit of measure] whether this be a longa, breve, or semibreve."*[20]

What we are to understand by the *principium perfectionis* is no longer a riddle (the beginning of every measure [i.e., unit of measure]). We also know, however, that in all *modi* the first part of the longa is that value which demands a consonance. The four main *modi* are, then, always to be interpreted as follows:

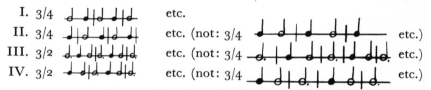

Franco expressly states that there is no internal difference between the first and second *modi* (there would be if in the first mode on the longa, and in the second on the breve, a consonance would be demanded); rather, one can proceed from the one to the other:[29] "If in the first *modus* (— ∪ — ∪) there is a rest of the value of an imperfect longa, then the first *modus* proceeds to the second *modus*":

(1. *Modus*)                              (2. *Modus*)

Also, Walter Odington's remark (Couss., *Script.* I:246) that one must

---

[28] "In omnibus modis utendum est semper concordantiis in principio perfectionis, licet sit longa, brevis vel semibrevis."

[29] (Gerbert, *Script.* III:9, Couss., *Script.* I:126): "Si primus modus, qui procedit ex longa et brevi et longa, pausam post brevem habeat longam imperfectam, variatur primus modus in secundum."

never be critical if a breve which appears before a longa is a dissonance, proves that the longa is always recognized as the beginning of the *perfectio*. Franco even goes so far as to assert that in one and the same *discantus* (composition) all *modi* may come together, since through the perfections (the *meter*) they become one and the same.[30] The identity of the first and fifth *modi* is, incidentally, already recognized by Anonymous VII (Couss., *Script.* I:379).

Walter Odington, the writer who most definitely remarked that originally the longa represented only two breves (Couss., *Script.* I:235), leads the triple longa back to the third and fourth *modi*,[31] which he represents in detailed discussion as dactylic and anapestic meters. He also remarks that they, in comparison with the trochaic first and iambic second *modi*, move in longer values, i.e., he feels that actually the entire foot [or metrical unit] should demand only one instead of two perfections, i.e.:

$$3/4 \quad \text{♩. ♪ ♩} \quad \text{instead of } 3/2 \quad \text{♩. ♩ ♩ and}$$
$$3/4 \quad \text{♪ ♩ | ♩.} \quad \text{instead of } 3/2 \quad \text{♩ ♩ | ♩.}$$

wherein apparently the actual meaning of the *ultra mensuram* is to be sought. Actually, in the *metra* the length is duple; but it is permissible to extend somewhat a long syllable in order to cover the note which is given to it. In other words, the third *modus* was actually ♩ ♩ ♩, and the fourth ♩ ♩ | ♩. They were changed, however, to the form in which we know them now because of the one-sided emphasis on triple meter. If we take in addition the rather curious passage in Johannes de Garlandia (Couss., *Script.* I:107a) which says that in the third (and fourth) *modi* the two breves actually constitute only one value (the weak, imperfect) (see above,

---

[30] (Couss., *Script.* I:127): "Et nota quod in uno discantu omnes modi concurrere possunt eo quod per perfectiones omnes modi ad unum reducuntur."

[31] (Couss., *Script.* I:241): "Nor is the mode suitable, that is, the third and fourth; a longa is of three *tempora* and the *brevis altera* of two, and it may be said that the longa has the measure of two *tempora* because it is permitted to draw out a long syllable to whatever length is suitable to the tone. And similarly, not every *cantus organicus* is in poetry; but also most suitably the longa of three *tempora* is in these modes and the *brevis altera* of two because these modes consist chiefly of dactyls and anapests. Moreover, the dactyl is named from the finger, and the anapest is the opposite of the dactyl. For the finger, beginning with the longa mode, ends in two breves, the middle joint of the finger is twice the extent of the top joint and the third [lower] joint is equal to the two upper joints so that it [the dactyl] may be in this order [from top to bottom]: breve, *brevis altera*, and perfect longa in the likeness of the finger. So in these modes, a perfect longa takes its origin from the first and yet in these modes there is a *brevis altera*, for the second one is always an *altera*, as in the third mode, so in the fourth. For if there were a variety, it would offend the whole composition unless, perchance, it [the *altera*] was changed into two *rectae* or if the second were first, it would change to the first mode."

p. 139 f.), then the transcription of the third and fourth *modi* in 3/2 meter seems sufficiently justified.

It is to be regretted that—although this is understandable enough—the authors of the entire first epoch of mensural music dealt almost exclusively with involved explanations of precepts concerning the values of notes and the correct manner of writing *modi* and *ordines*, so that only a few remarks remain concerning consonances and their uses in discant. We must assume, therefore, that the same principles used in improvised counterpoint (*déchant sur le livre*) were applicable to polyphonic compositions in mensural notation. The discant rules extend far into the time of the first explanations of mensural notation. Franco (in the *Ars cantus mensurabilis*) expressly leaves it up to the authors of the *musica plana* to determine why one consonance is more consonant than the other.[32] It seems that Marchettus of Padua had this remark in mind when he entitled the first chapter of his sixth treatise of the *Lucidarium musicae planae* (1274) *De consonantiis, quomodo et quare una melius consonet quam altera.* It begins: "Quaeritur, quare una consonantia magis concordet quam altera . . . (As to why one concord is more consonant than another)," etc. Even he, however, does not arrive at a satisfactory solution of this question.

That mensural notation first spread from Paris seems established. Evidence already pointing in that direction receives full corroboration in the important testimony of Anonymous IV. He reports that the Spaniards (*Hispani et Pompilonenses*) and Englishmen did not know the difference between the *proprietas* and *perfectio* at a time when rules were already established in Paris.[33] He does not mention the Italians, although he might have considered them as included among the "*Pompilonenses.*" The formerly discussed English manner of notation (of [Thomas] Anglicus) was, therefore, probably not a real mensural notation (we are, perhaps, even at this time, dealing here with a metaphorical notation or the manner of reading the "sights"). But in Paris, even before the actual appearance of mensural notation, according to the remarks of Anonymous IV, the "longs" and the "shorts" were already discussed (and the *modi* were probably also distinguished) but without *materialis signatio*, that is, without designation of note values through the shapes of notes.[34]

[32] (Gerbert, *Script.* III:11): "As to why one concord is more consonant than another, this must be decided by plainsong."

[33] (Couss., *Script.* I:345): "In the books of certain of the older writers no such significance was paid to the notational forms. They were able to proceed only according to their understanding, always using forms which were *cum proprietate* and *cum perfectione.* Such notation is found in the books of the Spanish and the Pamplonians, as well as in the books of the English in different gradations, sometimes more, sometimes less. . . . The French or the Parisians had all of the above-mentioned methods of notating."

[34] (Couss., *Script.* I:344): "In the older books, there was an exceedingly large number

Even the discant rules of Anonymous IV (Couss., *Script.* I:356b) treat the differences between long and short tones only at random, while they are otherwise on the same level as those with whom we last dealt, those who treated thirds and sixths as consonances; they, therefore, need not be discussed further. We shall find it necessary to return, however, for certain special considerations.

---

of ambiguous note forms, since all of the *notae simplicies* had the same form. The musicians could only reason things out, saying: I know this note to be a longa, this one to be a breve, etc."

While reading the galley proof of this section, I received the small study "*Der Ursprung des Motetts*" of Wilhelm Meyer (1898) containing the very interesting information that a copy of the large collection of the oldest two-to-four-part compositions, mentioned by Garlandia and Anonymous IV, which were used at Notre Dame in Paris, has been preserved in the *Antiphonarium Mediceum*, Plut. 29, 1, of the Laurentian Library at Florence. This codex, written during the 13th century, assumes even greater interest in connection with the Cod. H. 196 of Montpellier.

Concerning the remaining contents of Prof. Meyer's study, one must await a further development of his "preliminary remarks" before one can come to any conclusions concerning the derivation of the motet from sequence-like paraphrases and intercalations of antiphons.

## APPENDIX

FOOTNOTE 10: (Couss., *Script.* I:271 ff.): "Sicut enim res quaelibet naturalis ad similitudinem divine nature ex tribus constare invenitur et in vocibus et sonis trina tantum (Couss. tamen) existat consonantia (octave, fifth, fourth, see p. 101), sic omnis cantus mensurabilis ad similitudinem divinae naturae ex tribus constare invenitur, cujus probatio patet in mensura, ubi ternarius numerus reducitur ad perfectam."

Franco, *Ars cantus mensurabilis* (Couss., *Script.* I:119): "Ex quo sequitur, quod illi peccant, qui eam rectam appellant (sc. longam imperfectam), cum illud, quod rectum est, possit per se stare."

FOOTNOTE 12: (Coussemaker, *Script.* I:103): "Item notandum est, quod ubicumque invenitur brevium multitudo, i.e., semibrevium, semper participant cum praecedente, quae praecedens cum eis non reputatur in valore, nisi pro una tali sicut et praecedens."

FOOTNOTE 13: (*Op. cit.*, p. 107): "Sed duo puncti sumentur hic (sc. in modo tertio) pro uno, et aliquando unus eorum ponitur in discordantia, propter colorem musicae et hic primus sive secundus. Et hoc bene permittitur ab auctoribus primis et licenciatur. Hoc autem invenitur in organo in pluribus locis et praecipue in mothetis."

FOOTNOTE 15: (Coussemaker, *Script.* I:359): "Iterato sunt quidam qui multiplicant multiplices discordantias ante unam perfectam concordantiam sicut ante diapason et nimis gaudent et videtur esse mirabile magnum inter ipsos quod hoc potest fieri sicut (hic)

in superiori: d   f   c   ♮   c   B♭   c   (Couss. ♭   c   ♭   c)

in inferiori:   D   D   E   F   E   D   C."

FOOTNOTE 16: (Couss., *Script.* I:91): "Est autem flos armonicus decora vocis sive soni et celerrima procellarisque vibratio...Longi flores sunt, quorum vibratio est morosa

metasque semitonii (!) non excedit. Aperti autem sunt, quorum vibratio est (nec) morosa (nec subita sed media inter ista) metasque toni non excedit. Subiti vero sunt, quorum quidem vibratio in principio est morosa, in medio autem et in fine est celerrima metasque semitonii (!) non excedit... longi flores fieri debent in prima, paenultima et ultima nota in ascensu semitonium intendente. Si vero aliquem aliorum modorum in descensu, constituunt flores apertos, quos et nota secunda syllabae debet habere. Sed flores subitos non alia quam plica longa inter quam et immediate sequentem notae brevissimae ponuntur ob armoriae decorum."..."cum non naturaliter sed vulgariter (!) loquendo quaedam voces sint pectoris, quaedam gutturis, quaedam vero sint ipsius capitis.... Voces pectoris valent in gravibus; gutturis in acutis, capitis autem in superacutis."...
"Quando enim aliquem cantum tangimus in organis, si aliquam notam eiusdem cantus florizare volumus, puta G in gravibus, tunc ipsa aperta immobiliterque detenta non sui inferiorem in medietate puta F grave, sed potius superiorem, a scilicet, vibramus acutum. Ex quo pulcherrima armonia decoraque consurgit quam quidem, florem harmonicum appellamus.

"Quando igitur clavis immobilis cum vibranda semitonium constituunt et ipsa vibratio est morosa, tunc est flos, qui dicitur longus. Quando autem includunt tonum et vibratio nec est morosa nec subita, sed media inter ista, est flos apertus. Quando vero constituunt quidem semitonium, sed vibratio in agressu sit morosa, in progressu autem et egressu sit celerrima, tunc est flos, qui subitus appellatur."

FOOTNOTE 17: (Page 166): "Videndum est de falsa musica, quae instrumentis musicis multum est necessaria specialiter in organis. Falsa musica est quando de tono facimus semitonium et e converso (see p. 212, Chapter XI). Omnis tonus divisibilis est in duo semitonia et per consequens signa semitonia designantia in omnibus tonis possunt amplificari."

FOOTNOTE 18: "Iterato sunt et alii modi prout modi supradicti frangunt brevem vel breves in duas, tres vel quatuor etc. prout in instrumentis.... Sonus sub uno tempore potest dici sonus acceptus sub tempore non minimo non maximo sed medio legitimo breviter sumpto, quod possit frangi veloci motu in duobus, tribus vel quatuor non plus in voce humana, quamvis in instrumentis possit aliter fieri."

FOOTNOTE 19: (Couss., *Script.* I:117): "Cum, inquiunt, de plana musica quidam philosophi sufficienter tractaverint ipsamque nobis tam theoretice quam practice efficaciter illucidaverint, theoretice praecipue Boetius, practice vero Guido monachus et maxime de tropis ecclesiasticis beatus Gregorius, idcirco nos de mensurabili musica, quam ipsa plana praecedit tamquam principalis subalternam, ad preces quorundam magnatum (MS St. Dié: 'magistrorum') tractare proponentes non pervertendo ordinem ipsam planam perfectissime a praedictis philosophis supponimus propalatam. Nec dicat aliquis nos hoc opus propter arrogantiam vel forte propter propriam tantum comoditatem incepisse, sed vere propter evidentem necessitatem et auditorum facillimam apprehensionem necnon et omnium notatorum ipsius mensurabilis musicae perfectissimam instructionem. Quoniam cum videremus multos tam novos quam antiquos in artibus suis de mensurabili musica multa bona dicere et e contrario in multis, et maxime in accidentibus ipsius scientiae deficere et errare, opinioni eorum fore existimamus succurrendum. Et ne forte propter defectum et errorem praedictorum scientia dicta detrimentum pateretur, proponimus igitur ipsam mensurabilem musicam sub compendio declarare, bene dictaque aliorum non recusabimus interponere erroresque destruere et fugare, et si quid novi a nobis inventum fuerit, bonis rationibus sustinere et probare."

FOOTNOTE 21: (Couss., *Script.* I:118): "Modi autem a diversis diversimode enumerantur. Quidem enim ponunt sex, alii septem; nos autem quinque tantum ponimus, quia ad hos quinque omnes reducuntur. Primus enim procedit ex omnibus longis, et sub ipso reponimus illum, qui est ex longa et brevi, duabus de causis: prima est, quia isti duo in similibus pausationibus uniuntur, secunda est propter antiquorum et aliquorum modernorum controversiam compescendam."

FOOTNOTE 22: (Couss., *Script.* I:98): "Sed aliqui volunt, quod quintus noster modus sit primus omnium. Et bona est ratio, quia per istum modum praecedit (sic) omnes nostros modos. Sed quoad tempora cognoscenda prius est modus rectus quam obliquus, et sic non valet quod dicitur, quod quintus est primus."

FOOTNOTE 23: (Couss., *Script.* I:96) regarding the first mode: "Pausa vero utriusque (sc. tenoris et moteti [in three-voice settings]) valet unam brevem, nisi simul pauset uterque cum tripla: et tunc pausae cantus ecclesiastici tenentur ad placitum." Anonymous VII (Couss., *Script.* I:378) writes: "tanta est pausa quanta est penultima" (cf. also p. 379).

FOOTNOTE 25: (Couss., *Script.* I:236): "Sicut ergo longa in breves, et brevis in semibreves dividitur, ita semibrevem primo divido in tres partes quas minutas voco, figuram retinens semibrevis, ne ab aliis musicis videar discrepare. Verum cum brevis divisa in duas semibreves sequitur divisam in tres partes vel e contrario in tres partes et duas, divisionem pono sic:

"Cum vero in quatuor vel quinque aut ulterius divisa fuerit, non dicta divisione, sed tali parvulo circulo cognoscetur, qui similiter signum est divisionis, sic:

"Suntque duae de quatuor priores (Couss. prioribus) semibreves minores; duae vero posteriores minutae sunt, quasi minimae seu velocissimae, et sic de aliis."

FOOTNOTE 26: "Omnis proprietas brevis; improprietas longa. Opposita proprietas duas facit semibreves, quia una non ligatur, nec plures quam duae. Unde si plures (notulae) evenerint usque ad divisionem (that is, when a ligature encompasses more than two notes) sic fiunt: omnis perfectio longa; imperfectio autem brevis omnis vero media brevis excepta ea quae oppositam proprietatem semibreviatur. In his sicut in simplicibus contingit longas perfici et imperfici; breves autem rectas fieri et alterari."

FOOTNOTE 27: (Couss., *Script.* III:228): "Quod si noscere vis cujus mensurae sit aliquis cantus tibi propositus, debes ipsum cantare, vel aliquid sibi proportionale facere, sicut ipsius contrapunctum numerare, et per hoc infallenter in notitiam mensurae cujuscumque cantus tibi proposti devenire poteris, si laborare voles."

FOOTNOTE 31: (Couss., *Script.* I:241): "Nec est modus conveniens scilicet tertio et quarto; longa enim trium temporum, et altera brevis duorum, licet prius dictum sit longam in metris duorum esse temporum, quia syllabam longam licitum est quantumcunque protrahere voci aptatae. Et similiter non omnis cantus organicus est in carmine; sed et convenientissime in his modis est longa trium temporum et brevis altera duorum, quia hi modi constant principaliter ex dactylis et anapaestis. Dactylus autem dicitur a digito et anapaestus est dactylo contrarius. Digitus igitur a longiori modo inchoans in duas desinit breves. Media junctura digiti dupla est ratio extremae; duabus vero extremis tertia est aequalis ut sit iste ordo: brevis, brevis altera, longa perfecta (!) ad similitudinem digiti...ideo in his modis longa perfecta primo traxit originem, et tamen in his modis est brevis altera; semper autem secunda est altera, tam in tertio modo quam in quarto, ne, si diversitas esset, congregationem offenderet, nisi forte in duas rectas redigatur, vel si prior altera esset, in primum modum transiret."

FOOTNOTE 32: (Gerbert, *Script.* III:11): "Quare autem una concordantia magis concordat quam alia, planae musicae relinquatur."

FOOTNOTE 33: (Couss., *Script.* I:345): "Sed in libris quorundam antiquorum non erat materialis signatio talis signata, sed solo intellectu procedebant semper cum proprietate et perfectione operatoris in eisdem velut in libris Hispanorum et Pompilonensium et in libris Anglicorum sed diversimode secundum magis et minus....Gallici vero Parisiis habebant omnes istos modos..."

FOOTNOTE 34: (Couss., *Script.* I:344): "In antiquis libris habebant puncta aequivoca nimis, quia simplicia materialia fuerunt aequalia, sed solo intellectu operabantur dicendo: intelligo istam longam intelligo illam brevem."

## CHAPTER IX

# Composition in Three and More Parts

THROUGHOUT the entire 13th century the rules which theorists established governing composition in more than two parts are remarkably vague. In fauxbourdon (see Chapter VII) we met with a style of counterpoint in more than two parts formulated in a manner which seems acceptable even today and which was definitely established in the 14th century.*¹ The older organum (diaphony) remained counterpoint in two parts, even with octave doublings in both voices. The strict parallel organum of the *Musica enchiriadis* and its *Scholia* cannot lay claim to these characteristics, since continually accompanying octaves and fifths, after all, add only dynamic color to the unison, not actual contrast. The strict *déchant* in contrary motion, as it developed gradually from organum during and after the period of Guido of Arezzo and Johannes Cotton, is definitely two-part. It excludes the possibility of employing two different voices as a simultaneous discant over the same *cantus firmus*. With the attempt to add a third voice to two voices, one of which is the discant of the other, strict discant, which excludes all parallel motion and admits only octaves (unisons) and fifths (twelfths) throughout, is again relinquished. Not the extreme contrary motion discant, therefore, but rather the free discant which grew out of the organum of Johannes Cotton and the Milan Anonymous, etc., under the growing influence of English musicians and theorists, and contemporary with the *chant sur le livre*, must be regarded as the actual basis for counterpoint of more than two parts.

The earliest commentator on three- and four-part composition (aside from the *Discantus positio vulgaris*, which speaks only at random of the existence of three-voiced compositions), Johannes de Garlandia, is an Englishman who taught in Paris. His report shows unmistakable leanings in the direction of the theory of the three "sights" which we met in Lionel Power, who lived almost two hundred years later. For this reason we can probably attribute a very early date to this theory. Garlandia emphasizes, in writing of the *quadrupla* of Perotinus, that Perotinus, as well as other contemporaries, does not keep the normal distance from the tenor; because of this remark the origin of the treble sight and quatreble sight moves even further back than Garlandia, bordering on the 12th and 13th century. It proves at the same time, however, that the Parisian masters set about three- and four-part composition without leaning toward fauxbourdon. The characteristic of the English treble and quatreble —the position above the discant as a third higher voice and a fourth voice even higher—is therefore not applicable to the *triplum* and *quadruplum* of the Paris masters. Furthermore, we also have reason to assume that the bass voice which was added to gymel and fauxbourdon by Guilelmus Monachus is not of English but of French origin and is derived from the Paris *tripla* and *quadrupla*.*[2]

The meager remarks of Johannes de Garlandia concerning composition of *tripla* and *quadrupla* read:[1]

Triplum is a well-ordered connection between three notes according to the six consonances, unison, octave, etc., in the same *tempus*. More accurately: *triplum* is a well-ordered melody which fits and harmonizes with the discant, that is, a voice which is added to other voices (*cantus firmus* and discant) as a third one.... Triplum in its stricter sense (the English treble) must be consonant, though at a greater distance, with the first and second voice, if one does not represent the intervals

[1] (Coussemaker, *Script.* I:114): "Triplum est commixtio trium sonorum secundum habitudinem VI concordantiarum, scilicet unisonus, diapason etc. et hoc in eodem tempore....Specialiter autem sic describitur: Triplum est cantus proportionatus aliquis conveniens et concordans cum discantu. Et sic est tertius cantus adjunctus duobus. Unde prima regula: Triplum specialiter sumptum debet ex remoto concordare primo et secundo cantui, nisi fuerit concordantia insimul per sonum reductum (!) quod sibi aequipollet. Proprium est diapason et infra, remotum est duplex diapason et infra usque ad diapason, remotissimum est triplex diapason et infra usque ad duplex diapason." (*Ibid.*, 116): "The normal position of the *quadruplum* lies between the triple octave and below, which scarcely occurs, aside from instrumental music, thus all longas in the first *modus* are consonant with all of those which have already been mentioned, that is, the three voices which have already been composed, in either simple or composite concords. But the particular qualities about which we have already spoken are observed in some, as is apparent in all the *quadruplae* in the great book of Master Perotinus." (Compare here the reference to the *Magnus liber organi* of Leoninus (abbreviated by Perotinus) in Anonymous IV, and also the reference to Perotinus' own excellent *quadruplae* (Couss., *Script.* I:342). "These great *quadruplae* will be found to be preserved in proportion as well as in *color* as will be apparent and manifest from them. But the quadruplum [the fourth voice] as it is commonly made (and which we are presently inclined to do) observes the height and depth of the *triplum* [the third voice] and in general only occasionally goes beyond these limits. Such a *quadruplum* with the three voices with which it is associated may also be called a *duplex cantus*, because for the most part one hears two voices alternately, either this pair or that pair. This can be best observed in instruments....The first rule is that in the first *modus* all longas of the *quadruplum* must be consonant with the three voices which have already been set, in the best manner as we have said. Another rule: if you ascend or descend with one of the voices in the same interval [*proportione*], either two should ascend afterwards, or descend with the remaining voices and in this way change the ascents and descents, now with one [voice], now with another, until the end is reached."

reduced by one octave, which, however, means the same (here we encounter the remark referring unmistakably to treble sight).*[3] Under medium range we understand the intervals up to the octave, under "wide" range those from the octave to the double-octave, and under "widest range" those from the double octave to the triple octave.... The normal position of the *quadruplum* actually lies between the double and triple octave, which, however, aside from instrumental music, rarely occurs.... The *quadruplum*, as it is generally written, customarily retains the range of the triplum in height and depth and only at times exceeds it. Such a *quadruplum* voice with its three companion parts is also called a "double discant" because one hears two voices, mostly in alternation, sometimes this pair and sometimes the other (!). The main rule is that in the first *modus* all longas of the *quadruplum* must be consonant with all other voices. Another rule is that the *quadruplum* must rise and fall in the same motion with one voice and then in turn the other voices.

(This is followed by short rules governing coloration which are, however, not worded very exactly and in connection with which the assistance of instruments is again mentioned. At the end, the term *clausum lay* again appears; we shall refer to it in another section (p. 178).

Franco's rules are even more vague than those of Garlandia:[2]

Whoever wishes to compose a *triplum* must have the tenor and discant in mind and see that the *triplum*, whenever it is dissonant with the tenor, be consonant with the discant, and vice versa. It must proceed in consonances ascending and descending with the tenor, then with the discant, but not continuously with one of the two. Whoever wishes to compose a *quadruplum* or *quintuplum* must pay attention to the other voices which are already completed (it is always assumed that one voice is composed after the other), so that if there is a dissonance with one, it will be consonant with another, and that these do not continuously rise or fall with the same voice, but sometimes with the tenor, sometimes with the discant.

It is striking to see here permission to add dissonances at will to one or more of the voices in question, since Garlandia demands consonances on accented values (longas) for all voices; perhaps Franco is mainly thinking of sixths, which according to his rules are dissonances, or he may be using the term *concordantia* in its limited sense of *concordantia perfecta*.*[4]

Walter Odington also limits himself to general remarks:[3]

[2] (Couss., *Script.* I:132; Gerbert, *Script.* III:13): "Qui autem triplum voluerit operari, respiciendum est tenorem et discantum, ita quod si discordat cum tenore, non discordet cum discantu vel e converso. Et procedat ulterius per concordantias nunc ascendendo cum tenore vel descendendo, nunc cum discantu, ita quod non semper cum altero tantum. ...Qui autem quadruplum vel quintuplum facere voluerit, accipiat vel respiciat prius factos, ut si cum uno discordat, cum aliis in concordantiis habeatur, nec ascendere debet semper vel descendere cum altero ipsorum, sed nunc cum tenore, nunc cum discantu," etc. (Here a reference follows to the necessary *aequipollentia*, that is, the correspondence of the number of perfections in all the voices.)

[3] (Couss., *Script.* I:246): "Quod compositioni cantuum (Couss. *cantum*) organicorum quidem omnium sunt circumstantiae convenientes, scilicet ut principaliter in consonantia

...that for all kinds of polyphonic composition the conditions are the same, namely, that they always rest upon consonances.... (Concerning the composition of the *rondellus*,) the second and third voices must be so placed that they proceed in consonances, that is, the second in contrary motion to the first, the third in such a manner that it does not (together with one of the first two, but sometimes with one, then the other) ascend or descend at the same time.

Anonymous IV is more explicit; however, he does not go any farther than Garlandia in his main points. He probably gives us a key for the understanding of Franco's curious rule which says that one may use dissonances in one voice at will, but he does not allow this for the *triplum*, although he does allow it for the *quadruplum*. The entire passage reads:[4]

The rules governing the *triplum* are: In the first *modus* all uneven-numbered notes (the first, third, fifth, etc., note) must be placed against the uneven-numbered notes of the discant as well as the tenor in a consonant manner, so that all three voices among each other sound consonant on the strong values.*[5] All even-numbered notes (weak values) shall be composed as seen fit. Good composers, however, also take care to consider the weak values as far as the melody is concerned and have the *triplum* move in the same motion with the discant and, in turn, the tenor, but always moving two, at the most three, steps with the same voice. It is regarded as bad practice when one voice follows any other voice in

(Couss. *inconsonantiae*!) fiant..." (Page 246): "Aptentur alii cantus in duplici aut triplici procedendo per consonantias, ut dum unus ascendit, alius descendat, vel tertius ita ut non (semper cum altero tantum [supplemented from Franco]) simul descendat vel ascendat."

[4] (Couss., *Script.* I:359): "Regulae triplicium tales sunt; si fuerit in primo modo, omnia puncta imparia debent concordari cum omnibus imparibus dupli, ita quod primus primo, tertius tertio, quintus quinto et sic de singulis. Sic etiam dicimus quod omnia puncta imparia debent concordari cum omnibus imparibus tenoris, primus primo, tertius tertio, quintus quinto et sic de singulis. Tunc sic colligimus: duplum concordat cum primo omni imparitate sua, triplum simili modo cum primo, et triplum cum duplo semper cum omni imparitate sua: ergo quilibet cum quolibet et quibus cum aliis duobus, quare omnes tres ad invicem concordabunt et concordabuntur. Omnia paria puncta in triplici indifferenter ponuntur et hoc in concordantia vel extra. Tamen boni cantores ponunt paria puncta prout melum competunt et conveniunt et cum paribus in duplo et cum paribus in primo, ita si duplum ascendat, triplum descendit et e contrario. Et hoc semel vel bis vel ter ad plus. Simili modo faciat triplum cum tenore semel vel bis, vel ter ad plus. Quum inter tales reputabitur vituperium si unus ascendit nimis cum altero de quocunque genere....Eodem modo intellige de quadruplo adjuncto cum praedictis: si fuerit de primo modo omnia puncta imparia debent concordari cum omnibus imparibus in triplo et duplo et primo; si nunc ascendat cum uno illorum hoc bene potest fieri bis vel ter, sicut de aliis supradictis; sed opponere se debet nunc cum triplo nunc cum duplo nunc cum primo vel convenire cum eisdem in unisono....Sed nota quod quadruplum quandoque potest enim ponere in discordantia cum aliquo praedictorum, quod triplum cum suis subditis non potest facere, sicut si posuerit se in ditono vel semiditono cum tenore vel duplo et alii tres fuissent concordabiles vel concordantes in diapason, diapente, diatessaron. Et sic de necessitate erit una sexta discordans, si ditonus vel semiditonus fuerit ea tenore tertia supra, et hoc est valde mirabile."

the same motion for too long a time. The same rules are applicable to the *quadruplum*; only three voices are concerned here against which it can move in contrary motion, or move together to the unison. It is to be kept in mind that the *quadruplum* sometimes may form a dissonance with one of the other voices, which is not allowed to the *triplum* (!). For instance, when the *quadruplum* together with the tenor forms a major or minor third and the other voices, intervals of the octave, fifth, and fourth:

    Sixth!

Then necessarily a dissonance appears, namely, the sixth.*[6]

Shortly before, he says:[5] "Here we see how such a worthless and unpleasant dissonance as the sixth (!), which in general is to be rejected, becomes as the penultimate interval, immediately before the octave, the very best consonance."

A rather risky combination of the old parallel organum (organum at the fifth *supra voce* with octave doubling of the *cantus firmus* or of both voices) with one discant is suggested by Simon Tunstede (Couss., *Script.* IV:276). In this combination the two or three upper voices of the organum cover up the false (!) parallel movements through figuration ("*frangere debent et florare notas prout magis decet mensura servata*"— notes ought to be split up and ornamented as is suitable to the observed measure) while the discanting voice moves in imperfect consonances (thirds, sixths, tenths) with the tenor. One certainly agrees with Tunstede that experienced discantists are needed if something good is to come of this.

After the rise of mensural notation a number of different art forms, or actually ways of composition, gradually developed for which descriptions are scanty and not at all clear at first.

The *Discantus positio vulgaris*, the early age of which (12th century) we found corroborated thus far by its contents, and confirmed by the testimony of Hieronymus de Moravia, divides all polyphonic compositions (*discantus*) into separate species at the beginning of its second part (Couss., *Script.* I:96):[6]

---

[5] (Couss., *Script.* I:359): "Et sic patet, quod vilis discordantia sive tediosa, quae est sexta, et refutabilis ab omnibus in majori parte et ipsa est penultima ante perfectam concordantiam quae est diapason, optima concordantia fit sub tali ordinatione et positione punctorum sive sonorum."

[6] "Discantus vero alius pure discantus, alius organum. Quod est duplex, scilicet organum duplex et quod pure organum dicitur. Item alius conductus, alius mothetus et alius est ochetus. Discantus ipse et idem in prosis (Couss. pausis) sed diversus in notis

I. Pure discant

II. Organum, that is,    a. *duplex*
                         b. *purum*

III. *Conductus*

IV. *Motetus*

V. *Ochetus*

In pure discant the rests are the same [the text is the same*7] in both voices but the notes are different, if the discant uses the fifth, octave, and twelfth (!) with an ecclesiastical melody.

In organum duplex the rests also coincide [the text also coincides] but not the notes, because the tenor has extended longas (perfect) against which the discant uses two notes each, in this way establishing a consonant second melody which deviates from the tenor.

*Organum purum* is used when every note of the *cantus planus* (which moves in [perfect] *longae ultra mensuram*) corresponds to two notes of the discant, namely, one longa and one breve or something equivalent to these (*aequipollens*) as was previously discussed (Couss., p. 95: each note of the *cantus firmus* equals at least two notes of the discant, namely, one longa and one breve or an equivalent number of notes, i.e., four (!) breves or three breves with one *plica brevis*).

The *Conductus* is a multivoiced consonant composition in one meter which also allows secondary consonances (*secundarias consonantias*).

The *motetus* is a multivoiced consonant composition over given notes of a *cantus firmus* in mensurable values (that is, *longae rectae* and *breves rectae*) or in *ultra mensuram* (perfect longas, namely, when the *cantus firmus* is mensurated after the third, fourth, or fifth *modus*) and shows agreement between the voices neither in the note values nor in the rests [text]. For the *motetus* there are six basic rhythms (the *modi*, discussed on pp. 135 ff.).

Combinations of *modi*, in the rules of the *Discantus positio vulgaris*, are still limited to contrasting the fifth mode (all perfect longas) with one of the others, or the agreement of the *modus* in all voices. "The *ochetus* is a multivoiced consonant composition above a tenor without rests [a text](?) in any one of the *modi*." Here we see that any mention of the intrinsic

---

consonus cantus, sicut cum aliquis ecclesiasticus in quinta, octava et duodecima discantatur (!). Duplex organum est idem in prosis (Couss. pausis) non autem in notis, eo quod ductae longae sunt in tenore, in discantu vero duplex et a primo diversus consonus cantus. Pure organum est, quando cuilibet notae de plano cantu ultra mensuram existenti correspondent de discantu duae notae, longa scilicet et brevis vel his aliquid aequipollens. ...Conductus autem est super unum metrum multiplex consonans cantus, qui etiam secundarias recipit consonantias. Motetus vero est super determinatas notas firmi cantus mensuratas, sive ultra mensuram diversus in notis, diversus in prosis (Couss. pausis) multiplex consonans cantus. Cujus quidem modi sunt VI....Item ochetus est super tenorem uniuscujusque modi mothetorum absque prosa (Couss. pausa) diversus et consonus cantus."

nature of the *ochetus* is missing, which makes the possibility that part of the text is missing more probable; at any rate the *truncatus*, which is not missing in any of the later definitions, is missing here.

The *Discantus positio vulgaris* does not mention the number of participating voices. The remark, however, that in the *motetus* the lengths of rests of the discant and tenor can be as long as may be desired (see above, p. 144) when both are at rest at the same time with the *tripla*, shows that the *motetus* is regarded as being at least a three-part composition. All *moteti* which are given as examples in the *Discantus positio vulgaris* are, incidentally, available in the Codex H. 196 of the Archive of the Medical Faculty at Montpellier, and are printed by Coussemaker in *L'art harmonique aux XIIᵉ et XIIIᵉ siècles* (1865). His attempts at transcription, in the light of the results of our investigations, must be regarded as questionable. See also the excellent study of Oswald Koller in the 4. *Jahrgang* of the *Vierteljahrsschrift für Musikwissenschaft* (1888, p. 1 ff.).

Anonymous VII does not explain the forms, observing only that in the *motetus* (*motellus*) the tenor is the basis and the most valued part of the whole composition; for this reason the *modus* of the entire *motetus* is to be established according to the *modus* of the tenor.[7]

On the contrary, Johannes de Garlandia again brings us something new, namely, the first mention of the *copula*:[8]

> The *copula* is very important for the discant, which no one can properly understand without it. *Copula* is the connecting link between organum and discant or, expressed in a different manner, *copula* is that which is presented in a well-measured manner in place of the unison or, as follows, *copula* is an accumulation of notes which is always made known by two parts, whenever it occurs, a turning away (*aversus*) and a return (*conversus*), each of which contains a large number of notes.

This is, admittedly, rather obscure, and the remaining passage does not help to make it more easily understandable ("unde tractus fit, ubicumque

---

[7] (Couss., *Script.* I : 379): "It should be noted that the *motellus* of whatever mode it may be ought to be judged as the tenor is judged. The reason for this is that the tenor is the foundation of the *motellus* and the worthier part, and a thing ought to be named from its worthier and nobler part."

[8] (Couss., *Script.* I : 114): "Dicto de discantu dicendum est de copula, quae multum valet ad discantum, quia discantus numquam perfecte scitur nisi mediante copula. Unde copula dicitur esse id, quod est inter discantum et organum. Alio modo dicitur copula: copula est id quod profertur recto modo aequipollente unisono. Alio modo dicitur; copula est id, ubicumque fit multitudo punctorum. Punctus ut hic sumitur est, ubicumque fit multitudo tractuum. Et ista pars dividitur in duo aequalia. Unde prima pars dicitur antecedens (Couss. aversus), secunda vero consequens (Couss. conversus), et utraque pars continent multitudinem tractuum."

fit multitudo specierum ut unisoni aut soni secundum numerum ordinatum ordine debito").*8

Even more difficult to understand is Garlandia's remark concerning
organum:[9]

Organum itself (*per se,* that is, as an individual voice) is a voice presented
according to the pattern of a certain *modus,* regardless of whether its mensuration
is *recta* or *non recta* in comparison with the discant. In the *modus non rectus,* the meter
is determined according to longa and breve, as in the first *modus,* but only *ex
contingenti* (= *per aequipollentiam?*). The organum is called *non rectum,* when it is
based upon a *cantus* which does not carry *recta mensura.* In such an organum the
tenor remains upon one note until the other voice converges with it again on a new
consonance.*9

The major portion of the treatise deals with the treatment of different
combinations of the *modi.*

Pseudo-Aristotle at first [10] differentiates only between *discantus, hoketus,*
and organum and limits the two- and three-part discant to the three
consonances of the fourth, fifth, and octave (the fourth, however, only for
the three-part combination). He then speaks of the difference between
*cum littera* (with text) and *sine littera* (without text), which until that time
had not occurred. *Cum littera* are the figures (single notes or ligatures) in
the *motelli,* etc., *sine littera* the ligatures (*neumae*) of the *conducti,* etc. Figures
*sine littera* should, if at all possible (*quoad possunt,* that is, unless tonal
repetitions make it impossible) be joined into ligatures. On the other

---

[9] (*Ibid.*): "Organum in speciali dicitur dupliciter, aut per se aut cum alio. Organum
per se dicitur id esse, quidquid profertur secundum aliquem modum rectum aut non
rectum. Rectus modus sumitur hic ille, per quem discantus profertur, non rectus dicitur
ad differentiam alicujus rectae, quae longae et breves rectae sumuntur debito modo
primo et principaliter [specialiter]. In non recto vero sumitur longa et brevis in [non]
primo modo, sed ex contingenti. Organum autem non rectum dicitur, quidquid profertur
per non rectam mensuram, ut dictum est superius. Et ejus aequipollentia tantum se
tenet in unisono usque ad finem alicujus puncti, ut secum convenit secundum aliquam
concordantiam."

[10] (Couss., *Script.* I:269a): "There are only three types of measurable music, that is,
the discant, hocket, and organum. The discant is a singing in two or three different voices,
in which there are only three consonances, that is, the *diatessaron,* the *diapente,* and the
*diapason.* Through the composition of long and short notes and according to two measurements (that is, *localem* [pitch] and *temporalem* [duration]) it remains naturally proportioned.
A note is a representation of sound according to its own mode and according to the
equivalence of one [note value] to another. Notes of this kind are set down with text [*cum
littera*] and sometimes without text [*sine littera*]; with text as in *motelli* and the like, and
without text as in the ligatures of *conducti* and the like. Those [notes] which are without
text ought to be bound one to another as much as is possible, but the propriety of this is
sometimes overlooked because of the text associated with these notes."

hand, Aristotle discusses the *hoccitatio* (hoketus) at length,[11]*[10] pointing out that this manner of performance, interspersed with rests, is always given in such a way that two voices continually take turns so that an actual gap never occurs. For this reason it requires at least two parts. While all later writers give short note values to the hocket and refer it to the sixth (fifth) *modus*, Aristotle teaches it with longa and breve rests, and rules that by placing the rest close to the body of the longa it will clearly specify whether it absorbs the beginning or the end of the perfection.

Walter Odington, who wrote later than Franco but apparently did not yet know his version of this theory, is therefore a probable representative of the time of Petrus de Cruce and of the older Franco (if he was not the author of the *Ars cantus mensurabilis*). He writes the following, speaking generally:[12]

Diaphony is the harmonious difference between lower and higher voices and is so called because it does not continually progress in consonances, but rather dissolves the preceding dissonance, which had caused aversion and dullness, by means of a consonance. It is also generally called organum.

Further on, he is more detailed:[13]

[11] (Couss., *Script.* I:281): "Disconnected [cut-up] music, that is, *hoccitatio* ('that which is commonly called hocket'—shortly before this), is that which is made of tones which are present or omitted, of course, when a *tempus* is cut out from some part of the whole. And I speak of this in two ways, for sometimes this cutting out is from some part in the beginning and sometimes from some part of the end. This is just as in writing where it [the cutting-out] is clearly marked as an abbreviation with lines and figures which take the place of a verb. Whenever a *suspirum* (here generally used for rest!) is found between two longas not in the middle but close to the side of one of the notes, that note to which it is closer gets the rest. For if a line is closer to the preceding note it is taken from the end of that note's value, and if it is nearer the following note it is taken from the beginning of that note's value. By this it must be understood that no line should be drawn midway between the two figures...for the truncation is made only from these two, by alternating the two voices as many times as one can, so that between a pause or a rest a vacuum does not remain."

[12] (Couss., *Script.* I:235): "Diaphonia (!) est concors discordia inferiorum vocum cum superioribus, sic dicta,...quia concordia sequens tollit offensionem discordiae prioris, et haec Organum communiter appellatur. (Circa istam igitur partem tria attenduntur, scilicet: consonantia...quae sunt voces consonantiae, inaequalitas temporum in carmine [=metro]...et inaequalitas temporum in vocibus consonantibus...quae notis exprimitur fitque ut his in unam melodiam concurrentibus, mira suavitate reficiatur auditus)."

[13] (*Ibid.*, p. 245): "Est autem unum genus cantus organici in quo tantum attenditur cohaerentia vocum immensurabilium et Organum purum appellatur; et hoc genus antiquissimum est, et duorum tantum (!) aliud genus est in quo attenditur consonantia vocum et mensurationum in duplici, triplici et quadruplici et dicitur Discantus, quasi duorum cantuum ad minus.... Habet quidem discantus species plures. Et si quod unus cantat, omnes per ordinem recitant vocatur hic cantus Rondellus, id est rotabilis vel

There exists a kind of polyphonic chant in which only the succession of notes, the value of which is not indicated, is of importance. This is called *organum purum* and is the very oldest form, being always two-voiced. In a second kind, which is called *discantus*, we are concerned with the consonance and mensuration of a second, third, and fourth voice; this kind is in at least two parts. *Organum (purum)* is sometimes two-part, but then again sometimes a single part, namely, when the tenor, waiting for the appearance of a new consonance, is silent. The *discantus* consists of several kinds. If that which is sung by one voice is also sung in turn by other voices, then the form is called *cantus rondellus*,*[11] that is, a round or round-singing. This occurs with a text, but also without it. If such taking over of the melody of one voice by the other does not occur, but if each voice takes its own course, then it is called *conductus*, that is, a simultaneous progression of several melodies, in harmony with each other. There is also another kind of discant, which proceeds according to the manner of the second *modus*, but more rapidly in binary ligatures and has as its beginning a longa of uncertain duration: this is called *copula*, because of the continued ligatures. Another kind of *copula* has only individual notes (*puncti*) but proceeds more slowly than the sixth *modus*; this one is so named, however, because it does without the ligatures. Another kind considers the harmony and measurement of the tones and the poetry; this is called *motetus*, that is, movement of the melody in short values (*motetus* as diminutive of *motus*).[14] The last kind of discant, which occurs with text as well as without, is that in which the voices pause in turn. This is called rightly hocket, or "chopped singing."

The special rules for composition in the individual forms which are found in Odington offer very little which is new. For instance, a remark occurs in the rules governing organum[15] that in the *moteti colorati* dissonances may sometimes be excused if they appear because of the repetition of a melodic member above the sustained tenor (!):

circumductus; et hoc vel cum littera vel sine littera sit. Si vero non alter alterius recitat cantum, sed singuli procedunt per certos punctus, dicitur Conductus, quasi plures cantus decori conducti. Estque alia species quae procedit per binariam ligaturam, sicut secundus modus, sed velocior est, et longam immensuratam accipit in principio quae copulatur; dicitur nomen habens a re. Est et alia Copula quae singulos habet punctus, per se morosior quam sextus modus, dicta per contrarium, quia non copulatur. Et alia quidem species attendit consonantiam et mensuram vocum ac carminum, quae Motetus dicitur, id est motus brevis cantilenae. Alia vero discantus species est cum littera vel sine littera in qua dum unus cantat, alter tacet, et e contrario; et hujus modi cantus truncatus dicitur a rei convenientia, qui et Hoquetus dicitur."

[14] Gerbert points to a probably more correct derivation of the word in *De cantu et musica sacra*, II:129 (*motet* as a diminutive of the French *mot*).

[15] (Couss., *Script.* I:246): "Alio modo excusatur discordia, ut in motetis coloratis, quum scilicet super certum tenorem aliqua pars cantilenae iteratur."

(Apparently this remark refers to the two imperfect consonances
$\overset{c'}{a}$ and $\overset{e'}{c}$.) *Organum purum* shall move in consonances, and if desired, in
imperfect consonances (*discordiae concorcordes*) above a tenor of only a few
(two or three) notes from the *cantus planus*, and must always begin in the
octave, fifth, or fourth (!) and end in the octave, fifth or unison.

In the *rondellus*[16] as beautiful a melody as possible should be invented
which is put into rhythm according to one of the *modi* (with or without
text), and which is presented by each voice in turn. In addition, for the
second and third voice other consonant melodies are composed in such a
manner that only two of the three voices ascend or descend at the same
time and two are always in contrary motion. These contrary voices
(although this is not expressly said), which are introduced only as a
continuation of the main idea, as today in the canon and the fugue and
earlier in Fornsete's *Sumer is icumen in*, shall proceed through all the
voices, i.e.:

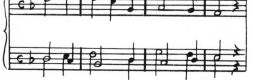

This short example suffices to illustrate the manner of composition of
the time. The two-part section (when the beginning is taken over by the
second voice) is a discant according to the rules of the time, and would
even pass today. The third voice, however (with the third group of four
measures of the first part), creates parallels (fifths) which, according to
the theory of the Franconian epoch, are not regarded as wrong, and in

[16] (Couss., *Script.* I:246): "Excogitetur cantus pulchrior qui possit et disponatur
secundum aliquem modorum praedictorum, cum littera vel sine, et ille cantus a singulis
recitetur; tamen aptentur alii cantus in duplici aut triplici procedendo per consonantias,
ut dum unus ascendit, alius descendit, vel tertius ita ut non simul descendant vel ascendant, nisi forte tamen majoris pulchritudinis, et a singulis singulorum cantus recitentur."

two-part composition are even at times admitted (*propter cantus pulchritu-dinem* [Franco], *majoris pulchritudinis* [Odington]), and are regarded as permissible even as late as Johannes de Muris (de Francia).

The *conductus* differentiates itself from the *rondellus* in the absence of imitation (voice displacement) as well as by the fact that all voices begin at the same time.*[12] Odington admits the possibility of several *modi* for the participating voices, although his example shows all voices to be in the same *modus* (the first). The short explanation of the *copula* in Garlandia is corroborated by Odington's more thorough explanation. The *copula ligata* is usually based upon some long notes from plainsong, as in organum, but also appears in three-part settings (all three voices beginning with an extended longa and then proceeding in *ligaturae binariae*). If the first longa is followed by a dot, one is not dealing with a *copula*, but a composition in the second *modus* (!).*[13] The *copula* (either the *ligata* or the *non ligata*) is always, according to Odington (p. 248), used in the ending when it is not possible to lead all voices to a satisfying conclusion (a kind of coda?).

The *moteti* are, from the very beginning, of most importance. Odington prescribes[17] that any well-known and pleasing melody may be chosen as tenor and that this should be altered to conform to the rhythm of one of the *modi*. A middle voice (the *medius cantus*) should be placed above it in the same *modus* or a *modus* which combines easily with that of the tenor. It is particularly emphasized that the *medius cantus* must be pleasing in itself (*decorus*). The third voice (the *triplum*, here called *tertius*) is frequently composed in the sixth *modus* (that is, in shorter note values); according to Odington it is not practicable to add a *tenor* in the fifth *modus* to a *medius cantus* in the sixth.

The hocket (*truncatio*) is set above a composed tenor or above a (known) melody in such a manner that the voices pause in turn; in three voices two are always singing while one pauses. For the hocket all *modi* are possible, but with Odington the sixth (short notes) is preferred. This provides an occasion for him to mention his two kinds of *signa divisionis*

---

[17] (Couss., *Script.* I:248): "*Moteti* are made with texts, in any of the modes. Some *cantus* with a suitable melody is taken for the tenor and arranged in a certain mode. The middle voice [*medius cantus*] can be made in the same mode or another mode that would combine with the tenor. The fifth mode, being in all the other [modes], can be tenor; besides the *cantus medius* may be composed in the sixth mode. The first mode is suited to the sixth, likewise the third and fourth are suited to the second, but the *cantus medius* which was to have been in the sixth mode demands a tenor in the sixth mode, even as it is found to be elsewhere. And it is most clearly to be seen that the *cantus medius* must be fitting [*decorus*]. The third voice is frequently made in the sixth mode since every voice can be made in one or the other."

(cf. p. 147) and to use them. A special kind of hocket, which should actually be called *hoketus duplex*, figurates the notes in succession:

Franco's definitions[18] agree with those of Odington. The wording corresponds so little, however, that one must assume a mutual source rather than a direct connection between the two.*14

Polyphonic compositions [discant] either have the same text for all voices, as in *chansons* and *rondelli* and a kind of church chant (organum), or they have different texts in the different voices, as in the motets, which have a *triplum* or a tenor with a special text; or, finally, one voice has a text and not the other one, as in the *conduits* and a type of church chant, misleadingly called *organum*. In all of these, with the exception of the *conduits*, the basis consists of an already composed melody which is called the tenor, because it carries (*tenet*) the discant and the discant grows out of it. In *conduit*, however, *cantus* and *discantus* are both invented.

The discant may begin in unison with the tenor or at the distance of an octave, fifth, fourth (below), major or minor third, and then proceed further in consonances with occasional inclusion of dissonances in suitable places, in such manner that when the tenor ascends, the discant descends and vice versa. It is occasionally permissible, however, because of the beauty of the melody, to lead tenor and discant in the same direction, ascending or descending. It is also to be noted that consonances must occur in all *modi* at the beginning of each measure, no matter whether the beginning value is a longa, breve, or semibreve. The values

[18] (Gerbert, *Script.* III:12 ff.; Couss., *Script.* I:130): "Discantus autem aut fit cum littera aut sine et cum littera. Si cum littera, hoc est dupliciter, cum eadem vel cum diversis. Cum eadem littera fit discantus in Cantilenis, Rondellis et cantu aliquo ecclesiastico. Cum diversis litteris fit discantus ut in Mothetis, qui habent triplum vel tenorem, quia tenor cuidam litterae aequipollet. Cum littera et sine fit discantus in Conductis et discanto aliquo ecclesiastico qui improprie Organum appellatur. Et nota, quod his omnibus est idem modus operandi, excepto in conductis, quia in omnibus aliis primo accipitur cantus aliquis prius factus, qui tenor dicitur, eo quod discantum tenet et ab ipso ortum habet, in conductis vero non sic, sed fiunt ab eodem cantus et discantus...discantus incipit in unisono cum tenore...aut in diapason...aut in diapente...aut in diatessaron...aut in ditono...aut semiditono, deinde prosequendo per consonantias, commiscendo quandoque discordantias in locis debitis, ita quod quando tenor ascendit, discantus descendat vel e converso. Et sciendum, quod tenor et discantus propter pulchritudinem cantus quandoque simul ascendit et descendit....Item intelligendum est, quod in omnibus modis utendum est semper concordantiis in principio perfectionis, licet sit longa, brevis vel semibrevis....Notandum, quod tam in discantu quam in triplicibus etc. inspicienda est aequipollentia imperfectionus longarum, brevium et semibrevium, ita quod tot perfectiones in tenore habeantur, quot in discantu vel in triplo etc. vel e converso computando tam voces rectas quam omissas usque ad paenultimam, ubi non attenditur talis mensura, sed magis est organicus ibi punctus." (This reminds one of the "closing trills" which Garlandia mentions, as well as Odington's remark about the *copula* before an ending.)

of the notes and rests must be well measured, so that the number of perfections is the same in all voices. Only the *penultima* constitutes an exception; it is not strictly measured but, in the same manner as a note of organum (*organicus punctus*, organ point), is of indefinite length.

The explanation of the *copula* agrees almost entirely with that of Odington, but while Odington declares that the *copula non ligata* is slower (*morosior*) than movement in the sixth *modus*, Franco, on the other hand, requires it to be faster (*velocior*) than movement in the fifth (the old sixth) *modus* and emphasizes as a further difference that the fifth *modus*, at will, may be written with ligatures, while the *copula non ligata* naturally may not be.

Also, regarding the *ochetus*, Franco offers some additions which Odington probably would not have ignored, had he known them. Franco says that there are as many different manners of hocket possible as there are different divisions of notes. Consequently the division of the longa (*perfecta*) into longa (*recta*) and breve or breve and longa (*recta*) results in two kinds of hocket, because in the one the longa is always omitted, and in the other, the breve:

But the longa can also be divided into two breves and (the breve) into two, three, or more semibreves, and in all these manners of division hockets can also be sung. The different possible divisions of the breve result in further deviations. This curious style seems to have been in general esteem during the 13th century, for it is called *oketi vulgares* by Franco.

Simon Tunstede (1351)*[15] copies Franco's rules almost verbatim (Couss., *Script.* IV:294 ff.), which proves that at least one hundred years after Franco the same techniques were still in use. Tunstede, however, includes a special chapter (the 44th of the IV. *principale*) treating of the artistic delivery of the tenor, which proves that the bad habit (which is already evident in the *flores* of Hieronymus de Moravia—cf. p. 141 ff.) of diminuting and coloring the plainchant tenor when discanting has developed still further. Tunstede recommends that the tenor move pleasingly up and down, if it takes care not to get in the way of the discant, "although according to the rules of the *Curia* as well as according to the usage of the French discantists and all really musical singers, the tenors of *moteti*, *rondelli*, and other *cantilenae* should actually be sung unchanged." The further remark that "in certain regions singers go contrary to nature and sing the *triplum* in tenor range" could hardly refer, as claimed by W. Nagel (*op. cit.*, I:63), to fauxbourdon, in which, as the Englishman Tunstede very likely knew for certain, the *triplum* was imagined in a lower position [19] but not sung as such. Tunstede expressly states this as an abuse with reference to the singing of *moteti* and (three-part) discant, and it can hardly be doubted that he hopes to correct the misuse of boy's voices (see pp. 120–121, Power's "to informe a chyld his counterpoint") through the use of men's voices. Another possibility would be that he wanted, as Johannes de Garlandia already had, to recognize the difference between the French and English ingredients of the *tripla* and *quadrupla* (cf. pp. 158–160). That he calls singers or composers who do this "unmusical ballad-singers" (*cantores ministeriales*) probably points to the first explanation as being the correct one.

Tunstede differentiates between two kinds of *copula*, the *imperfecta* and *perfecta*; this can be explained by the fact that at this time (1351) the difference between the *tempus perfectum* and *imperfectum* had been established. At the same time, however, further light is shed on the *copula* of the Franconian epoch. To all appearances the ligatures of the *copula* are not to be interpreted as breve-longa, but as shorter note values, similar to the multitone ligatures of the first period of mensural notation. Only in this light does it become clear how those two otherwise incompatible types of *copula* were combined. In both we are concerned with an accumulation of shorter note values. Tunstede gives this definition: [20] "*Copula* is a rapid discant with ligatures of two notes, namely, the division of the breve into two semibreves or the semibreve into two minimas, which must be brought together into one perfection." It seems that the *copula imperfecta* of Tunstede, in which two semibreves are counted as one *tempus imperfectum*, corresponds to the older *copula ligata*. In another passage [21] Tunstede ex-

[19] A practical utilization of the possibility of reducing larger distances by imagining the octave as a unison is found, outside of English discant, in the *Compendium discantus Magistri Franconis* (Couss., *Script.* I:156): "And if a note would ascend above an octave, it could be imagined in unison with the tenor." *[16]

[20] (Couss., *Script.* IV:295): "Copula est velox discantus ad invicem copulatus, sicuti est brevis partita sive fracta in semibrevibus, et semibreves in minimis, quae copulari sive computari debent ad unam perfectionem. Copularum alia perfecta alia imperfecta." "A *copula* is truly perfect with three semibreves when their durations [*valor*] are reckoned in a *tempus perfectum* of either major or minor prolation. A *copula* is imperfect with two semibreves whose values are reckoned in *tempus imperfectum* and are made to be in major or minor prolation. The notes of a *copula* can be distributed over the text in the voice of the *discantus* called *motetus* and in the other *cantilenae* according to what is seen as fitting in the process of composition. And it must be noted in all modes of discant that it is applicable to have concords as the basis of all *copulae*, accompanying with perfect and imperfect consonances....And so the *copula* will not be execrable."

[21] (*Ibid.*): "Et sciendum quod in tempore Franconis non erat mentio de modo imperfecto, nec de tempore imperfecto, neque de minima. Tunc temporis pronuntiabatur longa et brevis ita velociter ut nunc tempus perfectum."

plicitly points out that in Franco's time the value of a *perfectio* (three *tempora*) was as short as the value of a *tempus perfectum* in his time.

Anonymous IV (Couss., *Script.* I) no longer considers the special attributes of the *copula, rondellus, conductus,* and *hoketus* (he still cites *hoketi*), but treats them all as one under the collective name of organum and discantus (*conduits* appear in both categories, as "a kind of organum" and as *laici conductus* [p. 360]). For him the main problem is the number of parts concerned (*triplices* and *quadruplices*). In this connection surprising things appear, for example, the joining of voices with different tempos as *diversitas altera secundae triplicis* (!): *tempus tardum, tardius, tardissimum; velox, velocius, velocissimum; mediocre, mediocrius, mediocrissimum.* Even though the author in this passage probably went a little too far, inasmuch as the possibility of assuming three degrees of *medium tempo* does not seem too plausible (with which tempo must the comparison be made?), there actually seems to be a differentiation between different tempi (the first example of which is the old *copula*).

Many remarks of Anonymous IV are unfortunately of no value to music theory because they are based on a practice of which we have too few details to aid us in interpreting its problems. Closer investigation of existing monuments of this early art, an investigation to which Oswald Koller (*op. cit.*) has given strong impetus, may lead to more essential facts for the interpretation of the individual rules of this Anonymous.

The most extensive treatment[22]*[17] of the compositional forms of his time is found in Johannes de Grocheo's *Theoria*.[23] Grocheo, who throughout refers to music as it was practiced in Paris, cannot have written long after Franco, whom he quotes, or long before Johannes de Muris, with whom he is not familiar. This places him about 1300. Nothing is known concerning his life, although a later source indicates the possibility that he taught at the Sorbonne. His treatise contains extensive material on secular forms, which had been so greatly neglected by other theorists but which he places in the foreground. When dealing with *musica ecclesiastica*, examples of *musica vulgaris* are often used for explanations.[24] Grocheo is, furthermore, the first theorist who, thereby breaking all tradition, explicitly writes for the young members of the intelligent classes of the people. He is not too concerned with music for the church and mentions only as much about *musica ecclesiastica* as the layman would be required

---

[22] The material on Johannes de Grocheo is by the editor of the second edition of Riemann's *Geschichte,* Dr. Gustave Becking, who undertook this publication after Riemann's death in 1919.

[23] Edition in Latin and German with introductory remarks by Johannes Wolf (*SIMG* 1899–1900, pp. 65–130).

[24] For example (p. 127): "The *Credo in unum deum* is an easily flowing ascending and descending *cantus* in the manner of a *ductia*."

to know;[25] his entire treatment shows that he was more familiar with the secular forms. The *Theoria* is significant also in that it always refers to living art forms[26] and omits old theories when they are not applicable to modern music.[27]

When classifying music Grocheo rejects separation of it into *musica mensurabilis* and *immensurabilis*. *Musica plana* is only *non ita praecise mensurata*, but not *immensurabilis*. In Paris three principal styles of music are in use: the simple (*simplex*) of the people (*civilis, vulgaris*); the composed, regular, canonic (*composita, regularis, canonica*) mensural music, which in each case according to its species is preferred for secular purposes in intelligent circles, or in the church or by country folk; and finally the (ecclesiastical) music which appears as a result of the coming together of the first two kinds and is meant for the church service. Within the category of popular music differentiation is again made as to vocal and instrumental forms. The first is divided into *cantus* and *cantilenae*. *Cantus gestualis, coronatus*, and *versiculatus* are further subdivisions which were brought into connection with the *chansons de geste, sirventes*, and *vers* of the troubadours by Johannes Wolf. *Cantilenae* are the *cantilena rotunda, stantipes*, and *ductia*.

The number of verses of which the species of *cantus* consists depends upon the amount of material and the desires of the author. Only in the *cantus coronatus*, which moves in nothing but longas and perfect notes,[28] is the number of verses established as seven.[29] The verses here, however, have inner subdivisions.[30] A similar situation exists in the *versicularis*. The *cantus gestualis* has short verses with the same rhyme scheme, and the music also repeats itself.[31] At times the final verse is different. The *canti* are, above all, differentiated according to their textual contents; the prize belongs to the *cornatus*. The *cantilena* has the same section, called the refrain (*refractorium, responsorium*), at the beginning and at the end.[32] In between are the *additamenta* (additions), which in the *rondellus* agree both in music and words with the refrain.[33] Long note values are characteristic

[25] Prout usui civium necessaria sit.

[26] Therefore two-part organum is only mentioned in the historical summary.

[27] (Page 100): "This type of singing (precisely measured) is used by the moderns in Paris. The ancients divided this kind of singing into many parts but we divide it, following modern usage, into three [*motetus, organum, hoquetus*]."

[28] (Page 91): "Ex omnibus longis et perfectis efficitur."

[29] "Vel eo circa" Grocheo limits his statement himself on p. 120.

[30] (Page 94): "*Versus*...which are made by *punctis* and *concordantiis.*"

[31] (Page 94): "Idem etiam cantus debet in omnibus versibus reiterari."

[32] (Page 92): "Cantilena...ad modum circuli in se ipsam reflectitur et incipit et terminatur in eodem."

[33] "In the *rotundellus* they sound in concord together and rhyme with the *responsorium* (that is, the appendages [*additamenta*])." On page 92 the *rotundellus* is defined as a *cantilena* which contains only one *cantus* which is different from the refrain. (Cujus partes unum habent diversum cantum a cantu responsorii...et longo tractu cantatur.)*18

of this species, which was performed in Normandy by young men and women on festive occasions. In the *stantipes* and *ductia*[34] the *additamenta* partially agree in rhyme and music with the refrain but sometimes differ from them. Together the *refractorium* and *additamenta* constitute one *versus*; the number of verses depends upon the subject matter and the author's desire. Both forms differ because of the fact that the performance of the *stantipes* is difficult (*difficultas*), while the *ductia* has series of tones which easily and quickly ascend and descend.[35] The performance of the *stantipes*, as well as that of the *cantus coronatus*, is followed by an *exitus* on the viol, which is called *modus* by the players.[36]

The section dealing with instrumental folk music again speaks of the *stantipes* and *ductia*. After the declaration that a good artist should be able to play all *canti* and *cantilenae* on his viol, only those forms which usually play a significant part during the festivities of the rich are further discussed: besides the *cantus coronatus* (here also as an instrumental piece) are the *stantipes* and *ductia*. They are called textless (*illitteratus*) in this passage. Although the human voice is able to perform them, they do not have *littera* and *dictamen*.[37] The following differentiation is important: *ductia* is a composition measured in a fitting meter. Its rhythms determine the movements of those who execute them [the rhythms] according to the rules of the dance.[38][*19] The melodic structure of the *stantipes* is complicated.[39] The beat [*percussione*], which we met in the *ductia*, is missing here.

[34] (Page 95): "In the *ductia* and *stantipes* some are different [from the refrain or *responsorium*] and some are alike. Also, in the *ductia* and *stantipes* the *responsorium*, together with the *additamenta*, are called *versus*, whose number is not fixed, but determined by the wishes of the writer and the abundance of the content."

[35] (Page 93): "Ductia vero est cantilena levis et velox in ascensu et descensu."

[36] (Page 122): "In viella post cantum coronatum vel stantipedem exitus, quem modum viellatores appellant."

[37] (Page 97): "I say without a text, even if it were performed by the human voice and represented by notes, for it cannot be written with a text, since it has neither text nor rhyme." On the contrary, on page 93 the *consonantia dictaminis* of the *stantipes* was mentioned. Compare also the *copia sententiae* in note 34 above.

[38] (Page 97): "The *ductia* is a composition without text but measured with a fitting beat [*percussione*]. I say with a fitting beat because the beats order themselves according to the movements of the executants and lead the understanding of the people through graceful movement in that art which one calls the dance, measuring their movements in *ductiae* and *choreis* (round-dances)."

[39] (Pp. 97–99): "Stantipes...habens difficilem concordantiarum discretionem per puncta determinatus...percussione, quae est in ductia, caret et solum punctorum distinctione cognoscitur. Partes autem ductiae et stantipedis puncta communiter dicuntur. Punctus autem est ordinata aggregatio concordantiarum harmoniam facientium ascendendo et descendendo duas habens partes in principio similes, in fine differentes, quae clausum et apertum communiter appellantur. Dico autem duas habens partes etc. ad similitudinem duarum linearum, quarum una sit maior alia. Maior enim minorem

The division into *puncti* which is also to be found in the *ductia*, is here the sole governing factor:[40]

The puncta is an orderly succession of concordances which join together to become a melody in ascending and descending manner. It consists of two parts which are similar in the beginning, but differ as far as the ending is concerned. The different endings are generally called half- and complete endings [*clausum* and *apertum*]. I say, however, that it has two parts, etc., which are like two lines of which one is larger than the other, since the larger one includes the smaller one and differs from the smaller one because of its ending. The number of *puncti* in the *ductia* is fixed as three, in reference to the three perfect consonances. There sometimes appear compositions, called *notae*, which have four *puncti* and may be based upon the imperfect *ductia* or *stantipes*. There also exist some *ductia* having four *puncti*.

Actual mensural music is polyphonic. Three species are to be observed: *motetus, organum,* and *hoquetus.* The *motetus* means for the festivities of learned people and art lovers what the *rotundellus* means to the common people. Each of the three or four voices has its own text, but the tenor may appear without a text. Two voices at a time always create one of the perfect consonances, the fourth, fifth, or octave.[41] The voice-leading, which reminds one of fauxbourdon, has already been mentioned on page 123. A *quadruplum* can also be added to the tenor, *motetus*,[42] and *triplum*, so that during rests or truncations of other voices consonances may sound.[43] Organum, as Grocheo defines it, carries a simultaneously recited text in all voices. If it is to be used for the festivities and banquets of the learned and rich, a new tenor is invented.[44] This kind of organum is called *conductus.*

---

claudit et est fine differens a minori. Numerum vero punctorum in ductia ad numerum 3 consonantiarum perfectarum attendentes ad 3 posuerunt. Sunt tamen aliquae notae vocatae 4 punctorum, quae ad ductiam vel stantipedem imperfectam reduci possunt. Sunt etiam aliquae ductiae 4 habentes puncta."

[40] According to this, the *stantipes* here can scarcely be meant as a dance. Cf. Hans Joachim Moser in *ZfMW* II, 4, pp. 194 ff.

[41] (Page 106): "Motetus vero est cantus ex pluribus compositus habens plura dictamina vel multimodam discretionem syllabarum, utrobique harmonialiter consonans...(tenor) in aliquibus habet dictamina et in aliquibus non...dico utrobique harmonialiter consonans, eo quod quilibet debet cum alio consonare secundum aliquam perfectarum consonantiarum, puta secundum diatessaron vel diapente vel diapason."

[42] The writer suspects (*Handbuch der Musikgeschichte* I, 2, 1905, p. 210) that the form derived its name from this designation of the voice. In the section in Grocheo dealing with the various voices, for *motetus* or *motellus* we also have *commotellus*. See p. 177 and note 46.[*20]

[43] "In many a fourth voice is added, in order that it may preserve the consonance, while one of the other voices pauses or by conjunct motion goes upward, or two voices reciprocally truncate one another [cut one another off]."

[44] (Page 107): "Organum as it is here understood is a harmonious combination of voices which has only one text and one differentiation of syllables. I say only one text

The choppy manner of presentation of the *hoquetus* corresponds to the taste of rural and young people. Actually, two voices are sufficient. Because of the *consonantia perfecta*, a third voice, the *duplum*, can be added which does not follow the manner of the other parts. Much depends upon the accomplishment of the performer (*decantare*), in leading it pleasantly in fifths and octaves with the tenor.[45]*[21] The composition of these species starts with the tenor, which, whether it be merely made over (*ordinari*) or newly composed (*componi*), must uphold the measure and mensuration (*modum et mensuram*). In organum the *modus* is often changed, if possible, while in motets and other forms one *modus* is more or less utilized. Textual difficulties, as in the case of too many syllables in one of the simultaneous texts, are conquered by the addition of breves and semibreves to the part which is lacking.[46]

The treatment of *musica ecclesiastica* is difficult, Grocheo explains, because of different customs in different churches. He discusses it only briefly, therefore, and speaks of its many forms for his lay readers only. He often refers to secular types, especially to *cantus coronatus, stantipes,* and *ductia,* for explanations. Most of the space is devoted to liturgical questions and the question of modes. In this connection we find, among other things, the remark that the ecclesiastical modes are important for *musica ecclesiastica* alone, and have no significance at all for folk music and actual mensural music.[47]

Compared with the abundance of explanation in Grocheo, the terse remarks of other theorists fade into the background. Marchettus of Padua

------

because all the voices base themselves upon this single differentiation of syllables. This kind of singing is made in two ways. There is one which is based upon a certain church chant; it is sung in churches and other sacred places for the praise of God and the honor of the Most High. This kind of singing is mostly called organum. The other one is based upon a *cantus* which is newly composed for this purpose. It is customarily sung at banquets and festivals of the learned and rich. Since the name is derived from its purpose, this kind of singing is called *conductus.*" Johannes Wolf has pointed out that in the Middle Ages *conductus* also meant banquet or meal.

[45] (Page 109): "The *duplum* is that part which produces dismembered sections above the tenor, and occasionally has the relation of a fifth and sometimes an octave with it, which requires much discretion of the performer of this part."

[46] (Page 110): "In the composition of organum one resolves to change the *modus* often, but in the composition of *motelli* and other forms one strives to preserve the unity of the mode. And since there are several texts on hand in *motelli,* one can, in case one of the parts exceeds in numbers of syllables, add breves and semibreves to the other part or parts to make them even."

[47] (Page 114): "The *cantus* (that is, the simple and measured *cantus*) is neither regulated according to the rules of the modes [*toni*], nor can it be measured in this way. And if it is measured in this way, one does not call this a mode [*tonus*] with which one can [measure], and it is never mentioned." (Page 115): "For through the modes we do not recognize popular music, as for example, the *cantilena,* the *ductia,* and the *stantipes.*"

(in the introduction to his *Pomerium in arte musicae mensuratae*, in Gerbert, *Script.* III:179) makes it easy for himself and for us by dispensing at once with explanations of special uses of organum and discant with the remark that "Master Franco has himself enlarged upon these at sufficient length."

The already mentioned compilation treatise of Robert de Handlo (Couss., *Script.* I) remarks (p. 402) when dealing with the fifth (that is, the pre-Franconian sixth) *modus* (consisting of nothing but breves and semibreves) only that it can be used for all *hoketi, rondelli, balladae* (!), *coreae* (!), *cantifractus* (variations?), *estampetae* (!), and *fioriturae* (!). The *Speculum musicae* of Johannes de Muris (Couss., *Script.* II:394), the identity of which our tenth chapter will discuss, and which must be dated around the middle of the 14th century, adds the *fugae* to these new names of musical forms but again offers only an excerpt from Franco with reference to the same. That Petrus de Cruce is called a successor of Franco (p. 401) is contrary to the testimony of the much older Anonymous IV and is probably simply an error (perhaps he is being confused with Petrus Picardus).

Aegidius de Murino (Couss., *Script.* III:124), who is much later but probably still belongs to the 14th century, names the forms *ballada simplex* and *duplex, vironellus simplex* and *duplex* and *rondellus. Vironellus* is probably the versified species (with refrain verse) which is otherwise known as the *virelai*,[48] as is apparent from its similarity to the *ballade* and *rondeau*. We can only guess at the meaning of what the author says concerning the musical structure of these three song species (unfortunately!), since with his usual brevity he presupposes a thorough knowledge of terminology. The term *clausum* (complete cadence? *clausula?*) recalls Anonymous IV (Couss., *Script.* I:57):

> Primo faciamus clausum vel punctum in communi horum, hoc est secundum ultimam partem.
>
> (At first we must make a *clausum* or a *punctum* at the same time, and this at the second and last part [unison on the *finalis*?].)

It even recalls Johannes de Garlandia (Couss., *Script.* I:117):

> Item loco coloris in regione cujuslibet pone cantilenam notam copulam vel punctum vel descensum vel ascensum alicujus instrumenti (see the theory of the *copula*, p. 164 above) vel clausum lay.
>
> (Likewise the place of the color is chosen at discretion in that area among the notes of the *cantilena* after the *copula*, either at the *punctum*, or in descending or ascending with some instruments, or at the *clausum lay*.)

[48] Perhaps the enigmatic *lovireli* (*lo vireli*) in Elias Salomonis (1274; Gerbert, *Script.* III:21), which apparently has some connection with a frivolous, secular vocal type, refers to the *virelai*.

Apparently we are concerned in all three passages with a well-known technical term used by practicing musicians—presumably secular musicians—which is in contrast to the term *apertum*. The supposition arises out of the context of Aegidius de Murino's work that *apertum* means a cadence which is not complete (half cadence, *distinctio*), concluding on another than the final tone, and that *clausum*, on the other hand, means the close on the *finalis* (see also p. 176, Johannes de Grocheo). Aegidius rules that[49]

A simple *ballada* (dancing song) must have the following structure: in the first part a half-cadence and a complete cadence, in the second part only a complete cadence. The *duplex ballada* receives in the first as well as in the second part a half-cadence and a complete cadence. The simple *virelai* has a half-cadence in its first part and a complete cadence in the second; the double (extended) *virelai* has in both parts a half-cadence and a complete cadence (*dimidium* is apparently a term for "part" and is to be added in the beginning to "primo.") The *rondeau* has a half-cadence in the first part (on e when C is the *finalis*; and also on e when a is the *finalis*) and a complete cadence in the second part.

Of course what we understand as a half-cadence and a complete cadence is not exactly what is meant here (as the definition of a half-cadence on the tenth for a *rondeau* in C shows). Half-cadences on tones other than the final (which have always been characteristic of Gregorian chant) have the same meaning as far as formal logic is concerned, namely, as an indication of a deviation from the final by remaining on another tone.

It is striking to note the special prominence of C (major) and A (minor) as finals for the *rondeau* (and probably not only for this form), which points clearly enough to the breakthrough of modern keys [*Tonarten*] in secular music. Zarlino (*Opere*, p. 411) says explicitly that most of the *balli* and *danzi* of his time are written in C major, and that this key is therefore called *modo lascivo*. We do not know how far back this preference for major keys in secular music goes. Isolated remarks by theorists, characteristics of musical instruments, and some documents of secular art (the dance songs of Nithart and other Minnesingers, troubadour melodies, as well as the "Sumer is icumen in") allow us to believe that it goes back to a distant epoch.

Aegidius de Murino also left us (pp. 124–127) rules concerning the composition of three- to five-part *moteti*. We unfortunately cannot gather

[49] (Page 128): "Isto modo debet fieri Ballada simplex: in primo (dimidio) fac apertum et clausum, et ultimo fac clausum solummodo. Item Ballada duplex habet apertum et clausum ante et retro. Item Vironellus simplex habet ante apertum et clausum retro. Item Vironellus duplex habet dimidium (!) apertum et clausum ante et apertum et clausum retro. Item Rondellus habet apertum ante, quando finitur in UT, et debet esse decima (!); et quando finitur in LA, debet esse quinta (!), et retro clausum."

much more from them other than that the tenor, *motetus* ( =alto), contra-tenor, *triplum*, and *quadruplum* must nicely harmonize with each other. On the other hand there is an interesting remark[50] to the effect that the text of the *motetus* must be divided into four parts; the remaining remarks are much too vague to enable us to draw any positive conclusions (for instance, the rules concerning the coloration of individual voices).

[50] (Couss., *Script*. III: 125): "After the *cantus* is made and set in order (!) then take the words which are to be in the motet and divide them into four parts. And so divide the melody into four parts that the first part of the words may be arranged above the first part of the melody as best you can, and so proceed to the end. When it is necessary to stretch many notes above a few words, or many words in a little time, let these be fitted together in any way that you can."

## APPENDIX

FOOTNOTE 1: (*Ibid*., p. 116): "Situs proprius quadrupli in triplici diapason et infra, quod vix in opere ponitur, nisi in instrumentis, ita quod longae in primo modo concordant cum omnibus praedictis, scilicet tribus cantibus praepositis, sive in concordantia simplici, sive composita. Sed proprietas praedicta vix tenetur in aliquibus, quod patet in quadruplicibus Magistri Perrotini per totum in principio magni voluminis.". . . (Couss., *Script*. I: 342): "Quae quadrupla optima reperiuntur et proportionata et in colore conservata ut manifeste ibidem patet. Sed quadruplum communiter sumptum, de quo ad praesens intendimus, modum tripli in altitudine et gravitate recipit, quamvis aliquantum excedat in aliquibus locis. Et sic tale quadruplum cum tribus sibi associatis ab aliquibus duplex cantus nuncupatur, quia duo invicem nunc cum uno, nunc cum reliquo audientibus tamquam esset duplex discantus. Percipitur tamen in instrumentis maxime completis. . . . Unde prima regula est, quod si sit de primo modo, ponendae sunt omnes longae in concordantia cum omnibus longis trium subpositorum ut diximus, suo modo. Alia regula: si ascendis cum uno vel descendis una proportione, vel duas ascende postea vel descende cum reliquo, et sic mutando descensionem vel ascensionem nunc cum uno nunc cum reliquo, donec veniat ad finem."

FOOTNOTE 7: (Couss., *Script*. I: 379): "Notandum est quod motellus, cujuscunque modi sit, debet judicari de eodem modo de quo est tenor. Et ratio est quia tenor est fundamentum motelli et dignior pars, et a digniori et nobiliori debet res nominari."

FOOTNOTE 10: (Couss., *Script*. I: 269a): "Tria tantummodo sunt genera per quae tota mensurabilis musica discurrit, scilicet discantus, hoketus et organum. Discantus vero est aliquorum diversorum generum cantus duarum vocum sive trium in quo trina tantummodo consonantia, scilicet diatessaron, diapente et diapason per compositionem longarum breviumque figurarum, secundum dualem mensuram (sc. localem et temporalem) naturaliter proportionata manet." (269b): "Figura est repraesentatio soni secundum suum modum et secundum aequipollentiam sui aequipollentis; sed hujusmodi figurae aliquando ponuntur cum littera, aliquando sine. Cum littera vero, ut in motellis et similibus; sine littera, ut in neumatibus conductorum et simisimilia. . . illae quae sunt sine littera, debent prout possunt amplius ad invicem ligari. Sed hujus proprietas aliquando omittitur propter litteram his figuris associatam."

FOOTNOTE 11: (Couss., *Script*. I: 281): "Resecata musica, id est ipsa hoccitatio ('hokectus vulgariter appellatur'—shortly before this) est illa quae fit secundum rectam vocem et omissam, videlicet quando ab aliqua perfectione tempus sit resecatum. Et hoc dico dupliciter, nam aliquando a parte principii fit resecatio, aliquando a parte finis; prout in scriptura plane sub breviloquio per tractus et figuras declaratur; verbi gratia: quandocunque inter duas longas figuras suspirium (here generally used for rest!) non in medio, sed juxta latus alicujus figurae positum invenitur, illa figura cujus tractus propinquior erit, suspirium obtinet; utpote si tractus propinquior figurae praecedentis extiterit a parte finis ejusdem sumetur, si autem propinquior figurae subsequentis extiterit, tunc a parte principii sumatur ejusdem ut hic: Et per hoc intelligendum est quod nullus tractus inter duas figuras medium tenere debet....Sed a duobus tantummodo fit truncatio, alternando unusquisque vocem suam, tam rectam quam omissam, ita quod inter eos pausula vel aliquod suspirium majus et minus non remaneat vacuum."

FOOTNOTE 17: (Couss., *Script.* I:248): "Moteti fiunt cum littera in aliquo modorum. Sumatur aliquis cantus notus pro tenore, aptus melo, et in certo modo disponatur. Medius cantus potest fieri in eodem modo vel alio, prout competens fuerit tenori. Nam quintus modus omnibus aliis potest esse tenor praeterquam in sexto modo compositis cantibus mediis. Primus etiam modus aptus est sexto, similiter secundus, tertius et quartus sunt secundo modo apti; verum medius cantus, cum fuerit de sexto, exigit sibi tenorem de sexto, etsi aliter aliquando reperiatur. Et maxime visendus est medius cantus ut per se sit decorus. Tertius vero cantus frequenter fit in sexto modo, cum omnis cantus fieri possit in uno aliquo."

FOOTNOTE 19: (Couss., *Script.* I:156): "Et nota quando volueris ascendere supra diapason, imaginabis (!) te esse cum tenore in unisono."

FOOTNOTE 20: (Couss., *Script.* IV:295): "...Copula vero perfecta est cum tres semibreves vel valor sive sint de majori prolatione sive de minori, pro tempore perfecto computantur. Copula autem imperfecta est cum duae semibreves vel valor computantur pro tempore imperfecto utrum fuerint de majori prolatione vel de minori....Copularum figurae distribui possunt super litteram in discantu motetorum et aliarum cantilenarum prout decens videbitur componenti. Et notandum est quod in omnibus modis discantandi utendum est semper concordantiis in principio copularum, prosequendo deinde per consonantias perfectas et imperfectas...et sic copula dampnabilis non erit."

FOOTNOTE 24: (Page 127): "*Credo in unum deum* est cantus leviter ascendens et descendens ad modum ductiae...."

FOOTNOTE 27: (Page 100): "Et isto cantu (sc. praecise mensurato) moderni Parisiis utuntur. Quem antiqui pluribus modis diverserunt, nos vero secundum usum modernorum in 3 generaliter dividimus...."

FOOTNOTE 30: (Page 94): "Versus...qui ex pluribus punctis et concordantiis efficitur."

FOOTNOTE 33: "In rotundello vero consonant et concordant in dictamine cum responsorio (sc. additamenta) (p. 94). On page 92 the *rotundellus* is defined as a *cantilena* which contains only one *cantus* which is different from the refrain. (Cuius partes non (Wolf: unum) habent diversum cantum a cantu responsorii...et longo tractu cantatur....)"

FOOTNOTE 34: (Page 95): "In ductia vero et stantipede differunt quaedem (sc. additamenta ab refractorio) et alia consonant et concordant. In ductia etiam et stantipede responsorium cum additamentis versus appellatur, quorum numerus non est determinatus, sed secundum voluntatem compositoris et copiam sententiae augmentatur."

FOOTNOTE 37: (Page 97): "Dico autem illitteratus, quia, licet in voce humana fieri possit et per figuras repraesentari, non tamen per litteras scribi potest, quia littera et dictamine caret."

FOOTNOTE 38: (Page 97): "Est autem ductia sonus...cum decenti percussione mensuratus. Dico...cum recta percussione, eo quod ictus eam mensurant et motum facientis
et excitant animum hominis ad ornate movendum secundum artem, quam ballare
vocant, et eius motum mensurant in ductiis et choreis (round-dances)."

FOOTNOTE 43: (Page 108): "In aliquibus vero quartus additur, ut dum unus trium
pausat vel ordinatim ascendit, vel duo ad invicem se truncant, quartus consonantiam
servet."

FOOTNOTE 44: (Page 107): "Organum prout hic sumitur, est cantus ex pluribus
harmonice compositus, unum tantum habens dictamen vel discretionem syllabarum. Dico
autem tantum habens unum dictamen, eo quod omnes cantus fundantur super unam
discretionem syllabarum. Cantus autem iste dupliciter variatur. Est enim quidam, qui
supra cantum determinatum, puta ecclesiasticum, fundatur. Qui in ecclesiis vel locis
sanctis decantatur ad dei laudem et reverentiam summitatis. Est cantus iste appropriato
nomine organum appellatur. Alius autem fundatur supra cantum cum eo compositum.
Qui solet in conviviis et festis coram litteratis et divitibus decantari. Et ex his nomen
trahens appropriato nomine conductus appellatur."

FOOTNOTE 45: (Page 109): "Duplum vero est, qui supra tenorem minutam facit
abscisionem et cum eo aliquoties in diapente consonat et aliquando in diapason proportione, ad quod multum juvat bona discretio decantantis."

FOOTNOTE 46: (Page 110): "In componendo vero organum modorum alternationem
quam plurimum faciunt, sed in componendo motellos et alia modorum unitatem magis
servant....Et cum in motellis plura sint dictamina, si unum syllabis vel dictionibus aliud
excedat, potes unum per appositionem brevium et semibrevium alteri coaequare."

FOOTNOTE 47: (Page 114): "Cantus (sc. civilis et mensuratus) autem iste per toni
regulas forte non vadit nec per eas mensuratur. Et adhuc, si per eas mensuratur, non
dicunt modum per quem nec de eo faciunt mentionem." (Page 115): "Non enim per
tonum cognoscimus cantum vulgarem, puta cantilenam, ductiam, stantipedem...."

FOOTNOTE 50: (Couss., Script. III:125): "Postquam cantus est factus et ordinatus (!),
tunc accipe verba quae debent esse in moteto et divide ea in quatuor partes, et sic divide
cantum in quatuor partes, et (ut) prima pars verborum componatur super primam
partem cantus, sicut melius potest, et sic procede usque in finem; et aliquando est necesse
extendere multas notas super pauca verba (vel multa verba) super pauca tempora,
quousque perveniatur ad complementum."

CHAPTER X

# The Restitution of Even Meters.
# Marchettus of Padua.    Johannes de Muris.

ON SEVERAL occasions we had the opportunity to observe that even during the 12th and 13th centuries instrumental music underwent a lively and multiform development, since music theorists repeatedly emphasized the narrower limits of vocal music in comparison with those of instrumental music. It is unfortunate that nothing remains of instrumental music prior to the middle of the 15th century.*[1] On this basis, the belief has often been expressed that instrumental music only gradually severed itself from absolute dependence upon vocal music. Several testimonials since Hucbald's time prove the opposite, however, and force us to conclude that up to the exclusion of instruments (with the exception of the organ) from participation in the music of the church (during the 13th century), this aspect of musical activity was vast and diverse. In the beginning of the 13th century instruments embellished simple settings with passages and trills in the same manner as at the beginning of the 17th century, which Michael Praetorius has so vividly reported.

It can hardly be doubted that throughout the entire Middle Ages independent instrumental notation existed, for it has been proved (cf. *Studien zur Geschichte der Notenschrift*, pp. 28 ff.) that Latin letter notation,[1] which appeared during the 10th and 11th centuries in theoretical treatises, was used also for instruments. In the beginning of the 14th century Johannes de Muris (in Gerbert, *Script.* III:214) vouches for the existence of instrumental notation when he says, "Habent sua propria signa notarum" (They have their own signs for notes), a remark which prob-

---

[1] It appears that I will have to relinquish the name of "Frankish" letter notation which I used in my *Studien zur Geschichte der Notenschrift* for A B C̑ D E F G̑ A (in the order of a major scale), since I found a reference in W. Christ (*Beiträge zur kirchlichen Litteratur der Byzantiner* [1870]) that the second below is absolutely necessary to the first ecclesiastical mode (on D) (cf. p. 32 of the *Studien*). As seen in the system of the ecclesiastical modes, this gives a natural explanation for beginning on C in the lower register of the organ and *rotta*. The latest research (cf. p. 20) seems to give us enough indication, however, to assume an independent north-European origin for this system of notation.

183

ably refers to all of the previously mentioned wind instruments (*organa, tibiae, cornua, siringae, flaiota*) and stringed instruments (*citharae, psalteria, organistrum, monochordum-clavichord,* and similar types); he possibly also is referring to the string instruments enumerated from then on:

Chordalia, quae solum auditu discernuntur, temperantur autem per consonantias diapason, diatessaron et diapente et per diversas digitorum interpositiones artifices ipsorum formant sibi tonos et semitonos.

(String instruments, which can be distinguished only by the ear, are tuned by means of the consonances of the *diapason, diatessaron,* and *diapente,* and by the skillful use of the fingers tones and semitones are formed.)

The glowing description by the 14th-century writer Arnulphus de S. Gilleno (Gerbert, *Script.* III:316–18) of the secular music of his time [2] increases our regret that nothing more of this secular art remains than the melodies of the troubadours, *trouvères,* and minnesingers, who today claim more and more of our attention. The melodic beauty of these melodies becomes astonishingly apparent when their rhythm is made solely dependent on the meter.[3][*2] Arnulph remarks that "Among those who cultivate secular music there are also some clerics who invent the most difficult musical passages on the organ (*in organicis instrumentis*) which would hardly be possible for the human singing voice, and who show marvellous proofs of native creative ability." Hieronymous de Moravia (*ca.* 1260), whose description of the *rubeba* and the *viella* (Couss., *Script.* I:152 ff.) is of such importance for the history of stringed instruments, gives precise instructions for tuning and the development of fingering

[2] (Gerbert, *Script.* III:316): "In truth a second difference is apparent in these lay singers, who may be expert in the whole art of music, but led by zeal for its sweetness, they offer their delicate ears to any kind of music. In fervently loving and associating with musicians, just as a bee is convinced by the sweetness of honey and with desire more eagerly pursues the flower spread before him, so do they collect their harvest, and exercising frequently in every musical kind, they become more expert, use and industry supplying what art they lack. And we see some clergymen who invent the most difficult musical passages on the organ [*in organicis instrumentis*], which the human voice would hardly dare to try, and through some miracle they bring out a prodigy of composed music born in themselves. The others, indeed, who record what is done and handed down [do this] hardly less laudably, and now and then the industry of the inventor acknowledges the industry of the recorder." He is even more enthusiastic in his hymn of praise for the singers, particularly for the female singers (pp. 317–318), which appears to be almost too glowing an admiration for a schoolmaster in holy orders!

[3] Cf. Paul Runge, *Die Sangesweisen der Colmarer Handschrift und die Liederhandschrift Donaueschingen* (1896). Through this publication, which merits highest praise, the treasure of available minnesinger melodies has grown considerably (up to that time only the melodies from the Jena Minnesinger codex and a number of melodies of Nithart's songs in the fourth volume of F.H. v.d. Hagen's *Minnesänger,* 1838–56, were available). Compare also my critical study, *Die Melodik der Minnesänger,* in *Musikalisches Wochenblatt* (1897), as well as my choral arrangements of Nithart's melodies.

technique (actually the first violin "method"). He points out that "special tunings for the *viella* become necessary for the execution of secular (*laici*) and other highly irregular melodies, which often want to run through the entire hand (the Guidonian solmisation scale)." Johannes de Garlandia (*ca.* 1225) points out the greater agility and richer chromaticism of secular melodies (Couss., *Script.* I:115) and stresses, on the other hand, that instruments are used for the execution of *quadrupla* of higher position (p. 116), speaking especially of instrumental passages inserted to replace the *color* of the singing voice (concerning chromaticism in instruments, see the *Introductio* following Garlandia, Couss., *Script.* I:166, as well as Anonymous IV, *ibid.*, p. 338).

Furthermore, if we keep in mind that since the end of the 15th century and the beginning of the 16th we meet instrumental tablatures simultaneously in the most widely separated cultured lands of Europe, and that these tablatures used several different systems of tonal designation but corresponding methods of notating rhythmical elements, we may readily come to the conclusion that this manner of designating note values must have been centuries old.*3

Therefore it was hardly by chance that of the many attempts made from the end of the 13th century to add smaller note values to the three values of *musica mensurabilis* which had been originally taken over from *musica plana*, only those found favorable reception which showed a striking relationship to the rhythmic values of instrumental tablatures. These tablature values are:

| | |
|---|---|
| ● (♦) | for the long note (whole note) |
| &#124; | for its half |
| ⌐ | for its quarter |
| ⌐̄ | for its eighth |
| ⌐̿ | for its sixteenth |

These conform entirely to the stems and flags pointing upwards which were given to smaller note values starting with the semibreve from the beginning of the 14th century:

| | |
|---|---|
| ♦ | semibreve |
| ♦ | minima |
| ♦ | semiminima |

A peculiarity of all instrumental notation around 1500, that is, at the time when mensural designations were brought to their height of artistic subtlety, is that everywhere and always each note is equal to half of the value of the next larger species; that is, there is no knowledge whatsoever of perfection, alteration, etc., or of ligatures and the entire apparatus of mensural music. It therefore appears entirely natural that instrumental music, even during the 12th and 13th centuries, did not subject itself to vocal music's one-sided limitation of triple meter, since the undoubtedly ancient distinction between walked dances (round dances in duple meter) and jumped dances (skip-dances in triple meter) would have forbidden this limitation. Even though actual proof is lacking, it is nevertheless highly probable that the reintroduction of duple meters into (ecclesiastical) art music (around 1300) took place without sensation and without fame for its originator, since it did not constitute any actual innovation but only a restoration which could not have been avoided for any length of time. Nothing else was necessary but that ecclesiastical vocal music should assimilate a small portion of the practice of instrumental music, and in general, that of the secular music of the time. Without doubt ecclesiastical vocal music was finally unable to resist the penetration of the fully developed and strongly influential elements of duple meter, which had made themselves known in instrumental music, in unsophisticated folk melodies, and in the artistic melody of the knightly minstrels (arising from this folk practice) which had no need of the artifice of mensuration.

Since tablatures, as far back as we are able to trace them, use the bar line, i.e., a clearly visible demarcation every two or three beat-groups, it is doubtful whether the older tablatures ever had a time signature—at any rate it was not absolutely necessary.[4]*[4] It is very probable, however, that practical instructions for playing instruments, and introductions for the comprehension of tablatures, differentiated between duple and triple meters; this could have been readily accomplished by a simple remark covering duple or triple number (two beats, three beats).

Marchettus of Padua, the earliest writer to discuss *tempus imperfectum* or duple meter, which had again found favor (*Pomerium in arte musicae mensuratae* [1309],*[5] in Gerbert, *Script.* III: 193), already knew of different manners of practical designation, namely:

I = *Tempus perfectum*          II = *Tempus imperfectum*

and:     3 = Triple Meter          2 = Duple Meter

[4] Since tablatures (also the German organ tablature) do not use different mensurations, this makes the transcription of pieces in perfect meter (with perfections, imperfections, alterations, etc.) from the mensural notation in the tablature a delicate and dangerous proposition. For this reason Virdung in his *Musica getutscht* (1511) recommends to beginners "not to tabulate any song other than that which is *de tempore imperfecto.*" This wise warning of the master to his pupils not to begin tasks which they are incapable of realizing has been misinterpreted in H. Löwenfeld's dissertation *Leonhard Kleber und sein Orgeltabulaturbuch* (Berlin, 1897), who assumed that it meant the ignoring or putting lesser emphasis on triple meters by the organ masters.

He knew of other designations, which were used by other composers at their discretion, but he does not describe them (!). Among them there were probably those which later on were universally accepted:

$$\bigcirc = \textit{Tempus perfectum}$$
$$\mathsf{C} = \textit{Tempus imperfectum}$$

It seems that the differentiation between perfect and imperfect mensuration through time signatures appeared almost simultaneously in different places and among different authors. One cannot but be convinced that this is an example of secular music passing on some of its characteristics to the music of the church.*6 There is no reason to repeat the history of meter signatures here, since I have devoted an entire chapter to it in my *Studien zur Geschichte der Notenschrift* (pp. 254 f.), and I would be unable to state much that is new.[5] I wish only to remark that Anonymous III of Coussemaker (*Script.* III) is not later but earlier than Marchettus and even earlier than Philippe de Vitry, because he cites the latter (p. 371).*7

I would like to point out again, however, the beneficial influence which instrumental music and secular music in general had upon church music, although the latter is the only style with which music theorists have dealt. I have attempted to show in detail that all polyphony developed apparently from folk singing and that secular art repeatedly had a correcting influence upon church music, which had through speculation gone astray (Hucbald's parallel organum, octave-fifth *déchant* in contrary motion). Now we see that the rapid growth of *musica ficta*, as well as the expansion of notation through the inclusion of smaller note values (without calling upon a theological-mystical Trinity as a reason for their grouping!), as well as finally reintroducing duple meter and giving it equal importance with triple meter, must be attributed to the influence of secular music. The process by which mensural notation assimilated instrumental notation was by no means ended; it continued to the beginning of the 18th century by gradually doing away with larger note values, the actual basis of mensural notation, in favor of the smaller ones (from ♦ downwards). The bar line was accepted (around 1600), and finally even the balken, with which it was possible to visualize smaller values within the scope of one larger one, was introduced (although it achieved a more general use only at the end of the 17th century).

Mensural theorists found themselves in a dilemma when confronted with the gradual division of the breve into more and more semibreves without the shape of the latter changing. This finally led to the acceptance of smaller values as well as to the introduction of two kinds of mensuration.

[5] Cf. Johannes Wolf, *Geschichte der Mensuralnotation von* 1250–1460 (1905) and *Handbuch der Notationskunde* I (1913).

The *signum divisionis,* used to group the semibreves together (Petrus de Cruce and Odington), already constituted a major step forward in this direction. Odington (Couss., *Script.* I:245) also talks about a semibreve which has a downward vertical stem, the altered semibreve ( =2/3 breve) to which Marchettus (Gerbert, *Script.* III:151) again refers. Other attempts are the oblique stem ( $\nearrow$ or $\diagup$ ) for semibreves of shorter value which begin a group (Pseudo-Aristotle, Couss., *Script.* I:271 f.). It seems almost as though the establishment of the shape of the minima, which is different from that of the semibreve, must be credited to Marchettus of Padua (the name was first coined by Walter Odington, as we have previously noted, although he expressly guards against changing the manner of notation). Marchettus finds it possible to divide the breve into twelve (!) semibreves (Gerbert, *Script.* III:155):[6] "If one divides the breve (the *tempus*) of the third order into twelve parts, it is always necessary to indicate those twelfths of the *tempus* by special note designations."

He then recommends placing an upward stem on the semibreve for that value which corresponds to the twelfth part of the breve. Marchettus, besides dividing the perfect breve (*tempus perfectum*) into three semibreves, also divides these perfect breves into six or nine by using divisions into twos or threes. He still calls them semibreves (as in Franco), and they are shaped in the same way. For divisions of sextuple breves in twos, however, he recommends a new note shape $\downarrow$ :

I. Tempus perfectum novenariae divisionis

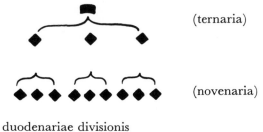

(ternaria)

(novenaria)

II. Tempus perfectum duodenariae divisionis

(ternaria)

[6] "Sciendum est quod si tempus dividatur in partes duodecim tertia divisione, oportet necessario, ut per scriptum possimus et debeamus praedictas duodecim partes temporis per duodecim notas rationabiliter figurare."

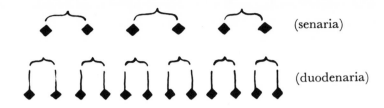

saying that ten semibreves should be read as $4+4$ *duodenariae* $+2$ *senariae*, and are also shaped as such, that is:

In the same manner $11 = 10$ *duodenariae* $+1$ *senaria*, etc. To this are added both forms of the division of the breve into two in *tempus imperfectum*, which Marchettus also establishes:

III. Tempus imperfectum senariae divisionis

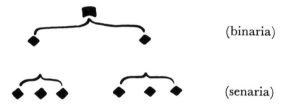

and   IV. Tempus imperfectum duodenariae divisionis

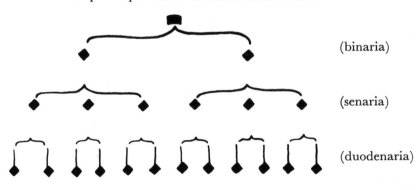

Marchettus in *tempus imperfectum* actually establishes a value as a higher unit which corresponds to only $2/3$ of a *tempus* and which in reality constitutes an incomplete *tempus*. We have in front of us, therefore, if we disregard the minimas (which are actually semiminimas), the four *prolationes* which are recognized as the invention of Philippe de Vitry:

1. Division of the breve into $3 \times 3$
2. Division of the breve into $3 \times 2$
3. Division of the breve into $2 \times 3$
4. Division of the breve into $2 \times 2$

One can only regret that Marchettus himself did not realize the importance of this clearly reasoned manner of division and therefore insisted upon the shape ♩ for the twelfth part of the *tempus*. Thus the renown for these two innovations did not become his, for quite justly that person who gave new shapes to those values which appeared as the result of the first division of the semibreve would have been regarded as the perfector of a new order in notation. This would have followed in the tradition of Philippe de Vitry (Philippus de Vitriaco).

It was not de Vitry, however, who invented the minima; he was still a boy at the time when Marchettus (1309) wrote the *Pomerium*. Perhaps Robert de Handlo's remarks (Couss., *Script.* I:397) are to be blamed for the legend of the "invention" of the minima by de Vitry.[7] De Handlo states[8] that the singers of Navernia (?) connected semibreves of different values (*minoratae* and *minimae*). This passage, of course, is far from a final explanation of the use of smaller values. Burney, who superficially read the commentary in Tunstede and interpreted Navarina or Navernia to be Arvernia, regarded Philippe de Vitry as one from "Auvergne." If we believe that Tunstede is correct when he says that de Vitry only sanctioned the minima but did not invent it, Anonymous VI (Couss., *Script.* I:369 ff.), whom Coussemaker dated around the end of the 13th or beginning of the 14th century (he is to be found in the same London codex as Anonymous IV), steps into the foreground. The manner in which this Anonymous, in the very beginning, treats of the minima as the smallest indivisible value[9] makes it appear as if we have here a new version of an

[7] Simon Tunstede (Couss., *Script.* IV:257) relates: "Concerning the minima, moreover, Master Franco makes no mention in his *Arte*, but only of the longas, breves, and semibreves. But the minima was invented in Navarina and was approved and used by Philippe de Vitry, the flower of the whole world of musicians. Those who declare that Philippe is said to have made the crochet, or semiminima, or dragma, or that he agreed with them, are mistaken, as is clearly evident to anyone who looks into his motets."

[8] "Admetus de Aureliana: The singers of Navernia join *minoratae* and minimas in turn, of their own accord." ( ♩♦ ?)

[9] "When figures and notes are here discussed and it is said what they are and their values are spoken of, let there be close attention. In the first place, they must be treated of by proceeding from the first note to the last....Since the smaller the value [*voce*] of the note, the first [i.e., the least] it is in value, it follows that the minima is the first value [i.e., the least value]...and its symbol, even by musicians in writing, is called the minima."

already established theory.*8 That the treatise is to be dated after de Vitry is apparent from the fact that it definitely rejects smaller values than that of the minima ("Quia minus minimo non est dandum in rerum natura—[That which is smaller than the minima is not given in the nature of things]"). The four prolations which are otherwise attributed to de Vitry are even more clearly presented by Anonymous VI than by Marchettus, so that de Vitry's accomplishments in this direction appear increasingly doubtful. Anonymous VI actually differentiates four divisions of the breve by their note values:

I. Brevis perfecte perfecta

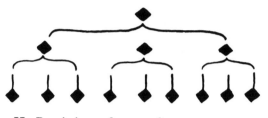

(3 × 3 minimas)

II. Brevis imperfecte perfecta

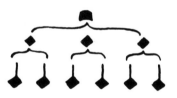

(3 × 2 minimas)

III. Brevis perfecte imperfecta

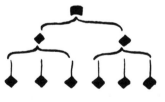

(2 × 3 minimas)

IV. Brevis imperfecte imperfecta

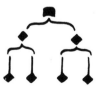

(2 × 2 minimas)

Anonymous expressly observes that the value of the larger notes (longa, maxima) depends upon the divisions of the breve.[10]

Concerning the shape of the smaller rests, Anonymous VI has some unusual ideas (also a sign that he belongs to the time before de Vitry); instead of a lengthy explanation, I will show the rests corresponding to the four divisions of the breve given above:

I.                II.                III.                IV.

This strictly logical but at the same time too highly refined system met with no approval, for the following periods always expressed the higher units (breves for two or three semibreves, semibreves for two or three minimas) with the same signs and made their values dependent upon the mensural signature:

I = *Brevis perfecta* and *imperfecta*, according to the signature

T = *Semibrevis perfecta* and *imperfecta*, according to the signature

Imperfect rests, with the relevant species of notes indicated by a signature as being in perfection, were always shown by placing two rests of the next smaller species next to each other:

TT = 2/3 *brevis* in *tempus perfectum*,

⊓⊓ = 2/3 *semibrevis* in the *prolatio major*.

The forms ⊓ and ⊔ were, however, dropped entirely.

I do not wish to omit pointing out that this treatise, according to Hawkins (*History* II:200) in the "Cotton MS" (Tiberius IX), carried the signature *Haec Odyngtonus* (!). Coussemaker, who assumed Odington to be identical with the archbishop of Canterbury, Walter of Eynesham (1229), overlooked this remark of Hawkins (*Script.* I:XV). Today, since we know that Odington was Professor at Oxford as late as 1316, his authorship does not appear at all unlikely. The treatise *De figuris sive notis*, however, must be regarded as having been written after the main work,

---

[10] "From this, therefore, it is evident that these four *mensurae* are sufficient (!) and that they are found first in the breve and later in others superior to the breve [of greater value than the breve]." The *brevis imperfecta imperfecte*, that is, duple division in two orders, is taught by Amerus (Bamberg MS litt. 115, Ed. IV. 6, dated 1271, published by J. Kromolicki, Berlin Dissertation, 1909, p. 9) as well as *Dietricus*, edited by Hans Müller, 1886 (Karlsruhe, Anonymous). Amerus is an Englishman.

*De speculatione musicae,* since in the latter Odington still rejects any in-novations concerning note value shapes (see above, p. 146 f.). The entire contents of the smaller treatise mày very well be regarded as a kind of supplement of the older work, although it nowhere refers to the latter.

Of apparently the same age as this treatise is the Anonymous II of Coussemaker (*Script.* III:364 ff.),*9 which Coussemaker oddly enough wants to date around 1400 (!). Internal reasons are entirely missing for such a date. The author of this treatise knows the differentiation between perfect and imperfect mensuration of the longa, breve, and semibreve, but does not mention any meter designations for them. He is not acquainted with the hanging rest for the semibreve, but still distinguishes, as does Pseudo-Aristotle, between a rest of 2/3 of a space and 1/3 of a space (!). He does not clearly perceive the order of the smallest values, but regards the possibility of the diminution (not in further imperfections) of an imperfect note by one which is at least two degrees smaller, for example, ◥◆ or ■ ♦ ( =○·· ♩), etc.

Johannes Verulus de Anagnia also belongs in the time of Marchettus, or at least not much later. His *Liber de musica* (Couss., *Script.* III:129–177), in spite of its unusual length, does not speak of anything but the division of the *tempus perfectum* and *imperfectum* into smallest parts (*athomi*), of which there are no less than seventy-two (!) contained in the *tempus perfectum majoris divisionis duodenariae majoris prolationis.* The following short excerpt proves how widely developed combinations of the smallest values were around 1325 (p. 161):

(*Tempus perfectum* and *prolatio major* = 9/8 measure)

(with syncopation *punctus*)

(with syncopation *punctus*)

etc.

Theodoricus de Campo (Couss., *Script.* III:177 ff.) in his short treatise *De musica mensurabili* refers to Joh. Ver. de Anagnia. This treatise shows that he was acquainted with Philippe de Vitry, and may therefore be dated around 1350. The semiminima ♩ is rejected by Johannes Verulus de Anagnia as being generally expendable; in Theodoricus de Campo it is still new, but accepted. Time signatures are not included by Johannes Verulus de Anagnia; Theodoricus knows only the following: O, C, ⊞, ⊡ .

Anonymous III, published by J. Adrian Lafage (1853), presumably belongs to the same time and is in a 15th-century codex in the Library Vallicellana, contained in the supplement to the *Compendium* of Nicholas de Capua. Anonymous III does not mention the semiminima but clearly explains the *prolatio major* and *minor* and is also acquainted with the making of imperfections by the use of the *remotae* ( ■ ♩ ). The time signatures are ⊟ and ⊟ for the *modus*; O C for the *tempus*; ∴ or ⁚ (in a circle) for the *prolatio.*

Philippe de Vitry, who lived between *ca.* 1290 and 1361 (cf. Couss., *Script.* II:XI following Tarbe, *Les oeuvres de Philippe de Vitry* [1850]), was Bishop of Meaux in his later years and was highly celebrated as a composer. We must therefore not be surprised if he also, as in the case of Guido, Franco, and others, received honors which he cannot fully claim. The often cited passage from a MS containing poetry of the 14th and 15th century (F. Wolf, *Über die Lais, Sequenzen und Leiche* (1841), p. 141):

Après vint Philippe de Vitry, qui trouva la manière des motés et des balades et des lais et des simples rondeaus et en la musique trouva les quatre prolations et les notes rouges et la nouveleté des proportions.

(Then came Philippe de Vitry, who discovered the way of writing motets, ballades, lais, and simple rondeaus, and who discovered the four prolations, red notes, and the innovations in proportions in music.)

is so exaggerated in its first part that one cannot attach much importance to the second. Motets, lais, and rondeaus existed long before de Vitry, and we have just discussed matters concerning the prolations. However, it is a fact that with de Vitry a new epoch of compositional practice, an *Ars nova*, appeared, which was probably given direct inducement by the title of a treatise ascribed to de Vitry (similar to Caccini's *Nuove musiche* of 1602, which by its title marked the beginning of a new epoch).*10

The *Ars nova Philippi de Vitriaco* (Couss., *Script.* III:13 ff.), however, asserts itself very definitely and introduces many new and interesting points so that at the end of an introduction, which is not very long (concerning monochord division and solmization table), the remark occurs that *musica falsa* (that is, the chromatic tones, with the exception of the well-known b♭ and b♮) is necessary since no motet or rondel can be sung without it.[11] Then the treatise skips at once to an explanation of the *tempus imperfectum* and introduces not only the minima but also the semi-minima:

♪ minima

♪ semiminima

These names, however, are not yet established; the author also mentions the names *semibrevis major, semibrevis semimajor,* and *semibrevis minima* for the various early types of semibreves. He hesitates about whether it would be better, in order to reserve the name *minima* (the smallest) for the smallest note value, to call minima rather by the name of *semiminor* and the semiminima simply minima. The minima of the *Ars nova* can be imperfected and altered (which is denied by Anonymous VI, however, who does not admit any semiminima). The *Ars nova* does not content itself as Marchettus did with designating the mensuration of the breve (with ○ or III at the beginning for the *tempus perfectum*, or C or II for the *tempus imperfectum*); it also wants to indicate the perfect or imperfect mensuration of the longa (by showing two or three small lines inside the circle; instead of the latter some also use the square for the *tempus*). The treatise does not have any signs for the perfect or imperfect value of the semibreve. Such a sign is designated, however, by the *Ars perfecta magistri Philippoti de Vitriaco* (Couss., *Script.* III:29), namely, for the *prolatio major* three dots in the circle or semicircle, and for the *prolatio minor* two dots. This treatise (of which the prefaced contrapuntal rules are not a part) is definitely not by de Vitry. This is not proved by the fact that the name Philippotus might either be written wrong or constitute a diminutive form of Philippus (similar to Jachet for Jacques), but by the fact that in the treatise (p. 29) Philippus is designated as the one [12] who for the most part with great subtlety brought about the innovations.

That the *Ars nova* was early attributed to de Vitry is apparent from the

[11] (Page 18): "You must accordingly know, as has been said, what the two signs for *musica falsa* are, namely, ♭ *rotundum* and, another, ♮ *quadratum*. And they have the following properties, namely, that ♭ *rotundum* makes a whole-tone of a semitone in descending, and a semitone of a whole-tone in ascending. And from the other sign, that is, the ♭, a semitone is made in descending, in place of a tone, and a tone is made in ascending, in place of a semitone.

"For at those places where signs are required, as has expressly been said, these are not false but true and necessary. For without these no motet nor *rondellus* could be sung."

[12] "While of the ancients...Franco is known to have bequeathed all, it is Phillipus who for the most part has with great subtlety brought about the innovations."

Anonymous VII of Coussemaker (*Script.* III:404 ff.), who expressly writes:

Item Dominus et Magister Philippus de Vitriaco ad confirmandum et declarandum artem praedictam in Arte nova ordinavit, quod est modus et tempus et quae sunt prolationes.

(Thus the Master and Teacher Philippe de Vitry confirmed and explained this renowned art, and codified it in his *Arte nova* which tells what the *modus, tempus,* and *prolatio* are.)

The four prolations of Anonymous VII completely correspond to the listings in the *Ars nova*, so that the identity of the treatise is beyond doubt. Since Anonymous VII was apparently not even acquainted with the semiminima, he must be regarded as approximately of the same age. (De Vitry is probably also meant on page 405 when Philippus Parisiensis is mentioned.)

As we have noted before, the *Ars nova* does not yet have a name for the mensuration of the semibreve which is later preferably called *prolatio*, but it regards the mensuration designations of the *modus* (longa) and the *tempus* (breve) as sufficient. (The same is the case with Anonymous V [in Couss., *Script.* III:379], who probably belongs to this time.) The *Ars nova* establishes only a *tempus perfectum minimum, medium,* and *majus*; and at the same time a *tempus imperfectum minimum* and *majus,* that is, five prolations, of which, however, the *tempus perfectum minimum* does not indicate other relationships between the note values, but only distinguishes itself by the tempo. It does not subdivide the semibreves, but takes them so fast that they correspond to the minimas of the other prolations. This is, then, an actual *allabreve* beat, and is the *diminutio temporis* for which the *Ars nova* had no symbol as yet. There is a reference to the old masters, with special mention of the name Franco. The naming of *prolatio major* and *minor* in the later sense appears only with the *Ars perfecta Philippoti* (de Vitriaco).[13]

Red notes also do not seem to have appeared first in the *Ars nova.*[*][11] The summary treatment of different occasions for the use of the *color* (p. 21) does not look as if this was an innovation, for examples are not added and only well-known compositions are mentioned. Red notes are employed, according to the *Ars nova* usage:

1. To indicate a change in mensuration,
2. To mark syncopation,
3. As a symbol of octave displacement,
4. To differentiate between the *cantus planus* and mensural notation.

---

[13] (Couss., *Script.* III:31): "I say this, that with semibreves one can make a distinction between a major and minor prolation. A major prolation is a large or wide measure giving to the semibreve the value of three minimas. A minor prolation is a short and moderate measure in which two minimas only can be offered for a semibreve."

The explanation of individual cases is by no means exhaustive and can be easily misinterpreted.

From [14] the first decades of the *Ars nova* in France there is another treatise which tries to deal in its own way with the mensuration problems of its time, the *Compendium de discantu mensurabili compilatum a fratre Petro dicto Palma ociosa*, which was made available through Johannes Wolf's publication (*SIMG* XV:504–534). Petrus was a monk of the Cistertian order in the Cherchamps cloister in the diocese of Amiens; he finished his treatise, according to the date of the manuscript, in the year 1336. In three chapters, which are in a somewhat disorderly form, he treats of the theory of discant, *falsa musica*, and the *flores discantus mensurabilis*, and each time emphasizes that the theory in this form is his own. He is especially proud of his twelve *modi* [15] with the aid of which he tabulates all possible combinations of perfect and imperfect longas, breves, and semibreves. In addition, *modi* 5–6 and 11–12 again restate the possible subdivisions of the breve without regard to the longas. With this work Petrus achieves a more complete theoretical division than a practical one, as is apparent in his examples. As he uses neither the meter signatures of de Vitry nor the note shapes of the Italians, it would not be clear throughout his treatise whether the longas were perfect or imperfect (and this would be true in many cases of the breves) if he did not indicate the *modus* in each piece by words in the beginning. The *color* is also not used; the sole mensural symbol is the *punctum divisionis*. He does mention the use of the *remotae* (■ ♦) to bring about imperfection. He lists the *minima* as the smallest note value, even though he is definitely familiar with shorter values, as is evident from p. 533:

Qui quidem 12 modi, possunt sufficere ad omnem vocis prolationem secundum artem cantus naturalis ita tamen quod unusquisque modus tam celeriter proferatur quam amplius ultra numerum sibi superius attributum minime valeat minorari.

---

[14] The following concerning the *Compendium* of *Petrus Palma ociosa* was added by Gustave Becking in the second edition of the *Geschichte*.

[15] (Page 516): "That which they call flowers [flores=diminutions, ornamentations] of mensural music [occurs] when many sounds, or small notes (which is the same thing), variously arranged according to the quality of a tone [unam vocem], are used in place of this one sound or simple note containing a quantity of these sounds in the right proportion.... I, according to the limited capacity of my genius, have compiled twelve modes or manners of mensural discant adorned with these diminutions. These modes or manners (as would appear proper to anyone) are arranged in perfect and imperfect *modi* and perfect and imperfect *tempi* and major and minor prolations....Let not this good gift, bestowed upon me by God, die or be extinguished in me, yea, let it be distributed in love by me to my brothers nearest me in Christ. Therefore, I feel that these twelve modes should be made known that they might shed greater light for all young men wishing to sing discants with distinction."

(At least, to this point there are twelve *modi*. These can suffice for the prolations of voices according to the art of natural song; however, each mode can so quickly enlarge itself far beyond the number which is its highest attribute that the value of the minima is lessened.)

The new theories are extremely clear and detailed in the *Liber musicalium* (Couss., *Script.* III : 35 ff.), but the authorship of de Vitry is insufficiently documented, as the Strassburg Codex, which is the only source for this treatise, belongs to the 15th century (1411). Due to the high esteem which was accorded de Vitry, many of the secondary sources based on his own reforms (*secundum Philippum de Vitriaco*) may have simply been labeled Philippi de Vitriaco by later writers.*12

If the *Ars nova* is genuine, the genuineness of the *Liber musicalium* does indeed seem problematical. It seems as improbable that an author would have written a work like the *Ars nova*, which contains so many new theories, without detailed explanations, as it is unthinkable that in such a clearly worded book as the *Liber musicalium* the same author would have appended a compendium which throws many theories into a new obscurity.

Possibly the *Ars nova* is not by de Vitry himself, but should be regarded only as one of those preliminary studies which Johannes de Muris (Normannus), as we shall see, opposes; in that case, however, the *Liber musicalium* could then be regarded as genuine. The testimony of Simon Tunstede, who certainly admits that Philippe de Vitry knew and made use of the minima, denies that he used the semiminima. This speaks against de Vitry's authorship of both treatises, of course, because both introduce the semiminima, even though only in connection with the first explanations of the notes. For this reason one could assume that the figure of the semiminima was later drawn in. Tunstede himself, although he is aware of the fact that, according to the opinions of many, de Vitry is said to have sanctioned the use of the semiminima, does not proceed beyond the use of the minima and also includes no representation of the symbol of the semiminima (i.e., *crocheta*, *dragma*), which must simply be regarded as a rejection of the necessity for these new values and symbols. (The *dragma* [♦] is first mentioned by Anonymous III in Couss., *Script.* III : 373; he is to be dated around 1350). It is also striking that neither Anonymous II (Couss. III) nor Tunstede makes any mention of red notes, and that Anonymous III (Couss. III) disposes of them in only three lines (p. 374). It is also striking that the *Liber musicalium* treats white and red notes as being of equal importance.16*13 With this in mind, either all evidence disappears for the assumption that the red notes are older than the white ones (cf. *Studien zur Geschichte der Notenschrift*, p. 280), or the probability

16 (Couss., *Script.* III : 44) : "When the note shape is changed into a white note or a red note, then either the *modus* or *tempus* or prolation is changed."

that the *Ars nova* was written before de Vitry becomes even more certain.

These controversial questions are, however, to be solved only with the aid of Johannes de Muris, if at all.

Who is the older, Muris or de Vitry?

According to Robert Hirschfeld's special study of Johannes de Muris (1884), it is no longer doubtful that Johannes de Muris is older if one regards as final proof the fact that the *Speculum musicae* was already completed by him in 1321 at an advanced age (Couss., *Script.* III:433, *aetatis fragilitas*).

My opinion is that Hirschfeld does not consider to a sufficient degree the evidence that there were two music theorists of somewhat the same age bearing the name Johannes de Muris, one of whom should more correctly be called Julianus de Muris, namely, the one who was elected rector at Paris University and who was a highly esteemed mathematician.*[14]

Since a Magister Johannes de Muris (Normannus) is mentioned, under a date of 1321, in an Oxford manuscript at the end of a mathematical treatise, and since at the same time it was reported that this author completed an extensive work concerning music in the same year (Fétis, *Biographie universelle*, article "Muris"), we have in our hands the key to solving the riddle as to how the author of the *Speculum musicae* could have opposed the author of the *Musica speculativa* and *Musica practica* (Hirschfeld, *op. cit.*, pp. 31 ff.). That the author of the *Speculum* could not have been the professor of long standing at the Sorbonne is proved as Hirschfeld correctly remarks in a narrative by him (Couss., *Script.* II:402): "He believed that in Paris he had once heard a composed *triplum* which was attributed to Master Franco, in which more than three semibreves occur for one *tempus*." If we hold to the viewpoint that approximately at the same time (in the first half of the 14th century) there were two musicians and mathematicians named Johannes (or Julianus) de Muris who were confused by posterity and perhaps even in their contemporary world (in the same way the two Francos were confused), then we can only assume from the way the theories of the *Musica speculativa* and *Musica practica* were attacked by those in the *Speculum musicae* that the latter work was written after the first two. What points most clearly to this is that the *Musica speculativa* is not yet acquainted with the semiminima, which is found in the *Speculum musicae*. Since the year 1323 as the date of authorship and the Sorbonne as the place is established for the *Musica speculativa* (Gerbert, *Script.* III:189 and 283), the *Speculum musicae* cannot be the same work completed in 1321 by Johannes de Muris. With this any reason to date the *Speculum* as early as 1321 is invalidated. The earliest definite year we find for Philippe de Vitry is 1343, in which year Leo

Hebraeus, "upon the wish of the outstanding teacher of the musical arts, Philippe de Vitry," dedicated to de Vitry a work concerning definitions of musical intervals (Couss., *Script.* III.X).*[15] Considering the negative attitude of the aged Johannes de Muris (in the *Speculum musicae*) toward the entire *Ars nova,* and the so far highly problematical friendship between Muris and Philippe de Vitry, proved by an extant letter from Muris (Couss., *Script.* III.VIII; the letter is also a mathematical treatise), it seems very understandable that the writer of the letter is at the same time the author of the *Musica speculativa* and *Musica practica.*

The author of the *Speculum musicae,* the Normannus de Muris, is a musician of highly conservative bearing, who, it seems, concerned himself as thoroughly with the music theory of the ancients as with the practical music of his time. Unfortunately Coussemaker in the *Scriptores* has printed only the two last books of the seven which comprise the voluminous work (vol. II:193–433!), although he does include the chapter headings of the first five books (I:76 chapters; II:125 chapters; III:56 chapters; IV:51 chapters; V:52 chapters!). From this it appears that this work is undoubtedly the most thorough of the entire Middle Ages. Why Coussemaker did not also print the third book which deals exclusively with intervals (*consonantiae*) and their division into consonances (*concordiae*) and dissonances (*discordiae*) I must confess I cannot understand. It is plainly a cruelty to arouse the curiosity of the music historian with chapter headings such as the following, when he cannot make further researches directly in Paris in the original manuscripts:

IV. 45. Cur semiditonum et ditonum aliasque prius tactas intermedias concordias ordinamus.

IV. 48. Assignatio causarum mediarum et imperfectarum discordiarum.

IV. 50. Concordiarum comparatio quantum ad cadentiam (!).

IV. 51. Concordiarum collatio quoad partitionem (!).

Will there ever be a Paris music historian or publisher courageous enough to make up for Coussemaker's neglect, and to make a work of such thorough scholarship available in its entirety? This work apparently not only comments upon the music theories of antiquity as based on Boethius, but goes back to the Greek sources themselves (Plutarch, Nicomachus, Ptolemaeus, etc.), even though the somewhat barbaric spelling of Greek names and technical terms seems to point to a yet understandably incomplete knowledge of the Greek language. The chapter register of the first book also points to a number of sections on instrumental music, the knowledge of which would be of the greatest interest (Chapters 15 and 19; these chapters are, however, probably very short).

That the author of this work is the "famous" Johannes de Muris can hardly be doubted, but this famous Muris had no part in the reversal which took place in the first half of the 14th century in musical practice.

Of the numerous works carrying the name Johannes de Muris, probably only the *Summa magistri Johannis de Muris* (Gerbert, *Script.* III: 190–248) may also be attributed to the author of the *Speculum*, a work which is written by turns in prose and hexameter couplets (860 verses in its final version). This might very possibly be the "exhaustive" work of Normannus de Muris, completed in 1321. The preference of the author of the *Speculum* for the earlier forms of vocal music, namely, the different kinds of organum, is also shared by the author of the *Summa*. The works concur in their detailed consideration of instrumental music. Far from being a thorough and erudite scholar like the writer of the *Speculum*, the author of the *Summa*, for instance, attributes (according to hearsay) to the Italians other solmization syllables than the UT, RE, MI, FA, etc., of the French, English, German, Hungarian, Slavic, Dacian, and other Cisalpine (!) peoples (this observation shows definitely that Muris is not an Italian).[17] His major authorities are Odo, Guido, Hermannus Con-

---

[17] It is certainly worth while to compare the three curious passages, the first of which (in John Cotton) is apparently a source for the second (in the *Summa*), while the third looks like a kind of correction or apology (the latter also proves that the author of the *Speculum* resided at times in Paris, but later did not live there). John Cotton writes (Gerbert, II: 232): "There are six syllables which we use for musical works, different indeed among different people. But the English, the French, and the Germans use these: UT RE MI FA SOL LA. The Italians use others, and those who want to learn them, let them ask of them." Muris writes in the *Summa musicae* (Gerbert III: 203): "So then, the first teachers of music came upon six syllables: UT RE MI FA SOL LA, which are the names of the six notes if they are considered from their alteration or mutation, for even if they are alternated above and below for all notes even unto infinity, they signify these notes and are their names. When notes are spoken of, they are called these names by the Gauls, the English, the Teutons, the Hungarians, the Slavs, the Dacians [Roman province between the Carpathians and the Danube river] and others on this side of the Alps. The Italians, however, are said to have other notes and names, and if anyone wants to know about this, let him ask them!" The corresponding passage in the *Speculum musicae* (Couss., *Script.* II: 281) reads: "There are, therefore, six notes, which are used in song, which some call syllables, because they are expressed by syllables and not by letters only (note here the reference to letter notation). These are indeed different among different people, according to the speech of each. I think I heard some at Paris say these names of the six notes: PRO TO DO NO NI A (!!) (TRI PRO DE NO TE AD is probably meant; see also *Handbuch der Musikgeschichte* I. 2., p. 183, and Gustave Lange, *SIMG* I: 543). But the Gauls, English, and Germans call them this: UT RE MI FA SOL LA." This certainly appears as if the *Itali alias habent* of the *Summa* met with well-founded opposition and for this reason fell into disuse, this being at the same time justified by the disclosure of another system of *solfeggio* (which receives no further testimonial).

tractus, and Salomon (probably Elias Salomonis). Nevertheless, one must not overlook the fact that the entire treatise deals only with *musica plana* (which is, however, not mentioned by this name), and that according to its contents it could definitely be dated in the 12th century, since not a single word mentions the existence of mensural music, and the term *discantus* is not even used.\*16 The chapter *De polyphonia* agrees entirely with the versions of polyphonic theory before the appearance of mensuration. Only *basilica dyaphonia, basilica triphonia,* and *tetraphonia* indicate an acquaintance with those kinds of organum which are treated by the authors of the Franconian epoch (*organum purum*). I shall, therefore, include some excerpts from the contents of this treatise (Gerbert, *Script.* III:239):18

18 "*Polyphonia* is nothing else than a manner of singing by a number of people keeping a diverse melody. Moreover, it is divided into three kinds, that is, *dyaphonia, triphonia,* and *tetraphonia*; that is, into double, triple, or quadruple singing. *Dyaphonia* is a way of singing in two modes, and is divided into *basilica* and *organica*. *Basilica* is singing a melody in two ways in which one continually holds one note, which is a *cantus firmus* for the song of the other singer. This other partner begins his song either at the *diapente* or at the *diapason*, sometimes ascending, sometimes descending, so that in the pauses [cadences] it agrees in some way with the one who keeps the bass. *Organica dyaphonia* is a melody, sung by two or more in two modes, so that when one goes up the other goes down and vice versa; yet in pausing they come together chiefly in the same place [interval]: the *diapente* or the *diapason.* . . .

*Triphonia* (*basilica*) is a melody or way of singing by three or more in three modes, in such a way, of course, that by one or more one note is held continually as the basis, and by another one or more the same song is begun at the *diapente*, singing in the same course to the end; by a third one or more the same song is begun at once at the *diapason*, and the course of the same song is correctly furnished by the first voice. . . . *Organica triphonia* is a melody or mode of singing by three or more, the three modes of singing being so divided that one or more hold the basis in the lower notes of the pauses; by another one or more a different *cantus organicus* is begun at the *diapente* or perhaps in the *diatessaron*; and by a third one or more a *cantus organicus* of a different form is begun at the *diapason* with a third part of the second *organica* going along with it. When the first part makes some kind of pause in a concord, either at the *diapente* or the *diatessaron*, it can even be that an *organica* and an unlike triple note may be sung at the same time by these three parts, and this mode is rightly called *organica triphonia*. The instructions concerning *tetraphonia* are similar; in this four different parts are varied. There is no doubt that the lower part begins among the lowest notes; the second part begins at the *diapente*, the third part in respect to the first begins at the *diapason*, and the fourth part, in respect to the second, begins a *diapason* from it. So four parts, by running through the song side by side, begin, pause, and end it, each in his own part as is ordained. *Organica*, as has been said, does not take its name from the vocal organ for the reason that as different *organa* sound differently, so also individual men have different individual forms. *Organica* is only a concord of unlike voices occurring in various ways as long as in the following species of song, if one part goes very high, the rest descend, and vice versa, and if they pause together, as has been said, they should pause either in the same pitch (clave) or at the *diapente* or at the *diapason*. If, however, they happen to pause anywhere else, which rarely happens, they

Polyphony is the simultaneous singing of several (voices) with different melodies. There are three special kinds: diaphonia (two-voiced), triphonia (three-voiced), and tetraphonia (four-voiced). The diaphonia is either basilica or organica....In the diaphonia basilica one voice sustains one tone continually as basis (basis) for the melody; the second voice, however, begins in the fifth or octave and moves up and down in such a manner that at all points of rest it sounds in consonance with the sustained note of the lower voice. The diaphonia organica on the other hand, consists of two voices (solo or chorus) which move separately, one of which ascends when the other descends and vice versa, while at the closes (pausando) both enter into the unison of the fifth or the octave. In the triphonia basilica the first voice shall again sustain a low note, the second shall start in the fifth, and the third in the octave and form (according to the better explanation given in the versified version) a kind of diaphonia organica above the basis, while becoming consonant with it at the closes. In the triphonia organica all three voices move freely, but in such a manner that they come together at the closes. In the same way we also differentiate between the tetraphonia basilica and organica, whereby the second voice starts a fifth above the first, and the third and fourth voices start in the higher octave of the first and second. In many instances the first voice has only a few notes, the second voice, however, many, in which case the first notes are prolonged and the latter are sung fast.

In spite of the striking correspondence of the diaphonia organica with the description of organum by Scotus Erigena, this description is obviously a very valuable addition to the most incomplete and obscure remarks of the first mensuralists, especially concerning the polyphonic settings of their time which were not actually mensurated. Since Muris himself had occasion to hear vocal music of this type (cf. above, p. 199), the report is almost as valuable for us as it would be had it dated from the Franconian epoch. (In passing it might be pointed out that the graceful and elegant terminology of this description speaks strongly for the identity of the author of the Summa with that of the author of the Speculum, who knew the Greek language.)

The Speculum musicae must be placed at the time of Philippe de Vitry, that is, around 1340–1360; however, a direct reference by Muris to de Vitry is nowhere evident, and attacks against the "modern teachers" may very well also refer to de Vitry's predecessors. In many instances Muris does not turn against the theorists, but against the composers, as in the case of his complaint concerning those who "do not keep the correct order among the consonances and use such intricate rhythms that no

---

should not pause for long, but suddenly move away. It often happens in organica that the lower part has few notes and the higher many; then the few must be sung slowly, the many swiftly, until at length at the end they run together into the same, as has been said, at the diapente or diapason [Gerbert: diatessaron]."

mensuration seems to be kept at all any more,"[19] or with his complaint against those who seem to see the good qualities of composition as being refinement, difficulty, and intricacy.[20] This might also very well refer to the composer Philippe de Vitry, whose works were already known to Tunstede who lived approximately at the same time (see above, p. 190).

We must not look to the author of the *Speculum* for any innovations after our previous conclusion, but at most for reports of advances made by others, which almost always take the form of attacks. Muris even regards the distinction between the *tempus perfectum* and *imperfectum* and the *mensura perfecte perfecta, imperfecte perfecta*, etc. (see also p. 191, Anonymous VI) as unnecessary complications of only speculative value and without value for practical usage.[21] The authorities of the *Speculum* are still in many cases Franco *teutonicus* (!) and *quidam qui Aristoteles nuncupatur*, as well as Petrus de Cruce. Muris is not even in favor of attempts to bring order into the many subdivisional values of the breve, a confusion which was already noticeable in Franco. Muris says, rather, that if the old masters were able to write without giving the semibreves any tails, then the new ones could do the same. He remarks, incidentally, that the new ones are not at all agreed as to how the new values should be formed.[22]

Thus Normannus Johannes de Muris, as far as we are now able to evaluate his main work, appears to have furthered neither the development of notation nor the theory of composition; his title to fame rests, rather, on his ability to conceive such an extensive work, in which he has treated in detail the music theory of the preceding epoch, a work which challenges the trend of his time throughout.

This is not so for the Parisian Johannes (or Julianus) de Muris, the friend of Philippe de Vitry, whom we must regard as the author of the *Musica speculativa, Musica practica*, the *Quaestiones super partes musicae*, and of the other treatises bearing the name Muris which are printed in the third volume of Coussemaker's *Scriptores*. He is the one who also belongs in the sphere of influence of the works which are inscribed *secundum Johannem de Muris*.

[19] (Couss., *Script.* II:388): "Now, moreover, some discantors or composers of discants observe none of the conditions that belong to discants, write compositions in which the correct order of consonances is not kept, write crudely, unpleasantly, with difficulties, intricately, and almost without measure."

[20] (*Ibid.*, 389): "But now some of the moderns who perhaps are considered among the greater in composing discants, seem to attribute the form and end of discants to the subtlety, the difficulty, and the intricacy of composition."

[21] (*Ibid.*, p. 395): "But what good is subtlety when usefulness dies?"

[22] (*Ibid.*, p. 407): "But these simple notes sufficed the ancients who wrote so many beautiful and distinguished works of mensural music. These could suffice modern singers if they were willing and if wanton curiosity and vanity, if it is right to say so, did not hinder it."

This Johannes de Muris de Francia (Gerbert, *Script*. III:307) is completely a man of the *Ars nova*; he regards the fourth as a dissonance, endorses *musica ficta* (for instance, starting a hexachord with D as UT in Gerbert, *Script*. III:307), and claims the possibility of imperfecting the longa through the semibreve, the breve through the minima, etc. We must regard the *Musica speculativa* (1323) as one of his first works, a glossary of sections from Boethius, individual sentences of which are opposed by the Norman Muris.

Perhaps we do not do an injustice to this teacher at the Sorbonne, who later on was Rector at the same institution, if we see in him the theoretical champion of the reforms of Philippe de Vitry, who left only a few, if any, theoretical works behind. If we consider the *Ars nova* to have been written before de Vitry, then there remains only the *Liber musicalium*, the genuineness of which is doubtful, since the *Ars contrapuncti* and the *Ars perfecta* were definitely not written before de Vitry.

Nevertheless it is unusual that two bearers of the name Muris who were so different in their theoretical approaches were not distinguished more sharply during their lifetimes, and that nowhere is there an existing reference to both at the same time. It is also strange that the only two known manuscripts of the *Speculum musicae* are in Paris, where, however, manuscript treasures from all parts of the world were collected![23]

This *excursus* has at least clarified our outlook to such an extent that we can again turn our attention to the further development of the theory of composition without having to fear that we will go too far astray in designating the periods of the various writers.

[23] The old dispute, whether Muris was by birth a Frenchman or an Englishman, is settled in the simplest manner by the evidence of there having been two writers bearing the same name. Presumably Normannus Muris lived and taught in Oxford and paid only brief visits to Paris for study.

### APPENDIX

FOOTNOTE 2: (Gerbert, *Script*. III:316): "Secunda vero differentia patet in illis laicalibus, qui licet sint totius artis musicalis expertes, zelo tamen ducti dulcedinis delicatas aures suas ad quaevis musicalia praebent, attentius adamantes et associantes musicos ut…et apis ob dulcorem mellis argumentat, in studium propositos studiosius prosequentes flores, et spicarum musicalium messis manipulos colligentes, quos possunt ut in plerisque cum cantoribus gratius garriendo concordent, et frequentius usitando in multis musicalibus quodammodo habilitentur, et reddantur experti, ut quod artis in eis deficit, usus suppleat et industria naturalis. Ex istis nonnullos videmus clericos, qui in organicis instrumentis difficillimos musicales modulos, quos exprimere vix praesumeret vox humana, adinveniunt atque tradunt per miraculosum quoddam innatae in eis inventivae musicae prodigium: reliquos autem, qui quae sic gesta sunt et tradita, paulo minus laudabiliter recordantur, et interdum inventoris laudem concinit gratialis industria recordantis."

FOOTNOTE 7: (Couss., *Script.* IV:257): "De minima autem Magister Franco mentionem in sua Arte non facit, sed tantum de longis et brevibus et semibrevibus. Minima autem in Navarina inventa erat et a Philippo de Vitriaco, qui fuit flos totius mundi musicorum, approbata et usitata. Qui autem dicunt praedictum Philippum crochetam vel semiminimam aut dragmam fecisse, aut eis consensisse, errant, ut in motetis suis intuenti manifeste apparet."

FOOTNOTE 8: "Admetus de Aureliana: Cantores de Navernia (sic) minoratas et minimas per se sic conjungunt ad invicem."

FOOTNOTE 9: "Cum in isto tractatu de figuris sive de notis, quae sunt, et de earum proprietatibus, sit intentio, primo est tractandum de prima nota procedendo ad ultimam. ...Unde cum quanto vox sit minor, tanto prior est in voce, sequitur quod minima vox prima est...et cum figura illius etiam apud musicos in scripto vocatur minima."

FOOTNOTE 10: (Couss., *Script.* I:375): "Ex isto (Couss. *istis*) igitur patet, quod istae quatuor mensurae sufficiunt (!) et quod primo in brevi inveniuntur et ex consequenti in aliis superioribus ad brevem."

FOOTNOTE 11: (Page 18): "Igitur scire debes sicut dictum est, quod duo sunt signa falsae musicae, scilicet ♭ rotundum et ista alia figura ♮ quadratum. Et talem proprietatem habent, videlicet quod ♭ rotundum habet facere de semitonio tonum...in descendendo, et de tono (Couss. *semitonio*) in ascendendo, habet facere semitonium (Couss. *tonum*). Et e converso fit de alia figura ista ♮, scilicet quod de tono descendente habet facere semitonium, et de semitonio ascendente habet facere tonum.

"Tamen in illis locis ubi ista signa requiruntur sunt, ut superius dictum est, non falsa sed vera et necessaria. Quia nullus motetus sive rondellus sive ipsa cantari non possunt."

FOOTNOTE 12: "Cum antiquitatem...Franconem notum est omnibustradisse, novitatemque Philippum in majori parte subtiliter invenisse."

FOOTNOTE 13: (Couss., *Script.* III:31): "Ita dico, quod semibrevibus idem est invenire (!) per distinctionem majoris prolationis et minoris. Major prolatio est larga vel lata mensura, dans unicuique semibrevi tres minimas vel valorem. Minor prolatio est brevis et modica mensura, sub qua duae minimae pro semibrevi tantummodo possunt proferri."

FOOTNOTE 15: (Page 516): "Dicunt enim flores musicae mensurabilis, quando plures voces seu notulae, quod idem est, diversimode figuratae secundum uniuscuiusque qualitatem ad unam vocem seu notulam simplicem tantum quantitatem illarum vocum continentem iusta proportione reducuntur....Ego circa capacitatem ingenioli mei XII modos seu maneries de discantu mensurabili floribus adornato compilavi. Qui quidem modi seu maneries, prout cuilibet competit, ordinantur sub modo perfecto et imperfecto et sub tempore perfecto et imperfecto et sub prolatione maiori et minori....Ne illud bonum a Deo mihi collatum in me mortificetur et extinguatur, immo proximis meis in Christo fratribus per me ipsum caritate distribuatur et benigne quidem summis desiderio affectibus, idcirco istos 12 modos ut clarius elucescant cunctis invenibus subtiliter discantare volentibus, sensui declarandos."

FOOTNOTE 16: (Couss., *Script.* III:44): "Quando figuratio mutatur in notis vacuis aut rubeis (!), tunc mutatur aut modus, aut tempus aut prolatio (!)."

FOOTNOTE 17: (Gerbert, *Script.* II:232): "Sex sunt syllabae, quas ad opus musicae assumimus, diversae quidem apud diversos. Verum Angli, Francigenae, Alemanni utuntur his UT RE MI FA SOL LA. Itali autem alias habent, quas qui nosse desiderant, stipulentur ab ipsis." Muris writes in the *Summa musicae* (Gerbert III:203): "Adinvenerunt ergo primi doctores musici sex syllabas UT RE MI FA SOL LA quae sunt nomina sex notarum si considerantur absque alteratione et mutatione ipsarum, si cogente necessitate alternantur supra et infra omnes notas usque in infinitum, (!) significant et nomina sunt earum. His nominibus, notae ut dictum est, appellantur a Gallicis, Anglicis, Teutonicis, Hungaris, Slavis et Dacis et caeteris Cisalpinis. Itali autem alias notas et nomina dicuntur habere, quod qui scire voluerit, quaerat ab ipsis." The corresponding passage in the *Speculum musicae* (Couss., *Script.* II:281) reads: "Sunt igitur sex voces quibus utuntur in cantu, quae ab aliquibus sillabae nominantur, quia sillabis et non solis litteris (! note here the reference to letter notation) exprimuntur. Hae quidem diversae sunt apud diversos sicut quidam dicunt (!); et ego puto me Parisiis (Couss. *Parisius*) a quodam audivisse sex vocum haec nomina: PRO TO DO NO NI A (!!) (TRI PRO DE NO TE AD is probably meant; see also *Handbuch der Musikgeschichte* I. 2. p. 183, and Gustave Lange, *SIMG* I:543). Sed Gallici, Angli, Alamanni has sic vocant: UT RE MI FA SOL LA."

FOOTNOTE 18: "Polyphonia...nihil aliud est quam modus canendi a pluribus diversam observantibus melodiam. Dividitur autem in tres species, scilicet dyaphoniam, triphoniam et tetraphoniam, id est, in cantum duplicem, triplicem et quadruplicem. Dyaphonia est modus canendi duobus modis; et dividitur in basilicam et organicam. Basilica est canendi duobus modis melodiam, ita quod unus teneat continue notam unam, quae est quasi basis cantus alterius concinentis; alter vero socius cantum incipit vel in diapente, vel in diapason, quandoque ascendens, quandoque descendens, ita quod in pausa concordet aliquo modo cum eo, qui basin observat. Organica dyaphonia est melodia duorum (vel) plurium canentium duobus modis, ita quod unus ascendat reliquus vero descendat et e contra; pausando tamen conveniunt maxime vel in eodem, vel in diapente, vel in diapason....

"Triphonia (basilica) est melodia sive modus canendi a tribus vel a pluribus et modis tribus, ita scilicet, ut ab uno vel pluribus teneatur pro basi continue nota una; et ab alio uno vel pluribus idem cantus incipiatur in diapente et in eodem cursu cantetur usque in finem; a tertio uno vel pluribus idem cantus in diapason continue incipiatur, et in prima voce cursus ejusdem cantus legitime finiatur....Organica triphonia est melodia vel modus canendi a tribus vel pluribus, modis tribus divisis ita, ut unus vel plures basim teneant in gravibus notis pausarum; ab alio uno vel pluribus cantus diversus (Gerbert: *distertius*) organicus incipiatur in diapente, vel forte in diatessaron; (!) et a tertio uno vel pluribus cantus incipiatur organicus diformis in diapason et pars tertia secundae organicae obviando cum ea; et cum prima utatur aliqua pausatione concordi vel in diapente, vel in diapason—potest etiam esse, ut organica et dissimilis triplex nota simul ab his tribus partibus decantetur et hic modus bene dicitur organica triphonia. Similis est doctrina de tetraphonia, in qua diversae partes quatuor variantur: pars nimiirum inferius incipit in gravibus; secunda pars cantum ejusdem incipit in diapente; tertia respectu primae incipit in diapason, et quarta respectu secundae incipit in diapason similiter; et sic partes quatuor cantum pariter percurrendo pariter pausent et pariter cantum finiant, ita ut parti cuilibet modo suo praedictum. Organica, ut dictum est, ab organo vocali nomen accepit, eo quod diversa organa diversimode resonant, quemadmodum et singuli homines singulas habent formas diversas. Organica nihil aliud est, quam dispar concordia cantus diversimode sibi occurrentis; dum enim in tali specie cantus pars una multum ascendit, reliqua vero multum descendit, et e contrario, et pausat pariter, ut dictum est, vel in eadem clave, vel in diapente, vel in diapason. Si autem eos alibi pausare contigerit, quod raro videtur, non debet vocem diu tenere, sed reptim resilire a pausa. Saepe tamen contingit in organica, quod pars inferior paucas (Gerbert: pausans) habet notas, et superior multas: tunc vero paucae tractim sunt, multae canendae velociter, donec tandem in fine concurratur vel in eodem, ut dictum est, vel in diapente, vel in diatessaron."

FOOTNOTE 19: (Couss., *Script.* III:388): "Nunc autem aliqui discantores vel discantuum compositores nullam harum conditionem observant proprietatem discantus, faciunt non bonae concordiae cantus, faciunt silvestres, male placentes, difficiles, intricatos et quasi immensurabiles."

FOOTNOTE 20: (*Ibid.*, p. 389): "Sed aliqui nunc novi, qui inter majores in discantibus componendis forsan reputantur, formam atque finem discantuum subtilitati, compositionis difficultati, intricationi videntur attribuere."

FOOTNOTE 21: (*Ibid.*, p. 395): "Et quid valet subtilitas ubi perit utilitas...?"

FOOTNOTE 22: (*Ibid.*, p. 407): "Hae autem simplices notule suffecerunt antiquis qui tot pulchra opera et distincta de cantu fecerunt mensurabili. Possent et hae cantoribus sufficere modernis, si vellent et non impediret hoc curiositas lascivia, vanitas, si fas est dicere."

## CHAPTER XI

# Counterpoint during the 14th and 15th Centuries

I N T H E first half of the 14th century, in place of the older designations—organum, *diaphonia*, and *discantus*—we see appearing for the first time the new term *counterpoint* used to describe note-against-note settings (*punctus contra punctum*).*[1] It is not known who coined this term; there is no doubt, however, that this change in terminology is one of the marks of the *Ars nova*. The oldest works of the Parisian Jean de Muris do not employ this term; therefore it may have been introduced by Philippe de Vitry personally. It is certain that the Parisian Muris used it soon after, and that it spread immediately to become common usage. It is not to be found in the treatise *Ars nova*, which gives us another reason for placing this treatise before Vitry, and it is also not found in the *Liber musicalium* (!). It occurs, however, in the *Ars contrapunctus secundum* (!) *Philippum de Vitriaco*; the *Ars perfecta* (Philippoti) is also prefaced by an *Optimae regulae de contrapuncto*. There is also an *Ars contrapuncti secundum* (!) by Jean de Muris, and the *Ars discantus secundum* (!) by the same author contains a section called *De compositione contrapunctus*. Coussemaker also includes in the third volume of his *Scriptores* an *Optima introductio in contrapunctum pro rudibus* by Johannes de Garlandia (!) belonging to a codex in the cloister Einsiedeln, dating back to the 14th century, which also contains works of Marchettus, de Vitry, and the Parisian Muris. It is not possible that this work is by the pre-Franconian Garlandia, especially since the *Dialogus* of Robert de Handlo, written in 1326, introduces by quotation a Johannes de Garlandia as the author of attempts at distinguishing the divisions of the breve by names (*semibrevis major, minor, minorata, minima*) and by shapes (♦ ♦). This leads to belief in the existence of a second Johannes de Garlandia (see p. 145 ff.) who must have belonged to the first decades of the 14th century. If the treatise found in the cloister of Einsiedeln rightfully bears the name Johannes de Garlandia, we must consider this second Garlandia as one of the first representatives of the *Ars nova*. The contents of the very short treatise[1] are as follows:

[1] (Couss., *Script.* III:12–13): "Volentibus introduci in artem contrapunctus, id est notam contra notam, considerare debemus, quod aliquae sint praenotanda. (Primo et principaliter, quod ab una littera quae clavis est usque ad suam similem proximam dicitur duplex vel octava.)

Whoever wishes to be introduced to the art of counterpoint, that is, note-against-note setting, must first be cognizant of the following:

1. *Cantus* and *discantus* must be led in contrary motion, unless good reasons require them to move otherwise.

2. There are nine intervals which apply in (note-against-note) counterpoint: the unison, third, fifth, sixth, octave, tenth, twelfth, thirteenth, and double octave. Of these, five are perfect, namely, the unison, fifth, octave, twelfth, and double octave (erroneously the third and sixth are also mentioned in this enumeration); these are called perfect because they are completely consonant to the ear. In simple note-against-note counterpoint (notes of the same value on different lines or spaces) two of these perfect consonances must never succeed one another, such as two unisons, two fifths, two octaves, two twelfths, or two double octaves. It is

"I. Primo quando cantus ascendit, discantus debet descendere, et e contrario quando cantus descendit, discantus debet ascendere, nisi aliis rationibus condignis evitetur. II. Considerando quod novem sunt species quibus utimur generaliter in contrapunctu scilicet nota contra notam, videlicet unisonus, tertia, quinta, sexta, octava, decima, duo-decima, tertiadecima et quintadecima. Istarum autem specierum quinque sunt perfectae scilicet unisonus...quinta...octava, duodecima et quintadecima; et dicuntur perfectae, quia perfecte et complective consonant auribus audientium et cum ipsis omnis discantus habet incipi et finiri. Et nunquam istarum specierum perfectarum duo debent sequi una post aliam, id est: duo unisonius, duae quintae, duae octavae, duae duodecimae et duae quintaedecimae non debent sequi una post aliam, sed duae diversae species imperfectae vel plures licite sequuntur una post aliam. III. Quatuor autem aliae sunt imperfectae videlicet tertia, sexta, decima et tertia decima. Et dicuntur imperfectae quia non ita perfecte (Couss. imperfecte) sonant ut species perfectae; et cum istis speciebus imperfectis possumus ascendere vel descendere in discantu cum tenore ad libitum; et interponuntur speciebus perfectis in compositione sine dissoluto. Et possumus duas species imperfectas ordinare ascendendo vel tres aut quatuor vel plures si necesse fuerit, descendendo autem duas vel tres vel quatuor vel plures semper speciebus perfectis sequentibus. IV. Etiam quanto cantus ascendit vel descendit per quatuor voces vel quinque, licitum est nobis, ascendere vel descendere in discantu per unam vocem tantum cum speciebus perfectis et non plures. V. Si autem cantus vel ascendit vel descendit per sex vel per septem, licitum est nobis ascendere vel descendere cum tenore et cum speciebus perfectis, ut discantus per duas voces. VI. Si autem cantus ascendit vel descendit per octo voces, licitum est nobis ascendere vel descendere cum tenore etiam cum discantu cum speciebus perfectis per tres voces. Et hoc secundum diversos ascensus vel descensus cantus. VII. Praenotandum est quod generaliter post unisonum sequitur tertia et aliquando quinta et aliquando sexta et etiam octava. Post tertiam sequitur generaliter quinta et aliquando octava. Post quintam sequitur sexta et aliquando octava et etiam unaquaeque species. Post sextam sequitur octava...et aliquando decima. (Post octavam sequitur generaliter decima et aliquando duodecima.) Post decimam generaliter sequitur duodecima. Post duodecimam generaliter sequitur tertia decima. Post tertiam decimam sequitur generaliter quintadecima. Post quintamdecimam sequitur tertiadecima, et e contrario et secundum diversos ascensus et descensus cantus. VIII. Praenotandum quod quandoque ordinantur duae tertiae (Couss. species) vel tres cantu ascendente, sequitur unisonus, cantu autem descendente sequitur quinta, ita ut superius dictum est. Post quintam (non) sequitur octava, nisi necessitas fuerit. IX. Quandoque ordinantur duae vel tres decimae cantu ascendente sequitur in fine octava; cantu autem descendente sequitur (duo)decima."

permissible, however, to use two or more imperfect consonances of the same value in succession on different lines or spaces.

3. The four remaining intervals are imperfect, namely, the third, sixth, tenth, and thirteenth. These are called imperfect because they do not sound with the same perfection as the others. Using these imperfect intervals, the discant may be allowed at will to ascend or descend in parallel or similar motion with the tenor voice. The imperfect intervals appear between perfect ones in simple note-against-note counterpoint (*sine dissolutu*—without figuration). Therefore one is allowed to use two, three, four, or more imperfect intervals of the same kind succeeding each other in ascending or descending motion, if necessary, providing that this is followed by a perfect interval.

4. If the *cantus* ascends or descends the distance of four steps (a fifth), the *discantus* may move in similar motion with it the distance of one step using perfect intervals (octave-fifth, fifth-octave).

5. If the *cantus* ascends or descends the distance of six steps (a seventh), the *discantus* is allowed to move in similar motion with it the distance of two steps using perfect intervals (twelfth-octave, octave-twelfth).

6. If the *cantus* ascends or descends by seven steps (an octave), then the discant may move with it in similar motion the distance of three steps using perfect intervals (fifth-unison, unison-fifth).

7. Generally when the *cantus* descends, the third follows the unison, though it may sometimes be followed by the fifth, sixth, or the octave. The third is usually followed by the fifth, but it may be sometimes followed by the octave. The fifth is followed by the sixth, occasionally the octave or some other interval, while the octave follows the sixth, or sometimes it may be followed by the tenth (the tenth follows the octave, and sometimes it may be followed by the twelfth). The tenth is usually followed by the twelfth, the twelfth is usually followed by the thirteenth, and the thirteenth is usually followed by the double octave. If the *cantus* ascends, the succession is reversed.

8. If the *cantus* ascends, the unison follows two or three (thirds), and if it descends, the fifth follows two or three thirds. The fifth is never followed by the octave, if at all possible.

9. If the *cantus* ascends, the octave follows after two or three tenths; if the *cantus* descends, the twelfth follows in the same manner.

Examples given as illustrations for those rules (the obvious errors in them are here corrected) are:

7a.

7b.

8.                                           9.

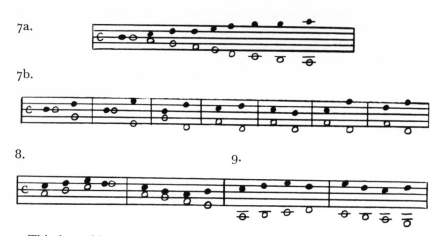

This is nothing else but a rectification of the strict contrary motion *déchant* through the use of the English manner of discanting with mene-sight and treble sight (parallel thirds with a close at the fifth, parallel sixths with a close at the octave), a compromise which we were able to follow in its several stages (see especially the theories of Anonymous V and XIII).*2

The *Ars contrapunctus secundum* (!) *Philippum de Vitriaco* (Couss., *Script.* III:23 ff.), which until now was considered (Couss., *Script.* III, XV) to be the work in which the term *counterpoint* first appeared, is apparently a revision of the *Optima introductio* of the younger Garlandia with the in-clusion of a new section (*tractatus primus* and *secundus*) and begins in the same way:*3 "Volentibus introduci in artem contrapuncti i.e. nota contra notam." After dealing at length with intervals, we read (p. 26):2

*Musica ficta* comes about when we change a whole-tone to a semitone or con-versely, a semitone to a whole-tone. For each whole-tone is divisible into two semi-tones and consequently the signs for semitones can be used for all tones (!)....
Wherever we find a ♭, we shall say FA, and wherever we find a ♮, MI.

(See p. 141 f., the almost verbatim citation from the *Introductio secundum* [!] by Johannes de Garlandia which we probably must also attribute to the younger Garlandia, as well as mention on page 114 by Marchettus, of Richardus Normandus.)

The *Tractatus tertius* which I include here for comparison with the *Optima introductio* of Garlandia II is divided in the same manner (I–II) and agrees line by line with Garlandia's except for a few changes in the

---

2 "Est ficta musica quando de tono facimus semitonium et e converso de semitonio tonum. Omnis enim tonus est divisibilis in duo semitonia et per consequens signa semi-tonia designantia in omnibus tonis possunt applicari."

wording.[3] The sentences which I have marked N.B.[1] and N.B.[2] are new:

[3] "I. When the *cantus* ascends the *discantus* ought to descend; this is a general rule that should be observed unless by means of imperfect species [imperfect consonances] or for other reasons it is avoided. II. It should be considered, as stated above, what the kind and quality of the thirteen species are, no more and no less, according to very learned doctors (Boethius, Guido, Master de Garlandia) and certainly according to Master Octo (Odo?), one most learned in this science.... Three of these species are perfect: unison, fifth, and octave (or *diapente* or *diapason*). They are called perfect because they bring a perfect, whole sound to the ears of listeners. With them [the perfect species] every *discantus* ought to begin and end, and these perfect species should, by no means, follow one another in a *discantus* in diverse lines or spaces. That is, neither two unisons, two fifths, two octaves, nor two other perfect kinds ought to follow one another, but this may certainly take place in one line or space where many such sounds may be found [repetition of perfect species permitted]. Moreover, two different imperfect species, or three, or even four, can follow one after the other, if it is necessary. III. Four of the aforementioned species are imperfect, that is, the ditone (with another name the third is perfect [that is, when the major third has the proportion 5/4]), the whole-tone plus *diapente* (with another name the sixth is perfect [5/3? a combination of 4/3 × 5/4. The Pythagorean designation for the major sixth is 27/16.]), the semiditone (with another name the third is perfect [6/5? The Pythagorean minor third is 32/27]), and the semitone with *diapente*, which is otherwise known as an imperfect sixth. They are called imperfect because they do not have so perfect a sound as the perfect species, for which reason they are placed among the perfect kind in composition. (N.B.[1]) Another six species are discordant, that is, the whole-tone, the semitone, the *diatessaron*, the tritone, the ditone plus *diapente*, and the semiditone plus *diapente*. Because of their discord, they are not used in counterpoint, but in *cantu fractibili* in the smaller notes. When a *semibreve* or a *tempus* is divided into more notes, that is, in three parts, then one of these three parts can be in the discordant species. (N.B.[2]) Further, it should be noted that in no way ought we to make the *discantus* ascend or descend with the tenor using perfect species while the *cantus* is ascending or descending stepwise. If anyone does this it will be false and contrary to art. We can, however, ascend or descend in imperfect species very well, as has been said. IV. Further, it must be noted that when the *cantus* ascends or descends through five steps (some masters feel compelled to say four steps), then we can make the *discantus* ascend or descend with the tenor only one tone using the perfect species, and not several times. V. If, however, it is with six or seven tones, then we can ascend or descend with the tenor using the perfect species, but only twice. VI. If, however, the *cantus* descends through eight tones, then we can make the *discantus* ascend or descend with the tenor using the perfect species through two or three tones but no more. VII. Take note that the unison requires the third, the third the fifth, the fifth the sixth, the sixth the octave; and this rules does not fail because always after the sixth the octave ought to follow because the rule is general that this should happen. Whenever after the unison the fifth follows, then the sixth and the octave follow, and the contrary, and whenever after the third the fifth sometimes follows, then the sixth and the octave follow, and the contrary. After the fifth any one of the species follows, and this accords with the different risings and fallings of the *cantus*. VIII. Notice that with imperfect species we can ascend or descend at will, and the same position they have in ascending they will have, in reverse, in descending. And just as the unison is related to the octave, so the octave is related to the double octave. IX. It is to be noted that‚ when two or three thirds ascend with the *cantus*, the fifth follows at once, and the same rule or custom is observed going from the octave even to the double octave, as has very often been said."

Dissonances are not allowed in counterpoint, but are used in figurate discant, i.e., when a semibreve or breve (the word *tempus* probably means beat; this may be the semibreve as well as the breve in the *Ars nova*) is divided into smaller values, namely, into three, one of which may be dissonant.*4

This is followed by an enumeration of special instances where the discant may move in similar motion with the *cantus* from one perfect consonance to another. The wording of "when the *cantus* ascends or descends five, or, as some teachers feel compelled to say, four steps" (following their usual manner of counting) points to Gui de Châlis (p. 86 f.) and other instructions for the strict octave-fifth-*déchant* (p. 88 f.) with their counting or omitting the beginning tone (fourth = the fourth step or = three steps upwards). At any rate, in giving the permissible movements in similar motion from one perfect consonance to another, those which are not given must be considered prohibited. The following types of voice-leading are therefore forbidden:

N.B.²                N.B.²

This seems to be, then, the first appearance of the rule that hidden octaves and fifths are not allowed, together with a number of exceptions (*licitum est* in Garlandia II, *possumus* in de Vitry [?]). Unfortunately the actual rule prohibiting them is missing; because even though the rule against a series of perfect consonances in similar motion is at first worded in such a way that it might refer to successions such as octave-fifth, fifth-octave, etc., both authors use the words *id est* and thereby mean definitely that we are here concerned with successions "duarum perfectarum ejusdem speciei." A succession of perfect consonances in similar motion is expressly forbidden when the tenor voice ascends or descends stepwise (N.B.²).

The *Optimae regulae contrapuncti* (Couss. III:28) preceding the *Ars perfecta* (Philippoti) also agrees with these two [Garlandia II and de Vitry] in its contents, but does not go as far as the double octave in its enumeration of intervals as Garlandia II does, or only to the octave as in the *Ars contrapuncti,* but goes as far as the twelfth. In this version there are also other minor deviations. The six rules are:[4]

1. Contrary motion between tenor and counterpoint (*sic*).

2. Beginning and ending with a consonance (see N.B. below), in order not to go against nature, as the *penultima* must always be a dissonance (imperfect consonance).

3. The prohibition of successions of (perfect) consonances of the same kind.

4. Alternation between consonances and dissonances (see N.B. below).

5. Several dissonances (i.e., imperfect consonances) are allowed if followed by a (perfect) consonance.

6. It is permissible to proceed from the twelfth to the octave, from the octave to the fifth, from the fifth to a unison, and vice versa (whereby contrary motion is probably meant). A happy medium is found by following the fourth rule. N.B. "Consonance and perfect consonance are synonymous. Dissonance and imperfect consonance mean the same."

The point of view from which these rules are written appears to be earlier than the one of the treatise which follows; perhaps they must even be dated before Garlandia II. As regrettable as it is that we have no source for the transition of the *déchantier* rules to the theory of counterpoint, we must nevertheless resist the temptation to regard Philippe de Vitry or the Parisian Muris as the discoverers of counterpoint, as is commonly done. We can now assume that only certain established compositional procedures evolved in musical practice which were crystallized during the first decades of the 14th century, known as the *Ars nova,* by de Vitry and the Parisian Muris, its outstanding representatives.*[5]

The terminology contained in the *Optimae regulae* is in striking agreement with the instructions for counterpoint contained in the *Compendium musicale* of the presbyter Nicolaus Capuanus (pp. 31–34), published

[4] "(Septem sunt species consonantiarum in discantu sc. unisonus, tertia quinta sexta octava decima duodecima).... I. Quando tenor ascendit, contrapunctus debet descendere et e converso. II. Semper incipiendum est ab una consonanti et nunquam in dissonanti, et sic finiri (debet) nisi aliter artaretur verum (quod penultima semper debet esse dissonantia vel imperfecta). III. Nunquam consonantia post consonantiam simul vel semel vel una et eadem consonantia replicari debet. IV. Semper una consonantia et altera dissonantia cantari debet. V. Possumus facere duas vel tres ad plus dissonantias et postea sequi debet consonantia. VI. Possumus descendere de duodecima in octavam et de octava in quintam et de quinta in unisonum. Et sic per ascensum. Sed mediocriter dicitur, quum una consonantia et altera dissonantia cantatur (cf. IV). Consonantia et consonantia perfecta idem sunt, et dissonantia et consonantia imperfecta pro eodem habentur."

separately in 1853 by J. Adr. de Lafage. Since this work dates back to
the year 1415, it cannot be used to prove the early age of the *Optimae
regulae*; however, it does prove that thirds and sixths, even fifty years
after de Vitry and the Parisian Muris, were still called dissonances by a
few scholars. Nicolaus Capuanus was by no means a scholarly writer,
since he attributes to Guido of Arezzo the idea (p. 31) that the *contrapunctus* is the *fundamentum discanti* (*sic*) and attributes to Boethius the concept of *musica ficta* (p. 34). Unfortunately, Lafage found rules concerning
counterpoint in only one of the two codices (in Vallicellanus) used by
him; otherwise he might have been able to reproduce the text more
correctly. The assumption that the rules themselves are not by Nicolaus
de Capua, but are much earlier, is based not only upon the omission of
the rules in the *Codex Casanatensis* but also upon the title of the compendium, which reads: "a multis doctoribus editum et compositum et per
presbyterum Nicolaum de Capua (*sic*) ordinatum." I shall restate only [5]
the most important sentences here in order to make the relationship to
the *Optimae regulae* clearer. Also of interest for us is the passage concerning
*musica ficta* (p. 32), which does not agree with the *Optimae regulae*: [6]

All dissonances shall carry the sign ♯ which is called *diesis* (!); this is used to
make the imperfect intervals perfect, namely the third, sixth, and tenth, or the
third before the fifth, the sixth before the octave, and the tenth before the twelfth:

[♯ in first measure apparently means b♮]

An explanation follows which is difficult to understand; it deals with
two kinds of counterpoint, which may be differentiated as *modus octavae*
and *modus duodecimae*; [7] the first adds counterpoint above the *hexachordum
durum* G a ♮ c d e, the second adds counterpoint above the *hexachordum*

[5] "It must be noted that there are seven species of counterpoint, namely: unison,
third, fifth, sixth, octave, tenth, and twelfth, four of which are consonant and three
dissonant. The consonant are these: unison, fifth, octave, and twelfth; the dissonant are
these: third, sixth, and tenth. It should be understood that we ought to begin and end
with consonance, but the *penultima* ought to be dissonant." (The prohibition of parallel
perfect consonances follows here, and permission to use parallel "dissonances," the text
of the latter unfortunately with the mistake "et neque" which distorts the meaning and
should read "namque.")

[6] "Et nota quod ad omnes dissonantias additur ista figura ♯ quae vocatur diesis, quia
ista figura ♯ habet perficere imperfectum, puta tertiam, sextam et decimam."

[7] "Now we must note that there are two modes in counterpoint: one is called the mode
of the octave and the other the mode of the twelfth. The first mode is sung through B♮

*naturale* C D E F G a (is this an indication of the treble sight and qua-treble sight?). The two manners of counterpoint are as follows:

a
*modus*
*octavae*

b
*modus*
*duodecimae*

[B *quadrum*] and is formed from G *grave* (!) following the order UT, RE, MI, FA, SOL, LA. Of this aforesaid counterpoint we have, moreover:

| Γ ut | sol mi | ut | G sol re ut | la | (!) sol mi ut |
|---|---|---|---|---|---|
| A re | la fa | re | a la mi re | la fa re | |
| B mi | sol mi | u(t) | (♭ fa) ♮ mi | sol mi ut | |
| C fa ut | la fa | re u(t) | c sol fa ut | la fa, re | |
| D sol re | sol mi | re (!) | d la sol re | sol mi ut (!) | |
| E la mi | la fa | mi(!) ut | e la mi | la fa re (!) ut | |
| F fa ut | sol fa | re | | | |

Also the second mode is through nature and is formed from c *acuto* following the order UT, RE, MI, FA, SOL, LA, and of the aforesaid counterpoint we have, moreover:

| C fa ut | sol mi | ut | c sol fa ut | la | (!) sol mi ut |
|---|---|---|---|---|---|
| D sol re | la fa | re | d la sol re | la fa re | |
| E la mi | sol mi | ut | e la mi | sol mi ut | |
| F fa ut | la fa | re ut (!) | f fa ut | la fa re | |
| G sol re ut | re (!) | mi sol | g sol re ut | sol mi ut (!) | |
| a la mi re | la fa | mi (!) ut | a la mi re | la fa re (!) ut | |
| ♭ fa ♮ mi | sol fa | re | a | | |

It must also be known that in ♭ fa ♮ mi we cannot have a *diapente* in these two modes except by *musica ficta*...for if the tenor is ♭ fa ♮ mi on the tone MI we ought to form suitable counterpoint from the *acuto* and then we have its *diapente*, that is, MI (fa ♯)

as here:    * [*sharp before b indicates a natural.] And so when we cannot have consonance through *rectae musica*, then we ought to resort to *ficta*, and apply it even though it is seldom used."

or, in other words, if I do not entirely misinterpret the author, we are here concerned with an interpretation of tones of the scale in a harmonic sense, which would appear as follows, if we would put them in triadic positions:

The "formatur in G gravi" and "formatur in c acuto" refer to the upper voice (the counterpoint); consequently the counterpoint of the *modus octavae* should assume as its main area of activity the hexachord G a ♮ c d e, and the *modus duodecimae* the hexachord c d e f g $\frac{a}{a}$, and should proceed from them in solmization and mutation. Therefore, the dual form of f is suggested for the first, and the dual form of b for the last.

Lafage's anonymous treatise (p. 35), *Musicae liber*, which he found together with the treatise of Nicolaus de Capua in the Codex Valicellianus, also belongs with this group, since he calls the imperfect consonances in counterpoint dissonances and does not mention the real dissonances at all. Here Boethius is credited with the authorship of counterpoint. Below [8] I am including the entire passage, since the works of Lafage have become rare. Further comment is not necessary.

The *Liber musicalium* attributed to de Vitry also contains rules regarding counterpoint (*regulae contrapunctus*).[*6] Interval definitions proceed up to the twelfth. The dispositions for counterpoint deal almost entirely with three to four tone neumes (Couss., *Script*. III:37 ff.). In the beginning the rule appears forbidding parallel or similar motion using perfect consonances

[8] "Notice that counterpoint is nothing else but setting one note against another note according to Boethius (he does not say you should set one for two but one for one). Hence we ought to oppose those singers who set two notes unless they set them dividing one note into two for the coloring of consonance, otherwise they go on in a gross manner. Note that counterpoint should always begin and end with consonance, but the *penultima* can be dissonant. There are four consonances in counterpoint: the fifth, octave, twelfth, and fifteenth, and there are four dissonances, that is, the third, sixth, tenth, and the thirteenth. Note that any dissonance in descending (with the tenor) requires its consonance as the third requires the fifth, the sixth the octave, the tenth the twelfth, and the thirteenth the fifteenth. Note that when the tenor ascends, counterpoint ought to descend, and vice versa. Yet this rule does not hold true with dissonances; we can ascend or descend with the tenor in as many as four dissonances, but not with consonances. Notice that two consonances of the same kind cannot be used, that is, fifth followed by fifth, and so on with the others. But. . .various consonances should be used when the tenor ascends as many as five [steps](!)."

and allowing progressions of imperfect consonances.[9] Then the following successions are given as being characteristic:

The text toward its end contains many errors; the words in parenthesis, for instance, must be added to the following sentence (p. 40):

Si velles ascendere vel descendere per tertias (tunc tertia revertit ad quintam; et si velles ascendere) vel etiam descendere (per sextas) tunc sexta (Couss. tertia) revertit ad octavam.

If you wish to ascend or descend in thirds (then the third will return to a fifth; and if you wish to ascend) or descend (in sixths) then the sixth will return to an octave.

The conditions under which parallel motion of perfect consonances is allowed are missing altogether in this passage. We find the categorical statement that (p. 37) "*Cantus* and *discantus* may ascend (or descend) only in imperfect consonances." The words "vel descendere" are missing in this codex and again show its faultiness.

In the [10] *Compendium* (1336) of Petrus Palma ociosa (*SIMG* XV:504–534) prominent use is made of the term *discantus*, while the term *punctus*

[9] (Couss., *Script.* III:37): "Two species, perfect in themselves, cannot be placed together, that is, a unison must not be used twice [in parallel motion] or a fifth or an octave or a twelfth. Note that the *cantus* and *discantus* should not ascend or descend together except with imperfect species."

[10] [This reference is made by Gustave Becking, who completed the second edition of Riemann's *Geschichte* following Riemann's death.]

*contra punctum* is used only once. On page 508 we find: "Simplex discantus, qui nihil aliud est quam punctus contra punctum sive notula
naturalibus instrumentis formata contra aliam notulam." (*Simplex discantus* is merely *punctus contra punctum*, or one note, formed by natural
means, against another note.) The unison and the octave are regarded as
perfect consonances, the fifth as an intermediate consonance (*media*),
and the two thirds as well as the major sixth as imperfect consonances.
The dissonances, to which the minor sixth is also relegated, are mentioned as *species discantus*, but may only be touched on in passing to the
consonant species.[11] Parallel or similar motion of voices is permissible:
1. *propter pulchritudinem*,[12] 2. *propter defectum vocis*, 3. *causa necessitatis*. It
must not occur, however, in the same *modus*, but instead must be figurated.
Admittedly,[13] movement of the tenor and *discantus* in the same direction
and with the same note values is allowed only with imperfect consonances.

Furthermore, a warning is given against the practice of literally repeating the same consonance (no matter what kind it is).

The rules for the *discantus simplex* are as follows:

The unison proceeds to all (consonant) species with an ascending
discant (the major third is not found in the examples).

The minor third proceeds:

1. to the unison (by contrary motion),
2. to the fifth (similar-descending motion).

The major third proceeds:

1. to the fifth,
2. to the major sixth,

(3. to the octave. This rule is missing here but appears on p. 514 in the
first example.)

The fifth proceeds to all species.

The major sixth proceeds:

1. to the octave (the tenor descends a whole step),
2. over a stationary tenor in the succession octave-major sixth-fifth,
3. over a stationary tenor in the succession fifth-major sixth-fifth.[14]

---

[11] "Notice that although we ought not to delay too long in these dissonances, yet we
can ascend or descend through them to all other kinds and differences of discant."

[12] See rule 9, p. 223.

[13] (Page 507): "Concedo tamen ascendere simul et descendere eodemque modo sive
divisione aliqua in speciebus sive differentiis imperfectis sicut est semiditonus, ditonus et
tonus cum diapente. Nec etiam in speciebus sive differentiis musicalibus praedictis
perfectis aut imperfectis neque in media consulo fieri eodem modo duas vel plures consonantias unisonantes in eodem spatio sive linea existentes."

[14] Among the examples (p. 511):

The octave proceeds to all species (the major third is again missing in the examples).

Above the octave the same relationships are repeated.

This very significant addition follows (p. 512):

> Insuper nota, quod licet omnes species discantus antedictae decentius stant et ordinantur in locis praedictis quam in aliis quibuscumque, possunt tamen ordinari et fieri, ubicumque volueris, hoc cautius observato, quod unicuique speciei discantus debitur numerus tonorum et semitoniorum observetur.

(Note above all, as has been stated, that although all species of *discantus* are placed and established in prearranged positions or in others, whatever these may be, they can be placed and arranged wherever you wish them, but here you must be warned, because in each species of *discantus* the number of the tones and semitones must be observed.)

According to Petrus, the *falsa musica* is always used when the steps required by the discant rules are not found in the "hand." Situations in which the minor third is enlarged to major,[15] the *tritonus* to a fifth, and the minor sixth to a major, and the B–MI (B♮) is lowered to a B♭ are especially emphasized. Transpositions indicated in the hand[16] are known to Petrus as UT = b♭ and UT = d. The following sentences point out apparent abuses (p. 514):

> Et si forte contigerit discantum fieri sub tenore, propter hoc minime mutabitur planus cantus...and: aliquotiens tamen reperitur contrarium in quibusdam motetis et rondellis, in quibus cantus planus in falsam musicam transmutatur. Sed non est intentionis meae in arte illa cantum planum in aliquod devium transmutare, sed pro posse meo communes ipsius regulas observabo.

(Perhaps the discant will be led under the tenor: for this reason the *cantus planus* will be changed very little...and: on the contrary, in certain motets and rondels one may find a *cantus planus* which has been changed by *falsa musica*. It is not my intention, however, to employ this means to change the *cantus* in any devious way, but rather to observe all of the customary rules.)

One of the oldest representations of contrapuntal theory (without using the term, however) is the treatise *De discantu et consonantiis*, which Gerbert includes in *Script.* III:306–307 and which bears the subtitle *Explicit tractatus de musica magistri Johannis de Muris de Francia*. This treatise was found in a St. Blasien MS by Gerbert and was the source used by him.*[7] Its contents are given here:[17]

[15] See rule 1, p. 225. (Line 1).

[16] See rule 12, p. 223.

[17] "1. Istarum praedictarum specierum quaedam faciunt consonantiam perfectam quaedam imperfectam....Unisonus, diapente et diapason faciunt consonantiam perfectam: 2. Et aliae species videlicet semiditonus et ditonus, tonus cum diapente faciunt

1. The perfect consonances are the unison, fifth, and octave.

2. The imperfect consonances are the minor and major third and the major sixth (the minor sixth is not mentioned). These imperfect consonances descend or ascend stepwise into perfect consonances, the minor third to the unison, the major third to the fifth, and the major sixth to the octave. The same rules apply to the compound forms of these intervals.

3. The beginning and end of the discant must have a perfect consonance.

4. The stepwise succession of two perfect consonances ascending and descending is, if possible, to be avoided.

5. Above a stationary tenor (*in rota*) there may be two unisons (Gerbert gives *notas* instead of *unisonos*) or two octaves, or also two sixths (if they are followed by the octave).

6. The sixth may be used only in simple discant (even here the term *punctus contra punctum* is not used) when it is followed immediately by the octave.

7. It is permissible to ascend with the tenor in thirds; [First sentence of Rule 8 in original] above a stationary tenor (*in rota*) several thirds may also appear.

---

consonantiam imperfectam, quia tendunt ascendere vel descendere in speciebus praedictis perfectis, scilicet semiditonus in unisono, ditonus in diapente, tonus cum diapente in diapason, ascendendo vel descendendo seriatim. Et quod ordinavi de semiditono, (et) ditono et diapente supra unisonum, sic supra diapason intendatis. 3. Sciendum est etiam, quod discantus debet habere principium et finem per consonantiam perfectam. 4. Debemus etiam binas consonantias perfectas seriatim conjunctas ascendendo vel descendendo, prout possumus, evitare. 5. Sciendum est notabiliter, quod nos (Gerbert: non) possumus duas notas ponere in rota vel in una linea, vel in uno spatio, et eodem modo duas octavas: item duas sextas eodem modo, si octava sequitur ultimam. 6. Item sciendum est quod sexta nullo modo potest poni in discantu simplici, nisi quod octava sequatur immediate. 7. Item sciendum est, quod nos possumus ascendere per unam tertiam, vel per duas, vel per tres, sicut placet, cum tenore. 8. Et etiam possumus licentialiter ponere duas tertias in rota, et in una linea, vel in uno spatio. Item possumus ponere duas quintas cum una tertia in rota, et duas octavas simili modo et duas quintas cum octava et tertia, et duas octavas cum quinta et tertia per ascensum vel descensum tenoris. Et istud supradictum non debet poni in discantu, nisi dum evitari non potest. 9. Item sciendum, quod nos optime possumus ascendere cum tenore de tertia in quintam, et sic de omni imperfecta specie in speciem perfectam, et e contrario eodem modo descendere cum tenore; et est valde pulcrum in discantu. 10. Item sciendum est, quod MI contra FA non concordat in speciebus perfectis, utpote in quinta, et octava, et...duodecima ac in unisono; sed in speciebus imperfectis, scilicet in tertia, sexta, et undecima licentialiter potest poni contra aliud. 11. Item notandum est diligenter, quod quando simplex cantus sive tenor, quod idem est, vadit in summo passu, utpote in passum tertium; si velimus discantare illum simplicem cantum, fingimus voces ipsi concordabiles in exteriori parte manus, utpote quintas et octavas, et sic de aliis speciebus, secundum quod bene licitum est. 12. Item sciendum est, quod quando velimus cantare per falsam musicam, oportet, quod discantando accipiamus istam vocem UT in D lasolre, et RE in E lamire, et MI in F faut et FA in G solreut et SOL in a lamire et LA in ♭ fa ♮ mi....Unde bene possumus per totam manum discantare per falsam musicam, dum tenor non sit concordabilis verae musicae. Sed quando per veram discantare possumus, per falsam illicitum est discantare.''

8. Two fifths and one third, or two octaves (and one third), or two fifths, one octave, and a third, or two octaves, one fifth, and a third are permissible above a stationary tenor, depending on whether it ascends or descends (afterwards), but only if this cannot be avoided.

9. It is possible to move easily from the third to the fifth in similar motion with the tenor, ascending or descending, or generally speaking, from an imperfect consonance to a perfect one, such movements being of great beauty in discant (this is in clear opposition to the now developing prohibition of "hidden" perfect intervals).

10. MI *contra* FA is discordant when used for all perfect consonances; MI *contra* FA, on the other hand, is allowed for imperfect ones, namely, the third, sixth, and tenth (Gerbert: *undecima*) (i.e., c FA against e MI or f FA against a MI and also in *musica falsa* [see below] G FA against ♮MI).

11. If the tenor moves in a very high position, namely, in the third octave (*in passum tertium* [?]), then the introduction of those tones which lie beyond the limits of the "hand" to make up fifths, octaves, and other consonances for the discant is allowed (as is known, the notes in the Guidonian "hand" extend only to our $d^2$, and even $e^2$ falls outside of the "hand." Here we find the first indication in theoretical literature which expressly allows the use of tones outside the "hand").

12. If the discant is used with *musica falsa*, then D should be regarded as UT:

| UT | RE | MI | FA  | SOL | LA |
|----|----|----|-----|-----|-----|
| D  | E  | F♯ | G   | a   | ♮  |

In this way it is possible to discant throughout the entire "hand," using these feigned (*falsam*) tones (by the use of customary mutations such as SOL = UT instead of FA = UT, and UT = FA instead of UT = SOL, which introduces c♯ and C♯ respectively).

What is here at first striking are the conditions attached to the prohibition of parallel perfect consonances (4). As a result, we may assume that the treatise belongs in the very beginning of the 14th century. The expression *in rota* is used enigmatically several times in context which one never finds in other authors under similar circumstances. That the canon (*rondellus, rotula, rota*) is referred to here is out of the question, since we are concerned only with intervals above a stationary tenor or a tenor which repeats the same tone. In the *Ars contrapunctus sec. Phil. de Vitriaco* (Couss., *Script.* III:27) we find in a similar section the following: "Sed bene in una linea vel spatio[18] ubi plures notae inveniuntur." These passages taken together provide an explanation for an even more puzzling section in Guilelmus Monachus (Couss., *Script.* III:290): "Sed nos bene possumus facere, si sint quatuor vel tres notulae, quod illae tres sint tres

[18] See p. 251 (*in eadem sede*).

quintae," etc. There remains, however, the question of the word-meaning to be answered, unless Gerbert by chance read *rota* instead of *nota* (*eadem nota*) or if the same passage used an entirely different word (*reiterata?*). One might possibly think of the English word "root" which is the term used today for the fundamental tone. *Rota* (wheel) might also have been a term for *repercussio*, although it is not found with this meaning in other sources. It is curious to note the continued vacillation of the treatises in their attitudes concerning the minor sixth. Its omission here must be interpreted in the light of Franconian rules (i.e., because it is a dissonance).

The *Ars contrapuncti secundum* of Jean de Muris (Couss., *Script.* III:59–60)*[8] also recognizes only three perfect and three imperfect consonances up to the octave: the unison, fifth, and octave; the minor and major third and only the major sixth. The movement tendencies of the imperfect consonances are brought into agreement with the frequently occurring requirements for progression to intervals which may be achieved by stepwise motion. These are no longer given as being absolutely fixed but with the qualification that "for the sake of variety in the chant" other intervals than those closest at hand may also be permitted. Here we meet with some interesting special rules:[19]

[19] "First it must be known that there is no species above the octave; whatever is made above the octave can be called reiteration or reduplication. Below the octave in all there are six species, three perfect and three imperfect. The first species which is the unison, although not consonant according to some, is the fount and origin of all other consonances according to Boethius, and it naturally demands a semiditone after (before?) it, that is, a minor third, i.e., RE FA, MI SOL, or the opposite [SOL MI, FA RE]. It can also have another imperfect or perfect species after it according to the variation of the *cantus. Diapente* is a perfect species and is called a fifth. It naturally requires a ditone after (before?) it, that is, the major third, i.e., UT MI, FA LA, or the opposite. It is possible even to have another kind of perfect or imperfect species, and this for the aforesaid reason. *Diapason*, that is, the octave, is a perfect species, and naturally requires a *diapente* plus whole-tone after it, which is, of course, the perfect sixth [*sexta perfectam*]. It can also have another perfect or imperfect species after it for the aforementioned reason. The semiditone, that is, the minor third, an imperfect species, naturally requires a unison after it. It can also be followed by another perfect or imperfect species, but then it should be altered to become a ditone. The ditone, that is, the major third, an imperfect species, naturally requires the *diapente* after it, that is, the fifth. It may also be followed by another species, perfect or imperfect, and this according to the variations of the *cantus*. The *diapente* plus whole tone, an imperfect species, naturally requires a *diapason* after it, that is, the octave. It can also be followed by another species, perfect or imperfect, this for the reason stated. It must also be known what sort of *cantus* ought to begin and end with perfect consonances; likewise, that the *cantus* must never ascend nor descend with the tenor in perfect consonances. It should be known that two like perfect consonances ought never to follow one another, but there can well be two, three, or four like imperfect consonances. Also, it should be known that when the *cantus* ascends the *discantus* should descend, and vice versa."

1. If the minor third does not proceed to the unison (but to the fifth), it must be changed to a major third (*sustineri*; see p. 107, remarks).

2. If the major third does not proceed to the fifth (but to the unison), it must be changed to a minor third (also *sustineri*).

3. Sometimes the major sixth does not proceed to the octave, but to the fifth, namely, when the tenor ascends by a major or a minor third. (N.B. 2 and 3 are only in the Codex Ferrariensis.)

The prohibition of parallels reads as follows:

The *cantus* must never ascend or descend together with the tenor at the interval of a perfect consonance. Two perfect consonances of the same type (*similies*) must never directly follow one another (*simul* = together); however, two, three, or four imperfect consonances of the same type may do so.

The treatise *Qualiter debent poni consonantiae in contrapuncto* (Couss., *Script.* III : 60 ff.), which immediately follows, has no connection with the rules in the *Ars contrapuncti secundum Jean de Muris* and deviates from them in essential points.[20] This treatise (by including intervals up to the twelfth) distinguishes four perfect and three imperfect consonances; the latter are the third, sixth, and twelfth; therefore:

1. The minor sixth is regarded as being of equal value with the major.

2. Parallel movement in perfect consonances of the same size is not allowed; without hesitation the twelfth may progress to the octave, the octave to the fifth, the fifth to the unison, and vice versa; whether this rule requires movement in contrary motion, however, is questionable.

3. Parallel imperfect consonances are allowed up to three; then, however, a perfect consonance must follow.

4. The counterpoint must not remain upon the same tone during two *tempora*, not even when the intervals are fifths or sixths (!), otherwise the tenor would be the discant, and this is expressly forbidden (!).

The second section of the treatise deals with the *diminutio contrapuncti* in a laborious but very lucid fashion; however, only note values in the perfect and imperfect mensuration of the breve and semibreve are discussed, while the treatise does not touch upon the kinds of intervals to be used. The musical examples are excellent and show that the practice of

[20] "Perfectae sunt unisonus, quinta, octava et duodecima, imperfectae sunt tertia, sexta et decima." (Page 61): " ... In suo contrapuncto non debet dare duas duodecimas nec duas octavas, nec duas quintas, nec duos unisonos, simul et semel, sed bene potest descendere de duodecima in octavam et de octava in quintam et de quinta in unisonum, et sic etiam per ascensum...talis potest in suo contrapuncto dare duas vel tres imperfectas ad plus, postea debet sequi perfecta...non debet dare in suo contrapuncto duas aequales notas quae sunt duorum temporum etiam si in prima sonaret quinta et in alia sexta....Ratio hujus potest esse, quia tenor discantaret, et hoc prohibitur expresse (!)."

counterpoint had already arrived at a gratifying stage of development, i.e.:

Finally, we must consider an *Ars discantus per* (!) *Johannem de Muris*[9] (Couss., *Script*. III:68) the first part of which (up to p. 70 where the questions begin) contains instructions for counterpoint which agree entirely with the treatise just discussed, although the presentation is somewhat different. Both major and minor sixths are of equal value and rank with the thirds as imperfect consonances. Doubt concerning the now permissible successions octave-fifth, etc. (possibly only in contrary motion?) is unfortunately not clarified in this version. The examples, however, contain a large number of hidden perfect consonances (see below). The sixth should be used only before the octave; however, if the tenor skips a fourth, the succession of sixth to tenth or sixth to third is permissible:

This first part gives the (very simple) examples in white notes; however, I cannot regard this as definite proof of a later period (though the codex was written during the 15th century).

The second part (p. 70: *Quot sunt concordationes*), when referring to the sixths (valuing both major and minor sixths as imperfect consonances), continues on the premises of the first part and energetically launches into an introduction to *musica ficta*[21] in the same manner as Jean de Muris' *Ars contrapuncti secundum.*

1. Wherever the minor third, with the discant ascending in seconds, enters into a fifth or another (!) perfect consonant interval, it must be changed to a major third (*perfici*, by ♯):

2. Wherever the minor sixth, with the discant ascending in seconds, enters into an octave or another perfect consonant interval, it must be changed into a major sixth:

The same (1–2) applies to the compound forms of these intervals.

3. Wherever a major third, with the discant descending (Couss: *ascendendo*) in seconds, enters into (the unison), the fifth, or another perfect consonant interval, it must be changed to a minor third (*imperfici*, by ♭):

[21] "Quandocunque tertia imperfecta, id est non plena de tonis immediate post se habet quintam sive etiam aliam quamcunque speciem perfectam, ascendendo solam notulam, illa tertia imperfecta debet perfici ♮ duro;" the other rules are similarly formulated, i.e.: "Quandocunque tertia perfecta, id est plena de tonis, immediate post se habet unisonum (Couss: quintam) sive aliam quamcunque perfectam speciem descendendo (Couss: ascendendo) solam notulam, illa tertia perfecta debet imperfici ♭ molli."

4. Wherever the major sixth enters into the octave or any other perfect consonant interval, with the discant descending by step, it must be changed to a minor sixth:

The same applies to the compound forms of these intervals.

Finally we meet on page 73 an explicit direction for the *subsemitonium*[22] in the following three instances:

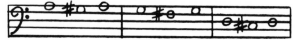

These are not meant for the upper voice, but rather, as is indicated on page 222 (Muris), the *cantus simplex* is to be interpreted to mean *cantus firmus* so that the *subsemitoniae* should apply to the tenor (they obviously already apply to the discant following the previous rules). For it is expressly pointed out that only SOL, FA, and UT should be raised (*sustinentur*) but never RE or even LA, and therefore the second example given with the first rule (N.B.) must be in error (d#).

This extensive treatment sheds different light upon the MI *contra* FA of the Muris treatise in Gerbert, *Script.* III:306, which we have discussed (p. 223), and the *Dissonantiae magis propinquae consonantiis* of Marchettus (Gerbert, *Script.* III:81. See our p. 112), instead of being theoretical sophistry, attains the level of very practical importance. Marchettus, who still regards thirds and sixths as dissonances, explains very plausibly that the sixth belongs less to the fifth than to the octave because both tones are dissonant and therefore require a resolution (p. 81); the smaller the steps which both voices have to make, the more satisfying the progression.[23] No further mention is made of the fact that with that statement he actually implies augmented thirds and sixths as even better than major.[24] *10

[22] (Cf. p. 224): "Whenever a LA SOL LA occurs in a simple *cantus*, the SOL should be altered and sung like FA MI FA," the same applying to the two other cases; ending: "It is to be noted that in counterpoint no other notes are altered but these three: SOL, FA, and UT."

[23] "This is so because dissonance is a kind of imperfection which requires perfection to finish it, but consonance is perfect of itself. The less a dissonance is removed from consonance the less removed it is from perfection, and the more it approaches perfection, and the more it has of the nature of consonance, the pleasanter it is to hear."

[24] Although the demand for an interval larger than a major sixth before the octave had never been made, nevertheless, F. X. Haberl (*KMJ* [1898], p. 35) may be justified in assuming that (at least later) singers regularly indicated the semitone [above, by raising it a half step] by singing an augmented sixth in such cases where the tenor made a Phrygian cadence.

Apparently this kind of chromatic change of sixths and thirds was already in use at the time when the *Lucidarium* was written (1274), although probably the ♭ was used more than the ♯; Marchettus does not endorse the latter, at least for sixths (*op. cit.*).

The continuation of the *Ars discantus per Jean de Muris* removes even the last doubt concerning our explanation of the "*in rota*" (see p. 222 f. above), although this author in no way agrees with the author of that treatise. He says, in connection with the rule prohibiting the succession[25] of perfect consonances of the same kind (Couss., *Script.* III:73): "If in the *cantus* two notes occupy the same line or the same space, then the discant is allowed to take any consonant intervals with the *cantus*, except two thirds or two sixths or sixth-octave." Further, he does not allow the succession fifth-octave above a *cantus* descending a second (because sixth-octave is the usual progression), or two thirds or sixths above a *cantus* descending a third. The same is true above a *cantus* descending a fourth, with the addition of the sixth-octave. The sixth-octave progression is not allowed above a *cantus* descending a fifth or sixth. When the *cantus* ascends a second he does not allow two thirds, two sixths, or the sixth-octave, and this is also true for the *cantus* ascending a third or a sixth. Successions of thirds and sixths are, in general, allowed only above tenors moving stepwise more than once. The sixth-octave progression is permissible if the *cantus* descends a step or by a fourth (the latter, however, "does not sound pleasant or lovely" for which reason it was even not allowed before).

Good:

Not allowed:

This, certainly, is an artfully contrived and thoroughly worked-out system which, however, never achieved general recognition, although it is undoubtedly based in its essence on the principles of English discant, a fact which should not be discounted.*[11] There is no trace here of any type

[25] "Item supra notulas in eadem linea vel eodem spatio sese sequentes sicut sunt LA–LA, SOL–SOL, etc., possunt poni omnes concordantiae, exceptis duabus tertiis et duabus sextis et sexta-octava cum suis aequipollentiis."

of liberal treatment; everything is based on a dry schematization. That
the Parisian Muris should be assigned the authorship of this treatise seems
doubtful to me. In spite of the use of *per*, this treatise is probably only a
development or extension of the teachings of Muris. Of special interest is
the section of the treatise dealing with three-part composition (pp. 92–95
in Couss., *Script.* III). This is probably the earliest attempt to designate
certain voice-leadings for the third voice (over a completed two-voiced
setting) in particular cases and to go beyond the meaningless phrases in
common use during the Franconian period (alternation of the voice
leading in similar motion in one of the two voices with consonance for
both, if at all possible). The rules are actually very well reasoned and show
the emergence of the chordal concept: [26]

1. Whoever wants to compose two counterpoints, that is, two discants above
the tenor, must be careful not to give consonances of equal value (*aequipollentes*) or
even the same (*consimiles*) to both, i.e., fifth and twelfth, or octave and double
octave, or third and tenth, etc., because in such a case not two different sounding
tones, but actually two tones of the same kind would result:

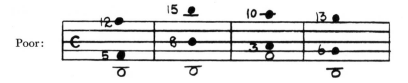

Poor:

2. He must also be careful not to give to one discant the fifth and to another
discant the sixth; the compound forms of these intervals also may not be joined

[26] (Couss., *Script.* III:92): "Quicumque voluerit duos contrapunctus sive discantus
componere super unum tenorem, debet se cavere ne duas aequipollentes sive consimiles
concordantias componat, ut in uno contrapuncto quintam et in alio duodecimam et e
contra; aut in uno octavam et in alio duplicem octavam et e contra; aut in uno tertiam
et in alio decimam; aut in uno sextam et in alio decimam tertiam et contra; et sic de
aliis, quia ibidem nulla esset diversitas, nec ibidem apparerent duo soni, sed tantum
unus. . . .Et debet etiam se cavere ut in uno contrapuncto ut componat quintam et in alio
sextam, et e contra aut in uno duodecimam et in alio duplicem sextam et e contra, aut
in uno quintam et in alio duplicem sextam et e contra, aut in uno duodecimam et in alio
sextam et e contra, quia totaliter discordarentur eo quod oriuntur ex secundis. . . .Et
dulce quod potest, poni est quando quinta ponitur in uno contrapuncto et in alio decima,
quia quamvis tenor taceret, illi duo contrapunctus insimul concordarentur sine tenore,
quia esset sexta. Item etiam dulce est quando decima in uno contrapuncto ponitur et in
alio duodecima, quia etiam sic tenore concordarentur et maneret tertia. Item etiam dulce
est quando sexta in uno contrapuncto ponitur et in alio octava, quia etiam sine tenore
concordarentur et sic dicendum est de suis aequipollentiis."

together, since they would be entirely dissonant because of the (even if transposed) second:

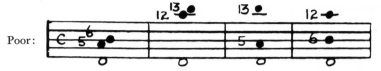

3. That which is most beautiful is when the fifth is given to the first discant and the tenth to the second because these two, even without the tenor, would constitute a consonance (the sixth). The same is true if one assigns the tenth to the first discant and the twelfth to the second, which two would also be consonant without the tenor (producing a third). One can also give the sixth to the first discant and the octave to the second, which two are also consonant without the tenor (third). The same applies to the compound forms (*aequipollentiae*) of the intervals mentioned:

(Even though example c seems less acceptable to us, we probably should not assume it to be in error, since perfect results may not always be expected from a first attempt.)

This direction for the chordal disposition of the tones of the *triplum* in the old sense (two discants above the tenor) is followed by another rule concerning the composition of three-voiced *moteti* or *carmina*, in which the third voice is almost always placed below the tenor and therefore called *contratenor*, while the discant is also called *carmen*:[27]

1. If the discant (*carmen*) is in unison with the tenor, the contratenor is given the third, fifth, sixth (which, however, does not sound as well), octave, or also the tenth below the tenor, but never the unison (!). If one disregards the sixth, there are three good concordances (actually, three possible combinations of consonant intervals, for example, in the case of c e g: c e, e g, and c g):

---

[27] "Ad sciendum componere carmina vel motetos cum tribus, scilicet cum tenore, carmine et contratenore primo notandum est quod quando unisonus habetur super principalem tenorem, tunc tertia sub tenore vel quinta sub vel sexta sub (quae sexta tunc non dulce sonat) vel (Couss: nec) octava sub; et decima sub potest poni in contratenore, sed eadem concordatio non potest ibidem poni.... Insimul sic sexta (Couss: quinta vel sexta) remota (Couss: remotis) manent tres bonae (Couss: binae) diversae concordationes supra quamcunque notatam...."

2. If the discant is a third above the tenor, the contratenor is given the third, sixth (which, however, does not sound as well), octave, or tenth below the tenor, but not the fifth below. The results are good concordances having three parts:

3. If the discant is a fifth above, the contratenor is given the sixth or octave below, but not the third, fifth, or tenth, so that good concordances having three parts result:

4. If the discant is a sixth above, the contratenor is given the third, fifth (this sounds best), octave, or tenth below, but not the sixth (!). The good concordances having three parts are therefore:

The following is missing (!) (5. If the discant is an octave above [the tenor], then the contratenor takes the third, fifth, sixth [which, however, does not sound so well], octave, or tenth below):

6. If the discant is a tenth above (etc., using the same intervals as with the third above, indicated under 2)....

7. If the discant is a twelfth above (etc., using the same intervals as with the fifth above, indicated under 3):

It is surprising to see here the conclusion that the sixth under the tenor is of doubtful value (with the exceptions of the desirable usage shown under 3) and that the six-four chord is directly rejected. The inclusion of the fifth among those intervals which are forbidden under 1 is apparently an error. Since the text is not without errors, which, however, are easily rectified, one can without hesitation delete the words *quinta vel.*

It is not very probable that these rules can be credited to the Parisian Muris. If Simon Tunstede (1351), who knew de Vitry's compositions, had seen these explicit rules, he very likely would never have copied Franco's meaningless rules for three-voiced composition. Tunstede, however, was somewhat familiar with the newer rules concerning two-voiced counterpoint, and he also affirms the alternation of thirds and sixths through ♯ and ♭, according to their contracting or expanding motion. The important passage is located where one would hardly ever look for it, in Chapter 14 of the III. *Principale* (Couss., *Script.* IV:227), which deals with the ecclesiastical modes:[28] "If the *cantus planus* (tenor) ascends and the discant descends, then the third which comes between the fifth and the unison must become a *semiditonus* [minor]; if the voices move apart through the third (to the fifth), the third must be a *ditonus* [major]." Tunstede is very concerned about this radical concept and proves it by expressly referring to it again in Chapter 19 of the IV. *Principale* (Couss., *Script.* IV:280):[29] "The *semiditonus* and *ditonus* [minor and major third] are altered in accordance with the ascending or descending *cantus*, as may be seen in the 14th chapter of the III. *Principale.*" The special rules for discant on pages 282–294 also contain many examples for using the ♯:

Unfortunately, these examples are not always dependable; as specimens, however, they sufficiently prove the great extent to which Tunstede was master of the technique of *musica ficta*. If we examine Tunstede's teachings concerning the prohibitions occurring in the *Ars discantus* of

---

[28] "Et nota quod quando duo cantores simul cantant, unus autem planum cantum et alius discantum: si qui discantat descenderit et gravis vox ascendat et tertia intersit, illa tertia habet fieri ex semiditono. Sed si cantant in unisono et unus recedit ab alio per unam tertiam vocem, illa tertia esse debet ex dytono. Decima...nota sive vox et tertia sunt ejusdem naturae."

[29] "Nam semiditonus et ditonus qui tertiam tenent vocem, diversimode variantur prout cantus ascendit et descendit, ut patet in Tertio Principali capitulo XIV."

Jean de Muris, we find only one point of opposition (Tunstede allows
$\frac{c}{F}\!\!<\!\!\frac{e}{E}$); Tunstede, however, almost throughout regards only contrary
motion as standard, and therefore similar motion with consonances does
not enter the picture. Parallels (p. 281) [30] are strictly forbidden in two-
part counterpoint and successions of fifths and octaves are allowed only
when a pause occurs between the two intervals (see p. 111 above,
Anonymous V, Couss. I). For three-part composition—and this is found
also in the Parisian Muris (see p. 223 above)—two octaves or fifths are
permitted by way of exception in order to achieve a better melodic effect,
when the third voice adds imperfect consonances to the progression, as in
the following example:

We meet another superior intellect in Prosdocimus de Beldemandis of
Padua who must have already attained full manhood around 1400, since his
extant theoretical works are dated from 1404 to 1413. In Padua Marchettus must have been esteemed even a hundred years after his death, for
Prosdocimus felt it necessary to dispute Marchettus' theoretical calling
(Couss. III, XXVIII), with which we are not at all in agreement today.
To us Prosdocimus simply seems more practical than Marchettus, whose
clumsiness in this direction can be easily overlooked in the light of some
of his theoretical concepts, such as the one discussed on page 115 which
explains chromatic deceptive voice-leading. The fact that Prosdocimus is
more lucid than Marchettus must not be regarded as an entirely personal
achievement, for he was able to use numerous other preparatory works
which were not available to Marchettus, especially those of the Parisian
Muris. Prosdocimus' first work (1404) is only an excerpt from Muris'
*Practica musica* (not printed by Coussemaker for this reason). His second
treatise, *Tractatus practice (sic?) de musica mensurabili* (Couss., *Script.* III:200)
refers to the first and still follows the teachings of Muris, deviating only in
minor points. He also speaks, for example, of the *diminutio*,[*12] the substitution of smaller note values for larger ones, not in reference to their

[30] "Two perfect consonances should never be used in succession either ascending or
descending unless a rest (*pausa*) intervenes or when the setting is in three parts [*quando
tres cantus simul modulantur*]. Otherwise, there is no good way in which two perfect consonances can come together either in ascending or descending, unless for better melodic
effect. If there are two diapasons in successions, the other [third] part may use imperfect
consonances, moving from the tenth to the sixth, or vice versa, or it may move two
tenths."

notation, however, but only to their execution.[31] Presumably these were already required by the ⊕ ₵ (*alla breve*) or, as in Anonymous X (Couss. III, see note) by the *color*. These were also called for by the syncope and required for motivic figuration (*color* and *talea*) following the instructions given in the *Libellus cantus mensurabilis* (Couss., *Script.* III:46–56). Prosdocimus otherwise speaks only of note values and does not deal with rules concerning the setting. Concerning the third treatise, *Summula proportionum*, dated 1409, Coussemaker commits an unusual error when he maintains that, for the first time since de Vitry laid down the precedent of employing *proportiones* in the place of the old *modi* (*proportiones* being the use of different mensurations for voices singing at the same time), these are explained in this treatise. The treatise contains in actuality nothing more than some elementary methods of calculation following numerous treatises which derive from Boethius. These deal with the *proportio multiplex*, *superparticularis*, and *superpartiens* and their inversions as the basis of teaching intervals. Not one word is to be found concerning rhythmic relationships, and all of the contents of the treatise are given with express reference to the "antique doctors" (*antiqui doctores*, p. 258).

The major work of Prosdocimus de Beldemandus is his *Tractatus de contrapunctu* (Couss., *Script.* III:193), written in 1412. The word *contrapunctus*, beside its narrow meaning of note-against-note, had already achieved the meaning current today (p. 194: "plurimarum notarum contra aliquam unicam notam in aliquo cantu positio"—"many notes against single notes in the same position in the song"). The treatise itself, however, only deals with note-against-note counterpoint.

Thirds and sixths are now undisputed consonances, even though they are still regarded as being imperfect. The fourth is dissonant, although it and its compound forms are less dissonant than the other dissonances, and it occupies a kind of intermediate position "for which reason, as is said, it was regarded by the ancients as a consonance (!)."[32] Prosdocimus

---

[31] Conclusive evidence that this was not a matter of the notation of small values but a matter of execution is found in Anonymous X (Couss., *Script.* III:415), a small treatise which may be placed in the same period. This treatise speaks of red and white notes in detail (and is of interest in that the *color* is also employed as a sign of diminution of the note values by half).

[32] (Couss., *Script.* III:195): "Also about these combinations you should know that certain ones are consonant, or concordant, or sounding good consonances to human ears just as there are unisons, the third, fifth, sixth, and their equivalents, namely, the octave, tenth, twelfth, thirteenth, fifteenth, and the like. And there are certain that are dissonant, or discordant, or sounding dissonances to human ears, such as the second, fourth, seventh, and their equivalents such as the ninth, eleventh, fourteenth, and the like. Yet you should know that the fourth and its equivalents make less dissonance than other dissonant combinations, indeed, they hold a middle ground between true consonance and dis-

classifies all consonances, with the exception of the unison, as being of two types (*major* and *minor*). The diminished fifth and the diminished octave, however, are real dissonances (p. 197): "Dissonances are never used in note-against-note counterpoint; they are used, however, in figural counterpoint in which the dissonances are not felt because of the short note values. The beginning and end of the counterpoint must utilize a perfect consonance." The rule against parallels is precisely worded; it is expressly said, however, that similar motion from one perfect consonance to another is allowed:[33]

> The counterpoint is never allowed to ascend or descend with the *cantus firmus* (whether the *cantus firmus* be placed higher or lower), using the same perfect consonant intervals (unison, fifth, octave). This is allowed, however, when the size of the intervals varies. The reason is: if one should sing the same as another person, which would be the case if the same interval were used consecutively, then the purpose of counterpoint would be disregarded, which consists of two voices presenting different melodies which are connected by good consonances, well arranged. (This is certainly an excellent reason!) Also, one should not lead the counterpoint with nothing but imperfect consonances without interjecting perfect ones (*contrapunctare* is already a technical term), because this would sound entirely too harsh.... It is best when perfect consonances interchange with imperfect ones (here the well-known chain of intervals follows: unison-third-fifth-sixth-octave-tenth-twelfth).

Prosdocimus interprets *musica ficta* very freely, although he warns, for example, against introducing E♭ in places where *musica ficta* would not be necessary, namely when one takes ♮ to E (p. 198). He adopts the view of Marchettus and his followers completely concerning the alteration of

---

sonance. This is true to such an extent that, according to what some say, they were numbered among the consonances by the ancients." (Page 197): "Discordantiae... nullo modo in contrapuncto usitandae sunt, eo quod propter ipsarum dissonantiam cordiali armoniae et naturae inimicantur, quae armonia finis hujus artis existere videtur. Usitandum tamen in cantu fractibili, eo quod in ipso propter velocitatem vocum earum non sentiuntur dissonantiae."

[33] (Page 197): "...Insimul cum cantu supra vel infra quem contrapunctamus (!) nunquam ascendere vel descendere debemus cum eadem combinatione perfecte concordante, ut cum unisono vel quinta majori, vel octava majori, vel cum his aequivalentibus, licet bene cum diversis vocum combinationibus perfecte concordantibus hoc agere possumus; et ratio hujus est, quum idem cantaret unus quod alter, dato quod in diversis vocibus insimul (eandem) concordantiam habentibus, quod contrapuncti non est intentio; cum ejus intentio sit, quod illud quod ab uno cantatur diversum sit ab illo quod ab altero pronuntiatur et hoc per concordantias bonas et debite ordinatas.... Contrapunctare non debemus cum combinationibus imperfecte concordantibus, continue nullam combinationem perfecte consonantem interponendo, quum tunc ita durum esset hoc cantare, quod in ipso nulla penitus reperiretur armonia."

thirds and sixths, according to their ascending or descending order. The example is quite radical (p. 199):

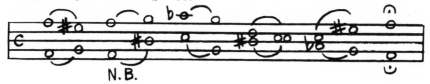

N.B.

It reappears, however, in the same way (employing the *tritonus* also at N.B.) in the *Libellus monochordi*, dated 1413 (Couss., *Script.* III:248), in which treatise the ♯ is called *crux* in passing. A second example in the latter work appears to be similar, but it is full of errors (three notes too many in the upper voice). This little treatise also continues the controversy (without naming names) over Marchettus' division of the whole-tone into five dieses and his establishment of the size of the chromatic, diatonic, and enharmonic semitone into four, three, and two dieses (p. 252; see also p. 114 above).[34] Prosdocimus clearly recognizes, at least according to tonal measurements then in use, that only two kinds of semitones exist; the difference in size he refers to as *croma* (i.e., a♭:g♯). He expressly states that this *croma* corresponds to a rational part of the whole-tone (the difference being known as the Pythagorean comma, a little more than 1/9 of a whole-tone).

Then Prosdocimus, with reference to the assistance of his beloved and highly cultivated "confrater" of the Doctors of Liberal Arts and Medicine, Magister Nicolaus de Collo de Conegliano, first develops two methods of dividing the whole-tone into semitones. The first introduces flats everywhere (b♭, d♭, e♭, g♭, a♭) the second sharps (a♯, c♯, d♯, f♯, g♯) and finally joins the two. With this we probably see for the first time someone of the Middle Ages[35] establishing an enharmonic-chromatic scale of seventeen

[34] "The outcome is that when the greater semitone (namely, 2187/2048) exceeds the lesser (256/243), the amount by which it exceeds (=531441/524288) is called the *croma*, which *croma* is not of the whole-tone (9/8) nor of the major semitone, but is evidently some part of the minor which has been left over, as some writers on music declare clearly. Some of those speaking on music have lied, saying that a tone is divided in five equal parts called *diesi* and that the minor semitonế contained two of these parts, the major three, and sometimes four. So when a semitone containing three [two?] of these parts is found it is called enharmonic because it is a lesser semitone, diatonic, which is greater, containing three of these parts, and chromatic when it is still greater and carries four of these parts within itself." As correct as Prosdocimus' objections are to Pythagorean tuning, those of Marchettus are closer to us in their musical sensitivity, corresponding in part to our present understanding of the differences in fifths and thirds.

[35] See p. 141f., however (and respectively, p. 212), where a sentence is given from the *Introductio secundum* of Johannes de Garlandia (II?) as it relates to the *Ars contrapunctus sec. Phil. de Vitriaco*, which maintains the possibility of employing chromatic signs for all steps of the scale. It intends only two forms for every step (c c♯, d d♯, e♭ e, f f♯, g g♯, a♭ a, b♭ b) and not three, as Prosdocimus intends (d♭ d d♯, g♭ g g♯, a♭ a a♯).

values within the octave:

| d♭ | c♯ | e♭ | d♯ | | g♭ | f♯ | a♭ | g♯ | b♭ | a♯ |
|----|----|----|----|---|----|----|----|----|----|----|
| c  |    | d  |    | e f |  | g  |    | a  |    | b♮ |

In this manner one achieves throughout the monochord two chromatic tones between each of the neighboring tones of the basic scale (*manus*), which are a whole step apart. Even though the last ones (d♯, a♯) will rarely appear in a good chant, it is nevertheless expedient to mark them on the monochord...in order that one could play a melody in which these tones appear, if it happens that such a melody was invented.[36]

The last treatise of Prosdocimus de Beldemandis to be included by Coussemaker, *Tractatus practice de musica mensurabili ad modum Italicorum* (*Script.* III:228 ff.), is of interest in the history of notation; it explains further those differences between the French and Italian manner of notation which were already indicated by Marchettus (see *Studien zur Geschichte der Notenschrift*, pp. 227 and 229). The Italians appear to have used the *punctus divisionis* continually and profusely, to group combinations of small note values, following the manner of Petrus de Cruce (p. 146). The treatise does not contain anything important concerning our subject.

In retrospect the rules of Anonymous XIII (Couss., *Script.* III, the "*appendans*") become highly significant in the light of the strong development of *musica ficta* during the 13th and 14th centuries (Odington, Marchettus, Muris [de Francia], de Vitry, etc.). We are, therefore, compelled to assume that these rules count upon the change of the minor sixth to major (before the octave) and the major third to minor (before the unison) at least as far as all closes and distinctions are concerned. This means for all musical settings in the first and second ecclesiastical modes a c♯ and for those in the seventh and eighth an f♯. Also, those tables concerning *conjunctae* (and *disjunctae*) in Odington and in the Anonymous XI of Coussemaker (*Script.* III; the latter treatise belonging to the 15th century), which were extracted and corrected for my *Studien zur Geschichte der Notenschrift* (pp. 52–55), may now be seen in their correct light.

Already in 1274 Marchettus (in *Pomerium*, Gerbert, *Script.* III:135) inveighs against the term *musica falsa*:[37]

[36] (Couss. III:257): "Et isto modo per totum monochordum habere poteris bina semitonia inter quaslibet duas litteras immediatas in manu musicali tonum resonantes ...et dato quod istae duae fictae musicae...(d♯, a♯) rarissime in cantu aliquo occurrant bonum, est tamen ipsas in monocordo ponere...ut cantum aliquem super tali monocordo pulsare possimus in quo cantu istae duae fictae musicae reperiantur vel saltem altera ipsarum, si talem cantum inveniri contingat."

[37] "Cum ergo tale signum sit repertum in musica ad pulcriores consonantias reperiendas et faciendas, et falsum in quantum falsum semper sumatur in mala parte potius quam in bona (quod est enim falsum, nunquam bonum est): ideo salva reverentia aliorum dicimus, quod magis debet et proprius nominari musica colorata quam falsa, per quod nomen falsitatis (vituperium) attribuimus eidem."

Since this sign (♯) in music was invented to achieve more beautiful harmonies, and the expression "false," on the contrary, is always used for something bad rather than something good (because something "false" is never "good"), I say with all due respect for the words of others, that music of such kind should better and more correctly be called "colored" (chromatic) than "false," because we would always attribute to it the blemish of incorrectness in calling it by the name of "false" music.

One might assume that this statement of Marchettus led to the changing of the name *falsa musica* to *musica ficta.* *13

Shortly after 1400 a decisive but gradual change in the appearance of notation took place, namely, the transition from the black–red to the white–black notation, i.e., the substitution of white notes for black for general use and the reservation of black notes (*nigredo*) for those exceptional cases for which red or white notes had been used. From Haberl's description of the Trent and Bologne mensural codices (*Bausteine zur Musikgeschichte* I, Guillaume Dufay, 1885) it may be clearly seen that these changes had become commonly accepted toward the middle of the 15th century. More precise dating is almost impossible, for between the appearance of this innovation and its general use there was a lapse of several centuries. Since Prosdocimus de Beldemandis knew nothing of this innovation, it cannot be dated around 1400, as has frequently been done, because of earlier incorrect dates for Dufay. Those theorists who used white notes must, therefore, more correctly be dated around the middle of the 15th century. This would at least establish an approximate external clue to the age differences of those authors of the 15th century with whom we shall further concern ourselves.

Black notes were still used, for example, by Antonius de Leno as well as by a number of *Anonymi* in Coussemaker's third volume of *Scriptores*. They are also used in the *Regulae* of the Carmelite Nicasius Weyts (Couss., *Script.* III:262–264). These treatises, however, do not contain anything of further interest to us except one last attempt to designate the mensuration of the *modus major* (for the maxima), the *modus minor* (for the longa), the *tempus* (for the breve), and the *prolatio* (for the semibreve) simultaneously through signs, as follows:

⊙ 3 3 ⎱ where the dot or its absence designates the *prolatio*, the
       ⎰ circle or semi-circle the *tempus*, the first number the *minor*,
C 2 2 ⎰ the second the *modus major*.

This is actually a rather sensible suggestion, which, however, was never established in practice. Only Anonymous XII of Coussemaker (*Script.*

III:493) clings to the circle as representing the mensuration of the breve and prefixes the number for the mensuration of the longa:

$$3 \odot, \; 3 \; \bigcirc, \; 3 \; \mathsf{C}$$

He does not use the number 2, but indicates the imperfect mensuration of the longa by omitting the number 3; he does not indicate the mensuration of the maxima. Anonymous XI (Coussemaker, *Script.* III:493), who uses similar indications, unfortunately gives no clue whether in $\bigcirc$ 2 the 2 signifies the *modus* or the *tempus*. On the other hand, John Hothby in *De cantu figurato* (Couss., *Script.* III:330) uses a reverse order:

$\odot$ 2 3 = *maxima perfecta* ($\bigcirc$), *longa imperfecta* (2),
*brevis perfecta* (3), *prolatio major* (•),

so that the mensuration of the semibreve is equivalent to the sign of the maxima (!).

The treatise *Tractatus de cantu organico* (Couss., *Script.* III:299), which is appended to the treatise of Guilelmus Monachus (though apparently not belonging to it), also shows a rearrangement of the two numbers (before and after the circle), 2 $\bigcirc$ 2, but does not tell us whether the circle is always an indication of the *tempus*. The only Anonymous in vol. IV of Coussemaker's *Scriptores* (p. 434), who probably belongs near the end of the 15th century, shows that in $\mathsf{C}$ 3 the semicircle indicates the *modus* (*modus minor imperfectus*) and the 3 the *tempus*. This Anonymous develops the *proportiones* (proportional notation) up to 5:4 and 6:1, and contains some other interesting details. In this work the ♯ is called *diesis*. The rules regarding voice-leading (p. 446) allow the succession of varying perfect consonances without exception; successions of thirds and sixths are allowed only in stepwise motion. Beginning with an imperfect consonance is allowed only after a rest (i.e., probably for the second voice, which starts later). Beginning and ending with an imperfect consonance is allowed for hymns and sequences, except in the first and last verses. The discant is only rarely allowed to make large leaps (fifths, sixths, sevenths, octaves). In general, a perfection must always end before a larger note value (maxima, longa, breve). The appended examples proceed from the discant as the first voice, to which are added several tenors, contra-tenors, and altos (*tenores acuti*)—very likely a proof that the treatise belongs close to the beginning of the 16th century.

Also of interest are the *Regulae de contrapuncto* of Anonymous VIII (Couss., *Script.* III:409), which unfortunately contain no notated examples, but probably belong before 1450 (from a 15th-century Florentine codex). This treatise allows fifths in contrary motion (5 $<$ 12, 12 $>$ 5), and the following hidden octaves and fifths

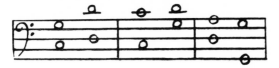

are allowed, following other teachers, but with the remark: "Regula non placet mihi (This rule does not please me)." Unfortunately, the text is not correct; although giving preference to the successions octave-fifth and fifth-octave, it appears that the author does not like being limited to the above cases. For endings he allows imperfect consonances in compositions of more than two voices, but does not allow the position of the sixth. He also warns of giving the fifth or third below the tenor (at the close) to the counterpoint (probably because of the resulting obscuration of the mode).

It may appear questionable to put the treatise of Antonius de Leno (*Regulae de contrapuncto*, Couss., *Script*. III: 307–328), which is written in Italian, into the period of black notation, since his notes always appear without mensuration as *puncti contra punctum* and he differentiates between the voices by the shape of the note and, furthermore, by the color. The consistency, however, with which he uses black notes only throughout the text (only once on page 326 does he use the $\lozenge$ for the division of the semibreve into eight parts; in other words, for the very smallest values, as in Marchettus) is probably proof enough that he knew nothing of white notation. The text contains nothing new (beginning and ending with a perfect consonance; parallels are not allowed; general recommendation of contrary motion and voice-leading in stepwise motion; allowance of successions of thirds before the fifth and succession of sixths before the octave; prohibition of the MI *contra* FA, etc.). Only on pages 312 and 315 is the following specifically prohibited: [38]

[38] (Page 312): "To these notes (namely, to D F of the tenor), if one were to say RE an octave higher to the first note, and if one were to say LA a tenth higher to the second note, it would be false." (Page 315): "If one were to say (F G of the tenor) to FA RE at the sixth, and to SOL SOL at the octave, it would not be good." The text which Coussemakêr has given is very faulty and shows no attempt to correct common transcribing errors. It is very likely full of errors incurred in the reading of the source.

The examples are exceptionally good throughout, even for counter-point with two and three notes against one, as in:

(The counterpoint in Coussemaker incorrectly uses the alto clef instead of the discant clef).

The *proportiones* following on page 324 (*sesquialtera, sesquitertia, dupla, tripla*) [39] are still not the combinations of different mensurations in voices singing simultaneously, which appeared later in the 15th century, but designate only the several possible ways of dividing the semibreve into four, six, etc., parts. For instance, the *proportio sesquitertia* (4/3) is the division of the perfect semibreve (i.e., *prolatio major* = 3 minimas) into four notes of the order:

♩♪ ♩♪   or   ♪♪♪♪   (quadruplets!) for   ♩ ♩ ♩

and in the same way the *proportio sesquialtera* is the division of the imperfect semibreve into three notes, i.e.:

♪ ♩♪   or   ♩ ♩ ♩   (triplets!) for   ♩ ♩

*Proportio dupla* is only the ordinary subdivision into minimas

(♪♪♪♪♪♪ = ♩ ♩ ♩), etc.

At any rate, here may be seen how later systems of proportions developed from the simple beginnings of duplet, triplet, and quadruplet formations (in the same voice). Philippe de Vitry might possibly have been the author of this *nouveleté des proportions*.*[14]

Similar rules are to be found also in the *Ars cantus mensurabilis* of Anonymous V, which Coussemaker places near the end of the 14th century (*Script.* III:379–398), but these are established with the help of the *color*. The author, who refers to Nicolaus de Aversa and Cechus de Florentia (Landino), is probably an Italian, and cites especially the Parisian Muris, as well as a Guilelmus de Mastodio (Machault?). He is probably identical with the author of the *Ars contrapuncti sec. Joh. de Muris* (see Couss., *Script.* III, XXXV).

We are led a little further by the Anonymous XI of Coussemaker (*Script.* III:416–475), the first part of whose treatise, which deals with *musica plana*, seems to bear close relationship with the *Summa musicae* of

---

[39] "And proportion *sesquitertia* is so called when there are four notes to the semibreve in major prolation, and four notes for three minimas."

Normannus Muris*[15]. (Gerbert, *Script.* III). It can be proved rather definitely that Johannes Hollandrinus, who is cited several times, is the same Muris. (A *canonicus* Jean de Muro is listed in Poncelet, Chartes de la Collégiale de St. Pierre de Liège [Brussel, 1903], approximately in the year 1324; see Steglich, *Quaestiones*, p. 187). The unrhymed hexameters of Anonymous remind one, in many places, of the rhymed poetic paraphrase of the *Summa* and seem partly intended for filling in the gaps of the latter by inserting sentences of the *Summa* in verses which do not appear there in verse (for example, the *unde claves octo graves*). A real (though mutilated) citation is probably the UT RE MI, etc. (Couss. III:418), in Muris (Gerbert, *Script.* III:206). Both verses read:

> UT RE MI FA SOL LA notularum nomina sena
> Sufficiunt notulae per quas fit musica plena.

The second portion dealing with *musica ficta* includes the fourth among the dissonances. The five "species" of counterpoint are the intervals: unison, fifth, octave, third, sixth (and their compound forms).

Dissonances are forbidden by all authors except in figurated singing; that is to say, for *minimae*, *semiminimae*, and *fusae*, in which cases dissonances are not felt because of the rapidity of their presentation. In other cases dissonance would bring great discomfort to the listener. Two consonances, however, should never appear in succession in these smallest values.[40]

(This probably means that for figuration the prohibition of fifths and octaves is still in force.) The word *counterpoint* already has taken on the meaning of polyphonic composition (p. 463:*[16] "Item 'contrapunctus' aliquando accipitur pro tota rundela, videlicet discantu, tenore et contratenore.") The rules for voice leading are as follows:[41]

---

[40] (Page 463): "Notandum de dissonantiis quod dissonantiae in omni cantu ab omni auctore prohibitae sunt, et dari non debent nisi in cantu figurativo scilicet in minima vel semiminima aut fusa, [in] quibus...dissonantia minus percipitur seu percipi potest ratione parvae morae seu velocitatis in pronunciando...verum si diceretur in aliis in quibus bene percipi posset, tunc talis dissonantia generaret displicentiam audientibus... item nunquam duae consonantiae dici debent nec in minimis nec in seminimis quamvis semiminimae unius minimae quantitatis sunt."

[41] (Page 463b): "I. Omnis contrapunctus et debet incipi et finiri in specie perfecta. II. Omnis contrapunctus non debet ascendere vel descendere cum tenore in specie perfecta nisi tenor ascendat vel descendat per quinque vel plures gradus, etc. (!) III. Contrapunctus non debet ascendere vel descendere cum tenore de specie imperfecta ad perfectam nisi tenor ascendat vel descendat per quatuor gradus vel plures (gradatim et sine saltu?) IV. Quinta non debet fieri post sextam. V. Contrapunctus debet capere proximas concordantias in quantum potest. VI. Quum tenor ascendit per plures gradus quam per duos tunc contrapunctus debet descendere, si saltem potest, et e converso. VII. Quum tenor habet MI in b FA ♮ MI tunc contrapunctus non debet habere perfectam speciem in FA et e converso; quum tenor habet FA in b FA ♮ MI tunc contrapunctus non debet habere

1. The beginning and ending must have a perfect consonance.

2. A progression at the interval (!) of a perfect consonance with the tenor is prohibited except when the tenor jumps a fifth or more (see p. 111, [Anonymous V]).

3. Counterpoint shall not be led in similar motion with the tenor moving from an imperfect to a perfect consonance (!), except when the tenor ascends or descends a fourth or more (stepwise?).

4. No fifth shall succeed a sixth (see below).

5. The counterpoint shall, if possible, move to the nearest consonance.

6. If the tenor skips, the counterpoint should, if possible, move in contrary motion.

7. MI *contra* FA is forbidden, with the addition: "Nisi sustineatur b duraliter," which does not mean a tied-over dissonance (*Halteton*), but rather the change of MI into FA by ♯ (or, vice versa, the FA into MI by ♭), since *sustinere*, as we know, is the term used to indicate chromatic changes (see p. 107).

8. If the tenor has the same tone several times (see the "*in rota*," p. 222), the sixth is allowed only at the end (probably because the octave should follow the sixth; see no. 12, p. 245).

9. In a tenor descending by step, the last step must lead to a perfect consonance (from the third to the fifth, from the sixth to the octave; Couss. gives *imperfectae specei* instead of *in perfecta specie*).

10. Successions of thirds and sixths (but only up to four or five) are allowed only when they lead to a perfect consonance and only when the tenor moves by step.

---

perfectam in MI, nisi sustineatur b duraliter (? probably rather 'b *molliter*;' ♮ *duraliter* should otherwise refer to the FA of the tenor!). VIII. Quum tenor habet duas vel tres notas vel plures in eadem linea vel spatio tunc in illis non debet fieri sexta nisi in ultima [si] saltem potest, etc. (?) IX. Quum tenor descendit per simplices gradus tunc in ultimo illius descensu debet fieri terminatio in perfecta specie. X. Plures tertiae et plures sextae possunt sequi una post alteram, ita tamen quod non fiant ultra quatuor vel quinque et post illas immediate sequatur perfecta species, et hoc fit quum tenor ascendit vel descendit per simplices gradus. XI. Tertiae bene possunt ascendere vel descendere cum tenore per simplices gradus nec (Couss. sed) non sextae. XII. Quum tenor habet duas vel tres notas ascendendo per simplicem gradum, tunc contrapunctus non debet haberi in ulla talium (?) sed prima potest esse octava vel tertia supra, secunda (scilicet nota) quinta vel octava, et tertia nota (Couss. non) debet esse tertia sub vel tertia supra (?). XIII. Quum tenor habet quatuor vel plures notas in ascendendo, tunc discantus debet habere mediam partem in sextis et residuum in tertiis ad unisonum. XIV. Quinta et sexta non debent simul stare in eadem linea vel spatio. XV. Nullus contrapunctus a tenore debet incipi infra octavam, nisi alte incipiatur, ut interdum fit; sic potest contrapunctus, id est discantus seu supremus chorus cum tenore incipi in unisono seu in quinta si placet. Similiter et dum tenor alte finitur potest bene discantus secum finiri in unisono seu in quinta. XVI. Omnis contrapunctus ad punctum motu contrario dari debet per se."

11. Stepwise successions of thirds with the tenor are good, as well as stepwise successions of sixths.

12. If the tenor has the same tone two or three times and then ascends a step, it may not take the sixth, but only thirds, fifths, and octaves, as shown here:

or:

13. If the tenor repeats the same tone four or more times before it ascends, it may use sixths in the middle and finally thirds, which lead to the unison.

14. A fifth to a sixth must not appear above a repeated tone in the tenor (see no. 4, above).

15. The counterpoint, which is the discant or *supremus* (Antonius de Leno also calls the discant *soprano*), is normally at the distance of an octave or more at beginning and end; only when the tenor begins (and closes) very high is it allowed to begin and end with the fifth or the unison.

16. In general, contrary motion is the obvious preference for counterpoint.

Additional rules are that perfect consonances must, if possible, alternate with imperfect ones, that the counterpoint must not repeat tones, and that the sixth is better after the fifth, but not before it (see 4 and 14).

The treatise following this collection of rules, which, however, probably does not belong with it, begins with *Ars cujuslibet discantus* (pp. 464–465) and contains nothing of importance for us, being apparently based upon older models. The text of the *Ars contratenoris*, following that treatise, is rather mutilated; it designates the following chords (○ = tenor, ● = discant, ◇ = contratenor):

etc.

The contratenor does not lie as the discant, usually one octave higher than the tenor, but generally it is in the same octave and sometimes lower. Between the discant and contratenor two fifths are allowed (!) when the contratenor lies above the tenor. The contratenor may also descend in parallel motion with the tenor from an imperfect to a perfect consonance (!).[42]

[42] (Page 465): "Supra notas tenoris non debemus numerare octo sicut in contrapuncto vel in discantu, sed simpliciter una, quia contratenor est ita gravis sicut tenor est, aliquando gravior....Discantus bene potest habere duas quintas cum contratenore et hoc quum contratenor est supra tenorem in acutis....Contratenor bene potest descendere cum tenore de specie imperfecta ad perfectam."

It is particularly emphasized "that the contratenor may also be a contradiscant," that is to say, it may not only appear below the tenor and between tenor and discant, but even above the discant. A rather naïve addition reads that the contratenor may be called tenor, when it appears lower than the tenor.[43]

Finally, as a conclusion to the older parts of the MS, there follows a second set of instructions concerning the composition of a contratenor in five rules (p. 466); the chords are ($\diamond$ = contratenor):

The final part of the treatise is of a later date and uses white notes. A rosette with drawings of all time signatures and a table of comparative note values is followed by a number of small specimens of the same, but then (after a fragment in hexameters which apparently again belongs to the first treatise concerning the *musica plana*) a section on proportional notation follows which is probably one of the earliest dealing with this subject.*[17] Another interpretation is not possible here because the note values are precisely established; for example, in regard to the *proportio sesquialtera* (p. 472): "This occurs when in mensural music three minimas are set against two," etc. On the other hand, a second treatise concerning the *proportiones* (pp. 474–475) ("proportio est duorum terminorum") has nothing to do with notation, but provides only the well-known basis for determination of intervals.

Anonymous XII of Coussemaker*[18] (*Script.* III:475 ff., from the same Trier Codex as the Anonymous XI) cites a Nicolaus Demuth (Demutis) as authority for his treatise on proportional notation, which is in agreement with that of Anonymous XI. The fact that Demuth himself is not given as the authority for Anonymous XI is proved by its considerable extention of the proportions (up to 9/8); Anonymous XII enumerates only 2, 3, 4, 3/2, 5/4, 6/5, and of these he discusses only 2, 3, 4, and 3/2.

One might be tempted to search for the origin of proportions in Germany if it were not for the *diminutio* of Anonymous V (see p. 242). Antonius de Leno also leads us in the direction of this practice. The use of several time signatures, in addition to triple, in the tenor of the Bolognese

---

[43] "For a contratenor can easily become a contradiscant...and it should be known that a contratenor which is lower than the tenor is called tenor."

mensural codices described by Haberl, indicates that proportions had become established before the appearance of white notes.

Anonymous XII's treatise also contains a somewhat short but very pointed set of instructions concerning counterpoint (p. 493):[44]

1. Beginning and ending should be with a perfect consonance, i.e., a unison, fifth (twelfth), or octave (double octave). Imperfect consonances: third, fourth (?!), sixth; not allowed: second, fourth (!), seventh. All intervals are determined from the top note of the interval to bottom, except the fourth, which is determined from bottom note of the interval to the top.

2. No perfect consonance is allowed to succeed itself, e.g., a fifth following another fifth, except when the singer takes the liberty of breaking the rules (*licentia cantorum*). A succession of two similar intervals is allowed only in the form of tonal repetition; i.e., $\frac{d\ d}{g\ g}$. All perfect consonances may be joined among themselves in any fashion; for example, the octave may follow the fifth, etc.

3. Imperfect consonances, namely, thirds or sixths, may succeed each other in any fashion, even three or four of the same kind.

This is concisely and reasonably expressed. John Hothby (approx. 1475) writes his *Regulae supra contrapunctum* (Couss., *Script.* III: 333)[45][*19]

[44] "De contrapuncto. Omnis discantus debet incipi et terminari in specie perfecta quoad tenorem. Species perfectae: unisonus. quinta...octava. duodecima. quintadecima. Species imperfectae: tertia, quarta (!) sexta. Species prohibitae: secunda. quarta (?) septima. Item...numeratio notarum pro his speciebus inveniendis semper fit a sursum deorsum praeter in quarta, ubi fit sursum. Item nulla species perfecta debet sequi se ipsam ut quinta post quintam nisi de licentia cantorum. Item omnes species perfectae possunt sequi invicem ut quinta post octavam etc. sed nulla sequitur se ipsam nisi in diminutione (!)....Item species imperfectae possunt se mutuo sequi scilicet (Couss. sine) ponendo tres vel quatuor tertias vel sextas."

[45] (Regulae essentiales) "I....discantum incipere et finire per consonantias perfectas. II....quando cantus planus sive tenor est gravis, contrapunctus sive discantus, cantare debet acutum, et e contrario; et si tenor sit mediocris, contrapunctus sit etiam mediocris. III....quando tenor in eodem loco firmiter manet discantum move et e contrario. IV....unam notam discantus juxta praecedentem ponere, et absque intervallo, si fuerit possibile,...(Regulae accidentales) I....cantare duas vel plures consonantias perfectas dissimiles tam ascendendo quam descendendo. II....duas vel tres vel plures consonantias [imperfectas] tam similes quam dissimiles cantare tam ascendendo quam descendendo. III....cantare discantum per gradum tam ascendendo quam descendendo quando tenor movetur per saltum, per consonantias perfectas (!). IV. quando tenor movetur per gradum tam ascendendo quam descendendo similiter potest se movere discantus. (Regulae placabiles) I....Si volumus in fine alicujus gradus descendentis facere unam quintam ante eam debemus facere unam tertiam vel plures secundum quantitatem graduum (us?). Si volumus facere octavam, ante eam debemus ponere sextam vel plures secundum quantitatem graduus. Si duodecimam etc. II. Si volumus in fine alicujus gradus ascendentis facere unisonum, ante eum debemus facere tertiam vel plures secundum quantitatem graduus ascendentiis. Si volumus facere quintam ante eam debemus facere unam octavam. Si octavam etc."

in the same categorical manner. For him the fourth is also a dissonance. (In Anonymous XII it is mistakenly taken for a consonance); MI against FA is not allowed; his four main rules are as follows:

1. Beginning and ending should be with a perfect consonance.

2. If the *cantus firmus* lies high, the counterpoint lies low, if the *cantus* lies low, then the counterpoint lies high, and thirdly, both can move in a middle position (this, however, involves many crossings and is a good rule only for equal voices).

3. If the *cantus firmus* sustains a tone, the counterpoint must move, and vice versa (this is a new principle, skillfully based upon the practice of composers; the treatise *Qualiter debent poni consonantiae* expressly forbids the cessation of motion in the counterpoint, when the *cantus firmus* moves; see p. 225 f.).

4. The counterpoint should, if possible, move by step. In addition to this, there are the following rules:

I. Perfect consonances of different sizes may succeed one another in any desired fashion.

II. (Imperfect) consonances of the same kind or of different kinds may succeed each other by two, three, or more.

III. If the tenor skips, the counterpoint may move by step to a perfect consonance.

And, finally, two suggestions (*Regulae placabiles*), one referring to step-wise succession of thirds before the fifth, and the other to successions of sixths before the octave (the first rule is full of errors; instead of *descendentis*, *ascendentis* is written). These are shown as follows:

The example under N.B. is important as a supplement (before ending on the fifth, the penultimate interval should, above an ascending tenor, be an octave).

All of the writers who have been discussed belong to the epoch following that of de Vitry and Muris and refer to these masters directly or to some of their famous successors. Even the English teacher-composers Chilston and Lionel Power, and Guilelmus Monachus, who probably also came from England (all of whom we discussed in Chapter VII), belong in this same period. The reason for our having discussed them earlier lies in the fact that the English manner of discant with its imagined intervals, small enough to be easily judged from the notation of the plainchant [*cantus firmus*], is undoubtedly of much earlier origin than 1400.

It is now necessary to discuss the later chapters of Guilelmus Monachus, in which he gives a detailed and clear account of the treatment of counterpoint in his time. It is he who, for the first time, gives us an indication of a more rational treatment of dissonances. More and more monuments of early 15th-century contrapuntal art are being gradually brought to light, which show that theory was able only gradually to comprehend and formulate the advances made by musical practice. This is to say that prepared suspensions were introduced by composers long before theorists allowed them in their rules. None of the theorists so far discussed allowed dissonances for note-against-note settings and permitted them only for figurated counterpoint where they "pass by so fast that they are hardly noticed." Now the time comes when the prepared dissonance, which makes its appearance as the syncope in a more ornamental style of counterpoint, is accepted. The fact that little mention was made of syncopation [46] during the period following the *Ars nova* proves only that

---

[46] The *Ars nova* (Couss., *Script.* III:21) is probably the earliest treatise which speaks of syncopation; however, it does not use this term but employs the word *color*: "Vel de rubris aliquando huc et illuc in Balladis, Rondellis et Motectis ponuntur, quia reducuntur et ad invicem operantur ut in 'plures errores'" (Red notes are used now and then in ballades, rondels, and motets, because they can be related to each other and mutually aid one another as in "plures errores"). The *Ars perfecta* (Philippoti) defines the syncopation as follows (p. 34): "Sincopa est divisio cujuscumque figurae ad partes separatas, quae ad invicem reducuntur perfectiones numerando" (a syncope is the division of some figure into separate parts, which in turn are made into perfections by numbering). According to the context, it appears that here also *color* indicates the syncope (the examples are not usable). The *Liber musicalium* (p. 48), on the contrary, has another means of making the syncope obvious to the eye, namely through the *punctus demonstrationis* which was placed next to the short note values at the beginning and end of the syncopated passage.*[20] The treatise speaks of only two or three minimas which belong with a semibreve but which are separated because of the syncopated notes and which are marked by two dots (·♩·). That the syncopation was really looked upon as being the displacement of a consonance is proved by the definition given in this treatise: "et illae semibreves (lying between the minimas which are marked by the *puncti demonstrationis*) debent cantari tardando, quia tardantur per minimam praecedentem" (and these semibreves [lying between the minimas which are marked by the *puncti demonstrationis*] should be sung with delaying, because the preceding minimas are also delayed). This is perhaps the most remarkable passage in all of the treatises ascribed to de Vitry in that it discloses a premonition of the true content of the following; namely, that a *retardation* is the holding off of a consonance by a preceding dissonance. Since none of the Muris treatises contain a similarly lucid definition, however, our suspicion as to the genuineness of the treatises can only be strengthened. The *Libellus cantus mensurabilis sec. Joh. de Muris* (Couss., *Script.* III) makes no mention of the *punctus demonstrationis*, and merely indicates several cases of syncopation, firstly, after a *punctum perfectionis* (actually *additionis*) (p. 53): "Item nota quod si punctus ponatur inter duas breves, dividit modum, nisi forte breves illae forent de tempore imperfecto, post quas vel ante quas reperitur aliqua semibrevis sola quae per sincopam reduceretur ad dictam brevem puncto perfectionis punctatam" (also note that a *punctus* divides the mode if it is placed between two breves, unless, by chance,

theory at first did not know what to do with the dissonances which had gradually appeared. The magic formula, "ad invicem reducuntur," meanwhile, provided assistance in face of the dilemma: the consonances appeared only as "somewhat displaced." There is a gradual change, to begin with, in Guilelmus Monachus, to whom we shall refer again.

Chapter VII (according to Guido Adler's division; Couss., *Script.* III:290) opens with an extensive discussion of the two- to four-part counterpoint of the French and English and states first that there exist two imperfect (these are mentioned first) and two perfect simple consonances: the third and sixth; the fifth and octave; all others are compound forms. Furthermore, the compound forms are also included, and six perfect and six imperfect consonances are found from the unison to the nineteenth (fifth of the double octave), and even the twentieth (sixth of the double octave), corresponding to the distance of the highest tone $\left(\begin{smallmatrix}e\\e\end{smallmatrix}\right)$ to the lowest ($\varGamma$) in the Guidonian monochord, is mentioned. In addition there appears the old rule, often met with, for the specific combination of these intervals: "The unison demands the third, the third demands the fifth, the fifth demands the sixth (above the same tone), the sixth demands the octave, etc. (and for the compound forms accordingly)." Here we find again that the sixth followed by the fifth is evidence of tonal repetition, that is, the tenor remaining upon the same tone (see p. 105). In the enumeration of this reversed order of intervals this is not especially

---

these breves are *tempus imperfectum*, after or before which a semibreve is found reduced by a syncope to what is called a dotted breve, dotted with a *punctus demonstrationis*). For example:

(It then follows the initial wording of the *Liber musicalium*, but without the *Liber*'s ingenious exposition and without the *puncti*). Even the *Ars discantus sec. Joh. de Muris* does not mention the *punctus demonstrationis*. The beginning of this treatise, "*Quaedam notabilia utilia,*" does not help to establish the genuineness of the *Liber musicalium*, although mention is made of a *Tractatus Magistri Philippi de Vitriaco* (p. 107). What is said about the syncope is very meager (p. 106): "Inveniuntur etiam aliquotiens in valore notularum, unicae semibreves, breves vel longas sequentes quae tamen eas nec augent nec minuunt, sed potius ad invicem reducuntur. Dicendum est quod si ponitur ibi per eas certa mensura, syncopetur, et tamen secundum aliquos deberent fieri rubrae vel vacuae" (single semibreves or breves following longas are also sometimes found in note values, which neither increase nor decrease them [the longas], but are rather reduced in their turn. It should be said that if, because of them, a certain mensuration is placed there, a syncope occurs. According to some they should be made red or white [vacant—*vacuae*]).

pointed out, but any doubt of it is hardly possible. The "in eadem sede" is, incidentally, another new synonym for "in rota" (p. 223).[47]

In the eighth chapter there are ten special rules concerning counterpoint:[48]

1. The beginning and ending must have a perfect consonance, and the *penultima* must be an imperfect consonance which can move by step to a perfect one (*aperta speciei perfectae*, corresponding to the *appendans* of the Anonymous XIII).

2. Stepwise succession of two perfect consonances is not allowed; unisons, fifths, and octaves of the same pitch may, however, follow each other in any desired number.

N.B. This passage has been completely misunderstood by G. Adler

---

[47] "A unison requires the third, the third requires the fifth, the fifth the sixth, in the same situation; the sixth requires the octave in various situations."

[48] "I....debemus incipere et finire contrapunctum per speciem perfectam, sed... penultima sit species imperfecta, aperta speciei perfectae. II....non possumus facere duas perfectas similes de linea in spacium tendentes nec e contrario de spatio in rigam; sed nos bene possumus facere, si sint quatuor vel tres notulae [i.e., in eadem sede!] et quod illae tres sint quintae vel tres unisoni vel tres octavae vel quomodocunque. III.... bene possumus facere duas vel tres species perfectas dissimiles sicut V$^{am}$ et VIII$^{am}$, VIII$^{am}$ et XII$^{am}$, XII$^{am}$ et XV$^{am}$ et e converso. Sed non possumus facere unisonum et octavam nec e converso, quia secundum Boetium unisonus reputatur [idem esse ac] diapason scilicet octava. IV....de speciebus imperfectis possumus uti ad libitum tam in ascensu quam in descensu de gradu ad gradum, sed quod talis species imperfecta post se habeat speciem perfectam qualem requirit etc. V....non possumus ascendere nec descendere per species perfectas nisi duobus modis scilicet per diapente et diatessaron, scilicet per V$^{am}$ et per IV$^{am}$. Per V$^{am}$ sic, si cantus firmus descendat quintam, contrapunctus potest descendere cum cantu firmo de perfecta consonantia in perfectam consonantiam sicut de quinta in octavam. Per quartam sic, si cantus firmus descendat quartam (Couss. quartam vel quintam) tunc contrapunctus potest descendere de imperfecto in suum perfectum sicut de tertia in quintam. VI....non possumus facere FA contra MI in speciebus perfectis propter semitonium. In speciebus autem imperfectis possumus facere quia dat dulcedinem. VII....in omni contrapuncto debemus semper tenere propinquiores notas sive proximiores, quoniam omne disjunctum est inconsonans. VIII....quamquam posuerimus duodecim consonantias tam perfectas quam imperfectas, tam simplices quam compositas, non obstante secundum usum modernorum consonantiae dissonantes aliquotiens nobis serviunt, sicut dissonantia secundae dat dulcedinem tertiae bassae (?), dissonantia vero septima dat dulcedinem sextae; dissonantie quarte dat dulcedinem tertie altie et illa tritoni (Couss. tertia [sic!]) dat dulcedinem quintae et hoc secundum usum modernorum. IX....quamquam dixerimus quod quinta debeat praecedere sextam in eadem sede et quod decimatertia debeat praecedere XV$^{am}$ in diversis sedibus (Couss. in eadem sede, which contradicts Chapter VII, 3), tamen aliquotiens est dulce sextam praecedere quintam [in diversis sedibus] et XV$^{am}$ praecedere XIII$^{am}$ in eadem sede (Couss. tam in eadem sede quam in diversis sedibus) propter dulcedinem. X. Item maxime vitanda est reiteratio hoc est rem unam bis vel ter reiterare sicut FA MI, FA MI; SOL FA, SOL FA, ita quod cantus firmus sic faciat."

and W. Nagel. Admittedly a more precise reference after *quatuor vel tres notulae* is missing, such as Muris offers in the passage in Gerbert III: 307, *in una linea vel in uno spatio*. Therefore one could, for this reason, assume that octave parallels permitted by Anonymous V (see p. 111) and Anonymous XI (pp. 243–245) are permitted in further stepwise movement. It is certainly impossible, however, that three or four perfect consonances of equal size would be permitted, and two forbidden.

3. The succession of two or three perfect consonances of different sizes is permitted, i.e., fifth-octave, octave-twelfth, twelfth-double octave, and vice versa. Only the successions unison-octave and vice versa are forbidden, since according to the teachings of Boethius (!) the unison is to be regarded as being of equal value with the octave. (That this passage, in referring to movements of fifth-octave, etc., does not concern similar motion is proved by the fifth rule.)

4. Stepwise succession of imperfect consonances is allowed ascending and descending in any number; the last one, however, must move by step to a perfect consonance.

5. If the *cantus firmus* falls a fifth, the counterpoint may move in similar motion with it from the fifth to the octave; if the *cantus firmus* falls by a fourth, however, then the counterpoint must move in similar motion with it from the third to the fifth.

6. MI *contra* FA is forbidden for all perfect consonances (because there would be a semitone missing or a semitone too much), but it is allowed for the imperfect ones, because in connection with these it sounds well (*dat dulcedinem*).

7. Stepwise movements are preferred because all skips are harder to understand.

8. Although we have established only twelve (perfect and imperfect) consonances as the basis for counterpoint, dissonant intervals often serve us as well, since the dissonance of the second resolves with pleasant effect to the third below, the dissonance of the seventh to the sixth, the dissonance of the fourth to the third above, and that of the *tritonus* to the fifth, following recent practice (instead of *tritonus* Coussemaker erroneously prints *tertia*).[*21] What is strikingly new here is that the third and sixth appear as resolutions of the dissonances of the second, fourth, and seventh. Whether the dissonances are regarded as being prepared or as passing is not mentioned.

9. We have ascertained that the fifth must appear before the sixth above a stationary tenor and the thirteenth before the double octave

above the tenor which moves by step, but the reverse is sometimes also possible with good effect:

(This is how the passage, which was completely misunderstood by Adler, though it is much corrupted, must be interpreted.)

10. Repetitions of the same melodic figures (*reiterationes*; Tinctoris: *redictae*, see p. 268 f.) are to be avoided, if possible, especially when they occur in the *cantus firmus*.

(not:                                                                    but rather:

We need not discuss again the detailed exposition of the treble-sight which then follows (without use of the term, however).

The tenth chapter again deals with gymel and fauxbourdon, but offers little additional information. The following passage is interesting:[49] "If this kind of counterpoint is to be sung in the manner used by the English, the *cantus firmus* must be read as the soprano so that the movement of the soprano regulates itself according to the notation."[*22] That this passage should be interpreted as referring to the technique of the treble-sight is also apparent from the following similar passages:[50] "The contratenor moves parallel with the soprano a fourth below, that is, in fifths (at the beginning and end) and thirds above the *cantus firmus*."[*23]

We (in contrast to the English) would be able to use this kind of counterpoint by substituting, for the various ways in which the soprano and contratenor are read, the actual notation of the intervals; furthermore, we could introduce syncopations of sixths and fifths; however, the *penultima* would have to be a sixth.[51][*24]

[49] (Adler, *op. cit.*, p. 19, Couss., *Script.* III:292): "Know that, if this style is sung as the English themselves sing it, the soprano must adopt the *cantus firmus*, and said *cantus firmus* must direct the soprano or *cantus*."

[50] (Adler, p. 21, Couss., *ibid.*): "The *contra* (tenor) is performed as the soprano, taking the fourth below the soprano, which generally results in the fifth and third above the tenor."

[51] (*Ibid*): "This mode of *faulx bordon*, however, can be taken differently among us, not observing the rules mentioned above but holding to the proper *cantus firmus* as it stands, and observing the same consonances mentioned above in soprano as well as contratenor, but making syncopations by sixths and fifths, the penultimate being a sixth."

In connection with this the question arises as to whether the author had in mind the intervals of the sights or those of the actual sounds, for in both cases such sixth-fifth syncopations are possible, as follows:

However, in both cases the result is not very gratifying. Perhaps we can use the *Regula circa cognitionem syncoparum* (Couss., *Script.* III:306) which appears at the end of the treatise, for explanation and correction. In any case it is of great interest to us, even though it might be of a somewhat later origin than the treatise itself.[52] We quote:

When the *cantus firmus* makes a curved movement, ascending at first a large number of steps, we can accompany it by syncopation with thirds and fourths below, that is, sixths and fifths above (!), while in descending with thirds and seconds below, that is, sixths and sevenths above:

This, then, gives a different impression. The suspension of the seventh before the sixth (this would, following the "sight," be seconds before the third below) might have constituted the starting point for later theories concerning the preparation of a dissonance. Even though we cannot

[52] "Concerning the recognition of syncopes. Notice that if a well-wrought *cantus* follows a curve by ascending from line to space, or on the other hand ascends ten or twelve tones by step, then we should make a syncope by a third and fourth below, or saying the same thing another way, through the sixth and fifth above, this truly in ascending. In descending we ought to syncopate by a third and second below, that is to say, through the sixth and seventh, so that the *penultima* is the sixth coming afterwards to the unison which is the same as the octave."

agree with Coussemaker's placement of the monk Guilelmus at the beginning of the 15th century,*[25] since he uses white notation throughout,
placing him in the middle of the century is still rather questionable,
although this would present a more complete picture of the state of music
theory as it was at the beginning of Tinctoris' activity.

The remarks concerning mensurations of this kind of counterpoint
(namely, that the measure is divided by three and the first note is twice
as long as are the following) are of lesser importance to us; on the other
hand, that several notes of the counterpoint may appear in transition or
in passing (*transitus, passagium*) over one note of the *cantus firmus* is a point
of great interest (Chap. X, 4 and 5).

The rules concerning gymel, which appear in more detailed form for
the second time (see p. 127), allow six consonances: the fifth, the third
above and below, the sixth, the octave, the tenth below, and the octave
below. This does not fit very well with the first instructions in Chapter V,
in which the unison is also demanded for beginning and ending, while
the fifth and tenth are not mentioned. Apparently this confusion resulted
from the designation of the sight, which was misinterpreted by the
copyist.

A new element is introduced by the monk Guilelmus with his rules for
leading a third lower voice to the gymel (which was touched upon briefly
in Chapter V), that is to say, a lower fourth to the fauxbourdon, upon
which the tenth chapter further elaborates.[53] The result is alternating
thirds and fifths below the tenor, a unison or octave below the tenor at
the beginning and end, and the penultimate note always a fifth below
the tenor. Since the usual close of the tenor is the step from the second
above down to the *finalis*, this rule concerning the fifth for the *penultima*
actually means the appearance of the regular bass cadence:

| | | | | |
|---|---|---|---|---|
| *Supranus* | a. | b.S. | c.T. | d. |
| *Contratenor altus* | | | | |
| *Tenor* | | | | |
| *Contratenor bassus* | | | | |

The eleventh chapter also emphasizes an important rule for composition in four voices (with contratenor *altus* and contratenor *bassus*), which

[53] (Adler, p. 23): "But if gymel accepts sixths and octaves as consonances after the
manner of *faulx bordon*, then the contratenor according to gymel can move like the contratenor of *faulx bordon* with thirds and fifths, or can take the fifth below for its *ultima*, and
the third below for its *antepenultima*...if, moreover, it holds to thirds and unisons...then
the contratenor will make the fifth below its *penultima* the third below or the octave below its *antepenultima*, or a unison with the tenor; the *ultima* being the octave below."

requires the distance of a fifth for the contratenor *bassus* in the penultimate chord. It repeats almost verbatim much of the tenth chapter (although the very sound limitation found in this chapter, which says that the *antepenultima* of the contratenor *bassus* may also be at the distance of an octave or a unison from the tenor, instead of the third, is missing (see example *d* above). Chapter X then goes into some interesting detail concerning exceptions:[54]

When the *cantus firmus* cadences with the soprano, the contratenor *bassus* is allowed to cadence with the tenor, that is, it may take the sixth or octave below the tenor. Then the contratenor *altus* keeps its course; that is, it cadences above the lower contratenor which is used as a tenor, with the succession third-fifth, in this way moving in fourths with the real tenor. The soprano then takes the fifth above the tenor as the *penultima* (the tenth above the lower contratenor which functions as tenor) and closes moving down one step:

S.
T.
CT. *altus*
CT. *bassus*

Or instead (in the same case) the contratenor *bassus* takes the third below the tenor as *penultima* and as *ultima* the octave below: then the soprano must take the third above the tenor as *penultima* and at the close, the unison, while the contratenor *altus* takes as *penultima* the sixth above the tenor and the third as final note:

CT. *altus*
S.
T.
CT. *bassus*

It cannot be proved, and it is hardly probable, that the bass voice

[54] (Adler, p. 24): "Exceptions are made to this rule, the first of which is this: If the *cantus firmus* holds firm to the mode of the *supranus* like FA MI MI FA, SOL FA FA SOL, LA SOL SOL LA, then the contratenor *bassus* can hold to the mode of the tenor, that is, it can make its *penultima* a sixth below the tenor and its *ultima* an octave below. But opposing this the *altus* will take the opposite mode, that is, it will make its *penultima* a third higher and its *ultima* a fifth higher than the contratenor (*bassus*) which will be a fourth below the tenor. The *supranus* will make its *penultima* a fifth above the tenor which will be a tenth above the contratenor *bassus*. In the *ultima*, it will be a third above the tenor, which is a tenth with the contratenor *bassus*. The second exception is this: If the *cantus firmus* or a *cantus figuratus* still holds to the mode of the *supranus*, that is, if it is FA MI (etc., as above), then the contratenor *bassus* can make its *penultima* a third below and its *ultima* an octave below the tenor. The *supranus* may make its *penultima* a third above the tenor so that its *ultima* is a unison with the tenor which will make an octave with the contratenor *bassus* below. A high contratenor will make its *penultima* a sixth above the tenor by making its *ultima* a third above the tenor."

descending by a fifth or ascending by a fourth, for the first time seen here as capable of effecting a forceful conclusion, has its roots in earlier English polyphony. For even if Chilston (p. 121 f.) stresses that many consonances of the discant lie below the tenor, neither he nor any other theorists dealing with the English discant (Power, Anonymous IV, Garlandia) make any mention of a voice which throughout is led lower than the tenor. The succession of fifth-octave, with the exception of the two cases in which the parts were changed, is entirely usual, and may even stem from the French *déchant*.

Before concerning ourselves with that group of theorists whose authority lasted about a century, similar to that of Franco during the 13th and 14th centuries and that of the (Parisian) Johannes de Muris for the 14th and 15th centuries, we must touch upon a treatise which treats only of *musica plana*. This treatise, however, contains some unusual initial moves in the direction of simplifying solmization and further information regarding *musica ficta*, as well as a brief treatment of counterpoint, although only from the viewpoint of *musica plana*. It is the *Ritus canendi vetustissimus et novus* of the Carthusian monk Johannes (J. Gallicus, J. Carthusiensis, J. de Mantua).*[26] Johannes Gallicus, following the testimony of his pupil Nicolaus Burtius (Coussemaker used Burtius' copy by his own hand in issuing the treatise in *Script.* IV:298–421), died in 1473 and was buried in Parma. He started his work under Pius II (1458–1462) and probably also finished it under him. Therefore his teaching activities must be dated before those of Johannes Tinctoris. The treatise itself indicates that Johannes Gallicus was born in Namur and studied in Italy under the humanist Victorinus Feltrensis (1378–1446, active from 1442 at the Gonzaga court in Mantua), and that he entered the order of the Carthusians in Mantua.

Since Johannes Gallicus, according to Burtius, achieved high repute in the musical world of his time (*multi inter musicos nominis*), the simplification of solmization, which is discussed in detail in Ambros (*Geschichte* II:81) and which Ambros found first perfected by Pietro Aron (1523), must be attributed to the suggestions of Gallicus. The good Carthusian gets very excited (p. 374) about the *nimia verbositus* of the solmization with its countless possibilities of mutation:[55]

How many tonsured men would vehemently thank God in church and would thank those with glowing enthusiasm who have dedicated themselves to God in

---

[55] (Couss., *Script.* IV:374): "Quot quaeso viri tonsurati Deum alacriter laudarent ardentique desiderio cantum illum eis qui Dei sunt suavissimum neque tamen lascivum quem nobis tradidere sancti addiscerent nisi tot ambages verborum, tot varii naturarum, ♮ quadrorum et ♭ mollium ordines totve non jam vocum sed sillabarum superfluae mutationes rudium animos ac ingenia fatigando debilitarent."

order to teach those lovely, but not secular, songs which have come to us from the saints, if not so many double names of tones, so many natural, hard, and soft hexachords and so much superfluous exchange of solmization syllables were present to tire out the heart and mind of God's followers and make them despondent.

With that, he makes a clean sweep and demands that stress should rather be placed on the correct distinction between whole-tone and semitone steps and that as basis for the entire solmization system only combinations of C–a and g–e be taken:

$$\Gamma \text{ A } \natural \text{ C D E}$$
$$\text{C D E F G a}$$
$$\text{G a } \natural \text{ c d e}$$
$$\text{c d e f g } \bar{\text{a}}$$
$$\bar{\text{g}} \ \bar{\text{a}} \ \natural \ \bar{\text{c}} \ \bar{\text{d}} \ \bar{\text{e}}$$

In all cases we must keep in mind the species of fourth which can be used only in one of the following three ways:

$$\text{UT   RE   MI   FA}$$
$$\text{RE   MI   FA   SOL}$$
$$\text{MI   FA   SOL   LA}$$

If a fourth ascending from FA were to appear, one must necessarily sing FA to LA. In other words, each tone is known by one syllable, and solmization with the former names G *sol re ut*, A *la mi re*, etc., is no longer used, nor is changing the syllable-name on one note, as LA = MI, etc. [mutation]. "Even if we present holy songs with square notes, we would be foolish to let them revolve in our mouths." [56] Actually only a single syllable should be sung on a single tone:

| $\Gamma$ ut, | A re, | $\natural$ mi, | C fa, | D sol, | E la |
|---|---|---|---|---|---|
| F fa, | G sol, | a la, | $\flat$ fa, | $\natural$ mi, | c fa, | d sol, | e la |

N. B.

| f fa, | g sol, | $\bar{\text{a}}$ la, | $\flat$ fa, | $\natural$ mi, | $\bar{\text{c}}$ fa, | $\bar{\text{d}}$ sol, | $\bar{\text{e}}$ la |

N. B.

Doing away with the *hexachordum molle* is, therefore, not firstly the work of Sebald Heyden (Ambros, op. cit.), but is clearly to be found here, at least half a century earlier. I presume that in practical usage complications of solmization or mutation were avoided even earlier. At

---

[56] (*Ibid.*, p. 378): "Nam et quando verba sancta sub nostris notis quadris proferimus, stulti videremur, si talia per os nostrum volveremus."

least the Louvain Anonymous (Couss., *Script.* II:484) and Anonymous XIII (Couss., *Script.* III:496) always use single syllables based upon the *hexachordum naturale* and *hexachordum durum*, and there is no mention of double syllables (see pp. 87 f. and 102 ff.).

Complete evidence for the fact that mutation with pronunciation of both syllables is impractical for mensural music, is contained in the Leipzig Anonymous which I published in the *Monatshefte für Musikgeschichte*, 1897–1898, and which was probably printed in the 15th century or at any rate before 1507, being therefore earlier than P. Aron. This evidence is contained in the chapter *De mentali vocum mutatione* (fol. 5ʳ) : [57]

> If only one syllable is pronounced, namely, that one *to* which mutation occurs, and the other, *from* which the mutation occurs, is only thought (which is the usual practice in mensural music, since, especially in highly figurated passages, it is not possible to pronounce both syllables), the pause which the two syllables cause would necessarily produce dissonances and bring disorder to the entire composition, as one can readily see. For this reason we say that ♭ is out of the question (in *cantu duro*) in ascending upon d and a RE, and in descending on a and e LA, but [not in] ascending in *cantus mollis* (with ♭) on d and g RE and [in] descending on a and d LA. In transposed singing (*cantus fictus*), however, as well as in singing which is not transposed, if the place which demands FA [the ♭ is used] is recognized, all else then follows naturally.

Here we find simple solmization fully developed.

Johannes Gallicus (similar to Prosdocimus de Beldemandis) carries on a sharp controversy concerning Marchettus of Padua's three kinds of semitones, and in general vehemently attacks him (see Couss. IV, p. 324). With reference to *musica ficta*, he writes (p. 385) : [58]

---

[57] "...quum scilicet una syllaba in mente servatur, altera in quam fit mutatio, exprimitur. Quae quidem mutatio est amica cantilenis mensuratis, ubi non permittitur, praecipue in diminutioribus figuris, quin ambae syllabae exprimantur, quandoquidem ista mora geminando syllabas gigneret dissonantiam, totusque concentus confunderetur ut quisque ex se ipso facile considerare potest...in cantu igitur duro ascendentes in d et a RE sumamus, descendentes vero in a et e litterulis LA capiamus; in cantu autem molli ascendentes in d et g RE sumamus descendentes vero in a et d litterulis LA capiamus. Verum in cantu ficto quemadmodum etiam in vero dumtaxat observandum est FA: quo habito reliquae syllabae sua sponte se offerent. Ex his liquet omnem solmisandi vim in eo existere ut sciamus quando MI quandove FA maxime in b clave modulandum sit; quo scito omnis solmisandi modus evidenter haberi possit."

[58] "Ipsa igitur eadem natura, quae tantam operante Deo nobis insinuat sonis et vocibus inesse virtutem, duas denuo prodit in omni perfecta consonantia simplici vel composita non dicam consonantias sed quasdam potius consonantiarum partes quae talem habent cum perfectis a quibus continentur et in quibus ortae sunt etiam consonantiis affinitatem ut nunquam ab illis nisi per tonum et minus semitonium vel quando plus per duos tonos integros distare valeant. Sed etsi quando separatae fuerint a suis perfectis,

Next to each perfect consonance is a...compatible dissonance (*dissonantia compassibilis*), the tones of which are a step removed, one a whole-tone step, and the other a semitone step, or both a whole-tone step. But even though it may be situated further away from the perfect consonance, it nevertheless strives with a sort of natural instinct to reach it so that it achieves an intermediate distance, namely one whole-tone and one semitone away or with one whole-tone in both parts, at the most.

(This sentence is hardly correct; at least it is not clear how a larger distance than that of the whole-tone is to appear before a perfect consonance. One would have to think of f♯ g♯ a, which around this time is common in closes on a, but which again would not give us a satisfactory translation.) Then follows the changing of minor thirds and sixths, already known to us, by the ♯ in transition to the fifth, the octave, etc., but license is also given to proceed occasionally from the major third to the unison and from the major sixth to the fifth. Further, on pages 394–395:

> You must never begin or end with such compatible dissonances; because these contain a certain suspended consonance (*suspensum quandam habent concordiam*), which is pleasing to the ear but never gives, as experience teaches us, the impression of complete satisfaction.

Although much of the contents are not new and the manner of expression is often bombastic, the treatise of Johannes Gallicus must, nevertheless, be counted among the most important works of the last decades before Tinctoris, and one may assume that he exerted much influence upon the manner of teaching during his time because of his energetic opposition to the atrophied solmization theories.

With reference to solmization, a direct antipode of Johannes Gallicus is his contemporary John Hothby (Fra Ottobi, died 1487), whose *Calliopea leghale* was printed first by Coussemaker in his *Histoire de l'harmonie au moyen-âge*. Until now unusual terminology made the treatise difficult to understand; only very recently was Dr. A. W. Schmidt able to clarify it (Dissertation: "*Die Calliopea legale* des Johann Hothby," 1897). Hothby

---

naturali quodam instinctu semper ad illas anhelant (Couss: hunelent) quandam videlicet imperfectam inter gravem et acutum suum retinentes concordiam, donec ad suas perfectas per tonum etiam ac per semitonium aut per tonum ad plus et tonum redeant, a quibus non aliter ut dictum est distare valuerat...est autem hic diesis quaedam toni duabus in partibus sectio per quam hujusmodi prolationem minoribus dissonantiis apothome quod major pars est toni desuper adjungitur, quod siquidem totiens fieri debet quotiens et ubicumque tales dissonantias ad suam perfectionem per tonum superius ac tonum inferius ire sentitur."

shifts the Guidonian hexachord to begin on F♯ = UT and D♭ = UT
(Schmidt, *op. cit.*, p. 35):

|     |     |     |     |     |     |     |
|-----|-----|-----|-----|-----|-----|-----|
| 1.  | C   | D   | E   | F   | G   | A   |
| 2.  | G   | A   | B♮  | C   | D   | E   |
| 3.  | F   | G   | A   | B♭  | C   | D   |
| 4.  | D   | E   | F♯  | G   | A   | B♮  |
| 5.  | B♭  | C   | D   | E♭  | F   | G   |
| 6.  | A   | B♮  | C♯  | D   | E   | F♯  |
| 7.  | E♭  | F   | G   | A♭  | B♭  | C   |
| 8.  | E   | F♯  | G♯  | A   | B♮  | C♯  |
| 9.  | A♭  | B♭  | C   | D♭  | E♭  | F   |
| 10. | B♮  | C♯  | D♯  | E   | F♯  | G♯  |
| 11. | D♭  | E♭  | F   | G♭  | A♭  | B♭  |
| 12. | F♯  | G♯  | A♯  | B♮  | C♯  | D♯  |

In none of his contemporaries do we find such an extensive tonal range
(other than that already discussed in Prosdocimus de Beldemandis; see
p. 237 f.). The riddle of terminology which Schmidt succeeded in solving
consisted of this: that Hothby, after the manner of German tablature,
called the flatted tones (all of them, even the B♭) by the names of their
neighboring tones below, but distinguished between the flatted tones and
their enharmonic sharp equivalents by establishing a second and third
series (*secondo ordine*: the flatted tones; *terzo ordine*: the sharp tones). For
instance, B♭ is called *A del secondo* (*ordine*), a♯ is called *A del terzo*, g♭ is
called *F del secondo*, etc. Raimund Schlecht's attempt at explaining the
*Calliopea* (Trier, *Caecilia*, 1874) failed because he read the *A del secondo* as
A♭. A further specialty of Hothby in the *Calliopea* of interest to us is a kind
of functional description of the tones of the hexachord:[59]

[59] Although they may have grown out of Hothby's views, Ambrosius Wilfflingseder's
characteristics of the six steps of the solmization hexachord ("*Teutsche Musica*" 1585,
fol. A.5) are, nevertheless, a significant extension of this system.

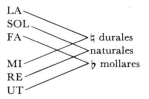

where LA as ♮ *duralis* is to be intended for the FA appearing above it, and UT as ♭ *mol-*
*laris* is intended for the MI lying below it (*subsemitonium*!):

$$B♮\overbrace{\phantom{x}}c \ \ d\overbrace{\phantom{x}}e \ f \ \ g \ a\overbrace{\phantom{x}}b♭$$

or:   f♯G  a b♮ c  d  e f♯ etc.

SOL ⎫
LA  ⎭        Demostratori

FA          Comite

MI          Principe

RE  ⎫
UT  ⎭        Demostratori

This is nothing but an attempt to indicate the special function of the steps of the hexachord by giving them names (note the special stress given the two steps forming a semitone by calling them "Prince" [*principe*] and "Count" [*comite*]).

In Johannes Tinctoris we meet a composer of distinction as well as a theorist of high repute. He lived from 1475–1487 in Naples as court musician at the court of Ferdinand of Aragon, and died in 1511 as a canon in Nivelles. His numerous treatises concerning various aspects of music theory suffer to some extent from excessive thoroughness and verbosity, an example of which is an almost endless treatment of voice leading in note-against-note counterpoint in the *Liber de arte contrapuncti*, written in 1477 (Couss., *Script.* IV: 76–153).[*27] These principles had long been in use and are here extended to the triple octave (!) with one chapter apiece for each interval. This treatise in its entirety is nevertheless very valuable, and of interest because of its fulness of detail.[60] Tinctoris remarks (p. 77) that according to competent judges, compositions worth listening to have been written only "in the last forty years." The names mentioned as composers of these compositions, John Dunstable, Gilles Binchois, and Guillaume Dufay, with their pupils Okeghem, Regis, Busnois, Caron, and Faugues, prove, however, that this remark should be taken seriously, and we may assume from it that the transformation in the style of musical composition around 1430 must have been a rather sudden one. That this transformation consisted, at least in part, of a different treatment of dissonances not yet defined by theory is proved in the many compositions extant from this time. Tinctoris, however, is the first to

---

I found something quite similar in Gottfried Keller's *Rules for playing a thorough-bass* (*ca.* 1700) where B♮, E, and A (under B♭) are called "naturally sharp notes" and F, C, and G (above F♯) "naturally flat notes". The first are then *principi* (MI's) and the latter *comiti* (FA's).

[60] Haberl first gives an account of a second printed work of Tinctoris, *De inventione et usu musicae* (printed after 1487) in the *Kirchenmusikalisches Jahrbuch* (1899), pp. 69 ff. K. Weinmann prints the fourth chapter in the *Riemannfestschrift* (1909) and gives it in its entirety (though it is only an abstract of a larger work no longer extant) in his *Joh. Tinctoris* (1445–1511) *und sein unbekannter Traktat "De inventione et usu musicae. Eine historisch-kritische Untersuchung"* (Regensburg and Rome, 1917).

elaborate on this new treatment of dissonances. He writes on page 135 of
the above-mentioned work (*Lib.* II, cap. 23):[61]

In similar counterpoint, note-against-note, dissonances are always forbidden,
in dissimilar counterpoint they are allowed under certain conditions (apart from
the works of the old masters, which generally contained more dissonances than
consonances). Almost all modern masters, not only composers but also improvising
discantors, when a consonance appears on the first or second part of the minima
while in *prolatio major*, or when a consonance appears on the first or second part
of the semibreve while in *prolatio minor*, use a dissonance on the note following,
whether it is an equal or a smaller value. In the *prolatio major*, as often as there
appears a contraction of two minimas belonging to different semibreves or two
such minimas repeat the same tone, or also on one minima, and in the *prolatio
minor*, as often as a contraction of two semibreves repeats the same tone, and when
immediately following a perfect consonance appears, a dissonance almost always
occurs on its first part [preceding the perfect consonance]. And when in the
*prolatio major* several minimas, or in the *prolatio minor* several semibreves descend
to a perfect consonance, very often a dissonance appears, as a result of syncopation, on the first part of each.

This, then, results in the following examples of passing (a) and prepared
(b) dissonances:

(Chapter 24, p. 137):[62]

[61] "In ipso autem simplici contrapuncto discordantiae simplicitur et absolute pro-
hibentur sed in diminuto cum ratione moderata interdum permittuntur, unde sciendum
est (ut veterum musicorum compositiones transeam in quibus plures erant discordantiae
quam concordantiae) quod fere omnes recentiores non solum compositores verum etiam
super librum canentes tam in prolatione majori supra primam vel aliam partem minimae
et in minori ultra hoc supra primam vel aliam etiam partem semibrevis posita concordantia discordantiam ejusdem aut minoris notae supra sequentem immediate collo-
cant. E contra vero tam in prolatione majori quam in minori supra primam partem primae
duarum minimarum in eodem loco existentium unitarum aut separatarum vel minimae
solius (?) et ultra hoc in prolatione minori supra primam partem duarum semibrevium
in eodem etiam loco unitarum aut separatarum perfectionem aliquam immediate
praecedentium discordantia fere semper assumitur. Imo si tam in prolatione majori quam
in minori per plures minimas vel ultra hoc in prolatione minori per plures semibreves
fiat descensus in aliquam perfectionem, discordantia super primam etiam partem cujuslibet earum syncopando frequentissime admittitur."

[62] "Besides those things which we have said about the admission of discords around

What is said here concerning the admission of dissonances for the parts of the
semibreve in *prolatio minor* is also applicable according to the rules of proportions, for the correspondingly larger note values of *allabreve* measure and all other
shortenings of species of notes. Also, if a consonance falls on a strong beat, a
dissonance may follow on a weak beat, and when a perfect consonance follows
in succession, a dissonance may appear on the first half of each note through
syncopation of the counterpoint.

In Chapters 25–28 extensive investigation is made of what limitations
are encountered in the freedom of dissonance treatment in certain cases
in proportional notation. In order to understand these subtle explanations,
one must above all clearly understand that during Tinctoris' lifetime two
meters provided the foundation for the ordering of beats, that which
used minimas as its basis (*prolatio major*) and that which used semibreves
as its basis (*prolatio minor*). To this the peculiarities of diminution and
augmentation (i.e., proportion) must be added; these, however, are not
of basic significance but may be regarded only as a reflection of one of the
main meters. Only the *allabreve* meter based on breves instead of semibreves and represented by ⊕ or ₵, the meter employed "by the ancients,"
deserves to be considered independently of the two others. Proportional
mensuration changes appear especially often in the tenor, while the other
voices continue in the same meter. If we encounter, for instance (Chapter
25), the entrance of the *proportio dupla* (twice as fast, i.e., two note values
of the previous meter to one beat in the same meter) after a beginning in
*tempus perfectum* with *prolatio minor* (corresponding to our simple 3/4
measure), then the value of the semibreve advances to that of the minima;
that is, two semibreves are now of the same value as before or, as in
another voice continuing in the previous meter, two minimas were used
as division of one beat. Now not three but only two semibreves belong to

---

parts of a semibreve *prolatio minor*, this must also be understood about discords around
parts of all notes and according to the requirements of equivalent mensurations, which
we are considering, also around parts of minimas whose prolation is in *subdupla* proportion, which is the same thing as when a tenor increases in *duplo*. It is also applicable
around the parts of breves in *tempus imperfectus*, *prolatio minoris*, in the *cantus* in the middle,
or through *proportio dupla*, and is also the same for singing around parts of longas in that
same *tempus* and mode of prolation, as it is for a minor imperfect in *proportio quadrupla*. It
is the same around parts of maximas of the same *tempus* and prolation in major and
minor mode, likewise in imperfect and *proportio octupla*. For when a concord is placed in
the same way on the first or another part of these kinds of notes, through the aforementioned modes, proportions and quantities of singing, discords of the same or of lesser
notes [notes on weak beats] may follow the above. And if two of these [lesser notes] are
united or separated in the same discord, and on the other hand are put together again
(that is, when one of the aforesaid notes descends to a perfect consonance), whatever of
them is above the first part [the strong or accented beat] frequently permits a discord to
be taken by syncopation."

the next higher unit, so that the order of strong and weak beats is now quite different:

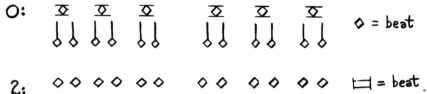

It is easy to see that in *proportio dupla* each of the two semibreves which belong to one beat demands the same treatment as each of the two minimas in simple *prolatio minor*. The semibreves are no longer values at the beginning of which dissonances may occur (through syncopation); rather, this quality belongs to the new value of the beat, to the breves which took the place of the semibreves, and these breves are divided into two parts. This is to say that the first of each of the two semibreves can become a dissonance because of syncopation. If instead of the *proportio dupla* the *proportio tripla* occurs, the semibreves keep their grouping of threes; they are not beats [they are not representative of the *tactus*] but subdivided values for which the rules given in the *prolatio major* apply to the minimas. It is not necessary to go into further detail concerning Tinctoris' premises. The principle is evident: each beat always demands a consonance or a prepared dissonance for its beginning, and freely entering dissonances (passing), as well as dissonances entering by step and proceeding by step, are allowed only upon the second half or the final third of a beat or on even shorter values.

In the twenty-ninth chapter Tinctoris further states [63] that some composers conscientiously avoid freely entering dissonances extending throughout the entire second half of the beat and allow them only on the third or fourth parts of the beat. This is more to be recommended than such liberties as appear in the music of Petrus de Domarto and Anton Busnois, who not only introduce the *semibrevis minor* (minima) in the *prolatio minor*, but also treat the entire semibreve as a dissonance (the example is given in values reduced by half):

Petrus de Domarto:

(The example from Busnois is full of errors.)

[63] (Couss., *Script.* IV:143): "Yet many so carefully avoid discords that they never assume the measuring of the discord to be directed over the entire half of a part [tactus]

The thirty-second chapter generally demands that as a norm all (passing) dissonances should enter by step and proceed by step,[64] so that the second appears after the prime or third, the fourth after the third or fifth, the seventh after the sixth (Couss.: fifth [?]) or octave; only in exceptional cases may a dissonant tone enter by a skip of a third. The return to the tone from which the dissonance is taken is allowed only when the dissonance is so short that it is hardly noticed. This is an exaggerated preference for the passing-tone over the simple neighboring-tone; it is probably based on the fact that the return to the beginning note is not melodic progression but only the ornamentation of a stationary tone. It is, however, not to be assumed that the reverse was also not used. Tinctoris generally enters into conflict with his productive contemporaries, despite his advances over earlier theorists. As a conservative schoolmaster he even scolds such a composer as Okeghem for the following harmless construction:

He bravely upholds the prohibition of MI *contra* FA in the perfect consonances, "which is the first rule to be impressed upon the pupils by masters," and calls offences against this rule made by people like Faugues, Busnois, and Caron "obvious errors" (*errores evidentes*):

The diminished and augmented forms of perfect consonances (*falsae concordantiae*) which appear because of the introduction of a ♯ must be avoided. They do appear, however, in the best masters, especially in

but over a third or fourth or lesser part. In my opinion such are more to be imitated than Petrus de Domarto and Anthonius Busnois, who in the first part of 'Et in terra' in the mass 'Spiritus almus' and in the cantilena 'Maintes femmes' not only make the half part of a note the measure of directing, being in the *semibrevis prolatio minor* in *tempus perfectum*, but make a discord of the entire semibreve."

[64] (Couss., *Script.* IV : 144) : "The rule for any kind of dissonance is this, that in ascending and descending it is always placed after some one of the concords to which it is nearest, as a second is placed after the unison or third, the fourth after the third or fifth, the seventh after the sixth or octave, and so of the others. And a concord by one or two degrees (although this latter is very rare) follows immediately after this very discord. So, if it ascends or descends by one degree, it must not return to the same discord without stopping unless this discord is so small it cannot be heard."

three- or more part compositions. Two-part examples (of which he does not approve) are given by Tinctoris on pages 121 and 127 as follows:

The third book of the *Liber de arte contrapunctus* lays down eight general principles (*generales regulae*) of counterpoint:[65]

[65] (Couss., *Script.* IV:147): "I. Omnis contrapunctus per concordantiam perfectam et incipere et finire debet...si tamen aliqua pausa cantum antecesserit cantus ipse [per] imperfectam concordantiam incipere poterit....Praeterea nonnulli quibus assentior dicunt non esse vitiosum si multis super librum canentibus aliqui eorum in concordantiam desinant imperfectam, quod tamen intelligendum censeo ubi plures fuerint concinentes quam concordantiae vocibus eorum contentae, ita etiam quod a sexta, tertiadecima vicesimaque supra notam inferiorem abstineant.

"II. Per concordantias imperfectas non autem perfectas ejusdem speciei cum tenore ascendere descendereque debemus...verumtamen ubi compositio trium aut plurium fit, nonnulli unam partem cum alia, inferiori dumtaxat excepta, per easdem species concordantiarum etiam perfectarum ascendere descendereque permittunt...immo si duarum partium ascensus aut descensus per concordantias perfectas ejusdem speciei fiat, dummodo aliqua intervenerit pausa, compositor a pluribus excusatur....Hujusmodi tamen ascensus vel descensus per concordantias perfectas ejusdem speciei multis quos imitari studeo displicet; et profecto nisi in compositione quatuor aut quinque aut plurium partium necessitate alicujus venustae perfectionis aut ordinatae progressionis eos minime censeo permittendos.

"III. Tenore in eodem loco permanente licet plures concordantias non solum imperfectas verum etiam perfectas ejusdem speciei unam post aliam continuo assumere... attamen, ubi aliae concordantiae possunt intermitti hujusmodi contrapunctus super cantum planum canendo diligenter est evitandus...in re facta vero praecipue si imperfectae fuerint concordantiae aliquando propter verba convenientissime permittitur.

"IV. Quam proximus et quam ordinatissimus poterit contrapunctus fieri debebit etiamlicet conjunctionibus longorum intervallorum tenor sit converso formatus; sed ab hac regula eximuntur qui magis contrapuncto dulciori ac venustiori student quam propinquiori....

"V. Supra nullam prorsus notam sive media sive superior sive inferior fuerit, perfectio constitui debet per quam cantus distonatio contingere possit (sumitur autem hic perfectio pro cujusque cantus media seu finali clausula per concordantiam perfectam regulariter efficienda)....

"VI. Super cantum planum canentes in quantum possumus redictas evitare debemus, maxime si aliquae fuerint in tenore...et quamvis ex omni parte in re facta regulariter etiam prohibeantur, aliquando tamen sonum campanarum aut tubarum imitando ubique tolerantur...redicta nihil aliud est quam unius aut plurium conjunctionum continua repetitio.

"VII. Super cantum planum etiam canendo duae aut plures perfectiones in eodem loco continue fieri non debent, licet ad hoc quodammodo cantus ipse planus videatur esse coaptatus...talis enim compositio cum redictis evidentissimam contrahit affinitatem, unde tamquam varietati contraria omnino est evitanda.

"VIII. In omni contrapuncto varietas accuratissime exquirenda est...hanc autem

1. The beginning and ending must have a perfect consonance. If the beginning starts with an upbeat, however (*si aliqua pausa cantum antecesserit*), one may start also with an imperfect consonance (third, sixth, tenth). Imperfect consonances are also allowed in a final chord in a polyphonic composition, but only the third and tenth, not the sixth (!) of the *finalis* or its compound form.

2. Parallel successions of imperfect consonances of the same size are allowed, but parallel successions of perfect consonances of the same size are not allowed. Some (as for instance Guilelmus Monachus; see p. 245) allow them, however, in compositions for three or more voices between discant and contratenor (but not with the lower voice), as in:

Nevertheless, many do not agree with this stand taken by Tinctoris. At best, this would be allowed in settings of four or five voices for the sake of a beautiful effect (*venustae perfectionis*) or as a result of strict imitation (*ordinatae progressionis*).

3. Above a stationary tenor the same perfect or imperfect consonances may be repeated if this is desired; however, some change is generally to be preferred.

4. The counterpoint shall, if possible, keep to itself and proceed by seconds, even if this sometimes entails a greater distance from the tenor:

This rule is not practiced, however, by those who would rather have a sweet and beautiful counterpoint than a smooth one.

5. A cadence shall be made on no note, neither a middle one nor a high or low one, which would make the mode of the melody uncertain.

6. Repetitions (*redictae*; see p. 253 concerning the *reiterationes* of Guilelmus Monachus) shall be avoided by the counterpoint, especially when they are already

diversitatem optimi quisque ingenii compositor aut concentor efficit si nunc per unam quantitatem nunc per aliam, nunc per unam perfectionem nunc per aliam, nunc per unam proportionem nunc per aliam nunc per unam conjunctionem nunc per aliam, nunc cum syncopis nunc sine syncopis, nunc cum fugis nunc sine fugis, nunc cum pausis, nunc sine pausis, nunc diminutive nunc plane aut componat aut concinat."

present in the *cantus firmus*. They are, however, sometimes used characteristically to imitate the sound of bells or horns, as in:

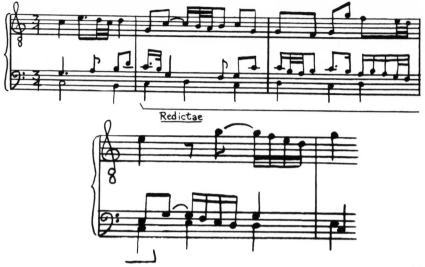

Redictae

7. Two final cadences appearing in direct succession in the same position are also to be avoided even though the tenor might be especially suited to it; this would only have a monotonous effect, similar to the *redicta*.

8. The counterpoint should attempt variety (*varietas*); but a song shall not employ as many devices (such as change of meter, modulation, proportions, alternating tones, syncopation, imitation, rests, embellishments, etc.) as a motet, and a motet not so many as a mass.

This is certainly quite different from the dry interval rules of the earlier theorists ˄f counterpoint. This is written by a man who practices composition and is its master [66] and who cannot conceive of the principles of voice-leading in any other sense than in connection with an organically developing work of art. The time of uncertain, probing attempts at polyphonic setting is now past and polyphonic music has come of age. The theorists now have completely different models from which they can study the laws of their art. From its concealed origin in England the art of controlled polyphony with truly independent voices quickly spread throughout all of Europe and flourished especially in the Netherlands. The fact that Germany was also in the forefront near the beginning of the flourishing of this art is proved by names such as Heinrich Finck, Heinrich Isaak, Adam von Fulda, Alexander Agricola, Paul Hofheimer, and Thomas

[66] Tinctoris is very well aware of his ability as a composer and points with satisfaction to his own works (p. 152): "Just as an unlimited number of compositions teach, not only those by me but also those by innumerable composers flourishing in the present age."

Stolzer—names which can be regarded as equally important to those of the great Netherlanders Binchois, Dufay, Busnois, Okeghem, etc., in the second half of the 15th century. Of these one is known also as a theorist, namely, Adam von Fulda. His *Musica* (Gerbert, *Script.* III) takes a special stand against the contrived settings of the Netherlanders, which Adam dislikes, but not without the honest admission[67] that formerly he was also intrigued by riddle canons, false proportions, etc. This type of device, however, does not serve any valid purpose. He says proudly (*op. cit.*, p. 354),[68] "The composer must be immune to all criticism, for he stands above other (musicians); he must never write anything of which he may repent later." He strongly condemns mere imitators.

Adam's rules for counterpoint are sketchy and without examples, but they are distinctly founded upon practical usage, similar to those of Tinctoris, and are not mere fundamentals. In the preface (p. 352) is a violent attack upon the disorderly manner of notation which had been introduced by instrumentalists.[69] It seems that this complaint applies principally to organ and lute music, for Adam speaks of arrangements in which pieces are "torn and corrupted" (apparently meaning replacement of the actual voices by chords and coloration of the melody). The rules are:[70]

---

[67] (Gerbert, *Script.* III:354): "For many, while they love obscurity, are laughed at by the learned because obscurity is rarely without error. But to tell the truth, I too have made use of this, showing my ignorance rather than giving any knowledge to artists. For he proves he is a miserable genius who uses inventions and not inventings. Therefore let him do as well as he can, for if one has done well, one can give authority to himself, as Socrates said."

[68] "Oportet ergo irreprehensibilem esse componentem, quoniam caeteris praeest: ne aliquid faciat, quod in posterum fecisse poeniteat."

[69] "Because alas! we see corrupt music by composers everywhere, and this happens because the worst usages of instrumentalists have flourished. These, although they scarcely understand two rules (O sorrow!), wish to compose songs—and would that it were only songs—but they even presume to attempt something great. And some of the others, scarcely understanding the shapes of notes (a modicum of what is suited to the art), correct every song, tear it to pieces, destroy it, and falsify every song that was ever composed. Those who prefer to stick to their depraved usage rather than yield to truth, let them teach actors and jesters that they would be scribblers of notes."

[70] "I. In omni cantu ad minus una vox dicitur aptari vero tono...scilicet [uni] octo tonorum (Gerbert: tonatos), id est clausulas pulcre localiterque ponere. Sicut enim accentus prosae per punctum ornatur, sic tonus perfectione (it must be called this in any case instead of 'per octo.' See Tinctoris' VIIth rule, p. 267).

"II. Omnis componens discat cantum distincte pausis ornare, quia varietatem faciunt. Non minus enim laudabile est pausare quam cantare, nec accentus prosae sine pausa sit.

"III. Omnis dissonantia, quoad fieri potest fugienda est (similiter tritonus cum semidiapente, quia discrepantia semitonii prohibetur) praeter in actibus, ubi eam perfecta continuo sequitur...."

1. At least one voice shall represent the mode in its pure form, namely, one of the eight ecclesiastical modes with correct cadences in the proper places.

2. The composer must learn to write rests at appropriate times, for they are an adornment and a pleasing change.

3. Dissonances are to be avoided, if at all possible (except at cadences where they are immediately followed by consonances). The *tritonus* and the diminished fifth are also to be avoided (this, however, is a rather insufficient statement).

4. The composer must keep in mind, when transposing, the correct distances between the individual tones which are to be arranged through chromatic changes (*conjunctae, musica, ficta*).

5. Each composer should be thoroughly familiar with the twelve intervals within the octave. Without this familiarity no melody can be composed.

6. He must also keep in mind the three main mensuration designations, the *modus*, the *tempus*, and the *prolatio*, according to which all rhythmic relationships can be exactly measured. He also must write the correct time signatures.

7. Successions of perfect consonances of the same size are not allowed: unequal perfect consonances may occur one after the other at will, such as the fifth following the unison, and the octave following the fifth (!).

8. Earlier only three to four imperfect consonances were allowed in succession; today longer series are also allowed, especially tenths, between which a middle voice occurs.

"IV. Componenti caute prospicienda erit clavium vera positio in toni transpositione, quia ibi conjunctarum obviatio est, quod Graeci synemnenon nostri vero musicam fictam appellare voluerunt.

"V. Omnis componens simpliciter memoriae tradet duodecim articulos, quia sine his nullus componitur cantus (the twelve *articuli* are the twelve modes or *species saltuum* explained in Gerbert, p. 349: semitone, whole-tone, minor third, etc., until the octave).

"VI. Componistae omnes singularem habeant respectum ad primos tres musicae gradus videlicet modum, tempus, prolationem, numeri gratia, ut cuique quae sua sunt aptent, id est verum signum pro agnitione et tactu.

"VII. Nulla consonantia perfecta suam similem perfectam sequi habet in arsi et thesi, sed quaelibet perfecta suam dissimilem digne imitari (comitari?) habet...ut post unisonum diapente, post diapente diapason.

"VIII. Licet olim veteres ultra tres aut quatuor imperfectas se sequi omnes prohibuerunt (Gerbert: prohiberent), nos tamen moderniores non prohibemus, praesertim decimas, cum ornatum reddant, voce tamen intermedia.

"IX. Diatessaron nunquam sola ponenda est nisi aut perfectam aut imperfectam moderetur: sed et nec simul ascendere nec simul descendere licentiam habet nisi sit... faulx bourdon, quod quidem fictum in hypothesi putant et in hyperboleothesi fieri posse (this probably means: though one might believe that that which was imagined for a lower position (treble sight) could be transposed into a higher octave, this is nevertheless a false conclusion!) sed hoc ratio non suadet, quia contra praecedentem (? probably the 7!) regulam esset (namely: successions of fourths cannot be approved as being inversions, because before inversion they would have been parallel fifths!).

"X. Discat omnis componens, contratenorem in hypothesi scilicet in gravibus potius perfectas ponere consonantias quam imperfectas, demta tertia cum ejus aequisonis, qui sonus consonantiae pari canore temperatur."

9. The fourth in two-voiced counterpoint is allowed only as an embellishment of the third or fifth. Successions of fourths can appear only as fauxbourdon (which, however, Adam still questions).

10. It is preferable that the contratenor create imperfect consonances with the tenor; thirds and tenths are also good (but not sixths).

In the *Introductorium musicae* (Leipzig Anonymous, *ca.* 1500, though there is no printer's name, and no place or year of publication is indicated), which I have published, there is a striking verbal correspondence with a number of Adam's definitions. This treatise may have been written by one of Adam's pupils; but whoever it was he was able to refer to the *Practica musicae* of Franchinus Gafurius; from the latter's rules of counterpoint (fol. 16ʳ) he extracted his own with few divergencies. The passage concerning cadences (fol. 17ʳ) is of interest, and I quote it in its entirety here:[71]

If at the close of a composition, or a section of a composition, one proceeds from an imperfect to a perfect consonance, generally the rule is to place the discant a sixth above the tenor and to have both move apart to the octave, the tenor descending one step, the discant ascending one step. The contratenor, as a rule, then takes as its penultimate note the fifth below the tenor, so that it is a tenth from the discant, but takes a unison with the tenor (a), or a fifth above (b), as its final note; it may also take the third below the tenor (c), but not at the close of the entire composition (!); here it is more satisfactory to take the octave below the tenor (d):

[71] "De cantilenarum conclusionibus. Quum ex concordantia imperfecta perfectam petimus concordantiam tamquam cantilenae terminationem vel alicuius partis eius, tunc semper penultima discantus in sexta supra tenorem quiescat et ambo contrariis motibus procedentibus sc. tenor unica voce descendens et discantus unica pariter voce in acutum intentus in octavam conveniant. Et penultima Contratenoris debet in quinta sub tenore constitui, qui tunc a discantu per decimam distabit. Verum ejus ultima notula poterit unisonum cum tenore aut quintam supra tenorem possidere; poterit item per tertiam sub tenore disponi et tunc cum discantu decimam personabit: hoc modo tamen in fine totius cantilenae deduci non poterit (namque ut predixi, perfectionem non principiis sed terminationibus attribuere debet); suavius tamen in octava infra tenorem commoratur. Verum si tenor clauditur in MI, penultima contratenoris debet in tertia collocari sub tenore discantu manente in sexta supra tenorem et sic ultima contratenoris in quinta sub tenore disponetur descendendo per quartam his syllabis SOL RE. Si autem tenor discantus formulam assumpserit capiat discantus speciem tenoris commeando cum tenore: aut ex tertia in unisonum stante penultima contratenoris in tertia sub tenore: aut ex quinta in tertiam: ita tamen ut ipse contratenor cum tenore ex sexta in octavam conveniat commeando cum discantu in decimis."

If the tenor closes on MI (Phrygian!), the discant also takes the third below as the penultimate note and the fifth below the tenor as the final note:

If, however, the tenor uses the discant formula at the end (moving one step up), then the discant descends one step, according to the manner of the tenor, into a unison with it, and the contratenor proceeds from the third below the tenor to the octave below (a); or the discant proceeds from the fifth above to the third above, and the contratenor, parallel with the discant, proceeds in tenths from the sixth below to the octave below the tenor (b):

(See the corresponding instructions of Guilelmus Monachus on pp. 255–256.)

Franchinus Gafurius (to whom this Anonymous apparently referred) was as a theorist probably one of the most important contemporaries of Johannes Tinctoris. According to the biography found near the end of his little treatise *De harmonia musicorum instrumentorum* (1518), he met with Tinctoris in Naples around 1480 and entered into public debates with him. Around 1480 we find a flowering of music theory in Italy which is without comparison: in Bologna, Bartolomeo Ramis and Giovanni Spataro; in Parma, Nikolaus Burtius, pupil of the recently deceased Johannes Gallicus, and Philippus de Caserta; in Milano, Franchino Gafori; in Lucca, John Hothby; and in Naples, Tinctoris. Not only by means of debates but also by means of heated polemical pamphlets all sorts of theoretical questions were brought closer to their solution, and foundations were laid for the last, but not least, part of music theory: the theory of harmony. This extraordinary activity in the realm of theory is obviously only a phenomenon accompanying the great upsurge which composition had been undergoing since the second third of the century and which had not yet reached its zenith. The subtle art of imitation, in much use in the Netherlands around 1475–1550, furnished many riddles for theorists, and the rapid development of the printing and sale of books promoted this even more. The overwhelming wealth of new materials was also the reason why actual compositions did not become the object of research to a degree which one would have expected following the initial stimulus given by Tinctoris. Discussions of changing the values of notes by different mensural designations, and especially combinations of the

same notes in different mensurations sung simultaneously, that is, in the
proportional notation which was so necessary for the canonic artistries of
the *Fugae quatuor vocum ex unica*, etc., absorbed much too large a part of
new books, so that the actual yield for our subject was relatively small.

Concerning proportional notation, as well as the entire apparatus of
manuscripts dealing with mensural notation at the peak of its intricacy, I
should like to refer to special works: Heinrich Bellermann, *Die Mensuralnoten und Taktzeichen im* 15. *und* 16. *Jahrhundert* (1858), Johannes Wolf,
*Geschichte der Mensuralnotation von* 1250–1460 (three parts; Leipzig, 1904),
and *Handbuch der Notationskunde* (2 vols.; Leipzig, 1913, 1919), as well as
my *Studien zur Geschichte der Notenschrift* (1878) and my *Kompendium der
Notenschriftkunde* (Regensburg, 1910), but especially Glarean's *Dodeka-
chordon* (1547), which is not too difficult to understand and which was
edited by Peter Bohn (German, with examples in modern notation [1889
as a publication of the *Gesellschaft für Musikforschung*, XVI–XVIII]); it
contains very instructive solutions of examples of all kinds of the Nether-
landish riddles.

## APPENDIX

FOOTNOTE 3: "I. Quando cantus ascendit, discantus debet descendere; et haec est
regula generalis semper observanda, nisi per species imperfectas sive aliis rationibus
evitetur. II. Considerandum, ut superius dictum est, quomodo et qualiter sunt tredecim
species et non plures nec pauciores, secundum doctores praelibatos (sc. Boetium, Guido-
nem, Magistrum de Garlandia cf. p. 23) ac etiam secundum Magistrum Octonem, in
hac scientia quondam expertissimum etc. . . . Istarum autem specierum tres sunt perfectae
scilicet unisonus quinta et octava (vel dyapente et dyapason). Et dicuntur perfectae,
quia perfectum et integrum sonum important auribus audientium et cum ipsis omnis
discantus debet incipere et finire; et nequaquam istarum specierum perfectarum debent
sequi una post aliam in discantu in diversis lineis vel spatiis, id est quod duo unisoni vel
duae quintae vel duae octavae, nec duae aliae species perfectae sequi debent una post
aliam; sed bene in una linea vel spatio ubi plures notae reperiuntur. Duae autem diversae
species imperfectae aut tres aut etiam quatuor sequuntur una post aliam, si necesse fuerit.
III. Quatuor autem praedictarum specierum sunt imperfectae, scilicet ditonus, alio
nomine tertia perfecta, tonus cum dyapente, alio nomine sexta perfecta; semiditonus, alio
nomine tertia imperfecta, et semitonium cum dyapente, alio nomine sexta imperfecta.
Et dicuntur imperfectae, quia non tam perfectum sonum reddunt vel important, ut
species perfectae, quare interponuntur speciebus perfectis in compositione. (N.B.[1]) Aliae
vero sex species, videlicet tonus, semitonium, dyatessaron, tritonus, ditonus cum dyapente
et semiditonus cum dyapente sunt discordantes. Et propter earum discordantiam ipsis
non utimur in contrapuncto sed bene eis utimur in cantu fractibili in minoribus notis, ut
quando semibrevis vel tempus in pluribus notis dividitur, id est in tribus partibus; tunc
una illarum trium partium potest esse in specie discordanti. (N.B.[2]) Ulterius notandum
est, quod nullo modo debemus ascendere neque descendere in discantu cum tenore cum
speciebus perfectis dummodo cantus ascendat de gradu ad gradum vel descendat. Si quis
fecerit, falsum erit et contra artem; sed bene cum speciebus imperfectis ascendere vel
descendere poterimus, ut dictum est. IV. Ulterius notandum est, quod quando cantus

ascendit vel descendit per quinque voces (et aliqui magistri dicunt per quatuor voces e hoc necessitate cogente), tunc poterimus ascendere vel (descendere) cum tenore in discantu cum specie perfecta per unam vocem tantum et non per plures. V. Si autem per sex voces aut per septem tunc possumus ascendere vel descendere in discantu cum tenore in specie perfecta per duas voces tantum. VI. Si autem cantus ascendit vel descendit per octo voces, tunc possumus ascendere vel descendere in discantu cum tenore cum specie perfecta per duas voces aut tres et non plures. VII. Praenotando quod unisonus requirit tertiam, tertia quintam, quinta sextam, sexta octavam; et ista regula non fallit, quod semper post sextam debeat sequitur octava, quia regula est generalis, quod semper post sextam sequitur octava, et quandoque post unisonum sequitur quinta, sexta vel octava et e converso, post tertiam aliquando sequitur quinta, sexta vel octava et e converso; post quintam sequitur unaquaeque species et hoc secundum diversos ascensus et descensus cantuum. VIII. Praenotando quod cum speciebus imperfectis possumus ascendere vel descendere ad libitum, et sicut species se habent ascendendo, sic se habent e converso descendendo. Et sicut se habet unisonus ad octavam, sic se habet octava ad duplicem octavam. IX. Praenotando quod quando duae tertiae vel tres ordinantur cantu ascendente sequitur immediate quinta; et eadem regula sive modus observatur in speciebus venientibus ab octava usque ad duplicem octavam ut saepius dictum est."

FOOTNOTE 5: "Notandum est quod septem sunt species contrapuncti scilicet: unisonus tertia quinta sexta octava decima et duodecima, quarum quatuor sunt consonantiae et tres dissonantiae. Consonantiae sunt istae scilicet unisonus quinta octava et duodecima, dissonantiae sunt istae scilicet tertia sexta et decima. Sciendum est quod debemus incipere et finire per consonantias sed penultima debet esse dissonantia. . . ."

FOOTNOTE 7: "Item sciendum quod duo sunt modi in contrapuncto: unus vocatur modus octavae et alius vocatur modus duodecimae. Modus primus cantatur per B quadrum et formatur in G grave (!) per ordinem usque ad UT RE MI FA SOL LA et de praedicto contrapunto (sic) habemus super:...Item secundus modus cantatur per naturam et formatur in *c* acuto (!) per ordinem UT RE MI FA SOL LA et de praedicto contrapuncto habemus super:...Et est sciendum quod in ♭ fa ♮ mi non possumus habere diapente per istos duos modos nisi per fictas musicas...nam si tenor est ♭ fa ♮ mi in voce MI opportet nos formare proprietatem contrapuncti id est de acuto (!) et tunc

habemus suum diapente scilicet MI (fa ♯) ut hic ...Et ideo cum non

possumus habere consonantias per rectam musicam tunc debemus recurrere ad fictam seu inusitatam et ea operare."

FOOTNOTE 8: "Nota quod contrapunctus nihil aliud est nisi ponere unam notam contra aliam notam, secundum Boetium (non dicit unam pro duabus sed unam pro una ponendam): hinc redarguendi sunt illi cantores qui ponunt binas notas, nisi ponerent cum bipartitione ad aliquam consonantiam colorandam, aliter grosso modo procederet. Nota quod contrapunctus semper debet incipi et finiri per consonantias, penultimam tamen debet esse dissonantiam. Nota quod quatuor (!) sunt consonantiae in contrapuncto videlicet quinta, octava, duodecima et quintadecima; et dissonantia sunt quatuor (!) videlicet tertia, sexta, decima et tredecima. Nota quod quaelibet dissonantia in descensu (tenoris) requirit suam consonantiam sicut tertia requirit quintam, sexta requirit octavam, decima requirit duodecimam et tredecima requirit quindecimam. Nota quod quando tenor ascendit contrapunctus debet descendere et contrario. Tamen haec regula fallit in dissonantiis quia possumus ascendere et descendere cum tenore per dissonantias usque ad quatuor, per consonantias vero non. Nota quod duae consonantiae ejusdem speciei non possunt poni scilicet quinta et quinta et sic de aliis. Sed . . . variae consonantiae ponendae sunt, scilicet cum tenor ascendit quinta tantum ( !)."

FOOTNOTE 9: (Couss., *Script.* III:37): "Duae species perfectae de se ipsis non possunt poni insimul, id est quod unisonus bis non debet poni, nec quinta nec octava, nec duodecima. Et nota quod cantus et discantus non debent ascendere (vel descendere) insimul, nisi cum speciebus imperfectis."

FOOTNOTE 11: "Nota quod, quamvis in istis dissonantiis non debeamus diutius commorari, possumus tamen ascendere et descendere per eas breviter ad omnes alias species sive differentias discantus."

FOOTNOTE 19: "Primo enim sciendum est quod supra octavam non est species; sed quidquid fit supra octavam, potest dici reiteratio vel reduplicatio infra quam octavam inclusive sunt sex species: tres perfecte et tres imperfecte. Prima species perfecta: scilicet unisonus, quamvis, secundum quosdam, non sit consonantia, est tamen, secundum Boetium, fons et origo omnium aliarum consonantiarum, et requirit post (prae?) se naturaliter semiditonum, id est tertiam minorem. Est autem semiditonus RE FA et MI SOL, et e converso. Potest etiam habere post se aliam speciem perfectam vel imperfectam et hoc secundum variationem cantus. Dyapente est species perfecta, et vocatur quinta; requirit naturaliter post (prae?) se ditonum id est tertiam majorem. Est enim ditonus: UT MI, FA LA et e converso. Potest etiam habere aliam speciem perfectam vel imperfectam, et hoc causa praedicta. Dyapason, id est octava, species perfecta, requirit naturaliter post (prae?) se dyapente cum tono, scilicet sextam perfectam; potest etiam habere aliam speciem perfectam vel imperfectam causa praedicta. Semiditonus, id est tertia minor, species imperfecta requirit naturaliter post se unisonum potest etiam habere aliam speciem perfectam vel imperfectam, sed opportet tunc tantum sustineri quod fiat dytonus. Dytonus id est tertia major, species imperfecta, naturaliter requirit post se dyapente, id est quintam; potest etiam habere aliam speciem perfectam vel imperfectam; et hoc secundum variationem cantus. Dyapente cum tono species imperfecta requirit naturaliter post se dyapason, id est octavam; potest etiam habere aliam speciem perfectam seu imperfectam, et hoc causa praedicta. Et est sciendum quod quilibet cantus debet incipi et finiri in consonantia perfecta. Item quod cantus nunquam debet ascendere neque descendere cum tenore in consonantia perfecta: sciendum est quod nunquam debet fieri simul duae consonantiae similes perfectae sed bene possunt fieri duae tres vel quatuor imperfectae similes. Item sciendum est quod quando cantus ascendit, discantus debet descendere et e converso."

FOOTNOTE 22: "Quandocunque in simplici cantu est LA–SOL–LA hoc SOL debet sustineri (cf. p. 224) et cantari sicut FA–MI–FA," the same applying to the two other cases; ending: "Et est notandum quod in contrapunctu nullae aliae notae sustinentur nisi istae tres scilicet SOL, FA et UT."

FOOTNOTE 23: "Hoc ideo est, eo quod dissonantia sit quoddam imperfectum, requirens perfectum quo perfici posset; consonantia autem est perfectio ipsius: quanto enim minus dissonantia distat a consonantia, tanto minus distat a sua perfectione, et magis assimilatur eidem; et ideo magis amicabilis est auditui, tamquam plus habens de natura consonantiae."

FOOTNOTE 30: "Nunquam duae concordantiae perfectae consequenter fieri debent nec ascendendo neque descendendo, nisi pausa intervenerit, aut quando tres cantus simul modulantur. Et non potest fieri aliter bono modo, quin duae perfectae concordantiae aut ascendendo vel descendendo concurrant, vel forte propter majorem melodiam, tunc unus illorum cantus fiet in concordantiis imperfectis, ut gratia exempli; si duae sint diapason consequenter, alius erit in decima voce et in sexta vel e contrario, aut fient duae decimae."

FOOTNOTE 32: (Couss., *Script.* III:195): "Item de istis combinationibus scire debes quod quaedam sunt combinationes consonantes sive concordantes sive bonas consonantias auribus humanis resonantes, sicuti sunt unisonus, tertia, quinta et sexta et sibi aequivalentes, scilicet: octava, decima, duodecima, tertia-decima, quinta-decima et hujusmodi. Et quaedem sunt dissonantes, sive discordantes, sive dissonantias auribus humanis resonantes sicuti sunt secunda, quarta, septima et sibi aequivalentes, uti sunt nona, undecima, quarta-decima et hujusmodi. Scias tamen, quod quarta et sibi aequivalentes minus dissonant quam aliae combinationes dissonantes, imo quodammodo medium tenent inter consonantias veras et dissonantias, in tantum quod, secundum quod quidam dicunt, ab antiquis inter consonantias numerabantur."

FOOTNOTE 34: "Excessus vero quo majus semitonium (namely 2187/2048) minus (256/243) excedit ($=531\ 441/524\ 288$) croma nominatur, quod croma nec totius toni (9/8) nec alicujus semitoniorum majoris scilicet et minoris pars aliquota existit, ut ipsi musicae auctores demonstrative declarant; et propter hoc mentiuntur quidam in musica loquentes, dicentes tonum dividi in quinque partes aequales, dieses nominatas, et minus semitonium duas illarum partium continere; majus vero tres et aliquando quatuor; sic quod ponunt triplex [duplex?] semitonium reperiri scilicet enharmonicum quod est minus semitonium, diatonicum quod est majus tres illarum partium continens et cromaticum quod est aliud majus in se quatuor illarum partium reportans."

FOOTNOTE 38: (Page 312): "A esse (namely to D F of the tenor) [se] dicessi (Couss: diresti) a la prima nota RE per octava se dicessi alla (Couss: dicesti alta) seconda LA per decima sarebbe falso." (Page 315): "Se dicessi (to F G of the tenor) al FA RE per sexta, et al SOL SOL per octava, non sarebbe bono (Couss: tono)."

FOOTNOTE 39: "Et proportion sesquitertia se chiama, quando sanno IIII note a la semibreva da mazore zo e IIII note per III minime...."

FOOTNOTE 43: "Quia bene fieri potest in contratenore contradiscantus...et est sciendum, quod contratenor in quantum est gravior tenore dicitur tenor."

FOOTNOTE 47: "Unisonus requirit tertiam; ipsa tertia requirit quintam; ipsa quintam requirit sextam, in eadem sede; ipsa sexta requirit octavam in diversis sedibus...."

FOOTNOTE 49: (Adler, *loco cit.*, p. 19; Couss., *Script.* III:292): "Si iste modus canatur secundum ipsos Anglicos, debet assumi supranum cantum firmum, et dictus cantus firmus debet regere supranum sive cantum."

FOOTNOTE 50: (Adler, p. 21; Couss., *ibid*): "Contra vero dicitur sicut supranus accipiendo quartam subtus supranum que venit esse quinta et tertia supra tenorem."

FOOTNOTE 51: (*Ibid*): "Modus autem istius faulxbordon aliter possit assumi apud nos non tenendo regulas supradictas sed tenendo proprium cantum firmum sicut stat et tenendo easdem consonantias superius dictas tam in suprano quam in contratenore possendo tamen facere sincopas per sextas et quintas penultima vero existente sexta."

FOOTNOTE 52: "Circa cognitionem syncoparum. Nota quod si cantus firmus semiuncem (sic) sequatur ascendendo de riga in spatium vel e converso et ascendat X, XII (?) notas gradatim, tunc debemus facere (syncopas) per tertiam bassam et quartam, quod idem est dicere: per sextam et quintam altas et hoc est verum ascendendo. Descendendo vero debemus syncopare per tertiam bassam et secundam quod (idem) est dicere: per sextam et septimam, altas ita quod penultima sit sexta veniendo postea ad unisonum quod idem est quam octava...."

FOOTNOTE 53: (Adler, p. 23): "Quod si Gymel accipiat consonantias sextas et octavas ad modum de faulxbordon, tunc contratenor de Gymel potest ire sicut contratenor de faulxbordon per tertias et quintas vel potest assumere suam penultimam quintam bassam et suam antepenultimam tertiam bassam...si autem teneat tertias et unisonos,...tunc contratenor faciet suam penultimam quintam bassam et suam antepenultimam tertiam bassam vel octavam bassam vel unisonum cum tenore et suam ultimam faciendo octavam bassam...."

FOOTNOTE 54: (Adler, p. 24): "Ab ista regula fiunt exceptiones quarum prima talis, quod (si) cantus firmus teneat modum soprani sicut FA MI MI FA, SOL FA FA SOL, LA SOL SOL LA, tunc contratenor bassus potest tenere modum tenoris, hoc est facere suam penultimam sextam bassam subtus tenorem, ultimam vero octavam bassam. Contra vero altus tenebit modum contra, hoc est faciet suam penultimam tertiam altam, ultimam vero quintam supra contratenorem (bassum), quae erit quarta subtus tenorem. Supranus vero faciet suam penultimam quintam altam supra tenorem quae erit decima cum contratenore basso, ultimam vero suam faciet tertiam supra tenorem, quae erit decima cum contratenore basso. Secunda exceptio talis est, quod si cantus firmus vel cantus figuratus teneat adhuc modum suprani, hoc est sic faciat FA MI (etc., as above), tunc contratenor bassus potest facere suam penultimam tertiam bassam subtus tenorem, ultimam vero faciendo octavam subtus dictum tenorem. Supranus vero faciat penultimam suam tertiam supra tenorem ita quod unisonus sit ultima cum tenore quae erit octava bassa cum contratenore basso. Contratenor altus faciet suam penultimam sextam supra tenorem, ultimam vero suam faciendo tertiam supra tenorem."

FOOTNOTE 62: "Praeter ea quae de admissione discordantiarum circa partes semibrevis prolationis minoris diximus hoc etiam de discordantiis circa partes omnium notarum et secundum directionem mensurae aequipollentium admittendis intelligendum est, ut circa partes minimae cujusvis prolationis in proportione subdupla vel ubi tenor quod idem est crescit in duplo; circa partes brevis temporis imperfecti et minoris prolationis in cantu ad medium vel per proportionem duplam, quod etiam idem est canendo circa partes longae ejusdem temporis et prolationis modi quoque minoris imperfecti in proportione quadrupla, et circa partes maximae eorundem temporis, prolationis et modi minoris ac modi majoris pariter imperfecti in proportione octupla. Namque posita similiter concordantia super primam aut aliam partem hujusmodi notarum per praedictos modos proportiones et quantitates canendarum discordantia ejusdem aut minoris notae supra sequentem assumi poterit. Et si duae earum unitae aut (Couss: et) separatae in eodem loco perfectionem aliquam praecesserint supra primam partem primae ipsarum discordantia e converso interdum collocatur, imo ubi per unam aut plures praedictarum notarum descensus fit in aliquam perfectionem quaelibet earum supra primam partem sui discordantiam syncopando frequentur assumi permittit."

FOOTNOTE 63: (Couss., Script IV:143): "Multi tamen adeo exacte discordantias evitant ut nunquam supra dimidiam partem integram imo super tertiam aut quartam aut minorem tantum cujusvis notae secundum quam mensura dirigitur discordantiam assumant. Et ut mea fert opinio tales potius imitandi sunt quam Petrus de Domarto et Anthonius Busnois, quorum ille in prima parte 'Et in terra' missae 'Spiritus almus,' iste vero in cantilena 'Maintes femmes' non solum dimidiam partem notae mensuram dirigentis hoc est semibrevis minoris prolationis in tempore perfecto immo totam ipsam semibrevem discordantiam effecerunt."

FOOTNOTE 64: (Couss., *Script.* IV:144): "Ordinatio autem cujuslibet dissonantiae haec est ut tam ascendendo quam descendendo semper post aliquam concordantiarum ei proximarum collocetur ut secunda post unisonum aut tertiam quarta post tertiam aut quintam septima post sextam (Couss: quintam) aut octavam et sic de aliis. Et hanc ipsam discordantiam concordantia uno gradu vel duobus tantum (quamvis hoc rarissime) distans ab ea immediate sequatur. Itaque si ab uno loco ascendatur vel descendatur per aliquam discordantiam ad eundem continuo non est revertendum, nisi ipsa discordantia adeo parva sit ut vix exaudiatur."

FOOTNOTE 66: (Page 152): "Prout infinita opera docent non solum a me verum etiam ab innumeris compositoribus aevo praesenti fluorentibus edita."

FOOTNOTE 67: (Gerbert, *Script.* III:354): "Multi enim dum obscuritatem amant peritis derisui sunt, quia rara obscuritas sine errore. Sed et ego ipse hac usus sum ut verum loquar plus ignorantiam meam indicans quam artis quid informans. Miserrimi tamen ingenii esse praedicatur qui utitur inventis et non inveniendis. Agat ergo quisque quantum digne potest; si enim bene egeris ipse tuae personae dabis auctoritatem, dicit Socrates."

FOOTNOTE 69: "...quia heu! corruptam a componentibus musicam undique cernimus: quod ideo fit, quia pessimus inolevit usus instrumentistarum qui cum vix duas intelligant regulas, proh dolor! componere carmina volunt et utinam solum carmina sed etiam quaeque grandia usu praesumunt. Caeterum aliqui vix notarum figuras intelligentes modicumve quid artis adepti omnem cantum corrigunt, lacerant, corrumpunt et recte compositum falsificant...qui vero mavult adhaerere pravo usui quam veritati obtemperare, discat mimos et joculatores fore componistas futuros!"

CHAPTER XII

# *The Revision of Mathematical Acoustics; The Consolidation of Contrapuntal Theory to Zarlino*

THE Spaniard Bartolomeo Ramos de Pareja, who taught at Bologna, is given credit to this day for having found the key to the theoretical derivation of the consonances of the major and minor third (*De musica tractatus* [Bologna, 1482], Lib. III, cap. 3).[1] One of the most surprising results of our research (p. 98 f.) is probably the fact that this credit should not go to Ramis, as he is usually called, but to the Oxford mathematician and music theorist Walter Odington, earlier a monk of the Benedictine cloister at Evesham, who lived about two hundred years before Ramis. Odington had already pointed out that the undisputed and generally recognized consonances of the major and minor third are based upon the harmonic division of the fifth (3/2) into the ratios of 5/4 and 6/5 (Couss., *Script.* I : 191–199). Odington, like Ramis, was confronted with the riddle of the syntonic comma $81/80$[2] by which the *ditonus* 81/64 (found by

---

[1] Unfortunately I am not able, despite all efforts, to give the contents of that part of this treatise which aroused so much attention. According to the information given me by the custodian of the only extant copy of this interesting manuscript, Luigi Torchi, Librarian of the *Liceo filarmonico* of Bologna, the Latin [script] of this manuscript is so difficult to read that no copyist known to him was able to make a copy of it for me. I hope that at some future time I will be able to supply this unfortunate omission. The manuscript of the treatise ascribed to Ramis (in the possession of the Berlin Library and earlier in Poelchaus' possession) which I have been able to inspect, thanks to the courtesy of the library staff, contains no trace of Ramis' innovations. For this reason the authorship of Ramis appears to me not to be beyond doubt.

In the meantime, through the efforts of Johannes Wolf, the above treatise of Ramis was printed in *Beiheft* 2 of the *JMG* 1901 [see bibliography].

[2] Fétis (in his article "Ramis" in *Biographie universelle*) maintains erroneously that Marchettus of Padua and Johannes Tinctoris emphasized the theoretical existence of the comma 81/80. Marchettus was acquainted with only the *diesis* (1/5 of a whole-tone) as the smallest interval and says nothing of a comma. Tinctoris calls the comma the part which is left over in a 9/8 whole-tone, when it is compared with a combination of two semitones of the proportion 256/243, in other words, the Pythagorean comma, which was common knowledge among all medieval theorists from the time of Boethius. On the contrary, Marchettus employs the harmonic division of the whole-tone 9/8 (although he does not appear to consider the harmonic division of the fifth 3/2 into 5/4 and 6/5) in

superimposing two whole-tones of the proportion 9/8) was larger than the ratio 5/4 (which corresponds to 80/64). The *semiditonus* (96/81) was also found to be smaller than 6/5 (=96/80) by the comma 81/80. This contradiction of traditional mathematical definition did not prevent Odington from adhering to his better judgment. He steadfastly maintained that thirds were considered consonant only because their actual sound as made by human voices did not agree with the sound of the *ditonus* and *semiditonus* according to the monochord, but corresponded to the naturally simple ratios 5/4 and 6/5 which appeared as a result of the harmonic division of the fifth.*[1] One must keep in mind the great authority which the Pythagorean system enjoyed throughout the entire Middle Ages in order to comprehend the audacity of Odington's new definition as well as his failure to bring this definition into harmony with the remaining interval designations. To question the ratio of 256/243 (the diatonic semitone) did not enter Odington's mind. He was also unaware that in addition to the conventional 9/8 whole-tone there was another of the proportion 10/9. Since he was convinced, however, apparently in consideration of the dominant role which major and minor thirds played in English discant—that thirds are consonances—and as a fine mathematician did not think a consonance possible without having a simple numerical ratio as its foundation, he had no alternative but to regard it as a tempering of the whole-tones, in order to achieve from two of them a major third of the ratio of 5/4.

For this mathematician a continuation of harmonic division would seem to have suggested itself:

Octave        1/2  (= 2/4), harmonic mean 3
                   (= fifth 2/3 + fourth 3/4)
Fifth         2/3  (= 4/6), harmonic mean 5
                   (= major third 4/5 + minor third 5/6)
Major third   4/5  (= 8/10), harmonic mean 9
                   (= large whole-tone 8/9 + small whole-tone 9/10)

Naturally he must have been deterred from taking this step by the apparent inconsistency that before the harmonic division of the third the harmonic division of the fourth should be effected. The latter would result in the following, however:

Fourth        3/4  (= 6/8, harmonic mean 7) (intervals would be 6/7 and 7/8)

---

the *Lucidarium* II. 9 (in Gerbert, *Script.* III: 75). Here he finds his own peculiar but not generally accepted definition of a larger semitone (diatonic ♭:♮), and a smaller one (enharmonic a:♭) as 17/16 and 18/17, and establishes a third kind of semitone (chromatic f:f♯) arbitrarily 4/5 of a whole-tone (four *diesi*).

which does not give any practically usable results. In the same manner the harmonic division of the minor third must be rejected:

Minor third     5/6  (= 10/12), harmonic mean 11 (intervals would be 10/11 and 11/12)

Odington probably retreated from this accumulation of smaller intervals, and rightly so. Still it is surprising and only to be explained in the light of his confidence in the consonance of thirds that Odington dared, in spite of these contradictions, to establish 5/4 and 6/5 as proportions of the thirds.

Ramis achieved similar results in an apparently much less independent manner, namely, by going further back to one of the tetrachord divisions of the Pythagorean Didymus (first century A.D.):*2

$$
\begin{array}{c}
\overbrace{3:4} \\[2pt]
\text{E} \quad \text{F} \quad \text{G} \quad \text{a} \quad (= 32:30:27:24) \\
\underbrace{15: 16: 18: 20} \\[2pt]
\underbrace{5:6} \\[2pt]
4:5
\end{array}
$$

This resulted, with the exception of the major third as 5/4, in an entirely different ratio for the semitone, namely, 16/15. Consequently, even if the tonal designations were not thought to be entirely correct, as we assume them to be today (the final step was reserved for Fogliano and Zarlino), nevertheless the Pythagorean semitone of the ratio 256/243 was finally eliminated and at the same time the distinction between a large and a small whole-tone established for the first time.*3

Ramis' innovations were violently disputed at first, as was to be expected. Nicolaus Burtius felt obliged to defend Guido of Arezzo against Ramis (*Musices opusculum* [Bologna, 1487]). He was subsequently set straight, however, by Ramis' pupil Giovanni Spataro (*Defensio in Nic. Burtii Parmensis opusculum* [Bologna, 1491]), who proved that Burtius was actually ignorant of the real problem, namely, the necessity of equalizing those contradictory whole-tones, found by steps of fifths and thirds, through some manner of temperament. Of course Ramis was in error in assuming that the definition of the whole-tone as 10/9 next to 9/8 and of the thirds as 5/4 and 6/5 instead of 81/64 and 32/27, and of the sixths as 5/3 and 8/5 instead of 128/81 and 27/16 was a form of temperament.*4 On the contrary, because of these designations, the number of contradicting values, whose compensation is the work of temperament, are only multiplied. The Pythagorean comma, by which the twelfth fifth is larger than the seventh octave, was not superseded by this new development, but the syntonic or didymic comma 81/80 (clearly indicated by Odington), by which the Pythagorean *ditonus* is larger than the 5/4 major third, found a place next to it. Perhaps we must suppose that Ramis proposed his deviations from a tonal system, regarded as irreproachable by the world, as concessions to aid musical practice. One must also not forget that we are not dealing with the rich enharmonic-chromatic system of today, but with tuning of the basic scale and inclusion of the intermediate tones which were then most used, namely, c♯, e♭, f♯, a♭ (g♯), and b♭. This is not an equal temperament, but the first attempt at the temperament of a pure tuning [unequal temperament].

Incidentally, even the mathematician Jacques Lefebvre (Jacobus Faber Stapulensis), to whose authority Franchinus Gafurius referred in his work *De harmonia musicorum instrumentorum* (1518) when taking an opposite stand to Ramis,[3] cannot but agree that 5/4 and 6/5 are probably the correct designations for the third. Faber's *Elementa musicalia* (a copy of the oldest edition, Paris, Johannes Higman and Wolfgang Hopyl, 1496, is owned by the Leipzig University Library) determines all intervals in the usual Pythagorean manner, but cannot avoid referring to the discrepancy which occurred between the mathematical proof for the dissonance of *ditonus* and *semiditonus* (as well as the Pythagorean major and minor sixth) and the practice of musicians, who used thirds and sixths as consonances, and rightly so:[4]

(*Elementum* III: 1):

The *semiditonus* (the minor third) lies between the ratios 6/5 and 7/6; although it is pleasing in sound to the ear, it is, nevertheless, not to be regarded as a consonance.

(*Ibid.*, in establishing proof for this):

[3] (Fol. 62ᵛ·): "Hence Bartholomeus Ramis the Spaniard thinks falsely (III:3) when he carelessly attributes the relationship of 5/4 to the interval of the ditone as found in the vibrating string. For as Jacobus Faber said (III:2), a ditone comes midway between 4/3 and 5/4."

[4] "The semiditone lies between the ratios of 6/5 and 7/6; although the semiditone makes a sound which is pleasing to the ear, it is nevertheless not to be regarded as a consonance (!)....The fact that a semiditone sounds pleasing to the ear is proved by one's experience in listening to musical compositions. It is not a consonance, however, because its ratio (32/27) is not superparticular, seeing that it cannot fall between the neighboring superparticular proportions 6/5 and 7/6 and have the external appearance of a superparticular." (El. III:2): "In the same way this is true of the ditone between the 4/3 and the 5/4; hardly music that can attain to a perfect harmony...even though in musical composition it is euphonius and sweet to the ear." (El. III:17): "The combination of a consonant *diapente* and a whole-tone is not admitted as a consonance as well as that of a *diatessaron* plus three semitones...even though this combination of sounds is still not consonant, musicians call it euphonius and suitable for harmonious composition."

The fact that the minor third sounds pleasing is proved by one's experience in listening to musical compositions: it is not, however, a consonance, because its ratio (32/27) is neither superparticular nor is it a complexity which can be reduced to a simple ratio.

The same is found in *Elementum* III:2, concerning the major third, which "sounds pleasing in composition, but still does not satisfy the requirements of a musical consonance," and *Elementum* III:17 concerning the major and minor sixth, which "sounds pleasing to the musician and seems suited for concordances."

Strangely enough Franchinus Gafurius relied upon this uncertain proof, which was actually nothing but a big question mark as far as the designation of the third as *ditonus* $(9/8)^2$, etc., was concerned. Nevertheless, Franchinus himself stressed the value of the major or minor third as the "medium tone" of the interval of the fifth in his *Practica musicae* (Milan, 1496):[5] "The fifth consists of the first two simple consonances (the minor and the major third); this combination results in a pleasing harmony between the two boundary tones, in actual imitation, as it were, of the harmonic division." Similarly, he knew how to evaluate other chordal formations, as e–g–c and c–e–g–c. In the already mentioned treatise of 1518, he carefully hid behind the riddle of "nature," by calling unison, fourth, fifth, and their compound forms the most excellent and perfect consonances; he developed the other intervals (major and minor third, major and minor sixth and their compound forms) more in a naturalistic manner than according to rational necessity.[6] He called these "irrational

[5] (Lib. III. cap. 2): "The fifth consists of the first two simple consonances, that is, the minor and major third; the concord results in a sweetness between the two extremities as if in actual imitation of adherence to harmonic division. Of this certain harmonic mean, if the interval extends to the top of the hexachord, the rising will contain this harmonic mean between its extremities, which is the *diapason* consisting of equivalent sounds. The sixth has only one tone in the middle and the accord brings a third in the lower part and the fourth sounds from the highest tone." (Here a most unusual passage follows, namely, that the fourth in such cases is inclined to a deeper intonation, in the direction of the fifth, as attempts on instruments prove!)

[6] This passage is worth quoting as an example of one of the earliest concerning "harmony" in the modern sense (Lib. III. cap. X, near the end): "What is harmony? It is, of course, the sweet and pleasant sounding of extreme and opposite voices with a common center (*medio*) embracing consonance....Hence those were mistaken who laid down the rule that consonance and harmony are the same, for although harmony is consonance, yet all consonance does not make harmony. Consonance is brought about by a high and low sound, but harmony, in truth, is made from high, low, and medium." (Cap. XI): "Three sounds are arranged as having something in common for harmony and these, sounding at once, bring about sweet agreement and harmony itself....The disposition of these three tones [*chordis*] is according to what they have in common for harmony (that is to say, the proportion of the lowest string has custody over the smaller. This very difference is of the largest to that which is the medium, and medium to the least, or the

consonances." Incidentally, Gafurius understood Ramis very well and even spoke of a division of the two-octave *systema teleion ametabelon* (*Perfectum et immutabile quindecim chordarum systema*) into twenty-four equal parts, that is, with twelve equal semitones within the octave.[7] He did this

interval made by the lowest and the medium strings is the same as the interval made by the medium and the highest) and is that which produces melody. That which we rightly called harmony is sometimes the agreement of two unequal consonances which are brought together from unlike proportions (the larger with larger numbers and the smaller with smaller numbers)....It is evident, therefore, that the *diapason* is called a consonance as a result of the [combination of] *diapente* and *diatessaron* and what is in the midst of them is called harmony from this circumstance." A harmony is, therefore:

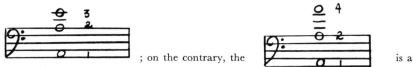

; on the contrary, the                                        is a *geometrica harmonia*.

(Cap. XII): "Concerning what the major and minor sixth and tenth have in common. There is also another mean in sounds which is not joined by the same limits or differences as in Geometry nor which is the equivalent of the diversities as in Arithmetic nor which is the equivalent of the extremities, limits, and differences as in harmony, but by these three, something else comes to be profoundly known, that is, harmonizing [*concinna*] and consonating [*consona*]. For as consonance is joined, *diapente* and *diatessaron* bring in another consonance (as has been proved), namely, an equal-sounding octave, as a mixture sonorous and sweet. This *concinna* is added to *consona* and produces another *concinna* which is well-suited to melody. Whence, as there are only two simple consonances, the *diapente* and the *diatessaron*, so there are also two simple *concinnae*, the major and minor third. For when the smallest consonance, the *diatessaron*, is superimposed on the major third, the extremities result in the major sixth, with a common tone [*chorda*] most suited and profitable to the *concinna*...but of the medium tone [*chordam*] itself: Ptolemy relaxes the third bordering on the ditone and *diatessaron* by the proportion 81/80 for a sweeter sounding of the music in the *concinna*. Superimposing a minor third (that is, a semiditone) on the consonance of a *diatessaron* produces a minor sixth which has a tone in common to fill out the *concinna*. Moreover, a common tone of this kind, which corresponds to the lowest tone with a semitone, they extend proportionately by 81/80 [that is, the Pythagorean minor third 32/27 plus the comma 81/80 becomes 6/5, the minor third resulting from Ptolemy's 'relaxing' of the major third]. Adding the consonant *diapente* to the major sixth (a common [tone] being preserved) produces the major tenth. In this same way a number of tones are found disposed diatonically in the vibrating string which are suitable for harmonizing [*concinnitati*]. And by adding a consonant *diapente* to a minor sixth (a common tone being preserved) a minor tenth is obtained for the *concinna*."

[7] (Fol. IV v.): "But some people distinguish a perfect and immutable system of fifteen tones [a two-octave diatonic scale] in twenty-four equal parts, and according to the proportionate annotation of these parts they dispose the consonances [i.e., the consonances are determined on a scale or gamut having such a division]. For, indeed, the *diapente* is a *sesquialtera* [3/2], the *diatessaron* is a *sesquitertia* [4/3]; the ditone is, in a disorganized manner, next to the consonant *diatessaron*, more exactly as a *sesquiquarta* [5/4], and a semiditone, which is less than a ditone, they make into a *sesquiquinta* [6/5] relationship. Again, they placed a *diapente cum tono* in *superbipartiente tertias* [5/3] relationship, and

by tuning the intervals as 3/2, 4/3, 5/4, 6/5, 5/3, 8/5, although he then disputed the correctness of this calculation.

Ludovico Fogliani (*Musica theorica* [1529]) is more lucid and perceptive than Ramis and dispenses with the last remnant of veneration for Pythagorean teachings, finding fault with its limitation of consonance to the octave, fifth, and fourth (Sectio II, fol. XIv.):[8]

> Even though these assertions are based upon highest authority, they nevertheless seem false to me because they run contrary to experience....Which human being who can hear at all can deny that besides these, there exist other consonances as well? Do we not find within the octave also the minor and the major third, the minor and major sixth, and, transcending the octave, the major and minor tenth, the eleventh which was already established by Ptolemaeus, and the minor and major sixth above the octave? That all these are real and very pleasing consonances can hardly be denied by anyone.

Fogliani accepts all ratios which Ramis established (5/4, 6/5, 5/3, 8/5), even the distinction between the large (9/8) and the small (10/9) wholetone. He further proceeds to a double listing of tones which differ by the comma 81/80, as in Lib. III, cap. 2, *De necessitate ponendi duo d solre et duo b mollia*, namely, two types of d: for the fifth above g and the minor third below f, and two types of b: for the minor third above g and the fifth below f. Furthermore, in fol. XXXIV[v] in the scale (B = chromatic tone) the following is found:

| C | B | D | D | B | E | F | B | G | B | A | B | B | ♮ | c |
|---|---|---|---|---|---|---|---|---|---|---|---|---|---|---|
| $\frac{25}{24}$ | $\frac{16}{15}$ | $\frac{81}{80}$ | $\frac{16}{15}$ | $\frac{25}{24}$ | $\frac{16}{15}$ | $\frac{25}{24}$ | $\frac{27}{25}$ | $\frac{25}{24}$ | $\frac{16}{15}$ | $\frac{16}{15}$ | $\frac{81}{80}$ | $\frac{25}{24}$ | | $\frac{16}{15}$ |

i.e.:

c    c♯    d    d    e♭    e    f    f♯    g    g♯    a    b♭    b♭    b♮    c′

(following modern designations of comma differentiations).

---

a *diapente cum semitonio* in a *supertripartiente quintas* [8/5] relationship. We will show the disposition of these to be without any good reason."

[8] "Even though these assertions are based upon highest authority, they nevertheless seem false to me, since they contradict sense...for who, except one who has lost his sense of hearing, denies that many other consonances can be found, besides the aforesaid five? [This should be three since only the octave, fifth, and fourth are referred to previously. The text, however, gives *quinque*.] For within the *diapason* is there not found, besides these, the semiditone, the ditone, the minor hexachord [sixth], and the major hexachord? Likewise, above the *diapason* is there not found the *diapason cum semiditono*, the *diapason cum ditono*, and *diapason diatessaron* (established by Ptolemy) and no less than the *diapason* with a minor hexachord and the *diapason* with a major hexachord? Moreover, these consonances which we are adding are those which are called minor third, major third, minor sixth, major sixth, minor tenth, major tenth, eleventh, minor thirteenth, and major thirteenth by those who practice them, all of which intervals cannot be denied to be true and very delightful consonances...the *sesquiquarta* [5/4] and *sesquiquinta* [6/5] which reduce the ditone and semiditone."

Zarlino might have appraised this more appreciatively than he did (*Opera* I:361). In fact, the modern tonal system, at least in its major concepts, finds its inception in Fogliano's time. Relationships among fifths and thirds are sharply differentiated, and the question arises as to how musical practice is to cope with the many values of "pure intonation." This means that an era of temperaments and assorted systems begins (Arnold Schlick, *Spiegel der Orgelmacher und Organisten* [1511]; Pietro Aron, *Il Toscanello in musica* [1523]; L. Fogliano, *op. cit.*; Giov. Spataro, *op. cit.*; Zarlino, *Istituzioni armoniche* [1558]; Francisco Salinas, *De musica* [1577]; etc.) and which ends with the final victory of equal temperament (Andreas Werckmeister, *Musikalische Temperatur* [1691]). Incidentally, Zarlino (*Sopplimenti musicali*, Opera IV:208–215) lists three ways of dividing the octave "direttamenti in 12 parti o semituoni eguali e proportionati." Fogliano also talked of such an equal division, and Zarlino (*Soppl.*, p. 160) expressed the thought that probably the founder of our keyboard (with five raised keys) was at the same time the founder of temperament, which is, up to a certain point, probably true. Organ and piano builders most probably acquired a routine technique of tuning their instruments before this tuning was established in theory.[*5]

What a long way there is from the first beginnings of a theory of polyphony, probably based upon the folk singing of northern England and the Scandinavian countries which moved mainly in thirds (organum during the 9th century), to the final, full recognition of thirds and sixths as actual consonances by academicians. What a revolution, for example, took place in the treatment of the fourth which the Greeks bequeathed to us as the principal interval of their scale division (tetrachord). This was then used by theory in its first timid attempts to bring polyphonic folk singing within the periphery of artistic forms, and achieved an unusual position as the preferred consonance, although this preference gradually diminished after the time of John Cotton. During the 14th century it was even thought to be an absolute dissonance by a large number of music theorists (for instance, the Parisian Muris) and even now is regarded sometimes as a consonance, sometimes as a dissonance. Is it not also truly remarkable that such a long time had to elapse between the instinctive handling of three-part composition based on intuitive recognition of triadic harmony, in the form of the English fauxbourdon (its age cannot be exactly designated), and the final, actual establishment of triadic harmony as the essence of polyphony? Walter Odington (*ca.* 1275) already stresses the pleasant sound of the major or minor chord with reference to the lowest tone (p.99 ), and from the time of the Parisian Muris more and more chord tables appear in the treatises. These threatened to divide the three-part setting rather uselessly into many single chords, since only single voices were heretofore kept in mind. At the most, an attempt was made to establish a relationship between two of the voices, the third being freely employed. Yet despite these trends, the actual establishment of a harmonic concept as a basis of musical hearing dates only from the middle of the 16th century (Zarlino). Before we turn to this development of harmonic theory, which constitutes the subject matter for our third book, we must briefly mention the contributions to contrapuntal theory made by theorists from Tinctoris to Zarlino.*[6]

Of special importance for us is Franchinus Gafurius' *Practica musicae* (1496), particularly the third chapter of the third book with its *octo mandata sive regulae contrapuncti*,[9] the contents of which I shall here state in brief:

1. The beginning of a polyphonic composition should be a perfect consonance (although Franchinus divided the consonances into *antiphonia* [octave], *aequisonia*

[9] (Lib. III. cap. III. De octo mandatis sive regulis Contrapuncti.)

"I. Principia uniuscujusque cantilenae sumantur per concordantias perfectas videlicet vel in unisonum: vel in octavam: vel in quintamdecimam: seu etiam in quintam ac duodecimam: quas et si perfectae minime sint: ipsa tamen suaviore sonoritate perfectis ascribunt. Verum hoc primum mandatum non necessarium est: sed arbitrarium: namque perfectionem in cunctis rebus non principiis sed terminationibus attribuunt. Inde et imperfectis concordantiis cantilenarum exordia Plerique instituerunt.

"II. Duae perfectae species ejusdem generis non possunt consequenter et immediate simul ascendendo vel descendendo in cantilena constitui: puta duo unisoni: vel duae octavae: aut duae quintaedecimae: sive etiam duae quintae aut duodecimae: quae et si perfectae non sunt, perfectis tamen, (ob quam sortiuntur suavitatem) connumerantur: ipsarum regulas atque mandata servantes. Haec enim regula non arbitraria est: sed legalis: omnem penitus exceptionem reiciens. Nonnulli tamen sunt arbitrati, duas quintas simul ascendentes vel descendentes pronuntiari posse: modo diversis protensae sint quantitatibus et intervallis: una scilicet perfecta: altera subtractione vel defectu semitonii diminuta: puta procedendo ab A re ad E lami: sive a proslambanomene ad hypaten meson: inde subsequenter et immediate ascendendo a ♮ mi gravi ad F faut: sive ab hypate hypaton: ad parhypaten meson, quod mea sententia falsum est: Namque quintam semitonio diminutam quae maxima et nota sit hujusmodi diminutio: cantilenae incongruam esse nemo dubitat. Hinc diapenticarum specierum ordinem a Proslambanomene duci non partitur harmonica medietas diatonice disposita. Tamen quinta ipsa (quod organistae asserunt) minimae ac latentis incertaeque quodammodo quantitatis diminutionem patienter sustinet, quae quidem ab ipsis participata (!) vocatur.

"III. Inter duas perfectas ejusdem generis concordantias diversis vel consimilibus motibus intensas aut remissas: una saltem imperfecta concordantia: puta tertia vel sexta et ejusmodi debet media constitui. Plures item imperfectae similies: atque etiam dissimiles ut duae vel tres vel quatuor tertiae et una aut plures sextae: inter duas ipsas perfectas ejusdem generis quam decenter disponuntur. Contrapunctus autem solam inter duas ejusdem generis perfectas concordantias consimilibus motibus ascendentes vel descendentes discordantiam continens, puta secundam vel quartam aut septimam: sive discordantia ipsa diminutiore figura notata sit ut...seminimina atque etiam minima: sive majoris quantitatis temporalem figuram imitatur semibrevem aut brevem: non

[unison], *emmeles* [fifth and fourth], and intermediate [thirds and sixths], and held to this general terminology when referring to these). This rule, however, is not binding, but arbitrary, for perfection belongs not to the beginning, but to the end (then follow examples of beginnings with third, sixth, and tenth).

2. Two perfect consonances of equal value must never follow one another in parallel motion. This rule is not arbitrary, but a law which permits no exception. Some allow the succession of a diminished fifth to a pure fifth, which I consider wrong, since a diminished fifth does not even belong in a real composition.

A short remark then follows concerning a very small diminution of the fifth which organists agreed the interval tolerated very well—perhaps the earliest observation concerning temperament.*[7] This was even given the

---

admittitur; namque si discordantia patens ac nota contrapuncto non congruit: imperfectae concordantiae locum ac vicem obtinere non potest: hinc et latens ipsa velocitate discordantia imperfectae hujusmodi concordantiae nequaquam poterit suffragari.

"IV. Plures perfectae et dissimiles concordantiae ascendentes vel descendentes possunt in contrapuncto consequenter deduci ut quinta post unisonum vel post octavam: et octava post quintam: ac reliquae eodem modo.

"V. Duae perfectae concordantiae similes possunt in contrapuncto consequenter et immediate constitui: modo dissimilibus procedant motibus atque contrariis, ut si duarum octavarum prima in acutum sit protensa: secunda in grave remissa: et e converso. Similiter quum fuerint duae quintae immediate succedentes quarum prima per thesim ducta sit secunda per arsim vel e converso...ultima semibrevis seu penultima notula contratenoris est quinta remissa sub tenore. Ultima vero notula ipsius contratenoris seu longa est item quinta sed intensa supra tenorem; quod in omnibus fere cantilenis evenire contingit.

"VI. In contrapuncto partes cantilenae scilicet tenor et cantus atque contratenor debent invicem esse contrariae in motu: ut quum cantus ascendit: tenor descendat et e converso, atque contratenor eodem modo se habeat cum altera ipsarum partium. Est tamen haec lex arbitraria. Nam saepe et multum tenoris notulae notulas cantus ascendentes aut descendentes consimilibus motibus subsequuntur: similiterque in contratenore proceditur: quod potissimum evenit: quum partes cantilenae sese invicem iisdem motibus fugant atque figuris.

"VII. Quando ex concordantia imperfecta perfectam petimus concordantiam tamquam cantilenae terminationem: vel alicujus partis ejus harmonicae: ad propinquiorem perfectam diversis utriusque partis motibus acquirendam concurrere necessum est. Ut exempli gratia quum tenor et cantus sextam majorem sonuerint videlicet diapenten cum tono: tunc ambo contrariis motibus procedentes scilicet tenor unica voca descendens: et cantus unica pariter voce in acutum intentus in octavam quae consyderata motuum contrarietate ipsi sextae propinquior est: illico convenient. Quod proprium est sextae majoris ad octavam scilicet transmeare. Minor vero sexta ad quintam frequentius revertitur unico motu: altera scilicet cantilenae parte immobili: altera mobili: contrariis vero motibus ad octavam item pertransit. Rursus quum cantus et tenor tertiam sonuerint: in unisonum (ducta prima motuum contiguorum contrarietate) convenient: Atque item laxati in contrarium ambo ad quintam transferuntur.

"VIII. Omnis Cantilena debet finiri et terminari in concordantia perfecta videlicet aut in unisono ut Venetis mos fuit (?) aut in octava aut in quintadecima: quod omnis musicorum scola frequentius observat gratia harmonicae mediocritatis perficiendae."

name which was in general use later (*participata*; *systema participatum* is the name used later on for equal temperament).

3. Between two perfect consonances of the same value, at least one imperfect consonance must be inserted, and according to discretion, also several of the same [imperfect consonances] or different sizes (thirds, sixths, etc.).

(The Leipzig Anonymous—*Monatshefte für Musikgeschichte*, 1897, no. 11 to 1898, no. 2—whose rules of counterpoint, incidentally, agree almost verbatim with those of Gafurius, has the following curious sentence: "Verum nunquam plures sextae ascendentes possunt in contrapuncto simplici constitui" (But several ascending sixths can never be set down in simple counterpoint) (fol. 15ʳ).

A counterpoint which uses only one dissonance between two perfect consonances of equal value, such as one second, fourth, or seventh, is not allowed, even though this dissonance enters upon a short note value. This is so because a dissonance, even though it were used openly and freely, would not add to the counterpoint and could never take the place of an imperfect consonance.

This is an excellent rule which says that figurative dissonance does not annul the mistake of writing a parallel. For instance, one must never write:

b a g c b g   g b a c d e
e – c, c – g, c – d, c – e, etc.)

4. Perfect consonances of different value may appear ascending and descending (*sic*), i.e., unison-fifth, octave-fifth, fifth-octave, etc.

(This sounds like an allowance of "hidden" perfect intervals, but in the examples such successions occur only in contrary motion).

5. Fifths and octaves which occur as a result of crossing voices are allowed, i.e.:

At the end, it is remarked that the skipping of the contratenor from the fifth below the penultima of the tenor to the fifth above the *finalis* is very common in all polyphonic settings.

6. Tenor and *cantus* shall move, if possible, in contrary motion to each other, and the contratenor shall move in parallel motion with one of these two voices, in

alternation. This rule is arbitrary in that the tenor often moves parallel with the *cantus*, especially in imitation, as in:

etc.

Gafurius, however, always recognizes the desirability of contrary motion.[10]

7. In closes, according to the rule, the progression should be from the "next neighboring" imperfect consonance to the perfect one; e.g., from the major sixth one moves to the octave by stepwise contrary motion. The minor sixth usually leads into the fifth by oblique motion (i.e., motion only in one voice), but it also can move to the octave (!). The third either contracts to the unison or expands to the fifth.

8. Each composition ends either with the unison (between tenor and *cantus*), as it was then the practice in Venice,[11] or with the octave, i.e., the double-octave, as may now be observed in the entire musical world for the sake of harmonic fullness (?!).

The fourth chapter of the third book is concerned with the treatment of dissonances. Even though there is an adherence to Tinctoris' teachings as far as the contents are concerned, the independence of Gafurius' formulation nevertheless merits its inclusion here:[12]

[10] (Lib. III. cap. IX): "But perfection is attributed to concords when they are reached by contrary motion, which is pleasant and delectable if it is perceived in a single movement."

[11] The Leipzig Anonymous: "As was the custom of the ancients."

[12] (Lib. III. cap. IV): "When and where discords may be admitted in counterpoint. ... A normal semibreve following a full measure of time should pulsate in the same measure as that of our breathing: in counterpoint one cannot connect discords as the masters of the art declare. Similarly, they do not admit a breve as a note for a discord, for this combination corrupts nature and sweetness by its discord, as is well known. That [discord] which is made by a syncope and by a very swift passing over may escape notice and be admitted into counterpoint. And this happens in almost all cantilenas as when we have imperfect concordance from which at once, by contrary or opposite movement of the voices, it proceeds to a perfect consonance near to itself. Then a minima or even a semibreve immediately preceding this imperfect consonance [or perfect] will be discordant, of course, when either the second comes into the unison from the third, or when the fourth goes on to the fifth, or when the seventh leaps forward to the equal-sounding octave. In this *concentus* (see the example) the first minima of the *cantus* makes a second to the tenor (revealing indeed a discord) and the second like minima of the *cantus* is a fourth to the tenor and is very noticeably discordant. These I should rarely concede to be admitted, for there is a noticeable discord in them, although it proceeds very swiftly and has the value of half a semibreve. Yet many, such as Dunstable, Binchois, Dufay, and Brasart, admit discords of this kind. The last semibreve of the *cantus* is divided into two minimas; the second minima makes a discord of the seventh with the last semibreve of the

Simple semibreves or even breves, appearing on the beat (not syncopated), must not be dissonant, because the exposed dissonance disturbs the naturalness of the harmony. On the other hand, the "hidden" dissonance, by syncopation or by passing quickly, is allowed in counterpoint. In almost all polyphonic compositions it may be found that in transition from an imperfect to a perfect consonance a dissonant minima or even a semibreve can occur, e.g., between unison and third a second, between third and fifth the fourth, between sixth and octave the seventh, as for example (the note values are reduced by half):

Here the minimas (quarter notes) of the *cantus* are dissonant at the asterisk (second and fourth) against the tenor, but I can seldom subscribe to this, for these dissonances are exposed, even though they pass quickly (only half a beat). This is written by many a composer, however, such as Dunstable, Binchois, Dufay, and Brasart, even in semibreves. The last semibreve ( + ) of the *cantus* becomes, through syncopation, a dissonant seventh on its second half, which, thanks to the syncopation, is not noticeable. In the same manner, the last semibreve of the contratenor creates on its second half a dissonant fourth against the tenor. Such dissonant minimas and even semibreves (!) must be allowed in counterpoint. Other dissonances also appear in counterpoint, but these are covered by a larger number of consonant voices (half-notes).

The fifth chapter deals with the consonant fourth (*De consentanea suavitate quartae*); if the discant lies an octave and the contratenor a fifth above the tenor, then contratenor and *cantus* constitute a fourth. In the same manner irreproachable successions of fourths appear, if the *cantus* moves in sixths and the contratenor in thirds above the tenor:

tenor, but if there is a syncope it is unnoticeable. Also, you will find in the last semibreve of the tenor, which, when it has been divided into two minimas, the second of these will make a discord of a fourth with the last semibreve of the tenor, though a hidden one. Wherefore a minima of this kind and also a semibreve are discordant; there is a necessity of admitting them to counterpoint. There is also a lurking discord in counterpoint besides the syncope which is contained in the parts of many cantilenas and is dulled by their concord. Moreover, a semibreve in double diminution and a breve in quadruple and the rest of those which are equal in quantity to a minima, if they were discordant, could be endured in counterpoint."

This type of counterpoint is called fauxbourdon. Even if Gafurius mentions this technique as suitable only for psalmody, his other examples (see the example above) as well as other extant settings from the middle of the 15th century (Binchois, Dufay, etc.) clearly indicate the great influence of fauxbourdon upon polyphony. The sixth chapter forbids the free entrance of the six-four chord, because in this the dissonance of the fourth in its lower position (directly above the tenor) is not covered ("iccirco in gravibus ipsis sonis quartae hujusmodi discordiam contrapunctus non sustinet"). In the fourth chapter we have already met with the prepared suspension of the fourth.

Considering these clearly conceived and, to a degree, very advanced views, it is strange to see that Gafurius did not recognize the sound basis of the rule, which was then just appearing (which he also sanctioned in his apparently lost work, *Flos musicae*), to let two voices singing simultaneously use the syllables of the same hexachord as much as possible in common, for example, to designate the octave C–c with UT–UT and not with UT–FA or UT–SOL. It proves how much the entire solmization and mutation system has been already discredited when he says in his intent to fight this rule: "The concordance or discordance of the syllables is not important, but only the actual distance of the boundary tones of the intervals."[13]

The twelfth chapter of the third book is again of great interest to us. Gafurius finds[14] that parallels are not sufficiently excusable even when a

---

[13] (Lib. III. cap. VIII): "There also are those who consider the last tones of the consonances by many sorts of names of vocal syllables, for they say that when the tenor pronounces UT, the *cantus* must similarly sing UT in unison, MI at the third, and SOL at the fifth and LA at the sixth in a single hexachord, but at the octave the *cantus* itself will sound UT equally with that of the tenor, and they think the remainder should be so called according to a consideration of this kind. We in truth (though even in *Flore musicae* we wrote this very arrangement) do not believe this should be regulated by any law, since neither the equality nor diversity of syllables but the sounding extremities of proper intervals at endings comprise the consonances. For when the tenor in $\Gamma$ has said UT, the *cantus* can not only say UT at the octave according to Guido's diatonic arrangement, but also even SOL and RE in G *solreut* below. For any syllable placed in G *solreut* below sounds equally at a perfect octave."

[14] "If from the perfect concord of the tenor with the *cantus* or of any part with another part, the same concordance occurs in another direction either up or down (a pause of a minima interposed in one of these parts of this same *cantilena*), I think it should by no means be praised. For they seem like two perfect concords, ascending or descending on account of the very small interruption of a very slight silence. There are some who, even when the interposed pause is that of a semibreve, do not admit two like perfect concords ascending or descending, although many disagree with them when a pause of a semibreve keeps a whole measure of time. So, in a pleasing manner, two or more pauses each having the value of a semibreve connect two similar perfect concords, either ascending or descending. Why, moreover, should we trust those who resist composers lest more than

rest the value of a *minima* is used in one voice, because this does not remove the impression of parallel motion. On the other hand, he thinks it an exaggeration to also forbid parallels after a pause of a whole beat or more. He calls it ridiculous not to allow the *cantus* to remain on the same note through several semibreves, "because in this case the tenor changes places with the *cantus*" (see the *Ars contrapuncti sec. Joh. de Muris*, our p. 226); it happens often enough that the composers lead the tenor and contra-tenor in a more lively fashion and the *cantus* in long notes, i.e.:

It is also preferable to lead the *cantus* and baritone ( =contratenor *bassus*) at the interval of the tenth, with the tenor in between using long notes, as in Tinctoris, Guilelmus Guarnerij, Jusquin Despret, Gaspar, Alexander Agricola, Loyset, Obrech, Brumel, Isaac, and many more composers of song, i.e.:

Finally, I should like to refer to the thirteenth chapter of the same book

three semibreves should be sounded as unisons in the *cantus* which they say is for this cause: that the *cantus* may not seem turned into the tenor or the tenor into the *cantus*? This, indeed, according to our opinion, is absurd, for very often composers of *cantilenae* denote the tenor and the contratenor by smaller notes and the *cantus* by slower ones, which more recent writers do very often."

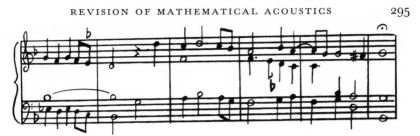

which deals with *musica ficta*,[15] giving us further proof of the gradual elimination of mutation, for it remarks that the *subsemitonia* are often not sung as MI [in accordance with solmization] but with the name of the unchanged step (a–G♯–a as LA SOL LA, G–F♯–G as SOL FA SOL).

[15] "To *musica ficta* of this kind we proceed by a triple consideration, that is, according to the chromatic genera, to the demonstration of the mixed genera and according to the division of the enharmonic genera, which are all called condensations of the diatonic genera and ornaments.... Moreover, in Guido's introduction to the diatonic system, *musica ficta* is shown by one interval of tone where b♭ of the hexachord displaces the tone FA which divides the tonal distance between A *lamire* and ♮ mi or between *mese* and *paramese* at the conjunction of the tetrachords. Wherefore they usually denote tones sharing a tonal interval of this kind by the sign ♭ *rotunda*, calling this by the syllable FA. Most people very often call SOL under LA at the interval of a semitone, when they proceed very definitely by beginning with these notes LA SOL LA in A *lamire*, and again by ending in the same, as in *Salve Regina*. Also between SOL and FA, beginning and ending in G *solreut* in moving as follows, SOL FA SOL, which the Ambrosians were accustomed to use for singing. For the syllable FA does not complete a semitone but is itself the dimension of a semitone, circumscribed by two sounds [i.e., the syllable FA does not bring about or stand for the half-tone F♯, but the F♯ is the result of dividing the distance between F♮ and G♮ into "two sounds" or two half-steps]. When, therefore, in the traditional Guidonian hexachords, you seek this fictitious progression you subtract a major semitone from single tones by describing these with the syllable FA and the sign ♭ *rotundum*, the change bringing about the transition of a tone to a semitone. Many people indicate the sound of a semitone by that which applies to the entire whole-tone, but when MI is changed to FA they write ♭ *rotunda* in the place of ♮ *quadra*, and when FA is changed into MI they place a ♮ *quadra* for a ♭ *rotunda*. Thence, if in E *lami grave* (*sic!*) you have changed MI into FA, FA is replaced by a major semitone below, whose hexachord has acquired ♮ MI *grave* (*sic*) as a beginning [i.e., if MI, that is E, is changed to FA, an E♭, the hexachord would take its beginning from a MI (♭) which is lowered to b♭].

                    B♭  c  d  e♭ f  g

But if in C *faut* you have changed a FA grave to a MI through a movement of the major semitone above (through a moving up of the leading tone), this kind of hexachord assumes as its beginning A *re*:

                    A  B  c♯ d  e  f♯

When, however, in ♮ MI *grave* you have changed MI into FA by the movement of a major semitone below (through a moving down of the half-step), a hexachord of this kind will begin on the F added below Γ, in the light of which it is not incongruous to call this *musica acquisita* [acquired music]. Also, by the introduction of the remaining tones one can bring about the conjunction of acquired hexachords. By this and by *musica ficta* you will easily understand the kinds of acquired consonances and tones."

"This is unimportant because the semitone appears not because of the syllable FA, but because of the correct measurement of the interval." Gafurius also develops the hexachords

Bb C D Eb F G     and     A B♮ C# D E F#

and farther down as *musica acquisita* the hexachord built on F under Γ,

F Γ A Bb C D.

Gafurius describes the *falsus contrapunctus* of the Ambrosian ritual, which was used even in his days in Milan, as a remnant of old times. It was used in ceremonial vigils in honor of the martyrs and in certain mourning songs and funeral masses; the second and the fourth are assigned major roles in this type of counterpoint. This testimonial is perhaps one of the strongest proofs of the continuing practice of primitive organum.[16] That this refers to an old ritual is further proved by the

[16] (Cap. 14): "Concerning false counterpoint. That which we call false counterpoint occurs when two singers proceed in dissonant intervals such as the major and minor second, the major and minor fourth, and the seventh and ninth of this sort, which intervals are by all reason and nature separate from every sweet harmony. For our Ambrosians use these in solemn vigils for the martyrs and in some canticles in masses for the dead, saying that this was instituted by the divine Ambrose. It is indeed a mournful singing in which the Church mourns the shedding of the blood of holy martyrs and for the assistance of the dead (who are lost).... Wherefore we can think that false counterpoint of this sort was introduced by those who were oppressed by a jealousy of music they did not understand. Only a singer with a rather high voice sings the notes of the plainsong, but two or three are joined into one sound following the notes of the plainsong in seconds and fourths in a fixed order, which, since they are separated from all reason in musical movement, I am ashamed to describe. When they begin a *succentus* [a singing together] of this sort in unison, they proceed with the plainsong in seconds and fourths even to the end or a certain termination, coming together to a unison. Very often they begin in seconds or in fourths, but they always end in unison, the process of which is shown in this example:

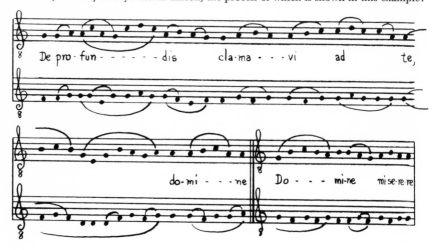

testimonial of Elias Salomonis (1274), who strongly expressed his disgust at the wailing in seconds which was so common with the Lombards.[17][*8]

Franchinus Gafurius, next to Tinctoris, occupied the highest place of authority in the first half of the 16th century and was cited by all the lesser intellects of his time.

The questions of pitch designation [*Tonbestimmung*] and temperament now become so important that the teaching of counterpoint was greatly neglected, as in the case of Ludovico Fogliano. Only in Pietro Aron, especially in his *Toscanello in musica* (1523, etc.), do we meet again a teacher who has originality;[*9] instead of repeating what others had said before, he had his own thoughts and defended his own opinions. The *Toscanello* is written in Italian, which is of value to us since it gives a number of technical terms in the form in which they were undoubtedly used by practising musicians, e.g., *contrabasso* for *contratenor bassus*, and *controalto* for *contratenor altus*, etc. The main contents of the *Toscanello* consists of points concerning musical grammar, i.e., the correct designation of measure (mensural designations), discussions of proportions, etc. Rules concerning voice-leading are not established until we come to the second volume. In the enumeration of intervals Aron proceeds to the *nondezima* and *vigesimaseconda*, that is, the fifth of the double octave and the triple octave (II:14). He begins the monochord with F under $\Gamma$ as the lowest tone; this is no innovation, however, for Tinctoris (1476) in his *Liber de natura et proprieta tonorum*, when he deals with transposing the ecclesiastical modes, descends below the limits of the Guidonian Hand (*extra manum*) for an entire octave (up to *contra* G; see Couss., *Script.* IV:37), and Adam von Fulda (Gerbert, *Script.* III:350) also speaks of the new practice of using tones lower than $\Gamma$ as well as going above $\frac{e}{e}$.

(He attributes this innovation to Dufay. See my edition of seven three-voiced chansons by Gilles Binchois in which I have pointed out that this composer also uses F and $\Gamma$.)

Concerning the prohibition of parallel perfect consonances (of equal value), Aron is very strict and not only turns against those who would occasionally allow a few fifths, but also combats—as Gafurius does—the succession from the perfect to the diminished fifth[18] since the latter is

[17] (Gerbert, *Script.* III:60): "Not, however, the song of the Lombards, who howl like wolves. It is quite evident that if one layman heard another layman sing in *primo basso*, he would not do well to jump directly into thirds nor by any means into seconds." This is said crudely enough, but we at least understand what he means.

[18] (Lib. II. cap. 14): "And thus, as a consequence, those who still use two fifths, one after the other, granted that one is perfect and one imperfect, according to our opinion run into error, because in the diatonic division such a diminished type is not permitted. Although organists in adding harmonies to voices take away some of their own from

never allowed anyway (as MI *contra* FA). Permitting any perfect consonances of different value to appear in succession seems to indicate that
Aron had similar motion in mind because of the *insieme*; that is, he seems
to allow the use of hidden perfect consonances.

Aron still uses the old rule that the perfect consonance must be preceded by its neighboring (*la più propinqua che si trova*) imperfect consonance;
that is, the octave must be preceded by the major sixth, the fifth by the
major third, and the unison by the minor third. In this connection, however, the necessity for chromatic change is pointed out when, for example,
the sixth before the octave is minor instead of major. It is not a requirement, however, that one must proceed from the major sixth or the minor
tenth into the octave. This is apparent because of the admission of the
succession fifth-octave, etc. The seventeenth chapter of the second volume
explicitly rules the interval successions: 1 ⟨ 3 ⟨ 5 ⟨ 6 ⟨ 8 ⟨ 10,
etc., or, vice versa, 10 ⟩ 8 ⟩ 6 ⟩ 5 ⟩ 3 ⟩ 1 as being obsolete, and
freely admits the successions 1 ⟨ 5, 3 ⟨ 6, 3 ⟨ 8, 8 ⟩ 5, etc., "because
many more beautiful and grateful songs are composed in this way than
are made in the antique manner in which one found himself more strictly
contained." [19]

Concerning beginning with a perfect consonance, he follows Gafurius
(*sara arbitraria*), and for the same reason regards the close with a perfect
consonance as obligatory. He allows imperfect consonances of the same
size in any amount, whether above a stationary or moving tenor. Concerning note values in figurative passages his rules are very free and
curious, inasmuch as he demands consonance for the first and last note of
such *diminutione* (that is, the first and last minima of a breve divided into
smaller values, and the first and last semiminima of a semibreve divided
into smaller values), while the middle values may be dissonant if the
natural course of movement demands it. [20]

---

them, they are tolerated more easily through the participation of other consonances....
Two, three, or more diverse perfect consonances can take place in counterpoint, one after
the other, ascending or descending, such as the fifth after the unison or after the octave,
and the octave after the fifth, or similarly the twelfth after, and all the other ways, without
any other note intervening."

[19] (Cap. 17): "And because manifestly such a method is not observed by the
moderns, free will will be conceded to us to be able to set a fifth after a unison, a sixth or
octave after the third, and the fifth after the octave (and as it will please you) I shall make
changes [*mutatione*] for one can see that many more beautiful and grateful songs are composed in this way than are made in the antique manner in which one found himself more
strictly contained."

[20] (*Ibid.*, cap. 17): "And I give this warning that in *canti diminuiti* the first note
and the last in such a diminuted passage must be consonant, and dissonance introduced
by diverse means as the natural flow of the music permits. Through the velocity by which
voices, thus diminished, move, there being in them some natural dissonances, these are

Concerning prepared dissonances, Aron makes no statement. It seems almost as though he did not recognize the progress made by Tinctoris in this field, for he does not mention this dissonance at all in his chapter about the *syncope* (I:37). He makes a rather important contribution, however, in correcting an aspect of the practice of syncopation by the rule forbidding the syncopation of semibreves over a rest which has the value of a breve. This should not be written

 i.e.,

but as below:

 i.e.,

His observation that a long sustained tone (but *not* a long pause between two long notes) has the effect of causing a lack of sensitivity to the meter, is certainly an excellent one.[21]

The compositional technique of imitation which achieved more and more popularity after the middle of the 14th century (Normannus Muris used the term *fuga*), and which developed into real canonic writing during the course of the 15th century, excluded the technique of writing each voice successively, which had formerly been the case. For the non-canonic setting, however, this technique continued to be used far into the 16th century. As far as I can ascertain, Aron is the first theorist who calls the successive-voice concept antiquated, emphatically pointing to the fact that the voices composed upon the tenor become more and more forced and impossible to sing, according to the order in which they are composed. He advises the beginner, however, to compose the voices, one at a time, in the usual manner, until he has gained the essential ability

not incommodious to the ear of the singer. And this is the mode and manner observed to the present time, as by examining the songs of the moderns, you will be easily able to understand."

[21] (Lib. I., cap. 37): "What is syncopation...those who syncopate a semibreve after a rest the value of a breve or a longa, or a minima after a rest the value of a breve are criticized by the general opinion of musicians because of the difficulty of utterance. But those who syncopate the semibreve in front of a breve or longa note [*figura*] observe the ordinary rule because singing and silence are contraries from which contraries are born, for syncopating which makes the note singable beyond the ordinary is arbitrary; and syncopation which makes the cantabile note [*figura*] bigger beyond the pause is not allowed. Therefore, if the semibreve and other similar notes are syncopated beyond the cantabile breve, such a procedure will not be disturbing because it proceeds with a flowing movement [*modulatione*] of harmonic concert."

to compose them simultaneously.[22] This is a good and wise council, which to this day is used, and rightly so.[23]

The eighteenth chapter, dedicated to cadences (*terminationi, cadenze ordinate*), makes it a duty for the composer to choose only those tones for closes and partial closes which are appropriate to the mode, namely, for the soprano (also for the tenor, if it is in unison, or in the lower octave):

| In mode | I: | d, f, g, a |
|---|---|---|
| In mode | II: | a, c, d, f, g, a |
| In mode | III: | e, f, g, a, b, c, d |
| In mode | IV: | c, d, f, g, a |
| In mode | V: | f, a, c |
| In mode | VI: | c, d, f, a, c |
| In mode | VII: | g, a, b, c, d |
| In mode | VIII: | c, d, f, g |

The normal cadences on the various notes are (those on b♮ in the soprano are missing because of the "fault of the woodcutter"):

---

[22] (Lib. II. cap. 16): "The fancy of many composers was such that first the *canto* should be composed, then the tenor and after the tenor the *controbasso*. This came about because they were lacking in order and awareness of that which is necessary in composing the *controalto*. Thus they rather made inconveniences in their compositions because it was necessary for the inconveniences that they put unisons, pauses, and ascending and descending skips there, difficult to the singer. Or else the utterance of the music [*pronontiante*] was in such a manner that the aforesaid *canti* remained with little sweetness and harmony. For in composing first the *canto* or the soprano and then the tenor, when the aforesaid tenor is composed there is sometimes no place left for the *controbasso*. And once the aforesaid *controbasso* is made, a number of notes of the *controalto* have no place, for which reason considering only part for part (that is, when the tenor is composed, if you expect only to accord that tenor, and similarly for the *controbasso*) it is inevitable that each part suffer in the concording places. Thus the moderns in this have considered better, as is manifest in their compositions in four, five, six, or more voices, each of which has a commodious part, easy and grateful, because they consider all the parts together and not according to the manner just described. And if it please you to first compose the *canto*, tenor, or *controbasso* in that order, the rule remains arbitrary for you (as has been observed by some up to the present who give the beginning to the *controbasso*, sometimes to the tenor and sometimes to the *controalto*). But because this would be clumsy and incommodious for you in the beginning, you shall begin part by part (!), and not until you shall have been somewhat practiced in the art shall you follow the aforesaid order and mode."

[23] Strangely enough (?) professional critics scarcely noticed that my *Lehrbuch des einfachen, doppelten und imitierenden Contrapunkts* (1888) attempts to use the successive technique again for training purposes. Aside from its great value as a training exercise, it is also significant in its application to fugal composition or to any composition which attempts to unite a counter-subject with a given theme. Above all it is valuable for accompanying music written with thorough-bass.

In addition, it is remarked that the same cadences are made with larger note values according to the demands of the composition; that the sixth (also where we are concerned with longer notes), which always resolves in the cadence to the octave, is preceded by the (syncopated) seventh. Only in very simple settings is this formation missing.[24]

An important addition to this discussion of cadences can be found in the rules contained in Chapter 20; this says that in closes where the tenor ends on e (third and fourth ecclesiastical modes) a final g with the tenor must be changed to g#:

[24] (Lib. III., cap. 18): "These cadences, according to the intention of the composer, are made in large note values, and the dissonant seventh is always placed before the sixth which precedes the octave except in that which is simply composed."

This tone, added to achieve a more pleasant sound, constitutes no
mutation, however; the raised g still uses the name SOL.[25] The addition
of the ♯ is necessary because inexperienced singers might otherwise intone
the minor third or tenth against the tenor. The remark proves that the
cadence with the major third was already common practice, even though
it would have "naturally" been minor!

Although Aron explains the successive-voice concept as being antiquated, he nevertheless gives instructions, like earlier authors, as to which
tones belong to the *controbasso* and *controalto*, according to what has been
placed in the tenor and discant. These instructions are also usable for
those who wish to compose in four voices simultaneously, since they can
only move tone-by-tone with the discant (from which Aron generally proceeds); whereby it follows that, above all, the relationship of the tenor to
the discant must always be first established. The possibility mentioned by
Aron, of using another voice than the first as the basis for writing (especially the bass) is, in any case, the rarer one. It suffices here to show
the results of each rule in an easily scanned arrangement (𝄽 = tenor,
♩ = discant, 𝆏 = low *contra*, 𝅘𝅥 = high *contra*. Aron at times calls the *controbasso*, *basso* for short and the *controalto* simply *alto*, in the same way in which
practicing musicians from the end of the 15th century used the Latin
names *bassus* and *altus*):

[25] (Lib. II. cap. 20): "From which it is necessary to note the figure of a *diesis* under the
syllable SOL of the aforesaid soprano, so that the minor tenth from the *controbasso*
(which was somewhat dissonant by being diminished a major semitone) by being raised
to its place is heard more sweetly. Although such an indication is not necessary among
the learned and practical singers, it is only placed there because, perhaps, the ill-practiced
and unintelligent singer would not give perfect utterance to such a position or syllable.
Since between MI and SOL there is naturally only a semiditone, that singer would not
sing otherwise than in his own way, unless his ear gave him aid, as one sees in some who
do this very well."

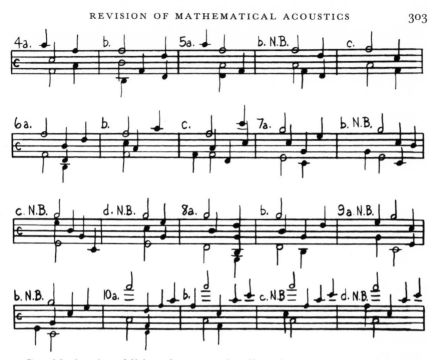

Considering in addition the general ruling that the composition must be arranged in such a way that the singers are spared uncomfortable progressions, and that intervals should be connected with each other in a manner suitable to each,[26] Aron's instructions for four-part writing seem in actuality very prudent and complete; for his time, one could not expect any which would be better. Among all available harmonies there is none with the fifth [of the chord] in the bass (six-four chord), and those few which have a third in the bass do not receive Aron's complete sanction. He expressly states that the sixth (thirteenth) between tenor and discant requires the fifth below the tenor or bass.[27] The *Toscanello* proves that around 1523 theory also began really to understand the significance of the triad; musicians had advanced this far in practice almost a hundred years before.

It would be asking too much to demand reasonable explanations of music theory for the logical interrelationship of harmonies already in existence around this time. The *cadenze ordinate* actually closes on the *finalis* and the usual final tones of the *differentiae* are still the only support

[26] (Lib. II. cap. 21): "And note that you must always accommodate the parts without passages disturbing to the singer and unite the consonances as closely one with the other as is possible, and this is given as a first rule."

[27] (Lib. II. cap. 30): "The thirteenth lacks the fifth below, as the sixth requires the same."

for tonal logic. This remained so for a long time, even after harmony became the main factor in composition and the system of ecclesiastical modes was replaced by the modern major-minor system. Although Walter Odington had already stressed the consonance of the (major and minor) triad with octave doublings of any three tones desired, and occasional remarks such as those made by Aegidius de Murino and even by the older Johannes de Garlandia point to a practice of harmonic formulation which follows certain paths, it was not until the 17th century that theory found certain clues for the explanation of harmonic logic; these, however, were still hazy at the beginning of the 18th century (Rameau).

Of the numerous theoretical treatises appearing in the time between Franchino Gafori and Zarlino, we must give special consideration to the *Ars canendi* (1537) of the Nuremberg cantor Sebald Heyden, especially because of its detailed treatment of the transpositions of the ecclesiastical modes then much used by composers of the second Netherland School, and to the greater usage of *musica ficta* these transpositions caused. Heyden completely ignores the *cantus naturalis* (p. 18) and differentiates only between the *cantus durus* and *mollis*, the former with a ♮ and the latter with a ♭ for the ♭fa♮mi step as actual basis. As simple and obvious as this may seem to us, it actually meant a big step forward from the Guidonian hexachord system to the system of the octave scales and to the modern system of the major and minor scales. According to Heyden, the most important thing to know is where a FA or a MI occurs; this is decided first by the accidental and second by the appearance of a ♭ or ♯ during the course of the composition. For the latter [♯ = MI] the use of the *sub-semitonium* at the cadences is unnecessary since we know (p. 295 f.) that it [the *subsemitonium*] does not require any mutation but is placed on the hexachords in its position [without changing the syllable] (p. 22):

If the accidentals (the ♭ or ♮) do not occur in their actual place (the note or step B), but on another, then the entire regular system is annulled and the order of the syllables arranges itself according to the following signs, i.e.:[28]

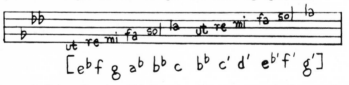

[28] (Page 23): "*Appendix prima.* If ♭ fa or ♮ mi is not written in its own place in the beginning, but in some other, then the position of the entire regular system is neglected from this one example, and the whole of the other syllables and order of voices will take another place below and above." The *appendix secunda* rules that an accidental which is not in the signature but rather appears during the course of the composition applies only to the single note to which it is prefixed.

The ♭ before e and b means that the syllable FA falls on those two tones, and the entire scale, in relationship to the *cantus durus*, appears one step lower (UT=b♭ and f). The ♯ designates the position of MI (we realize at the same time why the possibility of prefixing more than two sharps or flats did not enter the minds of the composers at that time because there are always only two places possible for the FA or MI within one octave):*10

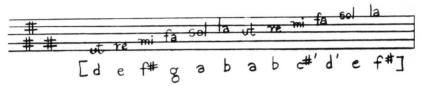

[d  e  f♯  g  a  b  a  b  c♯'  d'  e  f♯]

These possibilities of transposition were entirely sufficient to the needs of the time, especially since there was nothing to prevent further mutations during the course of a composition through the use of ♭a or ♯g.

Besides Heyden, only Glarean and Vicentino, whose works appeared just a few years before the first of those by Zarlino, command our attention and constitute the natural conclusion of this book. Glarean (or Henricus Loritus from Glarus, which is his actual name), the learned professor from Basel, was a pupil of Johann Cochlaeus in Cologne and a friend of Erasmus of Rotterdam, a versatile scholar of antiquity and the Middle Ages;*11 his *Dodecachordon* was published in the year 1547. The title of the work indicates the extent of his innovation, which aroused the interest of the entire musical world of his time: the increase of the number of the ecclesiastical modes from eight to twelve through the addition of two new authentic modes with their appropriate plagals:

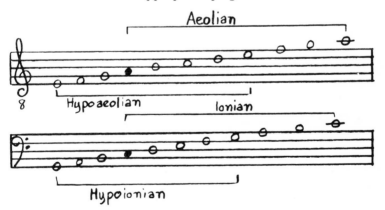

The C major and A minor scales had pushed themselves more and more into the foreground, especially in secular music, and music theory was hardly able to cope with this phenomenon. Glarean's explanation of his new additions, therefore, appeared at an opportune moment. He observed that each octave species admits of two kinds of division, the harmonic through the fifth and the arithmetic through the fourth:

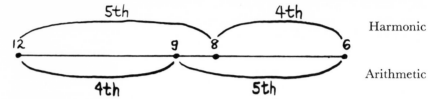

One of the seven octave species of the basic scale without chromatic alteration (♮, ♭) can be arithmetically divided only, namely, B♮–b♮, and a second f–f′ can be harmonically divided only, since B♮–f–♮ and f–♮–f divide the octave into a diminished fifth and a *tritonus* [augmented] fourth. The other five species, however, allow both methods of division, so that there are as a result six harmonic and six arithmetic divisions of which only eight correspond to the eight ecclesiastical modes; the four remaining are the two modes (and their plagals) which had so far not been recognized. Because of the significant role they had played for so long a time in actual practice, these new modes were generally and quickly accepted. Glarean selected the names *Jonius* (*Jastius*) and *Aeolius* in reference to the names of the later transposition scales (sharp scales) of Aristoxenos.

Incidentally, in spite of his classical education, Glarean did not recognize the error made by the author of the *Alia musica* (p. 11), who confused the octave species with the transposition scales. The opportunity to discover the error, therefore, passed unheeded. Both of the newly established final tones, on which, incidentally, the Guidonian hexachord finds its conclusion above and below (C D E F G a), follow the four which had already been in use, and the thought suggested itself to call C–G–c the first authentic mode and a–e–a the sixth authentic mode. This was actually tried later on by Zarlino, without any continued success, however. Glarean continued using the old names and numberings of the modes and designated the seven octave species in the usual manner, ascending from A:

I.    A  B  C  D  E  F  G  a    { authentic: Aeolius
                                { plagal:    Hypodorius

II.   B  C  D  E  F  G  a  ♮    { authentic not usable
                                { plagal:    Hypophrygius

III.  C  D  E  F  G  a  ♮  c    { authentic: Ionius
                                { plagal:    Hypolydius

IV.  D  E  F  G  a  ♮  c  d    {authentic: Dorius
                               {plagal:    Hypomixolydius

V.   E  F  G  a  ♮  c  d  e    {authentic: Phrygius
                               {plagal:    Hypoaeolius

VI.  F  G  a  ♮  c  d  e  f    {authentic: Lydius
                               {plagal not usable

VII. G  a  ♮  c  d  e  f  g    {authentic: Mixolydius
                               {plagal:    Hypoionius

The direct result of the new order meant even for Glarean a return to the strict maintenance of the age-old properties of the old eight tones and a reluctance to transpose them to the upper fifth.[29] Although earlier an ambitus a–e with g as the second below had been interpreted as a transposition of the first mode (*Dorius*) to the fifth above, or an ambitus c–g with ♮ as the second below as equivalent to the seventh mode (*Mixolydius*), Glarean now sharply opposes this with the remark that these are actually the new authentic modes, *Aeolius* and *Ionius*, which had not heretofore been recognized. The undisputed frequency of the ♭ in the fifth and sixth modes (*Lydius* and *Hypolydius*) he explains by saying that they are rather transpositions of the *Ionius* and *Hypoionius* into the upper fourth and formerly were most likely sung in the position C–c or Γ–g.

In addition, he finds it unnecessary to transpose an entire melody because of one single chromatic note and seems to prefer the elimination of transpositions.[30] The new formation of the *Aeolius* is explained by Glarean as being a result of composers of polyphonic compositions (*symphonetae*), who, drawn into this against their knowledge and volition, colored the upper fourth of the *Dorius* with chromatic changes (with a ♭ instead of a ♮), as they had similarly changed the *Lydius* into the *Ionius* by

[29] (*Dodecachordon*, p. 31): "From whence other universal rules [*katholicos canonem*] have been compounded. Every mode can, in truth, have another *confinalis* a fifth above the note [*finalem clavem*] which they call a final. This is in no way true, where the *diatessaron* clashes with it (namely, the fourth which extends from the fifth above the final to the octave, which indicates in the *confinalis* another position of the half-tone [for example, in the modes whose finals are on E, F, and G]). Yet this was a true rule [*canon*] and should be more considered. Also for the fourth note, through the diatessaron of any mode, the *cantus* may be used above the final, providing a FA has been used for the b♭."

[30] (*Ibid.*, p. 31): "Church composers, to be sure, make use of the transposition of cantilenas freely and excessively, from which they, at least, should find it possible to abstain. Why is it necessary, because of one chromatic note, to transpose the whole of the song? Especially when it could be introduced at this place by reason, after more familiarity."

such chromaticism (*lascivia*).[31] As far as the latter is concerned, he goes so far as to assume a regular conspiracy on the part of composers to transform all Lydian and Hypolydian melodies into Ionian and Hypoionian.[32] He says that around four hundred years ago, the then popular Lydian and Hypolydian modes were gradually replaced by the Ionian and Hypoionian, and that, therefore, many melodies, especially those from the graduals, were "contorted." Today, he says, the *Ionius* is the most esteemed of all the modes, even though it is removed from its rightful place and is transposed to the upper fourth. It is especially suited for dance pieces and was, therefore, in general use in most regions of Europe which he had visited.[33]

Apart from his energetic defense of the new modes, which he justifies, as we have seen, by reference to those of antiquity, Glarean is strictly conservative. The *musica extra manum* is extended downward to the *Digamma* |⁼ (great F, the lower neighboring step of the Γ) and upwards to the a (a²) of the harplike instrument he called the *cithara* (see pp. 56 ff. of the *Dodecachordon* for this and for a picture of this instrument, which he esteems greatly). The consonant intervals are enumerated only up to the double octave, but Glarean denies all larger intervals the ability to amalgamate.[34]

[31] (*Ibid.*, p. 256): "This mode certainly falls from composers involuntarily, and its nature guides and nearly compels this. For when men wished to change the Dorian in the upper fourth through wantonness, they unknowingly fell into the Aeolian, just as we said about the Lydian, which by the same wantonness they later distorted rather than deflected into the Ionian (compare this with the following citation)."

[32] (*Dodecach.*, p. 115): "The others namely, join notes in such a way that c *parvum* (= c′) is turned about to b♭...even though it is not permitted. Of course where the *cantus* goes up to e *parvum* (= é) it then goes to b♭ with a skip, although the tritone stands in the way. In these cases it is my opinion that a regular conspiracy exists on the part of such [composers] to turn all that is Lydian and Hypolydian into Ionian and Hypoionian, in order to achieve these wretched results. In such a way the *cantus* is contorted, particularly in the melodies of the graduals."

[33] (*Dodecach.*, p. 115): "Another kind of the third diapason [from C to c] is called the Ionian, harmonically divided, the first in its class, and of all the modes the most useful. But in our time it is removed from its rightful place by a fourth to the Lydian octave (the final of which is the note F) even if the *cantus* ends without a FA where the b is located. ...Further, this mode is especially suited for dance pieces and is therefore in general use in most regions of Europe that I have seen. Among the old church composers (*veteres Ecclesiasticos*) this mode is seldom found in their cantilenas. It is my opinion that around four hundred years ago the church singers were fond of it and many cantilenas in the Lydian mode...were changed to it [the Ionian], attracted by its sweetness and by its charm."

[34] (*Dodecach.*, p. 26): "Yet we are speaking about the intervals which are contained within the limits of the double octave. For the intervals which occur beyond it do not have a true blending and mingling of tones, even if some harmonize as the *decimaseptima*, *decimanona*, and *vicesima*; of these three they count the middle one among the perfect

He gives no instructions in counterpoint but remarks only in passing that the whole-tone which some of the ancients had counted among the consonances (?) is allowed only in the form of the syncope (this would be the name for this new [!] formation), but could not be heard there.[35] The fourth is allowed only above a fifth or third. Glarean's rule forbidding the major sixth as a melodic skip is new; the minor sixth he allows to remain as a peculiarity of the Phrygian mode.[36] Of the possibility of introducing the *tritonus*, the diminished fifth, and the diminished octave, Glarean knows nothing.

The explanation which he gives concerning the different use of measure signs (pp. 202 ff.) is important. The designations $\bigcirc$ 3 3, $\odot$ 2 3, etc., are gradually falling into disuse, he says, because it is recognized as a defect to show the *prolatio* in the sign of the mensuration of the *modus*. The manner of Franchinus (Tinctoris, according to present knowledge) came more and more into general use, namely, to reserve the circle for the *tempus* and to indicate the *modus* by rest lines[37] or only by *signa intrinseca*.

---

consonances and the extremes among the imperfect consonances. And the most skilled composers in our time use the *decimaseptima* rather frequently but the *decimanona* and *vicesima* more rarely, although as far as I can judge, they sometimes approve of this more for the reason that the highest voices may then play together, as if in the heights, and a true mingling of sounds be established."

[35] (*Dodecach.*, p. 25): "But in our time the whole-tone, which some have ascribed to the ancients, disappears from the number of the consonances and is allowed only in the *syncope*, as they call it (for that is the new name of this term), in which, however, it is not heard, just as it occurs in this concord of the contratenor before the half of the penultimate note of the tenor:

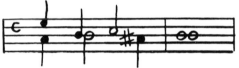

The diatessaron is again rejected unless a *diapente*, or a ditone, or a semiditone is placed below it."

[36] (*Dodecach.*, p. 20): "*Tonus cum diapente*...a perfect sixth...is scarcely ever allowed as a leap, for it is exceedingly hard, and within this interval Guido has constructed his hypotheses (hexachords)....*Semitonium cum diapente*, an imperfect sixth...is very familiar in the Phrygian mode and has a wonderful charm if used in the proper place."

[37] Cf. *Studien zur Geschichte der Notenschrift*, p. 263. Thomas Morley in his reliable work *A plaine and easie introduction to practicall musicke* (1597) still shows meter signs in the old manner, i.e., $\bigcirc$ 2 = *modus perfectus, tempus imperfectum*. The same author also shows in a long example, the differences between the manner of proportional notation used in England in his time and that used in Italy and Germany (p. 45): "If Glareanus, Ornithoparcus, Peter Aron, Zarlino, or any of the great musicians of Italy or Germany had had this example, he would have let it downe thus," namely, with the proportions of all kinds, the English by blackening the notes (*hemiola*) or with the addition of *sextupla*, *decupla*, or by inscribing 31 (= 3/1), 32 (= 3/2), etc., generally finding these sufficient for

It is rather amusing to read the description of the disagreement among composers in the matter of designating the *trochaica ratio*, that is, the triple measure (p. 214):

One composer shows it only by a number three, the other by    ⪚   3, Josquin de Pres by ◯ 3. Others assume a difference between *tripla, hemiola*, and *trochaica ratio* but are not able to distinguish between them. Because of the fact that the *tripla* is actually twice as fast as the *hemiola*, and the trochaic manner uses another mensuration as well as another manner of presentation, these are sufficiently distinguishable. Franchinus differentiates between the *semiditas* ( ⪚ , ⓞ) and *diminutio*, but others misinterpret his distinction, because they assume another value for the same notes, where Franchinus means only another kind of measure.

The most curious section of the *Dodecachordon*, which is, as is generally known, more significant as an anthology of contrapuntal showpieces of Dutch masters than as a theoretical work, deals with the simultaneous combination of different modes in the different voices of polyphonic composition (in the thirteenth chapter of the third book). This section is very characteristic of the period which pursued the principle of harmony and may be quoted here in part:[38]

The modes, among one another, show a certain hidden relationship, one generated by the other. This has not been established by composers of polyphonic music, but is in the nature of the modes. Thus, we see a tenor within the Hypodorian mode having a bass in the Dorian or even the Aeolian mode....*Cantus* and alto sometimes have the same mode as the tenor, while at other times they will deviate from it. If the tenor is Phrygian, bass and discant often fall into the Aeolian, but sometimes the *cantus* comes into the Hypophrygian. When the tenor

---

the writing of shorter note values ("more by custom than by reason"). A very enlightening explanation of complicated combinations of several proportions by placing parts one above the other, in score with measure bars (in partition), is found on pp. 34–35.

[38] (Page 251): "Modorum occultam quandam esse cognationem et alius ex alio generationem, non sane Symphonetarum ingenio quaesitam, sed rerum natura id ita disponente. Hoc enim fieri videmus quoties Hypodorii instituitur Tenor, ut ejus Basis sit Dorius, saepe etiam Aeolius....Cantus et Altitonans aliquando manent cum Tenore, aliquando evariant. Rursus quoties Tenor Phrygius est, Basis et Cantus saepe in Aeolium incidunt...nonnunquam cantus in Hypophrygium venit. Item cum Mixolydius in Tenore est, Cantus ac Basis Hypomixolydii quod Dorii est (!) Systema habent. Item, cum Hypoionicus instituitur, Ionicus venit in Basin. Denique si Tenor communem habet duorum Modorum diapente, Modi ipsi integri in extremis sunt vocibus, ut Authentus in Basi, Plagius in Cantu. In universum Baseos vox libenter ad Authentos inclinat, Cantus in Plagios, naturali quadam magis quam explicabili ratione. Sed ut in Dorii ac Phrygii Tenore Basis in Aeolium Systema uno dumtaxat semitonio a Dorio variegatum libenter incidit (!), ita saepe fit ut Basis Ionica Tenore nanciscatur Lydio...et contra Ionicus Tenor Basin Lydiam....Neque enim Cantores hoc studio aut suapte arte faciunt; excidit eis hoc magis naturae munere quam ipsorum voluntate. Nec tamen perpetuo, quod nunc dixi observatum est, sed ut plurimum, nam saepe contrarium reperias maxime in tortis cantibus."

is Mixolydian, *cantus* and bass keep within the range of the Hypomixolydian octave, which is that of the Dorian. If (for the tenor) the Hypoionian mode is selected, then the Ionian appears in the bass. If the tenor, finally, remains within the fifth which is common to a pair of modes, then the complete modes are likely to appear in the outer voices, the authentic in the bass, the plagal in the *cantus*. In general, the bass shows a preference for the authentic modes, the discant for the plagals. One recognizes this as natural, but is unable to explain it. But while the bass likes to go over to the Aeolian system together with a Dorian or Phrygian tenor, the Aeolian only distinguishing itself from the Dorian by a semitone (the minor sixth), it sometimes happens that below a Lydian tenor an Ionian bass appears or, vice versa, below an Ionian tenor, a Lydian bass....All this is not contrived purposely and artistically by the singers but happens naturally, more like a gift from nature than through their own will. That which I have said is, however, not of absolute validity, and often enough one may find another combination, especially in compositions which are distorted [Riemann: take chromatic turns].

How far Glarean is yet from recognizing the nature of harmony! That the authentic mode apparently likes to govern the bass is for him more curious than the opposite would be, because the plagals, according to tradition, seem more destined for the lower position.

The dispute concerning the correct mathematical designation of tonal relationships (Ramis, Gafurius, Fogliano, etc.) does not concern him; he does not mention a word about it.

In the same manner in which Glarean's work achieved special significance by the introduction of the new modes (which is basic to many details in the work and which distinguishes his work from all earlier ones), a work which appeared only three years before Zarlino's *Istitutioni*, namely, the "Reverendo Magistro" Don Nicola Vicentino's *L'antica musica ridotta alla moderna*" (Rome, 1555), has a special character.[*12] This work deals with the pet subject of its author, the attempt to infuse new life into the chromatic and enharmonic genera of the Greeks and the construction of a multikeyed keyboard instrument, the "archicembalo," upon which those genera could be reproduced next to the diatonic ones in all positions. The passages which deal with this subject, however, are the weakest ones in the book and are without interest for us. In order to explain the curious harmonic successions which were used by the chromatic madrigalists Cypriano de Rore, Vicentino himself, and others, it is not necessary to go to the antique genera, for since Marchettus of Padua a modern chromaticism had been developing more and more freely. This development is not at all in accordance with that of antiquity, since it was not influenced by the restrictions characteristic of the genera (leaving out certain steps of the tetrachords). It is, of course, not at all strange that admiration of the Greeks should take this form of expression. Glarean, for instance, fills long passages of his work with monodic (called *monades* by him) compositions in antique poetic meters with strict scansions (in which he had a predecessor, of course, in Peter Tritonius [1507] and others). Vicentino also tries earnestly to place his newly introduced three genera in practical use, and finally (toward the end of the century) there is an attempt to imitate the antique music drama, thus completing the resurrection of the artistic principles of antiquity. All this constitutes a closed circle of interrelated attempts by the musical Renaissance; to it we do not owe a revival of antique practice, but the definitive displacement of the ecclesiastical modes (which we know already as descendants of the antique scales) by the new major and minor scales and the new musical style of accompanied monody (which was also foreign to antiquity). Vicentino's *archicembalo* with its temperament of thirty-one steps[39] did not add anything to this, but the attempt to write chromatically did lead to new paths, and the already loose bonds of the old diatonic modes were completely shaken off.

Vicentino's *Antica musica*, however, deserves a place of honor in the history of music theory, not as a curiosity (in relation to what we said before) but because of the passages which deal comprehensively with counterpoint. Glarean's new modes are not known to Vicentino, nor does he take any notice of them, because he is more interested in his new enharmonic-chromatic system, the final purpose of which is probably the representation of all seven octave species on each of the seven steps of the basic scale. Vicentino (in fol. 126–127) notates these, using sharps to e♯, and flats to c♭; these two tones are used in the following instances:

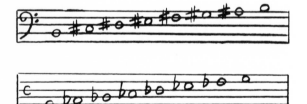

(Both are distorted by printing errors.)

Regarding tonal classification, Vicentino adopts Ramis' and Fogliano's

---

[39] Cf. my *Katechismus der Musikwissenschaft*, p. 47. Christian Huyghens (1629–95) in his *Novus cyclus harmonicus* (*opera varia*, Leyden, 1724, pp. 747 ff.) refers to the thirty-one tempered steps and the *archicembalo*, and accuses Salinas and Mersenne of not being able to recognize their exceptional value because of their ignorance of logarithms. Huyghens says that the fifths of this temperament are not too small by 1/4 of the syntonic comma, but 1/100 too large. According to my large table of tone values in logarithms (basis 2), however, the fifths are too small, and by 1/4 of a comma. I shall leave the final decision to the professional mathematicians.*13

position and always relates the consonances to the relationships which exist among the numbers 1–6 (fol. 34ᵛ), designating the major third as 5/4 and the minor third as 6/5.

His treatment of counterpoint is especially detailed, as we have said before, particularly when he examines the intervals singly for their value or lack of value (fol. 27 ff.). He declares the sixth, however, to be more dissonant than consonant.[40] This statement, appearing after Ramis, is rather unusual. Vicentino knows its value very well, however, in connection with other intervals. His remarks concerning dissonances are especially fine (fol. 29ᵛ):

In order that the composer may offer enough and varied fare to the ears, a new manner has been found to connect dissonances with consonances by introducing dissonances through syncopation. The syncope always draws two smaller values belonging to different larger ones together; then the second half of the syncopated note becomes a dissonance, i.e., a second, which through progression into a major or minor third finds at once its resolution. According to whether the syncopated note is a breve, semibreve, or minima, one distinguishes a large, small, and very small syncope. The note of resolution always must carry the value of the second half of the syncopated note, i.e.:

1. (large syncope)    2. (small syncope)    3. (very small syncope)

[40] "And in order that the composer may use enough variety of food for the ears, a means has been found of composing dissonances among consonances. And the aforesaid dissonances are made in the middle and in the favor of the syncope which will be as follows: that each time a note takes and binds halves of two notes, then the first half will be the second half of the first note and the other half will be the first half of the second note. Among composers it is usual to bind the syncope using three ways. The first way demands large [values] when the breve takes from two breves a half of each....I call small syncopation [syncopation involving small note values] that which occurs when a semibreve takes from two halves of semibreves and when the semibreve is sung at the raising of the beat [nel levare della battuta] (and thus it shall be the breve). The third way will be when the minima will take the half of two minimas with the aforesaid order, and this syncopation I shall call the smallest....Now the dissonance that is called the second will always be placed on the second half of the syncopated note and must always be descending to the consonance of the major third or minor by step [per grada]. And when the aforesaid syncopation ends, it must always end with a figure of one note which is worth the half lacking from the syncopated note. For example, if the syncope is the value of a breve, it must finish with a semibreve below by a step, etc."

The fourth is generally resolved to the third; it may also appear simultaneously with the syncopated second:

It can also progress to the fifth, with (a) or without (b) syncopation:

The augmented fourth (the *tritonus*) can also appear in this manner:

The syncopated seventh resolves to the sixth:

The strict rule covering passing dissonances (*dissonanze sciolte*) reads (fol. 32ᵛ):[41]

[41] (Fol. 32ᵛ): "Reader, know that from *tempus* to *tempus* one makes some gain, and one sees that in compositions which are not modern, composers have composed the resolved dissonance of a semibreve in one longa and have made the first good on the beat, and the second bad, on the upbeat. Afterwards, for a while, their followers have felt that that length was too long and thus it was abandoned, and through lack of discord to the ears [i.e., because dissonances are less perceptible in small note values] they used minimas; the first, good, on the beat, the second, bad, on the upbeat, and this order lasted a while. Now in our time we have abandoned the order of composing the minima on good and the other bad; and one has considered that the minima is a part which in our times is heard too much. And not only the minima but the semiminima is heard when it is not well placed; so that we are accustomed in compositions to make only the semiminima and

Formerly composers wrote passing dissonances by setting the first semibreve as a consonance (on the downbeat) on one longa (breve?) and the second semibreve as a dissonance (on the upbeat). Some time later it was realized that in doing so, too much time was allowed for the dissonance, and therefore only minimas were written as dissonances on the unstressed beat; this continued for some time. Today this has also been discontinued as it has been realized that the dissonant minimas are still too broad, so that only semiminimas and *cromae* (eighth-notes) are written as dissonances on the unstressed beats. Therefore, when four semiminimas appear on one beat, the first and the third ones falling on the downbeat and the upbeat are consonant. If two semiminimas follow upon one syncopated semibreve or a minima, then in descending the second one (?), in ascending the first one, must be consonant:

(note values reduced by one-half)

Even considered by today's standards it must appear far-reaching, although correct, to note the permission (fol. 32ᵛ) given to remove erroneous parallels through syncopation[42] (especially in compositions of more than five parts):

Vicentino is probably the first to note that syncopation without dissonance is also possible (*syncopa tutta buona*). No special rules are necessary to cover the consonant syncopation, and one must only be careful that not all

---

*chroma* [*fusa*] bad [that is, on the upbeat], (making, however,) the first good and the second bad and the third good and the fourth bad, beating at a rate of four semiminimas per beat so that the good will be on the beat and on the raising, following four semiminimas, the one behind the other. And then there are two near a syncopated semibreve or else a minima, and when they descend, the second must be good and not the first. And, on the contrary, when they are ascending the first will be good and the second bad, etc."

[42] "Practical music does not concede that in compositions, the practiced ear suffer any dissonance, or even two perfect consonances, either ascending or descending such as two or more fifths and thus of the octave. Since for everything there is some remedy, the composer will be warned that every time he sees fit to place a seventh in such a way that the composition will demonstrate that that seventh will have the effect of two octaves, they will not be. This way will be used for more than five voices because with a few voices such a seventh will be felt too much. And the same will be true of the unison, for what will seem to be two unisons and will not be; and when they will with the semitone, they will offend less the sense than with the tone, etc."

voices syncopate at the same time. At least one of the voices should accent the basic meter, because otherwise the syncopation is not noticed.[43] An example of such a consonant syncopation is:

The section which deals in detail with cadences (*cadentie*) (Lib. II, chapters 24–35, fol. 51ʳ–58ᵛ) mainly restates that which was said concerning syncopation. Unfortunately it loses some of its value—in spite of its detail—as a result of Vicentino's preconception that chromatically changed tones belong to the chromatic and enharmonic tonal species. For this reason he includes long tables of diatonic cadences only (without the self-evident ♯) in order to show their crudity and to demonstrate the necessity of the chromatic tones. In addition, he demands that all necessary accidentals be written into the cadences,[44] in order to avoid an otherwise inevitable misconception, as for example in the *cadentia dubbiosa* as in (a):

The introduction of the *subsemitonium* in the upper voice would make a minor seventh out of the sixth (! namely, the augmented sixth, b♭–g♯) and destroy the consonance. He even recommends a different ending

---

[43] (Fol. 33ᵛ): "One will be warned that in proceeding from more than one or two notes syncopating together, not to do it with all the parts; because it will not appear a syncope unless the syncope can be discerned at least by reason of one part which sings on the beat and the other parts which sing on the upbeat so that the differences of movement can be recognized."

[44] (Fol. 53ᵛ): "One makes a rule concerning cadences that all those which are to be altered [*sustenare*, which still has the meaning 'chromatically altered'] must be marked with the signs indicating a chromatic *diesis*, or with ♭ *molli* or with ♮, originated in order to prevent many errors made by singers (which can happen in compositions), thus to break the design of the composer who in such a note in the cadence wanted to demonstrate a *durezza* and the singer altered it and made the music sweet. And in doubtful cadences it would be a greater error to alter a major sixth, which would become a minor seventh (!) and would make great discord. The remedy to save doubtful cadences will be the following, that the diminution will deviate, or if one wants to make the entire, he shall make them [the voices] skip upwards and downwards.

(b and c) in order to save such *cadentie dubbiose* from arbitrary ruin which would result from the usual practice of singers.

Unfortunately Vicentino does nothing to remove any doubt as to whether in such cases as

at the asterisk g♯ and not g must be written. As obvious as this appears to be, it still seems strange that Vicentino, as well as theorists of the 17th century, did not consistently demand the ♯ (even the ♯ for the f♯ is often missing). We may probably assume that in the use of this figuration of rapid notes, they are naturally intoned according to the note which they embellish.

It is important to note Vicentino's admonitions to distinguish in style between compositions for church, chamber, or popular use.[45] This is probably the first place in literature where these styles are distinguished. The remark (fol. 84ᵛ) concerning composition for men's voices (*a voce mutata...cioe senza soprano*), which says that such composition achieves a solemn character because of the lower position and the limited range, should also not be overlooked.

The twenty-eighth chapter of the third book discusses composing for double choirs, which, as is certainly well known, was practiced for the first time on a large scale by Vicentino's teacher, Adrian Willaert. This chapter contains practical suggestions of lasting value: entrances of the second choir should be made on the second half of the final note of the section first sung by the first choir, and there should be a unison of both bass parts when both choirs sing simultaneously, because otherwise one choir lacks the necessary foundation which it cannot very well feel from the other; and also further suggestions. Also, the rules concerning the

[45] (Fol. 84ᵛ): "A great difference shall be observed in composing a composition to be sung in church from that which is sung in the chamber, and the composer must have his judgment finely formed and compose his compositions according to the subject and intent of the words...(here a comment follows to the effect that it is up to the judgment of the composer if he will begin a four-part composition and let the others enter gradually, or if he will let them come in in imitation)...and the order of composing popular [*vulgari*] compositions must be pleasant and understood without rules [*canoni*] and without too much subtlety of proportions, because such words [poems] as are madrigals will not succeed if not imitating nature in consonance and in steps applied to the aforesaid. And when one composes a composition *a voce mutata*, that is to say, without soprano, one will be warned that the extremities [of the range] should not exceed fifteen tones [that is, the range should not exceed two octaves] or at the most sixteen with a semitone."

setting of text (fol. 87) are important (new syllables should be introduced, if possible, only with skips).

Of special interest to us are the remarks concerning fugal writing, although not actually the fugue itself, which was not yet known to the 16th century, and also not the canon, but only the technique of imitation is here for the first time explained in detail. Vicentino rules[46] that a phrase must first be composed which is suitable for imitation by other voices. This must appear after a rest of the length of a semibreve or breve, but in no case longer than four breves (!), in all voices successively at an equal time distance. In order to "lead the listener astray," one can also enter one voice on the strong beat, the other on the weak beat. Imitation in unison and the octave is not regarded as the best because it has too little variety. The best order to follow is that in which the bass imitates the tenor a fourth below, and the alto and soprano imitate the tenor a fifth above, or the reverse, in which the bass imitates the tenor a fifth below, and the alto and soprano imitate the tenor a fourth above. If the imitating voice cannot continue its imitation strictly, it may move in free counterpoint. It is sufficient to imitate the first four or five [melodic] intervals exactly. This technique is usable for motets, madrigals, *canzoni Francese*, masses, and psalms (the strict canon being another case, as it is sung by two, three, or four voices all from one part). For imitation in contrary motion (*per ottava contraria*) the only requirement is that the skip of

[46] (Fol. 88ᵛ): "Desiring to begin the imitation [*fuga*], I shall elect a passage so that the other parts may say the same, and also the part that will enter after a rest or with a pause or two or three or four (and one shall not expect more than four pauses and they will almost be too many)...it will also be good to hear when all the parts of the imitation will enter in the same measure, the one after the other, as it would be, that with one pause or two or three or four a part entered and that so many pauses would make a part like the other...and sometimes to deceive the hearer it will seem good that one part enter with the imitation on the beat of the measure, and the other on the upbeat, and the third on the beat, and the fourth on the upbeat. And imitation, which can be made in various ways, will not be good at the unison or at the octave because these do not give too much variety...and when the bass in four tones makes an imitation with the tenor at the fourth, the contralto and soprano will come at the fifth, and on the contrary, when the bass and tenor make imitation at the fifth, the contralto and soprano will make it at the fourth....Then, when one will want to start an imitation and if the part which is to follow the imitation cannot follow it at length, the composer will accommodate it with a counterpoint above, and it will not be of much importance, because the beginning has been made in imitation in which the imitation of four or five notes has been effected... and if one shall want to make imitation by contrary octaves, that is to say that the beginning of one part shall skip to the fifth above, in this manner it will be bad procedure (namely, that the other voice skipped a fifth upwards), because it will appear to make the composition leave its mode, for when one part skips down a fifth the other must skip up a fourth, and when one skips down a fourth the other must skip up a fifth so that the formation of the octave will be just."

a fourth upwards must be answered by the skip of a fifth downwards and vice versa, because otherwise the character of the mode is destroyed. (Here we have for the first time a statement of the principle of the tonal answer.) Imitation at the distance of the second, third, sixth, and seventh is also quoted as possible and as having good effect, as well as the connection of two voices with two types of imitation.

So far Zarlino has been regarded as the one who first gave instructions in double counterpoint. This is incorrect inasmuch as Vicentino precedes him in this by three years. As both are pupils of Willaert, one may well assume that Willaert had already developed a certain technique of instruction in these higher arts. The thirty-fourth chapter of the third book of the *Antica musica* carries the title *Modo di comporre il contrapunto doppio overo compositione doppia* and speaks of double counterpoint at the octave and twelfth, with the additional remark that other types are also possible. It establishes the firm rule, especially for double counterpoint at the tenth, that successions of thirds and sixths must not be written[47] because they change, through inversion, into octaves or fifths. One of the illustrated examples is as follows:

But the possibilities of introducing the inverted voice after a rest, etc., are also discussed. Imitation in contrary motion with the shifting of the entrances through rests is taken into consideration. In short, Vicentino lets us take a look into the workshop of the complicated art of the Netherlanders, which we shall not deal with further, since it offers nothing new

[47] (Fol. 90ᵛ): "Many double counterpoints can be made in many ways...one can cause the singing to be at the octave, at the twelfth, and in other ways. It is sufficient for me to throw a little light for the ingenious disciple who by himself will find many things with effort and experience. And the latter will be warned that when a composition is composed above by a tenth [the original text has *duodecima*] one must not make either two thirds or two sixths consecutively, etc."

as far as the theory of compositional technique is concerned. The time during which such contrapuntal prestidigitation was regarded as the acme of artistry has come to its close, however, and we see no reason for regret that these masters of old tried to keep the secrets with which they were able to achieve this art. They did this to such an extent that we find hardly any remarks about these techniques in the writings of the theorists.

## APPENDIX

FOOTNOTE 3: (Fol. 62ᵛ): "Hinc falso arbitratus est Bartholomeus Ramis Hyspanus (III:3) qui integrum ditoni intervallum in chordotono sesquiquartae indifferenter ascribit dimensioni. Nam, ut Jacobus Faber inquit (III:2). Ditonus evenit inter sesquitertiam et sesquiquartam intermedius."

FOOTNOTE 4: "Sesquitonus (=semiditonus) inter sesquiquintam et sesquisextam collocatus est. Unde fit ut etsi sesquitonus jocunde suaviterque auditum feriat, nondum tamen consonantia ponendus sit (!)....Quod sesquitonus suaviter feriat auditum, cujuslibet musicis modulationibus intenti fidei fecit sensus; quod vero nondum consonantia sit iccirco evenit, quod sesquitonus (=32:27) in superparticulari ratione non consistit quandoquidem inter sesquiquintam et sesquisextam proximas superparticulares nulla cadit interstes mediaque superparticularis habitudo, etc." (*Ibid.*, El. III:2): "Itidem ditonus inter sesquitertiam atque sesquiquartam medius: minime musicam complet atque perficit harmoniam...etsi in musicis modulaminibus sit euphonus suaviterque auditum feriens," and (El. III:17): "Adjuncto ad consonantiam diapente tono, nulla parabitur...consonantia, item aeque ad diatessaron trisemitonio....Etsi hic sonorum congressus nondum consonantia sit, euphonum tamen musici nuncupant melo modulationibusque aptum."

FOOTNOTE 5: (Lib. III. cap. 2): "Quinta...componitur .n. ex duabus primis simplicibus scilicet tertia minore atque tertia majore, concordi medietate servata. Inde suaviorem ducit extremitatum concordiam quasi quae certa imitatione harmonicae adhaereat medietati (!). Hujus quidem medietatis chorda si in acutum exachordi intervallo fuerit intensa, acutiorem inter ipsas extremitates harmonica medietate conclaudet: diapason compositam perficiens aequisonantiam....Habet .n. sexta solam chordam mediam et concinnam quae sc. tertia est ad graviorem et diatessaron subsonat ad acutum."

FOOTNOTE 6: (Lib. III. cap. X, near the end): "Quid sit harmonia? Ea nempe est extremarum contrariarumque vocum communi medio consonantias complectentium suavis et congrua sonoritas....Hinc falso sunt arbitrati qui consonantiam et harmoniam idem esse posuerunt. Nam quamquam harmonia consonantia est, omnis tamen consonantia non facit harmoniam. Consonantia namque ex acuto et gravi generatur sono: harmonia vero ex acuto et gravi conficitur atque medio. Cap. XI: Tres soni harmonica medietate dispositi et simul sonantes dulcissimum concentum atque ipsam harmoniam efficiunt. ...Dispositis vero tribus chordis secundum harmonicam medietatem (ut sc. qua proportione gravissima chorda acutissimam sive major numerus parvissimum custodierit, ea ipsa differentia maximi ad medium; medii et parvissimi differentiam: seu intervallum gravissimae et mediae chordae intervallum mediae et acutissimae servet) ea tunc producetur melodia: quam proprie harmoniam vocamus: Haec nempe duabus consonantiis inaequalibus constat: quae ex dissimilibus proportionibus (majore quidem majoribus numeris: minore minoribus) conducuntur....Constat igitur diapason consonantiam per

diapenten et diatessaron harmonice mediatam nomen ab re harmoniam vocitari."
(Cap. XII): "De Sonora medietate Sextae et Decimae majoris atque minoris. Est
quoque alia in sonis mediocritas quae neque eisdem et terminorum et differentiarum
proportionibus commixta est ut Geometrica, neque aequalibus differentiis ut Arithmetica,
neque aequalibus extremorum terminorum proportionibus ac differentiarum ut Harmonica: sed his penitus tribus noscitur aliena quippe quae conjungitur ex communi
chorda sc. concinna et consona. Nam quemadmodum conjunctae consonae sc. diapente
et diatessaron aliam (ut probatum est) ducunt consonantiam videlicet aequisonantem
diapason atque permixtam sonoritatem et suavem: ita consonae addita concinna aliam
concinnam efficit quae ad melodiam recte coaptatur. Unde sicut duae tantum sunt
simplices consonae diapente et diatessaron, ita duae quoque simplices sunt concinnae sc.
tertia major ac tertia minor. Quod cum minor consonantia videlicet diatessaron super-
posita fuerit tertiae majori tunc extremi invicem termini sextam ipsam majorem communi chorda mediatam atque concinnitati aptissimam conducent...sed mediam ipsam
chordam: tertiam ditoniaeam et diatessaron continnentem sesquioctagesima proportione
relaxat Ptholomeus ad suaviorem concinnitatis modulationem....Superducta autem
tertiae minori (quae semiditoniaea est) diatessaron consonantia: sextam minorem communi chorda mediatam atque concinnam implebit. Mediam autem hujusmodi chordam,
quae ad gravissimam tonum cum semitonio correspondet: sesquioctogesima proportione
participanter intendunt....Verum apposita sexta majore diapentes consonantiae (communi medietate servata) decimam majorem: secundum sc. numerum chordarum in
chordotono diatonice dispositarum attinges concinnitati congruam. Atque eodem modo
superducta sexta minore diapentes consonantiae communi chorda mediante: decima
minor concinna concipitur."

FOOTNOTE 7: (Fol. IVv): "Verum nonnulli perfectum et immutabile quindecim
chordarum systema viginti ac quatuor aequis partibus distinxere: secundum propor-
tionabilem sc. ipsarum partium annotationem concordantias disponentes: namque
diapente in sesquialtera: diatessaron in sesquitertia: ditonum incompositum diatessaron
consonantia strictiorem in sesquiquarta: ac semiditonum qui ditono minor sit; in sesquiquinta distributione posuerunt. Rursus in superbipartiente tertias (5/3) diapenten cum
tono et in supertripartiente quintas (8/5), diapenten cum semitonio. Quorum disposi-
tiones...rationi minime convenientes monstrabimus."

FOOTNOTE 8: "Sed haec positio licet maxima innitatur auctoritate nihilominus mihi
videtur falsa, quum sensui contradicat....Quis enim nisi sensu aurium diminutus neget,
plures alias a praedictis quinque: inveniri posse consonantias? infra enim diapason nonne
praeter istas invenitur Semidytonus, Dytonus, Hexachordum minus et Hexachordum
majus, similiter supra Diapason nonne invenitur Diapason cum semidytono et Diapason
cum Dytono et Diapasondiatessaron (quam posuit Ptholomeus) necnon Diapason cum
minori hexachordo et Diapason cum majori hexachordo? hae autem quas addimus sunt
consonantiae quae a practicis appellantur Tertia minori Tertia major, Sexta minor,
Sexta major, Decima minor Decima major, Undecima, Tertia decima minor, Tertia
decima major: quae omnia intervalla esse veras et valde delectabiles consonantias non
potest negari...sesquiquarta et sesquiquinta quae dytonum generant et semidytonum."

FOOTNOTE 10: (Lib. III. cap. IX): "Verum concordantia perfectioni adscripta ad
quam contrariis motibus organizantes perveniunt suavior et delectabilior est quam si
unico⸰conciperetur motu."

FOOTNOTE 11: The Leipzig Anonymous: "Ut antiquis mos erat."

Footnote 12: (Lib. III. cap. 4): "Quae et ubi in contrapuncto admittendae sunt discordantiae)... Semibrevis enim recta plenam temporis mensuram consequens: in modum scilicet pulsus aeque respirantis: in contrapuncto discordantiae subjacere non potest: ut artis posuere magistri. Similiter et brevem notulam discordantem non admittunt, corrumpit enim concentus naturam et suavitatem ipsa discordantia, quum nota est. Quae vero per sincopam et ipso rursus celeri transitu latet discordantia admittitur in contrapuncto. Id enim in omnibus fere cantilenis contingit, ut quum imperfectam continemus concordantiam: ex qua immediate per contrarios organizantium motus ad perfectam sibi propinquiorem proceditur: tunc minima seu etiam semibrevis ipsam imperfectam [seu perfectam] immediate praecedens erit discordantia scilicet vel secunda quum ex tertia in unisonum pervenitur: vel quarta quum in quintam prodeunt: vel septima quum ad aequisonantem octavam prosiliunt.... In hoc concentu: (see the example) prima minima cantus secundam efficit ad tenorem (patentem quidem discordantiam) atque secunda pariter minima cantus quarta est ad tenorem notissime discordans: has ego raro concederem admittendas: est enim nota ipsarum discordia quamquam velociter gradiens dimidium tantum semibrevis obtinet. Complures tamen discordantes hujusmodi minimam atque semibrevem admittebant ut Dunstable, Binchois, et Dufay atque Brasart. Ultima vero semibrevis cantus in duas minimas distincta: secundam minimam cum ultima semibrevi tenoris septimam efficit discordem: sed latentem ducente sincopa. Idem quoque comperies in ultima semibrevi contratenoris: quae quum duas in minimas partitus fueris: secunda ipsarum ad ultimam tenoris semibrevem quartam discordem monstrabit sed latentem. Quare minimam hujusmodi atque etiam semibrevem discordantem: in contrapuncto admitti necesse est. Est item et latens discordia in contrapuncto: praeter sincopatam: quae scilicet inter plures cantilenae partes concordes continetur et obtunditur. Semibrevis autem in duplo diminuta et brevis in quadruplo ac reliquae ejusmodi: quod minimae figurae quantitate aequivaleant et si discordantes fuerint in contrapuncto poterunt sustineri."

Footnote 13: (Lib. III. cap. VIII): "Sunt et qui extremas concordantiarum chordas multimodis syllabarum vocalium denominationibus consyderant: dicunt enim quum tenor pronuntiat UT cantus in unisonum similiter UT modulabitur: in tertiam MI: et SOL in quintam: atque LA in sextam in singulo exachordo: sed in octavam cantus ipse similiter UT aequisonabit ipsi tenoris, atque reliquas secundum hujusmodi consyderationem existimant nuncupandas. Nos vero (etsi in Flore musicae hunc ipsum descripsimus ordinem) nulla tamen lege credimus id esse servandum: quoniam neque aequalitas neque diversitas syllabarum sed propriis intervallis disjunctae extremitates sonantium terminorum concordantias concludunt. Nam cum tenor in $\Gamma$ ut dixerit UT: cantus non modo poterit UT in octava exprimere secundum diatonicam Guidonis institutionem: verum etiam SOL et RE in G solreut gravem. Unaquaeque enim syllaba in G solreut gravi disposita: perfectam a $\Gamma$ ut aequisonat octavam."

Footnote 14: "Si ex perfecta concordantia tenoris cum cantu vel cujusvis partis cum altera ad aliam sibi similem concordantiam perfectam intensam aut remissam (interposita minimae notulae pausa in una ipsarum cantilenae partium) deveniatur: nequaquam sentio laudandum. Namque videntur duae perfectae consimiles concordantiae simul ac consequenter ascendentes seu descendentes ob parvissimam minimae taciturnitatis intermissionem.... Sunt et qui (interposita etiam pausa semibrevi), duas consimiles concordantias perfectas immediate ascendentes aut descendentes non admittunt: quamquam his complures dissentiunt cum pausa semibrevis integram temporis mensuram observet. Condecenter item duae aut plures semibrevium pausae duas consimiles concordantias perfectas consequenter ascendentes aut descendentes mediabunt.... Quid insuper credendum censemus iis, qui organizantibus obstant, ne plures quam tres semibreves in cantu unisonas pronuntient? quod propterea asservant: ne cantus videatur in tenorem conversus ac tenor in cantum: hoc nostra quidem sententia ridiculum est. Solent enim persaepe cantilenarum compositores tenorem atque contratenorem diminutioribus pernotare figuris ac cantum tardioribus: quod recentiores frequentant."

FOOTNOTE 15: "De Fictae Musicae Contrapuncto....Ad musicam hujusmodi fictam triplice consideratione proceditur, secundum scilicet chromatici generis dimensionem, secundum permixti generis demonstrationem et secundum enharmonici generis divisionem, quae omnes diatonici generis condensationes dictae sunt et ornamenta....In Diatonico autem Guidonis introductorio musica ficta unico toni monstratur intervallo ubi videlicet ♭ mollis exachordum quartam disponit chordam FA quae toniaeam scindit distantiam inter A lamire et ♮ mi seu inter Mesen et Paramesen instar tetrachordi conjunctarum: quare et chordulas hujusmodi toniaea partientes intervalla signo ♭ rotundae pernotare solent eas per syllabam FA pronuntiantes. Persaepe etiam plerique pronuntiant SOL sub LA semitonii intervallo: quum potissime proceditur his notulis LA SOL LA incipiendo in A lamire rursusque in ipsam terminando, ut Salve regina. Atque item inter SOL et FA incipiendo et terminando in G solreut hoc transitu SOL FA SOL: quod Ambrosiani plerumque modulari solent. Non enim syllaba FA semitonium perficit, sed ipsa semitonaei intervalli dimensio duobus sonis circumscripta. Quum igitur in Exachordis Guidonicae traditionis fictam hanc progressionem quaesieris: acutiores singulorum tonorum notulas majore subtrahes semitonio: eas FA syllaba ac littera ♭ rotunda describendo: permutatione ducente: quia fit ex tono transitus in semitonium. Plerique autem singulis tonorum intervallis hujusmodi vocem semitoniaeam inscribunt. Verum quum MI in FA permutatur loco ♮ quadrae ♭ rotundam ascribunt, quum autem FA in MI: loco ♭ rotundae ♮ quadram ponunt. Inde si in Elami gravem (sic!) permutaveris MI in FA; deponetur FA majore semitonio in grave: cujus Exachordum in ♮ mi gravem (sic!) acquiret exordium: B♭ c d e♭ f g. Quodsi in C faut gravem FA permutaveris in MI per transitum majoris semitonii in acutum (through a moving-up of the leading tone): Exachordum hujusmodi in A re initium assumit: A B♮ c♯ d e f♯. Quum autem in ♮ mi gravem: permutaveris MI in FA per transitum majoris semitonii in grave (through a moving-down of the half-step) Exachordum ipsum incipies in acquisitam F faut tono sub Γ ut depressam: quare non incongruum est vocum hujusmodi considerationem musicam acquisitam vocari. Per reliquas item introductorii chordas consimilem acquisitorum exachordorum deduces conjunctionem. Qua re et acquisitas consonantiarum species et tonos facile hac ficta musica comperies acquisitos."

FOOTNOTE 16: (Cap. 14): "De falso contrapuncto. Falsum contrapunctum dicimus quum duo invicem cantores procedunt per dissonas conjunctorum sonorum extremitates ut sunt secunda major et minor: quarta item major et minor: atque septima et nona ejusmodi, quae ab omni penitus suavis harmoniae ratione et natura disjunctae sunt. Hoc enim utuntur Ambrosiani nostri in vigiliis solemnibus martirum et in nonnullis missae mortuorum canticis: asserentes a divo Ambrosio institutum: lugubrem quidem cantum: quo ecclesia deploret effusionem sanguinis sanctorum martirum: ac mortuorum suffragia (quod absit)....Quare a nonnullis potius introductum falsum hujusmodi contrapunctum existimari licet quos ignoratae musicae livor oppressit....Solus quidem cantor acutiore voce pronuntiat notulas cantus plani: duo vero aut tres succinunt unico sono notulas ipsas cantus subsequentes in secundam et quartam vicissim certo ordine: quem quoniam ab omni modulationis ratione sejunctus est: me pudet describere. Quandoque incipiunt hujusmodi succentum in unisono cum canto plano procedentes inde per secundas et quartas ad finem usque vel ad certam terminationem in quam unisonantes conveniunt.

Plerumque item in secundam vel in quartam incipiunt, in unisonum vero semper termi-
nantur cujus processus hac notatur descriptione:..."

FOOTNOTE 17: (Gerbert, *Script.* III:6o): "Non tamen cantus Lombardorum, qui
ululant ad modum luporum. Quod manifesti patet; non si unus laicus audiret alium
laicum cantare in prima bassa, bene saliret recta in tertia non autem aliquo modo in
secunda."

FOOTNOTE 18: (Lib. II. cap. 14): "Et cosi per conseguente quelli li quali ancora
poneranno in uso due quinte l'una dopo l'altra, dato che una sia perfetta, et una im-
perfetta, secondo il parer nostro incorrono in errore, perche ne la divisione diatonica non
si patisce tal specie diminuta, benche gli organisti nel suo accordare le voci alquanto del
suo proprio ne togliono, ma più di leggieri essi sono tolerati per la partecipatione del
l'altre consonanze.... Due tre o più consonanze perfette diverse una doppo l'altra insieme
ascendenti, o discendenti possono in contrapunto tener luoco, come la quinta dopo
l'unisono, overo dopo l'ottava et l'ottava dopo la quinta cosi il simile la duodecima dopo
et ialtri medesimi modi, senza altra nota trammezzata."

FOOTNOTE 19: (Cap. 17): "E perche manifestamente tal modo non si osserva dalli
moderni, da noi sara conceduto libero arbitrio potersi fare dopo l'unisono la quinta et
dopo la terza la sesta, overo ottava, et doppo l'ottava la quinta et (come a te piacera)
farei mutatione, perche si vede, che molti più begli, et grati canti in questo modo son
composti, che non si fanno in quello antico ordine, nel quale l'huomo più stretto si
ritruova."

FOOTNOTE 20: (Cap. 17): "Et avertisci a li canti diminuiti, che sempre la prima nota
et ultima in uno discorso diminuito uuole esser concordante et li mezzi diversi alquanto
con dissonanze come il discorso naturale comporta nel quale per la velocita che in se
hanno le voci in tal diminutione, essendo in essa alcune dissonanze, non sono incommodo
allo udito del cantore. Et questo e il modo, et ordine al presente osservato, come essamin-
ando li canti delli moderni potrai facilmente comprendere."

FOOTNOTE 21: (Lib. I. cap. 37): "Che cosa sia sincopa.... Ma quelli che, syncoperanno
la semibreve dopo la pausa di breve, o di luonga et una minima dopo la pausa di breve:
sono ripresi dalla commune oppinione delli musichi per la difficile pronontiatione. Pero
quegli, che syncoperanno la semibreve nanzi la figura breve, o longa osserverano il
precetto regulare, perche cantare, et tacere sono contrarii: dalla quale contrarietà nasce,
che il syncopare che fa la nota oltra la maggiore cantabile: e arbitrario: et il syncopare,
che fa la cantabile figura oltra la pausa maggiore: non e conceduto....Adunque se la
semibreve et altre simili saranno syncopate oltra la cantabile breve, tale processo non
sara incommodo, perche procede con modulatione di harmonico concento."

FOOTNOTE 22: (Lib. II. cap. 16): "La imaginatione di molti compositori fù, che
prima il canto si dovesse fabricare, di poi il tenore, et dopo esso tenore il contrabasso. Et
questo aviene, perche mancorno del lordine, et cognitione di quello che si richiede nel far
del controalto et pero facevano assai inconvenienti nelle loro compositioni, perche bi-
sognava per lo incommodo, che ui ponessino unisoni, pause, salti ascendenti et discendenti
difficili al cantore, ouero pronontiante: in modo che detti canti restauano con poca
soavita, et harmonia, perche facendo prima il canto over soprano, di poi il tenore, quando
e fatto detto tenore, manca alcuna volta il luogo al controbasso, et fatto detto controbasso assai note del controalto non hanno luoco, per la qual cosa considerando solamente
parte per parte cioe quando si fa il tenore, se tu attendi solo ad accordare esso tenore, et
cosi il simile del controbasso, conviene, che ciascuna parte delli luochi concordanti

patisca. Onde li moderni in questo meglio hanno considerato come e manifesto per le compositioni da essi a quatro, a cinque, a sei, et a più voci fatte, delle quali ciascuna tiene luoco commodo, facile, et grato, perche considerano insieme tutti le parti, et non secondo, come di sopra et detto. Et se te piace componere prima il canto, tenore, o contro-basso, tal modo, et regola te resti arbitraria, come da alcuni al presente si osserva, che molte fiate danno principio al controbasso (!) alcuna vuolta al tenore et alcuna uolta al controalto. Ma perche questo a te sarebbe nel principio malagevole et incommodo, a parte per parte cominciarai (!) nondimeno di poi che nella prattica sarai alquanto esercitato, seguirai l'ordine et modo inanzi detto."

FOOTNOTE 24: (Lib. II. cap. 18): "Le quali cadenze secondo la intentione del compositore, si fanno di quantita maggiore, et sempre mai si oppone la settima dis-sonanza nanzi la sesta precedente l'ottava pur che non siano semplicemente composte."

FOOTNOTE 25: (Lib. II. cap. 20): "Delche e necessario segnare sotto a quella syllaba SOL del sopradetto Soprano, la figura diesis, accio che quella decima minore del contro-basso, quale era alquanto dissonante (!) per essere diminuta di uno semituono maggiore, essendo solleuata al luoco suo si senta piu soave. Benche tal segno appresso li dotti et pratichi cantore non e di bisogno, ma sol si pone, perche forse il mal prattico et non intelligente cantore non darebbe pronontia perfetta a tal positione, over syllaba, perche essendo naturalmente dal MI, et SOL un semidittono, senza quel segno esso cantore non cantarebbe altro, che il suo proprio, se gia l'orecchio non gli dessi ajuto, come si vede in alcuni, che questo molto bene fanno."

FOOTNOTE 26: (Lib. II. cap. 21): "Et nota, che sempre tu debbi accommodare le parti senza discorsi incommodi al cantore, et unire le consonanze piu prossime l'una a l'altra che sia possibile, et questo e dato per primo precetto."

FOOTNOTE 27: (Lib. II. cap. 30): "La terzadecima manca de la quinta disotto, come la sesta il simile desidera."

FOOTNOTE 28: (Page 23): "Appendix prima. Si ♭ fa aut ♮ mi ab initio, non in suo, sed alieno quopiam loco signatur, tum neglecta totius systematis regulari positione ex solo utriusvis loco totus omnium aliarum syllabarum ac vocum ordo infra supraque usurpetur."

FOOTNOTE 29: (Dodecachordon, p. 31): "Unde quidem Katholicos canonem prodiderunt. Omnem modum posse in quinta supra finalem clavem, aliam haberi confinalem, quam finalem appellant. Verum illud prorsus in nullo modo verum est, ubique enim diates-saron repugnat (namely the fourth which extends from the fifth above the final to the octave, which indicates in the confinalis another position of the half-tone). Atqui hic erat verus canon ac magis ponendus. In quarta quoque clave per diatessaron cujusvis modi cantum supra finalem finiri posse siquidem FA in b clave fuerit."

FOOTNOTE 30: (Ibid): "Ecclesiastici sane in transponendis cantilenis immodica utuntur licentia, qua utique carere poterant. Quid enim necesse est propter unam alteramve fictam voculam totum transponi cantum? praesertim cum hae consuetudine magis quam ratione introducantur."

FOOTNOTE 31: (Dodecachordon, p. 256): "Hic Modus sane excidit Symphonetis natura id monstrante atque propemodum cogente. Cum enim Dorium per lasciviam variare vellent in diatessaron superiore, imprudentes in Aeolium inciderunt, perinde atque de Lydio diximus quem eadem lascivia in Ionicum postea torserunt verius quam flexerunt."

FOOTNOTE 32: (*Dodecachordon*, p. 115): "Alii enim notulas quae c parvum (=c′) in his attingunt, in b torquent...est autem ubi non liceat, nempe ubi cantus ad e parvum (=e′) conscendit et in b uno relabitur saltu, obstat enim tritonus. Caeterum in ea sum opinione, conspirasse quosdam, ut ex omnibus Lydiis Hypolydiisque facerent Ionicos Hypoionicosque, at id parum feliciter processisse. Ideoque nunc tam tortos (!) esse cantus, praecipue in gradualibus."

FOOTNOTE 33: (*Dodecachordon*, p. 115): "Alter tertiae Diapason Modus Ionicus dicitur, divisus harmonicos, ideoque in hac classe princeps, omnium Modorum usitatissimus. Sed nostra aetate sede propria exulans per diatessaron in Lydii finali clavi hoc est F, non tamen absque FA in b clavi cantus finit....Porro hic Modus saltationibus aptissimus est, quem pleraeque Europae regiones, quas nos vidimus, adhuc in frequenti habent usu. Apud veteres Ecclesiasticos per raro ad hunc Modum cantilenam reperias. At a proximis quadringentis ut opinor annis, etiam apud Ecclesiae cantores ita adamatus, ut multos Lydii modi cantilenas...in hunc mutarint, suavitate ipsius ac lenocinio illecti."

FOOTNOTE 34: (*Dodecachordon*, p. 26): "Loquimur autem de intervallis quae intra disdiapason limites continentur. Namque quae ultra eveniunt intercapedines veram phthongorum crasin ac commixtionem non habent, etiamsi aliquae consonant ut decimaseptima, decimanona ac vicesima, quarum trium mediam inter perfectas numerant consonantias, extremas inter imperfectas: Et decimamseptimam nostra aetate doctissimi Symphonetae saepius usurpant (!), rarius autem decimamnonam ac vicesimam, immo quantum ego judico, magis hac de causa aliquando adsciscunt ut in sublimi celsissimae velut colludant voces, quam ut constet concentus ratio, atque vocum vera commixtio."

FOOTNOTE 35: (*Dodecachordon*, p. 25): "Nostra vero aetate, quem veterum quidam posuerunt, tonus, ex consonantiarum numero excidit, nec admittitur, nisi in Syncopis, ut vocant (nam id novae rei novum est nomen) ubi tamen non auditur, ut in hoc concentu Contratenoris antepenultimae notulae dimidium cum penultima tenoris consistit: (notated example). Diatessaron etiam rejicitur nisi subtentam habeat vel diapente vel ditonum semiditonumve."

FOOTNOTE 36: (*Dodecachordon*, p. 20): "Tonus cum diapente..., sexta perfecta...uno saltu vix admittitur, est enim oppido quam dura (the following addition is rather naïve: hac 'inductiones' suas Guido constituit!)....Semitonium cum diapente, sexta imperfecta ...Phrygio modo perquam familiaris, miram habet gratiam, si suo adhibeatur loco."

FOOTNOTE 40: "Eh acciò che il compositore possi usare assai varietà di cibo per gl'orecchi, si ha ritrovato un modo da comporre le dissonanze fra le consonanze et dette dissonanze si fanno passar con il mezzo, et il favore della sincopa laquale sara questa: che ogni volta che una nota pigliera et legara la metà di due note allhora la prima metà sara della seconda metà della prima nota, et l'altra metà sara la prima metà della seconda nota, et fra i compositori si usa legare la sincopa in tre modi. Il primo modo domando maggiore, quando la breve piglia di due brevi la metà per una...il secondo modo nomino sincopa minore...quando una semibreve piglierà die due metà di semibrevi, et che la semibreve sia cantata nel levare della batuttà (et cosi sara la breve). Il terzo modo sara quando la minima piglierà la metà di due minime, con l'ordine sopradetto et questa sincopa la dirò minima....Hora la dissonanza che si domanda seconda sara sempre posta nella seconda metà della nota sincopata et sempre deve essere discendente alla consonanza della terza maggiore o minore per grado. Et quando detta sincopa finisce deve sempre finire, con una figura de una nota che vagli la metà manco della nota sincopata, in essempio se la sincopa sara di una breve quella deve finire con una semibreve all'ingiù per grado."

FOOTNOTE 41: (Fol. 32ᵛ): "Lettore sappi che nella musica si fa qualche acquisto di tempo in tempo et si vede che nelle compositioni che non sono moderne; i compositori hanno composte le dissonanze sciolte di semibreve in una longa et hanno fatto la prima buona nella battuta: et la seconda cattiva nel levare; et di poi per un tempo i posteri hanno sentito, ch'era troppo longa quella durezza, tal modo fu abandonato e per manco discordo a gl'orecchi usorno le minime; la prima buona nel battere; et la seconda cattiva nel levare: et questo ordine ha durato un tempo. Hora in questi nostri tempi habbiamo lasciato l'ordine di comporre le minime, una buona et l'altra cattiva; et si ha considerato che la minima è parte che á questi nostri tempi si sente troppo, et non solamente quella ma anchora la semiminima s'ode quando non è ben posta; si che usiamo nelle compositioni far solamente le semiminime et crome cattive (facendo però) la 1. buona e la 2. cattiva et la 3. buona e la 4. cattiva, battendo a ragione di quattro semiminime per battuta che le buone saranno nel battere et nel levare, seguendo quattro semiminime, l'una doppo l'altra. Et quando sono due, appresso una semibreve sincopata overo una minima et che discendino: la seconda deve esser buona et non la prima; et per il contrario quando saranno ascendenti la prima sara buona et la seconda cattiva."

FOOTNOTE 42: "Il musico prattico non concede che in compositione l'orecchio esercitato patisca alcuna dissonanza ne ancora due consonanze perfette, ascendenti ne discendenti; come sono due et più quinte: et cosi dell'ottava, et perche in ogni cosa ci sonno qualche rimedio. Il compositore avertira ch'ogni volta ch'egli verra commodo, di porre una settima in modo che la compositione dimostrera, che quella settima fara effetto di due ottava et non saranno; questo modo s'usera a più de cinque voci perche a poche voci troppo si sentira tal settima. Et il medesimo sara dell'unisono o che parerano, due unisono et non saranno; et quando saranno con il semitono, offenderanno manco il senso che con il tono."

FOOTNOTE 43: (Fol. 33ᵛ): "S'avertira che nel procedere di più d'una o due note insieme sincopando non si facci con tutte le parti; perche non parera Sincopa imperò che la Sincopa si può discernere almeno per cagione d'una parte che canti nella battuta et l'altre parti cantino nel levare, accio si possi cognòscere le differenze del moto."

FOOTNOTE 44: (Fol. 53ᵛ): "Si da regola alle cadentie, che tutte quelle che hanno da essere sustentate, (N.B. still the same expression!) si debbono signare con i loro segni de Diesis cromatici o di b molli o di ♮ incitati per schiffare molti errori fatti dalli Cantanti, che possono occorrere nelle compositioni si per rompere di disegno del Compositore che in tal nota di cadentia volesse dimostrare una durezza (!) et ch'il Cantante la sustentassi et far la Musica dolce: et nelle cadentie dubbiose, sarebbe maggior errore sustentare una sesta maggiore, che diventarebbe settima minore (!) et farebbe gran discordo. Il rimedio di salvare le cadentie dubbiose, sara questo, che la diminutione le salucra, o se si vorrano far intiere, si fara che salteranno all' in sù o all' in giù."

FOOTNOTE 45: (Fol. 84ᵛ): "Gran differenza si fara a comporre una compositione da cantare in Chiesa, a quella che si ha da cantare in camera, et il Compositore dè havere il suo giuditio limato, et comporre le sue compositioni secondo il suggetto et il preposito, della parole...(here a comment follows to the effect that it is up to the judgment of the composer, if he will begin a four-part composition and let the others enter gradually, or if he will let them come in in imitation) et l'ordine di comporre le compositioni volgari, dè essere piacevole, et intese, senza canoni e senza troppo sottilità di proportioni, perche tali parole, come sono Madrigali, non ricerano si non imitare la natura di consonanze, et de gradi applicati a quelle, et quando si comporra una compositione a voce mutata, cioè senza soprano; s'avertira che gli estremi non passino quindeci voci et al più in sedeci con il semitono."

FOOTNOTE 46: (Fol. 88ᵛ): "Volendo far principiar la fuga, eleggero un passagio che l'altre parti possino dire il medesimo, et la parte ch'entrera con un sospiro doppo, o con una pausa, o due, o tre, o quattro (e non s'aspettera più di quattro pause et quasi che saranno troppo)...anchora sara buon sentire, quando le parti con la fuga entreranno tutte con una misura medesima una doppo l'altra come sarebbe che con una pausa o con due o con tre o con quattro una parte entrasse et che tante pause facesse una parte come l'altra...e qualche volta per ingannare l'oditore parera a buono fare ch'una parte entri con la fuga nel battere della misura et l'altra nel levare et la terza nel battere et la quarta nel levare. Et le fughe che si potranno fare in varii modi saranno buone ma non per unisono ne per ottava perche non daranno troppo varieta...et quando il Basso a quattro voci fara fuga col Tenore per quarta, il Contralto et il Soprano verra per quinta: et per l'opposito quando il Basso et il Tenore fugara per quinta, il Contralto et il Soprano fugaranno per quarta. Poi quando si vorra principiare una fuga et se la parte che havra da seguir la fuga non potesse seguirla a longo il Compositore l'accommodera con un contrapunto sopra et non importera molto, mentre ch'il principio habbi incominciato in fuga per che s'habbi fatto la fuga di quattro o di cinque note...et se si vorra fare delle fughe per ottava contraria, cioè ch'il principio d'una parte saltasse per quinta in più a questo modo sara mal procedere (namely that the other voice skipped a fifth upwards), perche parera che facci uscire fuore di tono la compositione, et quando una parte saltera all' in giù per quinta l'altra dè saltare all' in sù per quarta et quando uno saltera all' in giù per quarta, l'altra dè saltare all' in sù per quinta, accio che la formatione dell'ottava venghi giusta."

FOOTNOTE 47: (Fol. 90ᵛ): "Molti contrapunti dopii a molti modi si potranno fare...si potra far cantar all' ottava, alla duodecima et ad altri modi: a me basta dimostrare un poco di lume al discepolo ingenioso, che da se ritrovera molte cose, con la fatica, et con l'esperienza: et quello avvertira che quando comporra una compositione disotto per duodecima, non de fare due terze ne due seste."

CHAPTER XIII

# *Musica Ficta in the Notation of the 14th-16th Centuries*

TODAY one of the major problems encountered in the field of musicology is the contradiction between notation and musical practice with reference to the introduction of accidentals which gradually assumed more importance as the solmization system developed further.*1 The attempt to avoid the use of sharps, flats, and naturals in composition led to many rules which tried to base theory upon practice and which finally assumed such proportions that insurmountable difficulties were encountered when new editions were planned in our time—difficulties which the editors did not know how to solve. Many sharps, flats, and naturals in such new editions, therefore, appeared with a question mark above them, leaving decisions regarding chromatic changes up to the reader, decisions the editors did not dare to make. This irresponsibility is naturally to be condemned. Those who try to remove the ancient robing from compositions which belonged to epochs of former centuries must not be satisfied with using today's round notes instead of the former square ones, with scoring the single voices above one another, and with inserting measure bars (although even this demands much more knowledge than the layman ever dreams of); for the entire period of complicated mensural music of the 12th–16th centuries, a period extremely rich in works of art of highest beauty, the correct interpretation of rhythmic values, without a knowledge of which its transcription is impossible, requires the utmost familiarity with a highly complicated set of rules. Even correct transcription achieved with full technical command of the material still presents a strange-looking picture if the new editor does not keep in mind that the history of notation several times (around 1300 and 1600) makes sporadic transitions to the use of shorter note values, that the beat values during the 12th–13th centuries were breves ($\sqsubseteq$), from the 14th–16th centuries, however, minimas ($\circ$), and since the 17th century half-notes ($\downarrow$), quarters ($\downarrow$), and even eighth-notes ($\downarrow$). Therefore in order to see at once the correct note values for a given composition, it is necessary to shorten the notes to one-half, one-fourth, and even one-eighth of their value. In addition we have the not less important

329

(in fact, the probably more important) corrections of musical utterances by the introduction of chromatic alterations of tones, obvious to the practice of a period, according to the stipulations of its theorists. Even those who are complete masters of mensural theory are not capable of editing older works as long as they are not thoroughly familiar with *musica ficta* and able to round out their notation on the basis of general rules. It is the fault of the editors that, by neglecting to make these additions, a poor opinion of the harmonic value of 14th–16th-century settings came about, as though those settings were absolutely unbearable to listen to from the standpoint of our present-day feeling for tonality. The *chansons* of the Dufay epoch are hardest hit by these incorrect judgments; only when the missing chromatic changes are added to them is their grace and lightness of movement apparent. At this point it will be helpful to discuss briefly the various solmization rules as they developed in the practice of several centuries.

### 1. *MI Contra FA*

The oldest unwritten but nevertheless self-evident accidental is the MI *contra* FA, necessary for the correction of the *tritonus*. As is known, the scale basis of the solmization system consists only of six steps: UT RE MI FA SOL LA. The seventh step leading to the octave of the first step is without a name and can only be reached by transposing the entire system up a fourth or up a fifth. A fourth up from F leads to b♭, a fourth down from b♮ leads to f♯. The *tritonus* f–b or b–f is forbidden (MI *contra* FA, *diabolus in musica*). Whenever an augmented fourth or diminished fifth appears it must be corrected by the flat before b or the sharp before f. It is incorrect, however, to extend the strict injunction against MI *contra* FA also to the two tones sounding in accord. It can be proved that, at least during the time around the end of the 15th century (Adam von Fulda), the augmented fourth or diminished fourth in a chord was much appreciated when appearing directly before closes (cf. *Handbuch der Musikgeschichte* II. 1, p. 36). Intervals like the diminished fourth undoubtedly belong to those included by the injunction against MI *contra* FA; however, even they are accepted during the 15th century (*Handbuch der Musikgeschichte* II. 1, pp. 38–39). The editors are overanxious when, in not believing the evidence of the manuscripts, they have corrected instances as the ♯c–♮f (*DTÖ*, in Dufay's *Puisque celle*) and therefore destoyed its daring beauty.*[2]

### 2. *Una voce super LA semper canendum FA*

Also going back to the time when solmization first appeared, is the rule that the movement from the sixth step of the Guidonian hexachord to the seventh, with instantaneous return, must use the half-step above LA (b-*molle*) and not the whole-tone (♮ *durum*). This rule also remains valid up to the time of Willaert (16th century), who concluded the chapter of *musica ficta* with his liberal usage concerning modulating chromatic changes (cf. *Handbuch der Musikgeschichte* II. 1, p. 379, his two-voiced *Quidnam ebrietatis*).

### 3. *The Cadence-Forms of the Ecclesiastical Modes*

The difficulties which arise in connection with clarification of the nature of the ecclesiastical modes stem mainly from the fact that harmony, as long as it does not deviate from chordal formations true to the modal scale (the arrangement which is given by the individual tones on the hand), will not provide us with the strict cadences demanded by our present feeling for tonality.*[3] Harmony true to the Dorian scale lacks the subdominant, while it gives the position of a subdominant to the closing main chord of D minor:

$$d\text{–}f\text{–}a\text{–}c\text{–}e\text{–}g\text{–}b$$
tonic?

In the Phrygian mode, however, the subdominant is missing and the main chord of E minor itself appears as the minor dominant:

$$d\text{–}f\text{–}a\text{–}c\text{–}e\text{–}g\text{–}b$$
tonic?

In the Lydian mode the closing chord (F major) takes the position of a subdominant:

$$f\text{–}a\text{–}c\text{–}e\text{–}g\text{–}b\text{–}d$$
tonic?

In the Mixolydian mode (G major), however, it takes that of a dominant:

$$f\text{–}a\text{–}c\text{–}e\text{–}g\text{–}b\text{–}d$$
tonic?

This is the reason why a strict adherence of the harmony to the ecclesiastical modes has at no time been practiced. Instead, and in order to make satisfying closes possible, not only toward the end of compositions but also toward the end of all sections certain licenses were taken by theory ever since the appearance of polyphony. These gave the triad on the *finalis* a central position:

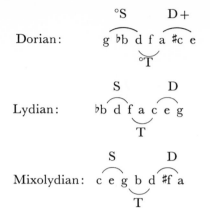

Only for the Phrygian mode was this kind of substitution not possible. Since the small step of a second f–e from the second scale degree to the first has an unfortunate closing effect, the introduction of a major dominant (b, d♯, f♯) was out of the question and the dominant quality [of the main chord] had to remain. However, it was the practice very early to build a major chord upon the *finalis* instead of a minor one:

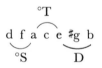

With this, however, the so-called Phrygian cadence became the actual half-cadence to which we are accustomed. The explanation given here for deviating from true scale harmony was obviously impossible in a period which did not yet know the concept of tonic, dominant, and subdominant. This could only have evolved later after the intuitive but instructive use of licenses to achieve more satisfactory cadential structures. The strange, colorful character of the harmony of those times with its cultivated manipulation of liberties at the cadences is based upon the fact that passages of strictly scale-wise harmony again and again led to cadences which altered the ecclesiastical mode to conform to our modern minor or major scale. These cadences, however, are not restricted only to the two places and forms in which they first appear as *clausum* and *apertum* (French *clos* and *overt*)—in Johannes de Garlandia (approx. 1150), and *clausum lay* in Aegidius de Murino (14th century) clearly in the sense of the complete cadence (*clausum*) and half-cadence (*apertum*) for the reprises (I[ma] and II[da]) of both parts of the *ballada duplex* (virelai, rondeau) (cf. *Handbuch der Musikgeschichte* II. 1, p. 208). Aegidius rules that in minor settings (*quando finitur in LA*) the half-cadence should occur on the fifth, in major settings (*quando finitur in UT*), however, on the tenth (!), and in this way explains those half-cadences (Phrygian cadences) at the end of many *chansons* which seem so strange to us. The half-cadence is in order in those cases, since after the second part the first one is again repeated for a final time. Besides these two main cadences, the questioning half-cadence in the middle, and the complete cadences at the end (both often marked with a ⌒), the compositions contain still other secondary cadences in other sections of the text similar to the *distinctiones* of Gregorian chant. In these secondary passages, any one of the steps of the hexachord temporarily achieves the significance of the *finalis*; only the seventh step is excluded, the one above LA, which during the solmization epoch was not named. For instance, a piece in the Dorian mode may cadence (except on RE—complete cadence; and LA—half-cadence) on UT, MI, FA, and SOL. For example, in the original (not transposed) position on a D minor chord (complete cadence on RE), A major (half-cadence on LA), A minor (complete cadence on LA), C major (complete cadence on UT), E major (Phrygian half-cadence on MI), F major (complete cadence on FA), G minor (complete cadence on SOL) may appear. In all these cadences accidentals are obviously required, especially the minor second below the fundamental tone of the simple chord (except in the half-cadence on MI). With this, then, the leading tones c♯ (before d) and g♯ (before A and as a third in the Phrygian cadence) appear in a D minor composition. The flat before b is naturally used in a half-cadence on LA.

The notation d c b ⓐ before the half-cadence on LA is meant as d c b♭ a, if a ♯ before the g in the upper voice does not make the ♭ impossible.

### 4. *Transposition of the Ecclesiastical Modes*

The Guidonian hand yields two transposed positions for each ecclesiastical mode, not including the original position, according to whether UT is c or f or g. In the *cantus mollis* (f = UT), not d but g is the *finalis* (RE) of Protus and of its plagal. With this the possible formations of secondary cadences are also. rearranged. For the Dorian on g ( = RE) the possible secondary cadences are rearranged as follows:*[4]

| UT | RE | MI | FA | SOL | LA | |
|----|----|----|----|-----|----|----|
| f+ | °d | a+ | b+ | °g | d+ | (°a) |
|    | =  |    |    |     |    |    |

that is, the two (Phrygian) half-cadences move to A major (MI) and D major (LA), and the cadence on SOL means C minor. The missing seventh step which has no cadence becomes the e-degree, namely, that which demands as highest note, without mutation, the *super* LA with a ♮ before c. The Dorian on a = RE would have the following harmonies:

| UT | RE | MI | FA | SOL | LA |  |
|----|----|----|----|-----|----|----|
| (g | a | b | c | d | e) |  |
| g+ | °e̲ | b+ | °g | °a | e+ | (°b) |

Here we even find a B major chord for the cadence on MI. Toward the end of the 15th century, however (John Hothby's *Calliopea legale*), the transposition of the ecclesiastical modes had already developed so far that even f♯ and d♭ take the place of UT, and therefore a Phrygian cadence on MI implies an a♯ major chord (for the Dorian, on g♯), and the cadence on FA the g♭ major chord (for the Lydian on d♭). Admittedly, the theorist must have been in advance of practice in this case. In the beginning of the 14th century, however, the Parisian Johannes de Muris teaches that sometimes in the *chansons* d or b♭ must be used in place of UT. Our exact manner of transposition by using accidentals in a key signature is still foreign to this time. We find only a ♮ and this often in one voice only, seldom two ♮'s (for b and e), this appearing also in one voice only. It would hardly be possible to find one's way through the maze of "foregone conclusions" if Adam von Fulda (1491) and Glarean (1547) had not given us a key in the simple explanation that there are only three characteristically different bases for melodic progressions, namely, major, minor, and Phrygian. Adam von Fulda formulates it by saying (Gerbert, *Script*. III: 343) that in any case one would have a *cantus* ♭ *mollaris* UT–FA or a *cantus naturalis* RE–SOL or a ♮ *duralis* MI–LA; Glarean even says it in a shorter and more precise way (*Dodecachordon*, p. 31): "Omnis cantus desinit aut in RE aut in MI aut in UT (Every *cantus* must end either in RE or in MI or in UT)," and explains the closing on UT, which apparently goes contrary to the ecclesiastical modes, by the addition: "Et quidem in UT vel connexo vel disjuncto (And, to be sure, in UT, either connected or disconnected)." That is to say, he identifies the *tritus* (Lydian) and *tetrardus* (Mixolydian) with the new Ionian mode which he himself introduced (major scale). Both authors agree in that they both insist on ascertaining in each concrete case whether the close of the entire composition is in major (on UT), in minor (on RE), or Phrygian (on MI). UT *connexum* or *conjunctum* is F (with a ♮ before the b; the old *trite synemmenon*), UT *disjunctum* is G (with ♮, the old *paramese—diazeuxis* above the *mese*). For a better understanding of Adam von Fulda's explanation, I should like to point out that among theorists there evolved gradually a characterization of the six *voces musicales* which classified these according to pairs, namely, UT and FA as ♭ *mollares*, i.e., those with the characteristics of the ♭; MI and LA as ♮ *durales*, that is, those with the characteristics of the ♯; and RE and SOL as *naturales*, which is to be interpreted that above LA as well as above MI the semitone is naturally to be used in order to avoid the *tritonus*. The half-step is necessary below UT as well as below FA for the same reason:

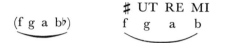

$$\text{(f g a b♭)} \qquad \begin{array}{c} \sharp \text{ UT RE MI} \\ \text{f } \quad \text{g } \quad \text{a } \quad \text{b} \end{array}$$

Next to the rule *una voce super LA semper canendum FA* a corresponding one could have been established to read *una voce sub UT semper canendum MI* to substantiate the *subsemitonium* in *tetrardus* (g–f♯–g) and naturally in all of its transposed positions. The same view is found around 1700 in Gottfried Keller's *Rules for Playing a Thorough-bass*, where b♮, e, and a are defined as "naturally sharp notes" and c, f, a as "naturally flat notes."

The stereotyped form of the discant cadence of the 14th–15th centuries,

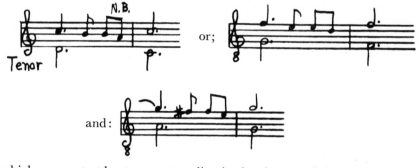

which we meet at least once every line in the *chansons* of the Dufay epoch, uses in all minor cadences not only the *subsemitonium* but also the raised sixth degree of the minor scale:

Both raised tones are, naturally, not indicated in the manuscripts, but are self-evident. Many cases occur where one must ask whether we have an *apertum* instead of a *clausum* or, instead of a complete cadence, a half-cadence where the tenor descends from the final to the fourth below (d c b♭ a). In such a case, the two raised degrees are superfluous for the discant

cadence and it becomes necessary to add a ♮ to the penultimate note
(which generally is not indicated):

Therefore it is not always clear, in spite of Adam's and Glarean's instructions, whether a piece ends on UT, RE, or MI.

The Parisian Johannes de Muris (*ca.* 1325) points out that wherever
the Guidonian hand is not sufficient, that is, where one meets with tones
which are not contained in the three positions of the hexachord (on c, f,
and g = UT), a transposition of the hand is in evidence. This, he says, is
what *musica ficta* is. The failure of the hand is to be understood in this
sense: if, for instance, a ♯ occurs before the note f or c, it is usually employed for the *subsemitonium* of a cadence ending on g or d, and the piece
closes with a complete cadence on d, excluding the possibility of the
mode being in Dorian. Rather, a ♯ (not in the signature), whether it
occurs in the beginning or later during the course of the composition,
indicates sufficiently that the mode throughout the entire piece must be
understood to be a Lydian on d, with d as UT. In the same way, a piece
with a cadence on f, in which a ♮ occurs before e or a and is not intended
as super LA, is not Lydian on f, but Dorian on f; i.e., f is not UT but RE,
the entire piece being not in F major but in F minor. Those *chansons*
transcribed in the *DTÖ*, which are taken from the Trent codices and
which belong to the epoch of Dufay, can be seriously questioned when
one approaches them with the apparatus of rules which are briefly
summarized here. Cf. my study "Verlorengegangene Selbstverständ-
lichkeiten in der Musik des 14.–16. Jahrhunderts" (instead of 15.–16.
Jahrhunderts), in *Musikalisches Magazin*, Heft 17 (Langensalza, 1907,
Beyer u. Söhne).

5. *Decline of* Musica Ficta *and Disintegration of the Mutation Theory*
*Caused by the More Frequent Appearance of Transposition Signs in Notation*
*(School of Willaert)*

Adrian Willaert (1527–1562), conductor of St. Mark's Cathedral (of
Venice) and his pupils (de Rore, Vicentino) were the first to free music
from the fetters of stereotyped cadences on the six steps of the hexachord
by unequivocably requiring a freer modulatory manner through the
more frequent use of accidentals. With this the earlier significance of
single sharps or flats during the course of the composition disappears,
namely, the indication of a transposition of the hand for entire settings.

Its place is taken by actual modulation during the course of the composition. For transposing the positions of the ecclesiastical modes in complete
compositions, the *chiavette* is employed with key signatures using one flat
(UT = F) or two flats (UT = E♭).*[5] This brings about the movement of

the four usual clefs  a third higher (low *chiavette*)

or a third lower (high *chiavette*)

The intention was that the pieces were to be sung in that position which
was indicated by the usual clefs, but with a rearrangement of the semitones indicated by the clefs. For example, in low *chiavette* the following

discant: would not begin with c', but with e♭'

or e', as if the discant had the c-clef on the first line, but with three flats
or four sharps.

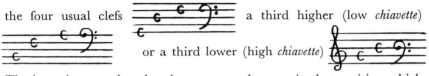

or

Therefore, in high *chiavette* the position is lower

by a (major or minor) third than it would be if the c-clef were on the first
line (with four flats or three sharps) as in A♭ major or A major. Since the
two kinds of *chiavette* also appear with one or two flats in the key signatures, six further transpositions of the ecclesiastical modes are available,
namely, to the fourth alone (with one flat) and a major second below
(with two flats) for each of the three notated types; in normal closes:
UT = c, with one flat; UT = f, with two flats: UT = b♭; in lower *chiavette*
without the flat: UT = e♭ or e, with one flat: UT = a♭ or a, with two
flats: UT = d♭ or d; in higher *chiavette* without the flat: UT = a♭ or a,
with one flat: UT = d♭ or d, with two flats: UT = g♭ or g.

# COMMENTARY

## CHAPTER I

# *Commentary*

*1. See Chapter I, Note *7, concerning this problem.

*2. The consonance of the fourth occupies a place of major structural importance in the formation of the Greater Perfect System. It is the smallest of the consonances, having the ratio of $4/3$ in the Pythagorean system of defining interval relationships, and is consonant, because consonance in that system is determined by the excellence of the relationship existing between superparticular combinations of the numbers 1 to 4 ($2/1 =$ octave; $3/2 =$ fifth; $4/3 =$ fourth). The third, having the ratio of $81/64$, is therefore representative of a dissonance. Cleonides writes in his *Harmonic Introduction*:

> The symphonic [consonant] intervals are the diatessaron, diapente, diapason, and the like. The diaphonic [dissonant] intervals are all those smaller than the diatessaron and all those lying between the symphonic intervals. The intervals smaller than the diatessaron are the dieses [a quarter-tone which is not necessarily an exact division of the half-tone; see Apel, Willi, *HD*, p. 211], semitone, tone, trihemitone [minor third], and ditone [major third]; those lying between the symphonic intervals are the tritone, the tetratone, the pentatone, and the like (Oliver Strunk, *Source Readings in Music History*, p. 38).

In the Greater Perfect System the two outer notes of the tetrachord ($=$ four strings) were fixed, and the two inner notes were capable of being varied to produce the three genera: diatonic, chromatic, and enharmonic. The diatonic genera consisted of a stepwise filling-out of the fourth (a G F E); the chromatic genera a sesquitone (minor third) plus two semitones (a F♯ F♮ E); the enharmonic genera a ditone (major third) plus two dieses (quarter tones) giving an F♮ F↓ E. For a comprehensive study of the three terms from a terminological as well as a historical standpoint, see the article "Diatonik-Chromatik-Enharmonik" in *MGG* III:403–426. Columns 409–415 deal specifically with material related to this study, i.e., the three genera and their influence on music theory throughout the Medieval and Renaissance periods.

*3. The hexachord also contains the two species of fifth free of the tritone (C̄ D E F Ḡ a) and may be seen as the TST tetrachord of the *Musica enchiriadis* with a whole-tone added above and below. Hypotheses such as these, however, as well as others concerned with origins, are not confirmed in any known sources. Concerning the history of solmization and hypotheses on origins of the hexachord system, see Lange's detailed study "Zur Geschichte der Solmisation," *SIMG* I:535–622. See also the article "Hexachord" in *MGG* VI:349–358, and Hans Oesch, *Guido von Arezzo*, pp. 63–70, where the solmization hymn *Ut queant laxis* is also discussed. A detailed discussion of the hexachord and solmization is found in J. Smits van Waesberghe, *De musico-paedagogico et theoretico Guidone Aretino*, pp. 86–113. A copy of the *Epistola de ignoto cantu*, in which Guido gives the first known description of the hexachord system of solmization, is translated into English in Strunk, *op. cit.*, pp. 121–125. Further, see Gustave Reese, *Music in the Middle Ages*, pp. 149–151.

Jacob of Liège in his *Speculum musicae*, lib. VI, cap. 62; Zarlino in his *Istituzioni harmoniche* II, cap. 30, p. 127; Kepler in his *Harmonices libri quinque* III, cap. X; and Calvisius in his *Excirtationes musicae duae* II shared the opinion that the hexachord was more perfect than the tetrachord because it contained all three species of fourth (Lange, *op. cit.*, p. 548). This relationship, also observed by Riemann (p. 3) is not in complete accord with medieval theoretical procedure, since the first species of fourth begins on the note A (or the note D) and the first species of fifth on the note D, whereas the hexachords (*naturale*, *molle*, and *durum*) begin on the notes C, F (with b♭), and G. Regarding the three hexachords as a practical means of obtaining scalar sequences into which most melodies would fit, the notes C, F, and G provided the beginning notes for similar patterns (TTSTT) which could be achieved in no other way. The hexachord pattern had the additional virtue of being free from a tritone relationship. The species of fourths and fifths in medieval theory had modal significance (see Reese, *op. cit.*, pp. 155–157), whereas there is no evidence of any such significance attached to the hexachord.

Riemann does not include any detailed discussion of this aspect of the hexachord-solmization system; therefore these references are given, out of chronological sequence, at this place.

*4. Riemann's exposition of the Greater Perfect System is here an admittedly sketchy one; it also fails to mention chronological development of this system as well as the relative importance of some of its concepts. The octave species as shown in the example on page 4 $\left(\text{projected on a diatonic system from A to } \frac{a}{a}\right)$ are a relatively late development. The original compass of the entire system was only one octave—the so-called Dorian octave e′–e. Gombosi, in his article "Key, Mode, Species" (*JAMS* IV:23), emphasizes that the compass e′–e was also the original location of the octave species. The octave species consisted of the various arrangements of tones which were placed within that octave by the *tonoi* or tunings (identified as transposition scales by Riemann on pages 5 and 6 and also referred to as keys). The tunings would not only change the functions of the notes within the octave (b which was *paramese* in the Dorian system would become *mese* in the Phrygian *tonos*), but would also transpose the entire Dorian system to a different location. The octave e′–e in the Phrygian tuning would not achieve a new modal significance. The removal of these octave species from the e′–e octave to any other portion of the system is, as was stated, a later development and opposed to the principle of tetrachord construction in which the tetrachord with the STT pattern is the only one employed. In other words, the double-octave A–$\frac{a}{a}$ containing a projection of the octave species could not be divided into tetrachords; Greek writers never speak, for example, of a Phrygian or Mixolydian tetrachord.

That the octave species may have been thought of as modes by the Greeks is strongly opposed by Gombosi (*op. cit.*, p. 21). The whole question of mode in Greek theory is discussed with great clarity in R. P. Winnington-Ingram, *Mode in Ancient Greek Music*. He concludes that it may have been possible that a kind of modal thinking might have existed in Greek theory and practice, but that no definite conclusions can be based on the extant evidence either in the theoretical writings or in the musical fragments. If mode is thought of as "a melodic pattern," which Gombosi suggests for want of a better term (see *JAMS* IV:280), then it might be said that the Greeks knew one mode (the Dorian) which they realized (at one point in the development of the system) in fifteen different keys (*tonoi*= tunings).

*5. Modulation, as it was supposedly understood by the Greeks, is explained by Cleonides in his *Harmonic Introduction* (Strunk, *op. cit.*, p. 45), where he says that modulation has four meanings:

> Modulation in genus takes place whenever there is a modulation from the diatonic genus to the chromatic or enharmonic, or from the chromatic or enharmonic to some one of the others. Modulation in system takes place whenever there is a modulation from the conjunct system to the disjunct, or vice versa. Modulation in tone takes place whenever there is a modulation from the Dorian tone to the Phrygian...or in general from any one of the thirteen tones to any other....Modulation in melodic composition takes place whenever there is a modulation in ethos from the diastaltic to the systaltic or hesychastic, or from the hesychastic to some one of the others....

Riemann, in speaking of a modulation to the "subdominant," refers to the fact, first recognized by Ptolemy (Reese, *op. cit.*, p. 41), that in modulating from the Greater Perfect System to the Lesser Perfect System (by the use of the tetrachord synemmenon) a modulation is effected to the key a fourth higher.

Dorian (with synemmenon) becomes Mixolydian *tonos*.

Lydian (with synemmenon) becomes Hypophrygian *tonos* (in a seven-*tonoi* system).

See also the article on "Ancient Greek Music" by Isobel Henderson in *NOHM*

I:354–357, for the Ptolemaic concept of modulation. A comprehensive study of modulation (= transposition) from the period of antiquity to Glarean is Frances B. Turell, *Modulation: An Outline of its Prehistory from Aristoxenus to Henry Glarean* (unpublished doctoral dissertation, University of Southern California, 1956).

*6. Aristides Quintilianus (2d or 3d century A.D.) attributed thirteen *tonoi* (keys, or transposition scales) to Aristoxenus (see *MGG* I:648), as did Cleonides (1st or 2d century; see Strunk, *op. cit.*, p. 44), apparently on the basis of Aristoxenian sources not known to us. The possible development of this system of keys, together with its subsequent history, is discussed in detail in Reese, *op. cit.*, pp. 28–44. The thirteen *tonoi* system is enlarged by Aristides and Alypios (4th century A.D.; see *MGG* I:399–401) to fifteen, having keys requiring up to five sharps and six flats. Gombosi (in his *Tonarten und Stimmungen in der Antiken Musik*, Copenhagen, 1939) and Reese (*op. cit.*, pp. 24–38) relate the development of the system of *tonoi* or keys to the demands of instrumental performance. This view is opposed by Isobel Henderson in *NOHM* I:340–363; she feels that the *tonoi* developed within the framework of Greek harmonic science after Aristoxenus and had no relationship to musical practice.

*7. Boethius gives the seven *tonoi* system of Ptolemy, but adds the Hypermixolydian, the so-called "eighth mode" of Ptolemy. Ptolemy does mention the possibility of an eighth *tonos* but denies it as a repetition of the first (see Reese, *op. cit.*, p. 38, and Gombosi, "Studien zur Tonartenlehre des frühen Mittelalters," *AM* X:156).

*8. Handschin in his *Musikgeschichte im Überblick*, p. 67, gives the following explanation which can be used as a basis for a discussion of the possible relationships existing between the antique and medieval tone systems:

> The medieval period, since it labelled the ecclesiastical mode on e as Phrygian, the mode on d as Dorian, and the mode on f as Lydian [c appears in the text instead of f] did not follow the sequence of the antique octave species, but took the transpositions as a point of departure, since in the same system the octave species, standing side-by-side, would be taken from bottom to top as Lydian, Phrygian, and Dorian. That the medieval period placed the Dorian, not on a, but on d, and the Phrygian not on b but on e appears to be the result of a particular circumstance: that in Boethius, who conveyed antique theory to the medieval period, a displacement of a fourth occurred, which as a result caused the series of *proslambanomenoi* to appear from A to g, rather than E to d (or at least one can understand Boethius to mean this).

Proslambanomenoi:                              become:

Otto Ursprung in his article "Die antiken Transpositionsskalen und die Kirchentöne," *AfMF* III:129–152, proceeds from a similar assumption. Ursprung believes that the naming of the ecclesiastical modes with the names of the antique *tonoi* occurred somewhere between Aurelian (9th century) and the *Alia musica* (10th century). Aurelian gives the characteristics of the tonal system based on Cassiodorus, and seems to take the names of the *tonoi* for tonal degrees (Ursprung, *op. cit.*, p. 147, and Gombosi, "Studien..." I:158). In the *Alia musica* (written by several authors) the eight *modi*, or *tropi*, or *toni* are determined, each mode being identified with an octave species and the initial tone indicated by a Greek name (see Wilhelm Mühlmann, *Die Alia Musica*, p. 12). These proceed from the Hypodorian to the Hypermixolydian, their outer limits corresponding to the Greater Perfect System on A. In this, however, the system becomes estranged from that of Boethius, and we have c instead of c♯ and f instead of f♯. This author of the *Alia musica* apparently had no understanding of the meaning of the *tonoi* and gives them a new meaning when he converts them into eight diatonic octave scales in a system extending from A to a. (This problem is discussed in great detail in Gombosi, "Studien...," a series of three articles appearing in five installments in *AM* X, XI, XII [see bibliography]; see also Reese, *op. cit.*, pp. 149–164, and footnote 17, p. 135). The possibility that the modal system may have evolved in part from a Byzantine system is discussed in Gombosi, "Studien..." II (see bibliography). Gombosi believes that the very first mention of the eight church modes in Alcuin is a conscious adaptation of a Byzantine system (*AM* XII:22), and that Alcuin is speaking of melodic formulas rather than octave scales which have their antecedents in the Byzantine *echoi*. The *echoi*

...existed in the same number—eight—as the Western church modes and were collectively referred to as *octoechos* (eight *echoi*). They differed, however, from the modes in that they were not abstract scale formations but melodic formulae which included the characteristic features (tonic, cadential endings, typical progressions) of all the melodies written in one *echos* (Apel, *HD*, p. 225).

The principle of eightfold modality is traced back to ancient Mesopotamian cultures by Eric Werner in his book *The Sacred Bridge*, pp. 373–409. Until mode became associated with octave species and came to signify a diatonic scale of eight tones, the outer tones of which made an octave, it referred to melodic formulas. The melodic formulas varied in different cultures, and even within the same culture. The major similarity was the existence of these formulas in eight types, the number eight having cosmic and religious significance. Werner attempts to show that the principle of eight modes is not an occidental concept but has roots in earlier Asiatic cultures.

*9. A brief summary of some aspects of the tradition of Greek theory as they appear in medieval theory before the *Alia musica* may be helpful here in comprehending the development of the medieval modal system. Boethius (*ca.* 5th–6th century), delineates the seven *tonoi* system of Ptolemy and adds an eighth (see Chapter I, note *8). Cassiodorus (*ca.* 5th–6th century), next to Boethius the most important early medieval source, describes the fifteen *tonoi* system (see Strunk, *op. cit.*, pp. 87–92), using as his source the lost Latin translation of Gaudentios' *Eisagoge* by Mutianus. Isidor (6th–7th century) bases his version on that of Cassiodorus and speaks of fifteen *toni* (*tonoi*) but does not enumerate them:

Key is a raised enunciation of the voice. For it is a difference and quantity of the harmony consisting in the intonation or level of the voice, of which musicians have divided the varieties into fifteen parts, of which the Hyperlydian is the newest and highest, and the Hypodorian the lowest of all (Strunk, *op. cit.*, p. 96).

There is no mention of anything resembling the ecclesiastical modes in Isidor. The modes were first codified by Alcuin (*ca.* 735–804), but in the sense of formulas (see note *8). Alcuin repeated Cassiodorus' definition of the *tonoi* but was uncertain as to their meaning; his uncertainty led to greater misunderstanding on the part of his successors. Aurelian (9th century) utilized three sources: Cassiodorus, Isidor, and Alcuin, using Alcuin as a source for his treatment of the ecclesiastical modes. Aurelian repeated the *tonoi* based on Isidor and Cassiodorus. "For a long period the *tropen* [ = *tonoi* ] appeared side by side with the ecclesiastical tones and were neither mixed nor mistaken for one another" (Gombosi, "Studien..." I:160). When we come to the *Alia musica* (10th century) we find no understanding of *tonoi* but rather an attempt to reinterpret them as octave scales (see note *8). Further, see Gombosi, "Studien..." I, II, III; the articles in *MGG* on "Boethius," II:49–57, "Gaudentios," IV:1469–1471, "Cassiodorus," II:892–897, "Isidor," VI:1435–1438, "Alkuin," I:325–327, "Aurelianus Reomensis," I:858–859; and Mühlmann, *op. cit.*

*10. See note *8 above.

*11. This is certainly a confusing mixture of systems, and Riemann increases the difficulty by misquoting Gerbert and giving the step designation *lichanos meson*, which should instead be (Gerbert, 127b) *lichanos hypaton*. The *proslambanomenos* of the Dorian scale would be D or *lichanos hypaton* of the Hypodorian scale based on A. The *mese* of the Dorian scale would be d or *paranete diezeugmenon* of the Hypodorian.

*12. See Reese, *op. cit.*, p. 154, footnote 19.

*13. For this, see Gombosi, "Studien..." II.

## CHAPTER II

*1. Riemann never accepted the conclusions in Hans Müller's *Hucbald's echte und unechte Schriften über Musik* (Leipzig, 1884), a work which is still considered authoritative by scholars today (see Reese, *Music in the Middle Ages*, pp. 125–126). Müller established that of all the treatises ascribed to Hucbald by Gerbert in vol. I of *Scriptores*, only one, the *De institutione harmonica*, is definitely his. It is therefore customary now to refer to the other treatises as Pseudo-Hucbaldian (see *MGG* VI:821–827). For a recent study of Hucbald and his contributions see Rembert Weakland, "Hucbald as Musician and Theorist," in *MQ* XLII:66 ff.

*2. The origin of the term organum is still unknown, and its derivation from the name of the instrument (organ) has neither been proved nor disproved (see Reese, *op. cit.*, p. 251). However, see W. Apel, "Early History of the Organ," *Speculum* 23:191–216, where this question receives its most comprehensive discussion.

*3. The treatise *De divisione naturae* is philosophical in nature and is concerned primarily with the science of *musica*, representing it in terms of dialectic, arithmetic, geometry, and astrology. Whether the quotation given by Riemann can be regarded as a description of a type of musical composition is by no means a certainty. Handschin interprets this passage to mean that tones, which in themselves are separate entities, are joined together according to rational principles governed by numbers and result in naturally beautiful concordances. *Musica* begins from its fundamental (*tonus*—the *principium*) and proceeds through simple and composite concordances, resolving these by finally returning to the *tonus*, following a kind of dialectical process. In view of the character of the entire treatise, Handschin feels this interpretation to be more comprehensible (see J. Handschin, "Zur Geschichte der Lehre vom Organum," in *ZfMW* VIII:321). It seems entirely possible that Erigena was indirectly influenced by musical practice, but the treatise itself is speculative and metaphysical in nature. For a summary of its contents see the article "Eriugena," *MGG* III:1492–1496. For further information on the origins of polyphony, and on organum in particular, see Handschin, *op. cit.*, 321–341, and Reese, *op. cit.*, pp. 249–258.

Dom Anselm Hughes believes that Erigena is referring to melodic successions (*NOHM* II:273) and interprets the phrase *intentionis et remissionis proportionibus segregetae* (separated by various degrees of pitch) as being a gloss on the word *discrepantibus*. The passage is quoted by Hughes from Migne, *Patrologia Latina*, cxxii:638, and is as follows (the wording differs slightly from Riemann's quotation. Hughes gives a translation of the text into English):

> Ut enim organicum melos ex diversis vocum qualitatibus et quantitatibus conficitur, dum viritim separatimque sentiuntur longe a se discrepantibus [intentionis et remissionis proportionibus segregatae], dum vero sibi invicem coaptantur secundum certas rationabilesque artis musicae regulas per singulas tropas naturalem quamdam dulcedinem reddentibus: ita universitatis concordia ex diversis naturae unius subdivisionibus a se invicem, dum singulariter inspiciuntur, dissonantibus juxta conditoris uniformem voluntatem coadunata est.

*4. The reason for the limitation placed on the movement of the lower voice is discussed at length and in connection with the *Musica enchiriadis* on pp. 17–30.

*5. See the discussion of this point in Reese, *op. cit.*, pp. 253–258.

*6. The possibility that quartal harmonization of medieval chant is more suitable to it, because of its pentatonic character, is developed in a series of articles by Joseph Yasser, "Medieval Quartal Harmony," *MQ* XXIII:170–197, 333–366, and *MQ* XXIV:351–385. The idea that medieval chant had a pentatonic structure had occurred earlier to Riemann (reference to him can be found in the articles). If one follows Yasser's assumptions (the articles are speculative to some extent), quartal organum would be a more characteristic form of polyphony based upon chant than, for example, a composition of Palestrina with its tertian sonorities.

*7. Riemann's assumption that Gerald here makes reference to singing in thirds has no definite foundation. The two-part singing of the English may have been a kind of organum in thirds, but it could have been singing in parallel fifths as well. Giraldus does not specifically mention thirds, only two styles of singing. His account, the *Descriptio Cambriae*, is dated 1198 in *MGG* V:160. Giraldus' account cannot be directly related to the gymel technique, since that term does not appear in a theoretical treatise until *ca.* 1430 (Guilelmus Monachus, Couss., *S.*III:289 and 292–293). Concerning a history of the gymel technique see "Gymel" in *MGG* V:1139. The composition *Nobilis, humilis* from the 13th century MS— Upsala C233—employing an "organum of thirds"—is dated around a hundred years later than Giraldus' report.

Comparative musicology has also not been able to establish definite evidence that the interval of a third is more natural in "folk singing" and in primitive cultures in the various stages of their development. Riemann's hypothesis that the third was rooted in the practice of "natural" or folk polyphony was questioned by Manfred Bukofzer in his *Geschichte des englischen Diskants und des Faux-bourdons* (Strassburg, 1936), pp. 102–103, as well as by Jacques Handschin in "Der Organum-Traktat von Montpellier" in *Festschrift für Guido Adler* (1930), pp. 50–57. For a history of polyphony employing the methods of comparative musicology see Marius Schneider, *Geschichte der Mehrstimmigkeit*, I and II (Berlin, 1934, 1936). Here again the third cannot be said to have preference on the basis of the evidence offered. That the neighboring fourth was substituted for the third in theoretical treatises dealing with early polyphony because of its authoritative role in antique theory can only be dismissed as pure conjecture. Even in later treatises the third appears only as a secondary interval occurring in part-movement before cadences on perfect intervals (see the treatises of Guido of Arezzo and John Cotton).

*8. This reference can be found in Gerbert I:191 and not 119, as is erroneously stated by Riemann. A translation of the *Scholia enchiriadis* can be found in Strunk, *Source Readings in Music History*, pp. 126–138; the reference in question is on page 132 and reads as follows:

Since there is always a reversion of the tropes or tones at the fifth and octave [reversion here apparently meaning a return to an original condition, i.e., in the organal voice, the trope or tone being reproduced exactly at the fifth or octave], and in the symphony of the diapente, since at the fifth the lower voice responds to the upper with the same variety of trope, we must respond to either voice from its octave with the same trope... in the symphony of the diatessaron, since at the fourth the lower voice does not respond to the upper with the same trope, we must respond to the principal and organal voices, not with the same trope, but to each with its own.

The term "trope" here must be defined as a melodic pattern expressing the mode by the manner in which it "fills up" intervals structurally characteristic of the mode (fifths or fourths).

*9. Attempts to establish an approximate date for the *Musica enchiriadis* have resulted in a number of conclusions. This treatise has been accounted for in more than forty MSS, and general opinion seems to place it in the 10th century (see the article "Hucbald" by Rembert Weakland in *MGG* VI:821–827). Handschin, however, feels that it belongs in the 9th century because of certain sentences in Scotus Erigena which seem to indicate relationship between the two. (See

Handschin, "Die Musikanschauung des Johannes Scotus," *Deutsche Vierteljahrs-schrift für Literaturwissenschaft und Geistesgeschichte* V:321.) It is very likely that a more definite determination of the date of the *Musica enchiriadis* will not be possible until existing MSS have been collated and a definitive version established.

*10. Martianus Capella (4th or 5th century) was born in Africa and received his education in Carthage and Rome. More exact dates for him are not known because of the lack of contemporary accounts. His works, which are encyclopaedic in content, are first found in 10th-century manuscripts and contain a treatise, *De musica*, highly valued as an instructional work in the Middle Ages (for further details see "Capella" in *MGG* II:802–805). The passage about which Riemann is speaking is found in Gerbert I:234 and is as follows:

> Quae omnia figurate Martianus in libro, quem de nuptiis Philologiae et Mercurii conscribit, in nemore Apollinis fuisse confingit, videlicet qui ipse est Sol moderator musicae coelestis. Nam, inquit, eminentiora culmina, id est, rami altiores perinde dis-tenta, id est, valde extenta, acuto sonitu, id est, subtili & gracili resultabant, id est, resonabant.
>
> Quicquid vero terrae confine & propinquum fuerat, rami videlicet inclinatiores & humiliores ac terrae viciniores quatiebat, id est, impellebat, repercutiebat rauca gravitas. At media, id est, mediae partes ipsius silvae, coniuncta sibi spatia concinebant duplis succentibus. Concentus est similium vocum adunata societas: succentus vero est, varii soni sibi maxime convenientes, sicut videmus in organo.

This passage, which is allegorical in character and by no means easily trans-lated, is here only paraphrased by Riemann. A more literal rendition is as follows:

> Of the things Martianus writes about in his book on the marriage of Philology and Mercury, he imagines all of these to have taken place in the grove of Apollo, who, of course, is himself the sun and the moderator of all celestial music.
>
> For the higher peaks, that is, the higher branches, are distended, that is, very much extended, with a higher sound; that is, they bound back with a subtle and graceful result, that is, they echo. Whatever, in truth, had been bounded by and neighboring to the earth, that is, the branches which are more slanting and lower and nearer to the earth, the rough heaviness (of the earth) shakes again and again. But the middle, that is, the middle parts of the woods itself, joined to each other, sing together with doubled sweetness. *Concentus* is the uniform fusion of the same tones; *succentus* truly is the best possible com-bination of different tones, which one can see in organum.

(Here Regino goes on to give an explanation involving intervals and consonance. He momentarily departs from his allegory, beginning with the sentence following "*concentus est...*" and his mention of organum seems to belong more to that which follows than that which precedes.)

The allegory of the branches in the grove of Apollo is part of a general attempt to relate the tonal system to natural phenomena. The glory of Apollo, the sun god and the moderator of celestial music, is reflected by his earthly kingdom. The sun falling with greater brilliance on the higher, lighter branches is like musical sounds of higher pitch, which "bound back with a subtle and graceful result." The lower-pitched musical sounds are like lower branches which are shaken again and again by the "rough heaviness of the earth." But those sounds of medium range are the sweetest of all when joined together. All these sounds make up the totality of celestial music and are called to life by the heavenly moderator, Apollo.

Riemann thought that the three levels referred to organum in which the octave represented a doubling of one of the voices, and that the term *media* referred to *mese* which would be a fifth below the uppermost tone. It is true that Regino refers to *mese* as *media* later in the treatise (Gerbert I:241); however, the general obscurity created by his use of allegory permits a great variety of interpretations, and it is not possible to approach this treatise as an example of or with any scientific exactness.

*11. Handschin ("Zur Geschichte der Lehre vom Organum," p. 329) interprets this passage to read "that in singing as well as in instrumental playing, not only is four-part organum possible but also six-part." A restudy of this passage, as quoted in Gerbert I:166, bears out his interpretation. The passage is as follows (including enough of the context to determine its meaning):

Sive namque simplici cantui duplex organum adjungas, quod potest significare primus versus ac tertius, qui ad secundum versum vicem tenent organi; sive ad duplicem cantum simplex organum referatur, quod versus secundus designat et quartus, organum in sui medio continentes, seu et organum gemines et cantum, sive etiam triplum utrumque socias, descripta ad invicem consonat ratione. Possunt enim et humanae voces, et in aliquibus instrumentis musicis non modo binae et binae, sed et ternae ac ternae hac sibi collatione misceri, dum utique uno impulsu, vel tribus in unum vocibus actitatis, totidem voces respondent organum.

(Either add two voices of organum to the chant melody which is to be found in the uppermost position during the first and third verse and which takes the position of the organum during the second verse; or add to a doubled chant melody [the chant melody and its octave] a single voice of organum as is found in the second and fourth verse and which has the organum in the middle; or double both the organum and the chant, or even triple both of them. They would all sound together in the manner described. It is possible that these same combinations be performed not only by human voices but also by instruments, two and two, or three and three, since if as many as three voices sing together at one point, just as many voices may answer as organum.)

*12. Riemann denies the existence of an independent system of organum in fifths in the *Musica enchiriadis*, but Handschin (*op. cit.*, p. 330) feels that an organum at the fifth does appear to be taught. The following is an attempt to review the *Musica enchiriadis*' teachings concerning quintal organum in order to determine which conclusion is valid.

Chapter VI treats of the characteristics of tones (how one may distinguish one tone from another) and their relationships to one another. The author remarks that every tone has another tone on either side of itself, five steps removed, which partakes of its quality. Since the early part of the treatise is concerned with its particular tonal system (the gamut whose significance was first noted by Spitta and which is discussed later in Chapter II by Riemann), its notational system (Daseian), and its solmization system, the reference to the interval of the fifth here must refer to the fact that in the *Musica enchiriadis* gamut all fifth relationships are perfect. Spitta, in his "Die *Musica enchiriadis* und ihr Zeitalter," (*VfMW*

V:451), remarks that the striking characteristic of this tonal system is the funda-mental significance of the fifth (the consonant quality of this interval is repeatedly emphasized in this treatise).

Chapter X discusses the symphonies (the simultaneous sounding of tones of different pitch level). They are enumerated in the following order: that of the fourth, the fifth, and the octave. It is not implied in the context that this represents a ranking of intervals, for the author writes following this enumeration, "One tone to another eight steps removed gives rise to the octave, which the other intervals (the fourth and the fifth) include in their range (when combined)."

Chapter X actually discusses, with examples, simple organum at the fifth, stating expressly that tones are consonantly answered by tones a fifth removed, and that this property is a particular characteristic of the fifth. The symphony of the fifth is again discussed in Chapter XII, with further examples. These chapters do not discuss the symphony of the fifth as a result of octave doubling, and it is our conclusion that the symphony of the fifth is of fundamental significance to the *Musica enchiriadis* and that this significance is borne out in the *Scholia*, which uses quintal organum as the basic type (see Strunk, *op. cit.*, pp. 128–129). Both the *Musica enchiriadis* and the *Scholia* begin with octave and fifth organum, then pro-ceed to quartal organum, which requires special consideration because of its irregularities (subsequently discussed in this chapter). See the discussion of the *Musica enchiriadis* in Jacques Handschin, *Der Toncharakter* (Zürich, 1948), pp. 316–327.

*13. See note *3 above.

*14. Only the Parisian and the Florentine MSS ascribe the *Musica enchiriadis* to "Uchubaldus," not the Bruges MSS, as Riemann states. See Handschin, "Zur Geschichte der Lehre vom Organum," p. 330.

*15. See note *3 above.

*16. Flaccus Alcuin does not speak of octave scales in his enumeration of the modes and probably thinks of them as formulas. His brief treatise containing this information is in Gerbert I:26–27; he states:

> Every musician must know that there are eight modes (*toni*) in music, for as a result of them all (melodic) combinations of tones (*omnis modulatio*) seem to be held together as if glued. The mode is the least part of correct music (*musica regulae*), just as letters form the least part of Grammar.... Their (the modes') names as we are accustomed to call them, have their origin for their authority as well as their sequence. [The *authentici* are so called for their superior authority, as the following sentence indicates, and the modes themselves are named for their sequence or place in the series, Protus, Deuterus, Tritus, Tetrardus.] For the first four are called *authentici* because their sound is higher and be-cause they are to be masters and leaders of the other four. For this reason the first ones are higher and the others lie lower.... The first one is called Protus,...the second Deuterus, the third Tritus, and the fourth Tetrardus (*tetrachius*) in the order in which they appear. The other four are called *plagii* (*obliqui, seu laterales*). This name is said to mean the lower part of these (Protus, Deuterus, etc.) because they (the *plagiis*) are four in number. They do not completely withdraw from the former and are lower because their sound is more depressed than that of the higher ones.

*17. In his article "The Psalmodic Formula NEANNO-E and its Origin," *MQ* XXVIII:93–99, Eric Werner concludes that these formulas are corruptions of Byzantine *epechemata* or *enechemata* (intonation formulas), which functioned either as memory aids or as ecstatic words for the intonation of the *octoechos* (the Byzantine tonal system). See also Egon Wellesz, *A History of Byzantine Music and Hymnography* (Oxford, 1949), pp. 250–252, and Gustave Reese, *op. cit.*, pp. 85–91 and 172–174. The formulas occur in a number of variant forms.

In Latin theory the formulas served the singers as memory aids or to indicate solmization. Werner emphasizes the important difference that solmization syllables became names of specific scale-tones, whereas the formulas in question continued to symbolize melodic patterns, or *pneumata*. Only after the 11th century did these formulas give way to the customary *alleluia* or *evovae*. Werner finds that the origin of *neannoe* may be found in the Hebrew word *Nin'ua'*, which is defined as meaning "quivering melodic movement."

*18. As already stated, the interval of the diminished fifth is not possible in the gamut of the *Musica enchiriadis*. Yet at certain points augmented fourths appear (see example, p. 27), giving rise to the rule governing quartal organum discussed on page 26 f. Despite this concern for the avoidance of the tritone, several examples of parallel quartal organum appear which contain augmented fourths, both in the *Musica enchiriadis* and the *Scholia*. Modern scholars generally agree that the examples should be emended to make all fourths perfect. See Strunk, *op. cit.*, pp. 127–131 (as well as footnote 3, p. 127), where the settings of "*Nos qui vivimus*" are given with a B♭. According to Strunk, the melody is the *tonus peregrinus*, which is given with the B♭ in the *Liber Usualis*, p. 117. *HAM* I:21 uses an F♯ instead for the same "*Nos qui vivimus*" setting. Lincoln B. Spiess, in his article "The Diatonic 'Chromaticism' of the Enchiriadis Treatises," *JAMS* XII:4, footnote 15, does not mention the similarity of the melody of this setting to the *tonus peregrinus*, but gives information concerning problems of melodic and textual identification. Spiess also uses F♯ to "correct" the augmented fourth. Reese, *op. cit.*, p. 254, example 67, gives an excerpt without emendation containing two augmented fourths. Since the chant setting of the *Te Deum* containing this excerpt, which can be found in the *Liber Usualis*, pp. 1832–1834, contains no accidentals, it would be necessary to add an F♯ in the *vox organalis* to obtain perfect fourths (assuming that the *organalis* followed the *principalis*). See also Ernst Ludwig Waeltner, "Der Bamberger Dialog über das Organum," *AfMW* XIV:175–183, concerning a treatise in a manuscript also containing the *Musica enchiriadis*. The *Bamberger Dialog* deals with free organum, which is described as being necessary in order to avoid tritones (the *Dialog* uses the Daseian scale and the rule specifying C and G as the limiting tones of the gamut). Its author augments the teachings of the *Musica enchiriadis* and the *Scholia*, for according to him, the organal voice can move under the limiting tones C and G if the respective segment of the *principalis* itself closes a second below one of these limiting tones (this rule is probably particularly concerned with G, since such a close below C would not be found). The lower voice moving in the tonal range around G may descend to F, but the *Dialog* requires the presence of the tone B♭ above.

*19. See Spiess, *op. cit.*, pp. 1–6.

*20. See Spiess, *op. cit.*, p. 2.

*21. See Willi Apel, *The Notation of Polyphonic Music*, pp. 21–22; Willi Apel, *Gregorian Chant*, p. 152; Siegfrid Wantzloeben, *Das Monochord als Instrument und als System*, pp. 60–68; and Gustave Reese, *op. cit.*, pp. 134–136 and footnote 17.

*22. See Reese, *op. cit.*, p. 173, footnote 28.


# CHAPTER III

*1. Berno was called as abbot to the monastery of Reichenau in the year 1008, and with his student and contemporary Hermannus Contractus, led the monastery school to high attainments. Berno's importance as a theorist, as Riemann subsequently states, is secondary to his achievements as a liturgist. Berno, for example, was a leader in the movement to include the *Credo* as a regular part of the Ordinary of the Mass. See "Berno von Reichenau" in *MGG* I: 1795–1796.

Brambach, in his *Die Reichenauer Sängerschule* II: 33, compares passages which are similar in Berno and in Hucbald, as does Riemann at the beginning of Chapter III.

*2. For a detailed discussion of Hucbald's *De Harmonica Institutione*, see Rembert Weakland, "Hucbald as Musician and Theorist," *MQ* XLII: 66–84.

*3. Questions concerning Odo's biography and authorship of treatises ascribed to him are examined in detail in Hans Oesch, *Guido von Arezzo* (Bern, 1954). Oesch's investigation resulted in his ascription of the *Dialogus de Musica* (in Strunk, *Source Readings in Music History*, pp. 103–116) and *De Musica* (Gerbert I: 265–284) to a writer in the Benedictine Abbey of Saint-Maur des Fossés, named Odo, who very likely had some correspondence in his lifetime with Guido of Arezzo.

*4. Pages 249b–250b in Gerbert I were placed there in error by Gerbert and actually do not belong to the *Prooemium tonarii.* (See Oesch, *op. cit.*, pp. 106–107. The "barbaric tone-names" have a Semitic appearance and some are even identifiable as being of Arabian derivation. *Scembs, Cemar, Asel,* and *Nar* are Arabian names for Sun, Moon, Saturn, and Fire. Three of these are also identified as such in *NOHM* I, p. 468.)

*5. The "dual aspect" of the ninth step may be explained as follows: In any melodic segment, it would be impossible for a "chromatic" movement to take place, such as b♭ to b♮, or vice versa. For this reason, b♭ and b♮ are never thought of as being related to one another, since this relationship was nonexistent. Either a b♭ or a b♮ could exist at the ninth degree of the Odonian gamut, but never both. If the ninth degree or "step" was a b♭, then the division between a and b would be smaller (a semitone); if the ninth degree was b♮, then the division would be larger (a whole-tone). Odo explains this as follows (see Strunk, *op. cit.*, p. 107):

Yet the first and second ninth steps, b♭ and b♮, form with respect to one another neither a tone nor a semitone, but from the first ninth step, b♭, to the eighth, a, is a semitone, and to the tenth, c, is a tone; conversely, from the second ninth step, b♮, to the eighth, a, is a tone, and to the tenth, c, a semitone. Thus one of them is always superfluous, and in each melody you accept one and reject the other in order not to seem to be making a tone and a semitone in the same place, which would be absurd.

*6. Oesch, *op. cit.*, pp. 100–104, in agreement with other scholars, regards this treatise as the work of the author of the *Dialogus*—because of the correspondence of their contents. The *Dialogus* is a presentation of the material of the *De Musica* (the treatise beginning with *Musicae artis disciplina*) in a form more suitable for instruction. See also Sigfried Wantzloeben, *Das Monochord*, pp. 69–76, for a detailed discussion of the Odonian monochord and the range extensions about which Riemann presently speaks.

*7. See the discussion on chromaticism in ecclesiastical chant in Willi Apel, *Gregorian Chant*, pp. 157–165.

*8. The division of the octave modal scale into a species of fourth and fifth is presented in its final and most polished form in the *Musica* of Hermannus Contractus. The concept of the species of fourth and fifth can be traced back to Aristoxenos, who indicated that it was possible to divide the various species of octave into species of fourths and fifths. Cleonides, though much later than Aristoxenos (Cleonides—first or second century A.D.; Aristoxenos—middle of the fourth century B.C.), apparently basing his *Harmonic Introduction* (Strunk, *op. cit.*, pp. 34–46) on an Aristoxenian source, also conveyed the manner in which octave species are divided (Strunk, p. 41):

> Of the *diatessaron* there are three species...thus in the diatonic genus the first species of *diatessaron* is that in which a semitone lies below the tones, the second that in which it lies above the tones, the third that in which it lies between the tones....Of the *diapente* there are four figures....In the diatonic genus the first figure is that in which the semitone lies at the bottom, the second that in which it lies at the top, the third that in which it is second from the top, the fourth that in which it is third from the top.

This concept was completely systematized by Gaudentios (see Reese, *Music in the Middle Ages*, pp. 42–44). That this particular division of the octave developed into the species of fourths and fifths of the medieval modal system cannot be shown. It must be remembered that octave species as such do not appear after Boethius until the 10th century (see Chapter I, note *8) in the *Alia musica*. Even in the *Alia musica* the species of fourths and fifths are not given in the authentic and plagal disposition of medieval theory (see Wilhelm Mühlmann, *Die Alia Musica*, in which the treatise is given in German translation with emendations, pp. 50–74). The section following Hucbald's *De harmonic institutione* (Gerbert I:104–121, ending with the sentence "*In hoc enim dumtaxat usque Spiritus Domini replevit*"), beginning "*In primo diapason C*" (pp. 121–125), is not a part of that treatise (Rembert Weakland, "Hucbald as Musician and Theorist," *MQ* XLII:82). It contains a description of the species of fourth and fifth in their authentic and plagal disposition (122a, line 7, to 122b, line 19), and Mühlmann believes that it must be based on the lost Latin translation of Gaudentios by Mutianus; Gerbert's *Anonymous I* (I:330–338) and the anonymous "Pseudo-Bernelinus" also deliver what seem to be earlier versions of the system perfected by the theorists of the Reichenau school.

*9. Hermannus Contractus represents a culmination in theoretical procedure and systemization rather than an originator of a new system or of new ideas. He was born in Swabia in 1013 and died in the cloister at Reichenau in 1054. This cloister was in its prime during his lifetime and was even visited by Pope Leo IX in 1049. Hermannus was a prolific writer, not only on music but also on history, mathematics, and astronomy. He was a composer and a poet as well.

His treatise has been translated into English by Leonard Ellinwood (Rochester, 1936) from a MS in the Sibley Library of the Eastman School of Music. The treatise is a detailed treatment of intervals, of the tetrachord division of the gamut, Hermannus' letter notation (which, as Riemann states at the conclusion of Chapter III, "met with little approval"), and a systematic exposition of the modes. As Brambach states in his *Theorie und Praxis der Reichenauer Sängerschule* (Part II of *Die Reichenauer Sängerschule*), p. 34, "Hermannus' theoretical exposition is simpler, clearer, and more consistent than those of his predecessors." Traces of Hermannus' writings on music are found in the works of Wilhelm of Hirsau (died 1091), Wilhelm's student Dietger (died 1120), Aribo (*ca.* 1078), and even as late as Engelbert of Admont (died 1331). "In correctness and clarity, it is surpassed by no other medieval system" (Brambach, *op. cit.*, p. 36).

*10. I have used Ellinwood's translation of this excerpt (Ellinwood, *op. cit.*, p. 56).

*11. In the *Enchiriadis* treatises the octave is always regarded as the duplication of the same tone in another region, hence the tones of the augmented octaves found in the characteristic *Enchiriadis* gamut bear no relationship to each other. The purpose of the *Enchiriadis* gamut differs from that of Hermannus in that the former is specifically designed for organum, whereas the latter is a fully developed tonal system applicable to the large *corpus* of chant, which was the most highly developed musical style of that period.

## CHAPTER IV

*1. The two most recent and comprehensive works on Guido are Joseph Smits van Waesberghe, *Guido Aretinus* (Florence, 1953) (in Latin) and Hans Oesch, *Guido von Arezzo* (Bern, 1954). Van Waesberghe is also the author of the article "Guido von Arezzo" in *MGG* V:1071–1078. The chapter on notation from Van Waesberghe's book is given in English translation in *MD* V:15–53.

*2. There is a recent critical edition of Guido's *Micrologus* published by the American Institute of Musicology, Rome, 1955, edited by Van Waesberghe. This edition is the result of a collation of 77 MSS in an attempt to arrive at the most definitive possible version of the treatise. It contains many emendations in the text and in the musical examples which have been utilized here in place of Gerbert's version (Chapters XVIII–IX of the *Micrologus*, Gerbert II:21–23) quoted by Riemann. The quotation in parentheses (footnote 1) is a later addition to the text. See Van Waesberghe, *op. cit.*, p. 200.

*3. The repercussion (*repercussio*) is the "main note of the recitation." This note is also called *tenor* and "is always the dominant of the mode" (Apel, "Psalm

Tones," in *HD*, p. 612). In the eight ecclesiastical modes the tone F occurs twice as a final (Modes V and VI) and once as a tenor (Mode II), and the tone C occurs three times as a tenor (Modes III, V, VIII). In the psalm tones the F occurs as a tenor (the tenor rather than the final being the main consideration) once (Mode II), and twice as a final (Modes V and VI). C occurs three times as a tenor in the present version of the psalm tones (Modes III, IV, and VIII), this version having remained unchanged since the period of John Cotton's *De Musica* (*ca.* 1100). In the case of Mode III and Mode VIII the original tenor was B (see Apel, *Gregorian Chant*, pp. 210–212, and also the article on "Choral," *MGG* II: 1282–1288), but was changing to C or had already changed in Guido's time. At any rate, the tones C and F occupied an important place in the psalm tones in Modes II, III, V, VI, and VIII as they probably existed in Guido's time.

As to the general importance of the tenor in chant, Apel says the following (*Gregorian Chant*, p. 136):

> The dominant [i.e., tenor] can hardly be said to be a characteristic of the mode, because the great majority of the melodies of a given mode fail to show any clear evidence of the dominant. Nor does the dominant occur in any of the medieval descriptions of the modes. Actually, the dominant is a characteristic property, not of a mode in general, but of a few special melodies associated with that mode, such as the psalm tones or other recitation tones. In these the dominant (more properly called the tenor) does play a prominent role as the pitch for the recitation, while, on the other hand, the basic characteristics of the mode, final and ambitus, are often absent.

*4. The melody in Example 6, however, closes on D. Riemann translates "Teilschluss auf dem Protus D," but the treatise (see p. 63, which follows Van Waesberghe's edition of the Micrologus) reads "Distinctio in proto A."

*5. Van Waesberghe's edition reads ♮ for the note in the *principalis* above *los* in *coelos* in Example 9 and gives b♭ where Riemann assumed a correction for Example 10. The explanation to Example 10 reads: "It may also be found that in the plagal Tritus the tone b♭ is added to c and d as the tone F is added to G and a." Riemann's Example 10 introduces the c to d relationship but this is not found in Van Waesberghe (Micrologus, p. 213). I have appended Riemann's version of the last four intervals in Example 10 following the emended version from Van Waesberghe. The use of ♮ or ♭ varies in the manuscript versions of the *Micrologus*. See Van Waesberghe (*Micrologus*, p. 226), where the variations are given.

*6. An investigation of the principles of Guidonian organum will be helpful at this point in understanding its further discussion by Riemann. First of all, the Guidonian organum gamut is as follows (Van Waesberghe, *Guido Aretinus*, p. 203):

| A | B | C | D | E | F | G | a | ♮ | c | d | e | f | g |
|---|---|---|---|---|---|---|---|---|---|---|---|---|---|
| I | II | III | I | II | III | IV | I | II | III | I | II | III | IV |

The rules governing the movements of quartal organum in the *Musica enchiriadis* no longer apply; the third sound or Tritus (III) in every tetrachord is now the limiting factor rather than the fourth (Tetrardus), this being the case in the *Musica enchiriadis*. The tritone in Guidonian organum is no longer a basic consideration, as it was in the *Musica enchiriadis*. In fact, in a progression of fourths in the above gamut only one tritone would occur: F up to ♮. Guido gives a rule covering the eventuality that ♮ occurs in the *cantus*. He says (see p. 65):

Finally we must remark that a perfect fourth lies below all tones with the exception of ♮; to all parts of the melody where this ♮ occurs the organum [which is still the lower voice] must add G.

Only if b♭ occurs in the *principalis* may an F be added below. Should the *principalis* descend from ♮ to F (by step, of course) or to G, the *organalis* (on G) would then move to F once the tritone has been avoided:

This principle may be seen in the following example from Chapter XIX of the *Micrologus* (Example 9 from Van Waesberghe, *Micrologus*, p. 213):

coe - los    un - de    de - scen - de - rat

A major consideration in Guidonian organum is the avoidance of half-step movement at the cadence. Of the cadence, Guido writes (see p. 65):

Such coming together of the voices [to the final, i.e., the concluding note] is done best with a whole-tone, less well with a major third, but never with a minor third (as a penultimate interval).

Returning once more to the limiting factor, which is the third sound or Tritus (see gamut), it can be seen that the forbidden half-step is encountered below the third step (III) in each case. For this reason Guido finds that certain modes (Tritus and Tetrardus on C, F, and G) are best suited for the introduction of whole-tones, major thirds, and fourths, whereas minor thirds and whole-tones are more characteristic of Protus on A and D. The Deuterus mode is most prone to the half-step relationships which Guido wishes to avoid. Example 5 illustrates two partial closes (*distinctia*) on Deuterus E.

Is there any attempt to rank or classify intervals in the Micrologus? Strangely enough, the fifth is omitted as an interval suitable for a "concord" despite its importance in the Pythagorean system which reigned in the Middle Ages. The Guidonian monochord follows the Odonic monochord (see Strunk, *Source Readings in Music History*, pp. 105–106, for its measurements; also see Smits van Waesberghe, *Guido Aretinus*, pp. 151–185) with its typical Pythagorean relationships ($2/1 = $ *diapason*, $3/2 = $ *diapente*, $4/3 = $ *diatessaron*, $9/8 = $ *tonus*). Guido's reason for avoiding the fifth was a practical one: the fifth was the characteristic interval of a type of organum (strict) which he did not prefer because of its "rigidity." An even further example of musical practice being at odds with a theoretical tuning system was the position of the third (major third $= 81/64$; minor third $= 32/27$ in the

Pythagorean system) in Guidonian organum. Guido himself remarks on the fact that thirds are not found on the monochord (Wantzloeben, *Das Monochord...*, p. 79):

> The divisions of the *semiditonus* [minor third] moreover, and the *ditonus* [major third], even if their sounds are joined in singing, are not admitted to the monochord.

The third must have constituted a problem for Guido, for in spite of its dissonant character in the tuning system, it appeared frequently in his organum. Wantzloeben remarks (p. 79):

> It must have struck a practicing musician like Guido that, on the monochord, the sound of the third, which was the result of the sum of two whole-tones, was intolerable, whereas it was not at all unpleasant in actual practice.

At one point in the *Micrologus* (Chapter XVIII) Guido states:

> We exclude the fifth and the semitone from the series of intervals available to us for concords, and allow outside of the fourth only the whole-tone and the major and minor third to be used. Of these the minor third has the lowest rank and the fourth the highest.

This certainly has nothing to do with any scheme of consonance and dissonance classification, for it places between the fourth and the minor third the intervals of a major third and a major second! Guido incidentally forbids the semitone as a "concord," yet one appears in Example 8, where it perhaps can be explained as a "passing" tone. When dissonances occur in Guidonian organum, they occur within a composition, representing an intermediate stage between the consonances of the fourth and the unison, the consonances being generally employed at main points (on accented syllables, at cadence points).

It is also interesting to note in the examples the prolongation of one tone in the *organalis* while the *cantus* moves around it, and also the crossing of voices (see page 66, and Reese, *op. cit.*, p. 260). Van Waesberghe discusses Chapters XVIII and XIX of the Micrologus in detail in his *Guido Aretinus*, pp. 200–225.

*7. See Chapter II, note *12. A "symphony of fifths" is taught in the *Musica enchiriadis*, and the *Enchiriadis* gamut appears to stress the basic importance of the fifth. Riemann, proceeding from his premise that organum in alternating motion (going from and returning to a unison) was the style of organum in practice and parallel organum a theoretical account of actual practice, discounted the references made in the *Musica enchiriadis* to organum at the fifth (see p. 20 f.) Erich Steinhard, in his article "Zur Frühgeschichte der Mehrstimmigkeit" (*AfMW* III:220–231), approaches the problem of precedence by restudying the treatises known to him, and concludes that both parallel and "motion" styles were in existence at the same time. Steinhard cites the *Prooemium Tonarii Oddonis* (Gerbert I:249–250) as stating that eight types of organum were in practice. It has been shown (Oesch, *op. cit.*, pp. 106–107) that this section of the treatise (249b–250b) does not belong to the *Tonari*. Whether the term "organum" here refers to a style of polyphonic composition is not known (see p. 43 f. above). It is true, however, that the organum treatise *Ad organum faciendum* (the Milan treatise —*ca.* last half of 11th century) mentions five organum "modes" (*quinque modi organizandi*). These "modes," however, do not deal with five individual types of organum but with means of setting organum at various points within the same composition (see pp. 70–72).

*8. Riemann at this point refers to the eighth example closing on G and using a b♭. Example 8 closes on F, however, and no b♭ appears (either in Gerbert or Van Waesberghe's edition); therefore he must be referring to Example 9. In Waesberghe's emended edition of the examples, however, the b is not ♭ but ♮. In connection with Example 9, see note *6 above.

*9. Accounts of the development of organum can be found in the following sources: Reese, *op. cit.*, pp. 249–271; *NOHM* II:270–286; and the article "Kontrapunkt" in *MGG* VII:1525–1528. These accounts discuss sources and give bibliographical references. The problem of organum and discant will be discussed in the commentary to Chapter V.

*10. On the *organistrum* (German: *Drehleier*; English: hurdy-gurdy) see the following: Reese, *op. cit.*, p. 258; *MGG* III:744–747; and Sachs, *The History of Musical Instruments*, pp. 271–273.

*11. Riemann translates the Latin "Quintus per multiplicationem oppositarum vocum augendo vel auferendo" as "ein fünftes Element bilden rhythmische Abweichungen des Organum vom Cantus durch Einführung längerer oder kürzerer Töne." This readily translates to "a fifth element consists of rhythmic deviations of organum from the *cantus* by the introduction of longer or shorter tones." Since "rhythmic" is used here in a descriptive rather than a historical sense it has been placed in parentheses in the text (p. 72). A more literal translation of the Latin reads: "The fifth manner introduces deviations [of the organum] against the *cantus*, longer or shorter."

*12. In organum treatises Riemann observed a development from parallel motion to discant (contrary motion organum), whereas he assumed that contrary and oblique motion were characteristics of actual practice. On p. 14 he writes the following of organum in practice:

It must, then, be understood that in no way is strict parallel movement of the voices in fourths or fifths characteristic of organum, but rather the distinguishing quality is an alternation of movements going apart and coming together to a unison.

He places much emphasis for this argument on his interpretation of a doubtful source, the *De musica* of Scotus Erigena, despite the fact that the language of Erigena's treatise is ambiguous and admits of a number of interpretations (see Chapter II, note *3). Parallel organum was, then, according to Riemann, an attempt by theorists to account for the practice of organum, and after having presented it as a theoretical concept they devoted much effort to the "alternating style" which more closely reflected actual practice.

Gustave Reese comes to similar conclusions (*Music in the Middle Ages*, p. 255), saying that it is likely that:

As given conscious application, the concept organum was linked primarily with the departing from and returning to a unison rather than with a mere bald progression of fifths or fourths.

And later (p. 258):

The impulse toward polyphony seems to come from *at least* two sources: the desire on the part of people with different ranges to sing at comfortable pitch levels, and the varying of a melodic line by people intending to sing it simultaneously (heterophony). May we not, then, be wrong in regarding parallel and free organum as two phases of the same thing? It is altogether likely that parallel organum was an outgrowth of the first source just mentioned and free organum of the second.

It has been suggested in this commentary, however, that parallel organum is by no means cursorily dealt with in the treatises, but that it is presented clearly, fully, and sufficiently in view of the lack of technical problems encountered in its performance (the parallel organum of the *Musica enchiriadis* and the *Scholia*). The gamut of these latter treatises actually seems to place considerable emphasis on the fifth. Steinhard (*op. cit.*, pp. 221–222) feels that since parallel and alternating styles of organum appear in the same treatises, one could assume that both styles existed in practice. He cites as evidence for the simultaneity of the two styles the eight types of organum listed in the *Prooemium Tonarii Oddonis* (Gerbert I:249–250), the mention by John Cotton of various types of organum being in practice (*De Musica cum Tonario*, edited by Van Waesberghe, p. 157), and Elias Salomon's report (Gerbert III:59) of organum practice in the 13th century similar to that described in the *Enchiriadis* treatises. (Concerning the eight organum modes, however, see note *7 above).

Later theorists, such as Guido, favor the alternating movement or contrary motion styles, and it is this which provides a basis for Riemann's theoretical evolution of organum from parallel movement to movement in contrary motion. The musical sources, being largely undecipherable, do not shed much light on this problem. Of fourteen sources from the pre-St. Martial period, only five are capable of transcription (see a list of these sources in Lincoln B. Spiess, "An Introduction to the Pre-St. Martial Practical Sources of Early Polyphony," *Speculum* XXII:16–17). The earliest musical source, the Winchester Troper, is written in undecipherable staffless neumes, note-against-note style, with evidence of contrary motion appearing rarely in parts other than the cadential sections (see Reese, *op. cit.*, pp. 260–261). It is dated from the early 11th century. Other sources show a striving for contrary motion (Reese, *op. cit.*, pp. 262–265). Survivals of parallel organum are noted as late as the 14th and 15th centuries (Reese, *op. cit.*, pp. 270–271; on the early musical sources see also *NOHM* II:280–285. Later organum treatises emphasizing contrary motion and including contrapuntal decoration will be discussed in the commentary to Chapter V). Discussions of the origins and character of early polyphony can be only speculative. It is very likely that the treatises represent observations on types of musical practice long in existence. That sources earlier than the *Musica enchiriadis* contain no definite mention of polyphony may also indicate that if such a musical practice was in existence, it had not yet attained a recognized status. The relation of early theoretical sources, such as the *Enchiriadis* treatises, to actual practice cannot be demonstrated by the known musical sources. See, however, *NOHM* II:282–285 in connection with later practice and theoretical sources.

*13. In his translation of Cotton's *De Musica*, Utto Kornmüller gives a musical example of organum from the MS Munich (StB. Clm 2599) fol. 92v ("Der Traktat des Johannes Cottonius über Musik," *KMJ* III:1–22). This same example is given in Van Waesberghe's new edition of Cotton's treatise (Johannis Affligemensis, *De Musica cum Tonario* [Rome, 1950]). Both voices are notated with neumes, the *vox principalis* in black and the *organalis* in red. Handschin ("Der Organum-Traktat von Montpellier," *Adler Festschrift*, pp. 50–57) does not believe this to be originally part of the treatise, since it sets several notes against one, although one could interpret the treatise to mean this. Examples of note-against-note organum are found in the following manuscript copies of Cotton's treatise: MS Erfurt Amploniana 93 and 94, both 14th century; MS Karlsruhe, K 505, and Leipzig (UB Ms 79, 12th century). On Cotton and his reidentification as Johannis Affligemensis, see Van Waesberghe, *op. cit.*, and *MGG* VII:115–119.

*14. Marius Schneider, in his *Geschichte der Mehrstimmigkeit* I:58, calls attention to the fact that the terms *duplicare* and *triplicare* are used in Cotton's treatise (in the passage beginning "animadvertere etiam debes...") in the same manner as the terms *multiplicare* and *duplicare* are used in the Florentine Anonymous (Magl. II, I, 406³) and the MS London Br. Mus. Egerton 2888 (a treatise completely based on Cotton), where they specifically refer to the doubling of voices (Schneider reprints Egerton 2888 in vol. II of his *Geschichte*). Schneider, therefore, rejects Riemann's interpretation of a "figurative treatment of the *organalis*."

## CHAPTER V

*1. The treatises discussed in this chapter deal with improvisation practice, one type of discant practice accomplished by the ornamentation of a liturgical melody chiefly in note-against-note style. Bukofzer (in "Discantus," *MGG* III:559–578) differentiates among three types of discant:

1. Discant referring to the style of the *clausulae*, with both voices moving in rhythm.
2. Discant as an improvisation practice (the type discussed in Chapter V).
3. "English" discant (see Chapter VII, Commentary).

The discant treatises in the second category "set forth the traditions of earlier organum, particularly the phase before organum became melismatic" (Bukofzer, 561). The following is an attempt to trace the development of organum in citing its most important sources and some characteristics of each one of them:

### Earliest Definite References to Music in Parts

Regino of Prüm (d. 915) gives a definition of organum in his *De harmonica institutione* (see p. 36 above) as well as a definition of consonance and dissonance from a polyphonic point of view (see Chapter II, footnote 35).

*Musica enchiriadis* (early 10th century) ⎫ These contain the earliest definite in-
*Scholia enchiriadis* (early 10th century) ⎭ structions on procedures in setting
parallel and free (movement from and to a unison) organum.

The Paris treatise, the Cologne treatise, and the Bamberg treatise (all early 10th century) employ the same gamut as the *Musica enchiriadis* and the *Scholia*. They do not deal with parallel organum but with free organum and employ the same restrictions limiting movement below the Tetrardus degree in every tetrachord. The Bamberg treatise does indicate exceptions to this limitation, however (see Waeltner, "Der Bamberger Dialog über das Organum," *AfMW* XIV:175–183).

### Later Treatises and Sources for Early Polyphony

*Micrologus* (11th century) of Guido of Arezzo. The chapters on organum (XVIII and XIX) are primarily concerned with free organum, though parallel organum is mentioned briefly at the beginning of Chapter XVIII. Organum is here called *diaphony* (as it is referred to in the *Enchiriadis* treatises. The Cologne and Paris treatises, however, are entitled *De organo* and use both terms, *diaphony* and *organum*. On terminology see Lincoln B. Spiess, "Discant, Descant, Diaphony, and Organum," *JAMS* VIII:144–147). The *vox organalis* is the lowest voice, as in previous treatises.

*Winchester Troper* (11th century) is a collection of 164 two-part *organa*, unfortunately undecipherable (see Reese, *Music in the Middle Ages*, pp. 260–261). Some contrary motion is in evidence in places other than the cadential sections, and the *vox principalis* is below the *vox organalis*.

MS Chartres 109 (11th century) contains a leaf of examples of organum of this period (reproduced in *NOHM* II:282–284). There is a great emphasis on thirds in these examples, with contrary motion predominating. Other musical fragments of this period are discussed in *NOHM* II:280–285, and a list of known sources is given in *Speculum* XXII:16–17 by Lincoln Spiess (Riemann bases his discussion of organum completely on theoretical sources).

The Milan treatise (*Ad organum faciendum*; second half of the 11th century) employs the *vox principalis* as the lower voice. Limiting tones are no longer observed to avoid the tritone, but a B♭ is employed instead. Contrary motion is employed as well as crossing of voices (see pp. 70–73 above).

The Montpellier organum treatise (MS Montpellier, Fac. de med. H 384, fol. 122–123; 12th century) delineates a style similar to that of the Milan treatise. The lower voice is the *vox principalis*, and the third is placed next to the fourth and fifth as a consonance. This treatise is discussed in detail in Handschin, "Der Organum-Traktat von Montpellier" in *Adler Festschrift*, pp. 50–57, and in Fred Blum, "Another Look at the Montpellier Organum Treatise," *MD* XIII:15–24. Blum includes a translation of the treatise into English with transcriptions of the musical examples.

*De Musica* of John Cotton or Johannes Affligemensis (12th century). Cotton uses three terms in his treatise, all having the same meaning: organum, diaphony, and discant. Contrary motion is the most desirable, and the *vox principalis* may be above or below the organum, i.e., the voices are permitted to cross.

The La Fage Anonymous (Adrien de La Fage, *Essais de Dipthérographie Musicale* [Paris, 1864], pp. 355–363) is a treatise from the middle of the 12th century and is important for its distinction between organum and discant. Discant is note-against-note composition, and organum describes the style of St. Martial organum, where the *cantus* or tenor (from the Latin *tenere*: to hold) consists of long held notes melismatically decorated by the *duplum* (formerly the *vox organalis*). See the article "Discantus" in *MGG* III:560. Handschin discusses this treatise at length in "Zur Geschichte der Lehre vom Organum," *ZfMW*: 321–341. It is now available in a complete edition (La Fage's was fragmentary), edited by Albert Seay ("An Anonymous Treatise from St. Martial," *Annales Musicologiques* V:7–42).

Vatican Library organum treatise (MS Ottobeuren 3025, fol. 46–50). This treatise contains nothing new in the formulation of its organum rules (31 are given) but gains significance through its 278 examples. Its style is characterized by highly melismatic movement over long values in the tenor, typical of St. Martial practice. The melismatic technique is apparently of the Gregorian variety and must have originated from the liturgical chant practice of the same period (see Rudolf Ficker, "Der Organumtraktat der Vatikanischen Bibliothek [Ottob. 3025]," *KMJ* XXVII:65–74). On the above two treatises see also Reese, *op. cit.*, pp. 268–269.

The Codex Calixtinus (first half of 12th century).

The St. Martial MSS (four early-12th-century MSS). These are the most important musical sources for the practice of this period. Two main styles or types are represented, one being primarily note-against-note, and the other having a melismatic duplum over sustained tenor notes. (For discussions of the contents of these MSS with musical examples see Reese, *op. cit.*, pp. 265–268; *NOHM* II:288–307; Heinrich Besseler, *Musik des Mittelalters und der Renaissance*, pp. 95–98.) One of the weaknesses of Riemann's discussion of the transition of organum from parallel movement to contrary motion to discant is pointed out by Manfred Bukofzer in the article "Discantus" (*MGG* III:561):

> Riemann attempted (*Geschichte der Musiktheorie*, p. 97) [p. 80 of this translation] to define the distinction between organum and discant as being that of parallel motion and contrary motion. The rise of contrary motion is, in fact, an important criterion in the history of polyphony; nevertheless voice-leading alone is not sufficient basis for a definition, and cannot be employed out of historical context. Riemann's definition is meaningful for only a small group of compositions, namely, the most primitive two- and three-part settings having almost exclusive parallel movement in fifths and octaves, which are found in late medieval German sources. These are, however, historically insignificant. What is more important is that Riemann failed to consider the development of organum to the melismatic style of St. Martial and then to the sustained tenor style.

The treatises on discant (as an improvisation practice), *Quiconques veut des-chanter* (Coussemaker, *Histoire de l'harmonie au moyen-âge*, pp. 245–246) and a Latin reworking of the same (Coussemaker, *Script.* I:324), are dated as 13th century by Bukofzer (see *op. cit.*, col. 571; discussed above, pp. 81–85). Bukofzer also dates *De arte discantandi* as 13th century; however, he places the treatise *De organo* of Guido de Caroli Loco (p. 86 f. above) in the 12th century as well as the Louvain *De organo*. The treatise *Quaedam de arte discantandi* (Coussemaker, *Harmonie*, pp. 274–294) is dated as 13th century in the article "Anonymi," *MGG* I:494, probably because of the sections dealing with mensural notation (Riemann, p. 89 above, dates it as 12th century). Anonymous II is dated as 13th century (*MGG* I:494).

*2. Ernest Ferand does not find the term *res facta* in any source prior to Tinctoris, where it occurs in his *Terminorum musicae diffinitorium*. The term had two meanings: first, "it signified a written, not improvised composition in plain or florid counterpoint"; second, "it signified...florid, not plain counterpoint, whether written or improvised. A third, inconsistent, meaning has been added to it in modern musicology, where the plain, unadorned version of a composition is often referred to as a *res facta* in contradistinction to its florid versions" (Ernest T. Ferand, "What is *Res Facta*" *JAMS* X:141–150; quote is from p. 149).

*3. See Chapter IV, note *14. See also p. 77 for the quotation from Cotton's treatise involving the verb *conglobare* as well as the translation given.

*4. Concerning Franco, see the article "Franco von Köln," *MGG* IV:688–698.

*5. See Anonymous IV, edited and translated into English by Luther Dittmer, Institute of Medieval Music, Brooklyn, N.Y. All further quotations from Anonymous IV are based upon this new edition; permission to quote was granted by the editor.

## CHAPTER VI

*1. See Chapter II, note *7. Riemann here refers to his opinion that Giraldus Cambrensis was describing singing in thirds in his late-12th-century *Descriptio Cambriae*. This cannot be proved, since Giraldus makes no definite reference to thirds, only to part-singing. It has been established, however, that singing in imperfect consonances appeared first in England but was not theoretically recognized until the 13th century (Anonymous IV). Gymel (i.e., *cantus gemellus*) refers to a characteristically English style of polyphony which moves predominantly or completely in imperfect intervals. Its existence cannot be shown earlier than the second half of the 13th century (the "*Nobilis humilis*" is from a 13th-century codex, MS Upsala C233) and it is not discussed theoretically until 1430 (by Guilelmus Monachus). Riemann here supposes the forms gymel and fauxbourdon to be predecessors of organum. Bukofzer, on the contrary, regards gymel as a specifically English development. It is certainly more accurate historically to observe the separate developments of these techniques rather than to regard them as being related. "Native" practices, while they must have existed in some form, can only be surmised; therefore, Riemann's continual references to "natural" or "folk" polyphony must be discounted in favor of more tangible evidence. See the article on "Gymel" in *MGG* V:1139–1146.

*2. The article "Konsonanz-Dissonanz" (*MGG* VII:1508) points out that the third in organum treatises is still a "transition" interval, i.e., it generally occurs in movement to and from perfect consonances. The 11th-century MS Chartres 109 (transcribed in *NOHM* II:282–284), however, shows a remarkable incidence of thirds. Hughes says, "There are as many as 67 thirds, 25 of these set in seven chains of three each and one of four" (p. 284). A recounting of the thirds in these examples showed there were 71 and that there were ten chains of thirds of three each, eight of which occur in parallel motion and two of which involve voice crossing. There is no example of a chain of four thirds in the transcription given by Hughes. While the examples of the Chartres MS show the third employed as an accented interval (corresponding to a textual accent) and as a transition interval, the organum treatises clearly require that the third be a transition interval. The Montpellier organum treatise (12th century) regards the third, next to the fourth and fifth, as a consonance; it teaches that one uses as a beginning interval the unison, octave, fourth, and fifth, occasionally also the third and sixth. It states immediately that the fourth and fifth appear oftener, however, because of their more beautiful sound. Handschin feels that the third spread into composition as a result of its use at the cadence (Handschin, "Der Organum-Traktat von Montpellier," in *Adler Festschrift*, pp. 150–157).

*3. These treatises are dated as follows in the article "Anonymi," *MGG* I: *Discantus positio vulgaris*, 12th century; Anonymous VII (Couss., *Scriptores* I:378–383), entitled *De musica libellus*, around 1200. Coussemaker's Anonymous IV is dated between 1270 and 1280. Luther Dittmer, in his edition of this treatise (see Chapter V, note *4), dates it as 1275 (p. 1).

*4. Heinrich Besseler, in his article "Franco von Köln," in *MGG* IV:688–698, concludes that only one Franco existed. He places Franco's important period in the middle decades of the 13th century (Reese, *Music in the Middle Ages*, p. 289, gives 1250 to after 1280 as the period of Franco's activity), because the motet-technique to which Franco's treatise *Ars cantus mensurabilis* corresponds is that of 1262–1269, with particular reference to the motets of Adam de la Halle. Therefore, the *Ars cantus* must have been written before 1262 (Reese, *op. cit.*, p. 289, dates it shortly after 1280). Besseler also points out the close relationship which existed between Cologne and Paris, with exchange of scholars and other notables a not uncommon occurrence. St. Thomas Aquinas, who studied under Albertus Magnus at the Dominican College in Paris (1245–1248), followed Albertus when Albertus went to Cologne, and remained there until 1252. When visitors came to Paris for a temporary stay they often took the surname *Parisiensis*. Therefore there is every reason to believe that Franco of Paris and Franco of Cologne are the same person. The *Franco Primus* mentioned by Anonymous IV cannot be brought into any historical connection.

There are supposedly two theorists who bear the name Johannes de Garlandia. Attempts have been made to identify these figures more closely, but without definite results. The elder Johannes is assumed to have lived around 1240 and the younger around 1300. The elder is credited with two treatises: 1. *De musica mensurabili positio* (Couss., *Script.* I:97–117), and *De musica mensurabili* (Couss., *Script.* I:175–182). The younger is also credited with two treatises: *Introductio musicae* (Couss., *Script.* I:157–175), and *Optima introductio in contrapunctum* (Couss., *Script.* III:12–13). See "Johannes de Garlandia," *MGG* VII:92–95. Heinrich Hüschen, the author of this article, does not make reference to Bukofzer's claim that the treatise *Optima introductio* is not by Garlandia the Younger, but is anonymous and belongs in the 15th century. The treatise is anonymous in the source used by Coussemaker (according to Bukofzer), and the other sources are vague (these are given in Hüschen's bibliography). On this question see "Discantus," *MGG* III:572; Reese, *Music in the Middle Ages*, p. 287; and Bukofzer, *Geschichte des englischen Diskants*, p. 111.

*5. Besseler agrees that the *Compendium* is not by Franco (*MGG* IV:693–694).

*6. Glenn Haydon (*The Evolution of the 6/4 Chord*, p. 127) disagrees with Riemann's interpretation of "una est perfecta, et non accidens," which Riemann takes to mean "Eine ist an sich konsonant, wird aber durch den Zusammenhang zur Dissonanz...." Haydon is of the opinion that Riemann reads too much into the passage, because the sentence in question is speaking of consonances and not dissonances. Haydon offers the following interpretation: "One [of the consonances] is perfect or imperfect [not-perfect] according to the context in which it occurs."

*7. The *Quatuor principalia* can no longer be attributed to Simon Tunstede. See Gilbert Reaney, "The Manuscript Chantilly," *MD* VIII:73, footnote 51.

*8. An English theorist, Theinred of Dover (last half of 12th century?), may be a predecessor of Odington in his evaluation of the third. He writes (*NOHM* II:339, note 4):

Ditonus qui sesquiquartae sonorum proportioni quae prima sequitur sesquitertiam adeo propinquis est, ut octogesima prima tantum parte maioris termini hic superet hand: quod auditu percipere difficile est.

(The ditonus which consists in sound of the proportion of a sesquiquarta [5/4] which is the next to follow the sesquitertia [4/3] is till then similar [5/4 is relatively the same proportion but 4/3], but the 81 goes beyond the larger number [the ratio 81/64 (the Pythagorean third) is larger than 80/64 (= 5/4) by 1]: this is very difficult for the ear to perceive.)

Thirds are still regarded by Odington as having the proportions 81/64 and 32/27, and he reports that thirds are used as consonances in practice because, due to the "skill of singers," their numerical relationships are closer to 5/4 and 6/5. Later in his treatise, in a compilation of intervals which he regards as "tolerable" (Couss., *Script.* I:202; III in error in *MGG* VI:1346), Odington gives the third with their Pythagorean ratios. See "Intervall," *MGG* VI:1344–1345. Martin Ruhnke, the author of this article, takes issue with Riemann on the identification of the formula given in Chapter VI, p. 134, footnote 11, as a major third. The numbers of the formula, however, actually represent both major and minor triads:

| 64. | 73. | 96. | 128. | 162. | 192. | 256 |
|---|---|---|---|---|---|---|
| | minor | | | major | | |

Riemann has corrected Coussemaker's version by replacing 73 with 81, in an attempt to make the numbers of the formula fit the designations of the diagram, which is as follows:

```
        diapason                              diapason
┌──────────────────────────┐      ┌──────────────────────────┐
      diapente                          diapente
┌──────────────────────┐          ┌──────────────────────┐
ditone    semiditone   diatessaron    ditone   semiditone  diatessaron
┌──────┬──────────┬───────────┬───────────┬──────────┬───────────┐
64       73        96        128         162        192        256
└──────────────────────────────────────┘
         diapason cum ditonus
     └────────────────────────────────────────────────┘
              diapason cum semiditonus
┌──────────────────────────────────────────────────────────┐
         diapason cum diapente
└────────────────────────────────────────────────────────────────────┘
                      disdiapason
```

The diagram seems obviously to require a ditone with a semiditone following; therefore, it seems that Riemann's correction of 73 to 81 is completely justified. See also *1, Chapter XII.

*9. Pseudo-Aristotle (Aristoteles) is now identified as Magister Lambert (see Reese, op. cit., p. 288).

*10. Bukofzer (article "Discantus," MGG III:571) believes that this treatise is dated too early by Riemann, and that it definitely belongs in the 14th century. Reese (op. cit., p. 295) dates it as "late 13th century," but as a conjecture. NOHM II:387 dates it as 13th century. Georgiades regards it as 14th century (Englische Diskanttraktate aus der ersten Hälfte des 15. Jahrhunderts, p. 58).

*11. The rule forbidding consecutive perfect intervals of the same type begins to appear in the treatises of the 14th century. Parallel movements of thirds and sixths are allowed only in groups of two or three. The 15th-century treatises place no restrictions on parallel movement of imperfect consonances, and it is for this reason that Bukofzer regards the Optima introductio, ascribed to Garlandia the Younger, as being a 15th-century source ("Discantus," MGG III:572).

*12. This treatise is apparently an English treatise concerned chiefly with "English discant"; it is very likely the earliest treatise to give an indication of this style ("Discantus," MGG III:576).

*13.

Den Beschluss bilden einige Anweisungen zur Vermeidung des MI contra FA, der unharmonischen Intervalle (relationes non harmonicae). Niemals soll eine Quinte, Oktave, Duodezime oder Doppeloktave als MI contra FA vorkommen (also auch die verminderte Quinte ist gänzlich ausgeschlossen).

*14. The date (1275) which Gerbert gives for the Lucidarium is from the Milan Bibl. Ambrosiana MS D5 and was apparently written in by a later hand. Pirotta, citing O. Strunk ("Marchettus de Padua and the Italian Ars Nova," MD IX:57–71), and Ludwig ("Die Quellen der Motetten ältesten Stils," AfMW V:289–315) have shown that 1275 is several decades too early. Their conclusions vary; the results are as follows:

| | | |
|---|---|---|
| *Lucidarium* | 1309 (Ludwig) | 1317/18 (Pirotta) |
| *Pomerium* | between | 1371/18 (Pirotta) |
| | 1309–1343 (Ludwig) | |

See "Marchettus von Padua," *MGG* VIII:1627.

*15. These ratios expressed in logarithms to the base 10 are as follows:

$$\log \left(\frac{25}{24}\right) \ = 0.01773 \qquad 70.7 \text{ cents}$$

$$\log \left(\frac{135}{128}\right) = 0.02312 \qquad 92.2 \text{ cents}$$

$$\log \left(\frac{16}{15}\right) \ = 0.02803 \qquad 111.7 \text{ cents}$$

*16. The "exact meaning" of the term *color* varies not only in different periods but within the same period. The meaning which Riemann discusses here is clarified by Gilbert Reaney in his article on "Color" in *MGG* II:1566–1567. Reaney writes as follows:

> The word *color* was employed (in the sense of an ornament) in place of *musica ficta*, particularly by Marchettus of Padua and Prosdocimus. This should not be surprising, for one of the reasons for the use of *musica ficta* was *causa pulchritudinis*, and a definition for *color* in use in the 13th century was *pulchritudo soni*. Prosdocimus explains that *musica ficta* was discovered for the purpose of ornamenting (*colorare*) consonances, wherever necessary (Couss., *Script.* III:198a, 251b).

## CHAPTER VII

*1. This chapter, and expositions of the same material in other of his works, have made Riemann notorious, for he misled students of music history for many years by his interpretation of *fauxbourdon*, until in the middle 1930's musicologists renewed investigation of this puzzling and yet important technique of 15th-century music. Riemann, with his predilection for the third as a "natural" sonority, placed considerable emphasis on the fauxbourdon style and assumed its origins to be earlier than they can be shown. This style was undoubtedly important and influential in the development of harmonic consciousness in the 15th century, or as Reese states (*Music in the Renaissance*, p. 65):

> Composers, influenced by its mellifluousness, were led to avoid the harsher asperities of earlier days and to smooth out the harmonic texture even when they were not writing in actual fauxbourdon.

Because of the controversial nature of this subject, a résumé of the findings of various specialists is given here in order to prepare the reader for the many inaccuracies of Chapter VII. Such a résumé may also be found in the article "Aux origines du fauxbourdon" by Susanne Clercx (*Revue de Musicologie*, XL:151–165). A bibliography may be found at the end of the article "Fauxbourdon" (*MGG* III:1897), and because a number of additional items have appeared since the publication of that article, these and others consulted have been placed in the annotated bibliography following the commentary, under the heading "Faux-bourdon and English Discant."

Riemann made no distinction between the continental and English practice of the "sixth-chord" style. Therefore it is necessary to give a definition of each before proceeding. The distinction was established first by Manfred Bukofzer in his *Geschichte des englischen Diskants und des Fauxbourdons nach den theoretischen Quellen* (1936), and Thrasybulos Georgiades, *Englische Diskanttraktate aus der ersten Hälfte des* 15. *Jahrhunderts* (1937) though independent conclusions were reached in both works. English discant (which is a designation by Bukofzer) is a style of im-provisation over a *cantus firmus* consisting of chains of sixth-chords with perfect consonances used at the beginnings and ends of phrases. The *cantus firmus* is the lowest voice according to the theorists of this style, and it must remain without ornamentation. This improvisation was accomplished through a system of "sights" (Riemann: *Leseweise*), which Bukofzer explains as follows ("Popular Polyphony in the Middle Ages," *MQ* XXVI:42):

> A sight is merely an expedient whereby the two improvising singers gauge the upper parts from a reading of the monodic chant alone. They start an octave and a fifth above the first note, with the apparent intention that they and the singer of the chant should all sing the liturgical melody at three levels. After the first note, however, each im-provising singer imagines that he drops to a level a third below what he sees. But since, in singing against the imaginary line, the improvisers preserve the same distance as, at the beginning, they maintained against the written one, the singer who started a fifth above the *cantus* will be singing a third above it, while the singer who started an octave above the *cantus* will be singing a sixth above it. At the cadence the improvisers return to the same distances as separated them from the *cantus* at the beginning of the phrase with the same intention as prevailed there.

There are no musical sources for this simple style, but when more contrary motion is introduced, then notation of compositions becomes necessary. In notated compositions it no longer becomes necessary for the *cantus firmus* to remain in the lowest voice; it appears occasionally in the top voice but most often in the middle voice ("Discantus," *MGG* III:573–577). The earliest treatise on English discant is the *Opinio* of Richard Cutell, which Bukofzer relates to the 14th century. Other treatises are the Pseudo-Chilston (which Riemann dates *ca.* 1375–1400) but which contemporary musicology dates as having been written after 1430 ("Chilston," *MGG* II:1194–1195), the treatise of Lionel Power (Bukofzer characterizes this treatise as an attempt to elevate the improvisation practice to a higher level. Parallel motion of imperfect consonances is restricted to three. Power allows three sixths and three tenths one after the other in his examples despite frequent contrary motion. Imperfect consonances are in the foreground in this treatise), and the treatises of Hothby and Guilelmus Monachus. The basic difference between continental discant and English discant is the preference of the former for perfect consonances, the latter for imperfect consonances.

The major study of fauxbourdon is Heinrich Besseler's *Bourdon and Fauxbourdon* (1950). Besseler believes that English discant and fauxbourdon are independent developments, though he admits the possibility of English influence as far as the

basic sonority (the sixth chord), common to both styles, is concerned. Fauxbourdon technique is characteristic of completed compositions rather than
improvisation; the *cantus firmus* is in the uppermost voice—the *superius*—and it is
treated as a polyphonic melody, usually with coloration. Besseler regards Dufay
as the founder of the fauxbourdon style, perhaps as a result of some indirect
contact with English practice. The designation *faux bourdon* occurs for the first
time in musical sources in a Dufay composition, the closing section of the *Missa St.
Jacobi*, which is marked as *post communio*. The tenor bears the marking *faux bourdon*
and there is an inscription by the *superius*:

> Si trinum queras / a summo tolle figuras
> Et simul incipito / dyatessaron insubeundo

> (If you would find a third part / take the notes from the highest
> And begin at the same time / proceeding at the fourth below.)

(There is a plate of the MS containing this example in Besseler's article on fauxbourdon in *MGG* III:1891–1892.) Parallel fourths were, of course, strictly forbidden as late as 1412 by Prosdocimus, but Dufay, using the device of the canon,
circumvented the prohibition of parallel fourths. The canon in Dufay's period
was an inscription or rule which gave "a clue as to the intended execution of a
composition which is purposely notated in an incomplete or obscure manner"
(*HD*, p. 112). The canonic inscription given above instructed the singer (or
player?) of the contratenor (the part omitted in the notated MS) to proceed in
parallel fourths with the *superius* or *cantus firmus*, following that voice with respect
to its rhythm, text, and melodic contour:

> Not to lead two voices in parallel movement contrary to the rules, but to *double* one
> voice through the use of an interval canon! This is the central idea of fauxbourdon
> (Besseler, *op. cit.*, pp. 16–17).

The composer placed himself under the restrictions of his canonic prescription,
removing himself from the jurisdiction of the usual methods and procedures, and
had to carry out the same interval succession from beginning to end.

Sources for fauxbourdon are given in Besseler, *op. cit.*, and also in a convenient
summary in Ernest Trumble, *Fauxbourdon, an Historical Survey* I: 6–12. Trumble
devotes space to an extended discussion of the canonic aspect of fauxbourdon,
suggesting that the combination of a Latin inscription plus a vernacular designation (*faux bourdon*) was not only unorthodox, but may have had a humorous or
cryptic meaning (see Trumble, *op. cit.*, pp. 16–23).

The main fauxbourdon controversy concerns itself with the origin of the term
and the roles which England and the continent played in its development.
Bukofzer and Besseler prefer to regard the English and continental developments
as separate and distinct, though Besseler grants the possibility of English influence. Georgiades (*op. cit.*) believes that both should be regarded as part of a
single unity, and that continental practice is an offshoot of English practice. A
numerous series of articles in *AM* gave testimonial to the fact that the question
was not a closed one. The two major contestants in the discussion were Rudolf von
Ficker and Heinrich Besseler, and one of the points of contention was whether

the term *faburden* was an anglicization of *fauxbourdon*. A philologist, Hermann M. Flasdieck, was called in by von Ficker to support his claim that the term *faburden* had an independent English origin. Flasdieck contributed a detailed article in *AM* XXV:111–127, which was, in turn, rejected by another philologist, Gustav Kirchner. Flasdieck's final contribution was another lengthy examination of the problem in the philological journal *Anglia* (74:188–238) which has not since been challenged (see also Brian Trowell, "Faburden and Fauxbourdon," *MD* XIII:43–78).

Another viewpoint on English discant is expressed by Sylvia W. Kenney in her article "'English Discant' and Discant in England," *MQ* XLV:26–48. This author feels that the use of the term "discant" in connection with an improvisatory three-voice parallel technique is a "fundamental contradiction." She is also unable to relate this technique to actual music by such composers as Power, which reveals no trace of the technique (there are some traces to be seen in the example by Power printed in *HAM*, pp. 67–69, but only traces). Bukofzer also remarks in his essay "The Music of the Old Hall Manuscript," *Studies in Medieval Renaissance*, p. 49:

> The scarcity of English discant [in the Old Hall MS compositions] is especially striking because most of the treatises describing it stem from precisely the time of O [ld] H [all], the early 15th century. However, the compositions of OH are examples of *res facta* and the improvised polyphonization of plainsong may have been practiced without being written down.

Discant is rather, according to Kenney, a style involving "contrary motion between two rhythmically equal voices" (p. 47) with the exclusive use of consonance. Power's discussion of sights, she feels, implies nothing more than differences in range (p. 34).

The result of many detailed investigations appears to emphasize, more and more, the separate development of English and continental styles which have the 6/3 chord as a basic sonority in common. Whether a fauxbourdon practice ever came to England from the continent now seems suspect in the light of findings described in the article "Faburden and Fauxbourdon" by Brian Trowell in *MD* XIII:43–78. These will be discussed in connection with the Pseudo-Chilston treatise quoted in part in Chapter VII.

*2. It is difficult to evaluate this source because Anonymous IV not only failed to mention the term for the practice he described, but did not indicate the exact intervals employed in this singing.

*3. The treatise described by Riemann is anonymous, and the authorship of Chilston was assumed by him because another treatise by Chilston occurs in the same MS (British Museum MS Landsdowne 763). Riemann brought Chilston into connection with fauxbourdon, regarding him as the first writer to describe this technique. The MS, which is a collection of theoretical writings, is dated as *ca.* 1450 by Besseler ("Chilston," *MGG* II:1194–1195). The anonymous Pseudo-Chilston treatise is reproduced in Sanford B. Meech, "Three Musical Treatises in English from a Fifteenth Century Manuscript," *Speculum* 10:235–269. Meech gives an emended version of this treatise (it was printed by Hawkins, *General History of Music*, in a corrupt version which was used by Riemann), as well as a translation. Meech's translation is not reliable, however, since it is based upon Riemann's interpretation.

*4. English influence is generally acknowledged not only by contemporary musicologists but by writers of the period. Tinctoris, writing in 1476, says:

At this time, consequently, the possibilities of our music have been so marvelously increased that there appears to be a new art, if I may so call it, whose fount and origin is held to be among the English, of whom Dunstable stood forth as chief. Contemporary with him in France were Dufay and Binchoys, to whom directly succeeded the moderns Ockeghem, Busnoys, Regis, and Caron, who are the most excellent of all the composers I have ever heard. Nor can the English, who are popularly said to shout while the French sing, stand comparison with them. For the French contrive music in the newest manner for the new times, while the English continue to use one and the same style of composition, which shows a wretched poverty of invention. (Strunk, *op. cit.*, p. 199.)

*5. According to Eitner (*Quellenlexikon der Musiker*) the name "Lionel Polbero" appears only in MS cod. 37, Bologna. The excerpt from Power's treatise is given here in translation; the original can be found in Meech, *op. cit.*, in a definitive version (Hawkins' was corrupt). Meech's translation of this excerpt is followed to some extent, but it has been altered at various points for greater clarity. Riemann gives the impression that Power's treatise is a fragment. The remainder of the treatise (Meech, *op. cit.*, pp. 243–258) deals with all of the sights and includes musical examples.

*6. The Landsdowne 763 (Pseudo-Chilston) is also in Meech, *op. cit.*, in a definitive version (Riemann used the corrupt version in Hawkins). It is given here in translation, utilizing Meech's translation to some extent, but departing from it when greater accuracy and clarity result. Because of the controversial nature of the section on *Faburden*, it has been given in a transliterated version (see note *7 below) from the article "Faburden and Fauxbourdon," *MD* XIII:47–48. It is in this section on *faburden* that Riemann made basic errors in translation. For example the following:

The sight of *Faburden* the which hath but two sights: a third above the plain-song in sight, the which is a sixth from the treble in voice, and an even with the plainsong in Sight, the which is an octave from the Treble in voice.

(The sight [mode of singing] of *Faburden* has but two sights: one imagined a third above the plain-song which is a sixth from [i.e., below] the Treble in actual sound and the other which is imagined in unison with the plainsong, which is an octave from the treble in voice.)

is translated by Riemann as:

Die Manier des Fauxbourdon...welcher zwei Leseweisen hat, die in der Unterterz des *Cantus planus*, welche eine Sexte effektiven Abstand für den Treble bedeutet, und die im Einklange mit dem *Cantus planus* welche eine Oktave Abstand für den Treble ergibt.

(The mode of fauxbourdon...which has two sights: that which is a third below the *cantus planus* and which is for the Treble in effect a Sixth, and that which is in unison with the *cantus planus* but which results in the interval of an octave from the Treble.)

In other words, Riemann has simply translated "below" for "above" and in doing so has turned the passage upside down as far as its meaning was concerned. He equated the position of the *cantus firmus* of English discant (in the lowest voice) with the position of the *cantus firmus* of fauxbourdon. We know now, however, that the *cantus firmus* of fauxbourdon is in the upper voice. We come, then, in relation to the quoted section on *faburden* in the anonymous Landsdowne 763 treatise to the question of the relationship between *fauxbourdon* and *faburden*. Brian Trowell (*op. cit.*) shows that *faburden* is actually not related to the continental practice, and in agreement with Flasdieck regards the term as well as the technique as having independent English origin. *Faburden*, then, is a practice which evolved from the practice of English discant. The vital distinction between *faburden* and *fauxbourdon* is the location of the plainsong in the middle voice, for the anonymous author writes: "These two accords (intervals) the Faburdener must rule by the Mean of the plainsong." Riemann interprets this to mean that the Mean must regulate itself according to the plainsong, but the author clearly writes "Mean *of* the plainsong."

Trowell writes further:

In a Faburden piece, the plain-song lies in the middle voice or Mean. Below it the tenor or Faburdener improvises in fifths and thirds by imagining unisons with or thirds above the written plainsong and pitching his voice a fifth below the imagined notes. He should begin with a sung fifth and move on in sung thirds, interposing fifths whenever he likes, provided that he does not sing two in succession; at the end of a word in the plainsong he should cadence by singing a fifth, preceded by as many as four successive thirds if the plainsong lies low. Cadences are to be avoided when the plainsong closes on b, e, and their octaves. The Treble doubles the plainsong Mean throughout at the fourth above.

*7. It must be emphasized here that the "sights" technique belongs to the improvisation practice of the English rather than continental fauxbourdon. A fauxbourdon composition is just that: a completed musical composition or a section of a musical composition which has been notated in two parts, the third part (the middle voice) being sung or played a fourth below the *superius*, which is the part bearing the plainsong.

*8. The translation of the Garlandia quotation in footnote 1 follows Riemann's translation of the same on page 159 f. A new translation of this puzzling passage, however, helps to clarify its content and show, at the same time, that it has nothing to do with the "sights" technique:

Triplum, in its stricter sense, must be consonant with the first [*cantus firmus*] and second [*duplum*] voice, though farther removed from them, if one does not at the same time represent it [the *triplum*] in the concordance by a sound which is the same as one of its (the concordance's) members.

Garlandia is not without difficult or abstruse passages; however, if in this case one attempts the most literal rendition of the Latin, the meaning becomes more evident. Garlandia is saying here that the *triplum* must be consonant with the *cantus* and the *duplum*, but it can also be in unison with one of these two voices. An examination of a three-part composition of Garlandia's period will show that this is a frequent occurrence (see the three-voice conductus *Hac in anni janua* in *HAM*, p. 41).

The testimony of Anonymous IV is much too vague to be adduced as evidence.

*9. According to Trowell the *cantus planus* would be in the middle voice and not the lower voice as Riemann indicates here. In the following paragraph Riemann attempts to find relationships to the Power and Chilston treatises in treatises by Anonymous V and Anonymous XIII. The question posed by such association is the extent of the relationship existing between English and continental discant practices. Bukofzer ("Discantus," *MGG* III:559–578) tends to separate the two developments, whereas Kenney ("'English Discant' and Discant in England," *MQ* XLV:26–48) implies a closer connection.

*10. The Reading Rota or "Summer" canon finds opinion again divided as to its date of origin. Bukofzer ("'Sumer is icumen in': A Revision," *University of California Publications in Music* II, 1944) revised the older view that the Summer canon dated from 1240, adducing evidence for redating it 1310–1325, as well as questioning the authorship of John of Fornsete. Handschin dates the Summer canon as the middle of the 13th century in his large and detailed study "The Summer Canon and Its Background," *MD* III:55–94 and IV:65–113. The piece itself is reproduced in *HAM*, pp. 44–45.

*11. About the life and activity of Guilelmus there remains no information ("Guilelmus Monachus," *MGG* V:1084–1087). Scholars have attributed various dates to him, but the last half of the 15th century seems to be most likely according to the contents of his treatise *De praeceptis artis musicae et practicae compendiosus libellus*. As Riemann states, Guilelmus used white notation, which came into general use in the last half of the 15th century.

*12. Bukofzer believes that Guilelmus is describing English discant under the incorrect heading of modus *faulxbourdon* ("Fauxbourdon Revisited," *MQ* XXXVIII: 22–40): Trowell, on the other hand, believes he is describing the *faburden* technique (*op. cit.*, pp. 64–65). Guilelmus does say that he is describing *Faulxbourdon* as practiced by the English; he also makes no reference to a *cantus firmus* but here only speaks of the "tenor."

*13. On this subject see "Gymel," *MGG* V:1139–1146.

## CHAPTER VIII

*1. It is very doubtful that enough evidence can be amassed to give certain knowledge about the rhythmic performance of early music. Most of our present information about this aspect of early music is based on deduction and conjecture; the question of its rhythm is still a controversial one. The performance today of ecclesiastical chant by various *scholae* may be aesthetically satisfactory yet a historical basis for these performance practices is not clearly established. The theories of rhythm in ecclesiastical chant are discussed in Willi Apel, *Gregorian Chant*, pp. 126–132, in Gustave Reese, *Music in the Middle Ages*, pp. 140–148, and in the article "Choral," *MGG* II:1288–1295. It appears to be evident that a rhythmic performance was characteristic of early ecclesiastical chant, according to Aribo who wrote in 1070:

> In earlier times not only the inventors of melodies but also the singers themselves used great circumspection that everything should be invented and sung in proportion. This consideration perished some time ago and is now entirely buried (quoted in Apel, *op. cit.* p. 132).

See also the quotations by Riemann on pp. 132–134.

The structure of hymn texts shows two characteristics that must have influenced their rhythmic delivery: first, all strophes were similarly constructed and could be sung to the same melody, and second, within each strophe the number of syllables for each verse remained the same or almost so. The order of the verse in early hymnology (before A.D. 600) was determined quantitatively, that is, through the longs and shorts of the syllables, the metric principle of antiquity. Around A.D. 600 the metric principle of the medieval period, determined by accented and unaccented syllables, was clearly visible as a basic system of order. A hymn melody could be used for a number of different texts, some melodies being typical of certain feast days. The exact performance of the rhythmic content of the hymn in the light of its very definite poetic order is, like ecclesiastical chant, still unestablished. Certain sources show attempts to indicate mensural values in the notation; codices from St. Gall, Einsiedeln, and Reichenau, *ca.* 1000, are the earliest that are interpreted to have such values (see the article "Hymnus," *MGG* VI:995–1018). It must be noted, however, that the above sources are in staffless neumes and the pitches cannot be read; the earliest decipherable sources are from the 12th and 13th centuries, other than a hymn melody *Aeterna Christi munera* contained in Daseian notation in the *Musica enchiriadis*.

In the older form of sequence,

> as a general rule there is no doubt of the priority of the melody, but this did not prevent the poet from expanding it or compressing it, or modifying its structure in the interests of his text (Handschin, "Trope, Sequence, and Conductus," *NOHM* II:158).

Rhyme was not used in earlier forms, but rather assonance at the beginning and the middle of a phrase.

> Since it was the rule that the text added to a melisma must be syllabic, it could not be metrical or in any regular rhythm: a group of syllables forming one or more words had to fit a group of notes forming a musical phrase (Handschin, *op. cit.*, p. 147).

Handschin assumes that the music of the trope and sequence was in "accordance with the taste of the times" (p. 148) and independent of the text. He also feels that this music had some affinity for the secular music of the time, in agreement with Riemann's supposition (*NOHM* II:149).

Changes of style occur around the 11th century.

The words are in regular verse form: there is a marked tendency to alternate accented and unaccented syllables, as well as to equalize the length of the lines, and the ends of the lines are distinguished by rhyme (Handschin, *op. cit.*, p. 161).

The priority of melody over text is no longer a characteristic. (For a complete study of the trope, sequence, and conductus, see Handschin, *op. cit.*, pp. 128–174, and Willi Apel, *Gregorian Chant*, pp. 429–464.)

*2. As far as ecclesiastical chant is concerned, this observation cannot be considered valid. One of the fundamental traits of Gregorian chant is the close relationship of text and melody (see Apel, *op. cit.*, pp. 266–275). Continuing, Apel says that agreement between textual and melodic divisions is also a "basic principle" but that some exceptions exist. These can be seen by taking a complete melody which is used for several different texts and observing the relationship between music and text. In some cases the textual and melodic divisions are not the same (see pp. 268–270); it is also not possible to say that poor adaptation is a characteristic of earlier or later periods, since examples can be found in both.

*3. Concerning these problems see Willi Apel, *Gregorian Chant*, Bruno Stäblein's article "Choral" in *MGG* II:1265–1303, and Gustave Reese, *Music in the Middle Ages*, pp. 164–193. For a view which differs in some points concerning Christian chant, see Jacques Handschin, *Musikgeschichte im Überblick*, pp. 95–153.

*4. Apel, in his summary of rhythmic theories of Gregorian chant, is of the opinion (*op. cit.*, pp. 126–132) that the neumes are justifiably distinguished as representing longer and shorter values but that these should not be forced into any rigid metrical scheme. Preferable would be "flexibility and variability" in the interpretation of note durations, with the realization that the rhythm of chant, like the rhythm of folk melody "is bound to undergo variations from individual to individual, and even more so from generation to generation" (p. 126).

*5. Hans Oesch (*Guido von Arezzo*, pp. 100–104) has shown this treatise to be a genuine Odonic treatise.

*6. Hieronymus (Jerome) de Moravia is, of course, a very late witness and hardly acceptable as evidence for any system of chant rhythm other than his own. Therefore the validity of his remarks for earlier practice is not established as well as the extent of its application to the chant of his period. Gustave Reese (*op. cit.*, pp. 145–146) gives clearer readings from Hieronymus' rules than Riemann does:

All notes, says Jerome, are of equal value with certain exceptions. Among these are the first note which, if it represents the final of the mode (but not otherwise), has twice the normal value; the second of several notes over one syllable of text, which likewise has a double value unless it is immediately preceded or followed by a note itself doubled as the result of some other exception to the rule; the last note before a pause, which, like the pause itself, varies in length according to the portion of the piece it concludes, the note always being longer than the pause to the extent of one normal time value. If from four to seven notes (or even more) are connected with one another musically (regardless of textual considerations), they consume nine time-values—these being disposed in groups of three—and the manner in which the available time is divided among the notes is clearly specified, some of the notes having three times the normal value, some (if there are more than four) less than the normal value.

*7. This is, of course, only an opinion. Riemann also does not consider the organa of St. Martial and Compostela with its characteristic notation in Aequitanian neumes. This notation, towards the end of the 12th century, changed to more definite shapes "characterized by the use of square forms" (Willi Apel, *The Notation of Polyphonic Music*, p. 217), which notation is now known as "square" notation. This notation contains single notes and groups of notes (ligatures) which Apel (p. 217) refers to as syllabic and melismatic notation. It was an innovation of the late 12th century to give these signs definite rhythmic values. William Waite (*The Rhythm of 12th Century Polyphony*, p. 8) ascribes this innovation to Leonin as a result of an influence (direct or indirect) from Augustine's treatise on metrics, *De musica*. These rhythmic values were contained in a system we know as the "rhythmic modes."

*8. For explanations of this system see Willi Apel, *Notation of Polyphonic Music*, pp. 220–281, William Waite, *The Rhythm of 12th Century Polyphony*, pp. 13–127, and Carl Parrish, *The Notation of Medieval Music*, pp. 73–107. This notational system is also discussed in Gustave Reese, *Music in the Middle Ages*, pp. 272–286.

*9. We are here concerned with a very difficult problem in the history of notation, i.e., whether binary or ternary meter is the earliest. Riemann is of the opinion that binary meter antedates the ternary, and this opinion colors his exposition in his chapters on notation. A great point of contention has been the interpretation of a passage from Walter Odington:

> Longa autem apud priores organistas duo tantum habuit tempora, sic in metris; sed postea ad perfectionem dicitur (ducitur), ut si trium temporum (The longa equalled two *tempora* among the first composers of organa, as in meter; later it acquired perfection in that it had three *tempora*...).

In this quotation from Couss., *Script.* I:235, *dicitur* (from *dicere*, to name or to call) is emended by Handschin ("The Summer Canon and Its Background," *MD* III:76) to *ducitur* (from *ducere*, to take on or receive) following the MS Cambridge Corpus Christi College 410, f. 30v.

Apel (*Notation of Polyphonic Music*, pp. 220–221) and Waite (*Rhythm of 12th Century Polyphony*, p. 24) regard as untenable the assumption that Odington here referred to binary rhythm, since the period prior to the one in which Odington wrote was the period of Notre Dame composition. In this period the binary longa always appeared with a breve, which combination results in triple time. A chronological consideration also enters into the discussion. The earliest presentation of the rhythmic modes is contained in the *Discantus positio vulgaris*, where they are presented in the form which may be seen on p. 135. The first, second, and sixth modes are called *rectus* in all of the treatises dealing with modal theory except the one written by Magister Lambert (Pseudo-Aristotle); the others are referred to as *ultra mensuram*. *Rectus* may be thought of as "normal," whereas *ultra mensuram* would represent that which was "beyond" the normal or characteristic measurement. At any rate, the first two modes are regarded as being the oldest (they are the most common in the Notre Dame repertoire), and the others (excepting the sixth mode) are assumed to be later additions. The *ultra mensuram* makes reference to the fact that in modes two, three, and four the longa is ternary rather than binary as in modes one and two:

| Mode I | ♩ ♪ ♩ ♪ | Mode III | ♩. ♪ ♩ |
|---|---|---|---|
| | L B L B | | L B B |
| Mode II | ♪ ♩ ♪ ♩ | Mode IV | ♪ ♩ ♩. |
| | B L B L | | B B L |
| | | Mode V | ♩. ♩. |
| | | | L L |

In this light Odington's statement has this meaning: that in the first modes to appear (one and two) the longa was binary (but always appearing in conjunction with a breve), but in later times, with the addition of modes three, four, and five, it received a ternary value as well.

The possibility exists, however, that Odington is referring to the musical practice of his country (England) rather than that of the continent. Luther Dittmer, following Handschin, feels that Odington is referring to a longa which underwent a transition from binary to ternary rhythm, and that Odington is stating that the use of binary rhythm is an older practice. See Handschin, "Summer Canon...," *MD* III:72–78, and Luther Dittmer, "Binary Rhythm, Musical Theory, and the Worcester Fragments," *MD* VII:39–57. Concerning binary rhythm see also Gustave Reese, *op. cit.*, p. 274.

*10. This author implies that, following the principles of the rhythmic modal system, a longa can only be imperfected when it is followed or preceded by a breve, or a combination of notes equal to a breve. A longa by itself is a ternary value, so a binary longa without the accompanying breve necessary to give it that value is an impossibility. His second complaint is that a ternary longa is said to "exceed the measure," i.e., is *ultra mensuram*. This complaint is justified in that the ternary longa is a perfect value and if it does exceed the measure (that is to say, if it goes beyond the "normal"), then an imperfect value would have to be regarded as perfect.

*11. The ligatures in the following example have rhythmic meaning in the modal system; they are *binariae* and are generally equivalent to a breve-longa (♪ ♩). In the case of additional repeated notes their values can become reversed, that is, to longa-breve. See Apel, *Notation of Polyphonic Music*, pp. 224–225.

*12. The ligatures in the following example are *ternariae*; their rhythmic meaning varies according to the mode. In the first mode they are equivalent to longa, breve, longa; in the second mode, breve, longa, breve; in the third and fourth modes, breve, *brevis altera*, longa (♪ ♩ ♩.); and longa, longa, longa in the fifth mode.

*13. See Chapter VI, note *4 on the identification of the two Francos.

*14. For a ligature to have propriety (*cum proprietate*) it must begin with a breve, and to have perfection (*cum perfectione*) it must end with a longa. For a ligature to be without propriety (*sine proprietate*) and without perfection, it must begin with a longa and end with a breve (see Apel, *Notation...*, p. 89).

*15. Riemann translates "Sed duo puncti sumentur hic (sc. in modo tertio) pro uno..." as "...dass in denselben zwei Noten für eine Zeit (nämlich die gerade, leichte) gerechnet werden..." (p. 167 of the second edition). First of all, this quotation from Garlandia applies to the third mode (♩. ♪ ♩), and he is saying, "But two notes (*puncti*) may be taken here (that is, in the third mode) in the place of one...." Riemann interprets this to mean "two notes for one value" (namely, the imperfect or unaccented value). If this is true, then the final *brevis altera* would be divided in two, resulting in ♩. ♫♪. Waite (*op. cit.*, p. 110) glosses this quotation with the explanation "two breves instead of a single longa." Since the longa is ternary in the third mode it could only be divided into a breve and a *brevis altera*; however, this is not clarified by Waite. Apel (*Notation...*, p. 244) cites the same passage out of context (that is, without the reference to the third mode), and his illustrations above the quoted passage show no relationship to this mode.

*16. The rhythmic modes should not be thought of in terms of beats, i.e., the feeling for a pulse characteristic of 18th- and 19th-century music. They are rather successions of patterns, the pattern of the first mode being ♩ ♪, the pattern of the second mode being ♪ ♩, the pattern of the third mode being ♩. ♪ ♩, and so on. Riemann's interpretation of the second mode as an upbeat mode is erroneous. Garlandia states (Couss. I:106):

Omne quod fit impari debet concordari cum omni illo quod fit in impari, si sit in primo, vel secundo, vel tertio modo (All odd-numbered notes [of one part] must form a consonance with the odd-numbered notes [of the other part] in the first as well as the second or third mode).

The odd-numbered note in the second mode is the first one, and it is on this note, and not the second, that a consonance is required. Apel (*Notation...*, p. 220) states that the second mode should "not be understood as the first mode with an upbeat; the accent falls here not on the longa but on the breve: ♪ ♩ ♪ ♩...."

*17. For an article on Franco see *MGG* IV:688–698. The *Ars cantus mensurabilis* is available in English translation in Oliver Strunk, *Source Readings in Music History*, pp. 139–159. The Latin text, wherever Franco has been here quoted, has been emended following the edition of the *Ars cantus* contained in the *Tractatus de musica* of Hieronymus de Moravia, edited by Simon M. Scerba, O.P. The translation of the Prologue to the *Ars cantus* contained in footnote 19 is from Strunk's English translation (pp. 139–140).

*18. This is, however, not true of the second mode. The terms *impares* and *pares* are more clearly translated as "odd-numbered" and "even-numbered." In the case of the second mode the first note (a breve) is odd-numbered and would be that part of the pattern (rather than beat; see note *16 above) for which a consonance is required.

*19. The term *tempus* is defined by Anonymous IV as follows:

A tone of one *tempus* may be said to be a tone receiving a time value [*tempus*] which is not the smallest, nor yet the largest, but which can be produced in a moderately short time, so that it can be divided in rapid motion into two, three, or four more [lesser values] by the human voice...(quoted from Waite, *op. cit.*, p. 15).

Franco defines the *tempus* as follows: "What we call a *tempus* is that which is a minimum in fullness of voice" (Strunk, *op. cit.*, p. 144). By this we must understand the *tempus* as the unit of musical time in the 13th century, equivalent to the quarter-note in our own time, that is, the breve. Riemann translates *tempora* (plural of *tempus*) as *Schlagzeiten* (beats), whereas one must think of patterns of values rather than beats in the modal system.

*20. Riemann translates *principium perfectionis* as "Anfang jedes Taktes" (the beginning of every measure [unit of measure]), when it is, more precisely, the beginning of every perfection. He is in error when he speaks of the first part of the longa as the value which demands a consonance, for we have seen that this is not true for the second mode, which he interprets incorrectly (see notes *16 and *18 above). His representation of modes two to four is also incorrect.

## CHAPTER IX

*1. See the commentary for Chapter VII on the subject of fauxbourdon, as well as the items in the bibliography under the heading "Fauxbourdon and English Discant."

*2. There is no definite evidence for any identification of Garlandia (see "Johannes de Garlandia," *MGG* VII:92–95). Riemann, assuming that Garlandia was an Englishman, erroneously read traces of the "sights" technique into Garlandia's writings. The four-voice fauxbourdon called *falsobordone* by some contemporary musicologists (see Trumble, *Fauxbourdon*, p. 13, for this distinction and a discussion of the terminology) is a development of the early 16th century and cannot be brought into relationship with the *tripla* and *quadrupla* of the Notre Dame period of composition.

*3. See Chapter VII, note *8 for another interpretation of this passage.

*4. See Chapter VIII, note *16.

*5. Riemann translates *puncta imparia* as "*ungerade Zeiten*," which has here, in turn, been translated into English as "uneven-numbered (or odd-numbered) notes" for the sake of greater clarity, and to avoid the tendency to ascribe strong and weak beats to the musical style under discussion. Accent undoubtedly played a role in the rhythmic concept of this style, but groups of patterns of long and short durations rather than beats are more characteristic of it.

*6. Riemann gives a capsule translation of this lengthy quotation from Anonymous IV. It is given in full here from the English translation by Luther Dittmer (p. 65):

The rules for the *triplum* are as follows: In the first mode, all uneven-numbered notes must form consonances with all odd-numbered notes of the *duplum*. Thus, the first note will form a consonance with the first note, the third with the third, the fifth with the fifth and so on for all individual notes.

Then we also state that every uneven-numbered note must form a consonance with every odd-numbered note of the tenor; the first with the first, the third with the third, the fifth with the fifth, and so on for all individual notes.

Thus in summarizing, we find that the *duplum* will form consonances with the tenor on all uneven-numbered notes, the *triplum* similarly with the tenor, and the *triplum* with the *duplum*; thus any one note will form a consonance with any other note, and similarly this one with the other two, because all three notes must consonate and form consonances with each other.

All even-numbered notes in the *triplum* can be composed without regard to this; they may form consonances or not. Good performers, however, also consider the even-numbered notes and concern themselves with these, and consider their relationship to the *duplum* and to the tenor. Thus, if the *duplum* goes up in pitch, the *triplum* will fall, and vice versa. This is followed for one, two, three, or more steps.

In a similar fashion, they allow the *triplum* to move with the tenor for one, two, three, or more steps. It is, however, regarded as reprehensible if two voices move upwards excessively in parallel motion with one another, no matter which voices are involved....

In the same manner a *quadruplum* can be added to the aforementioned. If it is also conceived in the first mode, every odd-numbered note must form a consonance with the same uneven-numbered note in the *triplum*, *duplum*, and tenor. If it now moves upwards in parallel motion with one of the other voice-parts, it can be fashioned so that it will go well for two or three notes as stated above in regard to the other voices. It may, however, move in the opposite direction, proceeding obliquely now to the *triplum*, now to the *duplum*, now to the tenor, or it may move along in unison with one of them....

It should be noted that the *quadruplum* may occasionally form a discord with the other voices, which is not possible between the *triplum* and the voices presented below it. Thus, the *quadruplum* might form a major or minor third with the tenor or *duplum*, and the other three might form consonances of an octave, fifth, or fourth. Thus, it will be necessary to have a discordant sixth, if a major or minor third is formed above the tenor, and this is quite astonishing.

*7. The text of the *Discantus positio vulgaris* is emended from Simon Cserba's new edition (Hieronymus de Moravia, O.P., *Tractatus de musica* [Regensburg, 1935]). Cserba emends Coussemaker's unreliable version from *Discantus ipse est idem in pausis*, etc., to *in prosis* and makes a similar emendation in three further places. The resulting change in the translation has been made in brackets and the meaning becomes considerably clearer in all cases.

*8. Cserba's edition emends *aversus* and *conversus* to read *antecedens* and *consequens*. Riemann's translation of this excerpt is not completely reliable; therefore it is given again here with some emendations and additions, including a translation of the last sentence given only in Latin:

The *copula* is very important for the discant, which no one can properly understand without it. That which is called *copula* is between organum and discant or, expressed in a different manner, *copula* is that which is presented in *modus rectus* equivalent [*equipollente*] to a unison. Or, in another way, *copula* is a large number of notes [*puncti*]. *Punctus* means here wherever there are a number of lines and this part is divided into two equal parts. The first part is called the antecedent and the second part the consequent, and each part contains a number of lines. A line is drawn wherever there are a great number of species [=intervals] such as the unison or another kind, according to the number arranged in the intended *ordo*.

Just exactly what a *copula* is is certainly not immediately apparent from this quotation. The term *copula* is encountered in later treatises by Franco, Anonymous IV, the St. Emmeran Anonymous, Walter Odington, and the anonymous *Quatuor principalis* (Pseudo-Tunstede). William Waite has devoted a section of his book *The Rhythm of 12th Century Polyphony* (pp. 115–119) to a discussion of the meaning of Garlandia's description of the *copula*. According to Waite, *copula* is a style of setting which can be distinguished from the styles of organum and *discantus*, and that the three styles "are styles differentiated one from another by the specific relationship of one voice to another rather than on the basis of any special rhythmic differences" (p. 119). It is possible to interpret "Unde copula dicitur esse id, quod est inter discantum et organum" to mean "That which is called *copula* occurs between an organum section and a *discantus* section." (Waite interprets this to mean "Whence *copula* is said to be that which is between [that is, something which partakes of the nature of] *discantus* and organum" [p. 115].) Willi Apel appears to accept both readings in the article "Copula," *HD*, p. 184, though in his *Notation of Polyphonic Music* he favors the former (p. 234).

*9. This difficult passage is translated by Willi Apel in "From St. Martial to Notre Dame," *JAMS* II:149, and William Waite, *op. cit.*, p. 112. Both translations are accompanied by extensive discussions which differ at some points. A translation of the passage contained in footnote 9 is given here, since Riemann's is somewhat condensed:

*Organum in speciali* is spoken of in two ways, either *per se* [two-voiced organum or *organum duplum*] or *cum alio* [with another voice, i.e., *triplum* (Apel: *triplum, quadruplum*)]. *Organum per se* is said to be that which proceeds according to *modus rectus* or *modus non rectus*. By *modus rectus* we mean that *modus* in which the *discantus* proceeds. *Modus non rectus* is so called to distinguish it from *modus rectus*, for in *rectus* the longas and breves are taken according to the first or principal [special] mode (Cserba, *op. cit.*, emends *principaliter* to read *specialiter*. Both Waite and Apel follow the Coussemaker reading). In *modus non rectus* the *longa* and *brevis* are [not? Cserba's edition reads as follows: *non primo modo sed ex contingenti*] in the first mode but *ex contingenti* [without relationship to one another]. Whatever then is sung *per non rectam mensuram* [in an irregular manner] is said to be *organum non rectum*, as mentioned above. The relationship of the upper part to the lower is limited to a single tone [Garlandia: *unisono*] to the end of a *punctus* [Apel: a section based on one tenor note. Waite: a phrase or section within the piece] where both parts meet in a consonance.

Coussemaker's reading of this text is given in footnote 9, with Cserba's emendations in parentheses.

*10. On the possible historical derivation of hocket see the article "Hoquetus," *MGG* VI:704–706. See also *NOHM* II:397–399 and Reese, *Music in the Middle Ages*, pp. 320–322.

*11. While the *rondellus* is rarely encountered on the continent, it was apparently a manner of writing beloved of the English. Luther Dittmer ("*Beiträge zum Studium der Worcester-Fragmente*," *MF* X:29–33) writes of this form as follows:

Though this species of composition is found in very small numbers in France, it is cultivated so much the more in England, while a few examples may be found in Spain. For the musical output of the 13th century the southwest English school in the vicinity of Worcester remains the locale where the *rondellus* flourished...this species of composition is plentiful in the Worcester sources as well as in neighboring ones (p. 29).

*12. On the *Conductus* see the article "Conductus" in *MGG* II:1615–1626, which includes an annotated bibliography at the end of the article.

*13. This apparently refers to the *punctus divisionus*, which in this case served to mark off perfections.

*14. Riemann's translation of the quotation in note 18 is a paraphrase. A complete translation may be found in Strunk, *Source Readings in Music History*, pp. 153–156.

*15. See Chapter VI, note *7.

*16. Riemann again attempts (in footnote 19) to read the "sights" technique into a context in which it does not belong. Bukofzer (*Geschichte des englischen Diskants...*, p. 110) feels that this quotation is more correctly interpreted as representing a technical aid in performance rather than an example of "*ständige Sightlesung*."

*17. Grocheo's treatise is available not only in Wolf's edition (cited in footnote 23) but in a later edition based on two MSS: the British Museum, Harley 281, and Codex 2663 of the Hessische Landesbibliothek in Darmstadt. This edition is edited by Ernst Rohloff, *Der Musiktraktat des Johannes de Grocheo* (Leipzig, 1943). See also Ernst Rohloff, *Studien zum Musiktraktat des Johannes de Grocheo* (Leipzig, 1930), and the article "Johannes de Grocheo" in *MGG* VII:95–100.

*18. Rohloff emends "Cuius partes *unum habent* diversum cantum a cantu responsorii" to *non habent*, which alters the meaning of the sentence and invalidates the observation made in footnote 33. The *rotundellus* would have no *cantus* which deviated from the refrain following the emendation. The translated passage reads as follows: "The parts of which [that is, of the *rotundellus*] have no *cantus* which deviates from the *cantus* of the *responsorium* or refrain...it is sung in a long-drawn-out fashion."

*19. Rohloff emends (see footnote 38) *Est enim ductia sonus* to *est autem ductia sonus*.

*20. Rohloff emends *Et in commotellis* to *Et cum in motellis* (see footnote 46), which eliminates the mysterious term referred to in footnote 42.

*21. Rohloff emends *qui cum tenore minimam* to *supra tenorem minutam*.


## CHAPTER X

*1. Sources for instrumental music earlier than the 15th century have been discovered, but they are few in number. The earliest extant pieces notated for keyboard instruments are in the MS. Brit. Mus. Add. 28550 (The Robertsbridge fragment). Three of the pieces are in the form of *estampies*, and the others are transcriptions of motets. The notation is Italian rather than English (see Apel, *Notation of Polyphonic Music*, pp. 38, 384), the upper voice in mensural notation on a staff and the lower voice in letters (tablature; see the article "Klaviermusik" by W. Apel in *MGG* VII:1130). An organ *estampie* from the Robertsbridge fragment is reproduced in *HAM* I:62–63; the style of this piece is unusual because of the motion of the voices in parallel fifths. The codex is dated as early 14th century. An *In seculum* motet from a Bamberg MS (Staatsbibliothek Ed. IV. 6) is inscribed for "viellatores" (viols), though the idiom of this motet is not particularly instrumental (transcribed in *HAM* I:34). The *caudae* (a *cauda* is [*NOHM* II:326–327] "an embellishment which appears at the end of intermediate phrases and sections or even in a short emphasis upon important words, and at the beginning as well as at the end of a composition") of what Hughes terms the *conductus cum caudae* may have been performed with instruments (see *NOHM* II:326–337). There are some 13th-century dances preserved in the British Mus. Harl. 978, fol. 8ᵛ–9 (see *HAM* I:43–44 for transcriptions) and some 14th-century Italian dances for the *vielle*, also in a British Museum MS Add. 29987, fol. 63r–63v (transcribed in *HAM* I:63–64).

Undoubtedly instrumental performance played a great role in the musical life of the Middle Ages, but the few sources give only a fragmentary picture of that practice. The citation from Johannes de Muris given by Riemann on p.183 f. may refer to a notation like that found in the Robertsbridge fragment. It is likely that as far as the musical sources were concerned, the distinction made between instrumental or vocal performance of a part was sometimes vague, the two being interchangeable, and that combinations of instruments and voices were characteristic. It is, then, not a question of the dependence of instrumental music on vocal music; rather written music was probably realized idiomatically by the performing medium, perhaps embellished and ornamented or made the basis of improvisation. The practice of using voices and instruments interchangeably persists throughout the 16th century, but the awakening of a sense of idiomatic instrumental usage does not clearly manifest itself until the German organ tablatures and the keyboard and lute music of the 15th and 16th centuries. On instrumental music in the medieval period, see Reese, *Music in the Middle Ages*, pp. 323–330, 383–386.

*2. For arguments in favor of this viewpoint, as well as those opposing it, see *NOHM* II:225–228, and Reese, *op. cit.*, pp. 206–211.

*3. The origins of tablature are obscure, though it has been suggested that the practice may have been developed by peoples for whom the lute was an indigenous instrument (Oriental-Arabic) and brought into Europe through Venice when that city was under the domination of the East (G. Morphy, *Les luthistes espagnoles du XVIᵉ siècle*, I:xvii. Morphy was not a musicologist, however, but an enthusiast for the lute, and he explains that the above supposition is more intuitive than based upon actual evidence).

*4. The Robertsbridge example printed in facsimile in Apel, *op. cit.*, p. 38, or the tablature of Adam Ileborgh (1448; also in facsimile, *ibid.*, p. 41), contain no bar lines. The bar lines in tablatures of the 15th and 16th centuries should not be thought of as implying accents or "bar-line" rhythm, but rather as a means of marking off convenient areas for reading.

*5. See Chapter VI, note *14 on the dating of the *Pomerium*. De Vitry's treatise *Ars nova* is dated *ca.* 1325. It must be borne in mind that the Italian and French *Ars novae* are independent developments, de Vitry being one of the leaders of the French. See the article "Ars Nova" in *MGG* I:702–729.

*6. The influence of secular music on the music of the church has often been emphasized in historical writings, and Riemann in particular seems to regard secular music as a "correcting influence," a representative of forces based upon the natural and intuitive instincts of people, which only required time to make themselves felt upon the artificial and contrived stylization of ecclesiastical art music as mirrored in the theoretical treatises. Polyphony, the unique heritage of Western art music, came about through "folk singing" as well as the Western insistence on the harmonic third (as opposed to the perfect consonances basic to theoretical concepts and musical systems). These characteristics of Riemann's work are discussed at greater length in the introduction to this translated edition. The reader is therefore referred to this discussion in the light of the material on p. 185.

*7. Anonymous III (Couss. III:370–375) is dated after 1350 in the article "Anonymi" in *MGG* I:496.

*8. The invention of the minima is ascribed to the younger Garlandia by Johannes Hanboys (Couss. I:424). Anonymous I (Couss. III:46) says that "the minima was invented in Navarre and was sanctioned and used by Philippe de Vitry, the finest figure of the entire musical world" (Apel, *op. cit.*, p. 338). Navernia and Navarina are probably synonyms for Navarre. *Ars nova* notation is discussed in detail in Apel, *op. cit.*, pp. 338–384, in its French and Italian forms.

*9. This treatise is dated after 1350 in the article "Anonymi," *MGG* I:496.

*10. A German translation with Latin text of de Vitry's *Ars nova* may be found in Peter Bohn, "Phillip von Vitry," *Monatshefte für Musikgeschichte* XXII:141–179. A new edition of this treatise has been published by André Gilles, Jean Maillard, and Gilbert Reaney with a commentary on sources and attribution. The Latin text and commentary is in *MD* X:5–33. A translation into French appears in *MD* XI:12–29. The Latin text in footnote 11 was emended following this new edition.

*11. Red notes appear in known sources for the first time in the *Roman de Fauvel* (*ca.* 1310) and signify a change from *modus perfectus* to *modus imperfectus* in the tenor (see Apel, *op. cit.*, pp. 328, 331 for a facsimile showing this). See also the article "Color," *MGG* II:1567–1574.

*12. See Chapter XI, note *1. The *Ars nova* is the only treatise ascribed to de Vitry.

*13. Reaney, in the article "Color," *MGG* II:1567, explains that the use of white notes (*vacuae* or *cavatae*) and red notes served the same purpose, that of changing from *perfectus* to *imperfectus*, the reason for using white notes instead of red being that red ink was not available.

*14. The problem of the two theorists bearing the name Muris was resolved by Heinrich Besseler in his "Studien zur Musik des Mittelalters," *AfMW* VII:167–252. Besseler established that the author of the *Speculum musicae* was not Muris but a Jacobus of Liège (the name Jacobus was discovered in an acrostic described by the author of the *Speculum* in the first chapter of the first book. It can be found in the first letter of Chapter II of the first book and the first letters of the beginning chapters in the other six books). The establishment of Jacobus' identity resolved the problem of having two theorists with the same names and totally opposite viewpoints. Jacobus, whose encyclopedic *Speculum musicae* in seven books constitutes one of the most valuable references for medieval theory and practice, was a conservative, whose purpose in writing was that of opposition to the "modern" trends of his time. Johannes de Muris, on the other hand, was a major representative of these trends. On these theorists see the articles "Jacobus von Lüttich" (*MGG* VI:1626–1631) and "Johannes de Muris" (*MGG* VII:105–115). A complete edition of the *Speculum* has been planned, but only one volume has appeared (Jacobi Leodensis, *Speculum musicae Liber Primus*, edited by Roger Bragard. Bragard has published two articles on the *Speculum* and its author: "Le speculum musicae du compilateur Jacques de Liège," *MD* VII:59–104 and *MD* VIII:1–17, which discuss sources, contents of the work, references made to it in later works, descriptions of the MSS and their histories, how they are related to one another, the name of the author, and attributions concerning authorship from the 16th century to the present time).

*15. See Eric Werner's article "The Mathematical Foundation of Philippe de Vitry's *Ars Nova*," *JAMS* IX:128–132. Werner offers evidence that refutes Riemann's contention that *De numeris harmonicis*, a treatise by a 14th-century mathematician and contemporary of de Vitry, Leo Hebraeus, had to do with the calculation of intervals. The name of the treatise involved a mistake by the author in the translation into Latin of a Hebrew expression which should have indicated the meaning "musical numbers." This treatise actually supplied a mathematical rationale for de Vitry's attempt in his *Ars nova* to set imperfect and perfect mensuration on an equal footing. See also "Leo Hebraeus," *MGG* VIII:630–631.

*16. This treatise contains a mention of the Franciscan and Dominican orders, however, which did not come into existence until the 13th century (Gerbert, *Script.* III:244). See Besseler, "Studien...," *AfMW* VIII:207, footnote 2.

# CHAPTER XI

*1.

The etymology of the term *counterpoint* goes back to the 13th century which understood the single note, later to be known as the breve, as a *punctum*. *Contrapunctus* is a contraction of *punctus contrapunctum*, meaning note against note. The earliest preserved evidence of the use of this word is to be found in a series of treatises from the beginning of the 14th century, whose authors and dates are for the most part not clearly accounted for (article "Kontrapunkt," *MGG* VII:1522).

The following three treatises are among those cited by the author of the above article, Claude V. Palisca: an anonymous *Musice liber* in La Fage's *Essais* (p. 241), the *Optimo introductio in contrapunctum pro rubidus*, "incorrectly" ascribed to Johannes de Garlandia, and the *Ars perfecta* attributed to a Magister Phillippotus. The pseudo-Garlandia treatise, *Optimo introductio*, is regarded as a 15th-century treatise by Bukofzer because of its lack of restriction on parallel movement of imperfect consonances, which he believes is a basic distinction between 15th-century and 14th-century music theory (the latter restricts such movements from two to three). The relevant quotation in the *Optima* (the contents are given by Riemann, pp. 209–212) is: "It is permissible...to use two or more imperfect consonances of the same value in succession on different lines and spaces." And a few sentences later: "Therefore one is allowed to use two, three, four, or more imperfect intervals of the same kind succeeding each other in ascending or descending motion...."

If this treatise is 15th century, then it is dated much too early by Riemann, and also by Hüschen (*MGG* VII:92–95), who regards it as having great similarity to the *Ars contrapunctus* of de Vitry, saying that its author (Garlandia the Younger) stands on the threshold of the *Ars nova*. Gilbert Reaney, "Fourteenth Century Harmony," *Musica Disciplina* VII:130–131, also regards the *Optima* as being 14th century.

Among the other treatises mentioned by Riemann on p. 209 the only one which can be definitely ascribed to Philippe de Vitry is the *Ars nova* (Reese, *Music in the Middle Ages*, p. 340), yet Reese feels that the other de Vitry treatises were written under his influence. De Vitry and Franco were, with Guido and Boethius, the most cited authorities among the Anonymi (see *MGG* I:494), and the ascription *secundum Philippum de Vitriaco* is by no means proof of authorship. The *Ars contrapuncti secundum* and *Ars discantus secundum* of Johannes de Muris are very likely student works, probably by authors later than de Muris (see "Johannes de Muris," *MGG* VII:110).

*2. See commentary for Chapter VII.

*3. Georgiades (*Englische Diskanttraktate...*, p. 59) feels that just the opposite is the case; the learned *Ars contrapunctus* is not an enlarged reworking of the small, popular-styled *Optima introductio*, but the latter is a "modernized, simplified version of a learned work, such as the *Ars contrapunctus* represents."

*4. This is the so-called *cantus fractibilis*, a melodic line consisting principally of short notes, and the only condition under which dissonances could take place (the speed at which the parts moved allowed the introduction of dissonance). A *cantus fractibilis* occurs when a semibreve is divided into two or three minimas (Reaney, "Fourteenth Century Harmony," pp. 130–131. Riemann says into three only, following the directions of the *Ars contrapunctus*).

*5. For historical résumés see the article "Discantus," *MGG* III:559–562 (Section I, entitled *Allgemeine Begriffsbestimmung*, for definitions; and pp. 567–572, Section III, *Der improvisierte Diskant [Homorhythmischer Kontrapunkt]* on sources and historical development). Also the article "Kontrapunkt," *MGG* VII:1521–1523 (Section I, for terminology), 1525–1535 (on historical development of contrapuntal theory to the period of Vicentino and Zarlino). An outline history of contrapuntal theory in English may be found in Knud Jeppesen's *Counterpoint*, pp. 3–22, concerned with the period covered by Books I and II of Riemann's *Geschichte*. This outline does not go into the detail, however, which is characteristic of the *MGG* articles since its primary interest is centered in the Renaissance. In the sources already mentioned by Riemann in Chapter XI, it becomes increasingly difficult to distinguish between rules governing discant improvisation and counterpoint (having reference to composition). As is pointed out by Palisca in the article "Kontrapunkt," contrapuntal treatises in the 14th century treat primarily of the note-against-note style in two parts and bear a resemblance to musical composition of the period only as illustrations of basic structure. It is not until the 15th century that theorists such as Tinctoris and Gafurius treated of compositional techniques which reflected actual practice to a greater degree; however, in 15th-century practice we also see the increasing systemization of dissonance treatment in musical styles. When this occurred it became possible for theorists to offer more comprehensive generalizations concerning musical practice.

*6. The *Liber musicalium* is not by de Vitry. Bukofzer places it in the 15th century ("Discantus," *MGG* III:572).

*7. This treatise (which is part of a larger work, *Quaestiones super partes musicae*, Gerbert III:301–307) is regarded by Besseler as an authentic work of Muris ("Johannes de Muris," *MGG* VII:109). The St. Blasien and Parisian MSS used by Gerbert as sources are not known today, but other sources are extant (*MGG* VII:112).

*8. Besseler does not regard the *Ars contrapunctus* as an authentic Muris treatise (*MGG* VII:110). He writes:

> The *Ars contrapuncti secundum Johannem de Muris* concerns itself with practical questions and enjoyed favor as a compilation. Compared with the systematization and the comprehensive presentation of the *Libellus*, the *Ars contrapunctus* is more loosely constructed and indicates the work of a student.

*9. See note *1 above.

*10. Riemann's reasoning here is as follows: Marchettus, regarding the sixth as a dissonance (the major sixth is apparently under discussion), says that the octave is the more likely resolution because the sixth is closer to the octave than to the fifth:

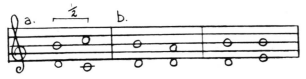

Example b is unsatisfactory because Marchettus regards both tones of the sixth as dissonant, therefore requiring resolution, and a movement from the sixth to the fifth would require one voice to be stationary and the other to move the distance of a whole step. Example a is satisfactory because of the half-step movement in one voice, making the sixth closer to the octave. Riemann's predilection for chromaticism and his penchant for heavily editing transcriptions of early music with accidentals brings him to assume that augmented sixths and thirds are *implied* in this treatise. For example, in thirds moving to fifths:

would be better as:

following the "implications" of the treatise. A sixth going to an octave

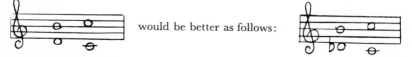

would be better as follows:

Such alterations are met in the 16th century in chromatic usages of certain styles of that period (see "Diatonik-Chromatik-Enharmonik," *MGG* III:411–416); however, a more conservative attitude towards *musica ficta* in earlier periods is generally characteristic of musicologists today.

*11. The treatise *Ars discantus secundum de Muris* is a later treatise, dated near the close of the 14th century by Besseler ("Johannes de Muris," *MGG* VII:110) because a discussion of *cantilena* settings contained therein becomes characteristic during this time. Bukofzer ("Discantus," *MGG* III:572) dates it as 15th century, giving it a position between 14th-century discant treatises and those 15th-century treatises which place no restrictions on parallel movements of imperfect consonances. The *Ars discantus* is the earliest treatise to provide musical examples with its discussion of the treatment of imperfect consonances. Bukofzer does not relate this treatise to the tradition of "English" discant.

*12. *Diminutio* is a term which can be defined as "means of ornamentation" generally by the introduction of smaller note values in the place of a larger value, or it may be regarded as being synonymous with *coloratura*. In the medieval period diminutions were probably, for the most part, improvised, and those which were written down very likely were attempts to avoid any excesses of ornamentation. *Diminutio* flourished in 14th- and 15th-century music and is discussed in the treatises as well (see "Diminution," *MGG* III:489–493 and 501–504).

The signs ⊕ and ⊄ are proportional signs. For a complete discussion of their significance see Apel, *The Notation of Polyphonic Music*, pp. 145–155; also Heinrich Bellermann, *Mensuralnoten und Taktzeichen*, pp. 55–107.

On Prosdocimus, see the article "Beldemandis" in *MGG* I:1575–1579.

*13. On *musica ficta* and *musica falsa* see the following: Reese, *Music in the Middle Ages*, pp. 380–382; the article "Musica ficta" in the *Harvard Dictionary of Music*, pp. 465–467; and Carl Parrish, *The Notation of Medieval Music*, pp. 197–200.

*14. For a history of proportions and a study of terminology see Apel, *The Notation of Polyphonic Music*, pp. 145–147. For material relative to the study of proportions see the article "Color," *MGG* II:1566–1578, and also the article "Diminution" (see note *12 above).

*15. The *Summa musicae* is not by Muris. On Muris sources see Heinrich Besseler, "Studien zur Musik des Mittelalters," *AfMW* VII:167–252 and VIII:137–258. On the identification of the *Normannus Muris* see the commentary on Chapter X, as well as the above article. Denes v. Bartha in his "Studien zum musikalischen Schrifttum des 15. Jahrhunderts," *AfMW* II:178, denies any resemblance between Anonymous XI (discussed in "Anonymi," *MGG* I:497) and the *Summa musicae*. According to Bartha the verse-types used in these treatises are differently formed, and not a single line of Anonymous XI is to be found in the *Summa*. The two verses quoted from the *Summa* (Gerbert III:204, and not 206, as given in Riemann) and those from Couss., *Script.* III:418 are as follows, for the sake of comparison:

> (Gerbert III:204):
> UT RE MI FA SOL LA notularum nomina sena
> Sufficiunt notulae per quas fit musica plena!
>
> (Coussemaker III:418):
>
> UT, RE, MI, cum FA, SOL, jungas simile et LA,
> Cunctas claudit odas manus ut plena docet illas.

*16. See the article "Komposition," *MGG* VII:1427–1435, concerning the term "composition" and the development of its meaning in the periods covered by this study.

*17. "The earliest mention of proportions is in the *Libellus cantus mensurabilis secundum Joh. de Muris* (CS III:58) a treatise of the mid-14th century in which *diminutio* (i.e., *dupla*) is discussed (Apel, *op. cit.*, p. 145)." Prosdocimus actually employs the terminology *proportio dupla, tertia*, etc., in his *Tractatus practice de musica mensurabili*, dated 1408. The treatise segment under discussion by Riemann is part of Anonymous XI, in Couss. III:416–475. It is dated around the middle of the 15th century in the article "Anonymi," *MGG* I:497–498.

*18. Anonymous XII is dated as mid-15th century in "Anonymi," *MGG* I:497–498.

*19. Biographical information and a full account of Hothby's work, as well as bibliographical references to editions of his treatises and other writings concerning him, may be found in *MGG* VI:771–782.

*20. The syncopation is a particularly complex problem in theoretical treatises. Its first appearance in a treatise may not be in a French source, as stated by

Riemann, but in an English source, the treatise of Robert de Handlo, completed in 1326 (Reese, *Music in the Middle Ages*, p. 414; this treatise is now available in an English translation by Luther Dittmer, *Robert de Handlo*, Institute of Medieval Music [1959]. See the footnote on page 34 of this edition concerning the possibility of syncopation as well as the passage in question.) The earliest meaning of the term refers to the division of a note such as a perfect breve or semibreve into several parts which are separated from one another by other larger note values, for example

the following succession:

to:

The device of syncopation was most characteristic in perfect mensuration, according to de Vitry and Muris, though Muris informs us that it is possible in imperfect (see Apel, *op. cit.*, pp. 395–402, for a study of syncopation in mensural notation). Carl Dalhaus, in his article "Zur Geschichte der Synkope" in *Die Musikforschung* XII:385–391, stresses what he feels is a vital distinction between the syncope of the 14th century and that of the 15th and 16th centuries. He emphasizes that the concept of the syncope as a retarded, anticipated, or displaced beat is erroneous for the 14th century; the displaced beat or *tactus* is rather a characteristic of 15th- and 16th-century music. The syncopation complex, such as the one shown in the example, Dalhaus feels, should be thought of as a rhythmic unity, but one not particularly affected by a feeling for a beat or an accent. Such complexes were combinations of values in which each value related itself to the other without the introduction of metric accent.

Dalhaus also disagrees with Riemann's statement (in Chapter II, footnote 46) that the passage "et illae semibreves debent cantari tardando quia tardantur per minimam praecedentem" (and these semibreves should be sung with delaying because the preceding minimas are also delayed) "discloses a premonition of the true content of the following: namely, that a retardation is the holding off of a consonance by a preceding dissonance." Dalhaus says (*op. cit.*, p. 385, footnote 4):

> The *Liber musicalium* does not say that the middle *semibrevis*, as a syncopation in our sense, retards the consonance; on the contrary it says that the middle semibreve, as the beginning of a perfection, is retarded by each of the already divided *minimae*.

*21. Coussemaker's version agrees exactly with the source which he used, the Codex 336 Ms. lat. 1581 in St. Mark's Library; therefore Riemann's correction of *tertia* to *tritonus* is misleading. The resolution of a *tritonus* to a fifth is also not typical of the period, rather a tritone, in a syncopation, usually resolves to a third.

Jeppesen believes that Guilelmus meant that "the syncopated upper fourth in the middle voice resolves into the third, which is followed by the fifth" (Knud Jeppesen, *The Style of Palestrina and the Dissonance*, p. 226). This is demonstrated by an example from Guilelmus' treatise, quoted by Jeppesen,

in which the middle voice resolves from the fourth (at the asterisk) into the third, which is then followed by the fifth (a typical cadence of the period; see Gustav Reese, *Music in the Renaissance*, pp. 44–48).

Another ambiguous phrase in rule 8 speaks of the dissonance of the fourth resolving to the third above. In this case the upper voice must be regarded as the dissonance, and the rule can read as follows: The dissonance of the fourth is resolved when the upper voice moves to the third.

*22. Riemann's translation is faulty here because of his mistake in interpreting fauxbourdon and "English discant" as being similar in execution (see commentary for Chapter VII, in which this is discussed in detail). A corrected version of the translation is given in footnote 49 for ease of comparison, the important difference being "the soprano must adopt the *cantus firmus* (the soprano is itself the *cantus firmus*)" rather than "the *cantus firmus* must be read as the soprano," as Riemann interprets it. Riemann interprets this passage and those following as reflecting the "sights" technique (discussed in Chapter VII and commentary), whereas Guilelmus is speaking of the fauxbourdon (see Manfred Bukofzer, *Geschichte des englischen Diskants*, pp. 3 and 71).

*23. Riemann incorrectly translates *tenor* as *cantus firmus*. See footnote 50 for corrected translation.

*24. See corrected version of translation. The translations in footnotes 49, 50, and 51 are from Ernest Trumble, *Early Renaissance Harmony*, Diss. Indiana University, pp. 236–238. See also Jacques Handschin, "Eine umstrittene Stelle bei Guilelmus Monachus," *Bericht über den Kongress der Internationalen Gesellschaft für Musikwissenschaft in Basel*, p. 148.

*25. Guilelmus may have written around 1480. See the article "Guilelmus Monachus" in *MGG* V: 1084–1087.

*26. See the article "Gallicus," *MGG* IV: 1296–1298.

*27. On Tinctoris see Reese, *Music in the Renaissance*, pp. 137–150, which gives biographical and bibliographical information, as well as a discussion of his compositions. In addition, the *Proportionale musices* of Tinctoris is given in English translation with commentary in Albert Seay, "The *Proportionale Musices* of Johannes Tinctoris," *JMT* I:22–75.


# CHAPTER XII

*1. Riemann may be exaggerating the importance of the 5/4 major third and the 6/5 minor third in Odington's treatise (see Chapter VI, note *8). In this treatise the Pythagorean system dominates, and Odington only reports that practice, deviating from the Pythagorean system, regards thirds as consonances because their sound as sung by voices comes closer to the proportions 5/4 and 6/5. In the diagram already discussed in the commentary to Chapter VI, the proportions are those of the Pythagorean system. Martin Ruhnke in his article "Intervall" in *MGG* VI:1345 mistakenly takes this diagram to represent the minor triad rather than the major triad as Riemann pointed out (p. 99). The diagram as it stands has a "minor" triad on the bottom and a major on the top (the major triad having Pythagorean relationships: 128–162–192 or 64–81–96). Riemann emended the 73 in the bottom group to 81 for good reasons: the diagram calls for a ditone, and the relationship of 73 to 64 as it stands results in a very flat minor third bordering on the whole-tone (73/64 = 227 cents as compared with 203.9 cents for the 9/8 whole-tone). The diagram as it stands would also have a very sharp major third (476 cents as compared with 498 cents for the 4/3 fourth) in the place where a semiditone is called for. Seventy-three is obviously an error and should be replaced by 81, resulting in a unified representation of relationships within a Pythagorean framework.

*2. Despite the fact that we can discover other types of third measurement before Ramis (see Murray Barbour, *Tuning and Temperament*, pp. 1–5 and pp. 15–24 *passim*), it is to Ramis that the impetus for the revision of theoretical concepts of tuning that took place in the 16th century should be ascribed. He apparently accomplished this by accident, for he was intent on discovering a tuning for the monochord that would supplant the more laborious "numbers and measurements" of Boethius (Ramis' monochord division from his treatise, the *Musica practica*, is given in Strunk, *Source Readings in Music History*, pp. 200–204). He did not intend to do away with the Pythagorean system, and it is likely that he was also not trying to resurrect Didymus. A comparison of the tunings of the E F G A tetrachords of Ramis' monochord (in Barbour, *op. cit.*, p. 90) and Didymus' Diatonic (Barbour, p. 20) shows the following:

| Ramis: | E | | F | | G | | A | | B |
|--------|---|---|---|---|---|---|---|---|---|
| | | 16/15 | | 9/8 | | 10/9 | | 9/8 | |
| | 0 | | 112 | | 316 | | 498 | | 702 cents |

| Didymus: | E | | F | | G | | A | | B |
|----------|---|---|---|---|---|---|---|---|---|
| | | 16/15 | | 10/9 | | 9/8 | | 9/8 | |
| | 0 | | 112 | | 294 | | 498 | | 702 cents |

the difference being in the placement of the 10/9 whole-tone. Ramis' tuning is actually a manipulation of the Pythagorean system which results in pure thirds being present at four important places: Bb–D, F–A, C–E, and G–B (each one a 5/4 third or 386 cents). The monochord is tuned in pure fifths from Ab–Eb–Bb–F–C–G, and the remaining six tones, also joined by pure fifths, D–A–E–B–F#–C#, "lie a comma higher than the corresponding notes in the Pythagorean tuning" (Barbour, pp. 89–90). Using the beginning point of Ramis' tuning (Ab) and a Pythagorean tuning using C as a beginning point, equivalent half- and whole-step arrangements are compared below (Barbour makes a similar comparison of these tunings [p. 90] which shows their relationships less clearly than the following):

*Ramis' Tuning:*

| Ab | Bb | C | C# | Eb | F | G | | Ab |
|---|---|---|---|---|---|---|---|---|
| 0 | 204 | 408 | 500 | 702 | 906 | 1110 | | 1200 cents |
| | 9/8 | 9/8 | *1 | *2 | 9/8 | 9/8 | 256/243 | |

*1: The difference between C and C# is 92 cents, which is two cents larger than a 245/243 semitone (90 cents).

*2: The difference between C# and Eb is 202 cents, which is two cents smaller than a 9/8 whole-tone (204 cents).

*Pythagorean Tuning:*

| C | D | E | | F | G | A | B | | C |
|---|---|---|---|---|---|---|---|---|---|
| 0 | 204 | 408 | | 498 | 702 | 906 | 1110 | | 1200 cents |
| | 9/8 | 9/8 | 256/243 | 9/8 | 9/8 | 9/8 | | 256/243 | |

The correspondence of the two systems is striking and clearly demonstrates their relationship. Further on Ramis see Barbour, *op. cit.*, pp. 89–92, and *MGG* VI: 1345–1346.

*3. The Pythagorean semitone 256/243 does exist in Ramis' tuning between the following intervals: C#–D (90 cents), and G–A (90 cents). See a representation of Ramis' tuning in Barbour, *op. cit.*, p. 90, where the various interval relations can be examined in detail.

*4. That Ramis thought of his system of tuning as a temperament is an interpretation read into his treatise by his successors. It was intended as a practical and simple division of the monochord and not a new theory of interval proportions. See Strunk, *op. cit.*, in which the extract given there makes this quite plain, as well as *MGG* VI: 1345.

*5. On the history of tuning and temperament, Murray Barbour's study *Tuning and Temperament* is the best general study. Barbour gives a comprehensive bibliography (pp. 205–217). On the calculation of intervals see the relevant articles in *HD*, and for historical information as well as methods of calculation see Martin Ruhnke's valuable article "Intervall," in *MGG* VI: 1326–1348.

*6. The assumptions of this paragraph have been discussed in Chapter II, note *7; Chapter VI, note *1; Chapter VI, note *8; and Chapter VII, note *1.

A very interesting discussion of the development of the meaning of *harmonia* can be found in *MGG* V:1609–1614.

*7. See Barbour, *op. cit.*, pp. 5–6 and also p. 25, where Barbour credits Riemann as having "discovered the first mention of temperament in a passage from Gafurius' *Practica musica* (1496)."

*8. The unusual practice of an organum in seconds found in use in the Cathedral of Milan by Gafurius is discussed in two articles (Ernest T. Ferand, "The 'Howling in Seconds' of the Lombards," *MQ* XXV:313–324, and Jacques Handschin, "Aus der alten Musiktheorie III," *AM* XV:2–15) and in the book *Die Improvisation in der Musik*, p. 138, also by Ernest Ferand. Riemann gave incorrectly the example from Chapter XIV of Gafurius' *Practica musica*, and it has been emended here (p. 296). The example as given shows a large number of seconds (but not as many as in Riemann's incorrect version), and also the ever-puzzling tritone (augmented fourth between F and B). Handschin calls attention to an earlier reference in Anonymous IV concerning the Lombards:

> Every penultimate note before the rest which is at the end of a section is a *longa*. If the penultimate note is a whole-tone above the tenor, as in *organa purum*, it will still form a good consonance, although the major second by itself is not a consonance. This method is quite often used by composers of *organum purum* and by the Lombard composers of polyphonic song. The difference, however, is that the composers of polyphonic song add the final note in their books—that is, the one after the penultimate note—and this note either forms a unison or an octave with the tenor. Certain Lombards, however, sometimes notate the final note and sometimes they don't, and they draw back down under the sound of the final consonance and then return to the same pitch; this does not correspond with the philosophy of consonances (From L. Dittmer, *Anonymous* IV, p. 63).

Handschin finds this style a variation of the predominant style of the *Musica enchiriadis*, in which the second, however, is not used as a passing interval, but stands next to the fourth and the unison as a chief interval (p. 4).

Riemann draws Gafurius' discussion of this "false counterpoint" into relationship with a citation from Elias Salomon's *Scientia artis musicae* (Gerbert III:60). Ferand, in a critical examination of Chapter 30 of Salomon's treatise, finds no trace of a contrapuntal style such as the one described by Gafurius. Suspicious passages are explained as follows: *novem punctos* (Gerbert III:59b) does not refer to the interval of a ninth, but rather to the octave (a fifth plus a fourth). The passage:

> Nam si unus laicus audiret alium laicum cantare in prima bassa voce, bene saliret recta in tertia [voce], non autem aliquo modo in secunda [voce]; vel e contrario de tertia in prima, sed nunquam in secunda.

is interpreted by Ferand (*Die Improvisation in der Musik*, p. 138) as follows:

> In four-part singing the first (lowest) and the third, as well as the second and fourth (highest), voices are easily confused by the laity because of the octave relationship which exists between the two pairs, not, however, the first with the second or the third with the fourth, because these are in the relationship of the fifth.

This should be compared with the more literal translation given in Chapter XIII, footnote 17.

*9. Pietro Aron (1480–1545/62) was one of the important theorists of the early 16th century and one of the few who forsook Latin and wrote his treatises in the vernacular. He was the first theorist to recognize the vertical composition of voices as opposed to the successive or horizontal technique of composition still practiced in his time. He wrote out of the experience of practice, and though he was well read in the literature of music theory, he preferred to deal with the problems of musical practice. He supported the views of Ramis, yet his system of temperament is the first example of mean-tone division (see Barbour, *op. cit.*, pp. 26–27, for a description of Aron's method, which is from his *Toscanello in musica*). Concerning the problem of modal identification, the excerpt from his treatise, *Trattato della natura e cognizione di tutti gli toni di canto figurato*, printed in English translation in Strunk, *op. cit.*, pp. 205–218, should be consulted. The *Toscanello in musica* with which Riemann concerns himself is probably the most complete compendium of counterpoint instruction before Zarlino. See also "Aron," in *MGG* I:665–667.

*10. Examples on page 304 f. were not correctly quoted by Riemann (*Geschichte der Musiktheorie*, p. 259) and have been emended after an examination of Heyden's treatise (available on microcards). See also Joseph S. Levitan, "Ockeghem's Clefless Compositions," *MQ* XXIII: 445–448, for an explanation of their meaning (as well as for the examples on p. 304 f.). The notes which these examples actually indicate are given in brackets below them.

*11. Heinrich Glarean, or Henricus Glareanus, was born in June, 1488 in Mollis in the Swiss canton of Glarus and died in 1563 in Freiburg. While he stands as an important figure in the history of theory, the influence of the *Dodecachordon* on later writers has not been adequately investigated to date (see the article "Glareanus," in *MGG* V:215–221). Scholars vary in their estimate of this work's influence. Strunk, in introducing the excerpt from the *Dodecachordon* included in his *Source Readings* (p. 219), says: "The *Dodecachordon*...had a tremendous influence on the changing concept of the modal system." Reese (*Music in the Renaissance*, pp. 185–186) describes the innovations of the *Dodecachordon* but refrains from any judgment concerning the work's influence. F. B. Turrell, in the article "The Isagoge in Musicen of Henry Glarean" (*JMT* III:97–139; this article contains a complete translation of a lesser known work of Glareanus as well as an extensive commentary), writes that the history of music theory in the first half of the 16th century was dominated by Glarean (p. 97). The *Dodecachordon* was published in 1547 as well as in abridgments in Latin and German (see *MGG* V:217) in 1557 and 1559. Hans Albrecht, author of the *MGG* article on Glareanus, feels that "apparently it [the *Dodecachordon*] had been soon displaced by Zarlino's more progressive publications" (217), and that it is still not clear to what extent the influence of this work was felt, even in the circle of music theorists in southern Germany. (Since this commentary was written, a new article has appeared in which Glareanus' influence on his contemporaries and on his posterity is further discussed. See Clement A. Miller, "The Dodecachordon: Its Origins and Influence on Renaissance Musical Thought," *MD* XV:155–166.)

The *Dodecachordon* is available in a complete English translation in Henricus Glareanus, *Dodecachordon*, in Clement A. Miller, "Henricus Glareanus: *Dodeca-chordon*" (unpublished doctoral dissertation, University of Michigan, 1950), which includes a commentary as well as transcriptions of the numerous musical examples which Glareanus included in this treatise (the translations contained in footnotes 31, 34, 35, and 36 are from Miller). A detailed study of modal theory in which the works of Aron, Agricola, Ornithoparcus, and Glareanus are examined is contained in a dissertation (Indiana University) by Helen Rogers, "Develop-ment of a Concept of Modulation in Theory. From the 16th Century to the Early 18th Century." Riemann tends to underrate the value of the *Dodecachordon*; how-ever, his interest in the *Geschichte* is focused more on the development of contra-puntal theory than on the tonal system itself. One could wish for more integration of these two aspects in Riemann's work, since they cannot be separated, nor one ignored in favor of the other.

*12. Vicentino (1511–1572) was a pupil of Adrian Willaert and known as an "apostle of advanced music," particularly because of his experiments in an attempt to revive the Greek diatonic, chromatic, and enharmonic genera. It must always be borne in mind, however, in the face of the humanist character of treatises like Glareanus' *Dodecachordon* and Vicentino's *L'antica musica* that know-ledge of the music of antiquity was nonexistent, though the antique treatises were beginning to be made known, and that theoretical treatises as far as the tonal systems were concerned are based upon concepts and terminology inherited from the Middle Ages. Vicentino's treatise was published in 1555 (three years before Zarlino's *Istitutioni harmoniche*), and though he deals with secular and instrumental music as well as sacred vocal polyphony, his work is by no means as comprehensive as Zarlino's.

*13. Huyghens (quoted by Barbour, *op. cit.*, p. 119) writes: "The fifth of our division is no more than 1/110 comma higher than the tempered fifths, which difference is entirely imperceptible, but which would render that consonance so much the more perfect." Barbour (p. 118) continues: "Riemann was confused by this remark, not realizing that Huyghens meant that this fifth was 1/110 comma higher than a fifth tempered by 1/4 comma." In terms of cents, Huyghens is saying that if the octave is divided into 31 equal parts (which would be 38.709677 cents per unit), 18 of these units would come to 696.578479 cents. The comma Huyghens is speaking about is the syntonic, or 21.5 cents. 0.195707 goes into 21.5 about 109.9 times.

Vicentino's 31-division tuning system is described in Barbour, *op. cit.*, pp. 117–118. Further on Vicentino's experiments see Henry W. Kaufmann, "Vicentino's Arciorgano; an Annotated Translation," *JMT* V, 2:32–53.

## CHAPTER XIII

*1. Riemann's introduction to one of the most controversial problems of con-temporary musicology, that of *musica ficta* (the addition of accidentals which were "understood" by the performers of music through the 16th century), must be read in the light of his desire as an editor to make earlier music conform as much as possible to a major or a minor tonality. This led him to make excessive use of accidentals in editing, a practice not generally condoned today. Theorists give some indications of the rules which are to be applied in the performance of *musica ficta* but these are often difficult to apply consistently in the sources. Some of these rules and other information may be found in the following: Gustave Reese, *Music in the Middle Ages*, pp. 380–382; Gustave Reese, *Music in the Renaissance*, pp. 44–48 (concerning conflicting signatures), p. 182 (concerning Aron's desire to have all accidentals indicated), p. 297 (concerning the avoidance of false relations), p. 665 (on *musica ficta* in German organ tablatures), p. 858 (concerning false relations in English virginal music); Willi Apel, *The Notation of Polyphonic Music*, pp. 104–107, 120 (the first edition of this work was the only available one for this note); *NOHM* II:369–373; and Carl Parrish, *The Notation of Medieval Music*, pp. 197–200. See also Chapter II, note *18; Chapter III, note *5; Chapter VI, note *16; and Chapter XI, notes *10 and *13.

Some idea of the complexity of the problem *musica ficta* and the controversies waged over it may be gained by reading the following articles in the order here indicated: W. Apel, "The Partial Signatures in the Sources up to 1450," *AM* X:1–13; E. Lowinsky, "The Function of Conflicting Signatures in Early Polyphonic Music," *MQ* XXXI:227–260; Richard H. Hoppin, "Partial Signatures and *Musica Ficta* in Some Early 15th Century Sources," *JAMS* VI:197–215; E. Lowinsky, "Conflicting Views on Conflicting Signatures," *JAMS* VII:181–204; and Richard Hoppin, "Conflicting Signatures Reviewed," *JAMS* IX:97–117.

Riemann's views on reducing time-values in transcriptions of early music are generally accepted and practiced today (see Apel, *op. cit.*, p. 97, and Reese, *Music in the Renaissance*, p. 18, footnote 88). His approach to notation transcription gives equivalent values in our notation to those of earlier periods as he explains on p. 329 f.

*2. The ♭ placed before the f may not have indicated an alteration but rather that the f so marked (actually f″) was "outside the hand" (one step higher than the gamut of Dufay's period) and therefore could be regarded as a *musica ficta* note, having no position within the limits of the tonal system (see Lowinsky, "The Function of Conflicting Signatures," *MQ* XXXI:254).

*3. The cadence is one of the major considerations in style analysis, and a detailed history of cadences is still lacking. As a factor in style analysis, it is incorporated into the essays in Bukofzer's *Studies in Medieval and Renaissance Music*. The evolution of the dominant-tonic cadence is discussed in Jacques Handschin, *Musikgeschichte im Überblick*, pp. 225–227. Lowinsky's "The Function of Conflicting Signatures" (see notes *1 and *2) discusses cadence forms at length (a summary of this article's findings is in Reese, *Music in the Renaissance*, pp. 44–48). The most comprehensive treatment devoted exclusively to the cadence is the article "Kadenz und Klausel," *MGG* VII:406–410 (for the periods concerned in Books I and II). Riemann's discussion of cadences applies most directly to 16th-century polyphony, and its weakness lies in its lack of references to specific periods and sources. Having emerged from the periods dominated by major and minor tonality, modern opinion differs sharply from that of Riemann in its evaluation of harmonic effectiveness, and is able to accept cadential structures outside of the major and minor realm as aesthetically and musically satisfying.

*4. The markings under the solmization syllables signify major and minor triads. The + stands for *Oberklang*, Riemann's theoretical term for the major triad arising out of the overtone series, and the ° signifies *Unterklang*, or minor triad, actually the reverse of a major triad proceeding downward from a fundamental. Riemann regarded the fifth of the minor triad as its fundamental tone; therefore °d is actually g b♭ d. The other *Unterklänge* in the examples should be determined in the same way.

*5. In connection with the *chiavette* the article "Chiavette" in *MGG* II: 1185–1190 should be consulted. Another important article (not mentioned in *MGG*'s bibliography) dealing with this question is Arthur Mendel, "Pitch in the 16th and 17th Centuries—Part III," *MQ* XXIV: 336–357. Mendel writes (p. 357):

Different combinations were undoubtedly often though not always used to imply transposition. Despite the generally accepted theory, however, not a shred of evidence has been produced to show that such transposition was by the interval of a third. The transposition frequently implied by the "high" *chiavette* was down a fourth or a fifth. No generalization that such a transposition was "always" or "never" implied can be made.

# BIBLIOGRAPHY

# *Bibliography*

### ENCYCLOPEDIAS AND DICTIONARIES

*Biographisch-bibliographisches Quellenlexikon der Musiker und Musikgelehrten der christlichen Zeitrechnung bis zur Mitte des* 19. *Jahrhunderts*, by Robert Eitner. 10 vols., 1899–1904 (reprint, New York: Musurgia, 1947).

> Important bibliographical and biographical source, particularly for information not found in other dictionaries (such as entries concerning obscure figures like Johannes Gallicus, etc.), but a work which must be carefully used since some of its information is in need of revision.

*Grove's Dictionary of Music and Musicians*. Eric Blom, ed. 5th ed., vols. 1–12, Macmillan and Co., Ltd., 1954.

> This work contains several articles of interest for the period under discussion, particularly the article on Greek theory by F. Winnington-Ingram. Generally, this dictionary is less detailed and informative on the subjects dealt with in the area of medieval and Renaissance theory, and provides little or no bibliographical information in the articles consulted.

*Harvard Dictionary of Music*, by Willi Apel. Cambridge, Mass.: Harvard University Press, 1947.

> A compact one-volume reference work of great value which is particularly helpful with regard to terminology.

*Die Musik in Geschichte und Gegenwart*, ed. Friedrich Blume. Vols. 1–8, Kassel: Bärenreiter, 1949–.

> The most comprehensive music encyclopedia now available, this work contains many excellent and detailed articles on music theory and theorists and subjects related to the material covered in the first two books of Riemann's *Geschichte*. Each article has an extensive bibliography. The bibliographies are valuable particularly for their references to European dissertations. A number of important American dissertations are not mentioned in pertinent articles, and occasionally an article from an American periodical is omitted from a bibliography. Nevertheless, the bibliographical coverage is extensive, and *MGG* is undoubtedly the most valuable single reference work on music and music history today. Pertinent articles have been cited in the commentary.

### OTHER REFERENCE AND HISTORICAL WORKS

Apel, Willi. *The Notation of Polyphonic Music*, 900–1600, with an appendix of transcriptions. Cambridge, Mass.: The Medieval Academy of America, 1949.

> The standard reference work in English on the notational systems of polyphonic music.

Besseler, Heinrich. *Die Musik des Mittelalters und der Renaissance, Handbuch der Musikwissenschaft*, ed. Ernst Bücken. Potsdam: Akademische Verlagsgesellschaft Athenaion m.b.H., 1931–35.

A history of the medieval and Renaissance periods which emphasizes the study of the musical sources and music's place within the general culture of the period. Theoretical works are only briefly mentioned in this study.

Carpenter, Nan Cooke. *Music in the Medieval and Renaissance Universities*. Norman: University of Oklahoma Press, 1958.

A study of music as a discipline in medieval and Renaissance universities which shows its relation to practice and learning. It becomes apparent in this study that these universities exerted considerable influence on composition and practice. Despite the extensive documentation of the work, the author has not included articles from *MGG* in her research (publications up to 1956 are cited) which would have clarified certain problems, such as the case of the two Francos. Simon Tunstede is also still retained as the author of the *Quatuor Principalia* (see Gilbert Reaney, "The Chantilly Manuscript," *MD* VIII:73, footnote 51).

Ferand, E. T. *Die Improvisation in der Musik*. Zürich: Rhein-Verlag, 1938.

A definitive historical study of the practice of improvisation and its relation to the development of the musical art. The great problem encountered in writing such a book is the transitory character of improvisation and the lack of sources. Such a history can be written from indirect sources alone, such as narrations, reports, rules in theoretical treatises, and other didactic writings. See also the article "Improvisation," *MGG* VI:1093–1135.

Handschin, Jacques. *Musikgeschichte im Überblick*. Luzern: Raber & Cie., 1948.

This work is an essay on music history rather than a detailed historical treatment; the author, calling upon his comprehensive knowledge and his keen perception of some of music history's most perplexing problems, writes a truly stimulating and rewarding book. Handschin is one of the great investigators of medieval music, and his discussion shows a fresh but profound understanding of this period.

———. *Der Toncharakter*. Zürich: Atlantis, 1948.

Subtitled an "introduction" to tone-psychology, this extraordinarily complex book contains many references to the literature of music theory examined from the point of view of the author's theories concerning tonal properties.

Haydon, Glenn. *The Evolution of the 6/4 Chord*. Berkeley: University of California Press, 1933.

A history of the treatment of the fourth in musical style from the 13th to the 17th century. Chapter XI (pp. 125–131) is concerned with the fourth in theoretical writings.

Hawkins, Sir John. *General History of the Science and Practice of Music*. 2 vols.; London: J. A. Novello, 1853.

A learned treatise on the history of music, written in the 18th century, with thorough and detailed reports on music treatises, including quotations from the sources. Portions of Boethius's *De musica* are translated into English, and a summary of the entire treatise is given. Hawkins' history contains corrupt versions of treatises by Lionel Power and the Pseudo-Chilston used by Riemann in Chapter VII. See commentary for Chapter VII.

*The Historical Anthology of Music*, vol. 1. Cambridge, Mass.: Harvard University Press, 1949.

A standard anthology of musical compositions from the medieval and Renaissance periods.

Machabey, Armand. *Genèse de la Tonalité Musicale Classique*. Paris: Richard-Masse Éditeurs, 1955.

Machabey raises opposition to the mathematical-acoustical approach to music and denies that this was of any significance in the development of the musical art. Why, for example, did the "experimenters" of antiquity stop suddenly at 4/3 instead of 12/11 or 119/118? The answer was given by them. Each of the three intervals 2/1, 3/2, and 4/3 was a consonance, and in stopping at the last ratio they abandoned the domain of acoustics and mathematics in order to return to that of pseudo-physiology; that is to say, the experimenters did not search to find an acoustical law which conditioned musical fact, but simply wrote numbers which expressed a fact already subjectively recognized. The evolution of tonality is traced by observing the development of the scale and the perfect cadence in practice through the 15th century. The theorists of the Middle Ages were actually more concerned with practice than with mathematical theory, according to Machabey. It was not until the Renaissance that theory returned to the camps of the mathematicians and acousticians.

*The New Oxford History of Music; Ancient and Oriental Music*, vol. 1, ed. Egon Wellesz. New York: Oxford University Press.

The first volume of the new and completely rewritten *Oxford History* covers primitive music, Oriental and Eastern music, and the music of ancient cultures. For the present discussion the chapter on Greek music by Isobel Henderson is of the most interest. The author, thoroughly acquainted with the literature of her subject, writes an exposition of Greek musical practice and theory which is clear and often stimulating. She differs extensively from the conclusions drawn by Otto Gombosi (*Tonarten und Stimmungen der antiken Musik*) and followed to some extent by Gustave Reese in Chapter II of *Music in the Middle Ages*.

*The New Oxford History of Music; Early Medieval Music up to 1300*, vol. II, ed. Dom Anselm Hughes. New York: Oxford University Press.

Articles in the volume concerned with our study were "Trope, Sequence, and Conductus" by Jacques Handschin, and the four articles by the editor beginning with the "Birth of Polyphony." This last group of chapters is not as comprehensive and detailed as one would wish for in a new history, but they do contain information of value (citations will be found in the commentary). The period covered by this volume, beginning with early Christian chant, extends to the *Ars nova*.

Parrish, Carl. *The Notation of Medieval Music*. New York: W. W. Norton & Co., 1957.

This is a second English work dealing with notation, from chant notation to the "mannered" notation of the late 14th century. It does not go into the detail characteristic of Apel's manual, but is very well suited as a text for the initial study of notation. It contains photographic facsimiles of manuscripts and a clear exposition of the subject material, providing helpful background for the reader of Chapters VIII and X of Riemann's *Geschichte*.

Pietzsch, Gerhard. *Die Klassifikation der Musik von Boetius bis Ugolino von Orvieto*. Halle: M. Niemeyer, 1929.

Riemann did not speak of the classification of music during the medieval period because it lay outside the area of his inquiry; however, a knowledge of this aspect of music theory may help to clarify the relationship of theory to practice during this period. Pietzsch believes that the treatises arose as a result of the needs of certain groups and were for their use only. The treatises dealing with *musica practica* are more difficult to classify but seem to be written with one of two groups in mind, the group which required instruction in chant or mensural notation, or dissertations directed toward the professionals. The speculative studies belong in the larger framework of scientific study. There are also treatises which attempt to embrace both the scientific and musical aspects. Pietzsch feels that the introductory sections of treatises should be given more attention; they are not given this attention because of the feeling that this material is only communicated by tradition and has no correspondence to musical practice. The preconception that all theory lags behind practice makes an effective evaluation of medieval theory more difficult. Pietzsch stands in opposition to Hermann Abert (*Die Musikanschauung des Mittelalters*), who approaches the study of the dependence of medieval theory on antique teaching by showing how antique theory was obscured by a gradual transformation. Abert regards the medieval period as a time of scientific, literary, and artistic decay. Pietzsch feels that Abert failed to observe the dependence of music theory on the general attitude of learning, and the value of *auctoritas* in the Middle Ages. The nature of scholastic method consists of the employment of reason to given teachings or truths or propositions of faith, in this way to bring human reason as close as possible to supernatural truths, and, if possible, to overcome objections or to banish them. The writers attempt to comprehend the teachings of predecessors and to uncover possible errors from which even the most renowned are not free. It is important in studying the writings of medieval thinkers to realize that they were unwilling to effect a complete rejection of authority.

Reese, Gustave. *Fourscore Classics of Music Literature*. New York: Liberal Arts Press, 1957.
    A short review of important music treatises, with a bibliography indicating translations of early sources into modern languages.

———. *Music in the Middle Ages*. New York: W. W. Norton & Co., 1940.
    This work is important in its detailed study of musical styles and literature, in its comprehensive discussion of medieval theory, and in its bibliography. A standard reference work of the greatest value.

———. *Music in the Renaissance*. New York: W. W. Norton & Co., 1954.
    Another standard reference work, unsurpassed in detail, with a comprehensive bibliographical coverage.

Sachs, Curt. *History of Musical Instruments*. New York: W. W. Norton & Co., 1940.
    A standard reference work on the history of musical instruments.

Schneider, Marius. *Geschichte der Mehrstimmigkeit*. 2 vols.; Berlin: J. Bard, 1934 and 1936.
    This work was planned as a three-volume history of polyphony, but only two volumes were completed. The author attempts to postulate the beginnings of polyphony by employing the methods of comparative musicology. His thesis is summarized by Reese, *Music in the Middle Ages*, pp. 256–257. After a study of polyphonic practices in primitive cultures (and related problems such as choice of intervals, imitation) he proceeds through the period of early organum (Guido, Cotton).

SOURCES

(In the original language of the treatise unless otherwise indicated.)

Adler, Guido. *Studie zur Geschichte der Harmonie*, in Vol. 98, Wien: Sitzungsberichte der kaiserlichen Akademie der Wissenschaft in Wien, phil.-hist. Klasse, 1881.
    One of the earliest studies of the problem of fauxbourdon, the conclusions of which are no longer tenable. Chapters 5 to 13 of Guilelmus Monachus' treatise *De praeceptis artis musicae* are reprinted in this work with German translation. The entire treatise may be found in Coussemaker, *Scriptores* III:273–307, with printing and reading errors corrected in Bukofzer, *Geschichte des englischen Diskants*, 153 ff.

Affligemensis, Johannes. *De musica cum tonario*, ed. Joseph Smits van Waesberghe. Rome: American Institute of Musicology, 1950.

The edition of this important treatise is the result of the collation of existing manuscript copies employing the methods of classical philology. The editor has also arrived at a new identification of the writer formerly known as John Cotton. See the article "Johannes von Affligem," *MGG* VII:115–119. See also Leonard Ellinwood, "John Cotton or John of Affligem," *Notes* VIII:650–659, and Joseph Smits van Waesberghe, "John of Affligem or John Cotton," *MD* VI:139–153.

*Anonymous IV*, edited and translated into English by Luther Dittmer. Brooklyn: Institute of Medieval Music, 1959.

The treatise of Anonymous IV is, in the words of the editor, "the most verbose, informative, and sagacious" of the known writers of the 13th century. The treatise is concerned with mensural notation and gives important historical information on personalities living in Paris in the 12th century. This edition contains a list of emendations of the Coussemaker version (*Scriptores* I:327–365). See also "Anonymi," *MGG* I:495 and a critique of this edition by Karl-Werner Gümpel in *MF* XIII:345–348.

Aribonis (Aribo Scholasticus). *De musica*, ed. Joseph Smits van Waesberghe. Rome: American Institute of Musicology, 1951.

This edition is the result of a collation of twelve manuscript copies. The treatise, by an 11th-century author, is particularly important for modal theory, furnishing "additional evidence of the importance of formulas in the modal concept" (Reese, *Music in the Middle Ages*, p. 156).

Aristoxenus. *The Harmonics of Aristoxenus*, the original Greek and an English translation with notes, introduction, and index by Henry S. Macran. Oxford: Clarendon Press, 1902.

Aristoxenus' *Harmonics* is a fundamental source in the study of Greek musical theory written from a definite empirical point of view. Macran's translation requires some alteration in terminology, and his notes do not represent the latest thinking on the controversial subject of Greek theory. See the commentary on Chapter I for specific bibliographical references on this subject.

Aron (Aaron), Pietro. *Toscanello in musica*, Venice, 1523.

This treatise is discussed in Chapter XII of Riemann's *Geschichte*. It is available on microcard reproduction, and there is a copy at the Library of Congress.

Blum, Fred. "Another Look at the Montpellier Organum Treatise," *MD* XIII:15–24.

An English translation of this treatise, as well as its musical examples, are included in this article. This treatise is discussed in note *1 to Chapter V. It was not known to Riemann when he wrote the *Geschichte*, or even at the time of its revision.

Boethius. *De institutione arithmetica*, libri duo; *De institutione musica*, libri quinque, ed. G. Friedlein. Leipzig: B. G. Teubner, 1867.

The Latin text of Boethius' important treatise on music; the result of a philological study of the sources known to the editor. This volume also includes a third treatise on geometry. The *Institutione musica* extends from p. 175 to p. 371.

Bohn, Peter. "Phillip von Vitry," *Monatshefte für Musikgeschichte* XXII:141–179.

This edition of de Vitry's famous treatise contains the original text with a German translation. See "Philippe de Vitry" in this bibliography for a reference to a more recent edition and translation.

Burzio (Burtius), Nicolaus. *Opusculum musices cum defensione Guidonis Aretini*. Bologna, 1487.

This treatise is discussed by Riemann in Chapters VII and XII. A copy is available at the Library of Congress.

Coussemaker, E. de. *Histoire de l'harmonie au moyen-âge*. Paris: V. Didron, 1852.

    This work, in addition to the sections which deal with the medieval period through the 14th century, contains the texts of a number of treatises with parallel translations into French. They are as follows: *Ad organum faciendum* (the Milan treatise), pp. 229–245 (discussed in Riemann, Chapter IV); *Libellus in Gallico de arte discantandi*, pp. 245–246 (Riemann, Chapter V); *Discantus positio vulgaris*, pp. 247–253 (Riemann, Chapters V, VI, VIII, and IX); *De organo* of Guido de Caroli Loco (Gui de Châlis), pp. 254–258 (Riemann, Chapter V); *L'art de déchanter* (*De arte discantandi*), pp. 259–273 (Riemann, Chapter V); *Quaedam de arte discantandi*, pp. 274–294 (Riemann, Chapter V); *La calliopée legale* of John Hothby, pp. 295–349 (Riemann, Chapters XI and XIII). Coussemaker's comprehensive compilations must be used with great care because the texts contain errors in printing and errors due to misreading of manuscripts.

————. *Scriptorum de musica medii aevi*. 4 vols.; Paris, 1864; reprint, Milan: Bollettino bibliografico musicale, 1931.

    A reference of fundamental importance for the study of medieval theory. In spite of the corruption of its texts, this work is still a basic reference tool for the music historian.

Fogliano, Ludovico. *Musica theorica*. Venice, 1529.

    This treatise is discussed by Riemann in Chapter XII. Fogliano was a follower of Ramis and an opponent of the authority of Boethius. See the article "Fogliano" in *MGG* IV:473–476. The treatise is available on microcard reproduction.

Gaffurio (Gafori, Gafurius), Franchino. *De harmonia musicorum instrumentorum*. Milan, 1518.

    This treatise is referred to by Riemann in Chapters XI and XII. It is available on microcard reproduction. In addition see the article "Gaffurius" in *MGG* IV:1237–1243, and Reese, *Music in the Renaissance*, pp. 178–181, on Gafurius and his contributions, not only to music theory but to composition as well.

————. *Practica musicae*. Milan, 1496.

    This treatise is discussed by Riemann in Chapter XII. It is available on microcard reproduction, and a copy may be found in the Library of Congress.

Gerbert, Martin. *Scriptores ecclesiastici de musica*. 3 vols.; Typis San-Blasianis, 1784; reprint, Milan: Bollettino bibliografico musicale, 1931.

    A basic collection of medieval treatises, which together with Coussemaker's *Scriptores* constitutes an almost complete library of treatises from the Middle Ages and the early Renaissance.

Gilles, André. "L'Anonyme III De Coussemaker, Scriptores III," *MD* XV:27–38.

    A new edition of the Latin text of this treatise.

Glareanus, Henricus. *Dodecachordon*, with five additional pages of *errata*. Basel, 1547.

    This treatise is available on microcards, and a copy may be found in the Library of Congress. It is of great importance for the study of the modal system as viewed by one of the most prominent of Renaissance humanist scholars. Riemann discusses this treatise in Chapter XII. See also note *10, Chapter XII.

————. *Dodecachordon*, translated into English with a commentary by Clement A. Miller. Unpublished doctoral dissertation, University of Michigan, 1950.

    This translation is available on microfilm reproduction.

————. "The *Isagoge in Musicen* of Henry Glarean," translated with an introduction by Frances Berry Turrell, *JMT* III:97–139.

    The Miller translation of the *Dodecachordon* and Turrell's translation of this earlier work make Glarean's two important music treatises available to the student who has no command of Latin. The *Isagoge* was published in 1517 as a preparatory work to the *Dodecachordon* and is addressed to students, whereas the latter work is for the musician and scholar. The work cites Boethius, Guido, and Gafurius, and is in agreement with the Pythagorean system. Turrell's introduction provides a comprehensive background for a reading of the treatise.

Guidonis Aretini (Guido d'Arezzo, Guido Aretinus). *Micrologus*, ed. Joseph Smits van Waesberghe. Rome: American Institute of Musicology, 1955.

This is a new edition of the *Micrologus* prepared from a collation of seventy-seven extant manuscript copies of this work. The chapters of the *Micrologus* on organum are discussed in Chapter IV and in the commentary where additional bibliography is cited.

Hermannus Contractus. *Musica Hermanni Contracti*, translated into English with a commentary and introduction by Leonard Ellinwood. Eastman School of Music Studies, 1936; reprint, 1952.

This important treatise is discussed in Chapter III and in the commentary. Ellinwood's edition contains a definitive text prepared from an MS in the Eastman School Sibley Library, as well as the translation.

Heyden, Sebald. *De arte canendi*. 1st ed., Nuremberg, 1537; 2nd ed., 1540.

Heyden's treatise is discussed in Chapter XII. Its contents have never been carefully investigated and discussed in any publication. See the article "Heyden" in *MGG* VI:361–366. This treatise is available on microcards, and is also in the Library of Congress.

Hieronymus de Moravia O. P. *Tractatus de musica*, ed. with an introduction by Simon M. Cserba O. P. Veröffentlichungen der musikwissenschaftlichen Institute der Universität Freiburg i.d. Schweiz, Reihe 2, 1935.

The only source for the life of this author is his treatise. He was born in Moravia, and around the beginning of the 13th century was a member of the Dominican order. He thought of his treatise as a compilation from theoretical works already existing. He wished to avoid the usage of too many Greek terms, and designed this treatise as a book containing all the information a student would have to know. Only Chapters 24, 25, and 28 are his independent work. He sometimes does not indicate his sources, for Chapter 19 is quoted from John Cotton without citation. Most of his citations are given literally, and he quotes most extensively from Boethius, the *Tractatus* containing sixty-six chapters from *De musica*. He also quotes the treatises of Johannes de Garlandia, Franco of Cologne, Petrus Picardus, and the anonymous *Discantus positio vulgaris*. Hieronymus' treatise is contained in Coussemaker, *Scriptores* I, but in an unreliable version. See also "Hieronymus de Moravia" in *MGG* VI:376–378.

Jacobus Leodiensis (Jacobus of Liège). *Speculum musicae Liber Primus*, ed. Roger Bragard. Rome: American Institute of Musicology, 1955.

This treatise is discussed in Chapter X. See Chapter X, note *14. The *Speculum musicae* is a veritable encyclopedia and an invaluable source. Unfortunately it is only available in part in this edition; several of its books are printed by Coussemaker.

Jan, Karl von. *Musici scriptores graeci*. Leipzig: B. G. Teubner, 1895.

This work contains the texts of the writers of late antiquity. A preface and a critical report on the sources is given in Latin. Each treatise contains a preface by the editor in Latin. The texts are as follows: Aristotle, *Loci de musica*; Pseudo-Aristotle, *De rebus musicis problemata*; Euclidus, *Sectio canonis*; Cleonides, *Isagoge*; Nichomachus, *Manual*; Bacchii Gerontio, *Isagoge*; Gaudentios, *Harmonica introductio*; Alypi, *Isagoge*. On texts of Greek writers see Reese, *Music in the Middle Ages*, pp. 17–19.

Johannes de Grocheo. *Der Musiktraktat des Johannes de Grocheo*, original text edited and translated into German, with commentary by Ernst Rohloff. Leipzig: Reinecke in Kommission, 1943.

This treatise is discussed in Chapter IX. Rohloff's edition is based upon the two existing MSS, London, BM, Ms. Harley 281 and Darmstadt, LB, Ms. 2663 (and not the Darmstadt MS only, as stated by Gilbert Reaney in his article "Johannes de Grocheo," *MGG* VII:95–100).

Johannes de Grocheo. "Die Musiklehre des Johannes de Grocheo," ed. with commentary and a translation into German by Johannes Wolf, *SIMG* I:65–130.

Wolf's edition is based on the Darmstadt MS alone. There are a number of differences in the two MSS, some of which are discussed in Chapter IX, notes *18, *19, *20, and *21.

Kornmüller, Utto. "Der Traktat des Johannes Cottonius über Musik," *KMJ* III:1–22.

This article contains a translation into German made from the version published in Gerbert's *Scriptores*.

La Fage, Adrien de. *Essais de Dipthérographie Musicale.* Paris: O. Legouix, 1864.

La Fage regarded his compilation as an attempt to preserve written monuments of the musical art in order to aid the understanding of past practices. At first this collection was to have included only sources from the library of his friend and teacher Joseph Baini, but this would have produced only a thin volume. La Fage's plan was then extended, and after making research in different libraries he amassed the material for the *Essais*. The title refers to parchments made from the skins of animals. The following works are contained in this collection:

*Tracti cantus per anni circuitum. Fragmenta musica Guidonis Aretini opera.* 13th century or late 12th century. This MS contains a hymn, *Versus de Sancta Maria*, notated on colored lines. There is a typical exposition of the Greek theoretical system, the ecclesiastical modes, and the division of the monochord follows Boethius. There is also an enharmonic and chromatic division (pp. 67–79).

*Joannis de Sacrobosco, Tractatus de sphaera; Odonis, Guidonis, Isidoris Seviliensis et aliorum opuscula musica.* This MS contains three distinct parts which do not appear to be the same handwriting or of the same epoch: 1. *Tractatus sperae M. Ioannis de sacro buschi anglici.* 2. This contains part of the *Enchiridion* of Odo. 3. This is a group of excerpts from Boethius, Guidonian fragments (from the *Micrologus*, and the *epistola* to the monk Michael), and fragments from Isidor (pp. 87–92).

*Musica disciplina magistri Ugolini Urbevetani.* A handsome MS from the beginning of the 15th century (pp. 116–180).

*Bibliothèque Nationale Manuscrit latins* no. 7211. Contains works of Hucbald, Guido, and Odo (pp. 180–195).

Philippi de Vitriaco, Joannis de Muris, Nicolai de Capua *et aliorum opuscula et fragmenta. Libri ascetici.* Rome, Bibliothèque Vallicellani B 83 (pp. 239–248).

Guidonis Aretinio *Opera.* Odonis *Dialogus et Tonarium*; Isidori Hispalensis *ex libro Etymologiarum*; Notkeri *Prologus sequentiarum*; *excerpta et fragmenta musica.* Florence Bibl. Mag. not in catalogue, provisional number 565. A 12th or 13th century MS (pp. 273–289).

Nicolai Capuani *Compendium Musicale.* A poorly written 15th century MS given in its entirety (pp. 308–338).

Boeth, Hugbaldi monaci, et *Anonymorum scriptorum Opera musica.* This MS contains an important anonymous organum treatise (pp. 355–362. The organum treatise begins on p. 360).

Rabanus Maurus, *De origine rerum.* MS Monte Cassino, Archives no. 152. The section of this treatise dealing with music is given here (pp. 363–372).

Joannes Presbyter. *De musica antica et moderna* (pp. 392–408). In addition to excerpts from authors from Hucbald, Guido, and Odo, this treatise contains a *vocabularium musicum*.

LeFebvre, Jacques (Jacobus Faber Stapulensis). *Arithmetica et musica* (*Elementa musica* begins on fol. 62). Paris: Joannes Higman et Wolfgangus Hopyl, 1496.

    This treatise is discussed in part in Chapter XII. A copy is available in the Library of Congress.

Meech, Sanford B. "Three musical treatises in English from a 15th century MS," *Speculum* 10:235–269.

    Three treatises are published in a form revised from the corrupt versions published in Hawkins' *General History*. Meech utilizes the Landsdowne MS 763 and gives a philological commentary on the texts and a translation. He interprets these texts on the basis of Riemann's Chapter VII. His conclusions, therefore, are also erroneous. The texts are the treatise of Lionel Power, an anonymous treatise—the so-called Pseudo-Chilston treatise—and a short but unimportant treatise by Chilston, *Of Musical Proportions*.

Mühlmann, Wilhelm. *Die Alia musica*. Dissertation, Leipzig, 1914.

    A study of the treatise printed in Gerbert I, resulting in the conclusion that this treatise was actually written by several authors. Gerbert's text is emended and a translation of the treatise into German is given. The treatise is discussed in Chapter I.

Philippe de Vitry. *Ars Nova*, ed. André Gilles, Jean Maillard, and Gilbert Reaney, *MD* X:13–33 and *MD* XI:12–29.

    This new edition contains a revision of the original text as well as a translation into French. The treatise is discussed in Chapter X.

Robert de Handlo. *Regulae*, ed. and translated into English by Luther Dittmer. Brooklyn: Institute of Medieval Music, 1959.

    Discussed in Chapter VIII. This treatise, according to the editor, was probably completed in 1326, and is concerned with the principles of mensuration of polyphonic music.

Schlecht, Raimund. "Micrologus: Guidonis de disciplina artis musicae," *Monatshefte für Musikgeschichte* V:135–165, 167–177.

    A translation of the *Micrologus* into German. The second section contains a commentary dealing with difficulties of translation and interpretation. Schlecht follows the Gerbert text. The treatise is discussed in Chapter IV.

————. "Musica Enchiriadis von Hucbald," *Monatshefte für Musikgeschichte* VI:163–178, 179–191; VII:1–16, 17–30, 33–45, 49–61, 65–80, 81–93; VIII:89.

    A translation of the *Musica enchiriadis* as well as the *Scholia* into German. Schlecht's translation must be consulted in the light of present knowledge of this treatise, particularly with regard to the gamut of the *Musica enchiriadis*, which he interpreted incorrectly.

Seay, Albert. "An Anonymous Treatise From St. Martial, "*Annales Musicologiques* V:7–42.

    A new edition of La Fage's anonymous organum treatise (briefly described on pp. 361–362 of the commentary). Handschin first called attention to the historical importance of this treatise (*ZfMW* VIII:321–341); Seay's edition, based upon three 15th-century manuscripts, is the first complete one.

Strunk, Oliver. *Source Readings in Music History*. New York, 1950.

    This collection of source writings contains a number of important works covered in our study. These have been specifically indicated in the commentary.

Tinctoris, Johannes. "The *Proportionale musices* of Johannes Tinctoris," translated into English with an introduction by Albert Seay, *JMT* I:22–75.

This treatise was the ninth of a series of eleven treatises by Tinctoris and was published by Coussemaker in *Scriptores* IV. Tinctoris' purpose in writing this was, according to the translator, to give "a solid foundation to this branch of composition to those who plan to utilize proportion in their composition and to assist those who must perform works employing the various ratios as an element of counterpoint."

Tinctoris, Johannes. *Terminorum musicae diffinitorum*, original text with a translation into French by Armand Machabey. Paris: Richard-Masse Éditeurs, 1951.

The first printed dictionary of musical terms, this little work contains definitions of about three hundred terms.

Vicentino, Dom Nicola. *L'antica musica ridotta alla moderna prattica*, 147 folios, with an eleven-page table of contents. Rome, 1555.

This unusual treatise is discussed in Chapter XII.

Wolf, Johannes. "Ein Beitrag zur Diskantlehre des 14. Jahrhunderts," *SIMG* XV:504–534.

This article contains an introduction and the text of a document of the early *Ars Nova* concerning the technique of composition, the *Compendium de discantu mensurabili compilatum a fratre Petro dicto Palma ociosa*, written in 1336. This treatise is discussed in Chapter X.

————. *Musica Practica Bartolomei Rami de Pareia*. Leipzig: Breitkopf und Härtel, 1901.

An edition of one of the most influential treatises from the second half of the 15th century. This treatise is discussed in Chapter XII and in the commentary to that chapter.

## BOOKS AND ARTICLES
### Concerning Material Discussed in Book I

Abert, Hermann. *Die Musikanschauung des M.A. und ihre Grundlagen.* Halle: M. Niemeyer, 1905.

Abert believed that music theory of the medieval period carried the burden of antique theory with it, in contrast to the Church Fathers (the founders of medieval music aesthetics, as were the Greek philosophers in antiquity) who stood in continual relationship with practice. The testimony of the Church Fathers shows that music played no subordinate role in the Church of the early medieval period; their writings contain no mechanical rehash of old teachings but an independent assimilation and extension of material fundamental to the actual practice of the art. The earliest writers, such as Boethius and Cassiodorus, have only antique theory in mind (and this is not clearly understood in all points), and their writings are alien to the practice of their time. They treat of the aesthetic aspect of music only from the standpoint of the Greeks. It is not until we come to Odo and Guido that we find theorists who develop their premises out of the living practice of their time.

Andrews, Frederick S. *Medieval Modal Theory.* Unpublished doctoral dissertation, Cornell University, 1935.

This dissertation is concerned with a study of modal theory that has particular reference to plainsong. The author finds that the theory of modal practice has been reconstructed by modern writers based upon a critical study of the music only. The writers of the *Scriptores* seem to have had only a tenuous relationship to the music upon which they commented, but these writings contain a large number of references that modify our understanding of modality to a great extent. The writer feels that the medieval theorists "were not only aware of the peculiar features of their musical language, but of the many points at which it escaped the symmetrical framework of their theory." The pedagogic approach in the treatises is their most important feature and contains the most valuable evidence. The early formulations of theory had primarily a liturgical purpose. We are so prone to associate mode with scale that it is difficult for us to see that a smaller unit than the octave was the basis of musical "feeling" in the medieval period.

This dissertation is an important contribution to our knowledge of modal theory.

Apel, Willi. "Early History of the Organ," *Speculum* 23:191–216.

This article is important for students of Riemann's *Geschichte* for its discussion of the connection between the organ and organum (see p. 11 and Chapter II, note *2).

———. *Gregorian Chant*. Bloomington: Indiana University Press, 1958.

The first comprehensive book in English on Gregorian chant covering such aspects as tonality, form, liturgical function, and related chant dialects such as Ambrosian and Old Roman Chant.

Appel, Margarete. *Terminologie in den mittelalterlichen Musiktraktaten*. Berlin: Buch- und Kunstdruckerei W. Postberg, 1935.

A study of terminological usage during the medieval period and of value to the student of this period. In addition to the studies, this work contains an alphabetical index of treatises and one of the terms discussed.

Brambach, W. *Die Reichenauer Sängerschule: I, Die Musikliteratur des M.A. bis zur Blüthe der Reichenauer Sängerschule*. Karlsruhe: n.p., 1883.

Brambach was of the opinion that the writers of antiquity and those of the medieval period differentiated completely between the science of music and its actual practice. Boethius depicted the system of antiquity, but medieval writers from the Carolingian period assumed that Boethius was representative of the living music of the Christian church. Various theorists and treatises of this early period are discussed, to figures like Hucbald, Odo, and Pseudo-Bernelinus.

———. *Theorie und Praxis der Reichenauer Sängerschule* (Part II of *Die Reichenauer Sängerschule*). Karlsruhe: n.p., 1888.

Chiefly a study of the works of Berno and Hermannus Contractus.

Chailley, Jacques. "Le mythe des modes grecs," *AM* XXVIII:137–163.

An article which attempts to show that the idea of a mode was a medieval one and not applicable to antique music. The author's definition of mode requires that the following conditions be met: the choice of an octave type, a fundamental unity; the identity of the function of the sound reproducing that of the octave; the determination of a tonic, identified by the first sound of the octave; hierarchy of the other degrees in relation to the tonic; indifference to ambitus.

Crocker, Richard L. "*Musica Rhythmica* and *Musica Metrica* in Antique and Medieval Theory," *JMT* II:2–23.

A study of rhythm and meter in the early Middle Ages, through Guido.

Ficker, Rudolf v. "Der Organumtraktat der Vatikanischen Bibliothek (Ottob. 3025)," *KMJ* XXVII:65–74.

This is a study of a short organum treatise (fols. 46–48, 49–50 of MS cited in the title) which, as far as its rules are concerned, is similar to other organum treatises. It gains its significance from the large number of musical examples it contains (278), including a table of 67 short *formulae* for organum. All the refinements of a virtuoso technique of improvisation are utilized; the melismas are apparently of the Gregorian variety, and the highly melismatic style does not seem to have originated from organum practice, but from the liturgical chant practice of the period.

Fox-Strangways, A. H. "A Tenth Century Manual," *Music and Letters* XIII:183–193.

A summarization of the contents of the *Musica enchiriadis*.

Gombosi, Otto. "Key, Mode, and Species," *JAMS* IV:20–26.

A penetrating discussion of the three terms by an outstanding writer on the subject of Greek music. See commentary for Chapter I.

———. "Studien zur Tonartenlehre des frühen Mittelalters," *AM* X:149–174; XI:28–39, 128–135; XII:21–29; XII:29–52.

An important study of the possible transformation of Greek theory to that of the medieval period, including an investigation of the possible influences of Byzantine origin. See commentary for Chapter I.

———. *Tonarten und Stimmumgen der antiken Musik.* Copenhagen: E. Munksgaard, 1939.

A stimulating exposition of Greek theory, relating it to the development of Greek musical practice. Gombosi adopts the theory advanced by Curt Sachs that the Greek notation system was not a pitch notation, but a fingering or positional notation invented for the cithara.

Grutchfield, E. J. "Hucbald: A Millenary Commemoration," *Musical Times*, 1930, pp. 507–510 and 704–710.

This article in two parts contains biographical material as well as information on treatises like *De harmonica institutione* and *Musica enchiriadis*. The author gives a detailed account of Daseian notation.

Handschin, Jacques. "Der Organum Traktat von Montpellier," in *Adler Festschrift*, Universal Edition. Vienna, 1930.

This article concerns an organum treatise discovered by Handschin in an MS Montpellier, Fac. de med. H 384, on fols. 122–123. Handschin gives an account of its contents and discusses it in relation to other treatises proposing a revision in the lineage of certain of these. See Chapter V, note *1.

———. "Zur Geschichte der Lehre vom Organum," in *ZfMW* VIII:321–341.

An article of fundamental importance for the student of the history of organum. See commentary for Chapter II, where this article is cited in several instances.

Kornmüller, Utto. "Die alten Musiktheoretiker," 1886, *KMJ* I:1–21; II:1–21; IV:1–19.

A readable summary survey of the treatises in Gerbert and several from Coussemaker, though in need of correction at some points. Despite its age this group of articles contains much worthwhile information and is written in a very objective and lucid manner.

Laloy, Louis. *Aristoxène de Tarente et la musique de l'antiquité.* Paris: Société Française d'Imprimerie et de Librairie, 1904.

A detailed study of the life and works of Aristoxenos. Mention of this work is not to be found in the bibliography of the article "Aristoxenus" in *MGG* I:653.

Lange, Georg. "Zur Geschichte der Solmisation," in *SIMG* I:535–622.

An important study of solmization which discusses its origins, purpose, and various applications in theoretical treatises.

Müller, Hans. *Die Musik Wilhelm von Hirsaus*, Frankfurt A.M.: Commissionsverlag B. G. Teubner, 1883.

A study of the life and writings of Wilhelm of Hirsau who is represented by two extant codices. Wilhelm's treatise *De musica* shows particular dependence on the works of Hermannus Contractus and Guido of Arezzo.

———. *Hucbald's echte und unechte Schriften über Musik.* Leipzig: B. G. Teubner, 1884.

A collation of the MSS of the *Musica enchiriadis* and a refutation of Hucbald's authorship for all treatises in Gerbert but the *Harmonica institutione*. Müller's work is still regarded as authoritative, though Riemann never accepted Müller's conclusions.

Oesch, Hans. *Guido von Arezzo*, Publikationen der schweizerischen musikforschenden Gesellschaft, Serie II, vol. 4. Bern: Verlag Paul Haupt, 1954.

An important new study of the life and works of Guido of Arezzo and his relationship with Odo of Saint Maur, the author of *De musica* and the *Dialogus*, ascribed in
Gerbert to Odo of Cluny.
Reinach, Theodore. *La Musique Grecque*. Paris: Payot, 1926.
A study of Greek music and theory including transcriptions of all of the extant
fragments of Greek music. Reinach inclines to the belief that some kind of modal
perception existed in Greek music. The strings of the lyre were tuned to the *mese*,
and in this way the *mese* ruled the harmony of the strings (that is, their tuning). The
*mese* also directed the sounds of the melody. See Winnington-Ingram, *Modes in
Ancient Music*, and the same author's excellent article in *Grove's Dictionary*, 5th ed., on
this subject.
Sasse, Götz Dietrich. *Die Mehrstimmigkeit der Ars antiqua in Theorie und Praxis*. Dissertation,
Borna, Leipzig, 1940.
This dissertation gives a survey of theoretical treatises through the *Ars antiqua*
without enough exhaustive examination of these works in connection with musical
sources (such as one finds in William Waite, *The Rhythm of Twelfth Century Polyphony*).
Schneider, Marius. "Ist die vokale Mehrstimmigkeit eine Schöpfung der Altrassen,"
*AM* XXIII:40–50.
On the practice of polyphony in primitive cultures.
Sowa, Heinrich. "Textvariationen zur *Musica enchiriadis*," *ZfMW* XVII:194–207.
This article concerns itself with additional text found in a copy of the *Musica
enchiriadis* in a Paris MS, lat. 7202, fols. 50–56. This material augments the text as
given by Gerbert and more clearly explains certain problems through more examples.
A more detailed exposition of tone-positions on the Daseian gamut is presented.
Sowa believes the *Musica enchiriadis* and the *Scholia* to be by three different authors,
and also regards these treatises as by no means the earliest formulations of polyphonic
practice.
———. "Zur Handschrift Clm 9921," *AM* V:60–65 and 107–120.
Concerning a small treatise copied on the margins of this MS which has bearing
upon modal identification and transposition.
Smits van Waesberghe, Joseph. *De Musico-Paedagogico et Theoretico Guidone Aretino Eiusque
Vita et Moribus*. Florence: Leo S. Olschki, 1953.
A study in Latin of the life and works of Guido of Arezzo. See commentary for
Chapter IV. This study was awarded a prize by the *Comitato Nazionale per le Onoranze
a Guido d'Arezzo* in 1950.
———. "Guido of Arezzo and Musical Improvisation," *MD* V:55–63.
This article deals with musical improvisation as a teaching device as found in the
theoretical writings of Guido of Arezzo.
———. "The Musical Notation of Guido of Arezzo," *MD* V:15–53.
This is a translation into English from Smits van Waesberghe's prize-winning
essay on Guido (*Guido Aretinus*), written in Latin.
Spiess, Lincoln. "The Diatonic 'Chromaticism' of the *Enchiriadis* Treatises," *JAMS*
XII:1–6.
A study of the chromatic members of the Daseian gamut. See Chapter II, note *18.
———. "Discant, Descant, Diaphony, and Organum," *JAMS* VIII:144–147. An
abstract.
A study of terminology. The author believes that parallel and oblique organum
were its earliest forms and that contrary motion became standard practice in the
11th century. At the end of the 11th century the note-against-note style predominates
until a more elaborate type emerges which culminates in the extended Notre Dame

examples. The term *diaphony* in earliest sources refers to the note-against-note style of organum (the meaning of this term before the 9th century is in doubt). With the St. Martial period there is a distinction in the styles of organum, the term *discantus* applying to the simpler style, and *organum* applying to the ornate style.

Spiess, Lincoln. "An Introduction to the Pre-St. Martial Sources of Early Polyphony," *Speculum* XXII: 16–17.

A list of practical sources prior to the St. Martial period. Of the fourteen sources given, only five are capable of transcription.

————. *Polyphony in Theory and Practice from the 9th Century to the Close of the 13th Century.* 5 vols.; dissertation, Harvard University, 1947.

A comprehensive and detailed study which could not be made available to the writer for examination.

Spitta, Phillipp. "Die *Musica enchiriadis* und ihr Zeitalter," *VfMW* V: 443–482.

An important and basic study of the *Musica enchiriadis* in which the construction of the Daseian gamut is definitively established.

Steinhard, Erich. "Zur Frühgeschichte der Mehrstimmigkeit," *AfMW* III: 220–231.

Steinhard, in opposition to Riemann, believes that parallel organum and oblique organum developed simultaneously. His article develops this thesis, which involves the establishment of a new chronology for early organum treatises. Steinhard also adds a discovery to this group of treatises, in support of his point of view.

Turrell, Frances Berry. *Modulation: An Outline of Its Prehistory from Aristoxenus to Henry Glarean.* Unpublished doctoral dissertation, University of Southern California, 1956.

A comprehensive study of modulation (= transposition) from the period of antiquity to Glarean. Chapter V (pp. 416–538) is a survey of treatises relating to the topics of mutation and *musica ficta*. Modulatory devices in the writings of Glarean are discussed in the last chapter. A particularly informative and detailed work.

Ursprung, Otto. "Die antiken Transpositionsskalen und die Kirchentöne," *AfMF* III: 129–152.

A comparison of medieval and antique theories of tone systems and a hypothesis on the change from the antique to the medieval system. See commentary for Chapter I.

Waeltner, Ernst Ludwig. "Der Bamberger Dialog über das Organum," *AfMW* XIV: 175–183.

This article concerns a short organum treatise found in a manuscript (the HS Bamberg HJ-IV-20) also containing the *Musica enchiriadis*. The author believes that this treatise contains information which shows more clearly the transition from the *Musica enchiriadis* to the organum theories of Guido.

Wantzloeben, S. *Das Monochord als Instrument und als System.* Halle: Max Niemeyer, 1911.

The authoritative work on the monochord, not only in connection with its importance in theoretical systems, but also concerning its eventual transformation as an instrument into the clavichord.

Weakland, Rembert, "Hucbald as Musician and Theorist," *MQ* XLII: 66–84.

A study of Hucbald's contribution to music and music theory through a study of those works known to be his. The treatise *De harmonica institutione* is discussed in detail.

Wellesz, Egon. *A History of Byzantine Music and Hymnography.* Oxford: Clarendon Press, 1949.

This work is valuable for the readers of Riemann's *Geschichte* in its coverage of Byzantine music theory and the tonal system of Byzantine music.

Werner, Eric. "The Psalmodic Formula NEANNOE and Its Origin," *MQ* XXVIII: 93–99.

A study of formula words which had close connection in the medieval period with modality and solmization. These words actually referred to melodic patterns rather than single tones. Werner offers a hypothesis as to the origin of these words. See Chapter II, note *17.

Werner Eric. *The Sacred Bridge*. New York: Columbia University Press, 1959.

This work is important for the readers of Riemann's *Geschichte* in the chapter which traces the ancestry of eightfold modality. See Chapter I, note *8.

Winnington-Ingram, R. P. "Ancient Greek Music: A Survey," *Music and Letters* X: 326–345.

An article on Greek music by one of the best English writers on the subject. This article was reworked for the 5th ed. of *Grove's Dictionary* ("Greek Music—Ancient").

———. *Mode in Ancient Greek Music*. Cambridge: The University Press, 1936.

After surveying the literature of Greek theorists, the author can find no conclusive evidence that a functional modality existed in their system. For the student of Greek theory, this lucid book contains much information presented with the utmost clarity and simplicity.

Wiora, Walter. "Zum Problem des Ursprungs der mittelalterlichen Solmisation," *MF* IX: 263–274.

This article is devoted to a discussion of possible origins of the so-called "Guidonian solmization system."

Wolf, Johannes. "Die Musiktheorie des Mittelalters," *AM* III: 53–64.

A very readable survey of music theory and theorists from Boethius to the *Ars Nova*.

Wolking, Hubert. *Guido's Micrologus de disciplina artis musicae und seine Quellen*. Emsdetten (Westf.): H. und J. Lechte, 1930.

A study of Guido's *Micrologus*, its structure and sources. This work is superseded by Smits van Waesberghe's and Oesch's studies. The musical examples given by Wolking sometimes differ with those in the later Waesberghe edition of the *Micrologus*.

Yasser, Joseph. "Medieval Quartal Harmony," *MQ* XXIII: 170–197 and 333–366; XXIV: 351–385.

A series of articles in which the author attempts to show the pentatonic structure of Gregorian chant.

FAUXBOURDON AND ENGLISH DISCANT

Besseler, Heinrich. *Bourdon und Fauxbourdon*. Leipzig: Breitkopf und Härtel, 1950.

———. "Das Ergebnis der Diskussion über Fauxbourdon," *AM* XXIX: 185–188.

———. "Das Neue in der Musik des 15. Jahrhunderts," *AM* XXVI: 75–85.

———. "Dufay, Schöpfer des Fauxbourdons," *AM* XX: 26–45.

———. "Tonalharmonik und Vollklang," *AM* XXIV: 131–146.

Bukofzer, Manfred. "Fauxbourdon Revisited," *MQ* XXXVIII: 22–40.

———. *Geschichte des englischen Diskants und des Fauxbourdons nach den theoretischen Quellen*. Strassburg, 1936.

———. "The Gymel, the Earliest Form of English Polyphony," *Music and Letters* 16: 77–84.

———. "Popular Polyphony in the Middle Ages," *MQ* XXVI: 31–49.

Clercx, Susanne. "Aux Origines du fauxbourdon," *Revue de Musicologie* XL: 151–165.

Ficker, Rudolf von. "Epilog zum Fauxbourdon," *AM* XXV: 127–131.

———. "Zur Schöpfungsgeschichte des Fauxbourdon," *AM* XXIII: 93–123.

Flasdieck, Hermann M. "Fauxbourdon and NE. Burden 'Refrain,'" *Anglia* 74:188–238.
———. "Franz. faux-bourdon und frühneuengl. faburden," *AM* XXV:111–127.
Georgiades, Thrasybulos, *Englische Diskanttraktate aus der ersten Hälfte des* 15. *Jahrhunderts.* Munich, 1937.
Kenney, Sylvia W. "English Discant and Discant in England," *MQ* XLV:26–48.
Kirchner, Gustav, "Französisch faux-bourdon und frühneuenglisch faburden (H. M. Flasdieck). Epilog zum Fauxbourdon (R. v. Ficker). Eine Erwiderung," *AM* XXVI:85ff.
Trowell, Brian. "Faburden and Fauxbourdon," *MD* XIII:43–78.
Trumble, Ernest. *Early Renaissance Harmony.* Dissertation, Indiana University, 1954.
———. *Fauxbourdon*, vol. I. Brooklyn: Institute of Medieval Music, 1959.

For a survey of this literature, see the commentary for Chapter VII. For additional bibliography see "Fauxbourdon" in *MGG* III:1897.

BOOKS AND ARTICLES
Concerning Material Discussed in Book II

Adler, Guido. "Die Wiederholung und Nachahmung in der Mehrstimmigkeit," *VfMW* II:271–346.
A historical study of imitation, including a study of the term.
Apel, Willi. "From St. Martial to Notre Dame," *JAMS* II:145–158.
The first appearance of modal rhythm occurs in the works of Leoninus, in the sections of the *organa* which are called *clausulae*. The *tenor* of the *clausulae* usually moves in groups in the fifth mode while the *duplum* moves in the faster rhythm of the first mode. The problem is to what extent "this novel principle is also embodied in the 'pedal point' sections" of the *organa*. The possible interpretations of the *duplum* are discussed, and the author concludes that its movement is based upon the principle of consonance (i.e., that each note is long if it forms a consonance with the sustained note of the *tenor*).
Balmer, Lucie. *Tonsystem und Kirchentöne bei Johannes Tinctoris*, Berner Veröffentlichung zur Musikforschung, Heft 2. Bern: Verlag Paul Haupt, 1935.
This study examines the *Expositio manus* and the *Liber de natura et proprietate tonorum* of Johannes Tinctoris, the two works in which he treats of the tonal system and the ecclesiastical modes. Tinctoris' exposition is compared to those of other theorists so that the reader is made more clearly aware of Tinctoris' individual contributions in these fields. This work is extensive in its detail and includes many quotations from the treatises discussed.
Barbour, J. Murray. *Tuning and Temperament.* East Lansing: Michigan State College Press, 1953.
The standard and only available history of tuning and temperament.
Bartha, Denes v. "Studien zum musikalischen Schrifttum des 15. Jahrhunderts," *AfMF* I:59–82; II:176–199.
This is a philological study of musical literary sources of the 15th century. The problems of collating manuscripts, of establishing definitive versions of treatises, problems in the reading of manuscripts, and problems raised by treatises in Gerbert and Coussemaker which are now missing are discussed. The author believes that Riemann wrongly ignored treatises which dealt only with *cantus planus* and gives only a one-sided picture as a result.
Bellerman, Heinrich. *Mensuralnoten und Taktzeichen.* Berlin: Walter de Gruyter & Co., 1930.
This work, which deals with white mensural notation, was first published in 1858

and later in two further editions. It is still a valuable reference and is written in a very lucid style. Bellerman's transcriptions were in note values of the same form as the originals, whereas the practice today is to use reduced note values which are equivalent in duration, rather than in appearance.

Besseler, Heinrich. "Studien zur Musik des Mittelalters," *AfMW* VII: 167–252; VIII: 137–258.

Two important articles which discuss important medieval musical and theoretical sources.

Bragard, Roger. "Le *Speculum Musicae* du Compilateur Jacques de Liège," *MD* VII: 59–104; VIII: 1–17.

This study discusses the sources of the *Speculum musicae*, its contents, the work as it is referred to in later sources, such as in Mersenne, in Rousseau's *Dictionnaire de Musique*, descriptions of the MSS, history of the MSS, how they are related to one another, the identity of the author, the attribution of authorship from the 16th century to the present, and biographical material on the author.

Bukofzer, Manfred. "Speculative Thinking in Medieval Music," *Speculum* XVII: 165–180.

Bukofzer sees three main currents of speculative thinking in medieval music. One, the idea of music as an image of the world or as an imitation of the *musica mundana*; two, the Pythagorean doctrine of numerical proportions; three, the tendency toward interpolation as a commentary. These ideas are interrelated. The medieval classification of music is as much dependent upon the first idea as the justification of polyphony is upon the second. The trope, the sequence, and the motet are based mainly upon the third premise. In the isorhythmic motet all three ideas are united into a single work of art.

Dalhaus, Carl. "Zur Geschichte der Synkope," *MF* XII: 385–391.

A valuable and detailed article on a difficult subject. See Chapter XI, note *20.

Dittmer, Luther A. "Beiträge zum Studium des Worcester-Fragments: Der Rondellus," *MF* X: 29–33.

A discussion of the *rondellus*. See Chapter IX, note *11.

———. "Binary Rhythm, Musical Theory, and the Worcester Fragments," *MD* VII: 39–57.

Dittmer attempts to establish the fact that binary rhythm was an older practice in England and not the first appearance of the *Ars nova* there. The point of contention is the sentence in Odington's treatise on music beginning "*Longa autem...*" which has been the basis of much musicological discussion (see Willi Apel, *The Notation of Polyphonic Music*, and William Waite, *The Rhythm of Twelfth-Century Polyphony*).

Ehmann, W. *Adam von Fulda als Vertreter der ersten deutschen Komponistengeneration.* Berlin: Junker und Dünnhaupt, 1936.

Fulda's treatise is found only in Gerbert III, 329 ff. Ehmann discusses it in section IV and uses Gerbert's edition in his references. He treats of its philosophical aspects rather than those relating to practice.

Ferand, Ernst T. "The 'Howling in Seconds' of the Lombards," *MQ* XXV: 313–324.

This article concerns itself with information in Chapter XII of Riemann's *Geschichte* to which Ferand is taking an opposite stand. See Chapter XII, note *7.

———. "What Is *Res Facta*?" *JAMS* X: 141–150.

The term *res facta* had two different meanings. It signified a written, not improvised, composition in plain or florid counterpoint. It also signified florid, not plain, counterpoint, whether written or improvised. A third and inconsistent meaning has been added to it in modern musicology, where the plain, unadorned version of a composition is often referred to as a *res facta* in contradistinction to its florid versions. Neither *res facta* nor *chose fait* is mentioned in any source prior to Tinctoris (in *Terminorum musicae diffinitorum* and *Liber de arte contrapuncti*).

Handschin, Jacques. "Aus der alten Musiktheorie III," *AM* XV:2–15.
    Concerning the Ambrosian "singing in seconds." See Chapter XII, note *7.

———. "The Summer Canon and Its Background," *MD* III:55–94; V:65–113.
    This extensive article concerns itself not only with the famous "Sumer is icumen in" canon (which Handschin dates as mid-13th century) but also with related musical sources, including a section on binary rhythm. For Riemann, binary rhythm suggested great antiquity, but Bukofzer finds that binary rhythm is impossible before the beginning of the 14th century. It is true that the binary division of the *longa* does not occur before the late 13th century on the continent, being recognized in theoretical sources at the beginning of the 14th century. Handschin finds that Riemann's attitude toward the interval of a third is "romanticism," but that his conviction of the priority of binary rhythm may actually have some basis. Binary rhythm is "psychologically" the simplest. Handschin believes that it is more plausible to take Odington's statement ("*Longa autem...*") as it is expressed, to mean the transition from binary to ternary rhythm.

Jeppesen, Knud. *Counterpoint*. New York: Prentice-Hall, Inc., 1939.
    This book was actually written as a text, but it contains an outline history of counterpoint (pp. 3–53), part of which considers the material covered in this volume.

———. *The Style of Palestrina and the Dissonance*. London: Oxford University Press, 1946.
    While the topic of this monograph lies outside the area of this book, certain aspects of the historical background given are applicable to it.

Kaufmann, Henry W. "Vicentino's Arciorgano; an Annotated Translation," *JMT* V, 2:32–53.
    A translation of a document describing Vicentino's tuning experiments on the Arciorgano, accompanied by a detailed commentary.

Kornmüller, Utto. "Johann Hothby, Eine Studie zur Geschichte der Musik im 15. Jahrhundert," *KMJ* VIII:1–23.
    A discussion of Hothby and his works.

Krüger, Walter. "Aufführungspraktische Fragen mittelalterlicher Mehrstimmigkeit," *MF* X:279–286, 397–403, 497–505; XI:177–189.
    Though these articles deal primarily with problems relating to the performance practice of certain medieval musical forms, the author includes theoretical treatises in the province of his consideration.

Levitan, Joseph S. "Ockeghem's Clefless Compositions," *MQ* XIII:440–464.
    See Chapter XII, note *9.

Marquis, G. *Contrapuntal and Harmonic Tendencies in 14th Century France*. Unpublished doctoral dissertation, University of Southern California, 1950.
    This dissertation covers pre-*Ars nova* counterpoint and theoretical views, counterpoint in the Roman de Fauvel, counterpoint in the music of Machaut, late 14th- and early 15th-century counterpoint, and harmonic tendencies in the music discussed. Theoretical concepts are given in summary, and the Riemann *Geschichte* is the source for these. General rules of *musica ficta* in the period covered by the study are discussed.

Miller, Clement A. "The Dodecachordon: Its Origins and Influence on Renaissance Musical Thought," *MD* XV:155–166.
    This article attempts to show that "the *Dodecachordon*, if not immediately sensational, had a profound effect on the musical thought of the time, an effect which

was acknowledged either implicitly or explicitly not only by distinguished theorists but also by many Renaissance composers" (p. 156).

Paetow, J. L. "The Life and Works of John of Garland," in *Memoirs of the University of California* II: 77–145.

Paetow writes (p. 142): "In various bibliographies it is stated that John of Garland also wrote books on music.... The books in question are: *De musica mensurabili positio, Introductio musice plane et etiam mensurabilis, Optima introductio in contrapunctum pro rubidus*, and *Tractatus de cantu plana*...." There is no evidence other than the citation (by Coussemaker) from de Vitry's *Ars contrapunctus* that a John of Garland who wrote on music was a Master in the University of Paris.

Pirrotta, Nino. "Marchettus de Padua and the Italian *Ars Nova*," *MD* IX: 57–71.

This study is on Marchettus of Padua and his relationship to the Italian *Ars nova*. See Chapter VI, note *14.

Reaney, Gilbert. "Fourteenth Century Harmony and the Ballades, Rondeaux, and Virelais of Guillaume de Machaut," *MD* VII: 129–146.

Actually, this article is a study of the harmonic result of 14th-century counterpoint and is stimulating because of its unusual approach to the musical style of this period.

———. "The Manuscript Chantilly," *MD* VIII: 59–113.

Concerning the attribution of the authorship of the *Quatuor Principalia* to Simon Tunstede, see p. 73, footnote 51 of this article.

Rohloff, Ernst. *Studien zum Musiktraktat des Johannes de Grocheo*. Dissertation, Leipzig, 1930.

This dissertation is based on a study of two sources of Grocheo's treatise, the MS London, BM, Harley 281, and Codex 2663 of the Hessische Landesbibliothek zu Darmstadt. The author gives a careful and detailed exposition of the entire treatise, including textual variants in the two sources.

Rogers, Helen. *Development of a Concept of Modulation in Theory from the 16th to the Early 18th Century*. Unpublished doctoral dissertation, Indiana University.

An extensive discussion of the modal system as seen by Aron, Ornithoparcus, and Glareanus is of interest for the reader of Chapter XII in the Riemann *Geschichte*, and is contained in the first part of this dissertation.

Seay, Albert. "The City of Hothby and Ramos," *JAMS* IX: 193–195.

This brief article concerns the ties of the city of Florence to the two theorists, Hothby and Ramos.

———. "The *Declaratio Musice Discipline* of Ugolino of Orvieto: Addenda," *MD* XI: 126–133.

On additional sources, uncovered by the writer.

———. "The *Dialogus Johannis Ottobi Anglici in arte musica*," *JAMS* VIII: 86–100.

This article concerns the opposition which existed between John Hothby, a conservative and a Pythagorean, and Bartolomeo Ramos, the proponent of reforms in monochord division and in the Pythagorean system (see Chapter XII, note *2).

———. "Ugolino of Orvieto, Theorist and Composer," *MD* IX: 111–166.

This theorist is not mentioned in Riemann's *Geschichte* and was known only by the fragments of a treatise by him printed in La Fage's *Essais*. Seay gives a detailed account of Ugolino, including a discussion of sources, theoretical writings, and compositions.

Schmidt, Günther. "Zur Frage des *Cantus Firmus* im 14. und beginnenden 15. Jahrhundert," *AfMW* XV: 230–250.

The author attempts in this study to point out the direct influences which the *cantus firmus* exerted on musical procedures in composition during the period of the *Ars nova*, the late 14th century, and the early 15th century. The author points out, in connection with his discussion of 15th-century music, that the name *fauxbourdon* does not designate the position of the *cantus firmus* but is rather related to the absence of fundamentals for the harmonies.

Waite, William. "Discantus, Copula, Organum," *JAMS* V:77–87.

The material in this article is contained in Waite's book, *The Rhythm of Twelfth-Century Polyphony*. See commentary for Chapter IX.

————. *The Rhythm of Twelfth-Century Polyphony*; transcription of Wolfenbüttel 677 and Olim Helmstadt 628. New Haven: Yale University Press, 1954.

An important work on modal rhythm which stands in opposition to the solutions advanced by Apel in his *Notation of Polyphonic Music* and the article "From St. Martial to Notre Dame," *JAMS* II. See commentaries for Chapters VIII and IX for discussions of various aspects of this and related problems.

Werner, Eric. "The Mathematical Foundation of Philippe de Vitri's *Ars Nova*," *JAMS* IX:128–132.

See Chapter X, note *15.

## MUSICA FICTA
(Items not already cited in the bibliography)

Apel, Willi. "The Partial Signatures in the Sources up to 1450," *AM* X:1–13.

Hibberd, Lloyd. "Musica Ficta and Instrumental Music c. 1250–c. 1350," *MQ* XXVIII:216–226.

Except for the use of certain tones foreign to the range of Gregorian chant and for the possibility that certain modifications later introduced into the regular system may have been first discovered quite by chance on some instrument (e.g., by accidental fingerings on a stringed instrument), one must conclude that there is not the slightest reason for believing instruments as such to have played any particular role in the introduction of chromaticism into late medieval music (p. 126).

Hoppin, Richard H. "Conflicting Signatures Reviewed," *JAMS* IX:97–117.

————. "Partial Signatures and Musica Ficta in Some Early 15th Century Sources," *JAMS* VI:197–215.

Lowinsky, Edward E. "Conflicting Views on Conflicting Signatures," *JAMS* VII:181–204.

————. "The Function of Conflicting Signatures in Early Polyphonic Music," *MQ* XXXI:227–260.

Mendel, Arthur. "Pitch in the 16th and Early 17th Centuries—Part III," *MQ* XXIV:336–357.

See commentary for Chapter XIII.

# INDEXES

# INDEX OF AUTHORS AND TREATISES

# INDEX OF SUBJECTS

A NOTE ABOUT THE TRANSLATOR

Raymond H. Haggh was born in Chicago in 1920, receiving his advanced education at Northwestern University (B.Mus. 1949, M.Mus. 1950) and at Indiana University (Ph.D. 1961). In 1955–56 he held a Faculty Fellowship from the Fund for the Advancement of Education, studying at Harvard University, and was also the recipient of a Danforth Teacher Grant (1957–1958). He has written several compositions which have been performed by the Oklahoma City Symphony Orchestra and university and college ensembles in the southeastern United States. He is now an associate professor of music at the University of Nebraska.